All the Missing Souls

HUMAN RIGHTS AND CRIMES AGAINST HUMANITY
Eric D. Weitz, Series Editor

ALL THE MISSING SOULS

A PERSONAL

HISTORY

of the

WAR CRIMES

TRIBUNALS

DAVID SCHEFFER

PRINCETON UNIVERSITY PRESS
PRINCETON AND OXFORD

Copyright © 2012 by Princeton University Press
Published by Princeton University Press,
41 William Street, Princeton, New Jersey 08540
In the United Kingdom: Princeton University Press,
6 Oxford Street, Woodstock, Oxfordshire OX20 1TW
press.princeton.edu

Jacket photograph: *Nyanza Massacre Site—September 1997.*
Photo by James Stejskal.

Library of Congress Cataloging-in-Publication Data

Scheffer, David.
    All the missing souls : a personal history of the war crimes tribunals / David Scheffer.
        p. cm.
    Includes bibliographical references and index.
    ISBN 978-0-691-14015-5 (hardcover : alk. paper) 1. Scheffer, David. 2. Lawyers—United
States—Biography. 3. United States. Dept. of State—Officials and employees—Biography.
4. International criminal courts—History—20th century. 5. United States—Foreign
relations—1993–2001. I. Title.
    KF373.S338A3   2010
    340.092–dc23   2011032314
    [B]

British Library Cataloging-in-Publication Data is available

This book has been composed in Baskerville and Trade Gothic

Printed on acid-free paper. ∞

Printed in the United States of America

10 9 8 7 6 5 4 3

TO MY PARENTS,

    FOR THEIR STRENGTH OF CHARACTER

MY WIFE MICHELLE,

    FOR HER UNFAILING LOVE AND SUPPORT

MY DAUGHTER KATE AND SON HENRY,

    FOR THEIR PATIENCE AND GOOD CHEER

We heard Serb voices—"Come surrender!"—and whoever did, they disappeared.

A Bosnian farmer explaining why he fled his home in July 1995 as Srebrenica's Muslims were being slaughtered in a nearby warehouse

We have upwards of 100,000 men that we cannot account for.... We have no idea where those men are now.

The author describing the unknown fate of Kosovar-Albanian men on April 18, 1999

THIS BOOK HONORS THE VICTIMS OF ATROCITY CRIMES DURING THE 1990S—THE MURDERED, THE INJURED, THE DISPOSSESSED, AND THOSE MISSING FOR A DAY OR FOR ETERNITY. THEY ALL SUFFERED ON MY WATCH AS AMERICA'S FIRST WAR CRIMES AMBASSADOR, BUT THEIR SOULS WERE NOT FORGOTTEN IN THE TRIBUNALS OF JUSTICE BUILT DURING THAT DECADE.

CONTENTS

All the Missing Souls

INTRODUCTION

AMBASSADOR TO HELL

ISAIAH PROPHESIED, "AND THE LOFTINESS OF MAN SHALL BE BOWED DOWN, and the haughtiness of man shall be made low."[1] That prediction bore truth in my lifetime and on my watch.

I recall Freetown, Sierra Leone, in February 1999. A teenage girl named Nancy lay before me in the shade of a small overcrowded hospital where mutilated victims, some only children, waited for miracles that never arrived. Their bodies were grotesquely disfigured. Nancy, in shock, remained mute. Drug-crazed rebel boys had brutally gang raped her and poured molten plastic into her eyes during their rampage through the city. For me, Nancy's plight once again evoked the horror of atrocities that erupted at massive crime scenes throughout the 1990s.

I also remember a steep hillside north of Srebrenica in eastern Bosnia where, on a hot August day in 2000, I stood witness to the first day that forensics experts were examining hundreds of skeletons of Bosniaks (Bosnian Muslims) dumped from a winding dirt road after they had been massacred by Bosnian Serb militia at a warehouse in the valley below five years earlier. Only ethnic Serbs lived in the area after the fall of Srebrenica in July 1995, and nobody had bothered to report the existence of an entire hillside of human bones. One Bosniak refugee returning that month to his home nearby had immediately alerted war crimes investigators. Another returnee told me, "We have to return to our homes here. We can look at Serb eyes because they are the guilty ones. We'll always look at their eyes and they'll be ashamed." She described how the men and boys of Srebrenica fled north as she heard their cries from the woods, "Help me! Don't leave me here!" Then, she muttered, "the Serbs would ambush and kill them."

Often, while listening to senior officials sitting comfortably in the White House Situation Room explain why other national priorities trumped atrocities and the pursuit of war criminals, I wanted Nancy and the other mutilated bodies and missing souls of girls, boys, women, and men of Bosnia, Rwanda, eastern Congo, and Sierra Leone to file silently through that wood-paneled room and remind policy-makers of the fate of ordinary human beings. Who among the powerful would embrace the new imperative to confront *hostis humani generis*, the enemy of all mankind? Who would compel atrocity lords to heel before the bar of justice?

During the last decade of the twentieth century, one of the most ambitious judicial experiments in the history of humankind—a global assault on the architects of atrocities—found its purpose as mass killings and ethnic cleansing consumed entire regions of the earth. The grand objective since 1993 has been to end impunity at the highest levels of government and the military not only for genocide, which captures the popular imagination with its heritage in the Holocaust, but also for the far less understood offenses of crimes against humanity and even war crimes. Because such crimes coexist as heinous acts in almost every atrocity zone, and because the criminal tribunals built in recent years have bundled them together in complex prosecutorial strategies, I use the term *atrocity crimes*, which I describe in greater detail in the postscript concluding this book.

The futile slogan of "never again" after World War II collapsed under the weight of atrocity crimes occurring again and again. Yet, with some kinship to the postwar military tribunals at Nuremberg and Tokyo, an unprecedented number of international war crimes tribunals appeared during the 1990s to bring to justice the leading perpetrators of such heinous crimes and end any legal basis for impunity. Such justice may seem self-evident today, but in the last decade of the twentieth century the outcome was unknown. The challenges were colossal in those years, as hundreds of thousands of individuals participated in the murder and ethnic cleansing of millions. The vision of achieving justice was daunting. Often the easier path would have been to cut peace deals with the leading criminals. If the tribunals' work had been left to domestic courts, particularly in devastated societies, there simply would not have been any justice at all. A choice had to be made, and the international community finally was prepared to make that choice. Either there would be a court where leaders who planned and carried out atrocity crimes would be prosecuted, or they would walk free with impunity.

The task was not to construct a new legal order of perfect justice where every war criminal from the top leaders on down to the foot soldiers would be prosecuted. Rather, the challenge centered on building tribunals that would hold political and military leaders to account for the atrocity crimes unleashed on innocent civilian populations for which they were primarily responsible. By the turn of the century, it was no longer plausible to argue that there was a logical or moral basis for leadership impunity. Many political and military leaders undoubtedly will escape any reckoning before a court of law, but that will be for reasons other than the bankrupt theory of leadership impunity that used to enable them to commit the worst possible crimes against humankind.

I had the lead American job of building five separate war crimes tribunals. From 1993 through 1996, I was senior adviser and counsel to Dr. Madeleine Albright, America's ambassador to the United Nations, and wielded primary responsibility for her atrocity crimes work. In 1997, when Albright became the secretary of state, I was nominated by President Bill Clinton and confirmed by the Senate as the first-ever U.S. ambassador-at-large for war crimes issues. On the one hand, this initiative marked a sad commentary on the state of the world at the close of the twentieth century—fifty years or so after the Holocaust and the Nuremberg and Tokyo tribunals and two decades after the atrocity crimes that devastated Cambodia during the rule of Pol Pot. On the other hand, my ambassadorship demonstrated that the United States recognized the gravity of the situation and rose to the challenge. No other nation had seen fit to designate anyone as an ambassador to cover atrocity crimes.

At the age of forty-three, I embarked on one of the darkest possible diplomatic assignments. My job, in union with dedicated colleagues in New York and Washington and an ad hoc cast of foreign diplomats and government officials, was to build new courts of justice that would prosecute war criminals and deter further carnage. Some described me as the Ambassador to Hell, but in my more optimistic moments I was a carpenter of war crimes tribunals, each one requiring new architectural plans and novel attempts at credible justice amidst carnage and mayhem.

This book is the story of how the war crimes tribunals—the International Criminal Tribunals for the former Yugoslavia (the Yugoslav Tribunal) and Rwanda (the Rwanda Tribunal), the Special Court for Sierra Leone, the Extraordinary Chambers in the Courts of Cambodia (the Cambodia Tribunal), and the International Criminal Court—were conceived and built to end the impunity of political and military leaders. Initiatives to construct similar tribunals for the atrocities that occurred prior to or during my watch in southern Sudan, the Democratic Republic of the Congo, East Timor, Chechnya, and Iraq proved futile by the turn of the millennium. That is a different story. In this book, I write both as a diplomat who helped lead the tribunal-building project and as a scholar who strives to understand the legal and political significance of both the achievements and failures of the enterprise I call "credible justice."

More important, what follows is a historical narrative of how international justice evolved exponentially during the decade of the 1990s and into the twenty-first century and brought to an end the presumption of impunity for atrocity crimes. It is the story of the political decisions that shaped the tug-of-war between peace and justice during that dynamic period in world history. The tribunal era, launched in 1993, arose from the unleashing of colossal death and destruction that seemed almost surreal in the wake of the Cold War. During my eight-year watch in the United States government from 1993 to early 2001, failures far exceeded successes. Millions of noncombatant civilians perished, and thousands of settlements, towns, and cities were laid waste. Atrocity crimes exceeded the number of international peace agreements, new democracies, and major new symphonies and operas.

But in the twilight of a bloody century that had experienced the extinction of countless Congolese, the atrocities against the Armenians, the Stalinist purges, the Nanking massacre, the Holocaust, Chairman Mao's Cultural Revolution, Pol Pot's harvest of death, Uganda's suicide under Idi Amin, the Ethiopian nightmare under Mengistu, disappearances in Honduras, Chile, and Argentina, and Saddam Hussein's genocidal assault on the Kurds, there was much more death and destruction yet to come. Large-scale atrocities erupted in the Balkans, including Kosovo, and in Rwanda, Burundi, Sudan, Congo, Sierra Leone, Liberia, Ethiopia and Eritrea, Angola, East Timor, Iraq, Afghanistan, Burma, and Chechnya. A few of these were extensions of earlier conflicts and internal massacres. But most were freshly minted butcheries. Despite the information revolution, the economic prosperity, the military superiority of modern armies, and the enlightened diplomacy of the new world order following the Cold War, the killing, mutilating, and wanton destruction proliferated. Only a few atrocities met a rapid response from diplomats and civilized warriors.

While the killing machines kicked into high gear, the law that "governs" such atrocities grew during the 1990s. International lawyers and diplomats began to make good on the immediate post–World War II era when laws protecting civilians and other noncombatants were codified. My challenge was to enforce a revitalized set of laws against individual war criminals, including political and military leaders who had traditionally enjoyed de facto immunity from prosecution. So while the killing and mutilations and massive destruction erupted weekly across several continents, international law enforcement matured in parallel as a highly favored retaliatory response to some of the atrocities. International criminal tribunals became a reality, with their prosecutors forcing themselves upon governments to compel cooperation. Local prosecutors suddenly realized they too could project themselves onto the global scene if only they would indict someone like Augusto Pinochet of Chile under the rubric of "universal jurisdiction." International investigations of the Mafia and the Cali Cartel lost their luster as the world turned its attention to the chase for war criminals.

But a nagging challenge remained: would the creation of war crimes tribunals actually deter future war criminals? Cynics delighted in raising the deterrence question every step of the way during the 1990s. I repeatedly had to prove a negative—that would-be perpetrators of atrocity crimes stayed their hand because of the threat of an international prosecution. Deterrence is a relative concept. How effectively has the death penalty or the multiplicity of municipal, state, and federal courts deterred murderers in American society? Have the criminal courts of Detroit ended all violence and theft there? Seeking evidence of rapid deterrence in the war crimes tribunals is like the quest for instant gratification by teenagers and egotistical professionals—it is a bizarrely twisted objective fraught with inflated expectations and unpredictable outcomes. The Yugoslav Tribunal certainly was conceived with the goal of having some kind of deterrent impact on the fighting in the Balkans, but no one could predict how much it would influence the depraved minds at work in the region or whether there would result any sudden cessation of heinous violence.

I posit, but cannot prove, that after several decades, or even most optimistically after several years, a country once consumed by atrocities stands a chance of having learned the lessons of deterrence and being transformed into a society that holds war criminals in contempt and breeds them no more. The war crimes tribunals were not designed, and should not be burdened, with all responsibility for creating a culture of deterrence and hence of peace and stability. They can play an important part in that endeavor, but failed states and conflict-ridden societies require far more from the international community and from their own indigenous sources of modernity to establish progressive societies. Thrusting the burden of ending all atrocities on the backs of the tribunals is naive at best and dangerous at worst.

The defeated citizens of Germany and Japan after World War II largely despised the Nuremberg and Tokyo military tribunals, which themselves inspired no decisive break from the past in those societies.[2] But later generations absorbed the historical significance of the tribunals and became champions of human rights and justice. Germany's support of the International Criminal Court is unwavering today. I often observed German negotiators invoking the memory of Nuremberg as if it were their redemptive predicate for a permanent court. Japanese society appears even now more accepting of its soldiers' wartime atrocities. But Japan became a remarkably nonaggressive nation (at least militarily), joined the International Criminal Court, and strongly supports international justice initiatives such as the Cambodia Tribunal. Such projustice outcomes may be many years or decades coming for Sudan or the Democratic Republic of the Congo or Serbia. But imagine how differently events would have unfolded if the atrocity masterminds of the Balkans, Rwanda, and West Africa had not been isolated and brought to credible justice by the war crimes tribunals since 1993.

There already are signs of deterrence emerging from the work of the International Criminal Court. For example, the court's arrest warrants against leaders of the Lord's Resistance Army (LRA) in Uganda helped drive the LRA into serious negotiations and inspire defections. In the documentary film *The Reckoning*,[3] Patrick Makasi, the former director of operations of the LRA until his defection in October 2007, admits, "In the bush, ICC is always the main discussion. Sometimes they talk about it five times a day. We hear that once you are taken to the ICC, you are as good as dead, and we hear there are already people taken to face ICC trials.... We hear that once you're taken there you have no more choice. I guess that's why [LRA leader] Joseph Kony fears the ICC. Maybe he knows more. Joseph Kony is afraid of ICC." Fear does not necessarily translate to deterrence, but it is a powerful wedge on war criminals.

I write in this book of crime scenes and victims, of the corridors of power and how policy-makers confronted megacrimes, how war criminals were pursued, and how courts to prosecute these war criminals were created against daunting odds. My primary research tool was personal notebooks covering eight years of work. I also drew upon declassified State Department cables.[4] Make no mistake—building the war crimes tribunals was a collective effort with dedicated, indeed at times zealous, advocates for international criminal justice from other governments, the United Nations, civil society, and among scholars and jurists spanning the globe. But I represented the most powerful nation, the United States, under the leadership of President Bill Clinton and Ambassador (later secretary of state) Madeleine K. Albright. Their commitment to international justice made a significant difference in what unfolded during the Clinton administration, even though, as related on these pages, they sometimes weakened in their resolve.

No one, including myself, is blameless for the worst atrocities that took place, and this book will describe mistakes and lost opportunities bluntly. But I embarked on a mission for justice that drew from the lessons of the Nuremberg and Tokyo trials and yet proved more challenging—in law and enforcement—than the task that confronted my predecessors after World War II. Theirs was victors' justice; mine was the long tedious struggle for international justice often targeting indicted fugitives either on the run or shielded by their own power. No one could dictate the outcome.

A world burdened with atrocities can challenge the legality, morality, and even the honor of modern war as it seeks to end the killing. During the 1990s conventional warfare morphed into state-sponsored massive crimes. The political responsibility of governments bowed to the judicial accountability of tribunals. Christian notions of the "just war," which were revived during the Gulf War of 1990–1991 and again with Operation Iraqi Freedom in 2003, became hopelessly entangled with proliferating rules to protect civilians during hostilities. This tectonic shift initially caught everyone off guard. While the laws of armed conflict mandate civilized means of conducting warfare, during the last two decades a frightening number of combatants, led by a new cast of war criminals, fought in defiance of those laws, brutally assaulting large numbers of civilians, destroying private property, and obliterating the environment. Nothing was left to the imagination.

We struggle anew with the nagging paradox of law and war, a seeming conflict that humankind has confronted for centuries. The challenges of armed combat grow with the number and intensity of internal civil wars, the callous targeting of civilians as a war aim or to fulfill a quest for power, and the desperate need for nations to intervene militarily to stop atrocities. These challenges also are defined by how the U.N. Charter limits armed conflicts and with the possibilities presented by technologically wondrous weaponry. At the same time the legal code has grown to regulate warfare despite the emergence of new atrocities. The formula to end impunity for atrocity crimes is deeply rooted in the rules to regulate war between civilized and not-so-civilized armies and in the deepening influence of human rights law. As we venture deeper into the twenty-first century, there undoubtedly will be just wars to wage, but we must understand how to wage them justly. When President Obama invoked the "just war" doctrine in his acceptance speech for the Nobel Peace Prize in November 2009, he put the issue squarely on the table, once again.[5]

I learned through extraordinary journeys that *international justice* has as much to do with the vagaries of global politics and our own moral strength as it does with treaties, courtrooms, prosecutors, judges, and defendants. The modern pursuit of international justice is the discovery of our values, our weaknesses, our strengths, and our will to persevere and to render punishment.

My own journey to Hell and back had no shortage of "reality checks" framing the grim business of confronting atrocity crimes. My boss, Madeleine Albright, was the most powerful woman in the world at the time, and I was honored to work for her. She often construed herself as the "mother of the war crimes tribunals," and in our final days together she scribbled that I was the "father of the war crimes tribunals." Working for Albright took me into almost every corner of America's far-flung foreign policy during the first term of the Clinton administration (1993–1996). Her ambassadorship to the United Nations created a "candy store of issues," as she described it, that propelled us through every day. As her representative on the Deputies Committee of the National Security Council, I participated in practically every major foreign-policy decision of Clinton's first term, and played my role in how the other deputies and the principals debated the hundreds of options through the years.

Albright displayed great cunning in her public service, and she brilliantly mastered both the Washington bureaucracy and the U.N. behemoth in New York. I marveled at how she could coax the most obstinate opponent into conceding vital points, while pitching over the cliff those who dared to presume that she, a woman in a man's world of diplomacy, had a weak spine. Some of my most enjoyable moments were when I played a bit part in her theater of misperceptions. During my early years with Albright, I would witness a group of men (and typically only men) enter her office at the State Department in Washington and plop down on comfortable couches for a policy meeting with her, while I sat on one of the hard-back chairs to take notes and occasionally contribute a few words. Ambassador Albright would rise from her desk, greet the gentlemen, and ask if they wanted coffee. Invariably, some of the men would say, "Yes, please," and expect Albright to sit down with them and have either her secretary or me serve the coffee. But Albright strode over to a side table, slowly poured the coffee, and brought each cup, one at a time, to the anointed men. Our first test was to see whether anyone objected to the U.S. permanent representative to the United Nations personally serving him coffee. Sometimes the men simply thanked her. The second test was to wait for one of the kind men to object and offer to help carry the coffee cups. But she would stop the poor soul and say cheerfully to the entire group, "Oh, please don't bother. You know, I used to do this for a living when I was a housewife." From that moment forward, Madeleine Albright controlled the meeting as the men sunk a bit lower in those soft couches.

Among the many experiences that demonstrated Albright's character, one stands out for me personally. My daughter Kate was born on January 21, 1993, and thus was the first baby to arrive among the relatively few new staffers then working in the Clinton administration, which had commenced the previous day. I always could look at young Kate and see the longevity of the Clinton administration in her appearance. When my wife Michelle returned to evening classes at her law school, she handed baby Kate over to me at the entrance of the State Department for the few hours that overlapped between her need to be in class and my need to stay on the job. My office became Kate's way station for a few months. I would carry her on my shoulder to meetings with State Department colleagues and while working at my desk. Albright, the mother of three daughters, embraced the reality of my fatherly duties with good cheer and support. I am told that I broke a few molds at Foggy Bottom as astonished men and women watched me multi-task. Soon Kate was enrolled in a day care center, but I owe Albright and our colleagues in her Washington office my sincere gratitude for tolerating those unorthodox evenings.

The war crimes tribunals were conceived during the 1990s. Albright, herself deeply invested in the assault on atrocity crimes, delegated much of that portfolio to me and encouraged me to spearhead the issue within the government, using her dual power centers at the United Nations and in the State Department to persuade an anemic government. I often spent as much time fighting the Washington bureaucracy as I did negotiating in

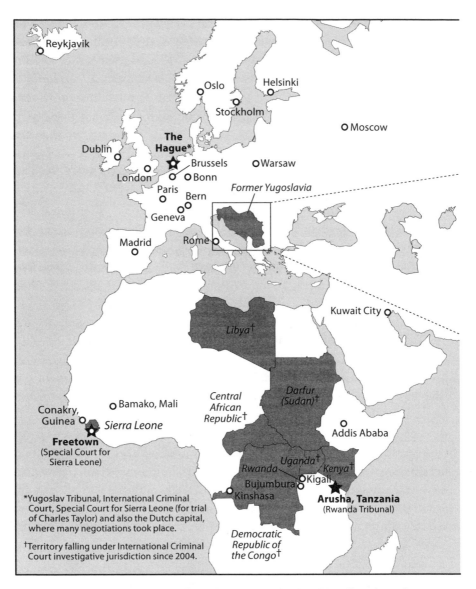

Figure 1. Map of atrocity regions, tribunal locations, and major cities where the author conducted negotiations.

foreign capitals and with U.N. officials (see figure 1). These were pioneering years as the killing fields multiplied across the globe. When Clinton's second term arrived in 1997 and Albright became secretary of state, support for the investigation and prosecution of atrocity crimes became an official diplomatic function in Washington with creation of the Office of War Crimes

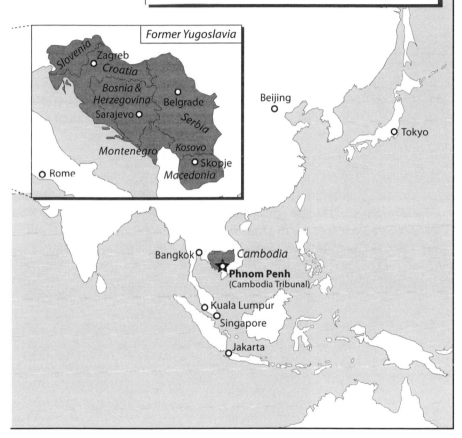

Issues in Albright's State Department. I led this office as an ambassador from the day it opened its doors in mid-1997 to the end of the Clinton era.

I witnessed firsthand the carnage of atrocity crimes in Rwanda, Bosnia, Croatia, Burundi, the Congo, Sierra Leone, Sudan, Guinea, and Kosovo. A numbness can descend on anyone who witnesses too many such horrors. But I was not just an observer. I had the job of doing something about these crimes. Often what I could do was pathetically too little and too late. In reality, I got used to mass graves being exhumed, to the sallow faces of the decomposing victims, to the grievously wounded victims populating the filthy wards of buildings that were called hospitals. But I never adjusted to the agony of children. Those who survived would gaze at me searching for answers and relief that I could not provide. I saw so much misery for so many years that my memories remain consumed by human suffering. Of course, thousands of humanitarian workers and noble soldiers witness far more misery arising from war, atrocities, and natural calamities every day. Their courage and selflessness in the face of seemingly impossible challenges far exceed my own efforts.

But this story only occasionally reveals the literal terror or personal impact of atrocities. Many others have written about the massacres, ethnic cleansing, and other human tragedies that I witnessed. My task, and what this book relates, was how to bring the masterminds of carnage to justice, however implausible it may have seemed to others. Sometimes, against enormous odds, the quest for credible justice stood a fighting chance. Each war crimes tribunal built during the 1990s is a story of trial and error, innovative lawmaking, political intrigue, and obstinate personalities. The cast of characters in each story includes war criminals, public and military officials, judges, prosecutors, international bureaucrats, and the ever-present victims. The memories in this book frame a decade of evil and justice, each struggling to ascend in a world of daily jousts between warlords and jurists.

PART I

CHAPTER ONE
AN ECHO OF NUREMBERG

There is an echo in this chamber today. The Nuremberg
principles have been reaffirmed.

U.S. ambassador Madeleine K. Albright speaking in the
United Nations Security Council on February 22, 1993

IN THE BEGINNING THERE WAS NO GRAND DESIGN TO BUILD A SERIES OF WAR
crimes tribunals culminating in a permanent international criminal court.
No one could foresee that there would be enough slaughter of innocents in
the 1990s to beckon forth judges and prosecutors for atrocity crimes trials
in courts scattered across the globe. But the atrocities in the Balkans in
1991 and 1992 prompted a reckoning for the perpetrators of the ethnic
cleansing, killings, and abusive detentions in that region.

Within the relatively short span of eighteen months, beginning with the
Serbs' siege of Vukovar, Croatia, in August 1991, an estimated 3,300 Croatians, 11,500 Serbs, and 30,500 Bosniaks perished.[1] Tens of thousands of
villagers and farmers—mostly Muslim—were ethnically cleansed from their
homes and farms. Strobe Talbott's column of November 25, 1991, in *Time*
magazine published a photograph of European observers comfortably seated
on lawn chairs, dressed in white, observing the targeted shelling of the historic Croatian city of Dubrovnik on the Adriatic Sea.[2] The picture epitomized
how the West failed an early test in the post–Cold War era. As the Soviet
empire crumbled, Yugoslavia descended into war, and the West watched as
innocents paid with their lives.

The public turning point occurred in the summer of 1992 with the por-
trayal of the Omarska detention camp, first by Roy Gutman of *Newsday* and

then by ITN television reporters and the *Guardian* newspaper. Scores of detention camps holding Bosniaks had been discovered scarring the east Bosnian landscape. Gutman's book, *A Witness to Genocide*, later told the much larger story of the ethnic cleansing of Bosnia and Herzegovina in 1992.[3] The United Nations Security Council created in October 1992 a five-person Commission to Investigate War Crimes in the former Yugoslavia to compile evidence of the atrocities sweeping across Bosnia and Croatia, with some expectation that the experts might recommend a criminal tribunal if the evidence so warranted.[4]

In August 1992, under the auspices of the Conference for Security and Cooperation in Europe (CSCE), a three-man team including Swedish judge and diplomat Hans Corell, who the next year would become legal counsel at the United Nations, launched investigative work that led months later to their recommendation that the international community "draft a convention that would establish an international *ad hoc* tribunal to deal with war crimes and crimes against humanity committed in the former Yugoslavia."[5] The CSCE Council of Ministers instructed the team by the end of 1992 to explore "the possibility of the establishment of an *ad hoc* tribunal."[6] Though the U.N. Security Council soon would leapfrog their initiative, Corell's group nonetheless submitted important draft concepts to the United Nations that helped frame the ultimate statute of the Yugoslav Tribunal. Other U.N. bodies—including the Commission on Human Rights and the General Assembly—raised the prospect for prosecutions of atrocity crimes, including the possibility of an ad hoc international criminal tribunal to prosecute perpetrators of "war crimes" in Bosnia and Herzegovina.[7]

Bill Clinton condemned the Balkans atrocities on the presidential campaign trail in 1992.[8] The last secretary of state of President George H. W. Bush's administration, Lawrence Eagleburger, declared on December 16, 1992, that the United States had provided the Security Council Commission to Investigate War Crimes with the names of five persons suspected of crimes against humanity. He boldly proclaimed: "We know that crimes against humanity have occurred, and we know when and where they occurred. We know, moreover, which forces committed those crimes, and under whose command they operated. And we know, finally, who the political leaders are and to whom those military commanders were—and still are—responsible.... [A] second Nuremberg awaits the practitioners of ethnic cleansing."[9] He named Bosnian Serb leaders Radovan Karadzic and Ratko Mladic and Serbian president Slobodan Milosevic. Eagleburger's bravado seized the headlines but did not jump-start any tribunal-building process in the final weeks before Bill Clinton became the forty-second president.

In my own transition work advising Madeleine Albright for her confirmation hearing to be the U.S. permanent representative to the United Nations, I focused more on the war and the peace process in Bosnia and Herzegovina than on any grand scheme for accountability. As Albright made her pre-hearing courtesy rounds in the Senate, no one suggested that pursuing justice would somehow solve the military or humanitarian challenges. However, newly elected Senator Paul Coverdell, a Republican from Georgia, and Senator Joe Biden, a long-serving Democrat from Delaware (and future vice president), spoke forcefully to her about the atrocities. Coverdell told her, "If war crimes are not pursued, then all Serbs will be culpable and it will continue to play itself out in a violent manner. We don't quite know where we are going in Bosnia, do we?" No senator yet pressed her for a war crimes tribunal. In these early discussions, Albright spoke of the "major failure of European institutions" and asked whether the arms embargo that had been imposed on Bosnia by the Security Council in 1991[10] should be lifted, and how the United States could lead a humanitarian intervention of some character. Senators listened, nodded, and wished her good luck.

A week before Bill Clinton's first-term inauguration, Warren Christopher, in his Senate hearing for confirmation as secretary of state, pledged that the new administration would support war crimes trials in the Balkans, but he clearly had not thought through how the task would be accomplished.[11] Christopher's commitment, however, opened the door for a growing chorus of support for judicial accountability. Albright's hearing for confirmation as ambassador to the United Nations, on the day following Clinton's inauguration, confirmed the point. She confronted the issue during an exchange with Senator Daniel Patrick Moynihan of New York, a former Harvard professor, American ambassador to the United Nations, and recent author on international law. Moynihan observed that genocide was taking place in Bosnia and Herzegovina and that there was a "systematic effort to destroy a population in order that a territory may be ethnically pure." He wanted Albright "to press the United Nations for war crimes tribunals," and she agreed to pursue a tribunal.[12]

Yet Albright remained cautious in those early few days. Shortly after the hearing, she responded to a written question from Senator Larry Pressler of South Dakota as to whether she would support the establishment of a U.N. war crimes tribunal to investigate Serbian government atrocities: "The

United States is actively supporting the investigation of atrocities in former Yugoslavia, including Serbian government atrocities. We [the former administration] proposed the establishment of the U.N. War Crimes Commission to investigate atrocities and prepare information useful for the prosecutions. It is imperative that persons responsible for atrocities be held individually responsible."[13] It would have been impolitic to have become so committed to the tribunal as Senator Moynihan had made her seem before Albright could arrive in New York and garner support within the Security Council to achieve just such an objective. Once confirmed, she moved quickly at the United Nations to make creation of the Yugoslav Tribunal her first major achievement.

War and justice, however, marched to different tunes in Washington. The Balkans war was spiraling out of control and seized the most attention. The quest for accountability more often was a sideshow, though of growing importance as the years progressed. Sometimes the two quests of peace and justice would intersect, but usually they advanced along separate pathways. Indeed, one of the common refrains in histories and commentaries about the Yugoslav Tribunal is that the effort to establish the war crimes tribunal served as a token alternative to the tougher choice of military intervention by Western powers during the critical years of 1993, 1994, and 1995. Some scholars believe that the Yugoslav Tribunal diverted into judicial investigations the policy decisions that leaders should have made to intervene with decisive military force to end the Balkan atrocities.[14] In other words, the "soft" option of an international criminal tribunal represented a form of action much less costly (but also less immediate in results) than the "hard" option of military intervention. If there was hope for the Yugoslav Tribunal, it was centered more on its potential to deter further atrocity crimes in the region. Since it took more than a year to hire a prosecutor, the real threat of the tribunal to actually force politicians and military commanders who are responsible for atrocities to stand trial did not materialize until late 1994. Even then, the genocide at Srebrenica in July 1995 demonstrated how fragile was the deterrent value of the Yugoslav Tribunal during its early years.

Explorations of military options in the Balkans were separate and highly complex exercises by policy-makers; the prospect of a criminal tribunal had very little to do with those decisions. Yet the erroneous logic persisted that the Yugoslav Tribunal served as the crutch upon which a timid Western alliance leaned to ease its conscience, while avoiding the risks (military, political, moral) that decisive military intervention would have incurred. The Clinton administration often proudly cited the Yugoslav Tribunal as an important initiative in the overall policy process for the Balkans. But discussions and decisions regarding military and other enforcement options (such as economic and diplomatic sanctions) were not propelled by the excuse that establishment of the criminal tribunal covered our backside. The failure to act militarily resulted from policies and circumstances that coexisted with the Yugoslav Tribunal but were not driven by its presence in The Hague.

In fact, military and sanctions strategists often resisted appeals for judicial resources and personnel and dismissed the importance of the Yugoslav Tribunal as primary leverage in negotiations. They offered to sacrifice it for the slightest concession by Serb or Croat leaders.[15] During March 1994, Albright, John Shattuck, who was the State Department's top policy maker on human rights, and a few other senior officials repelled a strong push by negotiators in the Bosnia Contact Group, which included the United Kingdom, France, Germany, and Russia alongside the United States, to grant amnesty from tribunal prosecution to Radovan Karadzic, Ratko Mladic, Slobodan Milosevic, and other Balkan leaders as bait for their cooperation in the sputtering peace talks [16] If the Yugoslav Tribunal had been the excuse for governmental inaction that some presume, then strict adherence to the tribunal's mandate would have been accorded far more importance and deference in policy-making as a panacea for inaction. But Albright, Shattuck, and I had to struggle every step of the way to sustain enforcement of the Yugoslav Tribunal's authority in deliberations over U.S. and U.N. policy in the Balkans.

Birth of the Yugoslav Tribunal

Before 1993, no war crimes tribunal had ever been established in the middle of the very armed conflict it was tasked to investigate for the commission of atrocity crimes. It was a novel experiment of dual-track justice and warfare, but a union that would become increasingly common with the advent of the permanent International Criminal Court. (Conflicts either raged on or smoldered in all the situations investigated by the permanent court in its early years.) The U.N. Security Council approved in late February 1993 the establishment of a tribunal under the most difficult circumstances, where brutal atrocities continued to bloody the soil and the lead perpetrators were men and women of enormous military and political power and hubris. They were not the vanquished, and the Security Council did not operate in any theater of victor's justice.

The Yugoslav Tribunal arose when no one knew who would prevail militarily, what territory the various warring factions would control, how many more atrocities—with their deaths, maiming, devastated towns, and revolting detention centers—would unfold in the years ahead. At the tribunal's inception, no one predicted that it would take seventeen months to agree upon a chief prosecutor for the tribunal, an essential step to any criminal law enterprise. In early 1993, a desperate hope to impose some measure of justice on the apocalypse unfolding in Bosnia and Croatia eclipsed doubts or uncertainties about the future.

The speed with which the Security Council initially authorized the Yugoslav Tribunal resulted primarily from the leadership of the United States and France within the council. The American lead relied almost exclusively on the new ambassador to the United Nations, Madeleine Albright. She seized the opportunity to make her mark quickly in the council on a subject that everyone could understand and which conveniently did not conflict with any other Washington priority for the new administration.

The notion of the Security Council using its power under the U.N. Charter to create an international criminal tribunal was novel because conventional theory argued for a treaty, entered into by governments, as the constitutional basis for establishing a criminal court that could prosecute and punish war criminals. Each ratifying nation would agree to the jurisdiction of such a tribunal and its power to render the ultimate sanction—to deprive individuals of their liberty. But time was not on the side of a multiyear endeavor to create a war crimes tribunal for the Balkans along the conventional path.

Within days of her confirmation as the U.S. permanent representative to the United Nations, Albright instructed me to begin moving the Washington bureaucracy toward a firm U.S. policy to establish a war crimes tribunal for the Balkans conflict. Much depended on whether the Security Council would take the decisive first step. Albright had set the stage for rapid action with a draft resolution recommending that the U.N. secretary-general prepare a report with a proposed statute for the tribunal, which would be acted on by subsequent resolution of the Security Council.

The early February surge of American support for a war crimes tribunal in the Balkans rested on several pillars: (1) that large numbers of Bosnians and Croatians were victims of systematic assaults on civilian populations; (2) that any tribunal created would neither be a victor's tribunal nor entail an indictment of any collective body of people; and (3) that the focus would be prosecuting the leading individual perpetrators of the atrocity crimes. The tribunal would enforce international law against individuals only and not against governments or groups of people. The latter traditionally was the task of the Security Council—to enforce international law against governments. Nations, at least in theory, shoulder some responsibility to ensure that their own citizens comply with the fundamental norms not only of codified law but of fundamental human decency and of civilization itself.

The legacy of Nuremberg and its focus on individual criminal responsibility reasserted itself as we labored to build a new tribunal. There was little difficulty in determining what constitutes an atrocity crime ripe for prosecution by the tribunal, for by 1993 the general framework of such crimes—genocide, crimes against humanity, and war crimes—was embedded in international law to a degree that welcomed a new age of criminal prosecution. The inevitable nuances would have to be sorted out by the judges in their reasoned judgments.

Justice in the Pursuit of Peace

The threshold question remained ever present: how could the Security Council, which is charged under the U.N. Charter to address threats to international peace and security, invoke any legal authority to establish an international criminal court? It had never dared to do so in the past, even avoiding the issue with Pol Pot and Saddam Hussein after their rampages. The Security Council wages both peace and war through deployment of peacekeeping forces or multinational "peace enforcement" troops, such as in the Gulf War intervention of 1991. Nowhere in the U.N. Charter is there any explicit authority to build criminal tribunals.

But often overlooked is a potent provision of the Charter, Article 41, which empowers the council to use nonmilitary measures to respond to threats to international peace and security. The nonexhaustive list does not exclude judicial measures, so the Security Council translated its Article 41 power into creation of the Yugoslav Tribunal.

Some nations, including Mexico, Brazil, and China, challenged the authority of the Security Council to create any international criminal courts, particularly the Yugoslav Tribunal and, almost two years later, the Rwanda

Tribunal.[17] These disgruntled governments agreed to contribute to U.N. General Assembly funding for the tribunals, but each did so under varying degrees of protest. The legal debate over the legitimacy of the Security Council creating an international criminal tribunal was not resolved until the Yugoslav Tribunal rendered its first major decision in the *Tadic* case in October 1995, in which the court determined that the council indeed had such authority.[18]

By February 1993, Washington had submitted five reports to the Security Council substantiating information about atrocities in Bosnia and Croatia.[19] It became increasingly implausible to submit such reports and somehow ignore the need for accountability.

Albright actively drove the Security Council toward approval of Resolution 808 on February 22, 1993.[20] With this resolution, the fifteen member states of the council unanimously authorized the establishment of the Yugoslav Tribunal in principle, but required that the secretary-general report back to the council with options for the governing instrument of the tribunal so that it could actually be set up to hold trials. If the secretary-general's report proved acceptable, then a subsequent resolution would activate the tribunal as an operating court. Albright spoke to the council:

> There is an echo in this chamber today. The Nuremberg principles have been reaffirmed. We have preserved the long-neglected compact made by the community of civilized nations 48 years ago in San Francisco to create the United Nations and enforce the Nuremberg principles. The lesson that we are all accountable to international law may have finally taken hold in our collective memory. This will be no victor's tribunal. The only victor that will prevail in this endeavour is the truth. Unlike the world of the 1940s, international humanitarian law today is impressively codified, well understood, agreed upon and enforceable. The debates over the state of international law that so encumbered the Nuremberg Trials will not burden this tribunal.[21]

Albright urged the secretary-general to prepare the report on the statute of the tribunal as quickly as possible. She offered the talent and resources of the U.S. government to help him prepare the court's guiding constitution. It was an exhilarating and somewhat unanticipated way to begin an administration that had been known for its focus on domestic priorities ("It's the economy, stupid"). In fact, it would take many more deaths in Europe and Africa in the coming years to focus President Bill Clinton on atrocity crimes and, in his second term, prompt Albright and him to create my ambassadorship.

Drafting Pangs

The Security Council required the secretary-general to deliver a draft statute, or governing constitutional document, for the tribunal to the council by April 23, 1993. While the U.N. lawyers were tasked to prepare the draft statute, ten governments, including the United States, and five organizations weighed in quickly with proposed language for it.[22] The State Department's deputy legal adviser, career lawyer Michael Matheson, who was assisted by Michael Scharf and other staff attorneys, prepared the American draft based on a common-law approach to criminal justice—which was no surprise coming from the U.S. government.[23] Matheson's draft set the standard for nations to comply with arrest warrants and to produce evidence requested by the tribunal.[24] Ultimately, the Security Council mandated such cooperation by states and approved a statute enabling the Yugoslav Tribunal to seek enforcement action by the council. At the time, the idea of the Security Council roping in governments actually helped smooth over criticism about the council's authority to create the tribunal and deprive individuals of their liberty in the first place. The rule that governments comply with tribunal orders was more akin to the conventional power of the Security Council over nations, something everyone could understand.

Albright convened a group of American legal experts on May 13 to review the U.N. draft alongside others, including the American draft, that had been submitted following Resolution 808. She identified important issues for discussion, including the definition of crimes and how the judges would be elected. We all knew the Russians wanted some give-and-take in the drafting, while the French wanted to accept the report unaltered unless the United States had fundamental problems with it. The British were full steam ahead. Albright invited human rights and international law experts to review the secretary-general's draft statute on the top floor of the old U.S. Mission to the United Nations on First Avenue in New York City. Each expert proved to deliver prescient comments on issues that would emerge for years thereafter. Telford Taylor, the former American prosecutor at Nuremberg who had just published his monumental memoir of the post–World War II trials,[25] reminded everyone of the importance of the documentary record at Nuremberg. He feared that, in the Balkans, the more obscure paper trail would not tell the whole story. Witness testimony would prove vital to the prosecution. International law professor Louis Henkin, author of *How Nations Behave*,[26] stressed the importance of deterrence and collecting evidence even if trials do not always result. The important mission must be, he said, to establish the record.

Aryeh Neier of Human Rights Watch pointed to the vast quantity of information held by U.N. peacekeeping forces in Bosnia and Croatia and by the International Committee of the Red Cross; ultimately, releasing such information to the tribunal would prove difficult. Allan Gerson, who had the same job as mine working for former ambassador Jeanne Kirkpatrick, doubted the tribunal's effectiveness without documentary evidence, and pondered whether the court was meant to achieve historic justice or the much narrower purpose of criminal justice. Professor Louis Sohn noted the contrast between the draft statute's reference to the crime of genocide and the more narrow U.S. definition of genocide (although the tribunal judges ultimately embraced the U.S. definition, which requires the intent to destroy all or a *substantial* part of a targeted group of people).

Both Henkin and Professor Diane Orentlicher, who became deputy to one of my successors, Stephen Rapp, in the Barack Obama administration, expressed grave doubts about the statute's constrained view of crimes against humanity, namely, that such acts must be associated with an armed conflict before they can be prosecuted by the court. That concern dated back to the Nuremberg Tribunal and its requirement for such a linkage.[27] In the intervening decades the old requirement that crimes against humanity be tied to an armed conflict, which originated from concerns peculiar to Nuremberg, had been largely abandoned in international law. Under modern law, crimes against humanity could be prosecuted even if committed during a time of "peace" (for example, as part of an internal campaign of terror and repression rather than an armed conflict with insurgents or foreign forces).[28]

Everyone in the room was deeply concerned that the tribunal statute was regressive in requiring the old linkage between war and crimes against humanity. Ultimately the technical relationship was maintained so as not to open up the draft statute to unknown amendments on other issues. The tribunal judges quickly overcame this issue by framing crimes against humanity within the overall context of the Balkans' multiyear conflict.[29]

The draft statute placed primary jurisdiction in the tribunal, rather than in the domestic courts of Serbia-Montenegro, Bosnia and Herzegovina, and Croatia. This meant that the tribunal prosecutor and judges could decide at any time that a case must be prosecuted before the Yugoslav Tribunal and not before any national court. Gerson found the formula too heavy-handed, but Neier pushed back, arguing it would be very dangerous to opt for "concurrent jurisdiction" with national courts without the fail-safe power of primary jurisdiction. He contended that the jurisdiction of Nuremberg was a different formula: trying only top Nazi leaders at the international tribunal in Nuremberg and leaving the four occupying Allied nations to set up other tribunals in their own zones of Germany to go after lower-ranked suspects from the Nazi era.

Former vice presidential candidate Geraldine Ferraro pressed a critical point, namely that the statute had to recognize rape as a war crime and a crime against humanity. She argued for amending the statute to make this clear. In the end, her suggestion was not accommodated. But the tribunal prosecutor and judges soon incorporated rape as a frequent war crime or crime against humanity, and eventually as a form of genocide.[30] Ferraro also argued for the need to employ qualified women, including some experienced with treating rape trauma, for the tribunal's staff. Albright willingly pressed that point hard in the early months of the Yugoslav Tribunal, insisting that either the prosecutor or the judge nominated by the United States be a woman.

Following the experts' meeting, Washington concluded that it would not seek any revision to the draft statute. Officials feared that the Russians and Chinese, as well as the Mexicans and perhaps even the Serbians, would seize the opportunity to weaken the tribunal, including knocking out its primary jurisdiction. The risks of opening up the statute to amendments were too great; fortunately, enough support gathered within the Security Council to accept the secretary-general's draft without change. But Albright and some of her colleagues on the council were determined to establish that the judges' future interpretations of the document should accord with the original intent of the Security Council members.

On May 25, 1993, the Security Council unanimously adopted Resolution 827, which locked in the secretary-general's unaltered draft statute as the guiding constitution of the Yugoslav Tribunal. Three preambular clauses of the resolution would resonate with both optimists and cynics in regard to the tribunal for years thereafter:

> *Determined* to put an end to such crimes and to take effective measures to bring to justice the persons who are responsible for them,
> *Convinced* that in the particular circumstances of the former Yugoslavia the establishment as an ad hoc measure by the Council of an international tribunal

and the prosecution of persons responsible for serious violations of international humanitarian law would enable this aim to be achieved and would contribute to the restoration and maintenance of peace,

Believing that the establishment of an international tribunal and the prosecution of persons responsible for the above-mentioned violations of international humanitarian law will contribute to ensuring that such violations are halted and effectively redressed....

These clauses set up the argument that the Yugoslav Tribunal would be a significant deterrent to further atrocity crimes in the Balkans and a key contributor to achieving peace in the region. In reality, they were idealistic visions of the future, and should not have been so optimistically stated in Resolution 827. At the time, however, it was understandable that there was so much hope invested in the enterprise as the military situation continued to deteriorate. Once the hard work of actually building the Yugoslav Tribunal began outside the media spotlight, and military strategizing again dominated policy discussions, the vision of deterrence and peace expressed in these clauses faded until the war ended two and one-half years later.

The operative provision of Resolution 827 that became the most challenging to enforce required all nations to cooperate fully with the Yugoslav Tribunal and to amend their domestic law to implement the resolution and the tribunal statute, "including the obligation of States to comply with requests for assistance or orders issued by a Trial Chamber under Article 29 of the Statute."[31] Throughout the Clinton administration I spent a great deal of my time ensuring U.S. compliance with that provision and coaxing other governments to do the same. The task gnawed at theories of sovereignty and challenged officials to use their own powers to advance the cause of international justice.

In her remarks following adoption of Resolution 827, Albright delivered several interpretative statements—as de facto legislative history—that, in retrospect, reveal useful foresight sustained in the judgments of the tribunal.[32] Some other views she expressed, looking back, were not well conceived.[33] But she was right to explain that the Yugoslav Tribunal could enforce key provisions of the 1949 Geneva Conventions and their 1977 Additional Protocols as part of the "laws or customs of war" because all those treaties had been ratified by Yugoslavia in prior years. This proved to be a critical step in broadening the character of war crimes the tribunal could investigate and prosecute. Second, she clarified that crimes against humanity would be prosecuted because they occurred "during a period of armed conflict" and thus were not necessarily linked to acts of war, which had been the Nuremberg standard. She opened the space for the judges later to dispose of the armed conflict linkage required at Nuremberg by simply concluding that all crimes against humanity occurred during the Balkans conflict, and then focusing on the actual crimes rather than analyzing everything through the prism of war.[34] The nexus to armed conflict was completely removed one year later when the crimes against humanity provision of the Rwanda Tribunal was drafted, and would be omitted in the statute of the Special Court for Sierra Leone, the law establishing the Cambodia Tribunal, and the Rome Statute of the International Criminal Court.

However, Albright went on to require that crimes against humanity must occur "as part of a widespread or systematic attack against any civilian population on national, political, ethnic, racial, gender, or religious grounds." The first part of this formula—"widespread or systematic attack against any civilian population"—was widely recognized and would be repeated through the subsequent statutes of the criminal tribunals. The second part listing numerous discriminatory grounds for such attacks (political, ethnic, racial, gender, or religious) was sourced back in part to Article 6(c) of the London Charter of the Nuremberg Tribunal in 1945, but thereafter the linkage of atrocity crimes to any of these grounds was not regarded as a prerequisite for a statute to achieve the status of customary international law. The fact that the Rwanda Tribunal and Cambodia Tribunal statutes repeated this discriminatory formula reflected the unique circumstances of the atrocity crimes in Rwanda and of the Cambodian government's insistence that the Rwanda Tribunal language on crimes against humanity be duplicated for the Cambodia Tribunal. The Rome Statute of the International Criminal Court clarified that the linkage to any discriminatory targeting—such as against an ethnic group—that the original formula suggested simply is no longer required when establishing a widespread or systematic criminal assault on a civilian population. Such discriminatory intent is a factor in defining persecution as a crime against humanity, just as the London Charter stipulated, but not when defining the many other crimes against humanity, such as extermination and sexual violence.

A Relatively Cheap Bargain

The murdered, mutilated, and displaced victims of the atrocity crimes covered by five war crimes tribunals number in the millions, and their devastated property is valued in the billions of dollars. These are megacrimes of the greatest complexity and size. Imagine investigating the 1.8 million individual murders that occurred in Cambodia, or the 300,000 killings in Bosnia, or 800,000 deaths, mostly by machete, in Rwanda. How does one do that on the cheap? Nonetheless, the relatively modest annual budgets of the five war crimes tribunals have invited repeated protests that international justice is too expensive and that such funding could be much better spent on domestic priorities in conflict-ravaged societies, including greatly strengthening national courts and law enforcement capabilities.[35] The sad reality is that national legislatures, including the U.S. Congress, simply do not appropriate foreign assistance in any significant amounts for the upgrading of foreign courts, prisons, or police forces unless, as shown in Iraq and Afghanistan, the objective is to detain alleged terrorists and others deemed threats to U.S. security interests. I repeatedly visited Capitol Hill to seek such money for Rwanda's and Bosnia's judicial systems and met countless deer eyes of indifference. No member of Congress wins votes back home for the building of courts overseas.

The United Nations financed the Yugoslav Tribunal's combined budgets from 1993 through 2008 of $1.48 billion and the Rwanda Tribunal's expenses from 1995 through 2009 of $1.26 billion. The United States, the largest funder of the two tribunals, covered about 25 percent of these bills and added about $17.5 million in voluntary contributions. The Special Court for Sierra Leone required $215 million of mostly voluntary funds, with the United States again being the largest donor. The initial five-year budget of voluntary funds for the Cambodia Tribunal totaled about $100 million, although Washington refused during the Bush administration to chip in until 2008 with a $1.5 million donation. Japan has been the primary donor for the Cambodia Tribunal. The member states of the International Criminal Court financed that body to the sum of about $377 million during its initial eight years. These numbers cover *all* prosecution and court administrative costs and most defense fees for all cases before the five tribunals. Thus, the total cost of the war crimes tribunals—roughly $3.43 billion from 1993 through 2009—fell below the program costs of two Stealth bombers and equaled the two-week budget of American military operations in Iraq. Expenditures for two flights of the Space Shuttle, or about 17 percent of the cash bonuses paid out by Wall Street firms in 2008,[36] could cover the entire international budget of the war crimes tribunals during this sixteen-year period.[37]

War crimes tribunals were created to pursue justice and, over the long term, influence the attitudes of would-be perpetrators and targeted victim populations. It is preposterous to assume that they would have significant short-term impacts on warring parties. Diplomacy, economic sanctions, and military actions have been far more important for the immediate pursuit of peace and stability. But the tribunals began a process that steadily produced indictments (which shame, delegitimize, and sideline war criminals), prosecutions, and historical records, all of which help build the peace over time.

In order to bring the most powerful war criminals to heel in real time, the verdict is in: we sometimes need war crimes tribunals, which are a relatively cheap bargain for the sake of justice and the future well-being of victimized populations.

"We Need to Break That Mold."

Throughout the 1990s, I fielded endless requests for support from international prosecutors and judges, persuaded federal agencies to cough up personnel for work at the tribunals, garnered evidence for the tribunals, lobbied Congress to appropriate the necessary funds and make voluntary contributions, and intervened with other governments to increase their support for the tribunals. Although other governments pitched in, the United States often became the convenient one-stop shopping ally of the war crimes tribunals. These endeavors were of such bureaucratic and mind-numbing doggedness through the years that I will spare the details. But one project entailed utilizing diplomatic initiatives to find a chief prosecutor for the Yugoslav Tribunal (who ultimately would be designated as prosecutor for the Rwanda Tribunal as well) and an American woman jurist, who was among the first judges to arrive in The Hague.

Not until June 1993 were efforts initiated to find qualified individuals to be the judges and prosecutor for the Yugoslav Tribunal. That date arrived more than three months after the initial Security Council resolution authorizing the court, when it might have been assumed the search should have begun. But it was unrealistic to begin the process until the constitutional structure of the tribunal was known and its authority to operate established. That point was reached with adoption of Resolution 827. The United Nations had established a new sixty-day deadline for nominations for the judgeships, which meant that names needed to be submitted by the end of July 1993. This would be a far different procedure than that experienced forty-eight years earlier at the Nuremberg Tribunal. The four victorious nations—the United States, United Kingdom, France, and Soviet Union—

that framed the London Charter and sat on the bench simply appointed national prosecutors and judges who arrived in Nuremberg prepared to take up their duties. President Harry Truman selected Supreme Court justice Robert Jackson as the American prosecutor without any election and without any lengthy consultation with other governments or with Congress.[38]

In New York, all would be different in 1993 and 1994 for the Yugoslav Tribunal. Judges were elected by the Security Council and General Assembly of the United Nations. The governments sitting on the Security Council had to agree upon the choice of prosecutor, but their collective approval would be anything but easy to achieve as the months dragged on.

Albright made it very clear, generally in her May 25 statement before the Security Council and more emphatically to me in private, that she wanted a woman nominated by the United States for a seat on the bench. If a woman could be selected as prosecutor as well, all the better. There never had been a woman judge on the highest court of the United Nations, the Permanent Court of International Justice and its post–World War II successor, the International Court of Justice located in The Hague. Albright simply said, "We need to break that mold." But there would be no aggressive campaign for women candidates, as that could backfire on Albright. She decided to wage a telephone crusade and to advance the objective behind the scenes. Few individuals worked the telephone more capably than Madeleine Albright. Nonetheless, she boldly told the United Jewish Appeal on June 7 that "the United States government is determined to see that women jurists sit on the tribunal and that women prosecutors bring war criminals to justice."

Recently retired federal judge Gabrielle McDonald, a tall and lean African-American Texan with a sonorous voice, impressed everyone. The Security Council and General Assembly elected her in the first round of voting for judgeships at the Yugoslav Tribunal. MacDonald knew little about international law and even less about international criminal law, but she proved to be a quick study and someone who easily brought her federal trial skills to bear on the Yugoslav Tribunal. She would become so successful in the position that she was elected president of the Yugoslav Tribunal in 1997 and served in that role for two years. Initially, she was joined on the bench by one other woman and nine men, each from a different country.

The hunt for a prosecutor proved far more difficult and would not be resolved until more than one year later, in July 1994. On June 2, 1993, I launched a search mission, tapping the Justice Department, the State Department legal adviser, and U.S. embassies overseas to generate a list of qualified candidates.

The first name that seized my attention came from Argentina. Luis Moreno-Ocampo had successfully prosecuted some of the Argentine generals responsible for the "Dirty War" of 1976 to 1983, taking the lives of an estimated thirty thousand "disappeared" citizens believed murdered by government agents and soldiers. I forwarded his name to Albright and recommended that she approach the Argentine ambassador to the United Nations, Emilio Cárdenas, to elicit his views and obtain Argentina's approval to advance Moreno-Ocampo's name. But Buenos Aires declined the opportunity as his investigation of government corruption soured official attitudes. At the United Nations, the disapproval of one's own government usually terminates any nomination to a U.N. post. (Political fortunes changed, and years later, in 2002, Moreno-Ocampo became the first prosecutor of the International Criminal Court.)

Other names began to surface, and an entire year of trial and error followed. The fifteen Security Council members reached a de facto agreement that any decision as to who would become the prosecutor of the Yugoslav Tribunal would be made by consensus only, thus requiring unanimous agreement. Unanimity proved elusive to the fifteen council members even though many candidates were considered.

Unfortunately, the convoluted search for a prosecutor left the impression that the United States and other major powers were talking the talk but not walking the walk, and using almost any excuse to slow down the Yugoslav Tribunal's early work. The delay elicited sharp criticism of the Clinton administration and the United Nations, with journalists such as Anthony Lewis of the *New York Times* and scholars venting their frustrations. They could not understand why it took so long to find a prosecutor and assumed something nefarious was afoot.

From Washington's perspective, nothing could have been further from the truth. The quest was thwarted because it took some time to figure out that Russia, in particular, definitively would block any NATO-country candidate and any Muslim. That knocked out Egyptian-American Cherif Bassiouni, a leading authority on international criminal law and chairman of the United Nations' initial investigation of the Balkans conflict, in August 1993 following Security Council consultations. Despite very positive signals from everyone, Charles Ruff, a leading Washington litigator who would lead the defense team in Clinton's impeachment trial years later, ultimately failed to gain Russian support. Other Security Council members insisted on a consensus candidate. Venezuela's successful candidate, Ramon Escovar Salom, wasted four months of everyone's time and effort following his appointment in October 1993 by opting to become interior minister in February 1994 rather than begin work as the tribunal prosecutor. Canada's nominee, though strongly pushed even by U.N. secretary-general Boutros Boutros-Ghali, never achieved enough credibility with Russia and France to garner the office.

Finally, in early June 1994, the South Africa desk at the State Department suggested the name of Richard Goldstone. At the time, Goldstone was a distinguished judge on the Appellate Division of the South Africa High Court, handling both civil and criminal cases, and had chaired the Commission of Inquiry Regarding Prevention of Public Violence and Intimidation in South Africa—a direct and timely assault on apartheid. He had been a practicing barrister for seventeen years, often as counsel for the prosecution. But a Goldstone candidacy was so heavily caveated that we paused in Washington. South African president Nelson Mandela was seriously considering Goldstone for the post of chief justice in South Africa, and it would be no easy matter to derail that particular train. Albright and I also were so immersed in how to create an international criminal tribunal in Rwanda in early June 1994 that we needed time to overcome Goldstone's domestic obstacles.

Luckily, independent of our own search, the Yugoslav Tribunal president, Antonio Cassese, began to circulate Goldstone's name as an excellent candidate for prosecutor following the suggestion of Roger Arrera, who was a judge on the French Conseil d'Etat. The Russian criteria would be met: no NATO ties, no Muslims, and, to make matters easier, no past history with the Balkans.[39]

Cassese called me to stress the urgency of selecting Goldstone, partly because several judges at the Yugoslav Tribunal believed that the deputy prosecutor, Graham Blewitt from Australia, did not have the legal authority, under the statute of the tribunal, to prosecute anyone in the courtroom. If only on grounds of common sense and practicality, I found this interpretation of the statute self-destructive, for it would prevent anyone but the chief prosecutor from arguing a case in the courtroom. But I had to take Cassese's view seriously, which meant getting Goldstone on the job as quickly as possible. Cassese, who had spoken to Goldstone repeatedly, told me that he was in touch with the French and that they would be prepared to support the

South African, while Russia's Boris Yeltsin would defer to Mandela's approval of a tribunal posting for his future Constitutional Court judge.

Thanks to Cassese's heavy lifting and our diplomatic appeals to Mandela and his vice president, Thabo Mbeke, Goldstone acceded to Nelson Mandela's request that he defer joining the Constitutional Court of South Africa for about two years in order to serve as prosecutor of the Yugoslav Tribunal. One might ponder why the chief judge of the Yugoslav Tribunal meddled so intrusively in the selection of the prosecutor. In fact, the independence of both the judges and the prosecutor might have been called into question if they were found to be so bonded in the early stages of the selection process. But the situation had become so dire in trying to find a prosecutor that no one, including myself, thought to question Cassese's motives. We were just grateful that an individual of Goldstone's character and nationality had been identified and stepped forward.

The die was finally cast. On July 8, 1994, the Security Council unanimously approved Resolution 936, which designated Goldstone, a short stocky man with a gentleman's demeanor and endlessly soothing voice, as prosecutor following Boutros-Ghali's recommendation. Thus, after fourteen long months, a white Jewish South African jurist finally was bound for The Hague and the most prominent prosecutorial role in the world. He would prove himself to be a brilliant diplomat as well, which is what the tribunal needed in its early years to garner support at the United Nations and among governments. Long after his work at the tribunal ended, Goldstone chaired a commission of inquiry about the Israeli intervention into Gaza at the end of 2008. He triggered both sharp criticism and praise for his team's conclusions that the Israel Defense Forces had committed war crimes and crimes against humanity against Palestinian civilians in Gaza.[40] I saw Goldstone shortly before he released his controversial report and experienced the same unflappable lawyer I had first met in 1994. The success of the Yugoslav Tribunal can be credited, in no small measure, to Goldstone's leadership at the outset, when so much of the new court's operations remained problematic as the Balkan conflict raged on.

The Americans Are Coming

In the State Department, we ascertained by early August 1993 that there would be a critical need to staff the Yugoslav Tribunal as quickly as possible with seasoned investigators and attorneys who had prosecutorial experience and some knowledge of atrocity law so that the hard work of the court could begin, even in the absence of a chief prosecutor. We began to focus on U.S. Army Reserve lawyers and assistant U.S. attorneys. By late August we decided to deploy, through the method of secondment, a group of such individuals to the Yugoslav Tribunal. But bureaucratic caution slowed the initiative. The Office of the Legal Adviser in the State Department was reluctant to begin identifying lawyers until the chief prosecutor was named, even though the whole point of the exercise was to fill a huge gap in resources that existed in the absence of the prosecutor. Ralph Zacklin, a stiff English lawyer in the U.N. Office of Legal Counsel, pronounced that all tribunal hires would have to be processed within the U.N. personnel system, which was and remains notoriously slow and inefficient. For such "volunteers," Zacklin claimed that a special services agreement would have to be drawn up, and that would take time to negotiate. Through the years, Zacklin proved to be stubborn in the face of judicial necessities of the criminal tribunals. He often threw a bureaucratic wrench into efforts to press forward with the urgent work of the tribunals. Complaints streamed into my office about his arrogant obstructionism, but I had to try to work out each problem with him, one frustrating phone call or meeting after another.

By late November 1993, at an interagency war crimes meeting in Washington, there was general agreement that U.S. personnel would be detailed to the Yugoslav Tribunal's Office of the Prosecutor, with their salaries and expenses paid by the U.S. government. The plan initially numbered the detailees at about ten investigators and five lawyers. The situation had become so dire in The Hague that speculation arose as to whether it would take Security Council action to ensure sufficient staffing for the tribunal. When word circulated in the U.S. Justice Department of the need to detail secondees to the Yugoslav Tribunal, an astonishing one hundred responses were received in short order from enthused department lawyers and agents at the Federal Bureau of Investigation.

I squeezed $3 million from the federal budget to cover the American secondees' salaries and expenses. The money came from a $25 million "drawdown authority" within the budget that my colleagues and I secured, of which a further $11 million would be allocated for a voluntary contribution to the Yugoslav Tribunal. By May 1994, a team of twenty government lawyers and investigators had assembled in Washington; they were deployed shortly thereafter to the tribunal. Goldstone has often claimed that the deployment of this initial team of lawyers and investigators enabled the tribunal to launch its work and that the Americans were instrumental in preparing the early indictments and trial work.[41] Some stayed on for many years of dedicated service and joined the tribunal payroll. One of them, Mark Harmon, became the longest-serving prosecuting attorney at the Yugoslav Tribunal. Several Americans who were direct hires as early as 1994 played leading roles in the prosecution of such defendants as Slobodon Milosevic, Momcilo Krajisnik, and Radovan Karadzic. One of the original American secondees, Brenda Hollis, who at the time was a lawyer with U.S. Air Force, ultimately became the prosecutor of the Special Court for Sierra Leone in 2010.

Early Struggles on Sharing Information

In early May 1993, a small corner of the Washington bureaucracy, which I occupied, began to organize and deliver various types of information about the atrocity crimes in the Balkans to the Yugoslav Tribunal. Some of it was unclassified, but much was classified. The intelligence community naturally was uncomfortable with sharing classified information with the Security Council's Commission to Investigate War Crimes in the former Yugoslavia, which had no fail-safe mechanism for protecting such information and no properly cleared personnel. The opening premise for sharing anything with the Yugoslav Tribunal was that such classified evidence had to be used by the prosecutor solely as lead or corroborating information, and not as evidence that would be disclosed publicly in the prosecution of a case in the tribunal's courtrooms. The sources for much of the material had to remain strictly confidential, and declassification or exceptional use of such evidence in the courtroom required Washington's express prior consent.

The American contribution of evidence had to be coordinated, particularly since it would entail tapping deeply into the intelligence community and determining what it could provide to the prosecutor. Deputy National Security Adviser Sandy Berger agreed to create an Interagency Working Group on War Crimes Evidence (the "Evidence IWG") on May 5, 1993. Berger directed that the Evidence IWG, which I cochaired with Jim O'Brien from the State Department's Office of the Legal Adviser, would need all available U.S. government information on alleged atrocity crimes in the Balkans, including information about who had authorized or permitted such heinous actions. O'Brien and I needed to build a "paper trail" tying atrocities to the military and civilian leaders at senior levels who had set large-scale crimes (such as systematic rape and torture, establishment of concentration camps, and "ethnic cleansing") in motion. The Evidence IWG had the task of coordinating, collating, and organizing information on a timely basis for use by the prosecutor at the Yugoslav Tribunal.

By late July 1993 intelligence analysts had briefed Evidence IWG members, first on ethnic cleansing and then on the "order of battle," which was an essential body of evidence to establish chain of command and superior responsibility in connection with atrocity crimes. As ethnic cleansers, the Bosnian Serbs moved very fast and in small units; they were good at concealing the origin of their orders. Ethnic cleansing in the Srebrenica area, which began years before the genocidal assault on the town in July 1995, constituted total destruction. The analysts were able to point to homes destroyed or damaged because of their proximity to the fighting and shelling. Structures that had been blown up by dynamite were widespread, from one hamlet to the next. Tanks had been poised to fire from their turrets directly into homes. In Sarajevo, the Bosnian Serbs had bombed entire apartment complexes and damaged electrical power facilities. Such destruction appeared intentional and far beyond what was necessary to carry out any military mission.

Still lacking, however, were enough trained individuals in the intelligence community to examine the considerable overhead imagery that had been collected and which could reveal the character and timing of the fighting and destruction on the ground. The Defense Department was not focused on imagery for the purpose of ascertaining commission of atrocity crimes, as its analysts were still locked into Cold War tank-counting skills and old habits that would take time to turn around.

The Evidence IWG determined that the best way to assist the tribunal with collection of evidence would be to set up leads, carefully examine facts suggesting direction from a higher authority, discover indicators of coordination, determine political structures, and explore whether civilian and military leaders took seriously their duty to punish perpetrators of atrocity crimes. All would depend, however, on whether the various agencies of the intelligence community assigned qualified investigators to the task at hand, and satisfying that requirement proved agonizingly frustrating for years thereafter.

Impressive evidence of ethnic cleansing, particularly in eastern Bosnia, emerged in August 1993. Analysts had identified 250 detention camps, exclusive of whatever data nongovernmental organizations were generating.

U.S. personnel interviewed Bosnian internally displaced persons (IDPs) camped out in Tuzla in September 1993 and began to gather significant accounts of atrocities that ultimately would be provided to the Yugoslav Tribunal.

By November 1993, the Evidence IWG had finally begun to make its mark in the bureaucracy. The need was growing to declassify information so that it could be shared with the Yugoslav Tribunal, but staffing remained too slim to fully accomplish the task. American interview teams had recorded accounts by hundreds of refugees from Brcko who had arrived in Copenhagen, Berlin, and Frankfurt. Though the interviews were well recorded, they could not be used in raw form by the tribunal. Rather, they would serve as lead evidence that tribunal investigators had to follow up with their own interviews to create viable records for the courtroom. Enough had been learned, however, to begin creating cases against individual perpetrators and local leaders.

U.S. investigators tried to uncover the trail of ethnic cleansing in Bosnia. The Bosnian Muslims driven from their homes had been made to sign away all their earthly possessions to the relentless Serb cleansers. Those documents, and the receipts held by the dispossessed, evidenced a very organized expropriation of the Muslims' property and the Bosnian Serb army's direct participation in the ethnic cleansing. The receipts constituted a paper trail of evidence.[42] Investigators also discovered at this stage that when there was a formal demarche or media report regarding an atrocity allegedly committed by Muslim forces, the Bosnian government reacted and tried to correct the situation. But when Serb-generated atrocities were reported, Bosnian Serb authorities did not react even if the crime was widely publicized.

The Evidence IWG briefed Albright and other State Department officials on the work accomplished up to December. By then, State Department personnel had interviewed over four hundred witnesses located in Europe. I lugged the almost four thousand pages of recorded interviews to the Yugoslav Tribunal during our first visit there the following month. Six months later, I learned that analysts within the intelligence community kept getting drawn off on other priorities. This dilemma constantly dogged our intelligence-sharing efforts throughout the 1990s. As much as I and others pounded the doors at CIA headquarters and the Pentagon, the atrocities agenda never rose to the level of priority that would have sustained uninterrupted work by a sufficiently staffed and dedicated team of analysts. As one

Cold War analyst scowled at me, "Real men don't do this." Real men massacre the innocent, but this hotshot thought bringing them to justice was a fool's errand.

By September 1994, at least 3,600 settlements had been targeted by ethnic cleansing, and 3,550 of those by Bosnian Serb Army (BSA) or paramilitary forces loyal to them. The ethnic cleansing had destroyed religious and cultural buildings in addition to tens of thousands of homes.[43] So much ethnic-cleansing data was piling up in Washington that I concluded with the State Department's top intelligence official that an ethnic-cleansing report had to be made available to Goldstone so long as classification and security concerns were addressed. In early 1995, Goldstone signed a statement of understanding designed to protect the confidentiality of certain information provided by the U.S. government.[44]

Such confidential information would be used solely as "lead information," namely, offered solely for the purpose of generating new evidence, and thus would be unconditionally guaranteed confidentiality. No disclosure to the judges, defense counsel, or anyone else could be made by the prosecutor without the prior written consent of Washington. The information had to be stored and used in accordance with U.S. security procedures. Access would be limited to the chief prosecutor, deputy prosecutor, chief investigator, and others approved by the U.S. government.[45]

The gathering of evidence marched on as the killing and ethnic cleansing continued. In recent years a fairly accurate count of the total number of casualties in Bosnia and Herzegovina has been established. From 1992 to 1995 the death toll numbered about 102,000 military personnel and civilians (compare this with the intelligence estimate of 145,000 that I relied on in April 1995), with the large majority being Muslims.[46] Tens of thousands of civilians became victims of ethnic cleansing, most of which occurred in territory that would be controlled by Bosnian Serbs. It was difficult to get precise numbers at the time because the Serbs, for obvious reasons, did not volunteer such information.

Goldstone complained about the U.S. intelligence agencies, claiming they did not want to be "tasked" on tribunal requests. This obviously was a major source of confusion: the agencies would not assist the tribunal without such requests, and yet when the requests came in, they complained about being told what to do. The Defense Intelligence Agency proved to be the biggest obstacle, requiring the National Security Council to intervene with the Defense Department to unwedge its resistance to atrocity crimes work.

The National Security Council finally instructed the intelligence community to provide full support to the tribunal, including the provision of classified information. This followed months of discussions we had already had with the tribunal on the handling of classified and "lead" information. But now the intelligence community decided to conduct a further, communitywide review of procedures for providing information. This stopped the sharing of classified information just as it was about to flow with new resolve. After that review was completed, in May 1995, Washington felt confident enough to share more of its classified information with the prosecutor of the Yugoslav Tribunal. I reminded Goldstone that it would greatly help for him to narrowly define his requests and clearly indicate which ones were urgent. Secretary of State Warren Christopher reported to Congress on April 21, 1995, in an unclassified report, that the United States had made arrangements to provide classified information to the tribunal, a pledge that would be fulfilled with this fresh procedure.

During the summer of 1995, the State Department sought agreement from other governments to cooperate with the Yugoslav Tribunal, particularly with respect to the arrest warrants of July 25 issued against Radovan Karadzic and Ratko Mladic. On August 4, the tribunal ordered governments to provide any information they might have on the whereabouts of indicted fugitives, including travel plans, in order to help the tribunal decide whether to issue additional arrest warrants, particularly in countries where the indictees were suspected of traveling.[47] The Clinton administration stepped up border control, made arrangements to cooperate with INTERPOL, and urged Congress to enact legislation providing for cooperation with the tribunal, including the transfer of persons to the tribunal.[48]

High-level discussions at the State Department focused on support for the tribunal and revealed considerable nervousness about the indictments' consequences for peace negotiations in the aftermath of the Srebrenica genocide. I weighed in with three points. First, indictments and negotiations are compatible with each other until proved otherwise. Second, we should ask Milosevic to strip the Bosnian Serb leaders of their political power in exchange for relief from sanctions. Third, no one should confuse peace negotiations in the near term with peace over the long term. The tribunal was important in laying the foundation for a meaningful long-term peace. Despite much concern voiced among civil society representatives and by Goldstone about U.S. resolve to render justice as well as make peace, over the subsequent critical months there was no backtracking by Washington on the tribunal's indictments.

In September 1995, the so-called outer wall was at risk of collapsing during the run-up to the Dayton peace negotiations. The U.S. position had been clear up to that point: Washington would not permit states (or subnational entities such as Republika Srpska) to enter the international community until they established a track record of cooperation with the tribunal.[49] Clinton had endorsed this position, which found wide support in Congress. It also was part of the multinational "Contact Group" position presented to Serbian president Milosevic earlier in the year, and no one had retracted it. Among the elements of the outer wall, the carrot of "entry into the international community" meant the entering government would enjoy (1) access to funds from international financial institutions as well as bilateral and multilateral assistance; (2) participation in international institutions such as the United Nations and the Organization for Security and Cooperation in Europe; and (3) bilateral relations, including diplomatic relations and informal ties. Albright worried about the risk of a policy decision that Serbian cooperation with the tribunal would be a condition of gaining relief from the outer wall of sanctions. She reminded national security adviser Tony Lake that well-calibrated economic sanctions should serve as *leverage* to force Belgrade's cooperation with the tribunal.

Meanwhile, Goldstone sent a letter to Washington complaining to the intelligence community that all the information it had provided in connection with the Srebrenica massacres had been useless. We considered this a highly inflated accusation, but to address his concern, the State Department conveyed to the tribunal an impressive package of information on Srebrenica shortly after receiving his letter. Nonetheless, Goldstone had a point that Washington had to address. In late October 1995, I brought to Albright's attention the reality that there needed to be more internal coordination of both policy and intelligence for war crimes matters. My prime example was the Defense intelligence community. Since early 1995, the Defense Department had been specifically tasked to provide information, but bureaucratic fumbling was preventing efficient responses. My colleagues in the State Department had made repeated requests for information, particularly witness statements, but to no avail. The main problem seemed to be the cumbersome bureaucracy itself, as well as insufficient staffing. Although progress on future information-gathering projects had been made by later in the year, a large volume of material from 1992 through to 1995 had not yet been examined. There was gridlock in the Defense Department, which clearly needed more personnel and more explicit instructions to accomplish the mission.

In early November 1995, prior to the conclusion of the Dayton talks, the Security Council unanimously adopted Resolution 1019, which addressed the Srebrenica massacres and other atrocity crimes that still were occurring in Bosnia and Croatia. The council demanded that all nations and all parties to the Yugoslav conflict fully comply with their obligation to cooperate with the Yugoslav Tribunal. Prior to the council vote, a gathering stream of data confirming the worse-case scenario at Srebrenica and its bloody aftermath had bolstered the council's resolve. Moreover, we now had strong reason to believe that the Bosnian Serbs had exhumed one of the six possible mass graves identified after the fall of Srebrenica. If that proved true, then such tampering with, or destruction of, evidence would violate the resolutions of the Security Council and the statute of the Yugoslav Tribunal.

The exhumation of the possible mass grave, identified in early August, appeared to be nearly complete on October 20, and we had imagery to prove it. We juxtaposed three photographs taken by a U.S. reconnaissance aircraft. On July 27, the probable burial site lacked any vegetation compared with the normal agricultural field that had been visible only months before. On October 20, another image revealed heavy excavation work consisting of an irregularly shaped, large trench between thirty and fifty meters in length. Analysts estimated that this activity, most likely exhumation, continued for about one week. By October 30 the site had been smoothed over, and the heavy equipment was gone. The last photograph suggested that something other than dirt had probably occupied considerable space in the trench. The suspected mass grave was the largest one identified, and it was the closest one to Srebrenica. The use of a heavy excavator, as evident in one of the photographs, suggested lack of concern for forensic evaluation of exhumed bodies and probably a desire for speed. This activity, and the absence of vehicles normally seen with the U.N.-affiliated or nongovernmental organizations active in Bosnia and Herzegovina such as the International Committee of the Red Cross, indicated that the operation had been conducted by the Bosnian Serbs to dispose of evidence of mass executions. At that point no excavation had been observed at the other five possible mass graves associated with the fall of Srebrenica.

With the Dayton Peace Agreement finalized and more evidence accumulating on the Srebrenica massacres, the Security Council adopted Resolution 1034 on December 21. The resolution strongly reaffirmed support for the Yugoslav Tribunal and confirmed its relevance to the Dayton accord. The council again demanded full cooperation with the tribunal, requiring this time that the Bosnian Serbs grant tribunal investigators access to atrocity sites (including Srebrenica) and that all parties, particularly the Bosnian Serbs, leave evidence undisturbed and preserve it. It also demanded that all detention camps throughout Bosnia be closed immediately.

Despite Albright's effective use of aerial imagery in the Security Council to reveal evidence of the Srebrenica atrocities, the American relationship with the tribunal on intelligence -sharing matters remained vexed. A great deal of Goldstone's November 1995 visit to Washington was consumed by this issue. He again learned from officials that he needed to better prioritize his requests for information. They learned from him that their performance on the delivery of information was far from stellar. Though Washington claimed that tribunal requests were a high priority, resources were limited. The key issue for the intelligence agencies, which also affected how many analysts would be dedicated to atrocity crimes work, was whether to be proactive and voluntarily search for and deliver relevant information to the Yugoslav Tribunal, or only react to specific requests for assistance. The Goldstone meetings in Washington that month made important headway on information sharing. Goldstone told me he was "happy that everything that could be done would be done," and he publicly welcomed the newly confirmed arrangement with the U.S. government. Thus, in the immediate aftermath of Dayton, there seemed to have been progress made toward calming the waters and sharing more intelligence with the tribunal.

Some long-standing problems, however, remained. In early January 1996, Senator Arlen Specter of Pennsylvania visited the Yugoslav Tribunal and claimed that one of the tribunal's prosecuting attorneys complained about the slow provision of intelligence. Just one month earlier I had been assured that tribunal staff had no such complaints. American analysts were asking practical questions, and tribunal staff had responded in mid-December, admitting there were more issues for the tribunal to address in order to sharpen their requests and elicit better cooperation from Washington. This type of confusion arising from disgruntled analysts and lawyers on both sides of the Atlantic unfortunately was common fare for years.

For example, in March 1996 I had to press a senior official in the Office of the Chairman of the Joint Chiefs of Staff to release more Srebrenica-related imagery. He attributed the delay to the large amount of imagery to process, and caustically noted that he and the Pentagon did not need the criticism. The official alluded to a policy within the Defense Department and among the Joint Chiefs of Staff to tread cautiously when there was danger of creating a public splash, and perhaps inflaming passions within Bosnia and Herzegovina, which they believed might happen with release of the inflammatory Srebrenica pictures. This was yet another day among so many where the Pentagon continued to place cooperation with the Yugoslav Tribunal on a lower peg of priorities, almost scoffing at any tasking. Additionally, protocol required that the director of the Central Intelligence Agency personally clear any declassification of imagery to the tribunal. Whatever rationale might lie behind the need to obtain such high-level approvals, it resulted in the kind of bureaucratic slowdown that could prove harmful to the prosecutor's efforts and to overall American cooperation with the tribunal.

Goldstone lodged an increasing number of requests in Washington for intelligence he could use in the trials, sometimes in ways that bred inefficiency. Washington misstepped also, notably in its failure to obtain and use timely intelligence to activate an arrest strategy. Beyond that, I was distressed, though not surprised, to learn that key intelligence agencies still lacked minimal staffing to work on collection of information about atrocity crimes in the Balkans. During a visit to the Yugoslav Tribunal on June 17, 1996, staffers told me that scores of their requests made to the U.S. intelligence community were still outstanding. However, in the case of many of these requests, Washington had submitted information to the tribunal but left the actual requests open, in order either to receive more detailed information from the tribunal about what was needed or to transmit additional information based on the tribunal's requirements. Investigation of mass graves demonstrated the problem, often requiring three to six months to obtain all the necessary information from the intelligence community. As a result, a number of requests remained pending, and hence the impression of noncooperation lingered.

During the first term of the Clinton administration, the American effort at intelligence sharing with the tribunal was a mixed bag of tardy responses that led to unending angst in Washington's relations with the prosecutor.

The intelligence community initially resisted the challenge to deliver more information faster, and some agencies remained stubbornly lackadaisical for a very long time. There were days when it seemed as if I was the lone crusader trying to move the system toward better performance.

Regardless, out of this experience emerged an intelligence-sharing arrangement that influenced what later would be expected for the Rwanda Tribunal, and would greatly instruct similar procedures for the International Criminal Court. Much of the American-generated evidence ultimately made its way, directly or indirectly, into trials and proved very helpful. These early experiences with intelligence sharing also demonstrated to Albright and others the critical utility of having someone coordinate that task as well as other matters with the war crimes tribunals, and that greatly influenced the creation of my ambassadorship and the Office of War Crimes Issues in the State Department in 1997.

CHAPTER TWO

IT'S GENOCIDE, STUPID

> We did not immediately call these crimes by their rightful
> name: genocide,.,. It may seem strange to you here, especially
> the many of you who lost members of your family, but all over
> the world there were people like me sitting in offices, day after
> day after day, who did not fully appreciate the depth and speed
> with which you were being engulfed by this unimaginable terror.
>
> *President Bill Clinton, speaking to genocide survivors in*
> *Kigali, Rwanda, on March 25, 1998*

THE VISITOR TO RWANDA MARVELS AT THE BEAUTY OF ITS ENDLESS TREE-
covered hills before pausing at fields of wooden crosses—thousands of
sticks nailed or lashed together to mark the graves of the genocide victims
of 1994. I visited such makeshift cemeteries often during my journeys to
Rwanda. I always found survivors nearby. Each had a different story of escape, but one common thread wove them together: their families occupied
the gravesites before me. At the Ntarama church in central Rwanda, hundreds of Tutsi bones and pieces of bloody clothing lay undisturbed as an
open grave site among the shattered pews, exactly where the people who
once wore those clothes were massacred by Hutu. During my first trip to
Rwanda as war crimes ambassador in September 1997,[1] I had walked inside
this same Ntarama church, stepped carefully, smelled the rot of death,
viewed the human bones, and imagined the enormity of the crime. I had
arrived at ground zero of the genocide.

The *New York Times* later published a page one photograph of me leaning
over to straighten a cross at Nyanza Cemetery on that September day.[2] It

accompanied a story by veteran reporter Steven Lee Myers describing my journey through the atrocity sites of Africa and the Balkans. The picture and article happened to be published on the morning of President Clinton's annual appearance before the U.N. General Assembly. An agitated State Department spokesman called me from New York, claiming that Clinton and Albright were upset about the photograph, which detracted from the president's own publicity during his stay in New York. The spokesman speculated that I had orchestrated the publication for that particular day, which was absurd, as I had no influence over the *New York Times*. Somehow the positive coverage of the Clinton administration's new war crimes ambassador on the job in Rwanda had little standing. It struck me as fitting, complementary rather that detractive, that such an article fortuitously appeared on the same day that Clinton pronounced before the General Assembly his aim to have an international criminal court built before the end of the century. But I learned quickly never to assume magnanimity from the White House.

American leadership in the building of the Rwanda Tribunal cannot be appreciated without first examining the American failure—shared with so many others—in confronting the genocide that Rwanda suffered. There have been many accounts written about the Western collapse in the face of the Rwandan genocide; most are serious efforts to establish the historical record. But I believe it is critical to provide a fresh perspective about what transpired during policy-making in Washington and New York, for only then can there be a proper understanding of the initiatives that Albright, John Shattuck, who was the top human rights official in the State Department, and I pursued by mid-1994 to build a tribunal and achieve some measure of international justice. This chapter relates that story of policy failure, which soon led to the imperative of building the Rwanda Tribunal, which is described in the next chapter. By the summer of that year, we were on a quest for redemption in the rivers of blood flowing out of Rwanda. The question that cries out for an answer, though, is how did we find ourselves in that shameful position?

Eight Thousand Hacked to Death Each Day

Over a period of about one hundred days commencing on April 6, 1994, an estimated 800,000 women, children, and men, most of Tutsi identity, were massacred.[3] That averages 8,000 murders per day. The killings were planned by the top Rwandan government, military, business, and media leaders and carried out by thousands of machete-hacking Hutu. It was a phenomenon that was unimagined at the time and remains almost surreal to this day. If anyone had speculated prior to the genocide that such a daily low-tech killing rate was even possible, he or she would have been labeled an alarmist. But history proved differently, and the resurgent genocide plagued the countryside for years thereafter. No other atrocity zone quite compared with the intense savagery of Rwanda during that period.

The United States failed in 1994 to respond effectively to the genocide that engulfed Rwanda. The reasons did not originate only with the brutal killings of eighteen American soldiers on the streets of Mogadishu, Somalia, six months earlier.[4] To be sure, that firefight had an enormously negative impact for years thereafter on Washington's attitude about military engagements in Africa or with anything labeled "U.N.," and it shaped the context for failing to intervene to end Rwanda's genocide. But Mogadishu was a distant scream that penetrated the subconscious thinking of policymakers. The real struggle took place over more contemporary issues that required immediate decisions for effective action but instead triggered a multitude of excuses and devastating delays. For those of us in the policy rooms at the time, the memory of our vacillation over the horror is sickening and will never be extinguished. I owe the victims and their families my soul every day.

During the Rwandan genocide, policy makers, including American, European, and U.N. officials, equivocated and made decisions with tragic consequences. The National Security Council failed to convene the Deputies and Principals Committees soon enough. They could have focused urgent attention on the genocide and sparked bold decision making and interagency coordination. While the Pentagon tied itself in knots reviewing performance criteria for peacekeeping operations, the State Department remained faithful to a failed peace process that was buried beneath the bodies stacking up throughout the countryside of Rwanda.

During a speech in Addis Ababa on December 9, 1997, Albright acknowledged that "we—the international community—should have been more active in the early stages of the atrocities in Rwanda in 1994, and called them what they were—genocide."[5] On March 25, 1998, during the first visit of an American president to Rwanda and four years after the genocide, President Bill Clinton echoed Albright's remarks: "The international community, together with nations in Africa, must bear its share of responsibility for this tragedy, as well. We did not act quickly enough after the killing began. We should not have allowed the refugee camps to become safe havens for the killers. We did not immediately call these crimes by their rightful name: genocide."[6] These words were very late in coming, but they had to be said for the sake of American credibility, and in fact they preceded by years the admissions and apologies of other key governments, such as France and Belgium.[7]

Conventional Responses

What happened? The United States responded conventionally to an extraordinarily unconventional crisis and thus lost opportunities to reverse the tide of killings at the earliest stages. During the initial months of 1994 and for several weeks into the genocidal rampage, diplomats analyzed the situation in Rwanda through the prism of a conflict between two sides—the Hutu-dominated government of Rwanda and the insurgent Tutsi-led Rwandan Patriotic Front (RPF). Both parties had signed the Arusha Peace Agreement (or Arusha Accords) of August 4, 1993, with strong international support.[8] Partly because of the tight schedule, partly because of continued fighting, deadlines were missed, prompting calls for speedier action by the parties. All eyes turned on how to salvage the Arusha Accords, not on body counts. The ethnic tension, which was starting to boil over, took second place to the imperatives of the peace accords, a process that was much more comprehensible to diplomats than the labyrinths of ethnic conflict.

A better understanding of the region would have alerted us that the interethnic slaughter of tens of thousands of Tutsi and Hutu in Burundi during the fall of 1993 could trigger further violence next door in Rwanda.[9] The international community's collective detachment from the reality unfolding in Burundi sent a strong signal to the extremist Hutu in Rwanda that the shooting gallery was open, free of charge.

One of my own shameful moments occurred shortly after the Mogadishu killings had paralyzed Washington. I briefed congressional staffers in November 1993 that our inaction to the massacres of tens of thousands of both Tutsi and Hutu in Burundi demonstrated the Clinton administration's reason-headed approach to peacekeeping. We were not going to rush into each and every humanitarian catastrophe, I confidently reported. Burundi, then Rwanda, proved that point in spades. When I visited a still violent Burundi years later, first with Albright and then as the war crimes ambassador,

I saw how mistaken the United States and other governments had been to react so meekly to the carnage in that country. The massacres there in fact had been genocide, as experts later concluded.[10]

In Rwanda, the American, French, and Belgian governments, represented by their ambassadors to Rwanda, responded conventionally to the now famous fax of January 11, 1994, from General Roméo Dallaire, force commander of the United Nations Assistance Mission for Rwanda (UNAMIR), to U.N. Headquarters. He reported information from a trusted source that Belgian peacekeepers would be provoked (violently enough to force their withdrawal), that men were being trained to kill Tutsi (at a rate of up to one thousand Tutsi in twenty minutes), and that a major weapons cache had been created.[11] U.N. officials instructed Dallaire to discuss his concerns subtly with Rwandan president Juvénal Habyarimana, even though Dallaire had planned a very aggressive demarche.[12] In Washington, there was no perspective that viewed the situation as a precursor of mass murder. The unreasonable view that everything must relate to the peace process prevailed.

The American, French, and Belgian ambassadors accompanied Dallaire to appeal jointly to Habyarimana on the need for retracting the cached arms and dismantling the local militia units called Interahamwe, meaning "those who attack together." In hindsight, the joint demarche informed the planners of the genocide about U.N. and foreign concerns, thus achieving precisely the opposite result than that intended. The Interahamwe were Habyarimana's own militia force, and he may have been a conspirator in the genocide plan. Relying on Habyarimana to provide an accurate report on the arms caches and training missions clearly was a mistake. A more innovative approach to the information in the Dallaire cable would have compelled the Security Council to stand behind the Canadian general and empower UNAMIR to fully investigate and then neutralize the arms caches.

Other warning signs met conventional responses. Violence increased in Rwanda in early February and then subsided around February 24. There were several political killings, each one followed by massacres of Tutsi. U.N. officials and foreign governments misinterpreted the signs and assumed that once the Arusha Accords were implemented, the killing would stop. U.S. officials continued to seek to persuade political leaders, in vain, to implement the accords. There were no high-level meetings in Washington to discuss any of these developments or to explore preventive actions.

By the end of March, further killings had poisoned the peace process. Diplomatic efforts to pressure the parties in the conflict to resolve their differences were faltering. Some speculated that a return to bloody ethnic conflict in Rwanda was possible. No policy initiative resulted, however, from that speculation. During these critical weeks before the genocide began, the Security Council emphasized that support for UNAMIR depended on implementation of the Arusha Accords.[13] U.S., U.N., and other foreign officials used the UNAMIR mandate's imminent termination and possible renewal as leverage on the parties to seek a compromise. The Belgians, who had the largest contingent of soldiers in UNAMIR, recommended extending it for only one month beyond its renewal date of April 5. Washington lobbied Paris to shorten UNAMIR's extension from five months to two, or possibly three, months.[14] On April 5, after lengthy debate, the Security Council agreed to extend the UNAMIR mandate for only four months and require a review after the first six weeks.[15] Such tactics were viewed as a strong political signal that further delays in implementing the Arusha Accords would not be acceptable, when in fact they set the stage for the genocide plotters' aim: the withdrawal of UNAMIR.

While diplomats focused on the Arusha Accords (and used UNAMIR as political leverage), ethnic tension remained untended. The militias were getting stronger and more vocal. Rwandan newspapers and a popular radio station, RTLM, incited killings of Tutsi and of UNAMIR soldiers or broadcast hate speech aimed at the Tutsi. Rallies held by extremists went largely unreported in the international media.[16]

The Genocide Begins

On April 6, 1994, President Habyarimana and Burundi's president, Cyprien Ntaryamira, were returning to Kigali from regional talks in Dar es Salaam, aimed at establishing a transitional government in Rwanda that would share power with Tutsi leaders, when their Falcon 50 aircraft received a direct hit after missiles were fired near the airport. They perished in a ball of fire. The responsibility for the attack has never been definitively established. But it proved to be a convenient pretext for Hutu political and military leaders to unleash their well-planned genocidal killings that night in Kigali and soon elsewhere in Rwanda.

Immediately, on April 7, the governments of Belgium, France, Italy, and the United States began evacuating foreign nationals and ill-equipped U.N. peacekeepers from Rwanda.[17] (There were between 3,000 and 4,000 foreign nationals in Rwanda, including about 1,500 Belgians, 300 French, 300 Germans, and 250 Americans.) That single objective swamped policy-makers in Washington, abroad, and at the United Nations, but it also liberated the genocidaires (as they have come to be known) to hack away.[18] The next day, April 8, Security Council members unanimously approved a nonbinding statement by that month's president of the council that emphasized the safety and security of the U.N. peacekeepers and reaffirmed the council's "commitment to the Arusha Peace Agreement" while urging "all parties to implement it fully and in particular to respect the cease-fire."[19] But the critical need to launch immediate planning for effective military and police intervention to stop the violence was delayed and obfuscated so long that the peace accord became useless.

I learned from colleagues at the U.S. Mission to the United Nations that U.N. officials on April 8 were hesitant to transform UNAMIR into a Chapter VII enforcement army, fearing such a move would only escalate the violence and that UNAMIR did not have the capability on the ground to engage in combat. U.N. officials also feared that if UNAMIR remained while foreign nationals departed, the peacekeepers would become a target for Rwandans seeking revenge. The U.N. undersecretary for peacekeeping, Kofi Annan, who said he was speaking for Secretary-General Boutros-Ghali, recommended that UNAMIR and foreign nationals be evacuated in the absence of any effective cease-fire. Annan sought a letter from interested governments requesting a UNAMIR evacuation so that Boutros-Ghali would not appear to be abandoning Rwanda on his own accord.[20]

Much of the information that flowed into Washington during these early days of the genocide focused on the military operations of the RPF and not on the killings of civilians. That partly was the consequence of having Defense Department attachés reporting to Washington rather than Foreign Service officers, who normally would report on a broader range of issues unfolding in a crisis. However, the International Committee of the Red Cross (ICRC) alerted U.S. diplomats in Geneva as early as April 12, six days into the genocide, to the kind of horrific detail that should have compelled everyone to switch from evacuation mode to "stop the killing" mode in the policy discussions. They reported an estimated nationwide death toll of up to twenty thousand Rwandans who had been killed within the first five days of violence:

> Complete mayhem has hit the streets of Kigali, leaving a heavy death toll and large numbers of wounded. Armed elements are on the rampage, going from

house to house killing and destroying.... Since [the airplane carrying Presidents Habyarimana and Ntaryamira was shot down] the bloodshed in the city has steadily grown in intensity. Today the fighting is still fierce, and the city is gripped by generalized looting and lawlessness. ICRC delegates in Kigali have described scenes of extreme violence, stating that there are thousands of casualties lying in the streets.... [and there are] rumors from a number of sources that massacres and destruction are going on in the south of Rwanda.[21]

As this report arrived in Washington, I joined a State Department meeting where we talked about "acts of genocide" appearing to unfold in Rwanda, and yet we were not prepared to conclude that "genocide" actually was occurring. I advised that this really was a distinction without a meaningful difference for the public. "Acts of genocide" are the physical acts that have to be paired with a specific (mental) intent "to destroy, in whole or in part, a national, ethnical, racial, or religious group, as such" in order to constitute the crime of genocide for which individual perpetrators can be held accountable. The physical acts are well known from the Genocide Convention: killing members of the group, causing serious bodily or mental harm to members of the group, deliberately inflicting on the group conditions of life calculated to bring about its physical destruction in whole or in part, imposing measures intended to prevent births within the group, and forcibly transferring children of the group to another group. Killing and serious bodily harm had been unleashed on great numbers of Rwandans, and I suspected at least some in the room understood that the identity of the victims was largely Tutsi.

"Our Opposition Is Firm"

Speaking for the Non-Aligned Movement before the U.N. Security Council on April 12, Nigeria argued that UNAMIR should be strengthened.[22] However, key diplomats and Washington officials decided to support the withdrawal of UNAMIR and thus accomplish what was assumed at the time to be the U.N. Secretariat's genuine objective. France and Britain argued that UNAMIR's mandate was not to enforce stability, and that the peacekeeping force did not have the capacity to do so even if it were so instructed. The United States, with Argentine and Spanish support, thought a withdrawal might be necessary but that a skeletal force could be left behind. This was due in large part to the African resistance to withdrawal and political concerns about what a full withdrawal would signify.

By the morning of April 13, the Belgians had begun to move swiftly to withdraw their 450-man contingent in the capital after ten of their peacekeepers were murdered and physically dismembered during the early hours of the genocide. That evening Secretary-General Boutros Boutros-Ghali sent a letter to the Security Council essentially making the case that unless a similar contingent could be found to replace the Belgians, UNAMIR's mandate would become "untenable."[23]

Advance word early on April 13 of Boutros-Ghali's anticipated letter had an important impact on critical Washington discussions throughout the day.[24] I did little but race down State Department corridors to briefings and policy sessions, trying to stay connected with Albright's team in New York while absorbing the pessimistic views of State and Pentagon officials. I heard from colleagues in New York that shutting down UNAMIR was rapidly becoming the unavoidable choice, and that at least one government on the Security Council had to take the lead, and ultimately the political heat, to accomplish that task. Some U.S. diplomats volunteered to step forward and recommend the withdrawal of UNAMIR, reflecting our knowledge of what Boutros-Ghali himself was recommending.

I called a political officer at the U.S. Mission to the United Nations about an April 13 draft by the State Department of a Security Council resolution dictating full withdrawal of UNAMIR. She responded immediately with disbelief and told me it would be absolutely impossible to get council approval for withdrawal of *all* UNAMIR personnel and that the effort would only gain us a great deal of ill will. Her insights bore truth in the months and years ahead. Even the French, who did not believe that UNAMIR had the capability to enforce stability if instructed to do so (but who also wanted Africans to see France as a staunch supporter), wanted to keep a substantial UNAMIR presence on the ground. The five Non-Aligned countries on the Security Council that year firmly argued for retaining UNAMIR and mandating the soldiers to protect civilians. Brazil and China joined them. That meant that eight of fifteen Security Council members would oppose the resolution that Washington sought and, worse yet, vote against it if Washington insisted on council action. So where were the nine votes and no vetoes we needed to pass it, she asked? The political officer bluntly counseled that there was no hope for the Pentagon's idea of terminating the UNAMIR mandate. She pleaded with me not to clear the cable, since the U.S. Mission would not be able to carry out the instructions.

I contacted the drafter of the State Department cable and warned her of the U.S. Mission's serious objection to the practicality of the resolution, explaining that it just would not fly in the council. Albright also cabled Washington confirming "that most Security Council members wanted to retain at least some elements [of UNAMIR]."[25]

Despite the political realities in the Security Council, many officials in Washington kept up the drumbeat that UNAMIR was inadequately mandated, trained, equipped, and staffed to respond effectively to the violence in Rwanda, that U.N. peacekeeping operations worldwide were already overloaded, and that UNAMIR could not satisfy the new criteria being developed within the U.S. government to guide peacekeeping and peace enforcement deployments. At a second peacekeeping core group meeting in Washington on April 13, officials recommended that Albright take a low-key approach in the council while Washington evaluated recommendations to leave a skeletal UNAMIR group behind in Rwanda or, in the alternative, to support total withdrawal if there proved to be overwhelming sentiment in the council. The smaller peacekeeping force would be approved to stay only if it could significantly contribute to the peace process, as if there was one to be revived.

The tide turned decisively when Susan Rice, who managed peacekeeping issues at the U.S. National Security Council, discouraged literal termination of the UNAMIR mandate but favored a troop withdrawal. Her boss, Richard Clarke, opposed any further peacekeeping presence that could not meet the stringent conditions of the imminent new peacekeeping policy of the Clinton administration. Their views enabled the State Department to close ranks and cable the U.S. Mission with instructions, namely, that Washington "shares Belgian concerns that the greatly changed circumstances in Rwanda have rendered untenable the continued presence of UNAMIR. We support a rapid but orderly withdrawal of UNAMIR forces and other UN personnel as required and urge the United Nations to resolve successfully the security of Rwandan nationals currently under UNAMIR protection."[26]

A subsequent cable on April 15 from Washington to the U.S. Mission reflected further internal discussions with the Pentagon and factored in the criteria for peacekeeping operations that we were finalizing for Clinton's forthcoming Presidential Decision Directive on Multilateral Peacekeeping Operations, or PDD-25, which was signed and publicly announced a few weeks later.[27] The cable stated that there was "an insufficient justification to retain a U.N. [peacekeeping operation] in Rwanda and that [the] international community must give highest priority to full, orderly withdrawal of all UNAMIR personnel as soon as possible." Then Washington pronounced its final judgment: "U.S. will oppose any effort at this time to preserve a UNAMIR presence in Rwanda. In the current environment, there is no role for UN peacekeeping. Our opposition is firm. It is based on our conviction that the Security Council has an obligation to ensure that peacekeeping operations are viable, that they are capable of fulfilling their mandate and that U.N. peacekeeping personnel are not placed or retained, knowingly, in an untenable position."[28] Joining the charge at the Pentagon for this abandonment of the Rwandan Tutsi was Lieutenant General Wesley Clark, the director of strategic plans and policy for the Joint Chiefs of Staff and who years later would lead the NATO military response to Serbian atrocity crimes in Kosovo.

I share equal responsibility. My clearance is clearly printed at the top of the instruction cable to Albright: "USUN/W:DSCHEFFER." As a coauthor of PDD-25, I embraced the logic of the argument, namely, that UNAMIR did not meet the criteria that should be applied to the new reality: the need for an enforcement (rather than peacekeeping) troop deployment in Rwanda. Despite that rationale, I cannot justify why I did not refuse clearance at that critical moment; I must have received a green light from the U.S. Mission to clear the cable, but in hindsight that is a weak excuse given what was unfolding in Rwanda with increasing ferocity. Perhaps I was persuaded by Deputy Assistant Secretary of State Prudence Bushnell of the Africa Bureau, who had fought in vain for a more effective response in the early days and whose judgment I respected, but who also cleared the cable. I cannot recall precisely how we arrived at the final decision to clear the cable, but I remember three factors that weighed heavily: (1) the deep influence on Washington officials of Boutros-Ghali's plea for a withdrawal, delivered by Kofi Annan on April 8, and the secretary-general's follow-up letter of April 13 to the council; (2) staunch Pentagon opposition to anything but full withdrawal and the National Security Council's recommendation to withdraw, both of which were essential components for any instruction cable on U.N. peacekeeping; and (3) the imperative of getting instructions to Albright before the U.N. Security Council's meeting on April 15.

Just prior to the contentious council informal discussions on April 15 and before the infamous instruction cable arrived in New York, the U.S. Mission indicated support for the British idea of a minimal UNAMIR presence in Rwanda that would protect U.N. staff remaining there.[29] The Belgian government had announced its plan to have all Belgian soldiers out of the country within three days.[30] France also announced the withdrawal of all five hundred French paratroopers deployed with UNAMIR. However, the Non-Aligned countries rejected the British proposal and supported Boutros-Ghali's latest recommendation, which by that afternoon was to maintain in place UNAMIR's force, minus the Belgians, at least for several weeks. Thus, the American tilt to the British proposal in the morning fell flat.

At the time, there was little knowledge or insight among key policy-makers in Washington about the special relationships that had long developed between, on the one hand, the governments of France and Belgium and, on the other hand, the Hutu government in Rwanda. The enormous controversy that erupted after the genocide over whether either of these European governments were complicit in the Hutu-orchestrated genocide of the Tutsi generated investigations and crippled French and Belgian relations with Rwanda. Rwandan president Paul Kagame implicated France repeatedly in policies and actions that allegedly facilitated the genocide—all attracting vehement denials by Paris. Not until late 2009 did France restore diplomatic relations with the Rwandan government.[31]

Albright and her deputy ambassador at the United Nations, Edward Walker, attended the consultations within the Security Council and dutifully followed the instructions from Washington. They dropped the bombshell that if a decision had to be reached, the United States sought *complete* withdrawal of UNAMIR. The room filled with murmurs of consternation and disbelief for several long moments. Nobody else lined up behind full withdrawal. Some pressed for a suspension of UNAMIR while keeping enough personnel in Rwanda to facilitate political negotiations and provide military expertise. Nigeria wanted UNAMIR restored to its original strength prior to the Belgian withdrawal to help save lives but without guaranteeing the safety of civilians. Argentina and China wanted to put everything on hold, without offering any clear idea about what to do next.

Albright wrote in her memoir that as she listened to her Security Council colleagues, "I became increasingly convinced we were on the wrong side of the issue." She called Washington to seek "more flexible instructions," but it would take many days for them to be forthcoming.[32]

Walker and his boss, Albright, were outflanked, shamed, and defeated even though they were not only doing Washington's bidding but also, more significantly, had taken the fall for Boutros-Ghali and the Belgians, who initially wanted a complete withdrawal of the peacekeeping force. We learned later from the release of a U.N. cable dated April 14, 1994, sent to Kofi Annan by the secretary-general's senior political adviser and special representative to the council, Ambassador Chinmaya Gharekhan, that "the Secretary-General 'at no stage' had recommended or favoured withdrawal [of UNAMIR]."[33] This seemed disingenuous. The mere fact that Gharekhan had to emphasize this to Annan reflected concern that earlier communications had doubtless left the impression—certainly with the United States—that the secretary-general supported withdrawal. Washington decision makers, lacking any knowledge of Gharekhan's after-the-fact clarification, moved solidly into the withdrawal column by April 15 and so instructed Albright.

The Security Council postponed a vote on the future of UNAMIR to facilitate further council deliberations. On April 21, Albright voted to adopt Resolution 912 requiring the reduction of UNAMIR from roughly 2,500 to about 270 personnel and adjusting the mandate to help secure a cease-fire, assist with humanitarian relief operations, and guard those Rwandans under direct U.N. protection.[34] This was an embarrassingly small number of peacekeepers to deter further genocide (and the mandate did not presume that they could), but it reflected political compromise within the Security Council. The council resolution was sharply criticized by the Organization for African Unity and by civil society as shortsighted and callous.[35] Given its earlier position advocating full withdrawal, the United States suffered irreparable harm to its credibility despite the fact that Washington joined others is approving a continued, albeit pathetically small, military presence. The verdict was in, right or wrong: the United States had abandoned the Rwandan Tutsi to their fate in the genocide.

The New Peacekeeping Policy

Meanwhile, at the State Department, Resolution 912 was viewed as an acceptable compromise. The resolution did not call the violence "genocide" but instead described "large-scale violence in Rwanda, which has resulted in the death of thousands of innocent civilians, including women and children." It demanded "an end to the mindless violence and carnage which are engulfing Rwanda." By then all recognized that a total withdrawal of UNAMIR was politically impossible. But there was little support, either in Washington or in the Security Council, for broadening UNAMIR's mandate to confront the raging genocide. Some believed the only role for the United Nations was to broker political reconciliation without any further peacekeeping duties. An expanded mandate and additional forces for UNAMIR capable of protecting the civilian population would have required setting down realistic criteria for both the operation and how to end it once deployed, and no one was stepping forward to do that.

Why the exit criteria? As demonstrated on April 15, the new U.S. peacekeeping policy, nearing completion in Washington, deeply influenced decision making on the future of UNAMIR. The killings of the U.S. Marines in Mogadishu did not launch this intensive exercise to develop a disciplined (and limiting) set of guidelines for U.N. peacekeeping operations. In fact, work on the new policy began in earnest in February 1993 and was largely finished before the "Blackhawk down" incident in Somalia eight months later. But that costly battle caused us to revisit the document for several additional months of relatively minor revisions and extensive consultations on Capitol Hill.

PDD-25 was officially launched on May 6, 1994, but its final wording already was completed and well known to U.S. policy-makers in early April when the Rwandan genocide began. We were compelled to follow the document's "factors" to consider U.S. support for and participation in U.N. peace operations. These "factors" included whether U.S. interests would be advanced; whether a cease-fire was in place and the consent of the parties obtained before a peacekeeping force would be deployed; whether the threat to international peace and security was considered significant in the case of a peace enforcement operation that might involve combat; whether the means to accomplish the mission were available, including the forces, financing, and a mandate appropriate to the mission; and whether there was a clear exit strategy. Any proposed direct American engagement triggered even tougher requirements.[36] As one of the staff authors of PDD-25, I was keenly aware of its use during the Rwandan crisis. In addition to the signals we received from U.N. officials, the criteria set forth in PDD-25 pointed toward the withdrawal option for UNAMIR because of the apparent inability to fulfill its mandate.

All was not lost. American officials gained much experience in the use of PDD-25 during and following the Rwandan genocide, a cataclysmic event that reminded everyone of the perils of focusing on peacekeeping criteria at the expense of humanitarian imperatives. Indeed, PDD-25's own recognition of humanitarian catastrophes as a key basis for U.N. peacekeeping, and its requirement that policy-makers consider the consequences of *not* deploying a peacekeeping force as well as the consequences of actually deploying one, took on new meaning and significance in later years.[37] So often in policy-making the consequences of not acting are ignored while the easier task of highlighting the risks of acting dominate the discussions. There were plenty of those blinkered moments in the Situation Room. The risks of *not* acting had to take on greater importance in all our decisions on peacekeeping and humanitarian catastrophes. But that lesson simply had not taken hold on April 15, 1994, when we decided in Washington to pull the plug on UNAMIR.

Nonetheless, blaming PDD-25 for having placed too many constraints on U.S. support for peacekeeping, and hence on confronting atrocities, overlooks the fact that the document was essential at the time to sustain congressional and Pentagon support for *any* U.N. peacekeeping operation. But in those early days of its implementation, PDD-25 and the conservative (indeed conventional) manner in which it was interpreted had the perverse effect of straitjacketing policy-makers into denying justifiable interventions or preventive measures when the lives of hundreds of thousands of innocent civilians were at stake. We learned the hard way that PDD-25 needed to be interpreted reasonably in light of the circumstances that can confront the international community and besieged civilian populations. Months later, at a congressional hearing on U.N. peacekeeping operations, Albright pointed to the PDD-25 analysis that retarded any rapid expansion of UNAMIR to meet the genocide. There was no way to satisfy the stringent criteria of PDD-25 quickly enough. "We're damned if we do and damned if we don't," she told Congress.[38]

High-Level Attention

On April 27, State and Defense Department officials discussed creating safe areas within Rwanda for displaced persons (mostly Tutsi) and using U.N. police to patrol the areas. We even considered asking neighboring Tanzania, flooded with refugees, to invade Rwanda as it had done in Uganda in 1979 to end Idi Amin's slaughterhouse rule. U.N. Charter Article 51's right of self-defense was all the legal justification the Tanzanians needed, some of us argued. Someone asked who would pay the Tanzanian government to

launch a full-scale invasion of Rwanda, and when no one from the Pentagon, State Department, or National Security Council volunteered a dime,
the discussion moved on as if the idea had never existed. At the U.S. Mission to the United Nations, we never had any money, so our leverage was nil
in such discussions.

The State Department spokeswoman, Christine Shelly, fielded tough,
but obvious, questions from the press corps on April 28 about U.S. policy
on Rwanda. She read from the press guidance prepared by the Office of the
Legal Adviser in responding to whether what was happening in Rwanda was
genocide. Instead of focusing on establishing a commonsense understanding that atrocity crimes of some character and of enormous magnitude
were occurring, and that we acknowledged that fact, Shelly delivered a dry
recitation of how to determine, from a lawyer's perspective, whether the
crime of genocide had occurred. The usual stumbling block of establishing
specific intent gave Shelly the opening to declare the "more complicated"
nature of the issue and that it required "very careful study before we can
make a final determination." Then, in response to whether the United
States had any obligation to take any particular action in response to genocide, Shelly pleaded the "no absolute requirement ... to intervene directly"
mantra of lawyer-speak. She opted to describe, again drawing from press
guidance, how the crime of genocide can be pursued in courts or by referral to the United Nations for its "competent organs" to take actions. The
entire exchange left the impression that the United States was scurrying
into the narrowest legal tunnel to avoid acknowledging the catastrophe unfolding in Rwanda and how to begin responding to it effectively rather than
rhetorically.[39]

Finally, on April 29, three weeks following the first wave of killings, the
Deputies Committee of the U.S. National Security Council convened to discuss the Rwandan crisis. The U.N. Security Council had met the day before
and was meeting again on the twenty-ninth, so I brought some fresh updates from New York. The Czechs and Argentines proposed a draft statement for the U.N. Security Council president blaming the government of
Rwanda for "genocide" or some comparable term, but that idea generated
a great deal of controversy over whether, and to what extent, to blame the
Kigali officials for the massacres of civilians. France, Djibouti, and China
firmly opposed blaming the Hutu-led Rwandan government, which happened that year to sit as a nonpermanent member on the council. Indeed,
the Rwandan ambassador to the United Nations spoke up during the April

29 consultations in New York for the first time in days, only to argue against blaming the Rwandan government for civilian massacres and to oppose an arms embargo on his country.[40]

The Deputies Committee members, including myself, entered the White House Situation Room generally aware of what was occurring in Rwanda and of their options. The newspapers and networks had covered the carnage extensively, and the White House and State Department had issued five statements over the preceding three weeks.[41] The latest White House statement mentioned specific military leaders who, human rights groups believed, were implicated in the slaughter.[42] The United Nations reported that more than 100,000 Rwandans had been killed, which was an astounding number to contemplate. Hate-radio stations called for more killing.[43] UNAMIR had drawn down to approximately 450 troops (although we were assuming it was 270 troops on April 29) who were focused on securing the safety of Rwandans under its protection at the Kigali Amahoro Stadium. About 500,000 refugees had fled to the borders of Tanzania, Uganda, and Zaire (later renamed as the Democratic Republic of the Congo). Many were blocked from crossing and needed humanitarian assistance. An interagency working group had identified short-term policy objectives, which centered on stopping the fighting, securing a cease-fire, resurrecting the Arusha Accords framework of peace talks, and preventing the violence from spreading to neighboring countries, including Burundi. The focus on Rwandan "fighting" still showed our failure to see the problem in terms other than government forces battling the RPF. The raw objective of stopping the slaughter (or genocide) was not articulated other than through diplomatic contacts and demarches.

I made the case for a U.N. genocide investigation, which was already being discussed in New York. On this point, I prevailed. The deputies instructed the U.S. Mission to support such an investigation combined with an inquiry into human rights violations. This meant the deputies had agreed to the first step in legal accountability, namely, a U.N. investigation of the crime of *genocide* in Rwanda. But the deputies did not discuss or approve the idea of publicly calling the killings "genocide" yet.

The story of how the term "genocide" was dealt with inside the State Department and at the United Nations reveals much about the failures in Washington and New York to confront the killings in Rwanda. It also explains the reason I later introduced the term "atrocity crimes" as a means of avoiding the worst errors of the Rwandan experience.

Clearly, the alarm bells should have been ringing incessantly within Washington policy circles over the rapidly mounting death count in Rwanda. I should have gone ballistic on April 26, when I saw in an intelligence report that the International Committee of the Red Cross was estimating between 100,000 and 500,000 killings of mostly Tutsi in Rwanda.[44] That was the critical moment—in late April—when the trumpet should have finally blasted to take forceful action and describe the killings as genocide, whether or not a legal determination could yet be made. I could have shouted out the point at the Deputies Committee meeting and insisted on more action and a public pronouncement of genocide. But I hesitated. I opted to press for one primary goal and ensure I achieved it: to obtain the deputies' support for a genocide investigation. I wonder to this day whether I could have accomplished more at that meeting.

In New York, on April 30, New Zealand's ambassador to the United Nations, Colin Keating, forged a nonbinding "presidential statement" in the Security Council that made no explicit reference to genocide.[45] The document asked the secretary-general to "make proposals for investigation of the reports of serious violations of international humanitarian law during the conflict."[46] This was code language for a genocide investigation, but it satisfied those on the council still nervous about invoking the word, not to mention the ever-present Hutu Rwandan delegation still sitting as a nonpermanent member.

Albright's focus then shifted to dispatching the U.N. high commissioner for human rights, Jose Ayala Lasso, to investigate the Rwandan atrocities. She practically had to drag him into announcing his trip on May 4.[47] Albright had been instrumental in creating the Office of High Commissioner for Human Rights several months earlier; yet its first occupant proved to be ineffectual and hesitant to act in the face of the very transgressions he was mandated to confront.[48]

The RPF slowed down the peacekeeping train in New York and by early May officially rejected intervention by U.N. or African peacekeeping forces in Rwanda. RPF officers asserted that their victory was the only way to stop the ongoing genocide. They believed that a peacekeeping force would create the perverse outcome of permitting those responsible for the genocide to go "unpunished" for their crimes.[49] The rebels made a concerted push to capture Kigali. In Washington, we thought the RPF might solve the Hutu-led genocide for everyone, thus deflating demands for a beefed-up U.N. peacekeeping force.

During the period of the Rwandan genocide, a number of other critical foreign policy matters competed mightily for the attention of policy-makers in Washington. This led to delay and weariness in addressing Rwanda within the bureaucracy, despite the obvious reality that something terrible was happening there. At the time, that relentless subconscious reminder of the Somalia debacle cast a pall over foreign engagements. Days were filled with meetings on China's human rights record and its most-favored-nation status, always a contentious issue during an election year. North Korean nuclear arms aspirations, which brought the United States to the brink of war in the spring of 1994, and the ongoing atrocities and fighting in Bosnia and Herzegovina and in Croatia occupied huge swaths of time. The needs of the Yugoslav Tribunal, final consultations with Congress about PDD-25, and the Middle East peace process took center stage. Refugee outflows from Haiti and the possibility of military intervention there, peacekeeping requirements in Angola, and even the final drafting by the U.N. International Law Commission of a statute for a new international criminal court kept everyone, including me, busy. The Rwandan debacle taught us, under the most horrific circumstances, that policy-makers must not permit other priorities and breaking events from distracting them from the need to respond swiftly to atrocities. The "walk and chew gum at the same time" principle should never be underestimated, particularly when so many lives are at stake.

John Shattuck, the assistant secretary of state for human rights, proved to be the most persistent high-level advocate for action and accountability in Rwanda. Following his visit to the strife-torn region in early May, Shattuck claimed that crimes against humanity and acts of genocide were being committed, and he sought an investigation by the omission. He and I joined together on the Rwanda challenge for years thereafter.[50]

Despite RPF resistance, the Security Council finally established a new platform for UNAMIR with the adoption of Resolution 918 on May 15, expanding its mandate and increasing its force (at least in theory) to 5,500 troops. The new mandate authorized UNAMIR to provide security and protection for displaced persons, refugees, and civilians at risk, including the establishment of secure humanitarian areas. UNAMIR also gained authority to provide security and support for distribution of relief supplies and humanitarian relief operations.[51] Back in Washington, I joined other officials in examining the new UNAMIR through the prism of PDD-25 criteria. It barely survived the scrutiny.

Lost in Translation

A persistent criticism of the Western response to the genocide in Rwanda has been how long it took to employ the term "genocide" to describe the carnage. Would simply labeling the massive killings "genocide" suddenly have compelled a government to invade the crime scene? No government would have ratified the Genocide Convention if the intent of its Article 1 were to require, as a legal obligation under the treaty, that all states that are parties to the agreement (called "states parties") must deploy their military forces onto foreign territory to prevent genocide whenever and wherever it occurs. Article 1 reads, "The Contracting Parties confirm that genocide, whether committed in time of peace or in time of war, is a crime under international law which they undertake to prevent and to punish." The undertaking to prevent and to punish is not specified. and nothing in the negotiating history of the convention speaks to precisely what is expected as measures of prevention. A state party's action could be diplomatic, economic, juridical, or military in character. While America's meager steps in the early stages of the Rwandan genocide were pathetic, there was no legal obligation to deploy U.S. military forces in Rwanda.

Nonetheless, a fair and politically realistic reading of the Genocide Convention requires that states parties do *something*.[52] In Washington my colleagues and I vacillated, found refuge in trying to revive the peace process, and subjected any strengthening or expansion of UNAMIR to the test of PDD-25 criteria that were not well adapted for either immediate decision making or the unorthodox tactics required to stem the tidal wave of killing in Rwanda.

The U.N. Security Council requested the secretary-general "to present a report as soon as possible on the investigation of serious violations of international humanitarian law committed in Rwanda during the conflict."[53] Many council members refused to use the word "genocide" in the resolution. By that stage, perhaps some 400,000 mostly Tutsi had been hacked to death. Member governments remained far more focused on the mechanics of a U.N. presence in Rwanda than on how to characterize what was occurring there.

Secretary of State Warren Christopher finally received, and then approved on May 21, a memorandum, signed by the assistant secretaries of state for African affairs, international organization affairs, and human rights, and by the department's legal adviser, authorizing use of the terms "acts of genocide" and "genocide" to describe the atrocities in Rwanda. There was no attempt in the memorandum to sharply distinguish between the two terms. The memorandum stated that some, but not necessarily all, of the violence in Rwanda was "genocide" within the meaning of the 1948 Genocide Convention and that the United States should declare that "acts of genocide have occurred in Rwanda" without triggering any particular legal consequences.[54]

Nowhere in the memorandum was there any suggestion that using the term "acts of genocide" or "genocide" would give rise to an obligation of the United States to respond militarily to the situation in Rwanda. The popular theory is that Washington refused to use the term for fear of being compelled to act with military force in Rwanda. That may have been a political perception among some, even in the State Department, at the time, but it certainly was not part of any legal analysis of the matter by State Department lawyers.

Interestingly, the legal adviser's supplemental memorandum concluded that all the factors of genocide were present in Rwanda and confirmed that the special intent requirement for the crime of genocide could be *inferred*.[55] Thus, although the term "genocide" was first used by the Deputics Committee of the National Security Council on April 29 to describe the "genocide investigation" they sought from the U.N. Security Council, it still took State Department lawyers and experts several more weeks—far too long—to analyze the information and the law, and then prepare the decision memorandum for Christopher authorizing public reference to "acts of genocide" and confirming that "genocide has occurred" in Rwanda.

Unfortunately, we did not go public with this finding of "genocide" quickly enough; word of Christopher's May 21 decision apparently did not filter through to all ranks of the State Department; and the official spokeswoman on June 10 created unnecessary confusion when she muddled and dodged her way through reporters' questions, leaving the impression that we still had not faced up to criminal genocide in Rwanda.[56]

The departmental press guidance proved incomprehensible and inconsistent with the clarity of the May 21 decision. The guidance simply left the wrong impression about the seriousness of "genocide" and "acts of genocide" and seemed to claim that the United States could walk away from any legal obligations, even if that were technically true with respect to genocide in Rwanda.[57] The correct press guidance and statement from the spokesperson should have read something like the following:

There is no practical legal difference between "acts of genocide" and "genocide." We use them interchangeably and Secretary Christopher approved use of both terms weeks ago to describe what is occurring in Rwanda. The use of either term has no different impact on our legal obligations under the Genocide Convention. Under Article 1 of that treaty, the United States is obligated, as a state party, to "undertake to prevent and to punish" genocide, but the article does not stipulate how that should be done. The United States has undertaken diplomatic and economic efforts and other measures, including support for an expanded peacekeeping mission, at the United Nations to confront the genocide in Rwanda and will continue to do so.

Even these words could not have overcome the fact that we had failed for more than two months to react quickly and effectively enough to the genocide. By June 1994, arguing technicalities about compliance with the Genocide Convention bordered on the obscene.

The State Department arrived at a determination of genocide by mid-May, prior to the word being uttered at the United Nations. There was no U.N. reference to "genocide" in connection with the killings in Rwanda until Secretary-General Boutros-Ghali's report to the Security Council on May 31, 1994, in which he concluded that "there can be little doubt that it constitutes genocide."[58] Then, on June 28, the Security Council first employed the term in a preambular clause of Resolution 925.[59] Two days later, on June 30, the U.N. Human Rights Commission special rapporteur on Rwanda, Rene Degni-Segui, issued his initial report concluding that hundreds of thousands of Rwandans had been killed in systematic massacres that constituted genocide against the Tutsi.[60]

The French Intervene

In mid-June, UNAMIR force strength still fell far below the authorized 5,500 personnel. Only 354 troops, 25 military staff personnel, and 124 military observers operated under General Dallaire's command.[61] On June 22, the U.N. Security Council approved France's offer to temporarily deploy thousands of French troops into southwest Rwanda, under U.N. Charter Chapter VII enforcement authority, and cordon off a humanitarian safe zone for Hutu fleeing the RPF.[62]

The United States did not join France's intervention, dubbed Operation Turquoise, to save the Hutu from RPF revenge in the wake of the genocide.

However, Washington committed almost four thousand troops, cargo aircraft, and humanitarian supplies to its own "Operation Support Hope," which undertook a massive refugee relief effort during July, August, and September.[63] Much of the attention of the Deputies and Principals committees during the summer was directed at the humanitarian plight of the hundreds of thousands of Rwandans, mostly Hutu, in squalid and overcrowded refugee camps in eastern Zaire and the tens of thousands of Tutsi refugees camped either in Zaire or Tanzania.

Ironically, the United States ended up committing its treasure and military assets to the survival, in significant part, of the genocidaires and their families after refusing to support or engage in tough military responses to the Hutu-led government's genocidal assaults on Rwandan Tutsi. There really was no choice but to reverse the humanitarian disaster unfolding rapidly in the refugee camps; if we had forsaken the refugees, the Clinton administration would have been criticized on two counts: for standing aloof during the Rwandan genocide and for abandoning hundreds of thousands of human beings in squalid refugee camps. However, Operation Support Hope demonstrated that, within a short number of weeks in July 1994, the United States had the capability to mobilize troops and cargo planes and fly them into the heart of Africa. In fact, the rapid evacuation of American citizens from Rwanda already had demonstrated how quickly the Pentagon could mobilize and act. The evacuation mission could have been executed with more personnel and firepower in April to effect the survival of significant numbers of Rwandan Tutsi if the political and military will had existed to do so.[64]

On October 5, 1994, UNAMIR Commander and Lieutenant General Roméo Dallaire visited Washington and spoke bluntly to me and other State Department officials about what had gone wrong and how to frame our future commitment to Rwanda. He said that policy-makers had to expect casualties in U.N. peacekeeping operations, and he complained that the United Nations simply did not have decision-making processes or the resources to react quickly to genocide. Dallaire urged that an expanded mandate for UNAMIR must include the authority to detain suspects. He believed that task was just as important to the aims of justice as the need to capture Hutu genocidaires in order to end their stranglehold over the refugees in the Zaire camps.

Timing Is Everything

The lessons from these tumultuous months influenced my own thinking and performance for the rest of the Clinton presidency. Violent humanitarian catastrophes may require unorthodox responses, speedy and innovative policy-making, and determined efforts to focus political will on the imperative of human survival. Atrocities do not wait for well-briefed discussions in regularly scheduled meetings of high-level officials. Atrocities do not fit well within rigid guidelines for policy-making. Atrocities, or the imminent launch of such atrocities, scream out for immediate, imaginative, and bold actions tailored to the unique threat. *Timing is everything.* The ultimate cost of atrocity crimes far exceeds what is required initially to face down the masters of the killing fields. For America, paying more attention to its global interests and strengthening the capacities of the United Nations, rather than fixating solely on narrowly conceived national interests, remains a good starting point.

Reliable information about atrocities can arrive from open sources, particularly nongovernmental organizations and the media. Policy-makers, however, remain wedded to intelligence information and diplomatic dispatches (or the lack of them) to shape their views. As a result, Washington too often seems adrift. Following the closure of the U.S. embassy in Kigali shortly after the start of the genocide, the U.S. government could monitor and analyze events in Rwanda only from outside its borders. With the exception of a couple of trips to assess the humanitarian situation, American personnel did not enter Rwanda until early July 1994, shortly after the French had occupied the southwest corner of the country. This long absence from the scene of the crime, which was belatedly recognized as genocide, severely restricted the flow of official information to U.S. policy-makers who fumbled all the data arriving from "open" sources.

Nonetheless, my work was only beginning. The next challenge in Rwanda was accountability for the genocide. Building a war crimes tribunal became my highest priority as I sought my own pathway toward redemption.

CHAPTER THREE
CREDIBLE JUSTICE FOR RWANDA

We could have gone unilateral, but we came to you.

A Tutsi negotiator addressing the author about American leadership in
building the Rwanda Tribunal on October 26, 1994

IN THE AFTERMATH OF THE GENOCIDE THAT RAVAGED RWANDA, THERE HAD
to be a judicial response at least as credible as that which the Balkans atrocities had inspired with the Yugoslav Tribunal. Thanks in large measure to
Albright's leadership at the time, serious planning for building a war crimes
tribunal for Rwanda commenced in mid-June 1994 as the genocide gave
way to the overpowering victories of the Rwandan Patriotic Front (RPF).
The highly trained and disciplined RPF militia, led by Paul Kagame, steadily
defeated Hutu army units and seized territory. By July, the RPF controlled
the capital of Kigali and most of the countryside. Kagame and his other
rebel leaders seized the reins of government, routed the Hutu politicians
and generals, and began to govern Rwanda.

Akin to the ongoing warfare in the Balkans during the creation of the
Yugoslav Tribunal, the killing in Rwanda had not ended before Albright
cabled the State Department and other key posts on June 15, 1994, recommending serious examination of whether the United States should propose
U.N. action to prosecute those responsible for the atrocity crimes.[1] Albright
mapped out three options for a prosecution strategy. The first possibility
was to build a new ad hoc tribunal for Rwanda, which "would be time-
consuming and involve considerable expenditure of resources." The second option, to expand the jurisdiction of the Yugoslav Tribunal to include

the situation in Rwanda, was described as perhaps "the most expeditious way of moving on this issue" and could result in "a small deterrent effect in Rwanda." Notably, the cable stated that "acting speedily will help blunt criticism of earlier USG reluctance to recognize that acts of genocide have taken place." But there were downsides to the idea as well, such as the fact that the Yugoslav Tribunal was only beginning its work and this could interfere with its ability to achieve its mandate. The third option was to establish an international criminal court, which would take years to realize and probably would not have jurisdiction over past atrocities. Albright requested that Washington inform her of its views quickly so that she could take action in New York before another government beat her to the punch. The same urgency that compelled her to act quickly in February 1993 for a court to address the Balkans' atrocities reasserted itself in June of 1994 for Rwanda's genocide.

Albright did not receive an immediate go-ahead from the State Department to push forward a resolution establishing a war crimes tribunal for Rwanda. Instead, the focus remained on supporting the creation of a commission of experts to investigate the crimes in Rwanda and thereafter make a recommendation, perhaps to build a tribunal, to the Security Council. A few weeks earlier the Security Council had begun to deliberate over a draft resolution to create a commission of experts to examine and analyze information on "violations of international humanitarian law" and "evidence of possible acts of genocide."

Spain, Argentina, the Czech Republic, and New Zealand initially cosponsored the resolution on a commission of experts, and the United States soon joined its list of cosponsors. The Security Council discussed the text on June 14 and finally approved it two weeks later.[2] We were mindful of what the special rapporteur on Rwanda of the U.N. Human Rights Commission had just concluded in his June 30 report: that genocide and war crimes had been committed and an international criminal tribunal should be established to prosecute such crimes.[3] The council resolution mandated the Commission of Experts to reach conclusions about the atrocities within four months, at which point the secretary-general would report the commission's conclusions and recommendations. Albright fully supported formation of the Commission of Experts but wanted to be prepared, through consultations with other governments, to act swiftly to create a tribunal if the commission found that atrocity crimes (including genocide) had taken place in Rwanda.[4]

Seizing the Initiative

The State Department mobilized quickly in early July to help staff the commission, fund it, and provide as much support as possible for its operation. U.S. diplomats in Paris approached the French government in early July to ensure that its collection of information from witnesses and others during Operation Turquoise in southwest Rwanda would be shared with the commission and ultimately a war crimes tribunal.[5]

All the while, Albright's June 15 cable, having received Christopher's support, proved to be the starting point for serious discussions in Washington for the establishment of a war crimes tribunal for Rwanda. On July 5, I spoke with the president of the Yugoslav Tribunal, Antonio Cassese, about the Security Council creating an ad hoc Rwanda tribunal. We both agreed that any duplication of talent and facilities would be a waste of money, so we wanted to explore what could be used in the Yugoslav Tribunal to help cover Rwanda cases. Short of creating a completely separate tribunal in all respects, we considered double-hatting Richard Goldstone as prosecutor of both tribunals, sharing the appeals chamber between the two tribunals, and creating a separate trial chamber and prosecutorial staff within the Yugoslav Tribunal to cover Rwanda cases.

By mid-July the writing was squarely on the wall that the United States would be pressing hard for a tribunal of some character to prosecute the perpetrators of atrocity crimes in Rwanda. The State Department instructed its diplomats that the United States would "support creation of an international tribunal ... if the Commission of Experts confirms that such violations [of international humanitarian law in Rwanda] have occurred. Such a tribunal might be structured along the lines of the tribunal set up for Yugoslavia, and the two tribunals might be combined in some respects."[6] The White House also issued a statement insisting "that those Rwandans responsible for genocidal killings and other crimes against humanity be brought to justice." It "hoped that the United Nations would act swiftly ... to create a war crimes tribunal."[7] Albright, impatient with a timeline dependent on the Commission of Experts, spoke before her Security Council colleagues on July 18 and called for quick action to establish a war crimes tribunal.[8] The British, however, remained noncommittal, waiting to see what the Commission of Experts would recommend.[9]

France reported to an international pledging conference for Rwanda on July 23 that the new Rwandan government, controlled by Tutsi RPF leaders, wanted a tribunal, cautioning that if the international community did not build one, the government would have to try the suspects in Rwanda. Within days, Washington accelerated the war crimes agenda for Rwanda. On July 26, cabled instructions to key posts requested the backing of other governments while advising them about U.S. support for an international tribunal for Rwanda. The U.S. position had matured quickly. The cable instructions provided the first clear summary of what I and others spent July intensively hammering out as the U.S. initiative, which was to support the establishment of an international tribunal that would be commensurate with the Yugoslav Tribunal. We proposed expanding the jurisdiction of the Yugoslav Tribunal to include Rwanda, adding new prosecutorial staff to deal with the Rwandan genocide, using the same appeals chamber, employing the same chief prosecutor, and sharing facilities and resources in The Hague. We also pressed for detaining suspects of the Rwandan atrocities and explored the types of legal authorities necessary to facilitate arrests.[10]

Several days later, I cochaired with John Shattuck, the assistant secretary of state covering human rights, the first interagency working group covering "war crimes," namely atrocity crimes, in Rwanda. The objective of our "Rwanda War Crimes IWG" was to create an expanded international criminal tribunal covering Rwanda with supremacy over domestic courts. The tribunal would treat detainees in accordance with international standards and prosecute them bearing in mind the goals of reconciliation and safe return of refugees. We also knew that the official creation of the Commission of Experts would drive much of our work in the coming weeks as the United States determined how best to assist the commission in collecting evidence of atrocity crimes. By early August we had explored a wide range of initiatives for justice, including getting the Commission of Experts on the ground in Rwanda with the help of American investigators who could channel to the commission information that our intelligence community, the nongovernmental organizations, and academics had collected about the genocide and its leaders.

The biggest headache was how to detain genocide suspects in Rwanda and neighboring countries. The easiest answer was found in the authority of an international criminal tribunal to issue arrest warrants provided the Security Council established such a court. Alternatively, we proposed that U.N. peacekeepers be granted authority by the Security Council to arrest genocide suspects, but the British expressed grave concern about moving in that direction. In the absence of a competent arresting authority, with the unwillingness of governments of bordering countries, and owing to the nearly nonexistent capabilities of the new Rwandan authorities, the very top genocide suspects were likely to achieve sanctuary, somewhere.

Nonetheless, the new Rwanda government, effectively led by Paul Kagame and a band of Tutsi warriors, claimed it had 110 perpetrators of genocide in custody, but there appeared to be no way to properly investigate and prosecute them, as most of Rwanda's judiciary and legal profession had been wiped out or were complicit in the genocide. Furthermore, prison facilities in Rwanda were squalid and vastly overcrowded (and remained that way for many years) as thousands of alleged genocidaires were detained indefinitely.

Bob Rosenstock, the astute American legal adviser in New York, advised us to give detention of suspects a second-place priority and focus instead on setting up the tribunal. The latter would be easier and attract Security Council support much faster than the detention challenge. To that end, the council heard from U.N. undersecretary-general Chinmaya Gharekhan on August 4 that the new Rwandan government strongly supported the establishment of an international criminal tribunal.[11] The Rwandan justice minister confirmed this view several days later in a letter to Secretary-General Boutros Boutros-Ghali.[12] On August 10, the Security Council issued a presidential statement welcoming the Rwandan government's support for the establishment of an international tribunal and urged the Commission of Experts to submit its conclusions as soon as possible.[13]

Later that day Rosenstock convened his counterparts from France, Russia, China, and Britain at the U.S. Mission to start talking about a tribunal. Only China opposed the creation of any international war crimes tribunal to address the Rwandan genocide. The Chinese were nervous that it was becoming too easy to build ad hoc tribunals and leaned instead toward prosecutions in Rwandan courts, with international assistance. The Russians veered far from the U.S. proposal for an expanded Yugoslav Tribunal (a court that they had been skeptical about from the beginning) and pushed the alternative of a separate tribunal with no linkages to the Yugoslav Tribunal other than sharing some facilities and personnel. Russia preferred a "Nuremberg-style" approach that would prosecute the higher-level offenders while letting Rwandan courts handle the lower-level perpetrators. The British straddled the Russian and American views, emphasizing that the most cost-effective means should be used and only the higher-level suspects prosecuted.

Meanwhile, during his trip to Kigali, Shattuck delivered to the new Rwandan government a draft letter endorsing creation of a war crimes tribunal by the Security Council, which we hoped would be the catalyst to galvanize the council action.[14] Then Shattuck and Crystal Nix from the Office of the Legal Adviser at the State Department met with the French in Paris on August 10 to press for the U.S.-proposed consolidated tribunal, but met resistance from French officials who argued for a separate tribunal for Rwanda. They expressed concern that expansion of the Yugoslav Tribunal eventually could lead to a de facto permanent international criminal court, an undesirable result from the French point of view.[15] In his talks with the British a few days later, Shattuck learned of their desire to discuss a complete judicial package for Rwanda, including international support for domestic judicial rebuilding, before adopting a resolution to create the Rwanda Tribunal. While such planning was certainly desirable, we knew that the Rwandan legal system was shattered and that rebuilding it would take years of multilateral assistance. Creating the Rwanda Tribunal had to be done on a faster track.[16]

Working the Problem

The Rwanda War Crimes IWG met on August 12, as it would repeatedly do for several months thereafter, to develop strategy for building the Rwanda Tribunal. The new government of Rwanda wanted three tiers of defendants: (1) those most directly responsible for genocide, who would be tried before the international criminal tribunal; (2) those directly responsible for implementing the killings, who would be prosecuted in Rwandan courts; and (3) those who had engaged in acts of violence, whose fate would remain undetermined at that time as the suspects numbered in the hundreds of thousands. The Rwandans insisted on a role in deciding how the first and second tiers of defendants were determined—a view that would challenge the independence of the Rwanda Tribunal as it was being negotiated and when it became operational.

By August 24, Washington's position shifted to accelerate the building of a tribunal. The State Department informed the American embassy in Rwanda that the prompt establishment of an international war crimes tribunal for Rwanda had become the highest priority. Such a tribunal would avoid the problems of perceived bias, unfairness, and ethnic revenge. We set our goal to establish the international tribunal no later than mid-September.

We also wanted the Commission of Experts to facilitate the creation of the tribunal by issuing an interim report as soon as possible.[17]

The Rwanda War Crimes IWG pushed forward intensively to find and deliver relevant information to the commission. Just as had been the case in the Balkans, the evidence and analyses compiled by the Commission of Experts would prove invaluable to the Rwanda Tribunal, assuming we could establish it. I met with Alison Des Forges from Human Rights Watch. She was a leading expert on Rwandan society and politics and had significant insight into what had transpired during the genocide. She helped guide me and others in the State Department to gather and understand evidence. In my many meetings with Des Forges, she never hesitated to graciously, but decidedly, shame me, with her sad and penetrating eyes, into acting on the priorities of justice in Rwanda. When she perished in a plane crash near Buffalo in 2009, I joined the global human rights community in mourning her death.

Shattuck and I launched an intensive effort through the Rwanda War Crimes IWG to strategize how to identify and apprehend genocide suspects. Governments would not detain or arrest Rwandan suspects absent clear domestic or international authority to do so. While some believed the mandate of UNAMIR, the U.N. peacekeeping operation in Rwanda, permitted U.N. peacekeepers to detain suspects, others were deeply troubled by the prospect. True to form, the Pentagon said any arrest function for UNAMIR sounded like Somalia and mission creep all over again. Prudence Bushnell, a deputy assistant secretary in the Africa bureau, did not think many of the leaders of the genocide were in Rwanda anymore and that the challenge really lay in tracking them down near Goma, Zaire (which later was renamed the Democratic Republic of the Congo), and in Tanzania. But the intelligence community could not locate them, which may have reflected the relative scarcity of its resources in eastern Africa. I directed a crash effort at compiling the names of leading suspects and working with Interpol to prepare arrest warrants, although we had not figured out yet the jurisdiction for their prosecution. I also requested that steps be taken immediately to prevent Hutu leaders from entering the United States, so we had to create a visa lookout for them at all U.S. consulates and entry points to the country.

To my astonishment, I learned that the visa application forms had never been revised to ask the applicant whether he or she had ever participated in genocide, crimes against humanity, or war crimes. The form used in 1994 simply asked about any association with Nazi Germany and persecution during that period. We were certain to run into trouble, and we did, with Hutu ringleaders who truthfully filled out their visa applications and legally waltzed into the United States to visit as tourists, some ultimately achieving green card status that would grant them permanent residence. Once on American soil, a genocide suspect from Rwanda could prove difficult to extradite to justice, especially if he or she held a green card.

In the following weeks, the working group pulled together about two hundred names for the visa watch list. These individuals were not necessarily prohibited from entering the United States, but they were subject to more intensive questioning at the border. We determined that all Rwandans needed to be asked specific questions that might elicit valuable information about their possible role in the genocide. So we cabled out immediate guidance to all embassies. Bushnell proposed excluding from the United States any religious minister from Rwanda, and to make that determination on foreign policy grounds alone. She knew that too many clergy were implicated in the genocide to take the risk. Her foresight bore out with Pastor Elizaphan Ntakirutimana, whose story will be told later.

Washington was alerted when any Rwandan applied for a visa. We got mired down in our working group discussions, however, over whether, in the absence of specific guidelines on admitting Rwandan citizens, suspicion of having committed genocide could be used as grounds to exclude anyone. Committing genocide had never been used to deny anyone a visa to the United States! Justice Department lawyers argued that a visa holder could challenge the factual basis for our claim of genocide in Rwanda and that, although Secretary of State Warren Christopher had determined genocide occurred, there was no official evidence that in fact it had occurred with the specific intent required under the Genocide Convention. We needed a test case, they said, so as to establish the premise for exclusion for genocide in Rwanda. The standard of proof, particularly for an alien seeking admission to the United States, was quite low, but it nonetheless required some evidentiary finding about genocide. A presidential proclamation would be too difficult to obtain. We finally decided to fingerprint each Rwandan citizen granted a visa to enter the United States.

The Resolution Takes Shape

By late August I heard that the U.N. high commissioner for human rights, Jose Ayala Lasso, was very upset with Washington for our allegedly heavy-handed efforts on Rwandan accountability, leaving the impression, he complained, that the operation was being run by Americans. I could only plead guilty, as Lasso had months earlier exhibited extraordinary weakness at a time when Albright struggled to get him to Rwanda to investigate during the worst weeks of the genocide. The last person I was going to defer to on what was necessary to move the process forward was Lasso.

On August 31, the U.S. draft for a U.N. Security Council resolution on establishing the Rwanda Tribunal sat at the U.S. National Security Council awaiting clearance. It would emerge at the United Nations two weeks later when Albright circulated it for consideration by her council colleagues. The United States wanted the council to establish the Rwanda Tribunal as soon as possible once the Commission of Experts issued an interim report or letter confirming that genocide or other war crimes (or, unspoken, crimes against humanity) had been committed in Rwanda. The plan was to amend the statute of the Yugoslav Tribunal to incorporate the requirements of investigating and prosecuting the genocide and other atrocity crimes in Rwanda.[18]

As we moved toward circulation of our proposed draft resolution in early September, the Russians continued to seek two separate tribunals, clearly not wanting to lend any more weight of authority to the Yugoslav Tribunal, which was targeting key military and civilian figures among its ally, the Serbs, for prosecution. France leaned toward the Russian concept, oddly arguing that there needed to be a separate tribunal for Rwanda to prosecute genocide because the Yugoslav Tribunal covered war crimes (which, of course, was only partially correct, as genocide and crimes against humanity had been part of the subject-matter jurisdiction of the Yugoslav Tribunal from its inception).[19] Nor did the French believe the same judges could be qualified to handle cases arising from either conflict. The Spanish also supported the Russian idea. China shifted into our column in support of a consolidated tribunal[20] as did numerous African states, including Rwanda, and the U.N. Human Rights Commission's special rapporteur for Rwanda.[21]

Efforts to build support for some kind of Security Council criminal tribunal thus took center stage in September. The U.S. embassy in Kigali learned early in the month that the Commission of Experts had completed their preliminary work and would file an interim report soon recommending the establishment of an international war crimes tribunal.[22]

On September 14, I met with Goldstone, who was adjusting to his new duties as prosecutor of the Yugoslav Tribunal. He argued strongly in favor of the U.S. proposal for one tribunal exercising jurisdiction over the Balkans and Rwanda. He believed that the Russian proposal—for two tribunals—would create a delay of at least one year in launching investigative and early prosecutorial work (which proved to be the case).

New Zealand Steps Forward

The first real turning point on the evolution of the Rwanda Tribunal statute occurred on September 26, when New Zealand proposed a compromise between the American proposal—one expanded tribunal—and the Russian and French preference for two tribunals. New Zealand's U.N. ambassador, Colin Keating, proposed that there be two tribunals sharing one appellate chamber (using the existing appeals chamber of the Yugoslav Tribunal) and that one prosecutor, Richard Goldstone, would work for both tribunals. The New Zealand approach intrigued us in Washington, as it conformed to one of the options we had looked at earlier and retained key consolidating features. We agreed to team up with New Zealand and push forward the hybrid concept of two tribunals sharing one appeals chamber and one prosecutor, as those were the primary collaborative goals of our original proposal. Too much time was passing by and we wanted to expedite the process, so a compromise of this character seemed acceptable. Given the French, Spanish, and Russian opposition to the American proposal of an expanded Yugoslav Tribunal, it would take some diplomatic heavy lifting to convince them that New Zealand's hybrid proposal was a significant shift from Washington's proposal.

Bushnell, just back from Rwanda, reported that the Rwandan people were totally traumatized. The stench of death was everywhere. She urged that we accelerate creation of the tribunal as there were cries for accountability and the Rwandan judicial system was in a shambles.

On September 28, the newly framed U.S.-New Zealand proposal to establish the Rwanda Tribunal sharing the prosecutor and appeals chamber with the Yugoslav Tribunal was circulated to the permanent members of the Security Council and to the rest of the council the next day. In meetings, led by Shattuck, that I joined in New York, the British, French, and Belgians signaled their acceptance of the New Zealand compromise and their desire that the tribunal be approved as quickly as possible. We met with Rwanda's new ambassador to the United Nations in New York to discuss creation of the tribunal. The Tutsi leadership could not share power with those who committed the atrocities, he said. While he was very grateful for U.S. support on building a tribunal, he insisted it be based in Kigali and asked that we trust his government. He strongly supported rapid establishment of the international tribunal but warned that the new government in Rwanda would more likely render "justice" itself—any way it could—if the tribunal were not established soon. Everyone agreed it was critical to send a "justice" signal among the Rwandan people—victims and perpetrators alike—with a Security Council tribunal.[23]

The Commission of Experts provided its preliminary report on October 1, 1994, recommending that a tribunal be established.[24] It proved to be a thorough preliminary report on the atrocities, and the door opened to push full steam ahead with creation of the Rwanda Tribunal. A draft of the Security Council resolution consistent with the U.S.-New Zealand compromise circulated to all council members a few days earlier on September 29 with the hope that it would be adopted by mid-October.[25] We were still pressing for The Hague as the seat for the Rwanda Tribunal both because of the shared appeals chamber and prosecutor and for the sake of cost efficiencies. We suggested holding some proceedings in Kigali, Nairobi, or elsewhere in the region as the need or desire arose.

Several days later U.N. secretary-general Boutros-Ghali announced that Goldstone should not be the prosecutor for both tribunals. In Washington, we were astonished at this sudden opposition to Goldstone and wondered whether Albright or Goldstone could bring Boutros-Ghali around to the compromise formula. Another complication was strong opposition from France, China, and Russia to having the tribunal cover Rwandans (mostly Hutu) committing crimes in neighboring countries. Further, Rwanda's representative in New York summarized his government's demands: (1) a July 1994 end date for jurisdiction, thereby exempting post-July actions by the new government's forces; (2) no coverage of war crimes, thereby arguably exempting the Tutsi militia and soldiers accused of attacking Hutus; (3) incarceration of convicted persons only in Rwanda; (4) no primacy for the tribunal, thus preventing it from seizing jurisdiction when a national court starts to try a suspect; and (5) trials in Kigali, giving the government physical control of the proceedings.[26] The Rwandans wanted the tribunal's jurisdiction to begin on November 15, 1992, to cover the alleged planning of the genocide.[27] Suddenly, we were confronted with serious roadblocks to creation of the tribunal.

Goldstone visited me in New York on October 19 to discuss strategy. He was strongly opposed to a separate prosecutor for the Rwanda Tribunal. We both agreed that it was critical to approach atrocity crimes in the Balkans and Rwanda with the same prosecutorial perspective so that cases would be litigated consistently with international criminal law as it existed then and would be developed in the years to come. Goldstone conceded that it would make sense to set up a deputy prosecutor's office in Kigali, which was accomplished in 1995. Ultimately, we successfully negotiated dual prosecutor responsibilities for Goldstone.

The Rwandans Object

The following day several U.S. officials, including myself, met with the Rwandan delegation in New York to thrash out their objections to the draft statute for the tribunal. The Rwandans revised their requested start date for the tribunal's jurisdiction to October 1993, or six months before the genocide began. As for the end date of the tribunal's jurisdiction, we argued it was premature to set it, as there remained a strong possibility of a recurrence of genocidal massacres in the refugee camps. The Rwandans were willing to have the administrative seat of the tribunal outside Rwanda but still insisted on the trials being held in Rwanda so that the government could convince its citizens that justice was being rendered. We told them that there might be a chance of some proceedings in Rwanda, but there could be no requirement that all trials be held there. We agreed to shift the focus of the crimes to genocide by placing that crime as the first one referenced in the tribunal statute.

The Rwandan justice minister, Alphonse Marie Nkubito, registered his government's demand that the Rwanda Tribunal permit the ultimate punishment upon conviction: the death penalty, which existed under Rwandan criminal law.[28] This appeared quickly as a deal breaker, for we feared Rwanda would vote against the resolution in the Security Council if the tribunal could not impose the death penalty. The Europeans, Latin Americans, and New Zealand—seven out of fifteen Security Council members— could not accept any resolution that endorsed the death penalty, so we knew this was an impossible demand to satisfy. (The Yugoslav Tribunal permitted only life imprisonment as maximum punishment, even for committing genocide.) As authentic Washington bureaucrats, we speculated about how to sweeten the deal for Rwanda to encourage them to stand down on their positions: more security and skilled investigators on the ground, voluntary contributions, support for an outpost in Kigali, jeeps from our stock in Mogadishu, and a lot of American detailees to the tribunal.

Rwanda's diplomatic team joined a drafting session in New York, where I was camped out on October 26. The Tutsi government wanted the resolution adopted and a Security Council tribunal established. "We don't want to miss this opportunity," they told me privately. "We could have gone unilateral, but we came to you." They argued that the atrocities by the Hutu had extended back for years in the country's history. But I joined others in arguing that the tribunal could not take on pre-1994 genocide allegations in Rwanda. The tribunal should not be perceived to be a Tutsi weapon against the Hutu; it had to be an entirely objective exercise. The Tutsi government might go after Hutu suspects with extreme bias domestically but not in an international tribunal. There could be a separate tribunal for Rwanda, we argued, and we would see what might be accomplished for a presence of some character (such as the deputy prosecutor) in Kigali.

The Rwandans then proposed a temporal jurisdiction of October 1, 1990, to July 18, 1994, which would wall off all the Tutsi security and retributive actions following the takeover of the government. After we pointed out the implausibility of going back to 1990, the Rwandans radically revised their proposal to cover April 6 to July 15, 1994. They obviously were prepared to sacrifice the genocide-planning period prior to April 6 in order to avoid liability for themselves after July 15. We countered with the dates of January 1 through December 31, 1994, and that ultimately became the approved temporal jurisdiction of the tribunal despite Rwanda's strong objection to post-July liability for what its troops were doing against Hutu following the genocide. The Rwandans, however, accepted many other compromise proposals for the text of the tribunal statute, and we embraced some of their ideas.

For example, we agreed to their preference for crimes against humanity to be described as being committed on "national, political, ethnic, racial, or religious grounds" even though that kind of limiting language was not used for the Yugoslav Tribunal. The central premise of crimes against humanity was crimes' widespread or systematic character and not their purpose. During the 1994 negotiations, the Rwandans wanted to stress the purpose behind the crimes against humanity and align that purpose as closely as possible with genocide.[29] Since the anti-Tutsi rationale of the killings was well established by then, we considered the qualifying language as acceptable for the circumstances of Rwanda. It helped the Rwandans sell the tribunal at home. and it was a relatively harmless add-on from our perspective.

The Rwandans also wanted to cover groups as well as individuals in the tribunal statute. This would have meant that mere membership in a Hutu group, such as the National Police, Coalition for the Defense of the Republic, Democratic Republican Movement, or murderous Interahamwe, would have subjected an individual to criminal liability.[30] The same tactic was employed in 1945 with the London Charter, which empowered the Nuremberg Tribunal to define as criminal any group or organization to which any defendant appearing in Nuremberg belonged. In the end, the Nuremberg Tribunal declared three of six organizations named in the indictment as criminal in character. These included the Gestapo, the Leadership Corps of the [Nazi] Party, and the SS (Schutzstaffel), which ran the concentration camps and cleared Jews and others out of the ghettos.[31] But no one else at the table wanted to go down that path in Rwanda, as it pointed toward collective culpability—precisely what we argued must not be the future of justice in the Balkans or Rwanda. The Rwandan negotiators backed down.

The Rwandans opposed the primacy of the Rwanda Tribunal in the draft statute, which mirrored the primary jurisdiction that the Yugoslav Tribunal had over domestic courts in the Balkans. But we persuaded them that it was necessary for the integrity of the international proceedings. Rwanda thought that domestic defendants had the right to appeal the judgment of national courts to the Rwanda Tribunal, but we assured them that such an appeal would not be possible.

The Rwandans insisted on their own judges sharing the bench with international judges, but there was strong opposition to that among Security Council members. The possibilities for bias and prejudice were just too great at that fragile moment in Rwanda's recovery from the genocide. I could sense the Rwandan negotiator knew he was asking for too much, and he quickly conceded the point.

We granted a major concession by permitting incarceration of convicted defendants in Rwanda as well as other agreeable countries. This was a hotly contested point among the council negotiators, since we knew that Rwanda's capacity to imprison a convicted defendant of the Rwanda Tribunal in accordance with international standards of due process was very doubtful. But we had to put the option in the statute in recognition of Rwanda's support for the overall process. Even if we had left Rwanda out of the text of this provision, the tribunal theoretically could have negotiated a detention right with Rwanda just as with any other country, so the reference to Rwanda was essentially harmless. It would be up to the judges to determine precisely where each convicted defendant was imprisoned, and their decisions would be subject to much scrutiny by the international community. Therefore, even if we put the option in the statute, it was unlikely a judge would choose to incarcerate a defendant in Rwanda. As it turned out, the convicted defendants of the Rwanda Tribunal who exhausted their appeals ended up in Koulikoro Prison in Mali or a prison in Italy. Although Benin, Swaziland, Rwanda, France, and Sweden also agreed to imprison those convicted by the Rwanda Tribunal, none had done so by 2010.

The Rwandans wanted to require that the government of Rwanda be notified in addition to the tribunal if the country where a convicted defendant was imprisoned decided to make him or her eligible for a pardon or commutation of sentence. That proved a bridge too far for the independence of the tribunal and we pushed the Rwandans back, insisting that any such notification would be made only to the tribunal. The tribunal's chief judge, its president, would make the call on whether the pardon or commutation of sentence should be granted by the national authorities.[32]

U.S. diplomats in Kigali demarched Justice Minister Nkubito on October 30. Nkubito surprisingly accepted December 31, 1994, as the end date of the temporal jurisdiction for the tribunal, which meant that Tutsi actions throughout 1994 would be subject to judicial scrutiny. (His superiors countermanded that view shortly thereafter.) However, Nkubito said the death penalty was the primordial issue for the Rwandan government, and we told him that it was unrealistic to press for that in a U.N. tribunal. We had not seen the flexibility Nkubito revealed in Kigali play out in his delegation's negotiating posture in New York, so we were puzzled. There was a committee of officials in Kigali who determined the final negotiating position, and while he was a member of the committee, he did not control its decisions. The committee consisted entirely of Rwandan Patriotic Front veterans except for himself, and it included RPF leader Paul Kagame. They were adamant about the death penalty issue and claimed that "90 percent of the Rwandan population" also supported the death penalty. Nkubito warned there would be no concession on the question of the ultimate punishment.

Shortly after this round of negotiations with the Rwandans, the gauntlet was dropped by the committee in Kigali. They believed their bottom lines—on the death penalty and the temporal jurisdiction—had not been honored by the other Security Council members. Further negotiations, they claimed, would be a farce. Not to be intimidated, council members believed they had no better option but to proceed to finalize the statute and authorize the resolution. On October 31, we learned that Rwanda would vote no on the resolution. The council sent a high-level team to Kigali to brief the government but not negotiate with it, thus delaying the New York vote by several days. Prospects did not look good for governmental support emerging from Kigali.

Plans proceeded to arrange a vote on November 7. The Rwandan government held firm on its belief in the primacy of Rwandan law for the tribunal. Irreconcilable differences eliminated even the option of an abstention by the Rwandan delegation.

We believed at that stage we had done all we could with the Rwandans. Kagame would not compromise on the most contentious points. The hardliners in Kigali had won with apparent ease. The political cost of any compromise on the death penalty was simply too high. However, I knew from my consultations that Rwandan officials intended to support the tribunal following the vote.

The Security Council Acts

The Security Council approved Resolution 955 on Tuesday, November 8, with one dissenting vote—that of the Rwandan government.[33] The United States never wanted such rejection by the new authorities in Kigali and, we sensed, neither had the surviving Tutsi. But domestic politics fueled much of the Rwandans' angst in the final days. They could not plausibly support a tribunal that denied the death penalty when plans were afoot to impose it on nationally convicted perpetrators of genocide. Nor could the case be made to expose their own Tutsi armed forces, who had liberated the country from a genocidal regime, to prosecution by the Rwanda Tribunal.

In the following weeks, a wave of meetings and initiatives in Washington set up concrete support for the new Rwanda Tribunal as it began to take on the trappings of a court. The State Department garnered $1 million as an initial voluntary contribution to help jump-start the tribunal. I spent much of my time seeking out other sources of federal funding to increase that amount. The U.S. voluntary contribution was used to establish two offices for the prosecutor, one in Kigali and the other in Arusha, and to pay for investigative work. (The initial U.S. voluntary contribution to the Yugoslav

Tribunal soon totaled $3 million, with about $2.3 million of it destined for computers and for investigations.) We also launched planning for legislation on Capitol Hill for authority to turn over suspects found on U.S. territory to the Rwanda and Yugoslav Tribunals. I had worked with the intelligence community to submit U.S. government reports to the Commission of Experts, including various subreports, other information received from civil society, and reports from the U.S. investigative team. This document dump for the commission also was destined for the new tribunal. I started to develop proposals for tribunal involvement in the refugee camps and cooperation with camp security forces.

Goldstone called me on December 7 complaining about a very difficult discussion he had just had with Hans Corell, the U.N. legal counsel, who claimed it was "inappropriate" for Goldstone personally to raise voluntary funds for the new Rwanda Tribunal, which desperately needed "jump-start" funding. Goldstone had secured financing from Switzerland to enable him to travel to Rwanda simply to do his job, but Corell chastised him because Switzerland was not a member state of the United Nations at the time. U.N. lawyers had objected to the many prosecutors and investigators provided free of charge by the United States to the Yugoslav Tribunal, objections that infuriated Goldstone. He was hoping on a hefty deployment of expert prosecutors and investigators from Washington for the Rwanda Tribunal. He argued, correctly, that the prosecutor was the individual who could make the most persuasive pitch for financial support and "in-kind" services from willing governments to help both tribunals achieve their mandated responsibilities.

I told Goldstone that Albright and I would intervene in New York to help him, and then I spent years doing exactly that with the ever-cautious U.N. lawyers. If it was not the Washington bureaucracy that scuttled or dangerously delayed one justice imperative after another, it was the U.N. bureaucracy. A great deal of my job was negotiating logistical problems raised by individuals who had very little stake in the pursuit of justice but loved to throw grenades into my office.

Arusha, Tanzania, became the leading candidate for the seat of the Rwanda Tribunal, and the Security Council consented in February 1995.[34] In Washington there emerged the belief that the Rwanda Tribunal would provide credible justice, help prevent another genocide between Hutu and Tutsi, and, with a strong reassertion of criminal law enforcement, assist with the reestablishment of the Rwandan judicial system. Still before us was the challenge of adopting a Security Council resolution requiring member states to arrest and detain fugitives indicted by the tribunal. That objective and much more would dominate my work with the Rwanda Tribunal in following years.

CHAPTER FOUR

ABANDONED AT SREBRENICA

We all assume the eastern enclaves are gone.

National Security Adviser Tony Lake speaking to the author and
other officials about the conflict in Bosnia and Herzegovina
on September 13, 1994

AS THE YUGOSLAV TRIBUNAL GREW FROM AN IDEA IN 1993 TO AN OPERATING
court issuing its first indictment in 1994 and finally to a trial court in 1995,
the war and its associated atrocity crimes ground on mercilessly. The tribunal coexisted with the relentless criminal assaults on civilians and prisoners
of war that defined the Balkans conflagration. Military strategizing had little to do with justice other than to recognize its potential once the fighting
was over and the shattered nations and peoples of the former Yugoslavia
could begin the long journey, still unfinished, toward restoration and reconciliation. One can easily place too much importance on the tribunal's
role in the Balkans conflict and misinterpret what was expected of it in the
early years. There was no simple way out of the Balkans imbroglio, and the
Yugoslav Tribunal had nowhere near the influence in the summer of 1995
to deter the worst slaughter on the European continent since World War II.
Any true understanding of the early years of the Yugoslav Tribunal, and
where to place the blame for continued atrocities as accountability struggled to take hold, must include the story of Srebrenica.

The Fate of the Enclaves

The last mass killing of the Balkans war, which ultimately triggered several
high-profile prosecutions before the Yugoslav Tribunal, occurred in July

1995 near the eastern Bosnian town of Srebrenica. For years it had been a refuge for tens of thousands of Muslims driven from their homes during the Serbs' ethnic cleansing of eastern Bosnia. The genocide that occurred there squarely challenged the deterrence value of the Yugoslav Tribunal. Bosnian Serb leaders, and probably Slobodan Milosevic, Serbia's president, seemingly ignored the growing reality that their heinous actions would fall within the tribunal's jurisdiction and lead to their indictments.

By the summer of 1995, about thirty-nine thousand lightly armed peace-keepers of the U.N. Protection Force (UNPROFOR) were patrolling parts of Bosnia and Herzegovina, Croatia, and Macedonia. UNPROFOR had been deployed since early 1992 and over the years had been tasked by the U.N. Security Council to negotiate and monitor cease-fires and zones of separation, help implement a no-fly zone, protect Sarajevo airport and humanitarian convoys destined for civilian populations, enforce a U.N.-mandated arms embargo on Bosnia and Herzegovina, and protect seven "safe areas" in the country (including Srebrenica). As U.N. peacekeepers, UNPROFOR soldiers acted only in self-defense and were not mandated to take sides between the combatants. In late May 1995, Bosnian Serb forces took hostage about four hundred UNPROFOR soldiers following two NATO air strikes on ammunition bunkers outside the Bosnian Serb capital of Pale. That single act of hostage taking, though relatively small in number compared to the overall UNPROFOR deployment, drove a stake into any credible argument in New York for supporting a lift and strike strategy, namely, a multilateral lift of the Security Council arms embargo on Bosnia accompanied by NATO air strikes on Serbian targets. The Europeans would not risk the lives of their own captured peacekeepers for the sake of air strikes. A few days later I met with Secretary of State Warren Christopher and Assistant Secretary of State Richard Holbrooke at the State Department, where we reviewed the Defense Department's Plan 40-104 on UNPROFOR withdrawal along with the prospect of getting a Rapid Reaction Force (RRF) of mostly British and French troops mobilized quickly enough in the event UNPROFOR stayed put and Plan 40-104 was canceled. UNPROFOR cost over $4.6 billion from 1992 to early 1996, with the United States paying almost one-third of that amount. The RRF would cost an additional $760 million (mostly paid by the United States) in its first year alone based on full deployment of a four-thousand-soldier brigade. That was an almost incomprehensible figure for a fatigued Congress to digest.

The prospect of actually achieving Plan 40-104 seemed increasingly re-mote. Holbrooke insisted we needed to "get a deal" with Milosevic, and that meant getting Milosevic and Bosnian Serb leader Radovan Karadzic to agree. Christopher recognized Holbrooke's point that if UNPROFOR with-drew, it would be a disaster for Clinton in the 1996 elections. But Christo-pher believed that if we simply muddled through another year, that also would be a disaster for Clinton in a year's time.

State Department envoy Robert Frasure, who had been shuttling back and forth to Belgrade, confided by mid-June that he could not carry his discussions with Milosevic any further. There was heavy shelling in Tuzla and Gorazde and fighting in Bihac. We could not revisit the Contact Group Peace Plan—the latest futile musings on peace with our allies and Russia—in the midst of the hostage crisis. That would only reward the hostage takers at Pale and undercut Milosevic in his dealings with the Bosnian Serb leader ship. And yet the only deal Milosevic wanted was with the United States, and not with former Swedish prime minister Carl Bildt, who represented the Contact Group. The Germans were strongly opposed to any communica-tions with Karadzic, although at that stage he had not yet been indicted by the Yugoslav Tribunal.

Albright met with Bildt in her State Department office for a revealing dis-cussion the next day. She admitted that we were in the middle of the end-game. The eastern Muslim enclaves were magnets, not safe areas. No one in the region seemed to want peace anymore. We understood UNPROFOR's commander, General Bernard Janvier, as saying that the Bosniaks could defend the enclaves themselves. Remarkably, Bildt simply said that the east-ern enclaves were a political perception only, not a real issue. So what hap-pens to the civilians in the enclaves, Albright asked? Demilitarizing the safe areas would be unfair, she said, because then the Bosniaks could not defend their own people. "Americans," Albright reminded Bildt, "are ones who go back to the basics. Bosniaks are victims in this war. People sometimes get mad at a rape victim who fights back. There is nothing worse than being mired down, or heading towards withdrawal. It is essential to get the Pale Serbs back to the table. We cannot suspend more on the sanctions than we already have. Milosevic has retreated from peace, emboldened by the hostage-taking." Bildt quickly changed the subject and pondered whether he could talk to Karadzic if the latter were to be indicted by the Yugoslav Tribunal. He was worried about the need to deal with Milosevic in the alter-

native and how to reach the Bosnian Serb leaders in Pale before the tribunal handed down its indictments.

By late June we were scrambling in Washington to react to the deteriorating situation in the eastern enclaves. We could not threaten NATO air strikes
without the agreement of the French and British, but their UNPROFOR
peacekeepers were in the crosshairs. The very effort to work on Plan 40-104
undermined efforts to strengthen and defend UNPROFOR. The endgame
strategy emerged: First, we had to recognize that any option had its costs and
risks. Second, we had to follow through on the RRF. If the RRF made no
discernible difference and the situation deteriorated further, then we would
know that the withdrawal plan had to be resurrected. If an UNPROFOR
withdrawal proceeded under NATO cover, the United States would press
for a multilateral lift of the arms embargo in the Security Council and use
its bilateral leverage with Russia (no trade, no grain, no financing) to force
at least an abstention on the vote. The size and cost of an extraction force
under Plan 40-104 was 110,000 troops at $3.2 billion. It seemed fantastical
and without any political legs.[1]

On June 29, a small humanitarian convoy reached Srebrenica. The situation there was desperate, but in Washington we could not determine precisely where the worst problem would erupt on any given day. The endgame
options we had been considering would not play out quickly enough. Jim
O'Brien, the State Department lawyer and Albright staffer who cochaired
with me the War Crimes Evidence Interagency Working Group, joined me
in devising strategy that identified the paradox of our policy. We submitted
our strategy paper to Albright on July 5, 1995, recognizing that the United
States intended to support the continued mission of UNPROFOR with a
robust RRF and an effective NATO air shield. But the delay in achieving an
effective NATO air shield was crippling the Clinton administration's ability to
sustain domestic support for continued deployment of UNPROFOR. We advanced some short-term goals: a robust RRF that would enable UNPROFOR
to act more credibly, an effective NATO air shield (which still required a
strategy to take out the Serb air defenses), and maintenance of a minimal
humanitarian safety net, including the new possibility of airdrops to enclaves
(like Srebrenica) at risk. It would be critical to keep UNPROFOR deployed in
Bosnia, particularly in the enclaves, but strengthened with the arrival of the
RRF. The alternative pointed to an abandonment of the eastern enclaves.

O'Brien and I proposed to supplement UNPROFOR with deployment of
a U.S.-led and NATO-supplied ground force to protect the safe areas, in-

cluding Srebrenica, and to put Bosniak forces responsible for the defense of the safe areas under NATO command. This would prevent the Bosniaks from diverting resources to other locations or launching offensive actions out of the safe areas. They would have to decide which safe areas should be protected by NATO and thus pursuant to NATO command. The Bosnian Serbs attacking them would be coaxed into cease-fires around the safe areas, and the Security Council would eliminate the U.N.'s role in sharing the power to unleash NATO air strikes so that NATO alone could determine military tactics. But even this short-term strategy proved too late as the war machine swept over Srebrenica.

Futile Plans

There were reports on July 3, 1995, of much greater civilian casualties in Sarajevo and of a worsening humanitarian situation in Bihac.[2] The humanitarian convoys were not getting through to the eastern enclaves. The Croats were building up their forces in Sector South. Two days later, access to the enclaves became increasingly difficult to achieve. Then heavy fighting and a worsening humanitarian situation descended on the Srebrenica enclave. The city itself was being shelled. Bosnian Serb general Ratko Mladic complained about Bosniak shelling of the Serb population in the Sarajevo area, and it appeared to us at the time that was why he had unleashed the bombing of Srebrenica—to retaliate for the shelling in Sarajevo. Defense Secretary William Perry reported that airdrops of humanitarian supplies into Srebrenica would not commence unless the Serb air defense system there was neutralized. That would require seeking the U.N. secretary-general's approval (turning his part of the "dual key") for NATO air strikes.

In retrospect, July 7 was a surreal day in Washington as Srebrenica came under attack. Albright and I spent hours at the Pentagon being briefed on the NATO extraction strategy for UNPROFOR, Plan 40-104, by Lieutenant General Howell Estes. The plan lost all meaning within days as the Srebrenica disaster unfolded. But one element of the briefing proved very timely. General Estes said NATO was the party now being denied flights over Bosnia in defiance of the original intent behind both Albright's no-fly-zone resolution adopted by the Security Council in March 1993 and NATO's Deny Flight mission: to ground all Serbian flights. That was being ignored as the Serbs flew fixed-wing aircraft and helicopters over their swath of Bosnia's territory. The United Nations, General Estes stressed, had only turned its master key for close air support and for preapproved air strikes. Even though NATO had turned its key in November to "seed" (take-out) any air defense systems, the United Nations had not yet done so. The integrated air defense system Milosevic relied upon across Serbia and Republika Srpska must not stand, particularly if NATO were to use airpower to defend the eastern enclaves. Albright needed explicit instructions from the White House to insist that the United Nations turn its key to enable NATO to resume Deny Flight. If Deny Flight had not been so denied for so long, NATO might have responded with effective and swift airpower to stop the Bosnian Serb advance on Srebrenica. It remains a pathetic footnote to the Srebrenica catastrophe that General Estes alerted us to a core problem three days before the end of the Muslim presence in Srebrenica, and yet in practical terms that was not enough time to achieve the diplomatic task of restoring Deny Flight.

As the Srebrenica situation rapidly deteriorated, I advised Albright to tell Lake that eliminating the air defense system in Bosnia must be priority number one, and that the situation in Srebrenica could be used as leverage to argue that if we had to evacuate the Dutch peacekeepers quickly, the United States would neutralize the air defense system with or without U.N. authority. The situation had become too tenuous to wait any longer. I purposely encouraged Albright to defy U.N. authority if necessary (namely, if U.N. secretary-general Boutros-Ghali failed to "turn the dual key" on use of air power) in her request to Lake. Srebrenica had changed the game fundamentally. But the imminent fall of Srebrenica made the points academic before they could even be argued.

I briefed Albright on July 9 for the next day's dinner with Clinton and House Speaker Newt Gingrich. She had to persuade Gingrich that a unilateral lift of the arms embargo remained a nonstarter for a host of reasons, one being that it would destroy any chance we had to achieve a multilateral lift in New York in conjunction with an UNPROFOR withdrawal. Milosevic would use a unilateral U.S. lift as his ticket to forge a Greater Serbia. The Bosnian Serbs would seize as much territory, including the safe havens, as possible before the Bosniak army could be sufficiently armed and trained. Gingrich had to decide whether he wanted a war strategy grounded in the unilateral lift, in which case he would have to support a belligerent combat role for the United States and the commitment of tens of thousands of American troops, or a peace strategy with all its complexities.

However, on the next day Srebrenica seized Washington's attention. I quickly advised Albright to tell Gingrich that but for UNPROFOR, Srebrenica already would be overrun. We might come under intense pressure to evacuate the Dutch peacekeepers, and we needed to address the plight of the Muslim population somehow if the Bosnian Serbs overwhelmed the enclave. But the atrocity surge in Srebrenica created facts on the ground faster than I or anyone else could devise strategy.

On the morning of July 10, we momentarily sighed when we learned that Srebrenica still stood as a safe haven and that while fighting continued, the Bosnian Serbs were not advancing further. The Dutch commander of the UNPROFOR contingent in Srebrenica was cautious. He reported that close air support would not be useful. Bildt had spent nine hours with Milosevic, and we awaited his detailed report on those discussions. The Pentagon concluded that its long-shelved contingency planning labeled "Daring Lion" to evacuate the eastern enclaves would take *at least fourteen days to organize.*[3] Officials asked whether they should start the clock running. (I simply laughed—did no one have the foresight in the Pentagon to do some *preliminary* planning for Daring Lion in, say, mid-June after the U.N. peacekeepers were taken hostage? Did they really need someone in the State Department to turn on their lightbulb?)

Since the Serbs had stopped advancing on Srebrenica, all eyes in Washington turned toward Sarajevo. The World Health Organization had reported 70 civilians killed in Sarajevo in May and more than twice that number (144) in June.[4] The fate of Sarajevo seemed more significant. Meanwhile, at Clinton's dinner with Albright and Gingrich that night, discussion of the Bosnian crisis was minimal. Two-thirds of the Senate might be prepared to vote for a unilateral lift, but Gingrich did not believe that two-thirds of the senators would override a presidential veto.

The Defining Moment

On July 11, I learned at a morning interagency gathering that the Dutch peacekeepers had decided to evacuate Srebrenica and had called for close air support. Two Dutch F-16s aimed for two Serb tanks, but neither was hit. The logistics of the Dutch desire to evacuate soon became apparent. Daring Lion, the emergency extraction plan, was nowhere near ready to execute, and the RRF was not yet fully deployed anywhere in Bosnia; the troops already in the field were in no position to do much yet. No helicopters were forward deployed. We needed a rapid assessment of the humanitarian impact if the Dutch were to pull out. The Serbs had just issued an ultimatum for the population of Srebrenica to evacuate the city. Who could replace the Dutch, we wondered? Sandy Vershbow, a sharp National Security Council official on loan from the State Department (and a future ambassador to NATO and then Russia), put it bluntly: "This is a defining moment."

In fact, a new Security Council resolution was not required for action. The U.N. secretary-general has inherent power to protect forces under his control. Boutros-Ghali could have called on NATO to do just that. He could have sent a letter to the Security Council informing its members of his request to NATO. The council could have responded by letter approving the secretary-general's action, thus avoiding any recorded vote on the matter. But none of that happened or was likely to unfold on such a short timescale.

Before the early morning meeting ended, the endlessly negotiated extraction plans had been rendered useless. Srebrenica had fallen. The Dutch commander had been taken hostage. We could not plausibly appear more interested in saving the Dutch peacekeepers than the people of Srebrenica, who by then were marching into the hands of the Serbs north of Srebrenica.

Berger convened the Deputies Committee later that morning, with Albright joining us from New York by video conference. The Pentagon confirmed that the second flight of U.S. F-16s did not locate their targets and the Serbs had fired an SA-7 missile at them. The Serbs had threatened to unleash hell on the Dutch peacekeepers unless the NATO air strikes ended. Predictably, all NATO flights were terminated. The Dutch said that their primary responsibility was the safety of their own peacekeepers and that their evacuation must be considered. Albright reported that she had not yet been asked in New York to secure the evacuation of the Dutch peacekeepers out of Srebrenica. Indeed, Boutros-Ghali's staff thought the Dutch could get out by themselves along an eastern route. One of his aides acknowledged, "Srebrenica is gone."

Peter Tarnoff, the undersecretary of state for political affairs, conceded there was no longer any way to retake Srebrenica, a view shared by the Pentagon. Indeed, neither the French nor the British had any capability in theater to save Srebrenica. Albright wondered whether the Bosnian government would permit the enclaves to be evacuated. Future NATO commander Wesley Clark admitted no one could raise the Pale Serbs (meaning Karadzic) on the phone. As for the RRF, it would take at least five days before it demonstrated any capability to intervene. It would take until mid-August before the full British unit planned for the RRF could deploy in Bosnia. Berger asked if there were any retaliatory options, but Tarnoff responded that there would be no support for that while any Dutch peacekeepers were held hostage. Oddly, the planning for Daring Lion did not anticipate this kind of situation, where the Bosnian Serbs already had overrun an enclave and cornered both the peacekeepers and the civilian population. Rather, Daring Lion had envisaged a *threat* of Bosnian Serbs taking over and an extraction of peacekeepers before the threat could be executed.

The Bosnian Serbs wanted to free their forces at Srebrenica (following its collapse) in order to attack Sarajevo. Karadzic and Mladic were convinced that the tide would turn in their favor. The stab at Srebrenica was retaliation for the Muslim offensive in Sarajevo. The Serbs also wanted to show the impotence of the much-touted RRF. The British and the French believed the eastern enclaves had become unsustainable. If Srebrenica in fact had fallen, as reports for the last twenty-four hours confirmed, the implications for the fate of Sarajevo seized everyone's attention.

Albright proposed more air cover for the enclaves. The Defense Department's Walter Slocombe simply replied, "No deal." He muttered, "This war has been a long search for the magic button to bomb." Tarnoff believed we would enter the war on the side of the Bosniaks if the Deputies Committee adopted Albright's proactive suggestion. If the United States lifted the arms embargo unilaterally, the British and French would abandon Bosnia altogether. General Clark added that the Dutch were not willing to risk their soldiers' lives and the British did not want to fight a war. When challenged, they backed off.

Berger wondered how to establish a firewall between Srebrenica and the towns of Gorazde and Zepa. We turned our attention to the worst case in Srebrenica. Leon Fuerth, Vice President Al Gore's national security adviser, asked what to do if the Serbs refused to release the Dutch peacekeepers. "What's at stake here," he said, "is an abject abdication of the institutions responsible for the security of the people."

Berger summed up by directing that we figure out what the British, French, and Dutch were willing to do to save Srebrenica. The State Department would contact Milosevic and the Muslim leadership to learn what options they believed still existed in Srebrenica and the other enclaves. Evacuation scenarios would be studied. Publicly, the United States would condemn the

Serb action and retain the right to force a NATO decision on close air support. We would consult with allies and express our belief that maintaining the safe area of Srebrenica was the best foundation for peace. The crisis strengthened the argument for speedy creation of the RRF. And Washington would state that NATO must be prepared to respond. Most of Berger's instructions, however, ended up in the dustbin of too little, too late.

Later on the same day, July 11, I met with a group of action officers from State, Defense, the National Security Council, and elsewhere to follow through on the deputies' meeting that I had attended. One of our taskings was to figure out how to save Srebrenica, however implausible that must seem in retrospect. The British, French, and German spines had stiffened over the course of the day, with the French proposing a Chapter VII resolution in the Security Council demanding a withdrawal of the Serb forces, restoration of the safe area, perhaps an augmented UNPROFOR force, and creation of a demilitarized zone, with help from the not-yet-ready-for-prime-time RRF. The Dutch complained about facing the overwhelming military strength of the Serbs. The Pentagon's Joe Kruzel, who would lose his life along with U.S. negotiator Robert Frasure on the Mount Igman Road near Sarajevo one month later while traveling with Richard Holbrooke and Wesley Clark, concluded there was no military option available to restore UNPROFOR in Srebrenica. What would be the point, he asked, of taking extraordinary steps now to create a concentration camp in Srebrenica, surrounded by the Serbs? "These enclaves are militarily indefensible," he said. "It is time to cut our losses there."

The Ukrainian battalion of UNPROFOR withdrew from Zepa, and its surrender to the Bosnian Serbs appeared imminent. CNN reported heavy fighting in Zepa. The State Department's Chris Hill (who would play a central role in the Dayton talks within months) believed we would jeopardize the northern region of Bihac and Sarajevo if we lost all the eastern enclaves. "We have no strategy," he continued, "so how do we deter the Serbs now?" A Pentagon official conceded, "We have no military options. Zepa is hopeless." At the highest levels, however, the British, French, and Germans wanted to defend the eastern enclaves. But the Russians did not want UNPROFOR to take sides, which made the peacekeepers' defense of the enclaves far more difficult.

Vershbow and the State Department argued for standing up to the Serbs where it really counted, in Sarajevo. Thirty thousand refugees from Srebrenica were heading north to Tuzla on a fifty-kilometer three-day walk. The

Dutch peacekeepers had pulled back to Potocari north of Srebrenica. As one of my colleagues put it, "Everyone is willing to fight to the last Dutchman." The Pentagon rejected using the meager troops of the RRF, saying it was never designed to be the savior of Sarajevo and the eastern enclaves. NATO could not revamp Plan 40-104 soon enough to evacuate the Dutch peacekeepers safely. At the close of the meeting, reports of heavy fighting in downtown Sarajevo filtered in. The capital of Bosnia had become a very dangerous place since the taking of Srebrenica.

The Debacle Looms

On July 12, the Deputies Committee convened again as Srebrenica and then Zepa were collapsing. General Mladic had arrived in Potocari and was screening all refugees to identify "war criminals." Bosnian Serbs were moving against Zepa. The Bosniaks had no strategic plan for the defense of Gorazde. The U.N. undersecretary for peacekeeping operations and future secretary-general, Kofi Annan, reported that Mladic's meeting with the Dutch commander had been very hostile. Mladic demanded that the peacekeepers in custody turn over all their weapons. He insisted that all Bosniak forces in Zepa lay down their arms immediately. The Dutch ambassador to the United Nations objected to any Security Council resolution that threatened the Serbs. The French lost some of their bluster overnight and leaned toward a political declaration. They sought, outside of NATO command, U.S. helicopter airlifts for the peacekeepers. The Pentagon quickly rejected such initiatives for bilateral assistance.

The British still argued that the eastern enclaves must not fall, fearing that the collapse of Srebrenica and Zepa would create a domino effect throughout Bosnia. One deputy in our meeting tartly barked that the British view had been overtaken by events and thus was now entirely irrelevant. Berger agreed that the United States could not alone respond to the French request for air support and airlifts for Srebrenica. But he wanted to tread carefully with the French and ask them what they were prepared to do. "We don't want to be responsible for killing any French effort to rescue Srebrenica," he said. Slocombe offered one possible outcome: that the Dutch peacekeepers and the Muslim refugees withdraw to central Bosnia while Srebrenica fell under Bosnian Serb control. It was implausible, he believed, to keep a Muslim civilian population in Srebrenica. But the Muslim-dominated government in Sarajevo was resisting the flow of refugees streaming north to

Tuzla, fearing it meant the end of Srebrenica and only one more validation of ethnic cleansing by the Bosnian Serbs.

Berger ordered that a demarche be fired off to Milosevic telling him to let humanitarian convoys through and permit refugees to reach Tuzla. He wanted some order to be brought to the entire U.N. diplomatic approach so that we knew who was negotiating with whom. The Bosnian government had to be told that the humanitarian necessity was to get refugees to safe territory. We needed to construct a firebreak to protect the other safe havens of Gorazde and Zepa. But Berger was quickly beaten back on Zepa, with even Kofi Annan conceding that the United Nations could do nothing to prevent it being taken over. There were no military options left to protect the enclaves. The State Department's John Kornblum (who soon became the U.S. ambassador to Germany) lamented that the imminent fall of Srebrenica and Zepa was already being portrayed as a major defeat for the United Nations and the Bosniaks. We should focus on humanitarian issues at this point, he said. Speculation abounded at the table that the Bosnian government had allowed the fall of Srebrenica and Zepa as a reason to kick out UNPROFOR and force Washington to lift the arms embargo unilaterally.

The deputies could only "manage" the situation in Srebrenica. We needed to consult with the French and British, ensure that the Dutch peacekeepers were protected and that relief supplies got to the civilians, maintain a firebreak at Gorazde, and argue that there was even more reason now to support the RRF and strengthen it. No one was yet aware of or predicting atrocities.

In a meeting later that day in Tarnoff's office, incoming data from Srebrenica was ominous. Up to thirty thousand refugees[5] remained with the Dutch peacekeepers but were starting to be transported in four groups to Tuzla: first the women and children, second the weak, third the less weak, and finally men of military age after being "screened" for war crimes by the Bosnian Serbs. Only later did we learn that mass slaughter, indeed genocide, wiped out the fourth group. They never made it to any detention camps for screening. Furthermore, support for a unilateral lift was building on Capitol Hill under Senator Robert Dole's leadership, which the administration would have to oppose given the immediate plight of the Dutch peacekeepers.

The State Department released a policy statement on July 12 summarizing Washington's condemnatory sentiments but also revealing the Clinton administration's unwillingness to act decisively and rapidly in the face of the bulldozers Karadzic and Mladic were driving at high speed through Srebrenica and Zepa.

Such pronouncements were only words when compared to the reality on the ground. On July 13, we convened again in Tarnoff's office and learned that 2,300 refugees had arrived in Tuzla and that 3,000 men were being held in Bratanov. For the almost 30,000 refugees still on the roads, this was the last day of food. The Bosnian government declared it was now a U.N. problem. Forty-eight Dutch peacekeepers continued to be held hostage by Mladic's forces. Bosnia's ambassador to the United Nations, Muhamed Sacirbey, told Albright that all males thirteen to sixty years of age were being separated out. The Bosniaks were demanding that the United Nations not evacuate those civilians who wanted to stay in Srebrenica. The Serb intention, they said, was to clean out the town.

Also that day, Assistant Secretary of State John Shattuck met with Jim O'Brien, Deputy Legal Adviser Michael Matheson, me, and others to examine options. Our group understood that the Yugoslav Tribunal was central to any plausible peace process. We debated whether we should talk to those under indictment (knowing that indictments probably were imminent against Karadzic and Mladic) and even whether we should speak to anyone who, in our judgment, *should* be under indictment. I proposed that Washington should find as many occasions as possible to talk about the Yugoslav Tribunal as part of the peace process, meaning that cooperation with the court was essential to building a viable peace in the Balkans. Prosecutor Richard Goldstone would be visiting the U.N. secretary-general on July 25, so I arranged to fly him to Washington shortly thereafter. Shattuck's meeting strengthened considerably the war crimes strategy for Bosnia and Herzegovina, but not in time for Srebrenica.[6]

The End of Hope

July 14 proved to be the end of any hope for Srebrenica and Zepa, and by then we knew it. The Serbs were still advancing on Zepa, and no plan existed to defend it. The Dutch Defense Ministry sought the immediate withdrawal of its peacekeepers, several hundred of whom were at Potocari, with many of them detained by Mladic's troops in two locations. Fighting had commenced around Gorazde. The British and French still disagreed on next steps. The British sought to demilitarize the remaining safe areas, while the French concentrated on reopening land routes to Sarajevo over

Mount Igman and sought helicopter lift assistance for Gorazde from the Pentagon. Several thousand Srebrenica refugees were unaccounted for, and the International Committee of the Red Cross had no access to any Bosniak males. Clinton committed to fighting the Dole amendment on unilateral lift, and he shortly thereafter vetoed it. Tarnoff noted that no American could deal with Mladic for fear of being trapped in a photo with him, a lesson General Wesley Clark had learned to his personal embarrassment in August 27, 1994, when he was photographed wearing a Bosnian Serb military hat alongside Mladic.

The principals met without their deputies.[7] The issues they had to address were so numerous that the best I could do was advise Albright as thoroughly as possible that morning before she attended the meeting. I recommended that (1) the State Department should plan immediately for the evacuation of Zepa; (2) the Agency for International Development should build adequate housing for the refugees streaming into Tuzla and help the U.N. high commissioner for refugees provide emergency food and medical relief; (3) the intelligence community should expedite the flow of information to the Yugoslav Tribunal following the court's announcement on July 12 that Goldstone was monitoring events in Srebrenica for possible atrocity crimes; (4) we should propose the defense of Gorazde as an achievable tasking for NATO and the RRF, and overall hold the line there as well as Bihac, Sarajevo, and central Bosnia; (5) the U.N. command should consolidate UNPROFOR in these defended areas; (6) Washington and its allies should forge ahead with a robust RRF and resume Deny Flight with strong pressure for turning the dual key in the secretary-general's office; and (7) with atrocity crimes probably occurring in Srebrenica, any talk of relaxing sanctions on Milosevic would be preposterous unless the town's restoration to its Muslim residents and refugees is added to the overall conditions for flexibility on sanctions.

Was there a smoking gun pointing to foreknowledge about the fate of Srebrenica? In other words, was the U.S. government alerted to the probability of a Serb assault on Srebrenica and the other eastern enclaves to cleanse them of Muslim populations? Was Washington informed in time to have planned to deter such military outcomes and forcible displacement of populations and thus prevent, in addition, the atrocity crimes that engulfed Srebrenica, including both ethnic cleansing and the genocide of eight thousand Muslim men and boys? I do not know, but there could have been information suggesting ethnic cleansing of the eastern enclaves (in other words, forced removal of Muslims) that seemed so self-evident to the ana-lyst of the day that it merited no particular urgency or need to alert officials in a timely fashion. I certainly had those suspicions by July 12, but events were overtaking us.

Still not knowing what was transpiring north of Srebrenica, where in fact thousands of Bosnian men and teenage boys were being slaughtered, I began on July 15 to launch U.S. assistance to the Yugoslav Tribunal relat-ing to the Srebrenica situation because ethnic cleansing already had been achieved. The intent was to interview witnesses, examine aerial imagery, and track troop movements and the latest flows of the refugees. Shattuck traveled to Tuzla to interview the refugees and find out what had happened and what could be done.

The Missing Men and Boys

The weekend intervened in Washington. Unbeknownst to policy-makers in Washington, the Serb-led genocide accelerated in the mountains and farm fields and abandoned warehouses north of Srebrenica. However, on Saturday, July 15, following up on the principals' meeting of the day before, I called George Tenet, who had just assumed his new post as CIA deputy director, and asked him to focus his agency's assets, including aerial surveil-lance, on Muslim men and boys detained near Srebrenica and on other developments that related to atrocity crimes in the region. He said he would immediately turn all keys and told me to call him again in two days. Tenet agreed with my suggestion that Goldstone formally request real-time infor-mation for the Yugoslav Tribunal, and I immediately conveyed that point to the prosecutor. In coming weeks, that targeted surveillance of the region north of Srebrenica proved vital as mass graves began to appear on the im-agery. Soon Albright was able to reveal such photographs before the Secu-rity Council, and the tribunal used them for prosecutions in later years.[8]

By the time officials reconvened in Washington on Monday, July 17, the killing had largely been accomplished, and yet we remained unaware of it as we planned next steps. We thought the missing men and boys were not among the other Bosniaks the Serbs had transported to Tuzla because they were being herded into detention for war crimes "screening" or, being the most capable of fleeing and having the most to fear from being captured, they had struck out on their own as the Serbs were closing in. Perhaps they were either heading toward Zepa or north into the mountainous terrain of central Bosnia. We also supposed that the Bosnian Serbs were aggressively tracking down those who might not be in their custody. Shattuck asked me to join him on his trip to Tuzla, but Albright requested I stay glued to the Deputies Committee meetings and interagency discussions during the critical days ahead. Tenet confirmed he had activated the entire system for humanitarian and war crimes information, and that the latter would be conveyed to Goldstone rapidly. Berger promised that the White House would put out a statement warning against commission of atrocities and reiterating strong support for the Yugoslav and Rwanda tribunals.[9] In retrospect such a gesture seems feeble, but at the time getting a White House statement strongly supporting the tribunals was profoundly important to efforts by Albright and me to press the war crimes agenda within the government, at the United Nations, and overseas.

I advised Albright that the so-called peace process was being pushed over the cliff by Carl Bildt. He appeared to regard the fall of Srebrenica as a minor irritant in his talks with Milosevic rather than an event significantly undermining Milosevic's credibility. As if blind to reality, Bildt plowed on while the eastern enclaves were either collapsing or coming under intense fire. He acted as if his negotiating package required no modification in light of the Srebrenica debacle. Bildt assumed Gorazde was manageable— that it would survive—and need not interfere with working out a deal with Milosevic. He chided Contact Group governments for scattered talk about military adventures, particularly to save Srebrenica. Indeed, his entire tone over the weekend had been to abandon the eastern enclaves so that his talks with Milosevic could succeed. I urged Albright to press the Contact Group to ignore Bildt's arrogant scoldings, even though they echoed those of Defense Department policy chief Walter Slocombe and some others in policy deliberations.

Frustrations

Albright called me from New York on July 18 to discuss air strikes in Bosnia: somehow the U.N./NATO dual key had to be dislodged. Jim O'Brien and I had earlier proposed to her how to remove the dual key and enable robust air support in Bosnia. She called it the "melting dual key" and wanted U.N. decision makers, such as Boutros-Ghali and his personal representative in the Balkans conflict, Yasushi Akashi, denied the authority to prevent turning the key. One option would be to require only one approval by the secretary-general to unleash air strikes. Thereafter, the initial approval would continue in force as the theater commander made individual targeting decisions without any further consent from New York. If that would give Boutros-Ghali political cover, it might work. That same day Goldstone took Tenet's bait and made a formal request for information about Srebrenica. His request enabled a much more focused effort back in Washington. Goldstone also reported he was sending three investigators to Tuzla to start interviewing refugees as witnesses to atrocity crimes.

Meanwhile, on Capitol Hill, Senator Robert Dole introduced his bill to unilaterally lift the U.N. arms embargo on Bosnia and Herzegovina. It quickly attracted support.[10] The Bosnian ambassador to the United Nations, Muhamed Sacirbey, actively lobbied in favor of it. However, oddly enough, Dole's bill would have replaced the arms embargo on Bosnia with customary standards for deciding on licenses for arms exports. Under those standards (which included risk of escalation, proliferation concerns, threats to U.S. citizens and military forces, and danger to allied forces), the administration could or likely would deny many, perhaps all, requests for licenses.[11] Thus the Dole bill would be an empty vessel or, if its supporters argued against applying the usual standards, potentially dangerous to allies and U.S. citizens. However, the prospect of such a dilemma could persuade members of Congress that voting for the Dole bill would be a politically cost-free gesture of humanitarian concern, burdening Clinton with figuring out how to administer it in the future.

On July 19 Zepa fell to the Serbs, its civilians fled in panic, and Mladic's forces still held the Dutch battalion at Potocari at risk of being slaughtered. Finally recognizing the ditch we had driven our foreign policy into, one official conceded to me that if all military planning was held hostage to the fate of real hostages, there would never be any military action to save peacekeepers or civilians.

There was only one bright note to the day. Jim O'Brien and I had a productive meeting at Langley. Tenet met us and conveyed one strong message: that the CIA stood prepared to respond to Albright's needs with the highest priority. That was music to our ears. Starting that day there would be a daily update on humanitarian and war crimes developments in the Balkans delivered to Albright and us. Tenet also stepped up to the plate on Srebrenica and pledged to gather information about its fate and to keep a sharp eye on Gorazde and Zepa. Though in retrospect this may appear the least the CIA could have done, at the time we were grateful that our long struggles to elicit this kind of cooperation from the intelligence community had finally showed some results, albeit it too late for tens of thousands of victims in the Balkans.

Meanwhile, Albright waged a lonely struggle to ensure that any formula for a sanctions-relief package on Serbia (to soften up or reward Milosevic for pressuring the Pale Serbs to stand down prior to the Dayton peace accords later in the year) maintained stiff atrocity crimes conditionality. Her major threat was Bildt, who seemed oblivious to any leverage associated with the Yugoslav Tribunal. Albright argued that neither the victims in Bosnia nor the American public would comprehend any sanctions relief without the cessation of atrocity crimes. Her efforts, as well as my own in the Deputies Committee, to hold the line on atrocity crimes conditionality for sanctions relief proved frustratingly difficult as officials at the State Department, Pentagon, and the National Security Council usually deprioritized or simply ignored the issue in favor of finding ways to coax Milosevic to do our bidding with the Bosnian Serbs, even if that meant turning a blind eye to the realities on the ground.

Albright Briefs the Security Council

As the Croatian offensive began to sweep forward to liberate Croatian territory under Serbian control in early August 1995, a significant amount of aerial imagery of the aftermath of the Srebrenica massacres was examined and then declassified so that Albright could bring such evidence to the Security Council in an informal session on August 10. Her initiative was reminiscent of Adlai Stevenson's display of missile sites in Cuba in 1962 and Jeane J. Kirkpatrick's airing of the intercepted Soviet aircraft communications following the shooting down of Korean Airlines 007 in September 1983. The fate of the thousands of Muslim men and boys isolated at Potocari and three thousand civilians from Zepa remained largely unknown. But there was enough information to conclude that the Bosnian Serbs had executed many of the refugees who fled north to Tuzla. Albright recounted harrowing tales brought back to Washington by Shattuck and married the eyewitness testimonies of survivors of mass killings with related aerial photographs showing groupings of people in fields and subsequent views of newly disturbed earth and vehicle tracks indicating mass graves. She called for all nations to cooperate with the Yugoslav Tribunal's investigations of the Srebrenica killings and for Boutros-Ghali to coordinate closely with Goldstone so that he would have access to whatever information the secretary-general uncovered for his report to the council. Albright concluded that all parties had an obligation to stop the crimes and, if they could not, to bring those responsible to justice.[12]

The Road to Dayton

Assistant Secretary of State for European Affairs Richard Holbrooke traveled to Serbia, where he had a vigorous discussion with Milosevic about the Yugoslav Tribunal. The American diplomat held firm with Milosevic that there would be no immunity for either Karadzic or Mladic if they set foot in the United States or any nation of the European Union. The indictments were nonnegotiable.[13] In some respects this situation would prove useful to Milosevic, as it gave him the upper hand with respect to his indicted colleagues in representing Serb interests during the negotiations. On September 22, Holbrooke was back in Washington and conveyed his impressions of the talks with not only Milosevic but also Mladic and Karadzic, who had suddenly entered the room in Belgrade. His eleven hours with the three men had been full of odd realities, he said. Mladic was everything Hollywood would typecast him as in a movie. Holbrooke observed: "He looked like a beaten man. He erupted twice and tried staring matches on me. We never spoke to him." Karadzic proved to be the group facilitator as Milosevic walked in and out of the room. Serbian references to NATO were endless. They did not like the Tomahawk cruise missiles, which proved to be a masterstroke, Holbrooke said. Half the time his hosts complained about NATO. The other half entailed real negotiations. "These are whining, self-defeated people. Therefore, the threat of a resumption of bombing is essential," concluded Holbrooke.[14]

After Albright explained the caution that still gripped the United Nations, Holbrooke bemoaned, "We're not committed to resumption of bombing if there's one attack on the road. Personally, I'd bomb if there is just one violation. It's the best thing for the peace talks. My greatest fear is getting lulled into an agreement followed by another Anschluss [alluding to the Nazi regime's de facto annexation of Austria in 1938]." The Bosniaks rejected elections until after suspected war criminals had been captured and removed from the political scene. The principals discussed how the Yugoslav Tribunal had proved more valuable than they had thought in the beginning. The tribunal's indictments gave Milosevic an excuse to keep Karadzic and Mladic

out of the peace conference, since travel for the two indicted fugitives was
nonnegotiable.

In late September, I traveled with Wesley Clark, Walter Slocombe, John
Kornblum, and others to Europe to negotiate the terms of implementation
of the anticipated peace settlement. I was tasked to develop and then help
negotiate the role of the high representative for Bosnia and Herzegovina,
who would be the civilian leader of the postconflict restoration effort. My
original recommendations for the post largely became reality in the wake of
Dayton. These were indispensable discussions about how to manage the
postconflict environment—an exercise that could have served the George
W. Bush administration well prior to the intervention in Iraq in 2003 and its
disastrous aftermath, when extremely deficient planning unleashed chaos
and an insurgency.

During our talks in Rome, the Italians told us that Holbrooke had made
it very clear to them that atrocity crimes were not part of the negotiations
for a peace settlement and that they were an independent and international process. The Italians may have misunderstood Holbrooke on this
point, as atrocity crimes were factored into the Dayton Peace Agreement,
albeit with less significance than some of us had sought. Nonetheless, by the
end of our European mission I had listed thirty-two issues as having been
prioritized for follow-through: atrocity crimes and the Yugoslav Tribunal
were nowhere on that list. They simply did not figure among my colleagues
and most of our European allies in the maze of political issues that had to
be married to military options for a successful end of the conflict.

Many meetings were held during October to iron out further details
prior to Dayton. At a policy meeting on October 20, the issue of what would
happen in the postsettlement period if there were military attacks on civilians arose as a critical issue. Deputy National Security Adviser Sandy Berger
argued that the task was not to create a civil order beyond the clear duty to
prevent gross human rights violations and to protect refugees. Civilian police needed to respond to human rights problems. The largely NATO Implementation Force (IFOR) would not run protection for civilian relief
convoys or investigate human rights abuses. This constipated view of IFOR's
range of duties would dog me for years, particularly during 1996 and 1997,
as I tried to help the Yugoslav Tribunal negotiate critical assistance first from
IFOR and then its reflagged successor, the Stabilization Force (SFOR), for
mass grave diggings and, most importantly, for apprehension of fugitives
indicted by the Yugoslav Tribunal.

By early November 1995, we were still trying to figure out precisely what had occurred in Srebrenica the previous July. So many of the thousands of Bosnian Muslim men and boys remained missing that the American intelligence community continued trying to determine what had become of them. More and more information was being collected, and facts were being reconstructed from witness statements. I proposed, futilely, that the peace negotiators in Dayton compel the Serbs to show where those men and boys were located, dead or alive. We naturally began to assume the worst regarding all of the missing. There was a déjà vu sense that descended on everyone as information about the same locations in Bosnia that had been in play since 1992, during the earliest efforts to determine the facts in the conflict, came to the fore again. The same detention camps were scrutinized. The ghosts of 1992—same place-names, same locations and buildings—haunted us.

The first long phase of the atrocity crimes endeavor in the Balkans drew to a close. Ahead lay five years of toil to secure the apprehension or surrender of the Yugoslav Tribunal's indicted fugitives and to confront the ethnic cleansing of Kosovo.

CHAPTER FIVE
THE PASTOR FROM MUGONERO

I question whether we are acting to subordinate U.S. sovereignty to the United Nations. I am particularly bothered by the potential harm of depriving this man of his freedom.... Little by little, we are losing the guarantees of those individual freedoms each time we give up a bit of our freedoms. It makes me, the grandfather of five little girls, worry about the future.

U.S. magistrate judge Marcel Notzon of Laredo, Texas, explaining why
he was releasing from federal custody Pastor Elizaphan Ntakirutimana,
indicted for genocide by the Rwanda Tribunal, on December 17, 1997

THE EARLY YEARS OF THE RWANDA TRIBUNAL WERE CHAOTIC AND FULL OF uncertainty as to whether international justice would prevail for the victims of the 1994 genocide. Corruption within the tribunal's ranks was a pervasive problem that occupied more of my time than practically any other of the tribunal's issues. But that story need not be related here. Ultimately, incompetent or corrupt tribunal staffers were sidelined, and the court got on with the business of investigating and prosecuting genocide suspects. The seemingly insoluble issues rested elsewhere. Would genocidaires hiding in the refugee camps be detained, and would indicted fugitives be tracked and apprehended in the vast reaches of Africa and beyond? How would tens of thousands of genocide suspects be brought to justice in Rwanda? Would animosity consume the relationship between the tribunal and Rwandan officials? Would genocide continue along Rwanda's western border and make the Rwanda Tribunal's temporal jurisdiction, limited to only 1994, seem far too brief for the demands of justice? Would the Clinton administration overcome challenges in the federal courts to extradite an indicted Rwandan pastor, residing comfortably in Laredo, Texas, to stand trial before the Rwanda Tribunal? None of these questions had easy answers. But each one posed a unique challenge to the Rwanda Tribunal and to the Clinton administration's redemptive efforts in the aftermath of the genocide.

Apprehending Genocide Suspects

For six months, from July 1994 to the end of that year of mass slaughter, Albright and other U.S. diplomats futilely tried to persuade the French government and key regional governments (such as Zaire and Tanzania) to detain Rwanda's genocide suspects in the refugee camps or wherever they might roam. Reports continued to flow in of genocide suspects hiding in the territory of other nations, particularly countries bordering Rwanda. Several governments had told Washington that they lacked domestic legal authority (as did the United States at that time) to detain such persons. France, for example, told us as early as July 1994 that it had no authority to arrest suspects for genocide, because the Genocide Convention had not yet been adopted into French law and because French soldiers did not have any authority to arrest war criminals in the region of Rwanda held by the French under Operation Turquoise.[1]

Fed up with the procrastination of key governments but determined to provide legal cover to those governments, Albright circulated among Security Council members in January 1995 a draft resolution requiring the apprehension of genocide suspects from Rwanda. The proposed resolution authorized governments to arrest leading genocide suspects, prior to their formal indictment, and to coordinate efforts to investigate and track them with those of Richard Goldstone, the prosecutor of the Rwanda Tribunal. The draft language also addressed ongoing violence in the refugee camps and continued planning by Hutu refugees to wage war against the new government in Rwanda. Such aggressive planning, while technically reaching beyond the temporal jurisdiction of the tribunal (which could only investigate crimes committed during 1994), threatened international peace and security and thus was fair game for the council's attention.

However, in early February 1995, French diplomats approached Goldstone for his opinion of the draft resolution only to indicate France's preference for a nonbinding statement by the president of the security council *urging* governments to detain suspects. Why, we wondered in Washington, were the French so skittish about apprehending the genocidaires, particularly if they had the legal authority of a Security Council resolution? Was the explanation really so simple as the fact that the Hutu had been their favored clientele in Rwanda for so many years prior to the genocide? Is that what Operation Turquoise was all about back in June?[2] I recall leaning back at my desk in astonishment—how gullible do they think we are? In two years I would be asking the same question regarding the mysteriously liberated status of fugitives indicted by the Yugoslav Tribunal, including Radovan Karadzic, living in the French sector of Bosnia.

Albright pressed ahead with the detention resolution in the Security Council. Washington wanted Paris finally to buck up and get on board. The aim was to detain suspects who were outside Rwanda until the tribunal could complete investigations and decide whom to indict. Goldstone needed time to build his cases, but meanwhile many of the genocide suspects were burrowing deeper into the countryside, wreaking violence among the refugees and launching counterassaults on Rwanda's borders. The draft resolution urged (rather than ordered) nations to arrest and detain suspects, pending prosecution by the tribunal or appropriate national authorities. The Washington appeal, targeted at the highest levels of the French government, aimed at overcoming their opposition in New York.

The French vehemently opposed the U.S. proposal and kept pressing their idea of a nonbinding presidential statement urging countries to detain suspects. After heated negotiations in New York, the State Department reluctantly acceded to France's anemic proposal as the best possible compromise but insisted on making it a formal resolution by the Security Council, with its greater legal impact, rather than a presidential statement. Anything less might be viewed by countries neighboring Rwanda as a compromise made to avoid stronger Security Council action. It was pathetic that it was taking so long to achieve so little. One of our closest allies appeared determined to act as an accomplice in facilitating the genocidaires' freedom.

Finally, on February 27, 1995, Security Council Resolution 978 was adopted, with language stating that the council "*Urges* States to arrest and detain, in accordance with their national law and relevant standards of international law, pending prosecution by the International Tribunal for Rwanda or by the appropriate national authorities, persons found within their territory against whom there is sufficient evidence that they were responsible for

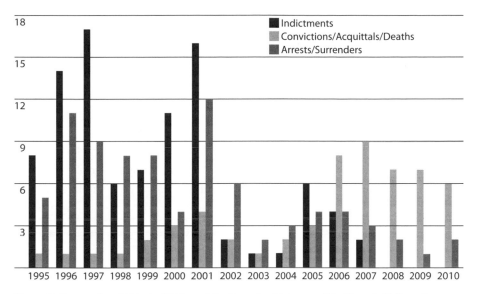

Figure 2. International Criminal Tribunal for Rwanda: Outcomes. The Rwanda Tribunal's record of indictments, arrests, convictions, deaths, and acquittals through 2010.

acts within the jurisdiction of the International Tribunal for Rwanda" and "Urges States who detain [such] persons ... to inform the Secretary-General and the Prosecutor of the International Tribunal for Rwanda of the identity of the persons detained, the nature of the crimes believed to have been committed, the evidence providing probable cause for the detentions, the date when the persons were detained and the place of detention."[3]

Despite the early stumble in getting a detention resolution out of the Security Council, the indictment and arrest record of the Rwanda Tribunal proved to be fairly impressive in the early years of its operation. As figure 2 shows, in the first three years of its operation (1995–1997), the tribunal issued 39 indictments and made 25 arrests. In the following four years (1998–2001), an additional 40 suspects were indicted while 32 indictees were arrested and transferred to Arusha. The trial work took much longer, with a paltry four convictions from 1995 through 1998, and only nine convictions from 1999 through 2001. Owing to the administrative and staffing problems that slowed down the work of the Rwanda Tribunal in its early years, such figures should not be surprising even though they were disappointing for an international venture of this character.

At the beginning of 1997, and after much diplomatic intervention by the United States, the indicted, fugitive general Théoneste Bagosora arrived in

Arusha to stand trial.[4] Prosecutor Louise Arbour praised U.S. cooperation and singled out our help in getting Bagosora to Arusha. Later that year, on July 18, 1997, the Hutu prime minister during the genocide, Jean Kambanda, was apprehended in Nairobi and pled guilty to genocide, which was an astoundingly positive development for the young tribunal.[5]

I traveled to Kigali and Arusha often during my ambassadorship to arrange U.S. assistance for tracking down the large number of indicted fugitives of the Rwanda Tribunal. During this time, the tribunal's tracking team succeeded far more than they failed, even if some suspects took years to locate and apprehend. Eleven indictees remained at large at the beginning of 2011.[6]

Local Justice

I learned a costly lesson in 1995. For one year, I had toiled with State and Justice Department officials and the American Bar Association to rebuild a credible domestic court system in Rwanda with prosecutors, judges, and defense counsel. We wanted to restore the rule of law to Rwanda, but with conventional courts, lawyers, and trials. That proved to be an impossible dream given the magnitude of the genocide, the large number of suspects, and the utterly devastated condition of Rwanda's judiciary. There was no possible way to rebuild the courts and train or inject enough lawyers and judges to even begin any conventional approach to justice. Part of the plan was to deploy foreign judges and lawyers to Rwanda to jump-start the domestic courts, but that was the height of folly. First, we could not identify enough of them willing to go to Rwanda. Second, the funds needed to support such a foreign influx were nonexistent. Third, Rwandan government officials were not happy campers about such a heavy dose of foreign influence on and control of their court system.

There had to be another way, and it was found through passage of a new local genocide law and promotion of an indigenous village justice procedure called *gacaca*, which is a community-based form of justice deeply rooted in Rwanda's history and designed to meld punishment with reconciliation at the discretion of grassroots courts. Ultimately, I regretted wasting one year following well-meaning but unrealistic advice to try to rebuild what simply could not be accomplished in such a short period of time while tens of thousands of suspects languished in overcrowded prisons.

The year 1996 proved tumultuous as I sought to provide adequate re-sources to the Rwanda Tribunal, dealt with accusations of internal corruption, and tried to assist the Rwandan government with its massive challenge of rendering justice to genocide perpetrators being detained throughout the country. By mid-April the Rwandan cabinet had approved draft legislation for the National Assembly to expedite adjudication of genocide violations and other atrocity crimes and establish a Specialized Chamber. But there already were more than sixty thousand cases to handle.

In August I met with Gerald Gahima, the deputy minister of justice, who was deeply immersed by then in moving the genocide legislation through his government toward approval. The draft law divided suspects into four categories, with category one covering high-level officials engaged in the genocide, making them eligible for the death penalty upon conviction. Categories two, three, and four included suspects of descending priority who would be subject to criminal prosecution or community-based justice that might entail acts of redemption (such as community service) rather than incarceration. Gahima spoke of the need for judges, prosecutors, and investigators to make the genocide law workable in the devastated judicial landscape of Rwanda. Critical problems included how to pay the salaries of the judicial staff, how to purchase the cars and motorcycles that would be needed for investigations, and how to build databases for the prosecutors where none existed. Gahima also desperately needed foreign funding for prison expansion. He said his government had received a large number of tents but needed money for constructing secure perimeters. "It takes more than tents to build a prison," he pointed out. There would be more arrests for years to come as refugees returned from Zaire and the genocidaires were weeded out and brought to justice under the new genocide law.

Gahima pointed to many misunderstandings about the Rwanda Tribunal and his government. Rwandan officials resented the fact that their own investigators would track down suspects outside Rwanda and then tribunal lawyers would arrive to claim jurisdiction. He claimed Kigali's right to prosecute them and believed the tribunal was being "insensitive and arrogant" toward the Rwandans. "We need some big fish to put on trial here!" Gahima began to lose his usual cool temperament: "The tribunal doesn't give much attention to what we do in Rwanda, all of the hard work we do to deal with tens of thousands of suspects." He was angry that he and his colleagues were shown no respect by tribunal authorities, or so he claimed. "In Arusha, they have ready-made cases of the leaders to prosecute. Our cases here are much tougher, but they don't care," he complained.

Gahima had held many meetings with tribunal officials, but, he said, they always came armed with their Security Council authority to stick in the Rwandans' faces. They rarely came to Kigali seeking evidence from him for their cases, which he found strange. Gahima complained that Goldstone infrequently visited Kigali and that his deputy, Honoré Rakotmanana from Madagascar, was nice but very weak running the Kigali outpost of the deputy prosecutor. He explained: "Everyone in that office does what they want. There is no firm leadership on top. Rakotmanana hasn't taken the time to build a firm relationship with the government. He only holds meetings with us when there is a crisis. They argue their points under the shield of Security Council authority rather than the mutual relationship we must have."

One could not deal with Rwandan officials since the genocide and fail to understand how fiercely proud they were of their own skills and achievements. They clearly had no patience for tribunal lawyers and administrators who acted with any degree of superiority or arrogance. In their view, the Rwanda Tribunal's primacy of jurisdiction did not mean primacy of character or political wisdom.

By September 1996, I was immersed in meetings with U.S. Department of Justice lawyers and the State Department's top human rights official, John Shattuck, to grapple with the increasingly precarious future of the Rwanda Tribunal. We fielded one crisis after another erupting over alleged corruption, long-delayed staffing decisions, favoritism for particular African nationalities, resistance from a host of governments on arrest operations, and chronic funding shortfalls. Relations between the tribunal's administrator, Andronico Adede, and prosecutor Goldstone and his deputy had deteriorated so badly I became the de facto middleman for communications among them. Adede interpreted his powers broadly, while deputy prosecutor Rakotmanana operated in a vacuum. He did not communicate with Adede, whom he considered a bully. I had to become the problem solver, as even Goldstone seemed unaware of all the problems erupting in Arusha or the extent of Adede's seeming incompetence.

Meanwhile, the prison population in Rwanda had jumped to eighty-four thousand, with six hundred to eight hundred arrests occurring weekly. Judges hesitated to prosecute under the new genocide law, because all were at risk of violent retaliation. Witnesses were being killed and intimidated.

Gahima could not even trust his own people in the Justice Ministry to secure witness protection. It was a mess.

Mudende and Resurgent Genocide

On my second visit to Rwanda after becoming the war crimes ambassador, I experienced one of the more horrific episodes of my exposure to atrocity crimes in that country. In December 1997 I flew into Rwanda with Albright to hold meetings with government officials. On our departure from Kigali, Albright's U.S. Air Force plane, which several months later plunged Commerce Secretary Ron Brown to his death on a hillside in Croatia, was rerouted suddenly to Lusaka, Angola, because of stormy weather over our destination, Kinshasa. Upon landing in Lusaka, the CNN reporter on our flight learned that a massacre of hundreds of Tutsi had just occurred in the northwestern corner of Rwanda at a camp called Mudende. This looked suspiciously like instant payback from the Hutu hiding across the border in the Democratic Republic of the Congo (the former Zaire) for Albright's high-profile trip to Rwanda and perhaps even my newly minted presence there as the war crimes ambassador. Albright ordered me back to Rwanda to investigate and report to her by the time she attended a NATO meeting in Brussels.

When I arrived on the scene in Mudende, the massacre site revealed its awful face and wretched smell. The dead had just been buried in mass graves. The wounded were at Gisenyi Hospital nearby. The other survivors, who had scrambled into the jungle during the rampage, were huddled at a warehouse down the road among other refugees. Many of the victims had been roasted alive within their tents, a tactic I would witness at other atrocity sites. Personal belongings lay strewn everywhere. Bullets and machetes were scattered in pools of blood. A container on the edge of the site, which a family had made into a home, was riddled with bullet holes and bathed in blood. Down the road was a rural prison, called a cachot, that had held 403 Hutu prisoners, most of whom were freed by the attacking rebels and fled with them back to the Congo, about ten kilometers to the west. At least 254 civilians were murdered at Mudende. Hundreds more were seriously wounded. A few thousand had fled the scene into the countryside during the nighttime attack.[7]

When I visited Gisenyi Hospital, one Congolese doctor, Patrick Kimpiatu, who was trained in the United States, had begun his forty-fifth hour of continuous surgery and medical care for 267 patients, 15 of whom had died since arriving after the massacre. Dr. Kimpiatu was the only doctor present with two nurses from Doctors Without Borders and few medical supplies. When I witnessed the victims of the machete attack for the first time, I could scarcely comprehend the carnage. I saw one child whose brain had just been stuffed back into his head by the doctor, without anesthetic. Another child was told his slashed leg would be amputated. His screams persisted throughout my visit and echoed within me for days. A beautiful teenage girl was lying motionless, forever paralyzed by a gunshot wound. An old woman was barely intact from machete slashes. Tents had been erected on the hospital grounds, crowded with the crippled and the dying. There had been no further medical assistance from any source. Blood and grime sloshed everywhere.

I had a recurring nightmare for years after Mudende: I would arrive at a massacre scene with the dead blanketing the killing field. But there always was a solitary tent, and when I entered it there was one hideously wounded survivor who pleaded for help. I would run from the tent screaming for a doctor. The doctor never arrived, and death overtook the victim.

After touring the atrocity site, I met Rosamond Carr, or "Raz," a remarkable elderly American woman who ran an orphanage at her home near Mudende.[8] (Her character was played by Julie Harris in the movie *Gorillas in the Mist.*) While girls and boys played hide-and-seek in her gardens, she told me that everybody had been terrified. Refugees streamed by her home all day long. Raz claimed that the shooting began at 11:45 p.m. and by midnight she saw the glow of the refugee tents ablaze. Shooting continued until 3:00 a.m. and then stopped. This information varied from what Rwandan officials had told me: they believed the battle was over in thirty minutes. I often found such discrepancies between official reports on atrocity crimes and what witnesses would recount to me.

Such was the case when I traveled down the road to the Nkirmira Transit Camp. Exhausted witnesses told me the shooting had started at 11:00 p.m. and ended about 3:00 a.m. They saw a lot of killing. Many women and children died, they said, and they claimed the total dead numbered 1,465, which was much greater than the number I had heard from government officials at the campsite. People died at different times, the survivors claimed, and 150 were allegedly abducted. The Hutu attackers used axes, machetes, spears, and rifles and sloshed flammable material on top of tents that they then lit ablaze. There had been too few soldiers to defend the camp for such a large number of attackers. When reinforcements arrived, they were slowed by a huge pile of stones on the road leading to the camp. The attackers left as the troops broke through. The refugees told me they wanted the attackers arrested and brought to justice. Victims always told me they wanted justice. Through the years I became quite skeptical of theorists and pastors who argued that all would be fine with simple forgiveness or reconciliation. No. The victims want justice.

My guide through all this was Richard Sezibera, a high Rwandan official who later became the country's ambassador to the United States. After we toured Gisenyi Hospital, Sezibera told me that Rwanda sought a partnership with the United States to fight the genocide. They needed more public statements and assistance to the military to confront the genocidaires entering Rwanda from across the border. It would be an antigenocide coalition of the United States, key governments in the region, and ultimately governments worldwide. Our talk that day found its purpose in the International Coalition Against Genocide, which I helped launch one year later.

In my report to Albright after the Mudende visit, I concluded that the number and severity of insurgent attacks on Tutsi constituted "a resurgence of genocide" in northwest Rwanda, which was vulnerable to the persistent threat of Interahamwe attacks from across the border.[9] The genocidal character of the anti-Tutsi attacks had become more prominent since August 1997. The poor treatment of the wounded from the Mudende Camp massacre reflected both the brutality of these attacks and the need for a much more rapid response capability by Washington and the international community. The Rwandan army's response to the Interahamwe insurgency had been brutal as well, and too often resulted in large numbers of civilian deaths.

I recommended that the State Department describe the massacres of Tutsi by insurgent militia as a continuation of the genocide of 1994 and thus as "genocidal attacks" by its perpetrators. Such a declaration would not impose an obligation on the United States to respond in any particular way (such as the use of military force), but I felt that using those words would imply that the United States should demonstrate an effective and responsive policy to crimes of that magnitude. Further, I recommended that the Office of Disaster Assistance had to improve its rapid response capabilities for medical emergencies arising from atrocity crimes. At the same time, Washington needed to press for investigations of Rwandan soldiers involved in illegal attacks on civilians. I recommended that the United States improve its military training program to the Rwandan army to enhance the military's compliance with the laws of war and human rights law.

The temporal jurisdiction of the Rwanda Tribunal, which covered only the year 1994, prevented the court from investigating the atrocity crimes that had occurred at Mudende and elsewhere in the years following the genocide. "Tribunal fatigue," a term I had coined years earlier to describe the Security Council's weariness of building more ad hoc tribunals or expanding the two that existed, rendered any suggestion of expanding the timeline of the tribunal implausible. But during those years of resurgent genocide, I often speculated on what could have been a far more powerful mandate if only the Rwandan government had not had a nonpermanent seat on the Security Council, and hence extraordinary influence in the negotiations creating the Rwanda Tribunal, in 1994.

The turmoil stoked by the genocide never subsided on my watch. One year later, in November 1998, on another visit to northwest Rwanda, I visited two camps of internally displaced persons who had been living there for about three months. They were local Rwandan Hutu who had fled to the security of the camps, which were guarded by government soldiers. The Interahamwe militia had threatened them for colluding with the Tutsi government. This was an odd reversal of fortune. I was used to visiting camps filled with Tutsi who had fled the Congo to avoid the Hutu militia there. As I entered the first camp, at Nyaratovu, I saw crowds estimated at 53,000 living in tents staked precariously into the steep hillsides. The scene was stunning and awful at the same time: thousands of tents and huts with a teeming population surviving in squalor and yet against the magnificent backdrop of the Rwandan hill country. I knew that a major rainfall could wipe out the camp, as the huts and tents surely would slide down the flooded slopes. At Nyamagoli, the nearby second camp I visited where 51,400 Hutu were crowded together, a courthouse had been converted into a small hospital. That symbolic transformation made me wonder whether, on the scales of human experience, perhaps the right to health trumped justice.

At Nyaratovu, the mother of a sick and malnourished child, like many others, had not heard about the recent Rwanda Tribunal rulings convicting Jean-Paul Akayesu and former Hutu Prime Minister Jean Kambanda. The fate of the leaders of the genocide had not filtered through to the masses of Rwandans who needed to learn that justice was being delivered, albeit in a far away court. But of what concern were distant judicial rulings when her child was dying in her arms? Who dared to prioritize justice over education, when other young children in the camp had to write on their legs for lack of paper in their makeshift schools?

The Pastor from Mugonero

The only indicted fugitive of any of the war crimes tribunals to have reached the shores of the United States during the 1990s was Elizaphan Ntakirutimana, a pastor in his seventies who was president of the Seventh Day Adventist Church in Rwanda in early 1994 and worked out of a church complex located in the Kibuye Prefecture. When he traveled to Laredo, Texas, after the genocide, Ntakirutimana had not yet been indicted. The Rwanda Tribunal did not even exist until November 1994 and only began issuing arrest warrants in 1995. So the pastor, who joined one of his sons in Laredo, received a green card visa from Washington and thus enjoyed permanent residency in the United States. Even though he was not a citizen, the green card gave the pastor considerable legal protection under U.S. law.

On June 20, 1996, the Rwanda Tribunal indicted Ntakirutimana on a full package of atrocity crimes, and later approved the first amended indictment against him on July 7, 1998, and a second amended indictment on October 20, 2000.[10] (Another son, Gerard, also was indicted and ultimately tried and convicted by the tribunal.)[11] The tribunal charged that Ntakirutimana had prepared and executed a plan by which large numbers of Tutsi were persuaded to seek refuge in his church and the adjacent hospital compound. He then collected armed Hutu, led them to the compound, and directed the slaughter of the Tutsi who had sought shelter there. The second indictment covered Ntakirutimana's use of armed gangs following the Mugonero slaughter, to ensure that the Tutsi who had escaped and survived were tracked down and executed.

Following the first indictment, Ntakirutimana was quickly located in Laredo, which sits opposite Mexico on the banks of the Rio Grande. U.S. marshals staked out the son's home and observed the pastor pack up a car on September 26, 1996, and start to drive north on the federal interstate highway. They pulled the car over before it traveled far and took Ntakirutimana into custody under the tribunal warrant. Back in Washington, the Justice Department briefed me hour by hour during the stakeout and arrest drama.

Our hopes for a speedy transfer to Arusha of the indicted Ntakirutimana dissipated as local justice took control of the case in the courtroom of U.S. magistrate judge Marcel Notzon. I sent a memorandum to Rwanda Tribunal prosecutor Louise Arbour explaining that Notzon was not going to trust either international law or the reality of the Rwanda Tribunal to protect the rights of green-card-holder Elizaphan Ntakirutimana. The pastor's religiosity played very well in Laredo, and Notzon clearly was in the "disbelief" column of how someone with Ntakirutimana's long career in the church could possibly commit genocide. He seemed far more willing to believe the indictee's protests of innocence than discover probable cause in the witness testimony backing up the transfer request. However, the Clinton administration looked to the case as an important precedent for its cooperation with the Rwanda Tribunal and as a means to encourage other governments to fully cooperate with the Rwanda and Yugoslav tribunals. So we could not afford to fail on this first test of our own resolve in American courts.

By October 16, new documentary evidence regarding witness testimony was certified and en route to Laredo from Rwanda. Ken Harris, one of the highly talented Justice Department attorneys responsible for the case, toiled away to file a lengthy memorandum with Notzon explaining the entire extradition process and the rationale behind it, which rested on the "Agreement to Surrender of Persons" entered into between Clinton and the Rwanda Tribunal and a statute that provided congressional approval of the extradition procedures.[12] Under long-established constitutional law, either an extradition treaty or a congressionally approved procedure suffices, and we undeniably had the latter. But Ramsey Clark, the former U.S. attorney general during the Lyndon Johnson administration, represented Ntakirutimana and engaged in beguiling discourses in the Laredo courtroom. Clark essentially argued that the Rwanda Tribunal was an illegally constituted court with no jurisdiction in the United States, that there was no extradition treaty with the tribunal, and that the evidence presented from Rwandan witnesses to establish "probable cause" was too unreliable to be trusted by the magistrate. It was hard not to wince at the courtroom arguments, but Clark was getting through to Notzon.

Not until December 17 of the next year, 1997, did Notzon deliver his long-festering decision on the fate of Ntakirutimana, and when he did, it was not a good day in either the Justice or the State Department. He ruled that the federal court in Laredo lacked jurisdiction to authorize the surrender of Ntakirutimana since the United States did not have a "valid extradition treaty" with the Rwanda Tribunal and because the genocide charges against him were not supported by probable cause given that the evidence was poorly substantiated. Notzon released Ntakirutimana, who returned to his son's spacious home in Laredo.[13]

Notzon's decision denying the government's request to surrender Ntakirutimana revealed remarkable misunderstanding and narrow-minded views about international law and constitutional practice in extradition matters. In Washington we marveled at how Ramsey Clark had pulled the wool over the good magistrate judge's eyes. We had a lot of work ahead of us, and it would not be easy. The end point would not arrive until the year 2000.

While Harris and his team of prosecutors retooled for a filing of the transfer request before a different judge in the federal courts of the southern district of Texas (a technical procedure under extradition law), I convened meetings with government immigration lawyers and Justice Department prosecutors to plot strategy. I posed a simple question to them: "If we lose on the transfer request, can you prosecute Elizaphan Ntakirutimana for the crime of genocide in federal courts, or at least deport him?" They deliberated and responded, uniformly, no. When Ntakirutimana entered the United States in 1994, he could truthfully fill out his visa application because it did not require any declaration of being involved in genocide or, for that matter, any atrocity crime. The declaration focused only on Nazi Germany and the Holocaust, which had enabled the Justice Department for decades to deport former Nazis implicated in the Holocaust who had lied on their visa applications. The law implementing the Genocide Convention in the United States explicitly provided for prosecution of genocide but only if the suspect was a U.S. citizen who had committed the crime anywhere in the world or an alien who had committed genocide on U.S. soil.[14] Ntakirutimana was neither—he was an alien who had waged genocide in Rwanda, so he had no connection with the United States as an agent of genocide. He walked free of any liability for the crime of crimes. America was a sanctuary for the Rwandan genocidaire!

I was so incredulous at the absurdity of the situation that I proposed amending federal law so that it would cover aliens in the United States who were accused of committing genocide in any foreign country. But there was resistance to the initiative both at the Justice Department (which considered it a very low priority among many tough issues requiring congressional support) and from Republicans in Congress, who appeared to have little interest in facilitating feel-good legislation from an administration that had just returned for four more years of governing. Many years later there was at least a revision in the I-94W Nonimmigrant Visa Waiver declaration, to ask: "Have you ever been or are you now involved in espionage or sabotage; or in terrorist activities; *or genocide*, or between 1933 and 1945 were involved, in any way, in persecutions associated with Nazi Germany or its allies?" (emphasis added).[15]

This still remains incomplete, as anyone who has been "involved" in crimes against humanity or war crimes, including torture or ethnic cleansing, can waltz into the United States unchallenged. Ideally, the content of the question will be amended one day to read: "Have you ever been or are you now involved in espionage or sabotage; or in terrorist activities; or genocide, crimes against humanity, war crimes, torture, or ethnic cleansing; or between 1933 and 1945 were involved, in any way, in persecutions associated with Nazi Germany or its allies?" (Of course, soon there will be no suspects from the Nazi era still alive and in sufficient health to question, thus negating the reason for focusing on Nazi Germany in immigration documents.) One decade later, in 2007, I consulted with Senator Dick Durbin of Illinois on the Genocide Accountability Act, which became law and achieved the objective of permitting the prosecution of any alien who arrives in the United States and is charged with committing genocide anywhere in the world. No longer would the United States serve as a sanctuary for genocide suspects.[16] If the Genocide Accountability Act had been on the books in 1997 and covered genocide committed in 1994, then we might have chosen simply to prosecute Ntakirutimana in federal courts if our effort to transfer him to Arusha had failed.

The Justice Department successfully argued the case before a different federal court judge, and on August 6, 1998, Judge John Rainey found that Ntakirutimana was properly extraditable to the Rwanda Tribunal for the offenses charged in the tribunal's indictment. The Surrender Agreement and the federal statute together constituted a constitutional basis for Ntakirutimana's surrender. There also was probable cause in the submitted evidence to sustain the indictment. Judge Rainey labeled irrelevant, for purposes of an extradition request, Clark's challenge to the authority of the tribunal under the U.N. Charter or his arguments of alleged inadequacies in the tribunal's procedures.[17]

Ramsey Clark and his client did not give up. They appealed to the U.S. Court of Appeals for the Fifth Circuit, sitting in Denver. Four of the five judges rendered a majority decision in favor of the Justice Department and validated the ruling of Judge Rainy. However, Judge Robert M. Parker, joining the majority, cautioned Secretary Albright, who would make the final determination on Ntakirutimana's transfer to Arusha, to look at the evidence very carefully. Parker believed the entire case was driven by political factors and that Ntakirutimana was innocent of the charges. He could not believe that a pastor could commit genocide. But he agreed with the majority that federal extradition law had been satisfied to require his transfer provided the secretary of state made the final decision to do so.[18]

Ntakirutimana filed a writ of certiorari with the Supreme Court, which denied it on January 24, 2000.[19] I prepared a memorandum to Albright arguing in favor of his immediate transfer to Arusha and discussed the issues with her. She approved transfer of Ntakirutimana, and he arrived at the Rwanda Tribunal shortly thereafter. He was tried and convicted of genocide and other atrocity crimes.[20] Ntakirutimana's trial proved how misguided Judge Parker had been. In Rwanda, many Catholic priests and nuns and Protestant pastors had been at the forefront of the genocidal assaults on the Tutsi, and they were convicted of heinous crimes by the Rwanda Tribunal and by national courts in Rwanda, Belgium, and France.[21] Ntakirutimana was sentenced to ten years of imprisonment and was released in December 2006. He died one month later.

Despite its many administrative and political setbacks, the Rwanda Tribunal rendered credible justice for the genocide that mercilessly swept through Rwanda in 1994. Never before has the rule of law been rendered so thoroughly against so many leaders responsible for atrocity crimes in Africa. The endeavor has proven its worth many times over.

CHAPTER SIX
UNBEARABLE TIMIDITY

If arrests are left to luck or stupidity, they aren't going to happen.

Yugoslav Tribunal prosecutor Richard Goldstone, during a meeting with Secretary of State Warren Christopher on January 26, 1996

FOR MORE THAN FIVE YEARS, FROM THE SUMMER OF 1995 UNTIL I LEFT THE State Department on the last day of the Clinton administration in January 2001, there was one high-profile challenge—the apprehension of indicted war criminals—that was excruciating to grapple with day after day. The future of the Yugoslav Tribunal sometimes hung in the balance, but more often the credibility of governments and armies committed to achieving peace in Bosnia suffered mightily in the years following the Dayton Peace Agreement. While arrest strategies were critical to the work of the Rwanda Tribunal and, after my own departure from government, the Special Court for Sierra Leone and the International Criminal Court, by far the most prominent challenge in the 1990s arose in the Balkans. The Yugoslav Tribunal had to rely exclusively on the reluctant cooperation of governments and of NATO forces in Bosnia to take into physical custody indictees who could be officially arrested by tribunal prosecutors. The unbearable timidity of the United States and its European allies to rapidly strategize and then implement an effective means of apprehending indicted fugitives from justice in the former Yugoslavia constituted an abdication of responsibility that will haunt the legacies of these governments and those who led them.

In Washington, political and bureaucratic resistance to tracking fugitives effectively and ensuring their arrest long delayed the rendering of justice by the Yugoslav Tribunal. There were endless inconclusive meetings within the State Department, among agencies, and by the Deputies and Principals committees of the National Security Council.

I suspect most Americans understand and expect that critical domestic policies—such as health care, energy, education, and taxes—have a Washington dynamic driven by interest groups, talking heads on cable television and the Internet, and most importantly political and bureaucratic jousts among the executive branch, Congress, and occasionally the Supreme Court. An unspoken code of conduct plunges everyone into a maelstrom of turf battles and political scoring that ultimately produces a policy result.

But where foreign policy is concerned, one might expect a different set of rules to apply. The "got ya" politics of Washington should defer to a more reasoned and determined effort to protect and project not only the national interests of the United States but also the country's global interests. The latter term describes the outer perimeter of U.S. foreign policy, which is the first line of defense against threats to the security of the nation but also the field of opportunity on which Washington can act to advance the values of the modern civilization that America shares with other nations. Our global interests demonstrate that we "get it" in terms of what needs to be done to improve the human and environmental condition of peoples throughout the world.

The relatively minor task of scooping up the architects of atrocity crimes in the Balkans in the last decade of the twentieth century should not have succumbed to mind-numbing excuses, prevarications, and fearful strategizing in the capitals of the major Western democracies. But it did, almost as if political and military leaders were confronted with the toxic dilemma of whether to raise the sales tax in Chicago. The good news is that despite overwhelming bureaucratic odds pitted against the challenge, by early 2001 almost fifty indictees of the Yugoslav Tribunal were in custody. Though many of the accused were arrested years after they were first indicted, and thus remained at large too long, each one of them nonetheless walked through the door of a trial chamber in The Hague.

The bad news is that Radovan Karadzic, the Bosnian Serb president charged with masterminding atrocity crimes in his own country, evaded arrest until July 2008, when he was located in Belgrade sporting a wizardlike gray beard.[1] Ratko Mladic, the Bosnian Serb general charged (along with Karadzic) with the Srebrenica genocide, was finally arrested in Vojvodina, a Serbian province north of Belgrade, in May 2011, and transferred to The

Hague to stand trial. Goran Hadžić, the president of several self-proclaimed Serb regions within Croatia during the Balkans conflict, was arrested on July 20, 2011. Their freedom from justice for so many years was no accident: there was no Herculean effort by NATO governments. Karadzic and Mladic defied the Yugoslav Tribunal because some officials on both sides of the Atlantic did their best to discourage or derail viable apprehension strategies. Among them were men of great power, including Defense Secretaries William Perry and William Cohen, Chairmen of the Joint Chiefs of Staff John Shalikashvili and John Shelton, Army Generals Ed Shensiki and George Joulwan, Admiral Leighton Warren "Snuffy" Smith, CIA Director John Deutch, and French general Bernard Janvier.

Other officials honestly wanted the arrests to take place, but did not commit enough of their political fortunes at critical moments to the difficult but not impossible task of bringing these two men and other fugitives to justice quickly and decisively. The highest State Department and National Security Council officials sympathetic to the goals of accountability sometimes slowed the effort and shifted their attention elsewhere, leaving me and other officials isolated. I never saw Clinton enter the ring to grapple with the toughest problems that, if overcome with his personal engagement, might have led to rapid arrests of Karadzic and Mladic during his presidency.

My job, first as Albright's senior adviser and counsel while she was at the United Nations and then as her war crimes ambassador after she became secretary of state, was to search for a formula that would put a full-court press on Karadzic and Mladic and achieve their arrest and transport to The Hague. How could I manage the key players in Washington and foreign capitals so that a viable strategy would emerge to take down these indicted fugitives? That was my tactical challenge for five years.

In the final two years—1999 and 2000—the task became even harder as Albright and I sometimes grew detached from each other's work. Her priorities as secretary of state predictably swamped her agenda each day. One of those was her admirable determination to protect the people of Kosovo and to prevent the ethnic cleansing of that land. I saw her interests shift more toward "genocide prevention" than doggedly pursuing the justice challenges of arresting indicted war criminals and assisting me to salvage a viable U.S. policy toward the planned International Criminal Court. Nonetheless, she stood firm with me at critical moments as I pressed the accountability agenda in Kosovo, Sierra Leone, and Cambodia during this period.

One of the most prominent justice struggles was keeping our eye on the prize of putting Karadzic and Mladic in the dock. It never came to pass on my watch. It was as if a pinball machine dictated American policy as officials debated the merits of arresting indicted fugitives and how to do so. Yet political and military leaders never found the formula to score the grand prize.

Fundamentals about Indictments and Arrests

In order to understand what went wrong with Karadzic and Mladic, and for too long with so many other indicted fugitives, one should understand the difference between indicting a war criminal and arresting one. The prosecutor of the Yugoslav Tribunal draws upon many sources of information to investigate an individual and, if the evidence points toward responsibility for atrocity crimes, to seek a trial chamber judge's approval of an indictment against the person. If the indictment is approved, the accused becomes an "indictee" of the tribunal and, if he or she remains at large and hence not in custody, the accused is an "indicted fugitive."

The prosecutor and his teams of lawyers, investigators, and forensics experts traveled throughout Bosnia and Croatia, and ultimately gained access to Serbia, to interview witnesses, retrieve documents, visit crime scenes, and excavate mass graves in search of evidence to prepare an indictment and, sometimes following its initial approval by a judge, to amend the indictment with additional evidence of atrocity crimes perpetrated by the same indictee. Such investigative work often proved very difficult, including obtaining access to certain areas and buildings and to witnesses. But the prosecutor and his staff kept at it until they could persuade the judge that there was "sufficient evidence to provide reasonable grounds for believing that a suspect has committed a crime within the jurisdiction of the Tribunal."[2] If the judge was so convinced, the indictment would be approved, and then two challenges confronted the prosecutor: arresting the indictee and proving his guilt before the tribunal beyond a reasonable doubt.[3]

Setting foot in the Balkans, however, for the purpose of investigating atrocity crimes and preparing indictments was far different from actually arresting the indictees who were targeted by that investigative work. Neither the Yugoslav Tribunal nor any of the war crimes tribunals employ skilled police or paramilitary units authorized to physically arrest indictees. The tribunal ultimately had a tracking team that sought to locate indicted fugitives so that an arrest could be made, provided someone was willing to

Figure 3. Map of Bosnia and Herzegovina. This map shows the three military sectors of Bosnia and Herzegovina established in the Dayton Peace Agreement of December 1995, one each commanded by American, British, or French forces. Also portrayed are the ethnic divisions of the country at that time.

apprehend the indicted fugitive. The Rwanda Tribunal also used an internal tracking team to locate its indicted fugitives. But the tracking team in The Hague had little to go on and needed the assistance of intelligence agencies of NATO governments in particular to help find the indictees. Once located, either by virtue of the tribunal's own tracking team or the efforts of others, someone had to detain the individual on national sovereign territory. The real problems arose in both achieving accurate and constant tracking of the indicted fugitives and then in devising some means by which they would be apprehended and formally arrested and transported to The Hague to stand trial.

A further crippling problem in Bosnia was the fact that following the Dayton Peace Agreement the country was divided into three major sectors (see figure 3): the North Sector (United States), the Southwest Sector (United Kingdom), and the Southeast Sector (France). The three major "occupiers" deployed thousands of troops to their respective sectors. Other NATO countries sent soldiers subordinated to the three main contributors. Polish, Danish, Russian, and Swedish troops deployed to the American sector. Canadian, Czech, and Dutch forces were stationed in the British sector. Italians, Egyptians, Spaniards, and Ukrainians served in the French sector. Arrest strategies and authorities devolved to each of these national forces, with varying degrees of engagement and oversight from partners in the particular sector. For example, the Italians had to coordinate with the French before launching any effort to apprehend an indicted fugitive physically present in the French sector and within the smaller patch of territory patrolled by the Italians. American soldiers could not migrate to the French sector to undertake an arrest operation. Nor could the tribunal prosecutor instruct the top commanders of the American, French, or British sectors to order their soldiers to find and arrest someone. The process of tracking an individual and arresting him was far more complex and fraught with delays, missteps, frequent unwillingness to take any risks, and the absence of an overarching strategy coordinated among the major troop contributors so that arrests could be made rather than just talked about year after year after year.

Both the tracking and arrest challenges proved extremely difficult for the prosecutor of the Yugoslav Tribunal. The simple reality, for better or worse, was that until a negotiated peace settlement could be achieved in Bosnia, arrests were put on hold. But by late 1995 that peace—however fragile—was emerging, and the task of bringing indicted fugitives to justice became a permanent feature of the international engagement with the Balkans.

Dayton and Impunity

In early September 1995, Richard Holbrooke, who shortly would head the U.S. delegation to the Dayton peace talks, attested that Slobodan Milosevic had appealed in talks with him for immunity for indicted fugitives Karadzic and Mladic so that, at a minimum, they could travel abroad for the imminent negotiations. Holbrooke denied the immunity plea and told Milosevic that if either indictee traveled to any foreign country or to the United States, he would be arrested.

The Dayton talks commenced two months later without Karadzic or Mladic in attendance. The stakes were high. Journalists, commentators, human rights groups, and even the Yugoslav Tribunal prosecutor, Richard Goldstone, speculated before and throughout the negotiations that the United States was prepared to sacrifice justice for peace.[4] Some outside observers worried in particular that amnesty would be granted to Karadzic and Mladic and guaranteed to Milosevic, who remained unindicted and would enjoy that status for four more years. Many also expected that the Dayton negotiating team would not insist that the parties cooperate with the Yugoslav Tribunal, including its orders to arrest indicted war criminals and transfer them to The Hague.

I wrote shortly after Dayton: "There was not a shred of truth to this speculation."[5] There was a bit of hubris in this declaration, as there certainly had been debate at Dayton over the issues of amnesty and cooperation, but in the end the essential requirements were met. John Shattuck, the State Department's top human rights official at the time, has described in gripping detail the battle that had to be waged at Dayton to protect the Yugoslav Tribunal from being undermined in order to secure the agreement of Milosevic and Croatia's leader, Franco Tudjman. Pentagon officials insisted that U.S. troops not be tasked to arrest the indicted war criminals. European allies and some top State Department officials wobbled on how cooperation with the tribunal and arrest issues would be finalized. But Albright and Shattuck, with Goldstone's key interventions from afar, made the critical difference in burying talk of amnesty and in securing cooperation language in the final documents.[6] Wesley Clark, the Pentagon's top negotiator at Dayton, later wrote that cooperation with the Yugoslav Tribunal on arresting indicted war criminals "was an aspect of the agreement that would cause many difficulties in the years ahead."[7] There are few better historical understatements.

U.S. negotiators incorporated the Yugoslav Tribunal into the General Framework Agreement at Dayton and eight of its eleven annexes,[8] thus creating a mosaic of obligations that confirmed—albeit only on paper—the tribunal's powers in Bosnia, Croatia, and Serbia. The originally drafted war crimes provisions were watered down during the negotiations, including deletion of an explicit requirement to comply with the Yugoslav Tribunal's orders. But the Dayton Peace Agreement proved that peace negotiations could coexist with the investigation and prosecution of atrocity crimes. Weeks before the signing of the agreement, Clinton said, "Some people are concerned that pursuing peace in Bosnia and prosecuting war criminals are incompatible goals. But I believe they are wrong. There must be peace for justice to prevail, but there must be justice when peace prevails."[9]

The administration's message for years had been "no amnesty." Clinton never signaled that the Yugoslav Tribunal's indictments were negotiable, and the administration's Dayton negotiators repelled contrary suggestions. Albright said of both tribunals that "the United States supports strongly the commitment ... to pursue any suspect, regardless of his or her rank, position, or stature, wherever the evidence leads. There is not, and there should never be, any statute of limitations on the force and effect of the tribunals' indictments."[10] Only the U.N. Security Council could entertain granting amnesty to an indicted war criminal, and the likelihood of it doing so was nil.

Goldstone influenced the Dayton talks, for the better. Just prior to his November 1995 private talks in Washington as the negotiations in Dayton were reaching their climax, Goldstone alerted me that he would reiterate behind closed doors what he had said publicly in recent days: There must be no "deals" at Dayton on amnesty or protection of war criminals from arrest. I advised Strobe Talbott, the deputy secretary of state, to be equally blunt in our response: In recent weeks the U.S. government had repeatedly pronounced its determination that there would be no amnesty and no "deals." No other government had so strongly opposed amnesty as part of any peace agreement, at Dayton or elsewhere. Albright, Strobe Talbott, Richard Holbrooke, and John Shattuck weighed in with similar statements. Albright's deputy at the United Nations, Skip Gnehm, emphasized before the General Assembly full cooperation by Milosevic with the Yugoslav Tribunal.[11] Why Goldstone continued to question the United States on the matter based on spurious rumors baffled me.

During his visit, Goldstone explained to me that, in his November 14 newspaper interview about the Dayton talks, he reacted to a journalist's questions about a report out of Belgrade that a deal had been cut on Karadzic and Mladic in Dayton. He stood by what he had said, but stressed that the journalist failed to include his further comment that the United States had repeatedly said there would be no deal on war crimes in Dayton. If in fact a deal had been cut, and he was only going on what the reporter had just said to him, then of course he would have a problem with that. I told him it sounded like one speculative statement built upon another, and he agreed. All the senior U.S. officials he met in Washington assured him that the rumors out of Belgrade were false and that no such deal was struck at Dayton. National Security Adviser Tony Lake and Albright emphasized to Goldstone the president's commitment not to compromise on this point.

Those who wanted the Dayton Peace Agreement to *guarantee* the enforcement of full cooperation with the Yugoslav Tribunal held unrealistic goals. No NATO forces were deployed to Croatia or Serbia, where so many indictees found sanctuary. Nor would there be immediate search-and-arrest missions against indicted war criminals. We were only at the very beginning of a long journey to figure out how to arrest the architects of ethnic cleansing and massacres in the Balkans.

In mid-November the Joint Chiefs of Staff pressed their "over the horizon" strategy of nonengagement in humanitarian crises during the Implementation Force (IFOR) deployment in Bosnia. (The United States deployed 20,000 of the overall number of about 57,000 NATO soldiers in IFOR.) I proposed that IFOR have the duty to respond to atrocities or other gross violations of human rights or serious threats to the safety of civilians. But Pentagon officials adamantly rejected any such duties. Their resistance on these issues foreshadowed a similar attitude toward tracking and arresting indicted fugitives.

The Principals Committee agreed shortly thereafter that some sanctions against Serbia would be suspended as soon as the entire Dayton Peace Agreement was signed in Paris, but that any permanent lifting of sanctions would be dependent on full implementation of the agreement. This accorded with Albright's long-standing view, which Holbrooke had challenged for weeks leading up to Dayton. The more significant discussion, however, concerned IFOR's mandate. The Dayton talks were muddled over IFOR's responsibility, if any, to respond to gross human rights violations, atrocity crimes, and interference with humanitarian agencies. Deputy National Security Adviser Sandy Berger reminded everyone that there had been agreement that IFOR would have the authority to respond, but that in Dayton the perception had grown that IFOR had no such duty. Berger said IFOR needed to be more forward-leaning on gross human rights violations. General Wesley Clark responded that, in Dayton, European allies had reacted very negatively any time American or Bosnian negotiators pushed for human rights or election monitoring responsibilities for IFOR. Lake reiterated Berger's point: the principals had agreed that when IFOR saw any major humanitarian problem, it would have the authority to respond, and he assumed in fact it would.

General John Shalikashvili, chairman of the Joint Chiefs of Staff, objected. He thought the principals had settled on IFOR *not* taking up routine police functions. Shalikashvili resisted the fact that atrocity crimes are not routine police events and they typically require strong military responses. But he conceded that the IFOR commander could respond to deliberate violence that exceeded the capability of local police. That would be different than saying it would be IFOR's mission to respond in the first instance. In effect, Shalikashvili argued that IFOR should be the default force that would respond only when civilian police personnel could not handle a gross violation of human rights. Berger turned to him and said bluntly that there had been agreement on IFOR's duty to respond. Shalikashvili stressed getting the maximum capability out of civilian police, or else the humanitarian taskings for IFOR would constitute the dreaded "mission creep." In my experience of countless such meetings, the "mission creep" mantra was the convenient fallback position for anything the Pentagon hesitated to assume responsibility for or viewed as unorthodox. Sadly, atrocities and other gross human rights violations had become the norm in the world of the 1990s, but the Pentagon was extremely slow to recognize that fact and respond effectively to it.

Another important atrocity crimes issue arose in Dayton on which John Shattuck, who attended the Dayton talks, attempted to hold firm. The suspension of sanctions against Serbia when Milosevic signed the Dayton Peace Agreement was contingent on performance of the terms of the agreement, failing which the suspension would be ended and sanctions reimposed. The trigger for that all-important leverage on the Serbs was originally conceived to be if the Yugoslav Tribunal prosecutor reported on a party's consistent failure to cooperate with the tribunal. Thus compliance with the tribunal and its orders needed to be in both the General Framework Agreement and in the new constitution forged at Dayton. This would place significant power in Goldstone's hands, a prospect that would not survive long at Dayton. Some wanted to impose a more general condition of gross and systematic violation of human rights before sanctions were reimposed, in which case the prosecutor would not be the trigger of that particular determination.

November 19 was the endgame for addressing atrocity crimes at Dayton. Shattuck was the last man standing who strongly pushed an atrocity crimes agenda. He told me by phone from Dayton that day that the requirement to comply with Yugoslav Tribunal orders had been removed from Article 9 of the General Framework Agreement[12] even though he had pressed the issue hard with Warren Christopher, his boss at the State Department. Shattuck asked me to urge Albright to weigh in. Some U.S. lawyers on the delegation, for instance Bob Owens, were arguing that the requirement to legally "cooperate" meant compliance with tribunal orders. I told Shattuck that for all three parties—the Muslims, Croats, and Serbs—to comply with tribunal orders, their "requirement" to do so should be explicitly stated in the agreement. The Serbs would try to take advantage of the new, watered-down language to avoid cooperation. I alerted Albright, but it was too late. Shattuck remained isolated as final drafting swept over the Dayton teams. The end product was still a positive achievement for tribunal equities, but it could have been so much more.

Further bad news arrived the next day from New York. The all-important sanctions resolution before the Security Council was stripped of war crimes conditionality except for nonbinding language in the preamble to the resolution.[13] The "outer wall" had disappeared. We were losing all traction both in Dayton and in New York. When Albright delivered her explanation of vote in the Security Council regarding the sanctions suspension resolution, she said that if there was manifest noncooperation with the Yugoslav Tribunal, then the United States would not hesitate to bring this to the attention of the IFOR commander and the high representative (the civilian leader for implementing the peace agreement) if the situation warranted. She spoke of the mosaic of obligations on war crimes found in the General Framework Agreement and in the new constitution.[14] This is the same theme I used in my *Foreign Policy* article shortly thereafter, with the intent of casting the most positive light on the exercise. It was, however, far short of where we had wanted to end up on war crimes conditionality in the entire Dayton process.

Seven months later, in June 1996, Goldstone confided to me that he had genuinely feared that the Yugoslav Tribunal would be sold down the river at Dayton. He was never invited to Dayton, and he was not consulted during the negotiations. His fears grew because of the lack of information, which he only got from newspapers. Nonetheless, he was greatly relieved about what was achieved there. "Holbrooke protected the interests of the tribunal," Goldstone told me. "The United States was the major power pushing for the tribunal and fully resourcing it," he continued. "But I had a great deal of healthy skepticism and lack of trust for the politicians. When I read the Dayton Peace Agreement, the tribunal is referred to in every possible place. There are references to the tribunal in areas where I would not have thought to see it." Nonetheless, he was deeply disappointed that IFOR was not granted proactive arrest authority. The compromise neither forbade nor required arrests.

Goldstone believed Dayton had led directly to changes in attitude by Zagreb and Belgrade. Croatia had just arrested Zlatko Aleksovski, an indicted fugitive, in Split. Before Dayton, Belgrade had refused to recognize the legitimacy of the Yugoslav Tribunal. But Milosevic, by signing the Dayton Peace Agreement, formally recognized the tribunal and permitted it ultimately to set up an office in Belgrade. The number of indictees in custody had jumped from one (Dusko Tadic) prior to Dayton to seven shortly after Dayton. As Goldstone cynically confided to me, "If today we had 56 out of 57 in custody, would the press still be saying it is '*only* 56'?"

Post-Dayton Labors

In late November 1995, top officials tasked me to prepare guidance for the North Atlantic Council (NATO's political masters) on the arrest of indicted war criminals. At a Deputies Committee meeting I pressed hard on atrocities coverage for IFOR, but other priorities were tumbling through the room, and war criminals were viewed more as a nuisance than a serious endeavor. Indeed, on November 27, Holbrooke said that there could be no commitment to remove Karadzic and Mladic from their positions of power prior to the signing of the Dayton Peace Agreement in Paris the next month. There was real fear of atrocities being unleashed on Serbs in Sarajevo. Thus the priority was to convince Bosnian president Alija Izetbegovic that he had a responsibility to protect the Serbs.

In Washington, some recognized the fundamental shortcoming of the Dayton Peace Agreement, namely, that it did not *explicitly* address either the civilian populations in danger or the arrest powers of IFOR. My colleagues on the atrocity crimes beat lamented the sad fate of these issues after they had been articulated repeatedly by the highest officials in Washington meetings. The Bosnian Serb situation on the eve of the Paris signing, December 5, was precarious. Mladic was ranting, which prompted National Security Adviser Tony Lake to caution that we would not renegotiate and would not give Mladic a veto on the process. "Tell Milosevic to tell them [the Bosnian Serbs and Mladic] to shut up," instructed Lake. He continued, "If Milosevic can't control them, then we are in deep shit." Albright reminded Lake that on the day the Dayton Peace Agreement is signed in Paris, Karadzic and Mladic must no longer hold any public office or military command. However, it would take longer, into 1996, to achieve that aim.

Regarding the Yugoslav Tribunal, agency heads agreed that Goldstone should be encouraged to exercise a right of full access to all areas in Bosnia, including Srebrenica. They were passing the buck to him, I thought. Goldstone would have to write to U.S. Army general George Joulwan, who was the Supreme Allied Commander Europe (SACEUR), and to Bosnian Serb authorities to gain access to crime scenes, mass graves, and witnesses. Rather than agree to use U.S. envoys to press the right of access issue, Washington assumed Goldstone could pry open the door himself. Lake, with a growing awareness of how little was indeed being accomplished, expressed blunt views about the shortcomings of IFOR's authority and the lack of political will to ensure arrests of indicted fugitives from the Yugoslav Tribunal.

With the arrival of IFOR, a distinctly incomprehensible term for the indicted war criminals appeared on the scene to burden me and everyone else for years. Someone in the Pentagon decided to call each indictee a "PIFWIC." This stood for "persons indicted for war crimes." PIFWIC was such a lame term it sounded as if the subject had sprung out of *Winnie the Pooh* and thus was unworthy of the attention of real soldiers. Further, it was inaccurate. The persons indicted by the Yugoslav Tribunal could be charged with only crimes against humanity, only genocide, only war crimes, or any combination of those three categories of crimes. Every time I heard someone in uniform, including NATO supreme commanders, speak of "PIFWICs," I felt like a piece of chalk was scraping up my spine. This was serious business, and it angered me that such a wimpy term could diminish the alleged evil of these indicted fugitives from the rule of the most fundamental precepts of law. Imagine a gung-ho commanding officer in the field being told that his mission for the day, or the week, was to track down a PIFWIC and arrest him. It sounded like they were planning games for a USO picnic. I refused to use this idiotic term during the 1990s and will employ it no more in this book, although many of the military officers I write about hereafter used the term liberally in their conversations with me.

The debate over amnesty for *indicted fugitives* continued to occupy some attention in late 1995, but it never pointed toward any real possibility. On November 16, during a meeting on Capitol Hill, Goldstone explained that the Yugoslav Tribunal had no authority to establish an amnesty for anyone. Only the Security Council could mandate an amnesty, he patiently explained to staffers who were mind-bending the problem into incoherent possibilities. In an interview with the *Christian Science Monitor* at the end of November, Albright confirmed that amnesty was never negotiated or agreed to in the Dayton talks.[15]

Setback in London

On December 6, 1995, the deputies pondered how any arrest "authority" could survive in the mandate for IFOR when so many NATO governments were balking at the prospect of IFOR apprehending indicted fugitives. My draft language for such authority had suffered cynical assaults by Pentagon officials. Instead, the deputies decided to pursue a U.N. Security Council resolution that would grant such authority, thus cornering hesitant NATO members with the "higher" diktat of the council. We agreed to deploy tribunal staff to meet with SACEUR George Joulwan and NATO lawyers to work through arrest procedures. Ideally, SACEUR would approve appropriate authorities for detention and transfer to The Hague, and the Security Council would confirm the SACEUR commitment with a Chapter VII enforcement resolution.

I flew to London to attend the peace implementation conference beginning on December 8. Before a room full of NATO, Balkans, and U.N. representatives, Deputy Secretary of State Strobe Talbott summarized the Dayton Peace Agreement, noting that Dayton at times had seemed like a European city and that there was unfinished business, which necessitated the London conference. He said that Dayton was based on the desires of the parties and that political will was backed up with the intent to use military force if necessary. Talbott pointed out the need for governmental authorities to respect and defend human rights. There would be no peace without justice and no justice without peace, he pronounced. Talbott stressed the consensus at Dayton to proceed with the prosecution of war criminals. Immunity and amnesty had never been negotiable at Dayton, and they were not negotiable in London, he said. "Our only remaining enemy is the war itself."

Joulwan emphasized IFOR's monitoring and enforcing duties under the military elements of the Dayton accord but remained disturbingly silent about war criminals. I thought, here we go again with the Pentagon equivocating on a central issue for Balkans peace. Joulwan stressed that it was not IFOR's intent to carry out humanitarian missions unless it was within the force's capabilities to do so. IFOR, he said, would be extremely busy at the outset with its primary duty to separate the warring forces. Carl Bildt was, to his credit, the only European official to stress full respect for the orders and directions of the Yugoslav Tribunal.

Sitting against the wall of the ornate London conference room, I scribbled: "I'm disturbed—any IFOR response to violence against civilians was dropped from the London document. Why? At whose initiative? Did the North Atlantic Council decision sheet address violence to individuals? In final hours, unbeknownst to me, it was dropped in London. Why didn't Joulwan explain this in his intervention?"

I asked Goldstone to call Joulwan, French officials, and Vitaly Churkin of Russia immediately to press on arrest procedures being addressed in the London document. Goldstone also would have to weigh in on the Security Council resolution. The Russian ambassador to the Netherlands called Judge Antonio Cassese, the president of the Yugoslav Tribunal, and Goldstone to press them to suspend the arrest warrants on Karadzic and Mladic, giving no reasons except that he was acting at the request of the cabinet in Moscow. We speculated that the reason may have been an effort on behalf of the Serbs to release two French pilots captured earlier in exchange for such a suspension. Cassese rejected the request outright, saying the judges would never entertain the idea.

In reality, the U.S. negotiating team in London helped strangle IFOR's capabilities on both atrocity crimes and protection of civilians. The final document tracked the Dayton language closely and Joulwan's statement at the conference, neither of which were strong endorsements of atrocity crimes priorities. The goal was to avoid "mission creep," and my colleagues actually took pride in achieving that. I informed Albright and State Department officials, including Holbrooke, that the final draft of the conclusion of the peace implementation conference omitted IFOR's important supporting task of protecting civilians, which had appeared in earlier drafts and was mentioned in British prime minister John Major's opening statement. Under "military implementation" (Section 9), earlier drafts had recited a key provision of the Dayton Peace Agreement: IFOR would have the right, within the limits of its assigned principal tasks and available resources, and on request, "to respond appropriately to deliberate violence to life and person."[16] When the section was revised simply to reflect what Joulwan had said in his London statement, that critical supporting task was omitted.

I was deeply distressed and argued that we needed to make certain that the full text of the key Dayton provision must be in the NATO Operations Plan, decision sheet, or other operative command document so that there would be no ambiguity about IFOR's authority to arrest indicted fugitives. This was arrest power I had worked on at the request of my colleagues, and it had been much discussed by the deputies and principals in Washington. I also advised that we needed to ensure both at NATO and in the Security Council discussions on the resolution authorizing deployment of IFOR that credible language survive on the authority of IFOR to arrest or detain indictees and transfer them to the tribunal. The forthcoming Monday was the critical day this issue would be determined for the NATO decision sheet then under discussion in Brussels. But in London, all efforts failed to insert meaningful and tough atrocity crimes language into the peace implementation plan. There were simply too many governments to compromise with, and there were NATO officers who seemed completely disinterested in the arrest of indicted war criminals who posed a risk to their troops *by remaining at large.*

On the margins of the London conference, Albright met with Serb leader Milan Milutinovic, who later would be prosecuted and acquitted before the Yugoslav Tribunal. He sought flexibility on the outer wall, asking, "Where is the end?" Albright described full cooperation with the Yugoslav Tribunal as one of two main pillars of the outer wall, the other being sufficient action on Kosovo and two other regions in Serbia. While the United States had agreed to suspend economic sanctions, Milutinovic's further pressure on Albright to leapfrog over the outer wall proved unpersuasive. She reminded him that Belgrade had ignored three recent letters from Goldstone seeking cooperation in investigations.

IFOR's Anemic Mandate

Back in New York, the Russians resisted incorporating any IFOR arrest authority in the U.N. Security Council resolution we were seeking in order to stiffen NATO's wobbly spine on the issue. The French also objected to explicit arrest authority and suggested that parties simply had an "obligation to hand over" the indictees. The North Atlantic Council, which politically oversaw the IFOR mission, waited for the Security Council resolution before addressing the arrest issue. The supreme allied commander, General

George Joulwan, expressing his views during a phone call with Wesley Clark, believed that IFOR would not arrest Karadzic even if he walked into a room full of IFOR soldiers.

Nonetheless, Goldstone told me on December 13 that he had just had a very positive meeting with NATO officials and had spoken with Joulwan earlier that day. Joulwan claimed the tribunal would get more meaningful cooperation than it had from UNPROFOR. But he did not want IFOR to hold an apprehended indictee for more than ten hours. Goldstone said he would be prepared to have tribunal officials in Bosnia for the handoff of any arrested indictee. Joulwan also assured him about security for tribunal personnel. This was all encouraging but did not reflect any firm IFOR commitment to follow through.

I learned the same day that Milutinovic would not sign the London agreement until Bosnia dropped its 1,200-page genocide case against Serbia before the International Court of Justice.[17] The threat proved to be nonsense, but it showed Belgrade's septic attitude about the atrocity crimes challenge ahead.

The Supreme Allied Command for Europe (SACEUR) proposed that IFOR transfer indicted persons to the Yugoslav Tribunal but detain an indicted fugitive only when IFOR troops came into contact with him in the execution of their assigned responsibilities. In other words, in the unlikely event that IFOR personnel happened to bump into an indicted fugitive while going about their official duties, and they had knowledge of his identity as an indicted war criminal at the moment of such an encounter, they would detain and hand him over. For several weeks in late November and early December, the North Atlantic Council discussed whether additional Security Council authorization was necessary for it to approve this anemic policy put forward by SACEUR. The U.S. delegation argued that no authorization would be needed beyond what was already established in the Dayton Peace Agreement and Security Council Resolutions 827 (1993) and 1031 (1995), and supplemented that rationale over the next several weeks with reliance on a December 16 North Atlantic Council decision, the tribunal's own order of December 27, and the express consent of the government of Bosnia and Herzegovina.[18]

By December 20, 1995, the Joint Chiefs of Staff were advising that the IFOR commander probably would not seek to arrest Karadzic and Mladic in Pale but might do so in Sarajevo, where there would be greater security. The U.S. commander entering Bosnia, Admiral "Snuffy" Smith, worried that he might meet Karadzic and Mladic outside Sarajevo, especially if he followed through on his announced intention to visit Pale quickly or if Mladic boldly engineered an "encounter" to embarrass him.[19] The State Department's attitude, held by its top policy-makers, was to favor a simple policy: the IFOR commander should personally avoid meeting Karadzic and Mladic unless he was prepared to transfer them to the Yugoslav Tribunal (and we knew Smith was not so prepared). Holbrooke noted that Milosevic supported IFOR arresting Karadzic and Mladic, but we could not take advantage of that sentiment unless IFOR exercised the fortitude to take down these indicted fugitives.

General Howell Estes III, who was director of operations (J-3) on the Joint Chiefs of Staff, said that indicted war criminals would be detained on the spot if IFOR soldiers came into contact with them. I posed to Estes the Pale hypothetical (a Snuffy Smith encounter with Karadzic or Mladic during a visit to Pale), and Estes backed up the standing order: detain them. I nevertheless was deeply skeptical that Smith or others around him understood their responsibility in such a crisp way, particularly since the modalities of such an action needed to be carefully considered. I needed to ensure that all IFOR officers and, to a reasonable degree, the soldiers they commanded were knowledgeable about the identity of the fifty-four indicted fugitives. So with Albright's support, I set in motion the circulation of mug shots, names, brief descriptions of their crimes, and their possible locations. Estes, whom I grew to admire, agreed to contact NATO quickly to explore how such information could be efficiently and widely conveyed to IFOR officers and soldiers.

On December 28, Talbott and other State Department officials agreed that any amnesty granted in Sarajevo to stabilize the situation there between Muslims and Serb residents must not compromise tribunal investigations and prosecutions. The issue was how to grant amnesty at the local level and isolate it only to Sarajevo, where the standoff between Muslims and Serbs remained on high alert. However, I ensured that atrocity crimes falling within the Yugoslav Tribunal's jurisdiction and their perpetrators would not qualify for any such amnesty.

Karadzic and Mladic

Without Bosnian Serb leaders Radovan Karadzic and Ratko Mladic standing trial before the Yugoslav Tribunal, the court could neither achieve its potential nor plot a realistic endgame to bring all indicted war criminals to justice. My task was to facilitate the arrival of Karadzic and Mladic, as well as all other indicted fugitives, to The Hague as quickly as possible and certainly long before the end of the Clinton administration's second term, during which I was ambassador at large for war crimes issues. There were times, however, when I questioned whether my own government and our European allies were truly committed to the mission of apprehending the indicted war criminals, particularly Karadzic and Mladic.

The exit strategy for U.S. troops in Bosnia depended, Albright and I argued repeatedly, on capturing the scores of indicted fugitives still roaming around the Balkans influencing their friends and remaining a threat to stabilization and ethnic harmony in the region. The short-term view, which dominated Pentagon and NATO thinking, was to ensure day-by-day protection for the deployed forces on the ground and lock in the "no casualties" boast for whatever commander had responsibility that week, month, or year. The long-term view, namely, the threat posed by indicted war criminals plotting havoc, stirring up ethnic divisions, engaging in black market operations, and confirming an attitude of impunity in the Balkans, seemed to be an afterthought in one meeting after another on arrest options.

No accounting of the Yugoslav Tribunal in its early years would be complete without some understanding of why it proved so difficult for so many years to bring these leading architects of the atrocity crimes in the Balkans to justice. That task framed the most visible challenge of ending impunity, not because the United States and its NATO allies could not accomplish the task, but because the political will to get the job done quickly and efficiently never materialized.

Arbour's Angst

The new prosecutor of the Yugoslav Tribunal, Louise Arbour from Canada, visited Washington in late January 1997 and told Defense Department officials that they needed to take the glamour out of indicted war criminals. She reminded my colleagues that, at their core, the indicted fugitives were common criminals with large body counts. The military told her that many of the indictees lived in the French sector of Bosnia. Without the French being engaged in the entire operation, it would be impossible to get the job done. Arbour described her plan to issue sealed indictments for those who might be harder to apprehend, thus enabling "track and snatch" operations to proceed against unwitting indictees. She wanted NATO's Stabilization Force (SFOR, the successor to IFOR) to plan for encounters and not just react to the unlikely accidental one. The Pentagon officials, seemingly oblivious to how fearful they sounded, told her to forget about changing SFOR's mandate.

Arbour admitted to Albright that she was trying to play down the apprehension card publicly. "The more people think the tribunal is in jeopardy, the harder it will be to get cooperation," she said. But without arrests in the near term, the tribunal would suffer a serious setback. She pleaded for an exemption from the no-growth budgeting that was overtaking the United Nations at the behest of Washington. If arrests were achieved, then prosecution of those cases would drain the tribunal budget quickly. Paradoxically, while Arbour needed to pursue sealed indictments more often, the more they remained sealed the harder it would be to request sufficient funds in the budget to cover trial work if arrests actually were made.

Officials of the Federal Bureau of Investigation (FBI) told Arbour that the military did not want to get involved because an arrest operation would be too risky. They parroted the Pentagon's risk-averse attitude. The FBI needed an on-the-ground assessment team to evaluate that risk. If *military* arrests were taking place in the British sector of Bosnia and Herzegovina, why would the FBI (rather than U.S. soldiers) be on the front line of arrests in the U.S. sector, they asked? Arbour responded, her back against the proverbial wall, that the military probably were more scared of Serb retaliation after an arrest than of the risks of the operation itself. Some of the indictees, she insisted, were easy targets. The tribunal staff moved around the region all the time with their own investigators.

Although FBI agents from the U.S. Hostage Rescue Team planned to visit Bosnia and Herzegovina soon and make an assessment, FBI officials expressed caution about their agents becoming too militaristic. They even cited the risk of stoking militia paranoia within the United States against the United Nations if the FBI effort were linked too closely to the international organization that, if one believed the extremist rhetoric, regularly sent black helicopters over Montana. Arbour sighed. She had had enough and shot back, "Everyone has a good reason why someone else should do it. We must break this entitlement to impunity!" Tracking down indicted war criminals still seemed like an alien responsibility to the tough-looking crowd at the FBI.

In her final Washington meeting, Arbour met with Sandy Berger, who had been elevated to national security adviser following Tony Lake's departure.

Berger, a short, burly, and fierce Washington lawyer and bureaucratic insider, knew exactly what was at stake. He agreed with her that the opportunity for deterrence would be lost if arrests were not made. However, Berger, echoing Clinton's own words, said no U.S. troops could be committed to the arrest strategy, although he said a way had to be found to achieve arrests. Arbour turned cross, vented her angst with me after the meeting, and remarked that she might have to rely on the Europeans to produce the right formula for arrests. She left Washington deeply frustrated with bureaucratic "nonsense."

Fractured Alliance

Nonetheless, with Albright's assistance, I kept pressing for action and joined senior State and Defense Department officials on a trip to Europe the first week of February 1997 to persuade our allies to join us in developing a viable arrest strategy. During the flight to Europe, on a small government aircraft, I mapped out for the team the legal authorities we would use to justify joint arrest operations with our allies in Bosnia and Herzegovina.[20]

The French, not surprisingly, proved more loath than either the British or the Dutch to embrace any arrest strategy. The U.S. delegation stated clearly to them that the United States sought French cooperation to establish a planning cell to elaborate a detailed operations plan but without any French obligation to participate in an arrest operation, even though so many of them would have to take place in the French sector of Bosnia. The French looked as if they were experiencing collective constipation. They were pained with our legal explanations and had difficulty with their own domestic legal authorities. For them, the risks included failure, the taking of hostages, the consequences for the peace process, the lack of secrecy, and the fear that French soldiers would be the first victims of any Serb retaliation. Their greatest concern focused on hostage taking among the French soldiers deployed in their sector if arrests went forward. French officials noted that U.S. forces had regrouped in the U.S. sector to avoid threats, whereas the European troops were scattered in their respective sectors and thus more vulnerable. They insisted on waiting until Albright's scheduled visit to Paris later in the month, which meant we lost three weeks for coordinated planning.

At the French Defense Ministry, skepticism and hostility swept over the discussion. One official said there would have to be an unassailable procedure, legally and operationally, to move forward, but then did not offer anything he thought would meet those high standards. The French would not commit until there was a real assessment about who undertook operational risks and who provided political oversight. They insisted on a clear distinction between the arrest forces and SFOR troops. They had no interest including the tribunal and Arbour anywhere in the chain of command for the operations. We pushed back on this point. The French criticized any strategy of arresting mid- and low-level indictees first and told us to prioritize apprehending Karadzic and Mladic. It was implausible, they said, *not* to go after Karadzic and Mladic. Hallelujah! But we Americans, seated comfortably in an ornately decorated Parisian conference room, wondered silently when the French would snatch Karadzic, who was generally known to frequent their sector of Bosnia, if they thought his capture was so important.

While in Europe, the American delegation met Arbour. She insisted, for good reason, on having the legal authority to say no to an operation and thus would have to be kept informed of planning for the arrests. That was precisely what the French opposed. However, when we met with the Germans in Bonn (which at that point was still the German capital), they expressed no major concerns but wondered about some of the legal arguments. They believed, correctly in my view, that just one successful operation would change the whole dynamic for multiple arrests.

In our meeting with Secretary-General Javier Solana of NATO on February 7, 1997, we told him that the arrest team would be designated as a "friendly force" and that SFOR's security responsibilities would fall within its mandate. Solana stressed that "success" would be hard to define without capturing both Karadzic and Mladic. He too worried about the sufficiency of the legal authorities. Because of ongoing NATO expansion talks, the timing of when to approach the Russians would be extremely important and sensitive. The Russians already were curious and agitated about arrest rumors, Solana told us.

Upon our return to Washington, high-level officials cogitated over an arrest strategy. There had been some progress in developing the planning cell, and more drafting was agreed upon. The Pentagon emphasized that protection of its military forces remained the highest priority but that indicted war criminals had been elevated to the third-highest military priority in Bosnia and Herzegovina. That was encouraging news since such rankings constituted the level of commitment the Pentagon would dedicate to developing and executing the arrest strategy. However, the intelligence community continued its foot-dragging habits and was far too slow in prioritizing information gathering on indicted fugitives. This only emphasized again why presidential intervention is sometimes required to shove midlevel officials back into line.

Early Arrests

By late May 1997, there still was no decision internally about how to proceed with an arrest. There apparently were "problems" with three secretly indicted individuals residing in Prijedor, located in the British sector, and with Arbour's position to arrest them sooner rather than later. Either there would be approval for an operation by mid-August, or we would wait until after the municipal elections to activate it. By that time there would have to be a new, proactive plan for arresting the Prijedor indictees even though in the month of May they were being tracked and could have been more easily picked up.

In late June, I held discussions with Hans-Peter Kaul, the legal adviser of the German Foreign Ministry. Kaul, a very polite and rigid-thinking German lawyer and diplomat, also was my German counterpart in the negotiations for the Rome Statute of the International Criminal Court. He later was elected as a judge to that court. He hinted that, as in Washington, there were serious divisions within the German government about arrests. But he shared our legal view that there was strong authority for the overall operation in paragraph 20 of Security Council Resolution 1088, which reads, "[The Security Council] [a]uthorizes Member States to take all necessary measures, at the request of SFOR, either in defense of SFOR or to assist in carrying out its mission, and recognizes the right of the force to take all necessary measures to defend itself from attack or threat of attack."[21] Kaul believed the indicted fugitives were a threat to the mission and to the troops of SFOR. In his view, the United States should ask General Joulwan to issue a request to member states for arrests. My German colleague felt this would rebut British criticism of legal insufficiency in the arrest strategy.

Kaul made a compelling argument. The United States rested legal authority on Resolution 827,[22] but also on Resolution 1088 as a supplemental rationale. Washington still needed to make the overall decision on proceeding with arrests. Officials were reluctant to engage SFOR in the arrest operation and argued for a separate operation. If SFOR were engaged, then the chain of command would reach to the North Atlantic Council, but in our view Joulwan did not have to go to that political body to make a Resolution 1088 request. Joulwan likely would not, on his own initiative, lodge such a request. Someone would have to shove him in that direction. I agreed with Kaul that Resolution 1088 bridged an arguable gap between Resolution 827 authority and the SFOR commander's mandate.

On June 26, 1997, I met with a very angry Arbour in The Hague. Two attempted snatch operations on the Prijedor three had just failed. She described Joulwan's recent talk with Deputy Prosecutor Graham Blewitt as disastrous. Joulwan had claimed that, operationally, the Prijedor situation was ripe for action. But SFOR had refused to "encounter" the three indictees. "It's an insult to my intelligence," Arbour scoffed. "These are idiotic military plans. If they have to wait for an encounter, that is just stupid. Why can't there be a creative approach to 'encounters'? [General William] Crouch [commander of U.S. Army Europe] will never permit a chance encounter. The whole thing is an absolute fraud." She told me that one SFOR lawyer had advised the tribunal that SFOR did not have a sufficient list of Bosnian lawyers to consult within the seven hours they needed to get the three fugitives out of the country, which she found outrageous obstruction. She threatened to expose SFOR's bungling ways. She could not contain her outrage any longer. Arbour claimed she would go public and expose the refusal of SFOR and the major powers to act on arrests. She fundamentally disagreed with appeals that she back off.

But the next day, the U.N. Transitional Authority in Eastern Slavonia (Croatia), led by a retired major general of the U.S. Air Force, Jacques Klein, brilliantly orchestrated the arrest of indictee Slavko Dokmanović and thus demonstrated that such arrests were not mission impossible.[23] (Klein remained in key posts in the Balkans for years thereafter and often pressed me to better assist him in the arrest of Karadzic and other indicted war criminals.) The Dokmanović arrest left no question as to the authority to arrest if forces acted under the general authority of U.N. Charter Chapter VII. With political will and military grit, SFOR or special forces could do the same in Bosnia and Herzegovina under the legal authority of Security Council Resolutions 827 and 1088 and the tribunal's Rule 59 bis, which permits transmission of arrest warrants "to an appropriate authority or international body or the Prosecutor."[24] This meant that NATO and any U.N. peacekeeping force, as international bodies, or even the prosecutor of the Yugoslav Tribunal, as "an appropriate authority," could receive an arrest warrant and act upon it. The latter became the favored procedure, as it enabled NATO or other special forces to detain an indicted fugitive briefly before the prosecutor arrived on the scene and made the actual arrest. Military forces traditionally have avoided criminal arrest functions, although the American intervention and occupation of Iraq in 2003 and thereafter cast that particular presumption aside.

Shortly thereafter, during an operation against the Prijedor indictees, Milan Kovaćevic was captured, Simo Drljaća died trying to evade arrest, and Milomir Stakic escaped, only to be arrested years later, on March 23, 2001.[25] The Prijedor operation would have been entirely eclipsed if a planned effort to arrest Karadzic at the same time had been implemented. The plan to take down Karadzic was a defining moment for our arrest strategy, but the operation was called off, probably because a senior French military officer, Major Herve Gourmillon, met secretly with Karadzic and was suspected of tipping him off.[26] Unfortunately, the Gourmillon affair scared off the Pentagon from coordinating any Karadzic arrest for a long time thereafter and gave the cynics within the Washington bureaucracy plenty of reason to back away from arrest strategies.

In July 1997, a man who was under sealed indictment by the Yugoslav Tribunal attempted to surrender to Dutch SFOR troops in Bosnia. The indictee contacted SFOR at midnight and said, "I want to surrender, at my home." Someone in the Dutch SFOR unit decided not to go to the house for fear it could be a trap. Later, when SFOR soldiers actually encountered the man, no one knew who he was or that he was indicted. They apparently did not understand how to handle the matter. The absurdity was palpable. Two days later SFOR futilely tried to invite the suspect to visit the SFOR base or to arrange some other kind of encounter with him.

The Principals Committee met in late July 1997, just as I was being confirmed by the Senate as the war crimes ambassador, to review and approve the long-awaited arrest strategy. The United States would take the lead in apprehending Karadzic and Mladic, but we would maximize the French role on Karadzic, provided we could overcome concerns arising from the Gourmillon affair. The identities of all sealed-indictment suspects would be communicated to the arrest team and the new NATO commander, U.S. Army general Wesley Clark, but not to SFOR until the operation on any particular individual was being executed. SFOR then would be fully engaged. There also would be a concerted effort to seek the surrender or arrest of top Bosnian Croat indictees, including Dario Kordic. Finally, an arrest strategy had emerged from the National Security Council.

The decision must have emboldened President Clinton, who described to Taylor Branch on August 13, 1997, "a blunt message to Milosevic through Holbrooke that crack NATO troops were coming to arrest Serbian leader Radovan Karadzic for war crimes. The 'soft' message was that Milosevic had a tacit option to remove Karadzic first. Otherwise, there would be no restraining ground rules, as there had been in Somalia, and any resistance would meet overwhelming lethal force."[27]

Meanwhile, the voluntary surrender of several Bosnian Croat indictees on October 3, 1997, demonstrated progress.[28] Dario Kordic, the most notorious among them, was charged with some of the worst atrocities of the Balkans conflict. State Department envoy Robert Gelbard, who had the lead in negotiating the surrender with Croatian authorities, had mostly succeeded in his task with great skill. But he went too far in promising speedy trials, which was a well-intentioned boast that I had to correct immediately by clarifying that the United States could not guarantee "speedy trials" at the tribunal.

Dead in the Water

By late October 1997, I learned that very little had happened to apprehend Karadzic. The Dutch Ministry of Defense concluded there would be no Karadzic apprehension, at least through winter. There certainly would be no arrest of Karadzic prior to the November 23 elections. However, by mid-November the legal rationale for a revived arrest strategy became clearer: First, SFOR would request assistance to ensure fulfillment of its mission. The prosecutor would request assistance in making arrests. Arbour already had issued an omnibus arrest order to SFOR and any associated forces. NATO secretary-general Javier Solana would direct further cooperation with the prosecutor. Special forces would act at the request of SFOR to assist in its mission, which included detention of indicted fugitives if the circumstances and tactical situation permitted. The special forces would create the encounter situation that ultimately delivered the indictees to tribunal lawyers for arrest, or so the plan suggested.

Arbour complained to me about inaction on arrest warrants against indicted fugitives. "Enforcement is so weak," she said, "because of a military culture unwilling to embrace its own body of law justifying armed conflict. It is astonishing that military leaders are unwilling to promote enforcement of the laws of war. International actors in Bosnia … put criminal justice at the bottom of their list. That is the wrong message to send.... It's only a sideshow to deny indictees public office [namely, lustration]. The main point is to arrest them and SFOR has repeatedly failed that test. SFOR won't even arrest indictees when they encounter them!"

I began to wonder whether the intelligence community had abandoned any serious arrest strategy. There was a systemic failure underway in Washington and at NATO headquarters in Brussels. The territory at issue in Bosnia and Herzegovina was about the size of Montgomery County in Maryland, and yet all efforts to track and apprehend the indicted fugitives roaming that patch of earth were failing. We had known since September that the French were holding back their support, and yet the State Department and the White House found political reasons not to challenge Paris.

By late May 1998, the arrest strategy was dead in the water. The British remained supportive, but the French appeared to have shut down, no doubt still chastened by the Gourmillon affair. There was no real operation against Karadzic or Mladic. Defense Secretary William Cohen proved to be so resistant that there emerged considerable tension between Cohen and Wesley Clark on apprehension issues. Many of the indicted fugitives had moved to Serbia, perhaps including Mladic. But some indictees occasionally returned to Bosnia, where they could be more easily snatched.

Once again, Cohen proved to be an obstinate barrier to any effective action. The arrest operation was moving at a snail's pace when it should have been on a speedway. Karadzic might have been located within days if a full-court press were applied to the challenge. But Sandy Berger now appeared to want the whole problem to fade way. I argued that Clinton would have several foreign policy successes if he ordered and then ensured follow-through on the apprehension of Karadzic and others, including Khmer Rouge leaders in hiding in Cambodia and some Rwanda Tribunal fugitives in Africa. Such arrests also would have greatly bolstered U.S. credibility as we headed toward the Rome Conference on the International Criminal Court. But that kind of thinking seemed too speculative and posed too many planning challenges.

By late August, the arrest strategy had transformed into a strictly no-risk operation. There seemed to be no political oversight of the planning cell. In NATO, General Clark was talking the talk and walking the walk, but nothing was happening. The operation was all American, with two types of soldiers—the can-do type who just needed to be told where to go and the bureaucrats who had to have every scrap of evidence before they moved in on an indictee, which meant that they never achieved enough confidence to do so. As one soldier told me, his boss wanted the number of tiles on the indictee's home triple-counted before even considering a raid. The French, Germans, and Dutch appeared unwilling to go after Karadzic. An Albright memorandum asking for more dynamic action on arrests remained perpetually with Berger and so had not reached Clinton. Karadzic and Mladic were the most wanted men in Europe, responsible for ethnic cleansing, the siege of Sarajevo, and the genocide of Srebrenica, and yet somehow the stars never aligned to hunt them down.

Evidence on Milosevic

The task of providing evidence about Slobodan Milosevic to the tribunal continued to gnaw at the American relationship with Arbour. Some of this clearly was the fault of the U.S. intelligence community and its failure to prioritize tribunal requests for assistance, that is, to assign enough staffing and resources, and to gather information that reached beyond simply protecting U.S. forces. Some of it was the fault of the prosecutor, who sometimes failed to seek specific information with specific requests, which is the methodology intelligence agencies work best with and respond to most efficiently.

Following many months of efforts by my deputy, Tom Warrick, and me to shove the bureaucracy and accelerate information sharing about Milosevic, the principals finally decided in late December 1998 on a comprehensive review of all existing U.S. government materials related to the Balkans conflict, including the crisis in Kosovo, in order to identify any information that could support or provide leads to developing indictments against Milosevic and his key associates. This was good if belated news, as the frustration level both in The Hague and within my own Office of War Crimes Issues had reached the breaking point. We needed a top-down and bottom-up scrub of all information on atrocities and tracking data from 1990 through 1998. It was a labor-intensive endeavor that was designed to provide the maximum amount of assistance to the prosecutor to help her indict Milosevic.

Much of the problem lay in the need for additional personnel and technology to work on this and other war crimes issues within the intelligence community. The prosecutor had informed us of her desire for intercepts, access to insider witnesses close to Milosevic whom we might know about, reports on the activities of Milosevic and other key figures, and copies of original documents relating to Milosevic. She also wanted us to speed up action on her requests for imagery and information and to permit access to U.S. diplomats who knew Milosevic well from their dealings with him. Karadzic, if arrested, might turn state's evidence against Milosevic. At long last, at least there was a principals' decision to prod the bureaucracy.

For months prior to the tribunal's indictment of Milosevic, the United States provided the prosecutor with an increased flow of relevant information culled from the intelligence community. Certain reporting had to be declassified or "sanitized" of extremely sensitive information for delivery to the tribunal under special "Rule 70 procedures."[29] There was almost always a time lag of weeks, if not months, to properly organize this information for transmittal to the tribunal, a process that increasingly frustrated Arbour and her staff. They had reason to complain.

American Credibility on the Line

On May 23, 1999, Arbour told me that she neither trusted nor believed anyone about Karadzic and his long-awaited apprehension. She was fed up. She believed, particularly in the heat of the Kosovo conflict being waged then, that an apprehension of Karadzic would send a powerful deterrent signal to Milosevic and the Serb leadership. From all that I could ascertain within the Washington bureaucracy, the problem remained the French. Either they would muster the political will to apprehend Karadzic, or they needed to stand aside to permit someone else to do it. During my visit to NATO headquarters the week before, I had asked Solana to speak directly to the French. He agreed that they were the problem and that he would try to reach President Jacques Chirac. Solana saw no reason at all for Karadzic to remain at large. There were good reasons why the U.S. government did not trust the French on this matter, he said. But he believed that Clinton also had to approach Chirac very soon and press him on the issue. We agreed that if the French balked, then they had to step aside and let other elements of SFOR operate freely to arrest Karadzic.

Warrick and I were still complaining in late June, in the aftermath of the Kosovo operation, that the principals' decision of December 1998 to ramp up information sharing on Milosevic was not sinking in with the intelligence community and that proper staffing had not been achieved. The crisis point arrived in late July. The entire intelligence bureaucracy, starting with the Intelligence and Research Bureau at the State Department, was stretched too thin, with too few staffers on atrocity crimes research. Many important issues were not being addressed, falling through the cracks, or being dealt with too late. Arbour's complaints kept coming. The problem appeared to be that responding to requests from the prosecutor still had not become a policy objective within the intelligence community. The Principals Committee had internally prioritized information sharing on Milosevic and had added Vojislav Šešelj, a high Bosnian Serb leader, to the top of our priority list, even though he too was not yet indicted.[30] But the principals' decision had been thwarted at all levels of the bureaucracy.

As I explained in chapter 1, the problem stemmed in part from the prosecutor asking intelligence officials, "Tell us what you know," to which they replied, "Tell us what you're interested in." Information requests from Arbour's staff sometimes were sloppy and reflected the stronger priorities of the internal tribunal advocate for a particular project. There persisted the outdated procedure, reaching back to December 1995, of the State Department's intelligence branch determining how its brethren in various agencies would handle tribunal and State Department taskings. That was because of the classified character of so much of the information and the need for the State Department to control the relationship with the tribunal. Fierce competition among the agencies to hold on to their control of the classified data blocked my efforts to shift some of that overall direction to the Office of War Crimes Issues, which had been tasked on September 23, 1997, to coordinate both the U.S. government's response to atrocity crimes and its support for the tribunals.[31] I had long identified critical staff shortages in the intelligence community and in the State Department. The failure to properly staff the evidence challenge was a systemic problem that we had tried hard to solve. But the internal response to my complaints produced lame excuses and new rounds of turf warfare.

I advised Albright how I saw the state of play within the U.S. government on atrocity crimes support, particularly regarding Milosevic and tracking information in the Balkans. Despite months of personal interventions by senior State Department officials and myself with relevant intelligence agencies, there had been no meaningful staffing or other resource decisions to strengthen intelligence support for the Milosevic investigations. The State Department's intelligence bureau had done its best to gain some additional personnel but only after enormous efforts within the federal bureaucracy. I told Albright that the criticism leveled at her and me by Congress, civil society, and commentators would prove true if we failed to act quickly. Our credibility was on the line more than ever before.

On arrests, I learned that the Pentagon (notably Defense Secretary William Cohen) simply did not want to engage in such operations and that if we tried to prioritize apprehensions, the Pentagon would shut down the entire arrest operation.

Clashing with the French

On October 12, 1999, I met with Ronny Abraham, the Quai d'Orsay legal adviser and future French judge on the International Court of Justice, in Paris and asked him to confirm that if ordered to do so by SFOR, the French would arrest Karadzic. I found it bizarre that I had to press for an order to the French before they would consider capturing Karadzic. Time and again as the American war crimes ambassador, I found myself prodding other governments to assume obvious responsibilities relating to accountability for atrocity crimes. Why, I would ask myself, am I here having to remind you—a top official of a major U.S. ally—about this?

Abraham agreed that if ordered, the French would arrest Karadzic provided the proper intelligence and security were in place. I reminded him of the strong reaction from the French government in June regarding my comments delivered to the international press corps in Djakovica, Kosovo, in response to Christiane Amanpour's question about why Karadzic remained at large.[32] I wanted to make sure his government understood that my response in Kosovo was identical to what I had been saying for years with no reaction from the French. My standard response was that Karadzic was generally believed to be in the French sector and that it was the responsibility of all military forces in SFOR to carry out appropriate operations within their rules of engagement in their sectors regarding indicted fugitives of the Yugoslav Tribunal. In its public reaction to my comments, the French government claimed that the chain of command pointed to U.S. commanders at both the SFOR and NATO levels. The French explained that they had never received any specific order to apprehend Karadzic. How bizarre, I thought, that Paris would need an "order" (from whom?) to carry out an arrest for which they had ample authority (and abundant political responsibility) under Security Council and tribunal mandates. But neither, as far as I knew, had the French ever approached SFOR commanders with any information pointing to an arrest opportunity for which they sought instructions.

Then, on November 3, one of the worst days of my ambassadorship descended upon me. Undersecretary of State for Political Affairs Tom Pickering called me into his seventh-floor office adjacent to Albright's and informed me that she wanted me to stand down on trying to apprehend Karadzic. Almost forty-one months had transpired since he was first indicted. Pickering offered no explanation to me other than the desire to tighten the information loop. Another aide to Albright, Michael Sheehan, would take over the project and Pickering would keep me briefed, although he said he might not know everything either. I surmised later that day that Albright may have acted to appease the French, who clearly did not like my meddling in their sandbox and perhaps had endured me one time too many in Paris the month before. Perhaps the Pentagon or the intelligence agencies, which doubtless were weary of my interventions on Karadzic, requested I be sidelined. Perhaps I was viewed as incompetent. I never discovered the real reason. I sat in my office pondering what had just happened and whether I should resign. I did not believe for a moment that cutting me out of the Karadzic loop was meant to enhance chances of apprehending him or was some signal that in fact the operational effort was narrowing in for the apprehension and only need-to-know officials were to engage. I had seen too much evasive and obstructionist conduct for years to accept that rationale.

I chose not to resign, because there were battles to wage on so many fronts that I could not in good conscience abandon the field, which included the International Criminal Court. I had gone through so many years of toil and setbacks on Karadzic and Mladic that I regarded this blow to my ego, to say the least, as yet another setback to overcome. The prize—custody of Karadzic and Mladic—still lurked out there.

One More Year of Excuses

Despite the decision to isolate me from arrest strategies regarding Karadzic, as the weeks progressed I got pulled back into apprehension issues even if I did not know of precise details about Karadzic and what was, or was not, being done to apprehend him. On November 17, 1999, I discussed with top Defense Department officials the reality that as arrests of various indictees were occurring in Bosnia, the reaction of the Serbs appeared relatively tame and not anything like what had been predicted by SFOR for years as the dreaded Serb backlash. That being the case, why would the French continue to fear retaliation if Karadzic were arrested? Yet any prospect of a unilateral U.S. penetration of the French sector to arrest Karadzic in a well-planned operation continued to meet certain Pentagon resistance.

By early 2000, there was no real political oversight of arrest priorities. No one could crack the whip and organize every component of the arrest strategy, although it hardly seemed like a strategy anymore. Speculation abounded that the French would not go after Karadzic because he would reveal collaboration between French general Bernard Janvier and the Bosnian Serbs during the U.N. Protection Force deployment (commanded by Janvier from March 1995 to January 1996). Would Mladic also rat on the French if he were captured? It had become a matter strictly of political will. Defense Secretary Cohen and U.S. Army general Ed Shinseki remained the biggest problems at the Pentagon. Few in the State Department thought that the U.S. military could leave Bosnia without the arrests of both Karadzic and Mladic. (As it turned out, many years later American forces left Bosnia, but European Union troops remained in a still fractured and potentially volatile Bosnian society, thanks in part to the impunity enjoyed for so many years by Karadzic and Mladic.) The dysfunctional relationship between France and the United States continued, with neither willing to exercise the necessary political will to arrest either Karadzic or Mladic.

On July 24, 2000, Pickering updated me on Karadzic. The old problems persisted. The Pentagon would not operate with the French. There would be "fratricide" if they did, he said. The U.S. military still did not trust the French on intelligence matters. Any American operation in the French sector would entail hundreds of soldiers owing to the need for self-protection. That fact alone inhibited working with the French.

The third Yugoslav Tribunal prosecutor, Carla Del Ponte, visited Washington two months later to press hard for arrests. Her highest priority, she told everyone, was the arrest of Karadzic. Cohen had the gall to tell Del Ponte and me in his Pentagon office that tracking indicted war criminals was not in the SFOR mandate and that he had told Congress he would not chase war criminals. That was five-year-old reasoning, and it fueled the fires of impunity. Cohen seemed oblivious to the risks that Karadzic continued to pose, not to mention the denial of justice, as long as he remained at large. I tried to steer Cohen and Del Ponte into some kind of constructive dialogue, but it was futile. Cohen's mind was shut down.

In contrast, although without any real explanation, Berger told Del Ponte that U.S. efforts had accelerated in the prior four months. His deputy, Donald Kerrick, had daily responsibility for it but claimed there was no actionable intelligence yet, as if this were some kind of new project he had discovered. Kerrick downplayed any effect that a change of Karadzic's appearance might have in tracking him. (We learned eight years later in 2008, when Karadzic was captured in Belgrade, that the change in his appearance had fooled a lot of people for many years.) Berger assured Del Ponte that Clinton wanted the arrests to happen before the end of his administration. I did not know what to make of such claims from the White House anymore, particularly when stacked up against Cohen's timidity.

At her meeting with Del Ponte, Albright told her that she hoped they could proceed with the arrest of Karadzic. There were some hurdles, but she wanted it done. There were so many agencies it was hard to get everyone to agree on how to execute the operation, she explained. Sadly, nothing had changed in five years to update that explanation, and on Karadzic she had frozen me out. Déjà vu overwhelmed me.

I joined Holbrooke in the U.N. Security Council on November 21, 2000, to receive Del Ponte's annual report on the Yugoslav and Rwanda tribunals. In response to her expected call for the apprehension of Karadzic and Mladic and the transfer of Milosevic to The Hague, Holbrooke confirmed the U.S. policy that these indicted fugitives should appear in The Hague as soon as possible and that the full implementation of the Dayton Peace Agreement could not be accomplished without such apprehensions. "The sooner the better," he said. He also noted: "Given the fact that the Federal Republic of Yugoslavia [FRY] has been and remains a sanctuary for these and other indicted fugitives, the new FRY must now accept a special responsibility to achieve this objective." He reported, "We have informed [Serb leader Vojislav] Koštunica that in order to receive further U.S. financial assistance, the President will need to certify to the U.S. Congress by April 1st of next year [2001] that the FRY is cooperating with the [Yugoslav Tribunal] on document production, witnesses, and transfer of indicted fugitives to The Hague."[33]

An arrest operation was planned for November, but the intelligence it was based on proved unhelpful and ultimately false. I labored to reinvigorate the State Department's long-standing rewards program on Karadzic, which offered up to five million dollars for information leading to the arrest and prosecution of indicted fugitives. Meanwhile, all eyes were on the next potential opportunity: Karadzic's travel plans for December 19 and 20 and where he might be seen on those dates. But nothing came of this final attempt by the Clinton administration to capture Karadzic.

Arrests and Trials, Finally

Given the domestic political changes afoot in Serbia, the fate of Slobodon Milosevic as an indicted fugitive gained new urgency just prior to the end of the Clinton administration. There were proposals to have Milosevic tried in Serbia for economic and electoral fraud crimes before being transferred to The Hague to stand trial for atrocity crimes charges. Del Ponte rejected that strategy outright. She argued the primacy of the atrocity crimes charges in the outstanding indictment against him and that it would be impossible for the tribunal to set up shop in Serbia to conduct a Milosevic trial. That would be a dangerous idea, although she believed some proceedings might be held in Belgrade. Del Ponte speculated that she could add some of the Serbian crimes to the tribunal trial, but the court's statute would have to be amended to accommodate such additional jurisdiction, and that never happened.

Milosevic was arrested by Serbian authorities in Belgrade on April 1, 2001,[34] and transferred to the Yugoslav Tribunal on June 29 of that year.[35] His trial for atrocity crimes in Bosnia, Croatia, and Kosovo commenced on February 12, 2002, and extended until March 14, 2006, a few days after Milosevic died in his jail cell and only a few months before the trial court was expected to render its judgment on the massive case.[36]

Although far too many years tolled before indicted fugitives began to be apprehended, scores of them either were arrested or voluntarily surrendered to the Yugoslav Tribunal during my watch as the war crimes ambassador (see figure 4). By the time I left office on January 20, 2001, there was a long trail of bureaucratic infighting, diplomatic jousting, planning, and finally action by American forces, British troops, and occasionally other allies in the field. The men and women who risked their lives to apprehend indicted fugitives in well-planned, albeit delayed, operations deserve the thanks of a grateful nation and international community. The trials of the indicted fugitives they brought to The Hague generated much of the juris-

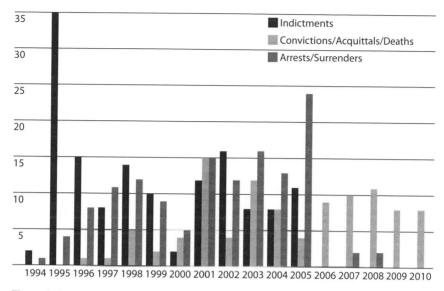

Figure 4. International Criminal Tribunal for the former Yugoslavia: Outcomes. The Yugoslav Tribunal's record of indictments, arrests, convictions, deaths, and acquittals through 2010.

prudence of the Yugoslav Tribunal and achieved a significant measure of justice for the victims of the Balkans war.

The real failure was back in Washington, where every top U.S. official, myself included, who tried to make headway with the Pentagon, the intelligence community, and even the White House on apprehending Karadzic and Mladic eventually was stymied and driven off the scent. The policy gridlock on capturing those two suspected war criminals, and the refusal to dig faster and deeper on the evidence against Milosevic, were inexcusable outcomes. They served only to salvage impunity for all three men for years while the Yugoslav Tribunal sought justice.

PART II

CHAPTER SEVEN
THE SIREN OF EXCEPTIONALISM

Before the century ends, we should establish a permanent international criminal court to prosecute the most serious violations of humanitarian law.

President Bill Clinton, before the 52nd session of the
U.N. General Assembly on September 22, 1997

THE FATE OF THE TRIBUNALS FOR THE BALKANS, RWANDA, SIERRA LEONE, and Cambodia is their temporary and limited jurisdiction. These courts were built as ad hoc judicial remedies for specific theaters of atrocity crimes committed during snapshots of time. They are each meant to close their doors soon, with their courtrooms and offices likely converted for regional justice or some other public endeavor. Years from now passersby may gaze upon the Aegon Insurance Building in The Hague and read a simple bronze plaque with these words: "Here justice was rendered by the International Criminal Tribunal for the former Yugoslavia, 1993–2014."

But what will happen if new atrocity crimes occur, as they will in the future, and nations fail in their duty to investigate and prosecute the perpetrators of such horrors? Does the Security Council overcome its tribunal fatigue? Do the fifteen nations represented there debate and grudgingly approve the costly construction of a new war crimes tribunal with a whole new cast of judges, prosecutors, defense counsel, and administrators? Does one of my successors once again negotiate directly or mediate among other negotiators the creation of another criminal tribunal designed for that specific atrocity situation, with all the costs associated with yet another new court and its personnel, not to mention the years it would take to finish the tribunal-building exercise? These questions matter because impunity is under siege, at least in theory and more frequently in practice. Therefore it may no longer be a question of whether a court will investigate atrocity crimes. The real questions are which court, at what cost, and within what time frame while the political will exists, witnesses and other evidence remain available, and victims and their relatives remain alive to prod the warriors of justice.

The likeliest courtroom for prosecuting the leaders of atrocity crimes already has arrived with the creation and trial work of the permanent International Criminal Court. It is located in The Hague and became operational on July 1, 2002, after more than sixty nations ratified its governing constitution, the Rome Statute. By 2007 the court's prosecutor had initiated investigations into four atrocity situations erupting in Uganda, the Democratic Republic of the Congo, the Central African Republic, and Darfur (Sudan). A fifth investigation, into election violence in Kenya, was approved in 2010, and the Security Council referred the situation in Libya to the court for investigation in February 2011. Probably none of the atrocity crimes committed in these countries would be under rigorous investigation followed by prosecution of leading perpetrators without the existence of the International Criminal Court. What is taken for granted today, namely, that the court stands prepared to launch quickly into investigating atrocity crimes unleashed in those parts of the world where it exercises jurisdiction, was by no means a certainty in the 1990s during my watch. A permanent war crimes tribunal, the idea for which began so problematically, generated years of high-stakes negotiations, attracted fierce resistance in powerful corners of Washington, and confronted head-on the indomitable spirit of impunity, which is the refuge of political and military leaders and warlords across the globe.

For the United States, the making of a permanent court extended over the entire eight years of the Clinton administration until its final days, and then continued despite the self-destructive policies and hyperbolic fearmongering of the George W. Bush administration. The entire exercise has proven to be an enigma for Americans from its beginning to the present day. The nation that forged the Nuremberg and Tokyo military tribunals after World War II and identified itself with bringing notorious war criminals to justice found itself awkwardly conflicted with a permanent International Criminal Court that would carry on the tradition but without the taint of victors' justice.

My goal was to defeat impunity. But there was no more difficult test of my fortitude and duty as a diplomat for the United States than the quest for the International Criminal Court. In this and the next two chapters I describe how the Clinton administration engaged in years of negotiations to build the permanent court; how, as the lead American negotiator, I rejected the final text of the Rome Statute in July 1998; but then, by the end of 2000, how President Bill Clinton decided that the United States would sign the Rome Statute on the last possible day. The story shines light on the strengths and weaknesses of the Washington bureaucracy in the making of treaties and in committing the United States to international justice and the means to enforce it. In 1993 I embarked on the most contentious struggle of my career. I probably made more enemies than friends in Washington over the battle for the International Criminal Court. But after eight years of perseverance to achieve American acceptance of the court, I ultimately realized some small measure of triumph.

The Exceptional Nation

The siren of exceptionalism enveloped the entire enterprise of the International Criminal Court on my watch and dictated the far more extreme policies under the George W. Bush administration. By "exceptionalism" in the realm of international law, I mean that the United States has a tradition of leading other nations in global treaty-making endeavors to create a more law-abiding international community, only to seek exceptions to the new rules for the United States because of its constitutional heritage of defending individual rights, its military responsibilities worldwide requiring freedom to act in times of war, its superior economy demanding free trade one day and labor protection and environmental concessions the next day, or just stark nativist insularity. We sometimes want the rest of the world to "right itself" but to leave the United States alone because of its "exceptional" character. The cynics of international law point to the realism of how nations act in their own self-interest. The United States, they argue, is a different nation of extraordinary attributes that simply cannot be lowered (or elevated) to the same level of performance as other nations.[1]

However, two basic building blocks of international law are the principles of *reciprocity*, that one nation should be entitled to exercise the same rights as those enjoyed by another nation with which it is dealing, such as for diplomatic privileges and immunities,[2] and of *equality of nations*, namely, that when nations create rights and duties among themselves, particularly through international treaties, they must do so bound by the same rules of the game and restricted to the same playing field regardless of their size or political, economic, or military might.[3] There is a heavy dose of utopia meandering through the principles of reciprocity and equality. But they have a core purpose in international relations: that no nation and no people have superior rights or exceptional privileges in the realm of international law—a purpose that is even more pronounced in the practice of international criminal law and reaches its zenith in the narrower field of atrocity law, where no perpetrator of atrocity crimes should be able to avoid justice.

There were often times in the negotiations to build the International Criminal Court when other negotiators would confront me with the general complaint that their governments had bent over backward to accommodate the United States when it refused to sign the Law of the Sea Convention in 1981.[4] President Ronald Reagan reversed course and demanded drastic changes to a treaty the United States had been the leader in negotiating throughout the 1970s under Republican and Democratic presidents. My fellow negotiators complained that Washington abandoned all of them after they had to bend their own wills to that of the new Republican administration in Washington. They spent more than a decade haggling over revisions that would conform the treaty to Reagan's vision. Then, swallowing hard, they agreed to amendments. Albright signed the Law of the Sea Convention in 1996.[5] But the United States failed to ratify the convention and so had not become a state party to it. How, the foreign negotiators would ask me, could they possibly trust the United States in the negotiations for the International Criminal Court? If they conceded anything to me, how could they be assured that ultimately the United States would join them in supporting the court?

I had to assure the diplomats that the Clinton administration sought ratification of the Law of the Sea Convention,[6] though it remains unratified as of this writing, and that Clinton was determined to support the International Criminal Court if we could achieve an acceptable structure for it in the negotiations. Nonetheless, imagine how uncomforting my words were to foreign cynics who had spent a large chunk of their careers accommodating the United States on the convention. The fact is that a small group of senators and far-right extremists believe that the Law of the Sea Convention, like so many other international treaties that have been signed but never ratified by the United States, somehow will rob the country of its sovereignty or will threaten federalism and democracy within our borders.[7] The Rome Statute of the International Criminal Court proved no different. Sometimes these fears arise out of ignorance about what a particular treaty requires of the United States and the way the treaty actually advances American priorities, and that was frequently the case with the Rome Statute. At other times they seemingly originate with nativism and fear of foreign influences. Whatever the basis, the end result is exceptionalism, and that does not advance U.S. interests very well with either friends or foes overseas.

Other governments were confused by and annoyed with the U.S. strategy in the talks for the International Criminal Court. As this chapter describes, that strategy ended up seeking to protect the United States as a nonparty to the treaty regardless of how its military might wage warfare on foreign territory. Because the United States deploys its armed forces globally, the Pentagon typically has been concerned that an international court exercising its jurisdiction on the territory of any state party to the treaty might try to prosecute U.S. soldiers who have to fight on such foreign land. That would not seem fair if the United States has not joined the court.

But from the foreign perspective, why should all the other negotiators, many of whose governments would become signatories and ratifiers of the Rome Statute, accord so much special attention to one nation's insistence that it be protected as a nonparty to the treaty, particularly one such as the United States, where certain members of Congress were determined to prevent the court from ever being established or, if established, from functioning? Why should not the United States stand up for its principles, ratify the treaty, be covered by it, and forget about its highly theoretical exposure as a nonparty, they asked me? Why was I obsessing over structuring a treaty to protect nonparties when the United States should be leading the court as a state party? It was almost counterintuitive at times—I had to argue for a treaty regime governing the International Criminal Court and at the same time had to achieve impunity for those who did not participate in the process, rather than focus on what the United States wanted in the court as an active member of it!

As a state party, the United States would have enormous influence in the court and see to it that deferral to national courts—the complementarity principle explained below—was strictly observed. Foreign negotiators found it difficult to square the U.S. position on nonparty protection with how that same privilege would be used by civilian and military leaders of other non-

party states and rogue elements to shield themselves from the court's jurisdiction and perpetrate atrocity crimes at will on the territories of states parties. The confusion only multiplied when I walked into the negotiating room
to argue for Washington's prior consent to any prosecutions of Americans,
even if the United States were to join the court. I appeared as the guardian
of impunity rather than its slayer.

Overcoming Tribunal Fatigue

Before I arrived in the State Department, the long post-Nuremberg
journey toward the establishment of an International Criminal Court picked
up steam only in 1989 after the prime minister of Trinidad and Tobago,
Arthur N. Robinson, proposed such a court to prosecute drug cartel leaders, which his own courts could not possibly bring down.[8] Washington
under the George H. W. Bush administration remained very cool to the
idea. Federal courts and various treaty relationships were doing just fine in
protecting highly sensitive intelligence about drug trafficking and seeing
to it that the kingpins were either prosecuted or extradited to jurisdictions
(such as the United States) eager to put them behind bars.

But as the atrocity crimes of the early 1990s swamped the news and as
tribunal fatigue undermined the will of the U.N. Security Council to reproduce an ad hoc tribunal with every mass killing, international lawyers and
governments began to get serious about what a permanent court would
look like and how it would function in the legal jungle of both national
and global laws. In my first six months with Albright I held three meetings
in my office to labor over the proposal for an International Criminal Court
under review by the U.N. International Law Commission (a group of thirty-
four independent experts from as many countries). One of the State Department's hard-working lawyers, Michael Scharf, summarily dumped a
thick three-ring binder of preparatory documents on my desk one day as he
was leaving for a teaching career, and wished me good luck. In September
1993 Senator Christopher Dodd, a Democrat from Connecticut whose father
had been a Nuremberg prosecutor, called Albright requesting that Clinton
speak favorably of such a court in his forthcoming address before the U.N.
General Assembly. That did not happen, until 1997.

But on October 13, 1993, the first full-scale meeting took place in the
State Department to discuss policy toward an International Criminal Court.
Almost two weeks later the U.S. National Security Council convened a high-

level interagency meeting to examine the options. The Treasury Department wanted to make sure drug enforcement cases got nowhere near the court. The Pentagon viewed the prospect of such a permanent court as strictly an adjunct to national prosecutions. If it could be limited to such a subordinate relationship and if it satisfactorily addressed American concerns about the crimes to be prosecuted, then the Defense Department could agree *in principle* to the court. It was an early signal from the Pentagon that something might be acceptable to the military brass and that we could look seriously at the proposal percolating in the International Law Commission.

The pace quickened. On November 22, I joined Defense and Justice Department lawyers to talk about the International Criminal Court. The lawyer from the Joint Chiefs of Staff saw the court as a last resort after the failure of national prosecutions. Jurisdictional arrangements must be fixed, he said, but he reconfirmed that in principle the Joint Chiefs of Staff wanted an International Criminal Court. I decided not to ignore the heavy hint.

Through the early months of 1994 a gray-haired, feisty Washington lawyer, David Birenbaum, whom Albright later selected as one of her subordinate ambassadors at the United Nations, assisted me with the conceptual framework for the International Criminal Court that the Clinton administration ultimately sought in the International Law Commission's final report. Birenbaum's early thinking about the court proved invaluable. He and I were determined to find a formula that would work for the United States. Another key player was Robert Rosenstock, the legal counsel at the U.S. Mission to the United Nations. He also was one of the "independent" experts on the commission. Rosenstock, a crusty, dandruff-flaking career lawyer who had served in the same counselor post since the Kennedy administration, often projected his own contrarian views on the subject in our many discussions with him. But he spoke frankly. He understood how other governments and experts were approaching the idea of a permanent court. I grew to admire him greatly and consulted with him throughout the administration. Rosenstock was my gut-check guy at the United Nations.

As early as March 1994, lawyers in the Justice Department's Criminal Division and at the National Security Council were rejecting any effort to include crimes of terrorism or international drug trafficking in the governing statute of the International Criminal Court. These were top priorities for a diverse group of Arab, Latin American, and European governments and, regarding narcotics, for Caribbean governments. But both sets of crimes already were covered by multilateral treaties that required prosecution or extradition to a jurisdiction willing to prosecute any suspect in the custody of a state party to the particular treaty.[9] As noted earlier, the investigation of these crimes involved a great deal of classified intelligence and undercover investigations that Washington had no interest in sharing with an international court. I always operated under tight instructions to knock out these two sets of crimes from further discussions about the International Criminal Court. Until the final days of the Rome diplomatic conference in July 1998, the United States objected to inclusion of drug trafficking and terrorism and, in union with many other governments holding similar views, prevented their incorporation in the Rome Statute.

In retrospect, the U.S. position may have been a mistake, at least regarding international terrorism. After the al-Qaeda attacks of September 11, 2001, the Bush administration's disastrous mangling of the rule of law in how terrorist suspects were detained and interrogated, and then how some were prosecuted before flawed military commissions, demonstrated some of the risks involved in national-only prosecutions.[10] A permanent International Criminal Court would have stood a better chance of depoliticizing the trials of major terrorist suspects. It would have established a judicial process that earned the respect of the international community in contrast to the scorn heaped on the United States, and the revulsion of so many Americans, to what Bush created at Guantanamo and secret detention centers and what his lawyers drafted in torture memoranda in Washington and argued in federal courts across the country when the legal challenges began to erupt. Technically, the International Criminal Court became operational on July 1, 2002, and could not have investigated the 9/11 attacks even if Washington had wanted to use it for that purpose. But as both an adjudicator and deterrent of future terrorist attacks of great magnitude, the court could serve a useful purpose.

By early 1994 I had become the de facto "go-to guy" within the administration on the International Criminal Court. Albright had encouraged me to pursue the issue. My position on the Deputies Committee of the National Security Council gave me unique access to the key agencies that would have to approve any U.S. policy regarding the court. But the issue also was a hot potato that no career bureaucrat felt was safe to handle and no other political appointee seemed interested in, given its long-term payoff or thankless demise. Having plunged head first into the Yugoslav Tribunal work, I had no doubts about taking on the issue but also recognized it was a high-stakes gamble.

At this early stage I received another encouraging signal from the Pentagon on March 20, 1994, when its lawyers conveyed two primary messages to me. First, I must ensure that the Status of Forces Agreements (SOFAs), which the United States had made with almost one hundred countries to govern the stationing of U.S. military forces on their respective territories, would be preserved. Criminal investigations and prosecutions of American soldiers deployed overseas are governed by the SOFAs, which ensure that U.S. military or federal courts will handle such cases and not the courts of the country where the crime allegedly was committed. This point was sacrosanct with the Defense Department. Second, Pentagon officials accepted that the Clinton administration could take a positive attitude toward the International Criminal Court provided fundamental changes were adopted in the court's governing statute, which the International Law Commission was drafting. Among those changes were the requirements that the U.N. Security Council would refer atrocity situations to the court, that the international court would take a case only after exhaustion of national efforts and extradition attempts, and that genocide would stand apart from war crimes. So I pressed ahead to find a workable formula for the structure of the court.

The next stop was the Justice Department and Deputy Attorney General Jamie Gorelick. She told me that her department must control access over the cases of concern to it and retain its power to compel other countries to do their duty to prosecute crimes in their own courts. The proposal for an International Criminal Court disrupted that neat division between U.S. and foreign courts and, she feared, could undermine the task of prosecutions. I emphasized that discussion centered on referrals by the Security Council or states parties of atrocity crimes only, and that major nations remained cool to the idea of including aggression in the court's jurisdiction.

In early May 1994, I joined officials representing the key agencies for a no-holds-barred discussion about the International Criminal Court. Strangely, the genocide in Rwanda was surging into its sixth week while, without a single mention of that calamity, we argued back and forth about whether to support the building of a permanent court that would cover any future Rwanda.

The Pentagon held to its relatively cooperative spirit about finding the right formula in order to support the court "in principle." Another strong voice at the table had grave reservations about promoting even the idea of an International Criminal Court. She believed the court would be susceptible to manipulation by adversaries who would use it for political purposes, would try to preempt national prosecutions, embarrass the United States for its use of the death penalty, undermine our multilateral treaties, and try to block Washington's request for extradition of suspects to the United States to stand trial. Would the international court question the discretion of U.S. attorneys? But her real concerns were about two sets of crimes that probably would not survive the process of defining the court's jurisdiction: drug trafficking and terrorism, which indeed were well covered by multilateral treaties.

Spirited discussion ensued about the value of granting the new court jurisdiction over crimes of international terrorism, with some of the administration's top lawyers acknowledging that there was some value in the idea. The challenge, in their view, was crafting the right balance between national and international prosecutions or terrorists. I shared the view of another official who reminded everyone that the Clinton administration already had shown the world that we took the rule of law seriously and that the International Criminal Court would be part of that same commitment. Those of us who worked within the United Nations system knew there was a head of steam behind the court in New York and that moving away from a positive attitude would risk setting up the United States for a major retreat from its leadership in the challenges of international justice.

One seasoned career lawyer emphasized the need to define far more specifically the war crimes jurisdiction of the court. He insisted on sticking to the Geneva Conventions and explicitly defining the other war crimes (drawn from customary international law) that would appear in the court's statute. He fretted that all the talk about a permanent court was derailing his own major concern, namely the creation of an international commission to investigate the war crimes of Saddam Hussein's regime in Iraq during the Gulf War. I smiled, as he and I were the only government officials who seemed to care deeply about setting up such a commission as a stepping-stone to an ad hoc international criminal tribunal to indict the Iraqi leadership. How different things might have turned out a decade later, in 2003, if we had had our way.

The meeting's outcome was better than I had expected, and it meant we had marching orders to stay in the court-building game. Over the following months Birenbaum and I worked with Rosenstock on the evolving statute being drafted by the International Law Commission. Rosenstock became increasingly determined to include the crime of aggression in the draft. He had been the U.S. representative to the long years of negotiations leading to the 1974 definition of aggression adopted by the U.N. General Assembly, and he was not about to walk away from the challenge of criminalizing aggression twenty years later.

When the commission approved a final draft statute for the International Criminal Court in the fall of 1994,[11] the end result did not meet all of Washington's requests. We had earlier set forth in detail our concerns, and many of our points were accommodated in the final draft: The role of the Security Council was enhanced in how cases arrived before the court. There was no more mention of customary international law as a vague basis for jurisdiction. There were significant opt-in procedures for all of the crimes other than genocide. Extradition treaties would be honored. The option of in absentia trials had disappeared. But problems remained. The crime of aggression remained, as did drug trafficking and terrorism crimes, albeit as optional possibilities. None of the crimes in the draft statute were defined, meaning that genocide, aggression, "serious violations of the laws and customs applicable in armed conflict," and crimes against humanity lacked any specificity for criminal prosecution.

Although states parties to the international court statute would be covered automatically by the crime of genocide, they would opt in for any of the other categories of crimes. In Washington, we had not yet determined any position on the automaticity of genocide for the court's jurisdiction. (Ultimately the United States accepted this automatic jurisdiction.) The draft statute also provided for state party referrals to the court, while we still preferred only Security Council referrals. But no prosecution could commence on a matter referred to the court by a state party if the case arose from a situation already before the Security Council, unless the council approved the referral. We were too blinded by our insistence on Security Council referrals to recognize the significance of this particular condition for state party referrals. However, we adopted it as a major U.S. position shortly thereafter and advocated it all the way to Rome in 1998. Also encouraging was the requirement that aggression could not be prosecuted unless the Security Council had first determined that an act of aggression had occurred between states.

The International Law Commission draft was imperfect, and the future remained unpredictable. Rosenstock alerted me that some of the countries in the "Western" group at the United Nations were interested in convening a diplomatic conference to examine the commission's draft statute. We concluded in Washington that rushing to a diplomatic conference to approve a treaty based on this draft was premature. Preliminary discussions at the United Nations first would be required, as there was too much work yet to accomplish on the draft statute. Some foreign governments, particularly Canada, and human rights activists misinterpreted our position as opposition to the creation of the International Criminal Court. That was grossly mistaken, and I spent months trying to make the simple point that we needed much more detailed work on the statute before formal steps could be taken to finalize a treaty. Among other governments, we certainly were not alone in that view. Eventually, the General Assembly approved the convening of an Ad Hoc Committee during 1995 where government representatives could slog through the commission's draft, negotiate differences of opinion about it, and consider the possibility of a diplomatic treaty conference.[12]

Letting National Courts Bat First

As we prepared to participate in the Ad Hoc Committee talks, Conrad Harper, the State Department's legal adviser, and I joined Albright for a meeting with Attorney General Janet Reno, Deputy Attorney General Jamie Gorelick, and the Criminal Division's Marc Richard at the Justice Department on January 25, 1995. Albright impressed upon them that the Ad Hoc Committee was a looming reality and Justice had to step up to the plate along with the State Department and Pentagon. Gorelick and Marc Richard saw the court as a direct threat to effective prosecution of narcotics and terrorism cases. Reno stressed that if drug trafficking crimes could be "pulled out, that would solve a big problem" she had with the court. Harper suggested keeping terrorism in if we could design an acceptable state consent regime for such cases that would serve U.S. interests. Reno tasked Richard to work with Harper and me to arrive at a compromise within three weeks. In discussions a week later, Marc Richard emphasized his department's deep concern that many countries would seize upon the court to avoid cooperating with the United States under the drug trafficking and terrorism treaties. Also, how would we identify the interest of any particular state to weigh in on jurisdiction over international terrorism? The world of genocide, crimes against humanity, and war crimes remained mostly alien to the day-to-day work or interests of our Justice colleagues.

I was designated as deputy chairman of the U.S. delegation to the Ad Hoc Committee. Ms. Jamie Borek, an experienced career lawyer and deputy legal adviser in the State Department, was the chairman of the U.S. delegation until I became the war crimes ambassador in August 1997, when we switched leadership posts and I headed the delegation thereafter. Following the first round of meetings in New York, I flew off with a small delegation of Justice, Defense, and State Department lawyers to Spain, Germany, and Italy in February 1995 for detailed discussions. At those meetings we laid out our rock-bottom requirement that the new court not imperil the Status of Forces Agreements between the United States and the scores of countries where U.S. forces were deployed. Air Force Colonel Steve Lepper, the military lawyer on my team, patiently explained all the reasons why the criminal law enforcement provisions of those many bilateral treaties and the multilateral one with our NATO allies must leave investigation and prosecution of American soldiers covered by the agreements with U.S. courts. We repeated this requirement in every negotiating forum until the final days of Rome in July 1998. What began as an explicit "carve-out" for the Status of Forces Agreements in the language we proposed for the statute of the court morphed into a generic description of "international agreements" that would require the consent of the "sending" state (such as the United States which "sends" soldiers abroad) before the suspect could be surrendered to the International Criminal Court for prosecution. That requirement became Article 98(2) of the Rome Statute.[13]

As early as the spring of that year I began to stress the importance of *complementarity* in the work of the court. That meant that the court should defer to national investigations and prosecutions of suspected war criminals and only when the nation that claimed jurisdiction proved unwilling or incapable of undertaking that responsibility would the court step in to pick up the case and seek or retain custody of the suspect. The United States helped lead on this idea throughout the years of negotiations.[14] Complementarity is such a powerful principle of deference to national courts that many of my negotiating counterparts thought it might be enough to bring the United States on board to support the final treaty text in Rome. The complementarity principle indeed was a major achievement for the United States in the negotiations, one that has resonated in how other war crimes tribunals essentially adopted it in their own work and how the future of international criminal justice is being plotted with complementarity as its fulcrum.

Joined by other negotiators, I began to push earnestly for the Security Council's referral of overall situations (in other words, entire conflagrations) of atrocity crimes to the court rather than referral of individual cases against particular suspects. The latter would prove an impossible bureaucratic nightmare and politically explosive prospect for the Security Council, and turn it into a master investigator and court clerk. The alternative, which proved acceptable and is required by the Rome Statute, is that the Security Council and states parties can refer only large-scale situations of atrocities to the court. Then the prosecutor investigates the situation and determines which individual suspects should be investigated and ultimately whom he or she should seek the judges' consent to prosecute.

In the spring of 1995, I told other governments that the United States would not yet state its position on whether to include the crime of terrorism in the court's jurisdiction. I emphasized that terrorism involves complex conspiracies, long-term investigations, classified intelligence for leads, coordination with the existing multilateral treaties that covered prosecution of terrorism in national courts, and the risk of hyping terrorist crimes as more than what they ought to be, namely, ordinary crimes of murder or destruction for political objectives.

Early Problems

Three seemingly irresolvable issues confronted us following the March 1995 talks. First, the opt-in procedure that empowered governments to select which categories of crimes their nationals would be exposed to before the court was losing favor to building automatic jurisdiction into the treaty for all the atrocity crimes, meaning that citizens of all members of the court would be open to investigation on *all* the atrocity crimes and not just genocide. The Pentagon was not yet prepared to accept that formula for war crimes and crimes against humanity.

Second, a debate unfolded in Washington over whether to require the consent of the state of nationality of the suspect before the court could prosecute him or her. The requirement seemed impractical, as it might cripple the court if governments could balk at consenting to prosecution of their own civilian or military leaders before it. But some Washington officials believed we needed it to avoid politically inspired prosecutions of the U.S. armed forces massively deployed across the globe. The alternative would be sole referral power held by the Security Council, but that option was losing favor in New York as diplomats pushed forward a right of state party referral of situations to the court.

Third, there was concern that negotiators had not yet figured out how to handle the option of offering domestic amnesties to war criminals to advance peace negotiations. The Clinton administration had recently accepted such a bargain to evict General Raoul Cedras and his cronies from Haiti in order to return President Jean-Bertrand Aristide to democratic power there.[15] Officials did not want to deprive themselves of that tool in the future.

By the end of August 1995 and another round of talks in New York, the U.S. position on the court remained positive but with caveats. We headed toward the annual meeting of the legal committee of the U.N. General Assembly in the fall with a position that approved further "interim" discussions in 1996 with flexibility as to what might follow, including a diplomatic conference to conclude the treaty. We publicly spoke of further examination and consultations about a statute for the court rather than bluntly stating we supported one, as we wanted to retain our leverage in those talks. Even though I spoke of the process being on "the right track," I knew many diplomats and nongovernmental groups would interpret this as American opposition to the court. But our intent was to slow down the process until we could prevail in our negotiating position on the structure of the court. We had decided by then to oppose inclusion of terrorism crimes as well as exclude drug-trafficking crimes and hold the line on Security Council control over referral of atrocity situations for investigation. We opposed inclusion of the crime of aggression in the court's jurisdiction because of the great difficulty in finding common ground with other governments to define it for the purpose of prosecuting individuals (rather than holding governments accountable). But internally I worked the possibility of Defense Department support for adding aggression provided the Security Council controlled any referral to the court.

On October 15, 1995, Clinton delivered an address at the opening of the Thomas J. Dodd Research Center in Storrs, Connecticut. I had been alerted to the preparation of this speech weeks in advance and, knowing that he would be speaking of Senator Christopher Dodd's father and his role as a Nuremberg prosecutor, I weighed in heavily for Clinton to support the idea of establishing the International Criminal Court and thus propel the process forward. When the day came, Clinton said, "By successfully prosecuting war criminals in the former Yugoslavia and Rwanda, we can send a strong signal to those who would use the cover of war to commit terrible atrocities that they cannot escape the consequences for such actions. And a signal will come across even more loudly and clearly if nations all around the world who value freedom and tolerance establish a permanent international court to prosecute, with the support of the United Nations Security Council, serious violations of international law."[16]

It was a beginning. In late January 1996, I learned that Clinton had indicated fresh interest in the negotiations and wanted the United States to express further support for an International Criminal Court. He wanted his negotiators to justify American positions to him in writing even though he was generally satisfied with what we already had advanced in New York. So during the early months of that year I spent weeks absorbed in meetings across Washington and in New York with foreign diplomats, Pentagon and Justice Department lawyers, senators and congressmen, international lawyers, and think-tank experts—all for the purpose of digging into the details of jurisdiction, the precise definitions for the crimes, the role of the Security Council, domestic amnesties in peace deals, and the overall structure of the court.

On June 28, 1996, I walked over to the White House for an interagency meeting convened by the National Security Council to assess the International Criminal Court. We decided to press for the diplomatic conference to be held in 1998, knowing that there would be much pressure at the United Nations to convene it in 1997. There were still many unresolved issues, however, and we continued to insist that the rules of procedure and evidence be completed prior to concluding the treaty. That project would take at least one year. Significantly, we confirmed our support for a state party referral of an atrocity situation to the court but only if it did not conflict with Security Council decisions, which translated into requiring council approval if the body already was "seized" with the conflict giving rise to the atrocities. (The International Law Commission had recommended this procedure in 1994.)[17] On complementarity, we favored the requirement that there must be a supermajority of judges who decide that a country's efforts on a case were not conducted in good faith before the court could seek to exercise jurisdiction over the investigation and prosecution.

Albright testified before a House of Representatives appropriations subcommittee in a closed hearing in early August and reconfirmed U.S. support for establishing an International Criminal Court. But she said that much depended on jurisdiction and on process. "We're not going to buy a pig in a poke," she declared. "We will not accept a raid on our sovereignty. The United States is very conscious about our sovereign rights. The key agencies have to feel comfortable." The subcommittee chairman, Republican congressman Harold Rogers, said the United States must not be subject to the jurisdiction of the court. Albright countered that we had to work out the limits of jurisdiction but when that was achieved, the United States would fall under the court's jurisdiction once it joined the treaty. But first, she cautioned, we were determined to make sure it was a good and credible court.

As another round of U.N. talks began in August 1996, I told delegations that Clinton had stated his vision for an International Criminal Court at the Dodd Center almost a year earlier. We wanted a court with broad membership that ensured due process for defendants, but much hard work lay ahead to make that a reality. The United States shared the objective of a diplomatic conference, but only when work on the statute of the court and the rules had progressed enough to ensure the success of the conference. We did not want an empty court to which few states would become party. I said it was irresponsible to skip necessary preparatory steps to a diplomatic conference. These were not popular words in the U.N. conference room, but they were honest expressions of hope and reality and of what it would take to make the process work.

Exploring for Flexibility

Reality arrived soon enough. By May 1997, I concluded that the United States was becoming increasingly isolated in the negotiations. Our longstanding position on Security Council control of referrals to the court, our refusal to embrace the crime of aggression unless it was specifically defined and activated within the statute to our complete satisfaction, and our opposition to any independent power by the prosecutor to initiate investigations of atrocity situations were some of the primary positions that distanced Washington from too many other governments deeply committed to setting up the court. I began to explore the possibility of some flexibility in the American stance.

I was mindful of two strongly held views split between two key agencies in Washington. One agency stressed the need for a complementarity regime that Washington would have confidence in over the years. How could it be strengthened in the negotiations, they asked me? Another agency wanted me to lock in the requirement of U.S. consent before any of our nationals appear before the court, in which case we could be more flexible on the requirement of the Security Council controlling referrals of situations to the court. Indeed, I understood the basic argument to be that if we could confirm the state consent requirement along with strong complementarity, then Washington should be able to withdraw its insistence on Security Council control and make do with the "Singapore compromise." That proposal was introduced by the Republic of Singapore in the talks to authorize the Security Council to temporarily shut down investigation of an atrocity situation initiated by referral of a state party or by the prosecutor provided no permanent member vetoed the relevant resolution. It was not an ideal outcome, however, for the option of requiring consent from the state of nationality of the alleged perpetrator of the atrocity crimes would undermine other U.S. laws exercising extraterritorial jurisdiction to capture drug traffickers, terrorists, money launderers, and other international criminals and authorize bringing them back to the United States to stand trial.

In late June 1997, I traveled to Bonn, Germany, to participate in a meeting with NATO allies to collaborate on the definitions for war crimes in the statute. One primary issue was the magnitude of war crimes that must occur before the court would exercise jurisdiction. I argued for a "gravity" test that would require both planning *and* a large-scale commission of war crimes to qualify for the court's jurisdiction. This was a Pentagon request, which I knew would ease my overall effort with the Defense Department if it could be achieved. However, many NATO governments represented at the Bonn meeting cautioned that stipulating a magnitude test so explicitly would undermine the future enforcement of the Geneva Conventions of 1949, under which individual soldiers could be held accountable for "grave breaches," namely very serious individual crimes during warfare such as willful killing outside of combat, torture or inhuman treatment, and unlawful deportations. They argued that requiring large-scale commission of the war crimes would lead, over time, to erection of a high bar for enforcing the Geneva Conventions even in national criminal courts and military courts.

The compromise language signaled the need for a magnitude threshold in the definition of war crimes for the International Criminal Court but did not require it explicitly. Thus, the long definition found in Article 8 of the Rome Statute opens with these words: "The Court shall have jurisdiction in respect of war crimes in particular when committed as part of a plan or policy or as part of a large-scale commission of such crimes." Even the absence of a comma after "war crimes" was meant to emphasize the particularity of the magnitude standard for prosecution. We could live with that formulation, although it would have made my job much easier in Washington and with the Pentagon if there had been a more explicit requirement for the widespread commission of war crimes. In the actual practice of the war crimes tribunals, including the International Criminal Court, war crimes typically have been prosecuted only when the gravity test was met.

The month of July 1997 proved to be one of intensive preparation for the next round of U.N. negotiations. I hoped to arrive at the August talks armed with a shift in the U.S. position so as to gain the upper hand in New York. But I could not break the logjam between Security Council control, which satisfied the Justice Department, and the precondition requiring consent of the state of nationality, which Justice rejected and the Pentagon strongly preferred. (The Pentagon also desired Security Council control over referrals as a supplemental insurance policy.) I had to settle on saying that the United States reserved its position on a consent regime for cases, meaning we could insist at some point on consent by the state (1) of nationality of the perpetrator, (2) of the victims, (3) exercising custody over the perpetrator, or (4) where the crime was committed. It was a weak card to play, as other delegations had much greater freedom to press hard on any combination of these consent regimes, leaving us in the dust.

The Pentagon never seemed to recognize how impractical their insistence on the alleged war criminal's government consenting to his prosecution sounded to the rest of the world. The Justice Department took far too long to recognize how toxic sole reliance on the Security Council to control all referrals appeared to almost the entire world save a couple of the other permanent members of the council (Russia and China). The Attorney General's lawyers recognized the value of complementarity, or deference to national courts, but saw it primarily as a bonus card shielded by the dominant role of the Security Council in referring situations to the court. Military lawyers cynically threw their grenades at the concept and insisted on seal-tight ways to immunize all soldiers from the reach of the International Criminal Court.

On August 5, 1997, I tried to make the best of it in my opening statement at the U.N. talks, which focused on complementarity. I had just been sworn in as the first-ever ambassador at large for war crimes issues by Bill Richardson, the U.S. permanent representative to the United Nations, before the U.S. Mission's staff—most of whom I had worked with for years as Albright's senior counsel. So I arrived in the U.N. Headquarters conference hall with some degree of pride and, I hoped, enhanced credibility to craft some compromises on the floor. I wanted to acknowledge where the United States shared the views of other governments in how to structure the court. My remarks, which I drew from handwritten notes, expressed these thoughts:

The issue of complementarity is of paramount importance to the United States. The end product of our work on complementarity will be exceptionally important to us when we all examine the issue of state consent [meaning, which state(s) must consent before a particular case reaches the court]. The objective is not to replace nations, not to cripple national prosecutions, but in fact to strengthen a state's prosecution so that accountability for international humanitarian law becomes an even more important element of state practice than it is today. The International Criminal Court is not a court of appeals from national courts. The objective is not to remedy every defect of national procedure. Nor is the objective to second-guess credible national prosecutions. But the court should decide if there is a serious problem and then act.

The United States agrees with the United Kingdom that the burden of proof is with the court to determine whether a nation has failed to properly investigate or prosecute crimes under the complementarity principle. Britain, Singapore, Canada, and Japan agree with us that national procedures should not be put on trial. The objective is not to intrude into sovereign judicial functions. Nonetheless, in the end it is the court that renders its own decision on admissibility.... The United States is flexible on making the standard for admissibility clearer. We believe "absence of good faith" in investigations and prosecutions is a workable standard. We are prepared to examine other formulations that focus on motive and that point to the unwillingness of a state to act on a case. We agree with Argentina and others that the complementarity principle needs a provision that addresses the inability of a state to act. The United States supports the French and Singapore proposal to ensure that a state decision was not motivated by a manifest unwillingness to relieve the persons concerned of any criminal responsibility....

Nor should the International Criminal Court exercise primary jurisdiction unless authorized under a U.N. Charter Chapter VII referral by the Security Council. A whole range of factors have to be factored into the process once a referral is made: the role of extradition treaties and Status of Forces Agreements, ongoing investigations by national courts, and peace negotiations that might involve amnesty deals. The United States joins Brazil in strongly requiring that the matter demonstrate necessary "gravity" to qualify for action by the court. The military needs to be assured that even after a matter has been referred, an individual case will be admitted only if there is sufficient gravity in the act itself.

I had to make another pitch for Security Council control in this floor statement because I was instructed to do so, but I knew the opposition to that position was so strong it was undermining our efforts on other negotiating fronts. I also circulated among all delegations a State Department paper on how amnesty deals with human rights abusers and war criminals in various countries, particularly in Latin America and Africa in recent years, had paved the way for peace agreements.[18] I did so at the request of Sandy Berger, the national security adviser, who wanted me to explore an option for amnesties in the work of the International Criminal Court so that Washington had some flexibility to play that card in order to end conflicts through negotiated peace agreements. The idea of amnesties seemingly flew in the face of the entire purpose of the International Criminal Court, which was to end impunity for atrocity crimes and hold war criminals accountable before the bar of justice. My point in circulating the paper was to force the issue before all the negotiators so that we could decide how, if at all, to address the probability of future amnesties in the work of the court. I never proposed a formula for drafting other than to suggest enough discussion to structure some recognition of the option in the court's statute.

However, my initiative initially proved disastrous with other delegations, particularly those representing governments that had caved in to amnesty deals in recent decades and thus were embarrassed when the American delegation's paper highlighted incriminating historical facts to everyone in the room. How could those governments dismiss the merit of considering amnesties when their own stability rested on prior invocations of the strategy in peace negotiations or the emergence of reform governments in their countries? One diplomat after another intercepted me, complaining about the tactlessness of the U.S. paper. That became a lesson learned on my part, but in the end the point was made. Although the Rome Statute does not include explicit language addressing how amnesties should be considered by the court, discretionary power by the prosecutor and the judges to take into account "the interests of justice" was understood to provide a basis for considering amnesties, particularly if they were granted to low and midlevel perpetrators who would not rise to the attention of the International Criminal Court in any investigation and prosecution guided by the Rome Statute.

However, there was enough push-back on formal recognition of amnesties to persuade Washington this was not going to be explicitly addressed in the court's statute and that impunity, certainly for leading perpetrators of atrocity crimes, was increasingly losing ground in the negotiations.

Scrimmages in Washington

Two months later I met at the Pentagon with Walter Slocombe, the undersecretary of defense for policy and someone I had sparred with in the Deputies Committee throughout the first term of the Clinton administration. He repeated the Defense Department mantra that the treaty would be unratifiable if there was any exposure of the U.S. military to the court. There had been six emergency embassy evacuations in Africa during the prior two years; 200,000 American troops were stationed overseas in forty countries; the United States was party to almost one hundred Status of Forces Agreements; enforcement operations with heavy U.S. commitments had been undertaken against Iraq, in Bosnia and Herzegovina, and in Haiti during recent years. That had to mean something in the negotiations. Slocombe said he would orchestrate a lobby campaign with foreign militaries to accept the U.S. position, which I said made little sense, as he would be arguing for immunity for our forces while exposing others to the court's jurisdiction.

Alan Kreczko, the National Security Council's counsel, told me that the Justice Department once again was weighing in *against* the Pentagon's love affair with the state consent requirement. Prosecutors argued that requiring the consent of the state of nationality of an alleged war criminal would be adverse to the long-advocated U.S. position rejecting legal rationales that a suspect's nationality grants his or her country a "protective veto" over prosecution for international crimes.

In Washington I met with civil society representatives, all of whom strongly supported the prospect of an International Criminal Court and could not understand why the United States was not joining the viewpoints of many European and Latin American governments, in particular, that were determined to minimize the role of the Security Council and treat American armed forces just like any other nation's soldiers. I explained that we still believed the Security Council had an important role to play in referrals and in enforcing the court's orders to governments. We spoke of a "matrix of safeguards" for U.S. interests and that the more civil society tried to knock down those safeguards, which included robust complementarity, precise definitions and thresholds of magnitude for the crimes, the right to reservations to the treaty, and preservation of our rights under Status of Forces Agreements, the more it forced us to fall back on the Security Council as the guiding hand of the court. I stressed our search for pragmatic and consensus-building approaches in the negotiations. The United States was constrained in its ability to lobby effectively among delegations, as we found it difficult to build coalitions for positions many other governments might be sympathetic toward but could not embrace publicly for fear of being identified with the United States.

Final Steps to Rome

In early February 1998, relevant government agencies focused on the U.S. negotiating position for the forthcoming final round of U.N. talks in March and the scheduled diplomatic conference in Rome during the summer. Two prominent views quickly emerged. One view held that state of nationality consent regime failed the laugh test and gutted the Court of all meaning. It had no future in the negotiations. The better course would be a complementarity regime that was robust enough to provide certainty that American suspects would not be hauled before the International Criminal Court.

A second view sought to package the state consent requirement within complementarity. If there was even a slim chance that American soldiers would be exposed to the Court's jurisdiction, then the state consent requirement would be the ultimate safeguard from prosecution. There also would be a firewall in complementarity that provided the Security Council with an override of a flawed domestic procedure or a perceived flaw in a decision by the judges to call up a case being handled domestically. I sought, and obtained, approval to determine what conditions we would insist upon if we conceded the state consent regime. This was the beginning of my "end game" thinking about a grand compromise prior to Rome.

I held scores of meetings in Washington and European capitals in my attempt to salvage the dangerously isolated U.S. policy on the court. No silver bullet emerged that we could use to make sure the Pentagon's insistence on virtual immunity for American soldiers could be locked into the treaty. My proposal to shift the American position away from state consent (by "reserving" on it in the talks) and to build a more robust complementarity regime attracted both supporters and opponents in the administration.

The alternative was to hold firm on Security Council referrals as the only means to trigger the court's jurisdiction. Some insisted on 100 percent protection from the court's jurisdiction for American military personnel, preferably through consent of the state of nationality of the alleged war criminal. At no point did the White House step forward to resolve the impasse.

The final round of U.N. talks prior to the Rome diplomatic conference commenced on March 16. Delegates focused on how the rules of procedure and evidence would be prepared, the merits of reservations, complementarity, the crime of aggression, and how amendments would be approved. Many of America's closest allies objected to permitting any reservations to the treaty, which proved to be a crippling blow to my own efforts to forge a compromise position in Washington. I spoke before the Twentieth Century Fund in New York on March 17 and set out the most fundamental elements of the U.S. position. I told the audience of increasingly cynical foreign diplomats that we had not yet taken a position on any state consent regime before a case could be investigated and prosecuted by the court and that we reserved on the point. I held firm that referrals of atrocity situations must be made by the Security Council or with council approval if a state party referred a situation that the council already was addressing on its agenda.

About one week later President Clinton visited Rwanda and publicly endorsed, once again, a permanent court to prosecute atrocity crimes. He declared, "Internationally, as we meet here, talks are underway at the United Nations to establish a permanent International Criminal Court. Rwanda and the difficulties we have had with this special tribunal [for Rwanda] underscores the need for such a Court. And the United States will work to see that it is created."[19] Those remarks so angered Senator Jesse Helms, the Republican chairman of the Foreign Relations Committee, that he immediately sent a letter to Albright (and released it publicly) stating that he was "unalterably opposed to the creation of a permanent U.N. criminal court" and that it would be "dead on arrival" in the U.S. Senate unless Washington could veto its decisions. He inaccurately aligned the court with the United Nations, even though it would be an independent court created by international treaty. Helms also crassly referred to a U.S. "veto" when no negotiated international treaty would bluntly yield so much power to any particular country, although he must have meant total control by the Security Council of the court's docket. He alienated 99 percent of the world when he put it that way. As Barbara Crossette reported in the *New York Times*, "The Senator's threats come as a team of American legal experts, led by David Scheffer, the State Department's representative for war crimes issues, is in critical talks here with more than 100 other nations over how the court will operate. In meetings this week and last, Mr. Scheffer has taken great pains, at the expense of criticism from human rights groups and other national delegations, to meet the objections not only of American politicians but also of the Pentagon, which fears legal action against American troops."[20]

I already had expended considerable political capital with other delegations by introducing another complementarity filter that became Article 18 of the Rome Statute. Under this provision, whenever a state party refers an atrocity situation to the court or the prosecutor independently seeks to initiate an investigation, the prosecutor must first notify all governments that "would normally exercise jurisdiction over the crimes concerned." That typically would include at least the country or countries where the crime was committed and those nations from which the suspected perpetrators and victims come. The notified countries have one month to inform the court that they are investigating or have investigated relevant individuals in their jurisdiction for the crimes identified in the notification. At that point, the court has to withdraw from the matter and let the country's courts proceed without interference. However, if the country proves unwilling or unable "genuinely" to take up the challenge, and the court decides that is the reality, then the prosecutor may get permission from the judges to forge ahead with the investigation and tee up the court for trials.

I rushed down to Washington in the middle of the U.N. talks in order to argue for my new complementarity proposal, which was clearly designed to open up some flexibility in the U.S. negotiating position on Security Council control and the state consent requirement in return for achieving support in New York for it. I obtained approval for my proposal, but with the caveat that I retain in brackets the need for the consent of the state of nationality of the suspect in the event the court's Appeals Chamber yanked a national case into the court's jurisdiction. Some officials strongly objected to any endgame for complementarity that would require state consent, but the die was cast thanks to the unbending will of the Pentagon on this issue. True to form, the bracketed reference to state consent greatly complicated my negotiations in New York after I returned from Washington, but at least I succeeded in getting the entire proposal locked in for final decision in Rome. Ultimately, in Rome, the bracketed language on state consent was deleted entirely at the insistence of most other delegations, as it would have defeated the court's power to accept a case that a government and its courts had utterly failed to take seriously despite having every opportunity to handle the case nationally.

Helms must have intended to undercut my leverage as a negotiator, because he essentially wrote that whatever was negotiated would never be approved by the Senate, and thus the United States would never join the court. He was blatantly trying to muzzle me as the American negotiator. Delegates spoke of little else for days thereafter as they asked me whether the United States remained a serious negotiating partner. Many foreign diplomats thought that Helms spoke for the United States government and thus was comparable to the voice of President Clinton on the subject. I patiently explained the separation of powers in the U.S. Constitution and that Clinton was committed to the establishment of the International Criminal Court, but Helms had succeeded in fogging up the entire negotiating arena in New York. Ironically, he made it impossible for me to achieve the very safeguards and terms in the treaty that he, at least in theory, wanted in order to support U.S. participation in the court. I knew from that day forward that he and his staff were not to be trusted and that his aim was simply to kill the court and any American role in it. Nonetheless, I drafted a conciliatory and explanatory letter to Helms for Albright to sign and have delivered to his Senate office.

While enduring the anger of countless foreign diplomats who read the Helms barrage as our final words, I wrote down an updated checklist of "where we are losing ground" on how to structure the court—areas where Helms's words made the unresolved issues only more difficult to overcome. Although we had made enormous gains in all these areas, there were too many brackets remaining in the negotiated text of too many provisions central to U.S. interests. They included how to maintain the secrecy of national security information, the infamous "trigger mechanism" on how situations would be referred to the court, the final details on complementarity, the status of the crime of aggression in the text, coming to closure on definitions for war crimes and crimes against humanity, the independence of the prosecutor to initiate investigations, precise terms for financing the court, how to ensure that highly qualified judges would be elected, drafting the elements of crimes, the status of nonparty states before the court, reservations, and entry into force and amendment procedures for the treaty. We would have to prevail with our desired bracketed language on these issues, or at least the most important among them, in order to succeed in Rome.

I advised Albright after the end of the U.N. talks in New York that the prognosis for U.S. success in Rome was not good. Most of America's major allies opposed our limited view of the court's powers. Britain had broken ranks with us on key issues, such as the role of the Security Council and state consent, and joined the "like-minded" group of more than forty-five mostly European and Latin American countries that opposed our fundamental positions. France still shared most of the American concerns, but I sensed it would shift away from us soon.

Several days after the U.N. talks ended in early April, I met with my French counterpart, Marc de Brichambaut. He alerted me that Paris would undertake a fresh appraisal of the International Criminal Court and pronounce a new position in Rome. He believed France would continue to oppose an independent prosecutor and wanted to form a coalition of countries to block it. De Brichambaut viewed the Pretrial Chamber as a sufficient means to oversee complementarity (without any need for state consent as a final backstop to keep cases from falling into the court's jurisdiction). "The Pretrial Chamber provides a reasonable degree of protection" from unwarranted prosecutions before the court, he said. He told me that Paris was prepared to accept the court's automatic jurisdiction over genocide and crimes against humanity, meaning that every state party automatically would be subject to scrutiny for those crimes. But exposure to war crimes prosecution should be an opt-in option for each state party. Only the Security Council could trigger the court's jurisdiction over the crime of aggression.

De Brichambaut claimed France would accept the Singapore compromise on Security Council intervention to stop investigations or prosecutions. The French also believed that the Security Council's role as promoted by the original International Law Commission draft of 1994 was superior to any state consent regime, which would give every government with a "dog in the fight" a veto on the court. He would join us in ensuring that internal conflicts (civil wars) also would be covered by the court's jurisdiction. The French diplomat warned me, however, that there was considerable pressure in Paris to announce strong support for the court before the diplomatic conference began and follow through with signing the Rome Statute immediately at the end of the conference. It was clear to me that France wanted to come out the leader in Rome and be viewed as such, even if (or perhaps because) it meant sacrificing some of America's sacred cows in the final negotiations.

At around this time the Pentagon sent out an arrogant cable to a large number of governments with which we shared considerable military ties, including large troop deployments on their territories.[21] It was a clumsy attempt by the Defense Department to pressure their military brethren to close ranks and stop the slide toward a court untethered from the Security Council and from a state consent requirement. I approved the cable, so I had to take full responsibility for it even though its inspiration and much of its blunt language originated from inside the Pentagon. I believed at the time that the U.S. military needed to vent with our friends and allies and make its case to them. The reality was that all the cables went straight to the foreign ministries and the diplomats with whom I was trying to negotiate and find common ground. The cable undercut my negotiating posture with other governments. I never saw any evidence that any government bent its will toward the Pentagon's demands as a result of the cable. Indeed, from what foreign negotiators conveyed to me, the cable only strengthened the opposition to us.

A New Strategy

I strategized a new approach that I hoped would satisfy the Pentagon, whose support I had to maintain prior to the Rome Conference. Unless I arrived there with a greatly improved U.S. position, we risked certain defeat on core issues. In my view, Washington would gain some much-needed momentum if it

- embraced the Singapore compromise,
- permitted the prosecutor to initiate an investigation provided he received a supermajority of votes of the judges in the court and provided he met the gravity test for the magnitude and seriousness of the atrocity crimes at stake,
- rejected the crime of aggression since it remained a work in progress,
- insisted on the right to file reservations to the treaty,
- required suitable war crimes definitions and finalization of elements of crimes before the court became operational,
- permitted withdrawal from the treaty with relatively short prior notification to other states parties, and, most significantly,
- *conceded that there would be no consent requirement for any state party but that such consent would be required for any nonparty state if its nationals were suspects, unless the Security Council overrode the nonparty state privilege with a resolution of referral to the court.*

In April 1998, I finalized this new U.S. strategy for the Rome talks. I had pondered and conceived it over such a long period of time that I could repeat it in my sleep. First, as a precondition to the court's jurisdiction in any particular case, the consent of the state of nationality of the alleged war criminal would be required *only* if the particular state were *not* a party to the Rome Statute. A referral of the atrocity situation by the Security Council would override any such requirement, even for nonparty states. The practical purpose would be that if the United States did not join the court, Americans would be protected from prosecution before it. Second, the state party that had custody of the suspect would not be required to transfer him or her to the court unless the court had determined that the case pertaining to the individual was admissible under the complementarity regime. The practical purpose would be that the United States could refuse to cooperate to transfer an American (in its custody) to the court provided the judges had not yet determined the case was admissible for prosecution before the court following the failure of national courts to handle the case.

Third, if the United States became a state party to the Rome Statute and the court ruled that the case was admissible under the complementarity regime, then the United States nonetheless could refuse to cooperate in the extreme case and accept the consequences. The only penalty specified in the treaty would be recourse by the states parties to the Security Council, which could be asked to order cooperation. Since the United States holds veto power in the council, this "penalty" would never be used against U.S. interests. Also, the United States always would preserve the right to withdraw from the treaty. On the flip side of this particular coin, however, the council could use its Chapter VII enforcement power to override all complementarity requirements and refer a situation to the court for prosecution regardless of the wishes of any state party or nonparty state. The United States, I proposed, should be prepared to lead in the Security Council to facilitate such referrals. Finally, the United States might need to make reservations to the treaty to protect its constitutional principles.

I aggressively advanced these points within the government for almost two months, until the end of the first week of the Rome Conference, in a bid to turn the tide toward a more realistic U.S. policy. But in the near term, lacking any approval yet to shift the U.S. position, I spent the month of May advancing the conventional party line as reasonably as I could with other governments and before the Council on Foreign Relations in New York, the Commonwealth Club in San Francisco, and a critical law conference attended by diplomats and civil society representatives in Trinidad and Tobago.

I flew to Paris on May 19 for an intensive day of talks with the French and British legal advisers. I learned that France would "more or less" sign the Rome Statute. The French would have to change their constitution in order to strip away the immunity enjoyed by the French president and cabinet officers for atrocity crimes. Paris clearly wanted to reach a consensus with Washington, and I was urged to join France in signing the treaty. The British conceded that nongovernmental groups were very activist and influential with government officials, in no small part because Whitehall had initiated a policy to be more open to civil society. The like-minded governments, I gathered, were less "like" than appeared on the surface, so differences of viewpoints still remained among them. The French were willing to press for a state consent requirement for prosecution of war crimes by the court, but London adamantly rejected any state consent privilege. I knew that British opposition to requiring the consent of the state of nationality of the suspect would doom that requirement in Rome. Few governments would understand the merit of the American argument for state consent when our closest ally, which was not shy about deploying its troops into hot spots alongside ours (and sometimes without us), rejected the entire concept.

The Freight Train Roars By

My final instructions for the Rome Conference reflected the gridlock that continued to bedevil the fate of the International Criminal Court within the highest reaches of the Washington bureaucracy. Discussions that preceded my boarding an aircraft at Dulles Airport bound for Rome on June 12, 1998, proved to be self-destructive exercises in what lawyers call the defendant's mentality. Repeatedly, every deliberation turned on the fear of prosecution of American soldiers and officials rather than considering the larger picture of ending atrocity crimes in our time.

Albright put my game changer for Rome on the table in Washington as a last-ditch effort to create a new dynamic that would advance U.S. interests in the talks. In my view, we needed to move toward a position that would enable me to persuade most governments that we were seeking credible safeguards for U.S. interests while also promoting an effective and independent court. We would not obtain 100 percent protection for U.S. citizens by advocating an unattainable Security Council position—our long-held "right of approval" requirement—or, even worse, an unattainable and inflammatory position on state consent for parties (in other words, that the state of the suspect's nationality must give prior consent to any prosecution even when the state was a party to the treaty). These positions, or variants, simply would not be adopted in Rome. Like-minded Europeans, Africans, and Latin Americans strongly opposed both Security Council and state consent options. The Non-Aligned Movement of over one hundred countries opposed any Security Council role with only a few exceptions. The state consent supporters in our corner were the most egregious human rights offenders, terrorist-listed countries, or other "bad actor" states. Pursuing such positions risked losing our credibility and undermined our ability to protect Americans even if the United States did not join the court.

The goal should have been to ensure protection for U.S. interests even if we did not join the court and, if we became a party to the treaty, to achieve as much protection as *realistically* possible. If we kept striving for 100 percent protection, particularly as both a nonparty state and as a state party, we would end up with much less protection than if we acted credibly to protect the totality of U.S. interests in the court whether or not Washington joined it.

The instructions I sought and which Albright advocated would permit two major revisions in our long-standing policy so as to gain the upper hand with other governments: First, I would fall off our Security Council approval position for state party referrals to the court and move toward the Singapore compromise of permitting the Security Council to block prosecutions. Second, I would abandon our "reserve" posture on state consent and push for state of nationality consent *only* for nonparty states unless the Security Council overrode the process with a referral of the situation to the court under Chapter VII of the U.N. Charter. The latter was the critical firewall we needed to build support for in the weeks ahead. Our long-held position regarding the Security Council was a wasting asset; it undermined our ability to win on other provisions in the treaty. The stubborn state consent position (even for states parties) was potentially explosive as well as utterly futile in the negotiations.

I also needed instructions to seek core U.S. objectives to protect individuals from unwarranted or undesirable prosecution by the International Criminal Court. Among these additional objectives were complementarity (that is, our proposal on deferral to national jurisdictions from the outset of investigations, which eventually became Article 18 of the Rome Statute), no crime of aggression unless the Security Council determined what situations of aggression reached the court (the Rome Statute punted the issue to further negotiations[22]), an acceptable list and definitions of war crimes with their elements for prosecution established by the negotiating governments (which all came to pass in the Rome Statute[23] and by June 2000 with respect to the elements of crimes[24]), and no self-initiating prosecutor or a substantially constrained one (the Rome Statute permits the initiation of investigation of a situation by the prosecutor but only after review and approval by a group of judges[25]).

In order to galvanize a shift in the U.S. position, policy-makers had to appreciate the complementarity rationale taking hold in the negotiations. Deferral to national courts able and willing to take on atrocity crimes investigations and prosecutions was fast becoming a bedrock principle for the operational structure of the court, and I argued that this should be seen as a highly credible basis upon which to build American engagement, if not support. Albright and I stressed the core objective of safeguarding military personnel from the court's scrutiny while the United States remained outside the court, since that presumably would be the reality for a long time to come. But some officials rejected all of my proposed strategy changes and pressed for full protection (through state consent) whether or not the United States became a party to the Rome Statute, and then they stated their firm opposition to the treaty regardless of what I could accomplish in Rome. Remarkably, some believed we could "roll over our allies" and force them to shift in our direction. Others reiterated their strong opposition to a state of nationality consent requirement in the treaty. They argued it would place into serious jeopardy the enforcement of the United States' bilateral extradition treaties around the world. I was confronted, once again, with policy gridlock that only Clinton could break, if he would just intervene to perform the nasty task.

During one heated discussion held by teleconference among the principals and me on a Saturday afternoon in late May, my peculiar location became prominently known just as a cabinet officer gravely remarked that he was calling from the West Point commencement ceremony, where he was speaking, and knew that many of the cadets were heading to Bosnia and Herzegovina to serve their country at extreme risk. He had no interest in exposing them to the court's jurisdiction. I happened to be on a rural stretch of road outside Suffolk, Virginia, calling from an outdoor phone booth lacking any door, near a crumbling roadside diner and railroad tracks. (We had to use available land lines for such weekend calls.) Suddenly, the deafening noise of a freight train roared by, completely swamping the phone line.

Somebody yelled, "What the hell is that?!" I screamed into the phone that I was standing next to a fast-moving freight train on a lonely road outside a diner in downstate Virginia. Laughter swept over the lines and lightened up the conversation after the freight train mercifully sped onward. But the end result remained in President Clinton's hands: he would have to decide on my instructions. I had to trust that Clinton, a master at political reality checks, would liberate me to negotiate a plausible package of safeguards and restore U.S. leadership in the Rome talks.

The Map Room Meeting

Almost two weeks dragged by after that freight train blasted through our high-level discussion about my instructions for Rome. We all awaited a decision from the Oval Office. Finally, I received a call to meet with the first lady, Hillary Clinton, at the White House on June 10 to advocate for the State Department proposal. James E. Baker, the legal adviser at the National Security Council, would present the Defense Department's position. Eric Schwartz, the multilateral affairs director at the National Security Council, would introduce us and moderate the discussion. I was being summoned for a slug-fest in front of Hillary rather than her husband, the president. He was being overtaken by the Monica Lewinsky scandal, which was raging by the early summer, and by preparations for his forthcoming visit to China. They overshadowed the endgame of the International Criminal Court negotiations, which may not have seemed as important at the time in his (or his chief of staff's) calculus but would prove critical in the coming years in terms of America's standing in the world. When all was said and done by the end of the summer of 1998, I concluded that the Lewinsky scandal grievously impaired U.S. national interests because Clinton and his closest aides did not focus enough on matters of state, and we all suffered for it.

Frank Berman, the British legal adviser, called on the morning of June 10 to inform me that he had obtained ministerial backing for a new British strategy in Rome, the details of which he could not yet share with me. I knew I was in trouble when my counterpart in London told me he was "confident that the British positions are coherent and well thought through, including protection for servicemen. The United Kingdom sees the court as a plank of the new international order." As I walked over to the White House, shoes freshly shined, the point sunk in that our common-law ally was going its own way—with the "like-minded"—and I was stuck with favorable nods from Russia and China but practically no one else given their hatred of Security Council powers. Would Clinton, through the medium of Hillary, understand what was at stake and how isolated we had become?

I met Hillary in the Map Room on the ground floor of the White House. Having spent so much time in the Situation Room, I knew the Map Room had been the de facto Situation Room during World War II for President Franklin Delano Roosevelt, who studied his war maps there. It was decorated and furnished as a sitting room in shades of red surrounded by white-painted walls decked with portraits, maps, and American landscape paintings, or so I recall from that day. The public knows the room from White House tours and from two notorious events. Later that summer Clinton testified in the Map Room to Independent Counsel Ken Starr on the Monica Lewinsky scandal, a devastating episode aired on television. President Barack Obama was sworn into office by Chief Justice John Roberts for the second time in the Map Room on January 22, 2009, with the correct recitation of the oath.

But on that day in 1998, Hillary entered with Melanne Verveer, her chief of staff. Schwartz, Baker, one of his deputy lawyers, and I took our assigned seats on the couch and assorted chairs. Hillary appeared tired and drawn, as if she had been through some kind of hell and back. I worried what that might mean for the fate of our discussion, but I plunged ahead explaining precisely what Albright had set forth in the late May teleconference as the shift we needed in the U.S. negotiating position. Baker then weighed in with the Pentagon's view to hold firm on the long-standing American requirements. Hillary asked how the negotiations had gotten so convoluted, with such complexities over jurisdiction. Why not, she asked, just have a global war crimes tribunal modeled on the Yugoslav Tribunal, which was created by the Security Council? When this all got started, she thought we would simply reproduce the Yugoslav Tribunal on a world stage. I explained why the International Criminal Court would be a treaty-based court independent of the United Nations and that after years of negotiations the situation had changed as governments expressed their largely negative views about the Security Council controlling a judicial process.

Hillary expressed her amazement that the French did not find the International Criminal Court abhorrent given that country's involvement in Africa and the exposure of their forces there. I explained that France was one of the most engaged governments in the negotiations and saw this as a means to lead in Europe and in the realm of international justice. (I also knew they were likely to sign the Rome Statute, perhaps even at the conclusion of the diplomatic conference.) She absorbed without flinching Baker's condescending warning that since the president *finally* understood the role of the military, if he were to support the Pentagon position President Clinton would earn the military's permanent respect and allegiance. And that meant he needed to back the current U.S. insistence on *full immunity* from prosecution by the court as both a nonparty state *and* as a possible future state party to the court. In rebuttal, I reminded her of the futility of trying to attain full immunity that would extend even to our status as a state party and that it was undercutting our credibility to achieve major objectives in the treaty. Hillary paused to reflect, thanked us, and told me she sympathized with how difficult my job would be in Rome. I saw that as a signal that she would advise the president to back the Pentagon's futile position, and that is exactly what he did.

I thus prepared for Rome with stale instructions that forced me to present the status quo, namely, the long-standing U.S. position as endorsed by the Pentagon and yet strongly opposed by the State and Justice Departments. Ironically, about one year later, long after the Rome Statute was put to bed, a top Defense Department official approached me. I knew him well, as he had dug in his heels during the Rome talks and blocked my efforts there to find workable compromises. But on that day he pleaded with me to negotiate an amendment to the Rome Statute so as to incorporate precisely the position I had presented to Hillary Clinton on June 10, 1998, namely to shield American soldiers from the court's jurisdiction while the United States remained outside the court. That became the Pentagon's tardy initiative in interagency discussions in late 1999 and 2000, and Defense Department officials pressed for it with surreal notions about what was and was not negotiable at that stage. I marveled at their cockiness despite the simple reality that they had so stubbornly rejected my proposal in 1998, prior to Rome, when Albright handed the option to them on a golden platter.

But by then, mid-1999, it was far too late. The Rome Statute could not be amended until a review conference that would be held seven years *after* the International Criminal Court became operational, which occurred on July 1, 2002. (The subsequent review conference was held in Kampala, Uganda, in 2010.) I nonetheless tried to seek a similar formula for the relationship agreement that later would be negotiated between the United Nations and the court, but that proved tough to gain traction on. I had to leave office at the end of the Clinton administration before I had the chance to make a final push on it.

Hillary Clinton's seeming perspective in the Map Room was resurrected in June 2002, when as a U.S. senator representing the state of New York she voted in favor of the American Service-Members' Protection Act, which was a blunt assault on the International Criminal Court that penalized (e.g., by withholding economic or military assistance) a large number of countries committed to supporting it. She voted against Senator Christopher Dodd's amendment to sunset the punitive measures of that law after one year. The deceptively worded legislation was the brainchild of top congressional Republicans Tom Delay and Jesse Helms and was warmly embraced by President George W. Bush, who signed it into law in August 2002. (The Clinton administration had strongly opposed the bill, introduced in 2000. I spent days persuading members of Congress to bury it, which they did on our watch.) The law inflicted great harm to American credibility, was derided throughout the world, and ultimately was rejected by many in the Pentagon because it decimated military-to-military relationships. By the end of 2008 all of its punitive sanctions had been repealed.[26]

Hillary Clinton's views evolved. After she became secretary of state in the Obama administration, she expressed "great regret" that the United States had not joined the International Criminal Court. During a public meeting in Nairobi, Kenya, on August 6, 2009, she was asked by a student how the United States could support the court's intervention in the investigation of electoral violence in Kenya when the United States had not subjected itself to the jurisdiction of the court. Clinton continued, "But we have supported the court and continue to do so. I think we could have worked out some of the challenges that are raised concerning our membership by our own government, but that has not yet come to pass."[27]

CHAPTER EIGHT

FUTILE ENDGAME

We labored under the paradox of being a leader for international justice but at the same time a leader for international peace and security.

The author, quoted in the Washington Post, *July 23, 1998*

THE DIPLOMATIC CONFERENCE ON THE INTERNATIONAL CRIMINAL COURT convened in Rome on June 15, 1998, during a very hot summer in the largely non-air-conditioned and Mussolini-era Food and Agriculture Organization building. It faces Circus Maximus, an open field where once stood the largest chariot-racing stadium in ancient Rome. As I entered the FAO building for the first time, I wondered whether America would have the fastest chariot.

I led the largest national delegation, which included lawyers and officials from all the relevant government agencies in Washington, most of whom had long worked with me in the United Nations talks leading to Rome. We camped out in the Holiday Inn (thanks to Washington's diktat that we fly and sleep American) on Piazza Maria Sopra Minerva and used the U.S. Mission to the Vatican as an official venue for our own diplomatic talks. Years later that particular Holiday Inn would be converted into a five-star wonder, the Grand Hotel de la Minerve, but we were not so fortunate. The Pantheon stood one block away. Almost every night during the five weeks of negotiations I returned around 11 p.m. and headed to Piazza della Rotunda, facing the Pantheon, for pizza and beer at a sidewalk café, where I continued to work and strategize with my delegation members. The early mornings always began with a staff meeting in the Holiday Inn to set the stage for the day's work assignments and plan of action.

Ambassador Hisashi Owada, who had represented Japan at the United Nations, headed the Japanese delegation for the Rome talks. (He later became a judge of the International Court of Justice in The Hague.) Owada proved to be sincerely interested in seeking a compromise formula that would bring the United States on board with the International Criminal Court, or at least allow me to join consensus on the final draft of the treaty text in Rome. When he first sat down with me in Rome, Owada said Japan would oppose the proposal for an independent prosecutor, support the American position on protecting national security information, and endorse our ideas on enforcement and cooperation with the court. But he signaled on the first day that the pathway out of the thicket for Washington was to press for the consent of the state of nationality only for nonparty states (unless the Security Council referred the situation to the court), and drop requiring it for states parties. The latter would be far too stringent on the Court's independence. This was exactly what I had proposed in Washington weeks earlier and what the Pentagon and the White House had shot down. Owada also said that Japan would support including the crime of aggression provided its definition was acceptable and there was a Security Council screen for determining whether an act of aggression had occurred.

By June 16, the British advised me to drop our long-standing requirement that the Security Council approve a referral by a state party of any situation that the council already was handling as a peace and security issue. In contrast, China and Russia were dissatisfied with the Singapore compromise enabling the Security Council to block investigations and prosecutions. They believed it did not fully preserve council powers. France finally tilted its hat toward accepting an independent prosecutor provided there was a Pretrial Chamber check on his or her decisions. As a supportive Swedish delegate put it, "We are not afraid of a Dr. Strangelove prosecutor, as there will be judicial review in the Pretrial Chamber." Mexico predictably railed against any Security Council role in the court's work, supported an independent prosecutor, and opposed our state consent position. Meanwhile, the Germans wanted the court to exercise universal jurisdiction over atrocity crimes, without any preconditions about state consent. Thus stood a fractured world.

Opening Shots

Bill Richardson, the U.S. ambassador to the United Nations (and later secretary of energy and then governor of New Mexico), flew to Rome to deliver the opening U.S. statement at the conference.[1] Given the fact that a great number of foreign ministers appeared in those opening days to press their governments' positions, Albright's presence would have been helpful. But she knew I had been delivered a very weak hand by the Principals Committee. We decided that our best opening shot was to come down hard against an independent prosecutor for the court, and Richardson pressed that point in his speech. It would take about two weeks before our opposition to an independent prosecutor, one who could refer atrocity situations to the court and then prosecute them, was overcome by the majority of governments supporting the idea. We undermined our own position by sticking so fervently to the Security Council as the controlling factor for referrals. Other governments regarded their support for an independent prosecutor as a means of bluntly opposing our fixation on control by the Security Council. I could count only on Israel, Indonesia, Japan, Tunisia, Turkey, Pakistan, the United Arab Emirates, Portugal, Uruguay, China, and few other governments to back our opposition to an independent prosecutor.

At the close of the first week of negotiations in Rome, President Clinton met with the Principals Committee at the White House to reconsider my negotiating instructions. The week had not gone well for our interests, and key Washington officials knew it. There remained great concern in Vice President Al Gore's office that if my proposed shift, which I was pushing, still left any Americans exposed to prosecution, how would those individuals be protected from the court's jurisdiction? Leon Fuerth, Gore's national security adviser and a member of the Deputies and Principals committees, understood we could not guarantee 100 percent protection of nationals, but what was the bottom line if the State Department's strategy was adopted? I told him that the strategy was clear: there would be no exposure for nationals while the United States was a nonparty to the treaty. That was 100 percent protection. If, however, the United States became a state party to the Rome Statute, and there was a decision by U.S. prosecutors and courts to permit an American suspect charged with planning atrocity crimes on a massive scale to avoid domestic investigation and prosecution, we would have to admit to serious problems with our system of domestic justice. Either we are the United States of America committed to the rule of law, or we have transformed into another kind of nation. If we investigated or even prosecuted a suspect but the court still demanded he or she show up in The Hague, the president could exercise the "nuclear option" and terminate U.S. participation in the treaty. That was the bottom line. But time was wasting.

Albright and I spoke by phone just prior to the White House meeting on June 20, 1998. I offered another round of talking points for our proposal and, as with Fuerth, assurances about the theoretical possibility of complementarity failing and an American being sought for international prosecution in the event the United States joined the court. I spent the rest of the day pacing before the Pantheon, talking with other delegation members, and waiting for my cell phone to ring. Eric Schwartz, the staffer overseeing the International Criminal Court issue for the National Security Council, finally called late that afternoon informing me there would be no change in instructions. The Pentagon once again had prevailed with President Clinton.

As I pondered the status of the negotiations over the weekend, I knew that I was unable to play real hardball with other delegations because I had no bottom line to deliver. I could move a lot of governments if I could say, "Look, we are reasonable. We know you have concerns about the Security Council and about state consent, and we will address those concerns. But for us to move in that direction, you need to assure us of your support for [the bottom line, whatever that is]." That bottom line could not be my current instructions, as those were hopeless, but where could I shift our position quickly enough to use it as leverage in the negotiations? I also was worried about morale on the U.S. delegation. The lawyers from the Pentagon were losing faith because they saw no way to budge the top brass to adopt a plausible, indeed winning position in the negotiations. All they heard were stubborn and losing propositions from the Pentagon. Gloom and doom began to set in. I knew that the second week of negotiations would be the critical break point. It was time to cut a deal, as the French were falling off the state consent requirement and we were quickly losing ground on the independent prosecutor option.

On June 22, I made a major push for my complementarity proposal at the conference. Delegates discussed the proposal at length and asked to see a revised U.S. text that accommodated their proposed edits. There was some progress, particularly with the Canadian diplomat, John Holmes, charged with marshaling the issue through the conference. I met with about thirty delegations and made revisions in the text that expedited appeals, ensured more targeted notifications to governments about referrals to the court, required only a majority (as opposed to supermajority) decision by the judges to haul a case before the court, and enabled the prosecutor to continue certain investigative responsibilities during the period when a state was handling the investigations itself. We were reaching a workable compromise on complementarity.

While a large majority of governments favored including the crime of aggression, the positions on a definition and trigger for it remained so diverse it was hard to see how any agreement would surface by the end of the conference. As the second week of negotiations concluded, there was no further support to be found for our primary position on Security Council control of referrals to the court and the consent of the state of nationality of the perpetrator in each case. I was beating a dead horse—a really dead horse—every time I brought it up in the conference. But my instructions remained unaltered, and the advantages I could have seized with my proposal of late May, which the White House had shot down, reconsidered, and shot down again, were fading very fast.

The detailed paper my delegation circulated among others on the independent prosecutor and the rationale for defeating it[2] bolstered Japan, China, and Egypt to join us, and even France seemed inclined to revisit the issue. Spain found the paper impressive and suggested the alternative of letting the U.N. General Assembly refer situations to the court for investigation. I also had to reinforce our position on protecting national security information, as that remained a tough slog with so many governments that cared little about protecting the classified intelligence of the major powers.

By July 1 the French abandoned their hopes to include corporate liability in the Rome Statute, as opposed to only individual criminal accountability. France sincerely saw the merit of investigating multinational corporations that too often fueled atrocity crimes with the "blood diamond" trade and illicit arms sales to the bad guys. But corporate criminal liability was virgin territory for international criminal law at the time and utterly unknown to atrocity law at that stage of tribunal jurisprudence. The Justice Department considered it far too novel and controversial a move for the court to expand its criminal jurisdiction to cover corporate behavior (other than investigating individual corporate officers). Many other governments agreed, and the option fell by the wayside. But corporate human rights responsibility and the criminal conduct that can result have become very potent items in the twenty-first century, and opportunities for civil liability have increased dramatically in national courts, including in the United States.[3]

Dinner Talk

The U.N. Security Council has five permanent members: Britain, China, France, Russia, and the United States. Any one of those "P-5" states has the power to veto any substantive draft resolution that comes before the council, which makes it virtually impossible for the United Nations to undertake any action that one of the P-5 nations opposes. On the first evening of July, I joined my colleagues from France, Britain, Russia, and China for a P-5 working dinner at the French embassy in Rome. We were surrounded by spectacular frescoes created by Annibale Carraci and walked through rooms designed by Michelangelo. It was a far cry from my late-night pizzas in Piazza della Rotunda, although the Parthenon is a nice backdrop to any menu. We immediately got down to business.

The British saw the crime of aggression as failing at Rome and thus doubted it would be included in the court's jurisdiction. My French counterpart, speaking with heightened confidence that evening, confirmed overwhelming opposition to Security Council control over referrals, and he identified India, Mexico, and the rest of the Non-Aligned Movement as the major culprits. The British negotiator firmly opposed any inclusion of the right to reservations to the treaty, while Russia insisted on it as a "must" requirement for its legislature, the Duma. I explained how essential it was for the U.S. Senate. The adoption of an introductory chapeau for the section on crimes against humanity, emphasizing the threshold requirements for jurisdiction and its applicability to internal situations as well as international conflicts, was fine with the British, French, and the United States, but Russia and China were still reviewing it (as they had initially opposed an ambitious section on crimes against humanity).

The French negotiator, Marc de Brichambaut, point-blank demanded I state the final U.S. position at Rome. It was an understandable question, as I had been asking it for months myself! I had to avoid his blunt query, as I had no final position. But I told all gathered at the dinner table that I could explore with them various parameters for a final deal. The British negotiator encouraged me to state a bottom line publicly, despite the fact that I was withholding comment to the press while we tried to reach agreement within the negotiating rooms. He believed that if I did so, governments would feel more comfortable shifting in our direction. I was putting Britain and France in a difficult position with my silence. Both admitted that the United States remained the key to the negotiations, and they did not want the court without us in it. But de Brichambaut cautioned that other countries did not feel the same way and would abandon the United States if necessary in Rome. I understood once again how disastrous was our failure to arrive in Rome with a fresh position to market, indeed one that had the bottom line I had proposed—requiring consent of the state of nationality only for nonparty states in the absence of a Security Council referral—which we would hold firm on and yet demonstrate flexibility regarding other issues of great importance to many governments.

My P-5 friends and I reviewed the bidding on war crimes and crimes against humanity and generally agreed where we wanted to end up. I elicited sighs of relief in the room when I declared that the Pentagon finally had relented in permitting use of the word "recruiting" in the war crime prohibiting the use of child soldiers. Armed services recruiters swarm through American high schools each year recruiting seventeen-year-olds to join the military and potentially enter combat once they are eighteen years old. But my need to uphold this recruiting practice proved much easier in Rome, as the bar was set so low—fifteen-year-olds—that the war crime became one of "[c]onscripting or enlisting children under the age of fifteen years into the national armed forces or using them to participate actively in hostilities."[4] Who could possibly oppose such a pillar of humanity?

We moved on to dessert and my admission that I still had not reached agreement with the Israelis on how to handle the crime of transferring, "directly or indirectly, by the Occupying Power of parts of its own civilian population into the territory it occupies."[5] The Egyptian-inspired inclusion of the words "or indirectly" in this standard war crime was meant to snare the Israeli practice of providing tax incentives to its citizens to move to the Israeli settlements on the West Bank and in Gaza, which most of the world regarded as occupied territory following the 1967 war. It was, however, a major roadblock for both the United States and Israel, as we believed it exceeded what customary international law and treaty law prohibited, namely, *direct* transfer of parts of its own civilian population.[6] My negotiating colleagues all were sympathetic with my plight, and one even suggested dropping the war crime altogether to avoid its explosive consequences.

Good Deeds

The next day, on July 2, 1998, I formally presented the updated U.S. complementarity proposal to the Rome Conference. Most delegations welcomed it.[7] Germany, however, remained unconvinced of its merit and thought my proposal was a ruse to postpone investigations by the court. If it was not Britain opposing us on reservations and France on state consent, now another major ally, Germany, was acting sanctimonious about my effort to establish a safeguard that potentially could enable us to fall off our long-standing positions on Security Council control or state consent filters. But I needed to demonstrate to Washington that there was strong support for this additional safeguard of national interests. Earth to Bonn, what were you thinking?

Events moved swiftly as the third week of negotiations neared completion. On Friday, July 3, Rolf Fife, the talented Norwegian negotiator, and John Holmes from Canada asked me to help on the penalties provision of the draft statute.[8] A sizable block of countries from the Arab world and the Caribbean insisted on the death penalty as the ultimate punishment for commission of atrocity crimes. The Europeans and Latin Americans were unalterably opposed to any invocation of the death penalty as matters of policy and law in their regions. Would I intervene with the death penalty advocates and persuade them to back down? Perhaps, given America's own enthusiasm for the death penalty, I could exercise enough influence to craft a compromise. I wanted to get something in return, of course, and at least locked in key support for the need for "elements of crimes" before the court could become operational. The elements of crimes is the all-important guide to the prosecutor, defense counsel, and judges that helps them interpret the characteristics of each crime, including those factors bearing upon criminal intent and the physical acts that define the crime. This was still a highly dubious proposition at Rome because most civil-law countries did not use "elements of crimes" in their criminal law. But my intervention on the death penalty helped garner key support for the requirement that the elements of crimes be completed in relatively short order after the Rome Conference and before the court began to investigate situations.

I met with leading delegations from the death penalty camp and spoke publicly before the working group on penalties. The United States well understood the rationale for the death penalty, I explained, as we applied it in sentencing frequently. (China led the world then and now in actual death penalty sentences and executions.) Nothing would prevent any country that still sentenced felons to death from continuing to do so with the arrival of the International Criminal Court. Under the principle of complementarity, any national court could investigate, prosecute, convict, and sentence a war criminal to death without any interference by the court. So the death penalty was available to those who supported it. But the court required a uniform sentencing policy, and that could not be achieved with any option for the death penalty given staunch opposition from Europe, Latin America, and Canada. The compromise we finally reached was full speed ahead with the death penalty in national courts under complementarity and life imprisonment as the ultimate sentence before the International Criminal Court. It felt good being a productive mediator in Rome rather than being on the defensive against a swarm of diplomats. The Arab and Caribbean groups clearly had miscalculated their strategy, thinking that I would go along with their perspective given America's continued reliance on the death penalty.

Punched in the Gut

By July 6, the situation was turning increasingly grim, certainly for our primary positions on how to control referrals to the court, on the right of reservations, and on the role of an independent prosecutor. I called Albright to discuss certain possibilities, such as permitting the court to exercise automatic jurisdiction for the crime of genocide (thus eliminating any state consent requirement before a case could be considered) and seeking to extend the negotiations beyond July 17, the scheduled end date, for another round later in the year. The secretary of state was busy and now obviously frustrated. She responded with exceptionally negative views about the negotiations and even about the concept of the International Criminal Court. I felt like I had been punched in the gut as I sought her support at a critical moment in the talks. I told her I needed to say we might be able to accommodate concerns on the Security Council and on state consent, but could then wield a big stick to meet core U.S. interests. Albright had talked with Berger and told me the view in Washington had turned quite sour. Albright asked, "What can we do to blow up the entire conference?" I was so stunned I hesitated, but then told her that the U.S. delegation could simply walk out and return to Washington or I could try to stall the endgame by seeking an extension beyond July 17. We chose the latter option, and I lobbied for resuming the conference in September or October so that I could reach a more accommodating position in Washington and structure some compromises with other delegations.

Later that evening I joined other key delegations in a meeting with Rome Conference chairman Phillip Kirsch, a Canadian diplomat-lawyer who later would become the first president of the International Criminal Court. He wanted to know what could be done to bridge the many gaps among the various governments represented in the room. I intervened with my conventional priorities: that we could explore automatic jurisdiction for genocide, that there should be a Security Council role regarding interventions to suspend investigations, and that we still supported consent of the state of nationality of the perpetrator. A wide range of other positions flowed through the evening as each delegation laid at least some of its cards on the table.

President Clinton's Instructions

On July 7, after a long day of negotiations, I spoke with Eric Schwartz at the National Security Council. I needed a clear position from Washington in order to take full advantage of Kirsch's gap-filling exercise of the day before. What I heard from him was not enough, but it was something. Schwartz spoke of requiring an opt-in for crimes against humanity and war crimes but permitting automatic jurisdiction for genocide. We might signal that the United States would accept the Singapore compromise on the Security Council and that we had some flexibility on Security Council referral power and the state consent requirement.

Schwartz reported to me on July 8 that President Clinton finally had decided on a new set of instructions. But before I could learn the details, I had to join a dinner meeting of the P5. Marc de Brichambaut of France posed three options for the future of the talks: a less ambitious statute with broader appeal, a more restricted statute of like-minded countries and some of the smaller nations, or a delay or postponement of the conference until critical issues could be sorted out. He wanted to press for the first option. To this end, I proposed that as an alternative to an independent prosecutor, he or she should have the power to brief the legislative body of the International Criminal Court—the Assembly of States Parties, consisting of representatives from each nation that ratifies the court statute—and alert them to an unfolding situation requiring investigation and perhaps prompt at least one government to refer the matter to the court. Russia and China voiced their strong opposition to an independent prosecutor while France, once again interested in the option, argued for a Pretrial Chamber of judges who would have to approve any initiative by the independent prosecutor. Britain already had jumped into the like-minded camp and voiced that group's primary concerns, which were to have an "effective" court built on fundamental principles of independence. Their view translated as support for an independent prosecutor.

When I returned to the Holiday Inn late that night, Schwartz called with Clinton's instructions for me, which constituted the first revision of my very long-standing Washington mandate:

1. The court would exercise no jurisdiction over nationals of nonparty states unless the Security Council referred the situation to the court or the nonparty state expressly consented to such jurisdiction.

2. Regarding the nationals of states parties to the treaty, the court would have automatic jurisdiction only over the crime of genocide and only if the court determined that the national government was unwilling or unable to prosecute (the complementarity principle). For crimes against humanity and war crimes, absent a referral by the Security Council, the state party would have to consent to prosecution by the court of its nationals, unless the state party had previously consented to (opted into) general jurisdiction by the court over its nationals for the crime in question.

3. I was authorized to signal U.S. interest in the Singapore compromise on the right of the Security Council to suspend investigations or prosecutions for at least one year. However, I was not to endorse it unequivocally, as it was hoped I could trade our firm support for it in exchange for acceptance of our primary objectives in the negotiations.

4. I could not commit to U.S. signature of the Rome Statute, but I could suggest that, if our key requirements were met, my delegation and I could consider recommending publicly that the United States sign the treaty. The final step of formally ratifying the Rome Statute (following signature), and thus obligating the United States under it, likely would have to wait many years before the constitutionally required two-thirds of the Senate would endorse it.

At least I had something new to run with—the "bottom line" my P5 colleagues were seeking from me—and I felt encouraged about the prospect of strengthening our position, but we had come too late to the party with our ideas.

On July 9, I supported a proposal before the conference, labeled "Article 7 bis," which would permit a state party to "opt in" to jurisdiction over crimes against humanity and/or war crimes, but every state party would be automatically covered by the crime of genocide.[9] (This formula originally had been adopted by the International Law Commission in 1994.)[10] I proposed that any state party would forfeit its right to refer matters to the court if it denied the jurisdiction of either of these categories of crimes. The Security Council could override any refusal to "opt in" with a Chapter VII referral to the court. I finished my statement by saying that if this procedure, along with some other approaches, could constitute an acceptable package for other delegates as well, then my delegation seriously would consider recommending that the United States should sign the treaty at an appropriate time in the future.[11]

Although twenty-two governments, including France and Russia, openly supported this approach, it failed to attract enough backing. So immediately, a major pillar of Clinton's instructions to me was shot down. The "like-minded" juggernaut of more than sixty governments had become entrenched with their views rejecting "opt-outs" and "opt-ins" and insisting on equality of coverage for all states parties to the treaty, and Britain had joined them. Indeed, Frank Berman pronounced Britain's view that all three core crimes—genocide, crimes against humanity, and war crimes—must form the jurisdiction of the court for each state party. "It's not a Chinese banquet," Berman remarked. He also was prepared to accept an independent prosecutor and the Singapore compromise. France, following the defeat of the earlier opt-in proposal, maintained that jurisdiction should be automatic for genocide, crimes against humanity, and aggression but that states parties should reserve the right to "opt in" for coverage of war crimes.

Owada's Gambit

Days of intense negotiation ticked by without significant progress on our primary issues. Then, on Sunday, July 12, Japanese ambassador Owada invited me and other key negotiators from Britain, France, Germany, Australia, Italy, Canada, and some other governments to a private meeting to try to find a formula that would garner U.S. support before the end of the conference. This was a critical gathering on an overcast and gloomy afternoon that spoke volumes about the endgame of Rome. Owada described the Rome Conference as a divided house. He said we could all satisfy ourselves with the progress made so far and take a break, resuming the conference in a few weeks. Or we could work out a "miraculous compromise." It would have to be a small package of common denominators attracting general agreement. And it would be a face-saving device to close the conference. The like-minded doubtless would be uncomfortable with it, or we could aim for a more ambitious package and attract their support for it. Owada preferred the latter.

There was, Owada said, an inherent contradiction in the entire exercise. We needed to build a court that was effective enough to capture and prosecute war criminals. The objective was not to harass governments but to prosecute the culprits. This might involve some departure from the traditional notion in international law of obtaining the consent of the engaged government. So Owada proposed a formula of "mutual sacrifice." First, we could not drag a national of a nonparty state before the court without the consent of that person's government either on an ad hoc or some kind of a priori basis. That would require a huge concession by the like-minded, which held onto the prospect of prosecuting any war criminal of whatever nationality who committed an atrocity crime on the territory of a state party to the court. Second, more specifically, Owada proposed that if either the state of custody of the suspect or the state where the crime was committed was a state party to the treaty, then the court could exercise jurisdiction over the individual unless the state of nationality of the suspect had not joined the court and not given its consent. In exchange, the United States would drop its "opt-out" proposal for crimes against humanity and war crimes, and France would drop its "opt-in" proposal for war crimes. A major concession by Washington would be to accept an independent prosecutor with "checks" on his or her power. The Security Council could override any rogue state that was not a party to the treaty by adopting an enforcement resolution under Chapter VII of the treaty and referring the situation to the court regardless of the nonparty state's wishes.

Owada's gambit was clearly something I wanted to work with, as it reflected the core of my own proposal of early June and it had the promise of turning the tide toward a favorable U.S. posture at the conference. The comments came fast and furious at our secluded meeting. Berman described those in the room as friends of the United States but added that all options looked disagreeable for the moment. Surprisingly, the German negotiator believed a compromise was within reach. The Italian representative rejected the idea of another conference; for obvious reasons the Italians wanted the Rome Conference to succeed by week's end. Owada pressed forward for the all-important right of a nonparty state to require its consent for prosecution of one of its nationals but expected the United States to acquiesce to the independent prosecutor provided he or she were held more accountable to the international community, particularly through the oversight of a Pre-trial Chamber. There also could be no discrimination between states parties and nonparty states on the use of the complementarity procedures. Berman cautioned against "protecting the villains," a key like-minded viewpoint that always confronted the issue of sovereign rights exercised by nonparty states. The German negotiator agreed with Berman's premise but reminded him that the Security Council would be able to refer situations to the court and this would create jurisdiction over nonparty states.

Given Berman's obstinacy, I gambled and suggested consideration of a carve-out for the permanent members of the Security Council (the P5), namely, a transitional provision that could be done in the form of a protocol and permit the P5 an opt-out privilege on war crimes and crimes against humanity for at least a certain number of years. This would recognize their special responsibility for maintaining international peace and security under the U.N. Charter and allow the United States, in particular, a testing period with the court while we maintained our vast overseas deployments of military personnel. But Berman argued for full cooperation with the court from the beginning and rejected the idea of a transitional period. De Brichambaut liked the transitional provision because it would have a definite time limit, as he believed it better for nations to join the court soon and not use the excuse of waiting to see how it functioned as a cover for failing to decide whether or not to join it.

Owada proposed a modification to his compromise and a wider application for my P-5 protocol idea. Owada said there would be broad acceptance of the court and the treaty obligations provided there was a protocol attached to it that allowed any state party to opt out of liability for its nationals on crimes against humanity and war crimes. Ratification of the treaty would mean full acceptance of it and then, if the government so chose, a separate signing of the protocol would enable that government to avoid investigation and prosecution for certain crimes. The shame factor in signing the protocol would be considerable and would give any government pause to consider the consequences before acting.

De Brichambaut described Owada's idea as a structure of Russian dolls and complained it was not "leadership readable." Owada emphasized that everyone had to find a satisfactory answer for nonparty states as well as states parties, and his ideas actually presented solutions even if explaining them required a few moments. De Brichambaut conceded he would be willing to look at the transitional-period idea. Chairman Kirsch said we had only forty-eight hours to get some traction on what we had been discussing and encouraged us to start marketing solutions. The Australian negotiator cautioned that so many delegations were insistent on automatic jurisdiction for all the crimes, with no opt-out possibilities, that he foresaw very rough sailing ahead.

I left the Owada gathering both encouraged and distraught. Owada had presented a workable formula, if only Washington would recognize that possibility. Getting the White House to modify my instructions always was a highly problematic venture. Yet I could sense from some of the negotiators that the like-minded group would bury the Owada proposal before we had a chance to inject it into the draft statute.

The Final Week Begins

The final week of the Rome Conference began with my hope that the few remaining days might finally propel agreement on a formula with which the United States could live, at least so as to avoid opposing the final draft. Maybe my original proposal, unwittingly cultivated by Owada, could finally take hold. However, I knew the forces arrayed against the United States were so formidable that we had a very steep climb ahead of us on Monday morning, when Kirsch was to lead a major public discussion of the various positions.

Austria delivered the statement of the European Union governments and expressed their unified support for an independent prosecutor who could refer situations to the court. The Vatican joined the European position, and Berman fully endorsed it for the United Kingdom. With that definitive European stance, any further U.S. opposition to an independent prosecutor would prove futile. India, in contrast, rejected any role for the Security Council, condemned the exclusion of nuclear weapons from the list of prohibited weapons, sought opt-in procedures for war crimes and crimes against humanity, believed that both the state of territory where the crime was committed and the state of custody of the suspect must consent before a case could be investigated by the court, and firmly rejected any independent prosecutor. Germany deplored the fact that after two years of its efforts to define the crime of aggression for inclusion in the statute of the court, it seemed it would be unsuccessful in getting this accomplished. So it pleaded for reflecting the crime in some other fashion in the statute (and that ultimately came to pass).

Owada held another meeting with key delegations that night. France proposed that there be automatic jurisdiction for genocide and crimes against humanity, with an opt-in right on war crimes during a transitional period of five to ten years following the opening of the court. Then there would be a review conference to reassess the opt-in privilege. Owada pushed back and argued for an opt-in privilege for both crimes against humanity and war crimes in an optional protocol to the treaty. Any government that signed the optional protocol effectively would protect itself from prosecution of such crimes unless it affirmatively "opted in" to such liability. Germany wanted a firm commitment at the end of the transitional period that the state party signing the protocol would be covered by all the crimes.

The delegate from Cameroon cried foul. He said nothing of what was being proposed had been seen before by most other delegations. "Can there be choices to punish the wrong?" he asked. "Are we creating sanctuaries for war criminals? The three core categories of crimes are being reduced to one—a court for genocide." He spoke passionately and reminded us that our strategizing to ease the way for certain nations, including the United States, was alien to most governments and likely unacceptable. Nonetheless, Owada plunged forward, telling the Cameroon diplomat that nonparty states could not be bound to the treaty and their interests had to be addressed. The Cameroonian responded, "Here we are facing evil. What we do here is a departure from international law, and it should be." At this point Berman interceded, saying that he "was profoundly moved by the Cameroon delegate. St. Augustine wrote, 'Give me charity, O Lord, but not just yet.'"

The next day Berman announced his opposition, on behalf of his government, to any opt-in procedure in perpetuity for the court. He would consider only some transitional period before all categories of crimes automatically applied to all states parties. Owada had a simple answer: if the optional protocol is terminated at the end of a certain number of years, the state party either can join the main architecture of the treaty or withdraw from the treaty altogether. According to Berman and the Australian delegate, Owada's proposal suggested that "a house half-built is not a house built." The Germans complained that it was becoming a rug sale. The Chinese delegate countered, "You can't ask those who don't live in the house to pay the rent." He was sympathetic to automatic jurisdiction for genocide but insisted on Owada's protocol idea for opting in on war crimes and crimes against humanity. It would, the Chinese diplomat urged, attract more governments to the court. But Berman countered that Owada's idea would create an unequal regime of those who fully accept the crimes and those who sign the optional protocol and perhaps opt in later (or not at all) for crimes against humanity and/or war crimes.

De Brichambaut stressed putting the minimum in the treaty, namely automatic jurisdiction for genocide, and then inviting those who want to be covered by other crimes to sign the optional protocol (the opposite of Owada's proposal for a protocol that, if signed, registered noncoverage of crimes against humanity and war crimes). I weighed in that the French proposal would be a workable compromise. But Britain's Berman was hell-bent against it. Norway's Rolf Fife presented my original proposal that any state party that did not accept automatic jurisdiction would forfeit its right to refer situations to the court. Later in the day, de Brichambaut told me that Paris would go as far as possible to seek a solution. He was encouraged by the new American attitude I had demonstrated. But the critical elements of flexibility, he feared, might not emerge from the like-minded and others to permit the permanent members to support the treaty (recognizing that we probably had lost the United Kingdom by then). He said France might abstain on the vote for the treaty in a few days and that Russia might abstain as well. There was little enthusiasm for delaying the conference.

I called Eric Schwartz at the National Security Council. He said that if universal jurisdiction trapping nationals of nonparty states inside the court's jurisdiction was *not* rejected, I would receive instructions to vote against the final draft statute. That meant that if nonparty states did not have the right to consent to prosecution of their nationals before the court, absent a Security Council referral of the situation, the United States would cast a negative vote. However, if we prevailed with our position on nonparty states, I probably would be instructed to abstain on the vote (or join consensus without recorded vote). If only, weeks earlier, I had been instructed to fight for that core priority—a position that anchored my proposed strategy but which President Clinton did not endorse until July 8, albeit with unsellable state party status conditions—Rome might have evolved far more favorably for the United States.

Schwartz, representing interagency views in Washington, also wanted to lock in protection of national security information and understand where things stood on automatic jurisdiction and whether it extended beyond the crime of genocide, how the court would be funded, the fate of the crime of aggression, and the final text of certain war crimes. He instructed me to hold a press conference the next day, Wednesday, July 15, to express Washington's desire to go the extra mile to find a solution provided that other governments demonstrate a cooperative negotiating spirit.

The Rise and Fall of the Wednesday Night Proposal

One of the longest days of my life—Wednesday, July 15, 1998—descended on me. I awoke to a scathing *New York Times* editorial that began, "It is hard to understand why Washington is sabotaging the creation of a permanent international criminal court that would serve American interests." It concluded by encouraging other countries to "proceed with the design and establishment of a serious court" if the United States remained opposed.[12] The French held a press conference expressing their full confidence in Chairman Kirsch to produce a balanced text of the treaty.

Schwartz arranged for President Clinton to reply to a letter from Italian prime minister Romano Prodi in which he sought "a constructive American attitude" at the talks. Once again, the meaning of "constructive" seemed to be that unless I conceded our primary positions to the Italian, and hence like-minded, view, I somehow was not being "constructive." Clinton's message turned the tables, claiming we had made significant concessions and it was time for other governments to demonstrate more flexibility. But Clinton's personal intervention was far too late to turn the like-minded juggernaut around, or even to shift its course by a few degrees.

I held my press conference to a packed room of journalists, delegates, and civil society representatives in the FAO building. In opening remarks, I said:

> Since early 1995, we have spared no effort to draft and negotiate a statute for a permanent International Criminal Court that would serve the interests of international justice, be realistic in its objectives, and operate as efficiently and effectively as possible.
>
> The United States has been a strong proponent of an appropriate court that it can back with its diplomatic, financial, and other resources. There can be no question in anyone's mind how significant such support could be, because the United States has demonstrated repeatedly its resolve to pursue international justice. No other country has shown as much support for the International Criminal Tribunals for the former Yugoslavia and Rwanda as the United States of America. We will continue to support these important institu-

tions. We also will continue to make every effort to bring all perpetrators of genocide, crimes against humanity, and war crimes to justice. We have been hoping, as a potential state party of an International Criminal Court, that the full weight of the United States could be used to support its critical investigations and prosecutions in the future.

At this conference, the U.S. delegation has engaged in the most intensive discussions with other delegates in order to achieve our common objectives. We have sought to find means to achieve fundamental U.S. requirements for the Court and also the objectives of other governments. In some instances our efforts have proven very useful in arriving at constructive language with broad appeal.

But we stand on the eve of the conference's conclusion without having found a solution. We fear that governments whose citizens make up at least two thirds of the world's population will find the emerging text of the treaty unacceptable. The world desperately needs this mechanism for international justice, but it must be a community, not a club. It will need the cooperation of governments to operate effectively, and it will not achieve its objectives by ignoring the legitimate concerns of many governments. The United States and other countries have critical responsibilities around the world that are crucial to the protection of civilian populations. A scheme that ignores these responsibilities is not going to serve the vital interest of the Court....

We hope that in these remaining days of the conference, we can still reach broader agreement among delegations. The United States stands prepared to engage in any discussions and any meaningful undertakings to achieve consensus on the document. There is still time to achieve our common vision for international justice.[13]

The follow-up questions kept assuming that if the United States opposed what the like-minded group wanted, we must be opposed to the whole concept of the International Criminal Court. That was simply false, as I had the task of trying to build the court on an alternative foundation. It was our fault, though. We had let others seize the high ground months, perhaps years, earlier, and I was left exposed to relentless incoming allegations of bad faith tactics.

Meanwhile, I had ensured that back in Washington my new proposal for the transitional period was being considered by everyone that day, particularly the Joint Chiefs of Staff, who met to examine what I had submitted. I recommended a transitional period of ten years during which a state party would have the right to opt in for crimes against humanity and/or war crimes, while liability for genocide would be automatic and not subject to any opt-out privilege. At the end of the ten years, the state party would either convert to automatic jurisdiction over all categories of atrocity crimes or withdraw from the treaty. Any state party that failed to opt in for both crimes against humanity and war crimes during the ten-year period would lose its privilege to refer atrocity situations to the court for the duration of the transitional period. Kirsch signaled that he was prepared to give us the ten-year transitional period and would recommend it to the final drafting session.

Unfortunately, support was gathering among the like-minded to hold firm to two alternative preconditions to jurisdiction, regardless of the fate of a nonparty state. In their view, if the consent of the state of either the territory on which the crime was committed or the state of nationality of the perpetrator was obtained, then the court could proceed with investigations and prosecutions. A state party would be deemed to have provided such consent in advance by virtue of ratifying the Rome Statute. Therefore, if a nonparty state national committed the atrocity crime on the territory of a state party, the court would have jurisdiction over that suspect even though his or her own government had not joined the court.

On the evening of July 15, I joined a long meeting at the Russian ambassador's residence in Rome with my colleagues from France, Britain, China, and Russia—the other permanent members of the Security Council. We were determined to find a common position that night, and we hammered out a provision for the treaty that protected nationals of nonparty states from the court's reach under certain circumstances and a protocol that would permit a state party to agree to be accountable for crimes against humanity and/or war crimes. Owada's efforts over the prior four days were clearly reflected in what we tried to accomplish that night. As we worked through the terms of what became known as the "P5 proposal," I sought approval in real time from the Joint Chiefs of Staff and the White House to agree to the terms, which I had previewed to Washington earlier in the day. The heads of the military branches met in the "tank" of the Pentagon to debate the terms while I labored in Rome at the Russian residence.

The final terms my counterparts from France, Russia, the United Kingdom, and China and I agreed upon included protection from the court's jurisdiction for the nationals of nonparty states provided the relevant nonparty state acknowledged that the activity allegedly constituting the crime

Photo 1. Ambassador Madeleine Albright's first recruits for her State Department office in late January 1993, with the author on the right, next to Albright; her chief of staff, Elaine Shocas, second from the left; and Kathy Klehr on the far left. The photo of President Bill Clinton was destined for a frame and a place on the wall. Image © Shepard Sherbell/Corbis.

Photo 2. The International Criminal Tribunal for the former Yugoslavia located in The Hague, Netherlands. Photo courtesy of Heidi Hansberry.

Photo 3. Ambassador Madeleine Albright donning U.N. protective gear before touring the devastated city of Vukovar, Croatia, with the author and others in January 1994. Photo courtesy of David Scheffer.

Photo 4. Richard Goldstone, the first prosecutor of the Yugoslav and Rwanda tribunals, on the right, addressing officials at NATO headquarters near Brussels, Belgium, in 1996. Christian Chartier, the spokesperson for the Yugoslav Tribunal, appears on the left. Photo courtesy of the ICTY.

Photo 5. Assistant Secretary of State John Shattuck examining atrocity sites near Srebrenica in Bosnia and Herzegovina on January 21, 1996. Photo courtesy of AP Photo/Rick Bowmer.

Photo 6. The author, on the right, standing beside stacked bodies of Srebrenica victims at a makeshift morgue near Tuzla, Bosnia and Herzegovina, where forensic experts sought to identify bodies with DNA testing and other techniques. Photo courtesy of David Scheffer.

Photo 7. Yugoslav Tribunal forensic experts excavating skeletons of genocide victims on a hillside north of Srebrenica in August 2000. Photo courtesy of David Scheffer.

Photo 8. A Bosnian Muslim refugee returning to her home near Srebrenica in August 2000. Photo courtesy of David Scheffer.

Photo 9. The author briefing the State Department press corps on March 2, 2000, about the Rewards for Justice program offering up to $5 million for information leading to the arrest and conviction of Yugoslav Tribunal indictees Slobodan Milosevic, Radovan Karadzic, and Ratko Mladic. Photo courtesy of the U.S. Department of State.

Photo 10. The International Criminal Tribunal for Rwanda located in Arusha, Tanzania. Photo courtesy of the ICTR.

Photo 11. The author at Ntarama Church in Rwanda in September 1997 viewing the bones and debris of hundreds of slain Tutsi who sought shelter there during the genocide of 1994. Photo by James Stejskal.

Photo 12. The second prosecutor of the Yugoslav and Rwanda tribunals, Louise Arbour, at a press conference in Arusha, Tanzania, in 1997. Photo by James Stejskal.

Photo 13. The author visiting the smoldering atrocity site at Mudende, Rwanda, on December 14, 1997. Resurgent genocide left hundreds of Tutsi refugees murdered or grievously wounded there. Photo courtesy of the Associated Press.

Photo 14. Rwanda Tribunal defendant Elizaphan Ntakirutimana, right, speaking with his American defense counsel, Ramsey Clark, left, on February 21, 2003, the day he was convicted for aiding and abetting genocide. Photo courtesy of the ICTR.

Photo 15. First Lady Hillary Rodham Clinton (on sofa, right) meets with the author (in chair, farthest back) and National Security Council staffers in the Map Room of the White House on June 10, 1998, to discuss U.S. strategy for the forthcoming Rome talks on the International Criminal Court. Official White House Photograph.

Photo 16. The author, with his back literally against a Roman wall, relaxing with members of the U.S. delegation to the International Criminal Court talks over a typically late dinner in June 1998. Photo courtesy of David Scheffer.

Photo 17. The author with U.N. secretary-general Kofi Annan in his New York Headquarters office on August 4, 1998, for discussions about the International Criminal Court and the Cambodia Tribunal. Photo courtesy of UN Photo/Eskinder Debebe.

Photo 18. The author signing the Rome Statute of the International Criminal Court on behalf of the United States at the United Nations in New York City on December 31, 2000. Photo courtesy of William Pace.

Photo 19. The International Criminal Court located in The Hague, Netherlands. Photo courtesy of Heidi Hansberry.

Photo 20. The author examining the bodies of two slain Serb policemen in Malisevo, a village in central Kosovo, in November 1998. Photo courtesy of AP Photo/David Brauchli.

Photo 21. Kosovar-Albanian refugees at the Macedonian border after being ethnically cleansed from Kosovo by Serb forces in early April 1999. Photo courtesy of David Scheffer.

Photo 22. The author interviewing Kosovar-Albanian refugees at the Macedonian border crossing of Deneral Jankovic in early April 1999. Photo courtesy of David Scheffer.

Photo 23. The author presenting a report about ethnic cleansing in Kosovo to the press at NATO headquarters near Brussels, Belgium, on May 18, 1999. Photo courtesy of Reuters/Benoît Dopparge.

Photo 24. Aerial photographs released by NATO that reveal before and after views of a mass burial site of Kosovar-Albanians massacred near Izbica, Kosovo, in April 1999. Photo courtesy of Reuters.

Photo 25. Carla Del Ponte, the third prosecutor of the Yugoslav and Rwanda tribunals, in her office in The Hague, Netherlands. Photo courtesy of the ICTY.

Photo 26. Mutilated victims at Netland Hospital in Freetown, Sierra Leone, in February 1999. Two brothers in this photograph had opposite hands chopped off by the rebels. Photo courtesy of David Scheffer.

Photo 27. The author during his meeting with President Ahmad Tejan Kabbah of Sierra Leone immediately following the atrocities in Freetown in February 1999. Photo courtesy of David Scheffer.

Photo 28. The Special Court for Sierra Leone located in Freetown, Sierra Leone. Photo courtesy of Will Romans.

Photo 29. The Extraordinary Chambers in the Courts of Cambodia located in Phnom Penh, Cambodia. Photo courtesy of Xander Meise Bay.

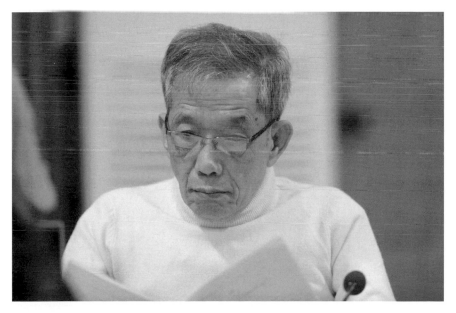

Photo 30. Kaing Guek Eav ("Comrade Duch"), the former head of the Khmer Rouge prison S-21 in Phnom Penh, during the first day of closing arguments of his trial before the Cambodia Tribunal on November 23, 2009. He was convicted of crimes against humanity and war crimes on July 26, 2010. Photo courtesy of the ECCC.

Photo 31. The author standing with Youk Chhang, director of the Documentation Center of Cambodia, on September 2, 1998, in a room full of documents Chhang had assembled about the atrocity crimes of the Pol Pot regime. Photo courtesy of David Scheffer.

Photo 32. The author walking through the cemetery at the Nyanza massacre site in Rwanda in September 1997. Photo by James Stejskal.

was an act authorized by that government. (Thus, a nonparty state unwilling to admit to the actions leading to the crime could not insulate its nationals from the court.) The nonparty state could consent to the court's jurisdiction voluntarily if it wished. The second major component of the P5 proposal was the protocol, which would remain in force for ten years after the court became operational. The duration of the protocol, however, could be prolonged by a decision of the Assembly of States Parties. A state party would have the option to sign the protocol and declare that its prior consent would be required in any particular case covering crimes against humanity or war crimes or both over its nationals. (Every state party would be subject to investigation for the crime of genocide, which would enjoy automatic jurisdiction under the treaty.) Thus, a state party could decline to sign the protocol and subject its nationals to liability under all the atrocity crimes in the Rome Statute or it could sign the protocol and require that its consent would be necessary before any of its nationals would be subject to prosecution for crimes against humanity or war crimes or both (depending on its declaration) for an initial transitional period of ten years. Thereafter, unless the Assembly of States Parties extended the period of the protocol by majority vote, the nationals of all states parties would be subject to investigation and prosecution for atrocity crimes.[14]

I awaited instructions from Washington before announcing American agreement to the proposal. An American official finally called and told me that "there was blood on the floor of the tank over this, David, and no one likes you anymore. But you have the approval of the Joint Chiefs of Staff for the P5 proposal. All the generals and admirals wanted me to convey this message to you: Do not even think about coming back to us with another compromise formula. This is our bottom line and you will not receive approval for anything less than this." Thus was the joy and agony of another round of decision making in Washington on the International Criminal Court. I turned to my colleagues with a smile and told them I had instructions from Washington to approve our collective proposal. There were a few slaps on my back as we reviewed every sentence before departing the Russian residence in the dead of the night.

The next morning Sandy Berger contacted his counterpart in Germany, Joachim Bitterlich, when it became clear that Germany was proving to be a major obstacle to a compromise deal, particularly the one we had just hammered out among the permanent members of the Security Council. The Germans insisted on denying explicit protection for nationals of nonparty states and immediately criticized the P5 proposal. Meanwhile, the Wednesday night group met with Owada to task him to present the P5 proposal to the like-minded and the European Union governments. We stressed to him that we could actively support the Rome Statute if the P5 proposal were adopted. Of course, the United Kingdom and France were playing both sides by then, knowing they could leap to the other side if the proposal were rejected. But we hoped that Russian, Chinese, and American support or acquiescence in the final text of the Rome Statute would mean enough to tilt the balance toward the P5 proposal. We still needed to see final terms on such other issues as the right to lodge reservations, confidentiality of national security information, state cooperation terms, how the crime of aggression would be addressed, funding for the court, oversight of the prosecutor, and the procedures for amendments to the treaty. But the major issues involved jurisdiction. If the P5 proposal were adopted, that would tip the scales toward our acceptance of or acquiescence in the final draft.

Owada, however, returned from his meetings Thursday afternoon only to report complete failure. The like-minded had an almost violent reaction to the P5 proposal and challenged Owada's credibility as an honest broker. Germany, as leader of the like-minded, led the verbal assault on Owada and the proposal. Time was running out. Once Owada reported the rejection, France and Britain split off, and the Wednesday night P5 coalition collapsed. I called Schwartz in Washington, and he encouraged me to present two alternative proposals the next day. I had been discussing them for weeks, but they were so extreme that we calculated they were lost causes. Friday, July 17, would be the day of lost causes, and Washington aimed to make it Scheffer's last stand.

Isolated in Rome

Late Thursday night, July 16, the small group of negotiators (excluding me but including the British) who had been tasked by Chairman Kirsch to create the final draft for the last day of the conference produced the "Bureau" draft. I saw it in the early morning hours of July 17. The Bureau draft included in Article 124 an opt-out right only for war crimes and only for seven years. There was nothing explicitly protecting nationals of nonparty states. The alternative preconditions for jurisdiction over any particular suspect required that the alleged crime take place on the territory of a state party or that the suspect be a national of a state party. Delegates from Egypt,

Italy, the Netherlands, Brazil, and Botswana rushed in to see me early Friday morning. The Dutch saw no reason to provide an opt-out right for any period of time for crimes against humanity. Italy tried to convince me that the Bureau had done a good balancing job. Brazil pleaded that the United States not actively oppose the treaty.

Then de Brichambaut and Berman visited. They were both mildly enthusiastic about the Bureau draft. De Brichambaut told me that Paris had satisfied its primary interest, namely an opt-out privilege on war crimes for seven years. He said, "David, I'm going to sign the treaty tomorrow because we know that no French national will ever appear before the International Criminal Court. We will ensure that our courts take the case first and dispose of it, nationally. We will amend what we have to, even our constitution, to guarantee that no French citizen ever ends up in The Hague." I told both of them that I was certain I would receive instructions to abstain on or even oppose the treaty text that had emerged from the Bureau. Everyone was still sound asleep in Washington.

I then met with China and Russia. China's delegate assured me of his country's opposition to the Bureau draft. The Russian negotiator said he would support the United States in opposing the Bureau draft, but within hours he fell silent. The German delegate walked in and told me that his government wanted the United States to join the court and that Germany had moved toward us on a couple of issues. But the bottom line for Bonn was no opt-in and no opt-out for any of the crimes, although the Germans would have to swallow Article 124. I told him we had expected more from Germany, particularly on the P5 proposal, and were deeply disappointed.

Shortly after that meeting, Jamie Borek from the State Department told me that she considered the preconditions for jurisdiction (Article 12 of the Rome Statute) especially perverse. They would expose U.N. peacekeepers from nonparty states operating on the territory of states parties to the court's jurisdiction, but grant impunity to genocidaires operating on their own territory provided it was part of a nonparty state. A nonparty state could lodge a declaration with the court inviting it to exercise jurisdiction over its territory or nationals in a particular situation. She noted, correctly, that as a nonparty state, Iraq under Saddam Hussein would be able to trigger the court's jurisdiction over coalition forces flying in Iraqi airspace in support of U.N. resolutions while he could gas his own people on Iraqi territory with impunity. (Two years later, in the rules of procedure and evidence [Rule 44(2)], I negotiated a partial fix to this problem by ensuring that if a nonparty state consented to the court's jurisdiction, it would have to expose its own conduct to investigation as well. A nonparty state might still take the gamble and accept the risk of investigation. It could hold another nonparty state's military operating under U.N. mandate on its territory accountable before the court by filing a special declaration [Article 12(3) of the Rome Statute].)

I spoke as soon as possible before the gathered delegates in the conference room that afternoon. I said, "We have a simple and reasonable proposal for [Article 12]. In Section 2 of [Article 12], we propose deleting the four words, 'one or more of' in the second line. This would have the effect of requiring that both the state of territory where the crime was committed *and* the state of nationality of the perpetrator would need to be states parties to the statute, or consent, before the Court could exercise jurisdiction. If this change could be made then the most fundamental concern of the United States would be accommodated and we would not have to consider any active opposition to the entry into force of the treaty or the operation of the Court once it is established."[15] I continued, "I deeply regret that we face the end of this conference with such profound misgivings and objections. This Court is the Court we and others warned of, strong on paper and weak in reality." These were fighting words, particularly to the like-minded, as they carried a threat of active opposition to the success of the treaty and of the court. But I had to play that card both to satisfy officials back in Washington, who were following my every word, and to try to shock the delegates into taking our proposal seriously or at least delaying conclusion of the conference in order to iron out a compromise. My direct appeal to U.N. secretary-general Kofi Annan to extend the conference had been rejected. A few days earlier he had criticized the United States and nine other countries that were not joining "others on one or more important issues or are insisting on certain points."[16]

Adriaan Bos, the Dutch diplomat who had earlier led the talks until he fell ill prior to the Rome Conference, intervened with an emotional plea that since the positions of governments would not change at this late hour in the conference, it was time to adopt the Rome Statute. "It's as far as we can go at the moment," he declared. His remarks garnered huge applause, and the stage was being set for the endgame. India jumped in with its own amendments to the statute to knock out any role for the Security Council in the referral of situations or suspension of work on cases and to add nuclear weapons to the list of prohibited weapons. Norway moved for no action on the Indian amendments. I voted no, namely supporting an actual vote on the substance of the Indian proposals, to keep alive the concept of getting to a substantive vote on the U.S. amendments. But 144 delegations voted yes, and thus the Indian initiative was dead and Norway had set a precedent it would employ against the United States shortly thereafter.

I then placed our final proposals before the delegates. These ideas were futile, but I had received instructions from Washington to put them to a vote. The first proposal, which I described earlier in the day, would have revised the preconditions for jurisdiction in Article 12 of the statute to require the express approval of both the territorial state where the alleged crime was committed and the state of nationality of the alleged perpetrator in the event either was not a state party to the treaty.[17] This proposal recognized the large degree of support at the conference for the consent of the territorial state but also remedied the dangerous drift of Article 12 toward near-universal jurisdiction over the nationals of nonparty states. In the alternative, our second proposal would have exempted from the court's jurisdiction conduct that arose from the official actions of a nonparty state when such action was acknowledged by the nonparty. This required a nonparty state to acknowledge responsibility for its actions in order to be exempted, an unlikely occurrence for regimes or established governments that have committed genocide or other heinous crimes.[18]

Neither proposal attracted sufficient support that afternoon to survive the final hours. Indeed, the vote on Norway's motion for "no action" on the U.S. proposals was 113 supporting no action, 17 opposing no action and seeking a vote on the substance of the proposals, and 25 delegations abstaining.[19] There was enormous applause and glee throughout the large room. Almost everyone stood and applauded and yelped, with civil society delegates in the room congratulating government delegates and the Italian delegation literally jumping up and down. They knew they had buried us, and they were ecstatic over achieving a treaty after so many years of tough negotiations.

I remained seated, however, as I could hardly stand and applaud my own defeat on the vote. I was filled with disappointment. Only Berman, seated one chair away from me, also sat, arms folded across his chest. He leaned over and told me he thought the conduct of the other delegates was shameful. I appreciated the gesture, despite Berman's responsibility for killing critical American proposals, and yet it remained a very painful moment. One of the members of my delegation from the Pentagon leaned over my shoulder and said his boss was extremely proud of my last stand. That Defense Department official had been a major reason why the military had been so obstinate for so long, so his aide's praise at that particular moment seemed obscene to me.

Following the debacle, the White House instructed me to request a written recorded vote on the final passage of the Rome Statute, thus showing precisely how many governments supported the final text, how many opposed it, and how many abstained. A recorded vote was a self-destructive gesture, as I knew we would lose it by a landslide. The better path, one I had argued for over the phone line with Washington, was to let the treaty text be adopted by oral consensus and no recorded votes, since we knew for certain it would be approved and no other country was talking about a recorded vote. I could deliver a tough statement afterward pointing out all of the problems we had with the final draft, as would other governments that disliked parts of the treaty but recognized the overwhelming numbers of delegations supporting it. Yet the Pentagon in particular insisted the United States had to go on the record opposing the final text, and the White House caved once again to its demand. I knew at the time we would go down in history as opposing the Rome Statute, even though we had tried so hard for so many years to support the creation of the International Criminal Court and we had contributed so much to the text of the treaty. All that we had accomplished would be swamped by the global memory of what I was about to do that night—vote against the Rome Statute.

So I called for a vote, which was recorded only by total numbers and not by how each government actually voted. Those countries in favor of the final text were 120 in number; 21 delegations abstained, and 7 voted against it.[20] Joining me in the "no" column were Israel and China, which publicly acknowledged their opposition. It appeared that the rogue's gallery of Iraq, Cuba, Syria, and Yemen also registered "no" votes. An annexed resolution to the treaty was adopted that kept the flame lit for adding drug trafficking and terrorism crimes to the Rome Statute as early as the mandatory seven-year review conference after the court became operational.[21] We thought we had put those crimes behind us long before Rome, and yet at the last moment they were resurrected for consideration in the relatively near future. Even the crime of aggression made it into the final draft as a prospective crime once its definition could be determined and the role of the Security Council settled. As someone on my delegation put it the next day, "They bought off everyone but us!"

In my final remarks at the plenary session late Friday night, and following the disastrous vote, I tried to strike a conciliatory tone with these words:

> Mr. President, the United States knows that all governments represented here tonight must be partners in the pursuit of international justice. We are deeply disappointed that some of our fundamental concerns were not addressed in the statute for the International Criminal Court. But the challenge of international justice remains and the United States will continue as a leader in supporting our common duty: to bring to justice those who commit these heinous crimes in our own time and in the future. Anyone who has stared into the face of a victim of such crimes knows that we must all carry out this solemn responsibility.... The contributions of the United States to this statute will stand, and for that I am grateful to the outstanding American delegation. Americans in particular can be very proud of what these talented officials have accomplished.

The Israeli delegate stated he would have voted for the Rome Statute if the crime of transfer of population into occupied territory had not been included with its novel language. China insisted that state consent should be the legal basis for the court's jurisdiction and, failing that, China had to vote no. Singapore, which appeared to abstain, pointed to the expedience of the treaty rather than to its soundness as law. Its representative objected to the withdrawal of chemical and biological weapons from the list of prohibited weapons at the last moment, something we also were deeply disturbed about, as we had long included them in the listing of war crimes. The exclusion arose as a bargained trade-off for excluding nuclear weapons, which angered India and the Arab world. If the major powers could use their nuclear weapons without criminal penalty, then, the argument ran, the nonnuclear states should be able to use chemical and biological weapons without criminal liability. It was a cynical maneuver the Bureau had made the night before in preparing the final draft, and we were stunned by the audacity of it.

I signed conference documents that enabled the United States to participate as an observer in future meetings of the Assembly of States Parties.[22] Afterward, long after midnight, I walked back alone to the Holiday Inn through the darkness of Rome's deserted streets. I had the opportunity as the sun rose to head toward the formal closing ceremony of the conference and the signing of the Rome Statute by a small group of governments, including Italy and France. But I felt utterly deflated, uninspired, and antisocial. I decided that no one in Washington would want me recorded in any photograph of the celebratory "signing" ceremony. So I walked to the Vatican and visited the Sistine Chapel, where I marveled at Michelangelo's spectacular frescoes. All that I had labored over seemed insignificant to me at that moment, as if the past five weeks were but a momentary passage that had brought me to this glorious masterpiece. It did not take long, however, for the memories to flood back as I made my way across St. Peter's Square.

CHAPTER NINE

ROME'S AFTERMATH

I guess we'll have to send someone up to New York to cross out that ambassador's name.

Senator Jesse Helms during the confirmation hearing for secretary of
state designate Colin Powell on January 17, 2001

DURING THE FLIGHT HOME FROM EUROPE ON JULY 19, 1998, I JOTTED DOWN my reflections on what had gone wrong during the Rome negotiations on the International Criminal Court. One example stood out. At the height of the conference, a mysterious set of devastating "talking points" reportedly prepared for Defense Secretary William Cohen landed in the lap of the *New York Times*.[1] The Pentagon denied any knowledge of the document, and its spokesman, Kenneth Bacon, said he believed it did not originate from within the Defense Department. But the talking points threatened that the United States might withdraw its troops from Europe if Germany kept pressing for universal jurisdiction for the court. It was an arrogant strong-arm tactic, ignorantly conceived and clumsily conveyed, that simply angered everyone I had to work with in Rome, particularly our NATO allies. They resented the threat, which totally backfired on me in Rome. I never learned the document's origins, but I despised whoever had written or used it, as those individuals did America no favors.

In the aftermath, I concluded that one reason the value of the U.S. military had not sunk in with friends and allies was the Pentagon's own reluctance to describe its changing role in the world following the Cold War. It had to market itself as relevant to foreign interests and not only to American interests and security. The Pentagon needed to stand in the shoes of other nations and see the world as our foreign friends viewed it. That meant developing a greater will to engage in international humanitarian and peace operations alongside other nations' armed forces. Granted, the United States took enormous risks with its military forces in major conflicts such as the Gulf War of 1990–1991, the Somalia intervention in late 1992, Haiti in 1994, and finally Bosnia and Herzegovina in late 1995. But too often those interventions were perceived by others as designed strictly to advance U.S. national security or economic interests rather than promote global interests that form the rationale for peacekeeping and humanitarian missions joined by many other nations. The Defense Department believed that such massive deployments justified exceptional protection for American forces, without understanding that other governments simply did not see it that way and, in fact, argued for stricter compliance with law by the U.S. military because of its heavy footprint.

The Pentagon gains if it understands the perspectives of other governments and then uses the U.S. military presence far more intelligently to persuade others to cooperate on such matters as treaty making. Indeed, I thought the Pentagon needed its own corps of diplomats, teamed with the State Department, to make the most effective case. We could not just say we needed international support for the protection of our military; we also had to say why the United States must have such protection. Unless the United States accepted a new set of responsibilities in peacekeeping and humanitarian initiatives, with boots on the ground alongside those of other nations, we would never convince others of the need for special protection. There had developed a disconnect between our military commanders and those of other nations because they were not confronting atrocity crimes with the same understandings. The Pentagon was stilled trapped in a Cold War mentality of essentially going it alone globally. That model no longer served our best interests.

Another failure that was systematic within the Washington bureaucracy was our inability to make policy decisions on complex treaties in a timely manner. Top officials needed to take the time to understand the issues so that knee-jerk reactions did not dominate policy discussions. However, decisions must be arrived at early enough at each stage of the negotiations in order to have an impact and maintain American leadership in the talks. There was a chronic failing, particularly prior to and during the Rome Conference, to arrive at early decisions that could make a real difference in the negotiations. I constantly had to push the process along, pleading for decisions by the Principals Committee and by President Clinton with enough lead time to allow me to work the new U.S. position with other governments.

The key turning point was the Map Room meeting with Hillary Clinton on June 10, 1998, for that was when the tide could have been turned for a dynamic new U.S. position at the start of the Rome talks. That new position was one that Japan's ambassador Hisashi Owada essentially replicated, at least in part, in the final week of the negotiations. But by then it was too late to deal with the vast majority of governments, whose positions had been solidifying during the conference. Without a White House decision that could have catapulted the United States to the head of the pack again, I was forced to play the highly unorthodox and self-serving card of trying to opt out of coverage of crimes against humanity and war crimes. Throughout the five weeks, there essentially was no leadership from President Clinton to support my efforts. The July 8 oral instructions from the White House arrived far too late for me to gain the necessary traction with dug-in delegations. Multilateral diplomacy cannot be conducted with delayed decision making or with spin control or military strong-arm tactics. We had to learn how to make hard decisions, of considerable complexity, early enough to transform the negotiations.

Finally, I was burdened prior to and during Rome with the frequent presence of staffers of Republican senator Jesse Helms, chairman of the Foreign Relations Committee, and his compatriot, Republican senator Ron Grams of Minnesota, in the negotiating room with me and floating around the corridors raising havoc with other delegates. I was under instructions to accommodate them as a courtesy to the legislative branch, but it was a very destructive process that constantly undermined my authority as a negotiator and, in my view, U.S. interests. Other governments were confused: who was speaking for the U.S. government? It was no surprise that when Helms pontificated from the Senate about the treaty being "dead on arrival" in that body and the dangers of an International Criminal Court, foreign officials and their publics thought he was Washington speaking to them. As I discovered during the spring 1998 talks in New York, Helms succeeded, paradoxically, in seriously undermining my ability to prevail on precisely the positions he wanted in Rome. Of course, his real aim probably was to torpedo the entire process. He held Albright, Clinton, and me hostage to his incendiary rhetoric, but I always had to play nice with him in return. That strategy proved to be the height of folly.

Anthony Lewis, the Pulitzer Prize–winning columnist for the *New York Times*, lamented the American failure in Rome. He quoted words I had uttered earlier in the year and then showed how I had failed to live up to them. I had said, "We live in a world following the cold war where mass killings, mass rapes and atrocities are occurring with shocking frequency. The rule of law, which the United States has always championed, is at risk again of being trampled by war criminals whose only allegiance is to their own pursuit of power."[2] But Lewis wrote on July 20: "One cannot read those words now without a sense of irony and regret. For the great disappointment at the Rome conference was the performance of the United States, It fought to weaken the court, using hard-boiled tactics to try to bring American allies around to that position." Though he correctly identified Helms as a major culprit, Lewis pinned the ultimate blame on Clinton: "[A] President with vision, and with a backbone, would not have let that undo America's championship of the rule of law. President Clinton had a great opportunity. His delegation won significant protections against frivolous prosecutions. He could have embraced the outcome in Rome as a victory for American principles—and then, if the Senate said no, waited for time to bring us in. After all, it took 40 years for the Senate to ratify the convention against genocide."[3] But that chance was gone, or so most thought at the time.

Rejoining the Talks

During my final hours in Rome and after I returned home to Washington, only one administration official contacted me to recognize my efforts in the negotiations. John Shattuck, the assistant secretary of state for democracy, human rights, and labor, called the day after I arrived home and said some very kind words. Neither Berger nor Clinton contacted me. Albright fell silent about Rome, and the next time I saw her in the State Department, she barely acknowledged me. I had to wonder whether I had blown it, for my relationship with her thereafter was more distant. Within weeks she was absorbed by the bombings of the U.S. embassies in Nairobi and Dar es Salaam, and I basically lost touch with her for months. (Albright omits any reference to the International Criminal Court in her memoirs.)[4] The only laudatory words I received, aside from Shattuck's decent gesture, came from Helms. After I testified before his committee on July 23 to explain the outcome of the Rome Conference, his aide, Mark Thiessen (who a few years later became speechwriter to Defense Secretary Donald Rumsfeld and then to President George W. Bush), took me aside to convey Helms's congratulations on the "outstanding" job I had done to reject the Rome Statute. I actually felt soiled with that remark and left the hearing room adrift in loneliness.

I told the senators that day that major U.S. objectives had been achieved in the Rome Statute.[5] But it was not enough, as I pointed out, and no one really knew what lay ahead for the United States and the fast-evolving court. From late July until the end of 1998, I encountered fierce resistance within the administration, particularly from the Pentagon, and from Capitol Hill to doing anything more on the International Criminal Court. There were to be years of further negotiations in a Preparatory Commission on all the supplemental documents that had to be finalized before the Court could become functional.[6] The United States had full privileges to be part of those negotiations as did all other governments that had participated in the Rome Conference, whether or not they supported the final text of the treaty. Initially, mine was the lone voice that argued for a return to the negotiating table to protect our interests in the further talks and to try to address our major concerns by obtaining "fixes" in the rules of procedure and evidence, the elements of crimes, and the relationship agreement between the United Nations and the court that would be drafted well into 2000. It was a long internal struggle that pitted me against my own department and every single other agency with a stake in the issue. Rumors surfaced that the Pentagon was trying to persuade Berger to fire me. Helms's staffers showed me no mercy as I maneuvered to rejoin the talks. But I persisted in my advocacy that we reengage.

Eventually, I prevailed and reconstituted my delegation to arrive at the United Nations in February 1999 to participate in a fresh round of negotiations on the supplemental documents. I was greatly assisted by William Lietzau, a Yale Law–educated Marine Corps military lawyer who advised the Joint Chiefs of Staff. Lietzau had long been on my delegation, including at Rome, and had been instrumental in persuading everyone of the vital need for the court to use an agreed-upon set of elements of crimes, which would provide the definitional guideposts for how the prosecutor, defense counsel, and judges interpret and enforce the atrocity crimes in the Rome Statute. We had hoped to have it drafted prior to Rome, but the compromise was to ensure must it must be negotiated and finalized before the court became operational. Lietzau prepared the initial draft of the elements of crime, which became the working document in the 1999 and 2000 talks. Guided by the skill of the Jordanian chairman of the working group on elements of crimes, Ambassador Zeid Ra'ad Zeid al-Hussein, Lietzau was deeply influential in those talks. Ably assisted by Major Michael Newton, U.S. Army, who was the military lawyer assigned to the Office of War Crimes Issues, Lietzau can be credited with the reason I joined consensus on June 30, 2000, in adopting the elements of crimes.

I also was assisted by Molly Warlow and her team of prosecutors from the Criminal Division of the Justice Department. Together they slogged through eighteen months of detailed negotiations on the rules of procedure and evidence, which were essential in order for the court to function efficiently and fairly. At every step of the way before, during, and after Rome, Warlow briefed me on whether the International Criminal Court was being structured so as to meet U.S. constitutional requirements. In the end those requirements were met, in no small measure because we returned to the talks and ensured that the rules of procedure and evidence met our interests.[7] With full interagency clearance, on June 30, 2000, I joined consensus in adopting them for the court.[8]

During this post-Rome period in my ambassadorship, I set out to achieve many of our unmet requirements in the rules of procedure and evidence and in the elements of crimes, and succeeded with my delegation in gaining approval for them.[9] I also plunged into finding some formula for the relationship agreement between the court and the United Nations that could address Washington's concern about the exposure of the U.S. military to the court's jurisdiction. The relationship agreement would be a binding treaty between the International Criminal Court and the United Nations, and thus I wanted to inject a clause into it that would address our most fundamental concern—the exposure of U.S. armed forces during the period when the United States would not be a party to the Rome Statute. On its face, the strategy was clever and would have changed the dynamic in Washington to one of relatively positive support for the court. I sought language that was intended to focus on the official actions of nonparty states, including those undertaken in U.N. peacekeeping and peace enforcement operations or in U.N.-authorized military deployments, provided they were acknowledged by the "directing" government, and to shield the military personnel engaged in such actions unless the consent of the nonparty state was obtained or such country already was penalized by a Chapter VII enforcement action of any character by the Security Council.[10]

I presented this concept informally to delegates in the March 2000 Preparatory Commission talks at the United Nations, and thereafter it became known as the "March proposal." Shortly after that session, I traveled overseas to key capitals to make the case for it there as well. It was not entirely surprising that the March proposal, which was really another means of carving out an exceptionalist enclave for the United States, attracted great skepticism and opposition from other governments worried that it would undermine the Rome Statute's authority to investigate nationals of nonparty states who commit atrocity crimes on the territories of states parties to the treaty. My response to that criticism pointed to the Security Council's power to refer situations to the court and thus ensnare nationals of nonparty states into the court's jurisdiction (as ultimately proved to be the case in the Darfur situation referred to the court in April 2005 and Libya in 2011). Nongovernmental organizations also lashed out at the idea.

I modified the March proposal in September 2000 by limiting the protection for nonparty nationals only to their engagement in international armed conflicts. I pledged to develop a formula that would protect only those nonparty states acting responsibly in the international community and honoring the principle of complementarity.[11] But my efforts failed to attract enough support, and with the administration winding down and a presidential election in full heat, I could not get cabinet officials, including Albright, to boost my effort by intervening with foreign leaders. Too many nonparty states were committing atrocity crimes, and that left supporters of the International Criminal Court disinclined to figure out an exclusion for the law-abiding governments that chose not to join the court quickly. There was too much cynicism directed against the use of U.S. military power globally to trust in a formula that granted virtual impunity from the court to American soldiers and their commanders.

Earlier, in March 1999, I lit a firestorm among international law scholars with a speech before the American Society of International Law's annual meeting. I explained that there was no established principle of customary international law, yet, that entitled a country that had joined the International Criminal Court to delegate to the court prosecution of a suspect from a nonparty state without that non-party state's consent, as opposed to prosecuting him or her in the state party's own national courts. The latter right of any country is indisputable. If an American, for example, commits a crime in Italy, Italian courts have full jurisdiction over that American citizen (unless, perhaps, the perpetrator is an American soldier covered by a Status of Forces Agreement between the United States and Italy). But Italy has no legal right to extradite the American to Syria, which has no connection to the crime or the suspect, to stand trial there for the crime committed in Italy just for the sake of political expediency. My argument was that for a treaty-based international tribunal like the International Criminal Court, there was no principle of customary international law that automatically sanctioned delegation of territorial jurisdiction over citizens of nonparty states to the court for prosecution without the consent of the nonparty state or in the absence of a Security Council referral to the court.[12] I was not alone in this view.[13] I conceded that someday such a delegation to a treaty-based court might rise to the level of custom and thus be enforceable globally, but that day had not yet arrived.

Unfortunately, my speech was misinterpreted by academics who thought I was trying to deny the age-old territorial jurisdiction a state has over a foreigner who commits a crime on that nation's territory and may even be subject to a legitimate extradition request by another nation.[14] Nothing was further from the truth, and indeed the Justice Department never would have cleared my speech if that had been the argument.

Despite the force of my argument, I knew it was too theoretical to carry much weight with other governments supportive of the Rome Statute, with nongovernmental organizations dedicated to forging ahead to launch an operational court, or even with my friends in the legal academy who had little patience with any reopening of such a sensitive issue.

Final Steps toward Signature

As the eighth year of the Clinton administration came to a close, so too did the opportunity for governments to sign the Rome Statute. The last possible day under the treaty's terms was December 31, 2000.[15] Thereafter, any nation that wanted to join the court would have to "accede" to the treaty rather than ratify the treaty as a result of its signature to the document. The technical procedures for accession were certainly possible for any country, including the United States. But symbolically the status of a signatory brought added credibility to a government's role in the process and would make ratification in the U.S. Senate someday an easier proposition than to accede to a treaty that Clinton had refused to sign. Also, signatory status would give the United States much greater credibility to persuade other governments to incorporate further "safeguards" in the supplemental documents, including not only the March proposal but other critical ones that I had successfully lined up, with significant support, for official consideration in 2001.[16] Clinton had sought the creation of the International Criminal Court by the end of his presidency, and we had achieved enough in the negotiations of 1999 and 2000 to make a good case for signing the Rome Statute. But again I was mostly alone in seeking such an outcome when I began, in September 2000, to advocate internally for a U.S. signature.

Morton Halperin, who was director of policy planning at the State Department, and Eric Schwartz at the National Security Council remained skeptical but counseled me on how to plot a signing strategy by the end of the year. Halperin laughed when I suggested that we try to obtain Clinton's signature on the treaty by November or early December, which was when I would be struggling to gain support for U.S. proposals in New York negotiations. He reflected that Clinton never made a decision until the last possible moment, and predicted it would be reached on December 31. He proved correct.

I was still trying to keep the March proposal alive in New York for the Preparatory Commission talks in late November. A new round of negotiations, focusing on the relationship agreement and other supplemental documents, would not commence until 2001. I joined a dinner in Washington with Charles Ruff, the wheelchair-bound White House counsel during the impeachment proceedings of 1998 and 1999. He told me he firmly believed the United States should sign the Rome Statute and that I should press hard to make it happen by the end of the year. His words were more encouragement than I had received in years from any White House official on any aspect of my job confronting atrocity crimes. I took him at his word and renewed my efforts to persuade Clinton on the merits of signing the treaty.

On October 27, I met with Alan Baker, the legal adviser in the Israeli Foreign Ministry. He surprised me with the news that his government was considering signing the Rome Statute despite renewed violence and the collapse of the peace process with the Palestinians. Baker conceded that the attorney general and Defense Ministry were still opposed because of the language in the statute making it a war crime to transfer population, directly or indirectly, into occupied territory. He and I had worked with Lietzau and others successfully to insert a footnote in the elements of crimes clarifying that the "term 'transfer' needs to be interpreted in accordance with the relevant provisions of international humanitarian law."[17] It was designed to remove novel arguments about indirect tax incentives to transfer a population into occupied territory. I advised Baker that an Israeli signature would not send shock waves through Washington. On the contrary, we should work together to ensure that both governments sign the Rome Statute.

As the New York talks got underway in late November and into early December, I lobbied other delegations on the March proposal in the hope I could build some support for official consideration in the next year. It would have been unwise to thrust it onto the negotiating floor prematurely, only to see those in opposition quickly bury it. On December 6, I received a call in New York from the Joint Chiefs of Staff, demanding that I immediately advance the March proposal in the talks. But I was not interested in any further institutional suicide on behalf of the Joint Chiefs, who seemed to have tin ears when it came to understanding the dynamics of the negotiations. The National Security Council staff backed me up, as they wanted no last-minute defeat either. The better tactic was to let the March proposal simmer for the time being and lock in other safeguards for consideration in 2001, which I accomplished with the support of several other mostly European governments.[18] I was determined to set the stage for final closure the next year on a range of issues that would better protect our interests. But I could not negotiate 100 percent impunity for the U.S. armed forces, which was the dream world so many still populated back in Washington. I firmly believed that if the United States acquired the credibility of being a signatory state, and if the next administration (be it led by Al Gore or George W. Bush) used that credibility to build in further safeguards in a cooperative spirit, we would be in a much better position to protect American interests even if the U.S. Senate never took the final step to ratify the treaty.

One morning during the New York talks, I ventured over to the Plaza Hotel on Fifth Avenue to have breakfast with an old friend of the president's, federal judge Richard Arnold from Arkansas. Charles Ruff had encouraged me to seek him out and see if he could help persuade Clinton to sign the treaty. Since Arnold was visiting New York City at the time, I spent almost two hours explaining the court and addressing his questions about it. The judge at times appeared sympathetic, but he also had his doubts and seemed uncomfortable with the whole idea of approaching Clinton on the subject. I quickly sensed that this was such an alien institution, merging common-law and civil-law procedures, that he could not find his bearings. Arnold never called Clinton, but I never regretted making the effort. The experience taught me that the complexities of the Rome Statute required a long educational effort in the United States, even for federal judges.

On December 8, the final day of the New York negotiations, I was seated in the United States chair in Conference Room 4 of the U.N. Headquarters Building preparing to make my final remarks. My beeper buzzed, and I read a short news flash that the Florida Supreme Court, by a vote of four to three, had just ruled in favor of Al Gore's challenge to the presidential election results in Florida and ordered a manual recount statewide.[19] Gore probably would win that recount, and I hoped I would have the opportunity to return to New York in February of the next year and resume our efforts, ideally armed with the credibility of a signatory nation supporting me. I daydreamed that the White House would call me any moment informing me that the United States indeed would sign the Rome Statute and that I was instructed to announce it before the gathered delegates that day. But the call, of course, never came.

It did not take long for Senator Helms to try to bulldoze my hopes for an American signing of the Rome Statute. On December 12, he published an op-ed in the *Washington Post* urging Clinton not to sign the treaty.[20] Alan Baker called me from Israel to alert me that Helms had published his article there as well, basically as a warning to Israel to stand down. Helms's aide, Steve Rademaker, confirmed that Helms would contact Israeli prime minister Ehud Barak directly and urge him not to sign. I told Baker that a letter circulated among other senators by Senator Patrick Leahy, a Democrat from Vermont, urged Clinton to sign the treaty and that it was picking up a fair amount of support. (Ultimately, seventeen senators signed it.)[21] I said Senator Helms did not speak for the entire U.S. Senate and that many of his colleagues strongly disagreed with him. Baker conceded that the Israeli military remained opposed to the Rome Statute but that his government might move on the matter very soon. He told me that some Holocaust survivor groups were weighing in seeking Israel's signature. We promised to stay in close touch during the coming days.

Clinton Makes His Move

On the morning of December 15, President Clinton read an op-ed in the *New York Times* coauthored by former defense secretary Robert McNamara and former Nuremberg prosecutor Ben Ferencz.[22] Leave it to the wonders of a prominently published op-ed to finally awaken a president to action.

Schwartz immediately informed me that Clinton had written on the margins of the op-ed that he wanted to be kept informed on the issue, as if I had not been trying to do that for years. One can write countless memoranda and hold the highest-level meetings on an issue, and yet what galvanizes a president is often what the rest of the world sees along with him on a cold winter's morning. I laughed and told Eric that I would give him as much information as the president could handle. But my experience with Judge Arnold reminded me that I needed to break the issues down to understandable nuggets for Clinton, despite his high intelligence, to digest in a relatively short time frame.

A top Pentagon official called to remind me that, at a February 28, 2000, White House meeting, Berger had pledged there would be no U.S. signature on the Rome Statute. I told him that as of February 2000 that was the position of the White House, but it was now December and much had transpired since then, including the rules of procedure and evidence and the elements of crimes that we supported. The official also suggested that the Bush transition team be consulted. I had long been lashed to Senator Helms's staff and knew that terrain very well. But I was instructed in December by the Bureau of Legislative Affairs at the State Department to let the White House and their experts handle both Capitol Hill and the transition team. I was told not to communicate on my own with either in these final weeks of the Clinton administration.

Baker called from Jerusalem to learn whether Clinton was moving toward signing the treaty. If he was, then Baker said it would facilitate advancing a similar decision in Israel. Whichever government opted first for signature would influence the other government to close ranks behind it. Meanwhile, I continued to prepare briefing documents for Clinton. My memorandum would be joined with the State Department's input while Berger marshaled memoranda from the Defense and Justice departments, the intelligence community, and his own staff for a thick briefing book destined for the president. On December 20, there was a flurry of activity as various diplomats sought to reach Clinton encouraging him to sign the treaty. Meanwhile, Justice Department lawyers told me that they were arriving at their own conclusion to recommend signature to Attorney General Janet Reno. They believed that the last two years of U.N. talks on the supplemental documents had generally worked in favor of U.S. interests and that while the treaty still had flaws, the document was not unconstitutional. There was no legal impediment to it under U.S. law, but it remained a policy decision whether to sign the treaty and ultimately join the court.

Defense Secretary William Cohen remained adamantly opposed to the Rome Statute. If the White House staff decided on recommending signature to Clinton, the Pentagon was determined to get a "kick ass statement" from Clinton expressing continued U.S. concerns. I conveyed to Berger the reality that the International Criminal Court would be operational someday soon. The Pentagon was still arguing that somehow we could ensure that it would not exist by being stubbornly opposed to it. I told Berger we had used up every ounce of goodwill on this issue and the Pentagon's strategy had exhausted itself. Another phone call with Alan Baker confirmed that he was still struggling with his own Defense Ministry. On Sunday, December 24, Barak heard a strong pitch from several in his cabinet not to sign the Rome Statute, as they feared it would open a new front for international criticism while fighting the Palestinians and could result in putting Israeli military leaders on trial. Baker told me that Barak was leaning against signature. He asked me to arrange for Clinton to call Barak. The only way this would work, Baker said, would be if both governments showed up simultaneously to sign the Rome Statute. I agreed but told him I was trying to get my own leader to recognize the merits of signing the treaty, so it might not be a good moment to ask him to lobby Barak.

I then went into high gear to ensure that Clinton heard from a range of influential friends, including Greg Craig, Vernon Jordan, and Stuart Eizenstat, about the value of a U.S. signature. I asked Harry Barnes, former U.S. ambassador to Chile and an administrator at the Carter Center, to contact former president Jimmy Carter, who had hosted me for a roundtable discussion on the court just before the Rome Conference. Barnes phoned back to say that Carter was not prepared to call Clinton. There had been too many occasions, Carter told Barnes, when he was asked to contact Clinton on other issues and the president never responded to him. But Carter sent Clinton a written message. Carter also contacted Vice President Al Gore. I reached out to the movie director Steven Spielberg, who knew Clinton and had produced the Academy Award–winning film *Schindler's List* in 1993. My effort to galvanize Spielberg annoyed Robert Rifkind of the American Jewish Congress. He exclaimed: "Spielberg knows nothing about the treaty. This needs to be rationally decided!" I simply responded, "Welcome to politics." I had spent years rationally deliberating the treaty, but now was the time for political clout.

The German negotiator, Hans-Peter Kaul, said Chancellor Gerhard Schröder had tried to reach Clinton by phone but without success. The iconic Philadelphia lawyer and human rights activist Jerry Shestack, who would soon become president of the American Bar Association and had observed me in action in Rome, contacted Elie Wiesel on my behalf. Wiesel told him that he would have to think about contacting Clinton because he also was seeking a pardon for somebody before the president left office. I kept trying to reach Nelson Mandela in South Africa through various contacts, including Richard Goldstone, the former prosecutor of the Yugoslav and Rwanda tribunals.

On December 28, I received a call informing me that Clinton needed to know within five minutes where Albright stood on signing the treaty. I was not aware at the time that she might not have signed the "approve" line on the decision memorandum sitting on her desk. In fact, she was gone for the Christmas holidays. I immediately called Undersecretary of State for Political Affairs Tom Pickering and pulled him out of a meeting with secretary of state designate Colin Powell. We agreed that I should disrupt Albright's vacation and seek her immediate approval for signature of the Rome Statute. A few moments later I reached Albright at her getaway in Colorado. She told me that she "favored signature" and actually had tried to reach Berger that morning with her view but had been unsuccessful. I conveyed that news to Eric Schwartz. One of his aides asked, "Well, does Madeleine *strongly* favor signature?" I just said "yes," as I was not about to call Albright back and ask her such a silly question. When Albright made a decision, she did not equivocate.

The next day I spoke again with Baker. His Defense Ministry was coordinating a "kill signature" campaign with the Pentagon, he told me. Given the Sabbath on Friday evening and Saturday, the Israeli cabinet would not meet again until Sunday, December 31. He had sent full powers of signature to the Israeli ambassador to the United Nations in case the cabinet approved signature. He told me the ball was in my court now and all depended on what I would convey to him on Sunday regarding the final U.S. decision.

Signing the Rome Statute

On Saturday, December 30, I was on the phone all day with the White House and Baker in Jerusalem. Clinton had taken his briefing books on the treaty to Camp David, and I fielded calls from aides asking me the president's steady stream of questions. The Defense Department, Joint Chiefs of Staff, and the intelligence community requested he not sign the treaty. The State and Justice departments, Ambassador Richard Holbrooke at the

United Nations, and Sandy Berger, as his National Security Adviser, recommended signature. Clinton had a split decision to resolve.

I drafted my own version of what Clinton should say if the treaty were signed and faxed it to Berger and Schwartz, who were feverishly working on the statement at Camp David and the White House. There was still no decision from Clinton as he performed his characteristic cram right to the last moment. Late Saturday night Baker called me to say he was still telling everyone there was no decision out of Washington as their Sunday morning meetings commenced in Jerusalem. His government was on hold, awaiting word from me. Reporters started to call me, but I ignored them. Late Saturday night Schwartz told me to go to Union Station early Sunday morning and board the earliest train for New York. A snowstorm had hit the eastern seaboard, air travel was grounded, and the highways were mostly impassable. Some of the phone calls I took that day occurred while I shoveled my home out from under the heavy snowfall. Neighbors witnessed me stop every so often and open my cell phone in the frigid outdoors.

Sunday morning arrived and, after a difficult drive in the darkness to Union Station, I was dutifully seated on the first Amtrak bound for New York City. I still had received no confirmation of Clinton's decision one way or the other. I would be the official to sign the treaty if that were in fact his determination, and so the requisite papers were drawn up at the State Department so that I could sign on behalf of the United States. They were faxed to the U.S. Mission to the United Nations on Sunday only after I had arrived there. While I was on the train, Schwartz called me continuously with final detailed questions about the treaty and to labor through the text of the presidential statement if the decision were a "go."

When I arrived at Penn Station midmorning, I was ascending the escalator out of the building when Albright called me to confirm that Clinton had just decided that the United States would sign the Rome Statute and that I was to perform the task forthwith. She warmly congratulated me for prevailing. The snow had immobilized the city, so I trudged in my hiking boots from Penn Station over to the United Nations, but I felt airborne. I reached Hans Corell, the U.N. legal counsel, by phone at his home and asked him to maneuver through the snow, open up his office, and permit me to sign the Rome Statute. Far from being put out, Corell was ecstatic at the news and said he would inform U.N. secretary-general Kofi Annan immediately. He told me he would rush to his office as quickly as the weather permitted.

Some hours went by before everything could be arranged for the signing "ceremony" at U.N. Headquarters, which was closed on New Year's Eve—a Sunday and a snow emergency day as well. As I waited at my favorite Irish pub on Second Avenue with my much-used cell phone plugged into the wall socket, I reached Baker in Jerusalem and informed him of Clinton's decision. He immediately presented the news to Barak and his cabinet, and they finally determined to join us in signing the treaty. I arrived late afternoon at the United Nations, still in my hiking boots, and made my way to Corell's office. There he had arranged a small ceremony, complete with flags and a signing table. William Pace, who headed the coalition of nongovernmental groups supporting the court, was on hand to witness the event, as were some journalists. Also present in Corell's office was the Israeli ambassador, who would follow me an hour or so later to sign the treaty. His government's signing statement cautioned against interpreting the treaty to deny Israeli key interests, and Corell regarded it as a de facto reservation. He halted the process and sought a retraction before he would permit the Israeli ambassador to sign.

I intervened and explained to Corell that the Israeli statement was similar to Clinton's, which also spoke of flaws in the treaty.[23] After much discussion Corell relented, and the Israeli ambassador signed the treaty. The United States thus became the 138th signer and Israel the 139th and final signer of the Rome Statute on the last possible day for signatures. What had begun in earnest in September became reality on that cold December evening. I caught the last flight to Washington as LaGuardia Airport resumed operations and arrived home after midnight into the arms of my wife Michelle.

The next morning, the *New York Times* reported on page one that I had signed the treaty.[24] While I received some congratulatory phone calls and e-mails, some from people I had not heard from for years, I also learned that Senator Helms was incensed with the outcome and with me. The senator who had applauded me after Rome now condemned me. The penalties descended swiftly. An international judgeship at the United Nations that Clinton had nominated me for in early January was yanked on January 31, 2001, in one of the first decisions reached by White House counsel Alberto Gonzales and President George W. Bush to reverse Clinton's legacy. Helms quickly pledged after my signature that it would be erased from the treaty,[25] and Bush and my longtime critic John Bolton, who became a high State Department official, tried to fulfill that ambition in May 2002 when Bolton sent a letter to the United Nations deactivating the legal effect of my signature.[26] In reality, my signature remains on the treaty but with an asterisk next to it referring to the Bolton letter. However, a new letter could nullify the effect of Bolton's missive and resurrect the legal authority of the signature on the treaty, thus identifying the United States once again as a signatory nation and preparing the way for ratification of the treaty someday by the U.S. Senate. So all was not lost, and I have never regretted signing the Rome Statute. In early January I joined a Washington dinner in honor of Harold Koh, the administration's top human rights official, who was departing Washington in the final days. I had attended college with Koh and worked closely with him during his tour at the State Department. Berger, Albright, and many other senior officials attended the dinner. Berger rose and gave an eloquent toast praising Koh. Then, to my utter surprise, Berger turned to me and told the gathered diners that one of his happiest moments in government service was January 1, 2001, when he opened the *New York Times*, saw my name reported, and read about my having signed the Rome Statute on behalf of the United States. Applause broke out. After eight long years, I had prevailed.

Curiously, Clinton never contacted me directly, even about the signing. I had always heard from Berger or Albright instead and conveyed views to the president through them. He had created my ambassadorship and gained considerable mileage from it as his foreign policy evolved over the years. I was relegated to shaking his hand occasionally, sitting in Principals Committee meetings in the Situation Room with him, or speaking with Hillary. I am certain this hurt our strategy on the International Criminal Court, as I needed to prod him into decisions at critical moments and never could gain access through his inner circle to do so directly.

What President Clinton's Signing Statement Meant

What disturbed me in the aftermath of the treaty signing was the way in which President Clinton's signing statement has been distorted by the treaty's critics. Clinton's December 31, 2000, statement was a precisely worded articulation of why the United States signed the treaty and what remained to be done in order to advance the prospect of serious consideration of ratification of it in the future.[27] There were three main points in the statement. First, Clinton reaffirmed "our strong support for international accountability and for bringing to justice perpetrators of genocide, war crimes, and crimes against humanity." Signing the treaty would sustain the "tradition of moral leadership" of the United States in advancing the principle of accountability from Nuremberg through the establishment of the Yugoslav and Rwanda tribunals.

Second, he emphasized the importance of the complementarity principle in the treaty and that the U.S. delegation had worked hard to achieve the limitations on the prosecutor that are part of the complementarity regime, which the United States believes "are essential to the international credibility and success of the ICC."

Third, President Clinton stated: "We are not abandoning our concerns about significant flaws in the Treaty. In particular, we are concerned that when the Court comes into existence, it will not only exercise authority over personnel of states that have ratified the Treaty, but also claim jurisdiction over personnel of States that have not. With signature, however, we will be in a position to influence the evolution of the Court. Without signature, we will not." The use of the term "significant flaws" was not easily arrived at during the final hours of the decision-making process at Camp David, in Washington, and on the Amtrak train on the morning of December 31. I believed there were flaws in the treaty, but I did not believe that a description of them as "significant" either was accurate or would improve our leverage as a signatory. Allied governments did not view as "significant" the flaws we had long identified. Further, the term would only provide ammunition to the opponents of the court on Capitol Hill and elsewhere, as it did, to recklessly bash the treaty, using our own words to do so. Our work in building safeguards into the treaty regime had diminished the significance of the flaws that I had identified before the Senate Foreign Relations Committee on July 23, 1998. Clinton's statement went on to recognize achievements in the post-Rome negotiations. But "significant" was the word that accommodated the skeptics within the administration, particularly at the Pentagon, so it remained.

Clinton recommended that his successor, George W. Bush, not "submit the Treaty to the Senate for advice and consent until our fundamental concerns are satisfied." This was consistent with the administration's longstanding position on ratification, and in any event it would have been impossible, with only twenty days remaining in his presidency, to prepare the treaty for submission for ratification to the Senate. That exercise alone usually takes years for any treaty. But thereafter critics distorted the language to say that Clinton signed the treaty without any intent to ratify it, which was not the case at all. The issue was when to ratify it and under what conditions.

The key concern was that "Court jurisdiction over U.S. personnel should come only with U.S. ratification of the Treaty." This reflected the rather complex and paradoxical point we had been making for years about the jurisdiction of the court. Despite the Pentagon's wish for full immunity regardless of whether the United States was a party to the Rome Statute, the central American concern had been exposure of U.S. personnel while the United States remained a *nonparty* to the treaty. We faced an awkward dilemma: *We argued for protection as a nonparty state in order to build domestic support for ultimately signing the Rome Statute and joining the court as a state party.* So we needed to see evidence of such protection *prior* to ratifying the treaty when, as a state party, we would lose it.

I soon came to understand, however, that the Rome Statute has, by intent or otherwise, a self-correcting mechanism on the exposure of nationals of nonparty states to the court's jurisdiction. The final days in Rome were chaotic, and provisions in the treaty that had been negotiated over several years and then jumbled in the endgame nonetheless created a surprisingly workable solution to the American problem with the court—and I doubt anyone, including my delegation, realized it on that final night in Rome. Several articles of the Rome Statute were drafted under the premise that a state and, in the context of the article, its nationals would only be covered by the statute as of a date sixty days *after* the state ratified the treaty. Under Article 11(2), the court can only exercise jurisdiction for atrocity crimes committed *after* entry into force of the Rome Statute for the ratifying state. Article 24, which prohibits *ex post facto* enforcement of the statute, only makes sense when read with Article 11(2) if it means, "No person shall be criminally responsible under this Statute for conduct prior to the entry into force of the Statute *for the State of nationality of such person.*" (I have added the italicized words to show the logical meaning of the provision.) Otherwise, any nonparty country such as the United States or China or India or Israel or Egypt would have to accept the proposition that a future ratification of the Rome Statute by any of them would be meaningless because their nationals have been covered by the statute since July 1, 2002, when the court became operational, anyway!

No government would ratify the Rome Statute if it was acknowledging by that act that its nationals were fair game for prosecution for actions reaching all the way back to 2002, long before it ratified the treaty. No existing member of the court has invited it to examine conduct of its nationals prior to its own ratification of the Rome Statute. Of the three state party referrals being investigated in 2011, all three countries (Uganda, Democratic Republic of the Congo, and the Central African Republic) ratified the Rome Statute prior to July 1, 2002. The Darfur and Libya situations were referred by the Security Council. The investigation of the postelection violence in Kenya in 2007 and 2008 was initiated by the prosecutor in 2010. Kenya became a state party to the Rome Statute in 2005. The whole incentive structure of the treaty was to assure countries that their past conduct would not be open to investigation, so that they could start with a clean slate of compliance with atrocity law and be judged on only their *future* performance and not their past sins (unless the Security Council had already tagged any one of them with a referral to the court or there had been explicit state consent for the court's jurisdiction).

The ratification procedure has to have some meaning, as negotiators intended it to have from the beginning, and that meaning is to subject a country's population to the jurisdiction of the court under any one of three scenarios: as a ratified state party to the treaty for alleged crimes committed after ratification (or perhaps with that state party's express consent for pre-ratification crimes); with the nonparty's explicit consent under a special declaration provided for in Article 12(3) for crimes that indeed could reach back to July 1, 2002; or following a Security Council enforcement resolution (such as occurred for Darfur in 2005 and Libya in 2011) that refers the atrocity crimes of a situation perpetrated by the nationals of a nonparty state or on the territory of a nonparty state to the court, again for any designated period of time provided it falls after July 1, 2002.[28]

Many would cry "foul" at my interpretation of the treaty, as it challenges an unvarnished application of Article 12, whereby the preconditions to jurisdiction are only if either the state of nationality of the perpetrator or the state of the territory on which the atrocity crime occurred is a state party. But Article 12 cannot extinguish the logical meaning of other articles of the treaty that were meant to separate nonparty states (and their nationals) from states parties. Acceptance of this understanding of the Rome Statute would vastly simplify the issue in the United States and other major nonparty states and enable everyone to focus on steps toward ratification and toward near universal membership in the court.

The second prong of Clinton's conclusion in his signing statement was that "signature is the right action to take at this point." He continued, "I believe that a properly constituted and structured International Criminal Court would make a profound contribution in deterring egregious human rights abuses worldwide, and that signature increases the chances for productive discussions with other governments to advance these goals in the months and years ahead." For the United States to have entered 2001 as a nonsignatory of the Rome Statute would have aligned the country, whether fairly or not, with such nonsignatory states as the People's Republic of China, Pakistan, North Korea, Egypt, Libya, Syria, Cuba, Vietnam, Indonesia, Iran, and Iraq as seeming rejectionists of international justice.[29] Bill Clinton continued to speak favorably of the court in the aftermath of his presidency.[30]

The End of Leadership

Regrettably, the incoming Bush administration abandoned the Preparatory Commission talks in early 2001. Bush also forfeited all the safeguard provisions I had lined up, with foreign support, for debate and likely approval in 2001, and he and his lieutenants trashed America's recognition of the value of the International Criminal Court after the Bolton letter arrived at the United Nations in May 2002.[31] Bush's signature of the American Service-Members' Protection Act a few months later constituted a direct assault on the court and all governments that joined it or dared to consider supporting it.[32] The American seat in further negotiations remained vacant throughout the Bush administration even though all an American diplomat had to do to take advantage of observer status was to sit, listen, and watch. As the years passed, most other major nonparty states appeared as engaged observer governments at meetings of the court's Assembly of States Parties, particularly in talks on the crime of aggression. But the American voice remained silent as Bush administration officials appeared too intimidated even to observe the court. The era of American leadership in the arena of international justice had passed.

PART III

CHAPTER TEN

CRIME SCENE KOSOVO

With the exception of Rwanda in 1994 and Cambodia in 1975, you would be hard pressed to find a crime scene anywhere in the world since World War II where a defenseless civilian population has been assaulted with such ferocity and criminal intent and suffered so many multiple violations of international humanitarian law in such a short period of time, as in Kosovo.

The author, speaking to the State Department
press corps on May 10, 1999

MORE THAN TWO YEARS AFTER THE DAYTON PEACE AGREEMENT, WHEN THE atrocity crimes being investigated by the Yugoslav Tribunal were thought to have ceased, brutality swept over the landlocked Serbian province of Kosovo, which is located south of Bosnia and Herzegovina, east of Albania, and just north of Macedonia. For several years, the Kosovo Liberation Army (KLA), which was a guerrilla force of Kosovar-Albanians of Muslim faith dedicated to the liberation of the Kosovo province from the sovereignty of the Christian-dominated Federal Republic of Yugoslavia, had waged a violent campaign against Serb civilians and Serb government offices in Kosovo. The KLA became an obvious target, and rationale, for Serb military and police interventions into Kosovo to confront its secessionist actions. Repressive Serbian tactics demonstrated little mercy to Muslim civilians caught up in the secessionist struggle. Slobodan Milosevic's mission of death and mayhem in his crumbling Yugoslavia was not finished in 1995. He had one more campaign of ethnic cleansing to wage.

The Kosovo conflict of 1998 and 1999 became a major test for the Yugoslav Tribunal and for those governments actively supporting it. The catastrophic conflict in the Balkans that generated the tribunal's mandate for justice had ended in December 1995 with the signing of the Dayton Peace Agreement in Paris. How could it be, several years later, that the Yugoslav Tribunal would be reactivated for another round of atrocity crimes, only this time in the southern reaches of the former Yugoslavia? The Serbian leadership in Belgrade and their Russian allies believed the tribunal's mandate ceased with the Dayton accords; Washington, London, Paris, and other capitals viewed the mandate quite differently, as there was no literal end date established for the tribunal and the same men who had laid waste Bosnia and Croatia had turned their attention to another geographical slice of the tribunal's territorial jurisdiction: Kosovo. The interlude between Dayton and the Kosovo conflict was notable, but irrelevant.

Milosevic and the senior Serb leadership may have ignored the Yugoslav Tribunal during the early years of the Balkans conflict, but they were doing so at their extreme peril by these final years of the 1990s. The leaders of the Kosovo assault (other than Milosevic, who was indicted and tried for the Kosovo crimes but died before judgment) were prosecuted, and all but one were convicted and are serving stiff sentences handed down by the Yugoslav Tribunal.[1] Meanwhile, by the time the assault began, many American officials, including myself, had learned hard lessons from the Rwanda genocide of 1994 and the Srebrenica genocide of 1995, and we were determined not to repeat our mistakes. By then, the tribunal was a potent judicial tool, and I had enough support from President Clinton, Secretary of State Madeleine Albright, Secretary of Defense William Cohen, and other top officials in Washington to wield it like a battering ram in the execution of U.S. and NATO policy.

The Killing Begins

In early March of 1998, Muslim refugees fled from Serbian-inspired violence against them that itself often responded to KLA attacks.[2] The magnitude of the Serbian actions in Kosovo appeared large enough to trigger the Yugoslav Tribunal's jurisdiction, and that is what we concluded in Washington. Louise Arbour, the Yugoslav Tribunal prosecutor, privately held this view but needed more facts on the ground to state it publicly.

Article 1 of the tribunal statute appeared straightforward and inviting in regard to the Kosovo situation: "The International Tribunal shall have the power to prosecute persons responsible for serious violations of international humanitarian law committed in the territory of the former Yugoslavia since 1991 in accordance with the provisions of the present Statute." Kosovo was part of the former Yugoslavia, and it had always been part of the larger discussion about the future of peace and security in the Balkans. Indeed, President George H. W. Bush had warned Milosevic in December 1992 not to assault Kosovo.[3] The security of Kosovo was a key component of Clinton's six-point plan of February 10, 1993, and a pillar of the "outer wall" of sanctions against Serbia, which Albright had long fought to maintain. Belgrade must have known that any assault on Kosovo, regardless of KLA provocations, essentially would be red meat for an American response and most likely NATO action.

In short order, on March 10, 1998, Arbour confirmed the Yugoslav Tribunal's jurisdiction over Kosovo and the violence unfolding there. On June 12 and again in July 1998, Arbour affirmed publicly that events in Kosovo constituted an internal armed conflict, which then gave her the factual prerequisite for bringing indictments against either Serb or KLA leaders for crimes against humanity or violations of the laws and customs of war.[4] Arbour requested that I transmit to the tribunal as quickly as possible Washington's intake of detailed information about developments in Kosovo so that she could strengthen her own investigations.

The month of August 1998 proved decisive. Fighting consumed most of Kosovo.[5] Belgrade denied me a visa to visit Kosovo. That snub only inspired me to organize a briefing for Arbour in Washington about the armed conflict, with evidence of Serb aggression and Serb-initiated killings and destruction mapped out along a timeline. The Serbs were trying to create a public record of attacking the KLA as "terrorists" rather than as an armed resistance in Kosovo. The reason for the distinction lay in the Yugoslav Tribunal statute, which invoked jurisdiction over crimes against humanity with respect to an armed conflict—the issue that had dogged the statute-writing exercise back in 1993. The prosecutor's determination that the Yugoslav Tribunal had jurisdiction over the fighting in Kosovo would be seriously undermined if the Serbs made a convincing case that the KLA was simply a terrorist organization engaged in terrorist acts of violence rather than an army of soldiers engaged in an armed conflict. Awkwardly, the senior U.S.

envoy to the region labeled the KLA a terrorist group as late as February 23, 1998,[6] which could have undermined Arbour's theory of jurisdiction and emboldened Belgrade in its denial of tribunal jurisdiction. But Washington lifted the terrorist label within days thereafter because the KLA had essentially transformed into the most viable opponent to Serbian military and paramilitary assaults into Kosovo. From Washington's perspective, the KLA needed to be an armed force locked in combat at that point to blunt the Serbian threat to Kosovo's autonomy. If there had been no Balkans conflict of the 1990s, there might never have been the metamorphosis of the KLA from terrorist organization to armed force in the eyes of Washington policymakers. But the history of Serbian-led atrocity crimes provided a compelling case for supporting a viable and growing opposition in Kosovo.

Getting to Yes on an Atrocity Crimes Investigation

Human rights activists sought indictment of Milosevic for the criminal assaults sweeping through Kosovo in the summer and fall of 1998. Meanwhile, the French claimed that Kosovo invited a very difficult assessment: while there was no doubt about evidence of wanton destruction, they thought it might not amount to ethnic cleansing. I knew the facts were beginning to challenge that assessment, but the French were right to be as rigorous as Arbour proved to be in the following weeks. Between July 26 and the end of August 1998, the Serb offensives in central and western Kosovo damaged over one-third of the villages, and about one-fourth of their structures suffered significant damage. No fewer than four thousand houses had been severely damaged or destroyed. Most of the destruction was caused by deliberate torching of structures—either as a punitive measure or to conceal looting—after civilians had fled and the area was secured by Serb forces. Fifty-nine towns sustained significant damage to 50 percent or more of their structures and at least 105 towns were less than 50 percent damaged. There was no evidence of detention camps or mass graves at that point. The numbers of internally displaced persons, however, were staggering. U.S. analysts gauged the total at 360,000 while Catholic Relief Services estimated 320,000. Kosovar-Albanians had been forced to abandon their homes. These forced evictions could not be justified under any military doctrine. Mosques also were being destroyed in a manner reminiscent of what had occurred to religious buildings during the ethnic cleansing of Bosnia and Herzegovina.

One nongovernmental organization estimated that eighteen thousand homes had been damaged, far exceeding Washington's assessment. The farmers could not harvest in devastated fields and were outcasts in their own homeland. A lot of medical aid was blocked systematically, and only about 5 percent of humanitarian needs were met. There also had been reports of firing on refugees. Meanwhile, civil society groups griped about Arbour and complained that she seemed profoundly disinterested in Kosovo. They accused her of refusing to launch any investigation unless she was certain of getting someone to The Hague to stand trial. In their view, she wanted a high batting average and thus was waiting to implicate Milosevic. Human Rights Watch called on Arbour to be more aggressive and to deter further crimes and abuses by launching investigations. The group also urged her to publicly hype the Yugoslav Tribunal and its jurisdiction over events in Kosovo. They wanted Arbour to confirm that Milosevic held command responsibility and was not outside the reach of the tribunal.[7]

The situation on the ground worsened. The Serb army and police burned more homes and sponsored sniper attacks on Kosovar-Albanians. The KLA, with a command and control and logistics infrastructure in Albania, responded as a combatant force would under such circumstances. There was wild speculation about the numbers of civilian deaths. But this much we could conclude: the damage was disproportionate to any combat requirement. Crop burning was widespread and nasty, with deliberate killings of livestock in the fields and barns. Suddenly, villages suffered significant damage, mosques were burned down, and, without any apparent military necessity, thousands of civilians were violently evicted from their homes.

On September 1, 1998, I consulted with Arbour in The Hague. Although she had earlier confirmed tribunal jurisdiction, she was not yet prepared to conclude, at least publicly, that the actions and the magnitude of atrocities in Kosovo actually rose to criminal conduct that would merit her formal investigation. She scoffed at the "amateurs in the NGOs [nongovernmental organizations]." Two weeks later Milosevic told the State Department's human rights assistant secretary, John Shattuck, that Kosovar-Albanian anarchy would be the Serbs' green light to invade Kosovo. The Serbian leader boasted that he would scorch the earth until the snow fell.

Later that month, we examined in Washington what might tie Milosevic to the violence in Kosovo. Aside from his boast to Shattuck, it was all inferential information. We knew his surrogates were out there in the field, but there was no evidence of daily phone calls, no note takers that we knew of at his meetings, and we had no meaningful intelligence on other fronts. Nor did we discover any grand strategic direction. There was no proof of his direct involvement or that he ordered specific criminal acts in the field. There was not even a cold, let alone smoking, gun. But Arbour had set her sights on Milosevic and prioritized investigative priorities to target him. It was still relatively early in the commission of atrocity crimes in Kosovo, and no one knew that the worst was yet to come.

The Principals Committee met in early October 1998 to discuss Kosovo. The massacres and humanitarian crises were self-evident departure points for discussion. The United States and its European allies had completed consultations for use of NATO airpower in Kosovo if that proved necessary. NATO had approved various measures and requisitioned more assets to stand ready for military action in Kosovo. But, beyond such preparations and approval, any action such as air strikes required an Activation Order, which would explicitly order military commanders to act in Kosovo. Albright later that day told me, "Kosovo is not Bosnia following Srebrenica. It's more complicated, and it will take time to get NATO activated on it."

Judge Gabrielle McDonald, who had succeeded Antonio Cassese as president of the Yugoslav Tribunal, confided to me that Karadzic and Mladic thought they could ignore Security Council orders, indirectly placing Kosovo at risk. She believed that Belgrade's noncompliance must be dealt with once and for all. Russia's view on the council was distressing, she said, for Moscow categorically opposed any special operations by NATO, arguing that they would violate the Dayton Peace Agreement. In addition, they contended, any forced seizure and arrest of indictees in Kosovo or Serbia would violate NATO rules prohibiting operations in those areas. They conceded that Belgrade always could be reminded of its obligations, but Russia would object to any resolution that violated Moscow's interpretation of Dayton. Russia recoiled at Arbour's description of "Serbian aggression in Kosovo." Moscow also opposed the use of sealed warrants and strongly complained about how arrests were being made in Bosnia and Herzegovina. We had known for months that Russia likely would veto any Security Council resolution authorizing the use of armed force against the Serb forces in Kosovo.

Meanwhile, the degree of criminality in Kosovo only worsened as summer turned to fall in 1998. There was a systematic character to the civilian destruction and mistreatment of internally displaced persons (IDPs), who suffered retaliation for any Serb deaths in Kosovo. The IDPs endured segregation and detention. Many were beaten. Some shootings were at very close

range, no more than ten feet away. In September, Milosevic launched a calculated offensive throughout Kosovo. When it was finished, villages burned
in its wake, and IDPs were streaming everywhere. There was agreement in
Washington that Richard Holbrooke, drafted back into service to negotiate
an agreement with Milosevic that would stop the Kosovo rampage, at least
for a while, needed to incorporate a strong Yugoslav Tribunal component
into his talks. The Organization for Security and Cooperation in Europe
(OSCE) Mission in Kosovo would have to be proactive and uncover human
rights abuses and atrocity crimes with the help of forensic and international
humanitarian law experts.

In November 1998, I visited Belgrade to attend a conference on, of all
things, war crimes. Lacking a special visa and without notifying the Belgrade
authorities, I joined U.S. embassy staff who drove me in the early morning
darkness south to Pristina, the capital of Kosovo. When we arrived, a firefight had just ended in Malisevo, a town southwest of Pristina, between the
Serbian Ministry of Interior Police (MUP) and the KLA. I traveled there with
a U.S. Kosovo Diplomatic Observer Mission (KDOM) team and saw two
Serb policemen who had been gunned down and were lying facedown on a
street. Some residents took us to a body, decomposing for an estimated
three weeks, in a well.

Outside the town of Golubovac, I met an old man who had witnessed
torture and murders while hiding behind a wall at his farm. He had seen
two Serb "commanders," one sitting on top of a mound of dirt while the
other crouched near some Kosovar-Albanian prisoners, who were farmers.
Serbian soldiers used a big stick to beat and stab them. They used a smaller
stick, converted into a pitchfork, to gouge out the prisoners' eyes. Both commanders then shot the prisoners dead after the soldiers had tortured them.
There were burial sites nearby, which would prove critical for forensics. The
prongs of the pitchfork that had been used to stab and torture were still at
the site. We told the witness to collect and save all evidence and produce it
only to the tribunal investigators. The old man worried about his safety and
said the French, Germans, and others had already been there, so he felt like
a marked man. I left him the business card of tribunal investigator Dennis
Milner and told him I would inform Milner to go to the farm to collect the
murder weapons, shell casings, and other evidence.

Startled Serbian authorities in Pristina with whom I met ("How did you get
here!?") claimed there was no combat, only clashes between terrorists and
police forces. There were, by their count, 306 villages where "antiterrorist

actions" had been necessary. As I tumbled along the rutted Kosovo back roads with a KDOM observer team, I saw countless burned-out farmhouses and demolished village neighborhoods. Kosovo was afire, and diplomats were trying feverishly to douse the flames. Slow-motion ethnic cleansing already was upon us.

Back in Washington a week later, I more clearly understood speculation that Kosovo was "hanging by a thread" and, later in December, that it was a "tinderbox." The Deputies Committee discussed the certainty, if it were put to a vote in the Security Council, of Russia vetoing Yugoslav Tribunal jurisdiction over the atrocity crimes in Kosovo. Belgrade claimed it was a violation of Serbia's constitution to surrender anyone to the Yugoslav Tribunal. The Serbs also asserted that the tribunal had no jurisdiction in Kosovo because no armed conflict existed. And they claimed that the Holbrooke-Milosevic agreement of October 1998 superseded the Dayton Agreement of 1995, which in any case said nothing about Kosovo. For all these reasons, in Belgrade's view, the Serbs did not have to cooperate with the tribunal.

Račak Massacre

As the new year dawned, Arbour attempted to visit Kosovo, but Belgrade still denied her a visa. In mid-January 1999, forty-five Kosovar-Albanians were massacred near Račak in Kosovo.[8] It appeared that Serbs had executed the Muslim farmers. William Walker, the American envoy to the Kosovo Verification Mission (KVM), concluded as much, publicly, during his visit to the killing site while the bodies still lay scattered in a gully. That blunt assessment inflamed the Belgrade authorities, who declared him persona non grata.[9]

I spoke with Arbour in the immediate aftermath of the Račak massacre. NATO had issued a strong statement on the need for Yugoslav Tribunal access to Kosovo. The NATO Activation Order was on a hair trigger. Arbour told me she had hoped the North Atlantic Council would say that if she was not permitted entry into Kosovo, then NATO would take her in itself. She was not hopeful that another banging of fists would accomplish anything. If Belgrade flatly denied her entry again, then someone had to help her and tribunal investigators physically enter Kosovo. She needed access to people who were eyewitnesses and thus had to cross the border to interview them. For example, five witnesses were in Pristina Hospital under MUP guard, and KDOM knew at all times the status of those individuals. She just needed to reach them in person.

Arbour traveled to Macedonia and waited at the border with Kosovo, trying to cross it.[10] She had been coaxed there by NATO governments and NGOs, but she was no happy camper as the hours and days ticked by. On January 20, Holbrooke called me while I was on a visit to Cambodia to say that Arbour was still languishing at the border. It had become a circus atmosphere, and Arbour rejected any compromise regarding what she would investigate once inside Kosovo. The Security Council had issued a strong presidential statement on Kosovo the night before, with China surprisingly being helpful in allowing language insisting on cooperation with the tribunal to be inserted in the text.[11] But Arbour never entered Kosovo that month, owing to the Serbs' intransigence at the border.

On January 22, in the aftermath of the Kosovo border fiasco, Arbour told me in The Hague that the handling of the Walker issue was abysmal. Washington had turned Walker into a matter of principle and insisted that he remain on duty in Kosovo even after Belgrade declared him persona non grata. But in standing firm on Walker, we had given the Serbs even more reason to keep Arbour out of Kosovo. She had advised the OSCE about how to monitor the situation in Kosovo so as to collect valuable information for the tribunal. But her instructions were never distributed to the KDOM monitors. She believed the Račak massacre occurred because the Serbs thought they could get away with it. The fact that Walker, representing the OSCE, had immediately fingered Serbs with responsibility for the massacre undermined her task. How could Serbs expect to see a fair trial if they were branded so quickly by such a prominent official, she asked? Even if an expected Finnish report on the massacre[12] proved to be a competent one, the tribunal investigators still needed to get into Kosovo to conduct their own inquiries. Arbour insisted she would need access to every KVM monitor who visited the massacre site and talked to the Finnish team. She also needed a complete chronology of the monitors' actions. My work was cut out for me.

By late January 1999, all NATO allies had agreed to the Activation Order on Kosovo.[13] The Serb military was on the move. NATO granted authority to its secretary-general to take military action. Albright's last-ditch peace talks on Kosovo were about to begin in Rambouillet, France, and would occupy the world's attention during the month of February.

Ethnic Cleansing

As the Rambouillet talks stumbled forward, it became increasingly clear that the Serbs would continue to deny Arbour and her investigators access to Kosovo. We had to find a back door. The Rambouillet agreement provided for "international organizations" to have access to Kosovo. The Yugoslav Tribunal in fact is an international organization. By reference to Security Council resolutions describing the tribunal's mandate, we could establish the hook for the tribunal and insist, for example, on the right to visas for its investigators. But the idea had no time to gain traction.

On March 9, the Serbs adamantly refused to accept a NATO force in Kosovo.[14] What did Milosevic want, we asked ourselves? Did he want only to instill in all of us the terror of his threatening a war, or did he really want to unleash his war machine on Kosovo? The answer came quickly. Intense fighting and looting erupted in Kosovo on March 19, 1999. The OSCE monitors and staff evacuated quickly, along with about fourteen hundred civil society personnel. The Serb offensive against Kosovo had begun with a ferocity that exceeded Deputy Secretary of State Strobe Talbott's earlier observation, delivered at his morning meeting with senior officials: "The Serbs are picking off a village a day in Kosovo." We had no doubts about who struck first in Kosovo and what would likely unfold if Milosevic were left unchallenged.[15]

Shortly thereafter, Holbrooke met with Milosevic in Belgrade for almost six hours. Talbott told senior officials in the State Department that if Holbrooke hit a stone wall, then NATO's airpower would be unleashed within days. Russia's foreign minister, Yevgeny Primakov, was en route to Washington. Julia Taft, the assistant secretary of state for population, refugees, and migration, reported that the humanitarian situation in Kosovo was deteriorating rapidly. Seventy thousand Muslims were homeless. But the policy was set that no U.S. troops would go into a nonpermissive environment. We knew airpower was our only viable weapon.

On March 22, the NATO bombing campaign began. The next day, Holbrooke reported no major breakthrough in his talks with Milosevic. Serbian missiles were being aimed at Tuzla and other U.S. bases in Bosnia, raising the stakes considerably in Washington. We learned later that by March 14 the Yugoslav Army (VJ) and the MUP knew that orders would arrive from Belgrade to launch an ethnic cleansing campaign against Kosovar-Albanians in Kosovo with the start of the NATO bombing. The Serbs recognized that they would lose men, equipment, and other facilities to NATO bombing, but in the end, they believed, the costs would be worth the benefit of the Kosovo problem being solved once and for all. They would premise their long-planned ethnic cleansing on the excuse that NATO bombing had somehow triggered the great exodus from Kosovo. Rarely has such a bogus excuse for atrocity crimes been dumped into the public marketplace.

Three days later, on March 25, Washington had majority support in the Security Council for the military response. But Russia's ambassador, Sergei Lavrov, invoked his view of international law to block the resolution. This prompted Talbott to tell me and others that he needed to use a stronger legal argument to rebut Lavrov.

In retrospect, a popular conclusion about the NATO bombing campaign launched in March 1999 in response to the Serb actions has been that it was "illegal but legitimate."[16] At the time, there were heated discussions within the State Department, the National Security Council, and the Pentagon about precisely how to justify the bombing campaign. The State Department's deputy legal adviser, Michael Matheson, conceded that there were two lines of possible reasoning. The first pointed to a clear violation of international law, due to the failure to obtain an explicit Security Council resolution authorizing the use of force against Serbia to protect the people of Kosovo. Russia was determined to prevent any such resolution from being adopted.

The second rationale provided an authoritative, albeit controversial, justification that consisted of a cluster of points invoking past Security Council resolutions addressing the Kosovo situation, solid NATO authorization to use airpower, and humanitarian concerns, but stopping short of invoking the age-old doctrine of humanitarian intervention. A more straightforward rationale, such as an appeal for collective self-defense from Kosovo's neighbors, Albania and Macedonia, inundated with Muslim refugees, would have established the "legality" requirement in the absence of a Security Council authorization. But the collective self-defense option, which I argued for within the State Department, was never employed.[17]

At Talbott's next morning meeting, reports of atrocities dominated the discussion. I raised the need for a strong public statement on accountability for such atrocities and also for saying that the United States was "eyes on" the violence and destruction sweeping across Kosovo, even though we had no one on the ground there. In his briefing to senators later that day, Undersecretary of State for Political Affairs Tom Pickering mentioned the possibility of a two-month bombing campaign. The senators considered such a long bombing run "impossible." It ended up falling just short of two months.

On March 27, 1999, reports arrived of a massive campaign of expulsions of ethnic Albanians from Kosovo. Five to seven abreast were flooding across the Albanian border. There were signs of hasty departures and movements to the border with little luggage. Women wore bedroom slippers, and children marched without shoes and socks. Refugees claimed that thousands more were in the mountains trying to reach Albania. They told the media that security forces had burned their houses, forced them into trains, and herded them toward the border. Few men were among the refugees. The Albanian press reported summary executions of military-age males and prominent ethnic Albanian intellectuals. The refugee flow toward Macedonia slowed, but we speculated that had occurred because of a lag in their internal processing by the Serbs.

Shortly thereafter, I spoke with Arbour about the KDOM and KVM monitors operating among the refugees and coordinating with the tribunal. Arbour wanted to keep their interviewing of witnesses low-key until she could get her own tribunal investigators and interviewers into Albania and Macedonia, which she planned to do as soon as possible.

Ethnic cleansing had enveloped the Pristina region of Kosovo. The MUP were requesting VJ assistance, so the two forces were beginning to undertake more coordinated efforts. Since the fighting had begun in earnest, 560,000 people, more than one-fourth of Kosovo's preconflict population, had been displaced. Among them, 280,000 remained in Kosovo, 20,000 were in Serbia, 62,000 had fled to Montenegro, 14,000 had made it all the way to Bosnia, and 75,000 had reached Albania. Another 26,000 Kosovar-Albanians were in Macedonia, 80,000 in western Europe, and 3,300 in Turkey. On March 23 alone, 15,000 refugees crossed into Albania, 14,000 into Macedonia, and 30,000 into Montenegro. The Serbs had deployed into Kosovo almost 41,000 troops, including 300 tanks, 300 armored vehicles, 180 pieces of artillery, 15,000 MUP, and 5,000 special police. Over the prior weekend, the Serbs distributed pamphlets in Pristina warning Kosovar-Albanians to leave Kosovo or be killed.

It was not difficult to conclude, as early as March 28, that ethnic cleansing had been unleashed on Kosovo. The Serbs were using the NATO bombing of military targets as a pretext to accelerate the ethnic cleansing campaign. There were significant forced expulsions, summary executions, and destructions of civilian housing of Muslim families. The violence appeared so widespread and systematic that the basis for the Yugoslav Tribunal's jurisdiction over crimes against humanity in an armed conflict had been met.

In Mitrovica, originally numbering seventy thousand residents, only a few ethnic Kosovar-Albanians were left. Kosovar-Albanians were expelled from Pec, Prizren, Suva Reka, Orahovac, and Dakovica. Serb forces confiscated all belongings, personal documentation, and license plates. Serb-distributed pamphlets in Pristina warned Kosovar-Albanians "to leave this country or we will kill you." Intense fighting was spreading from one settlement to the next. Special volunteers of the VJ had been readied to enter Kosovo and operate as discrete groups of "irregulars" only nominally under VJ control. The "Wolves of Vucijak," which had operated in Croatia in 1991 and then in Bosnia and Herzegovina, had departed for Kosovo. The paramilitary forces of Zeljko Arkan, a notorious Serbian war criminal indicted by the Yugoslav Tribunal in 1997, were seen in the Pristina area and along the Albanian border committing massacres.

The American ambassador to Macedonia, Christopher Hill, and General Wesley Clark, who commanded NATO, requested that I fly into the region to bear witness to atrocities occurring in Kosovo. I flew to Ramstein, Germany, and then hopped aboard a U.S. military aircraft to Skopje, Macedonia, where, on March 31, I met with Ambassador Hill. He was deeply concerned that war would spill over into Macedonia and that the country might not survive the onslaught. (I asked him, rhetorically, what more was required for a legal claim of "collective self-defense"?) He believed other countries simply were not interested in the plight of the Kosovar-Albanian refugees. We talked about a U.N. trust territory or NATO protectorate for Kosovo. (Within several months Kosovo would become a U.N.-administered entity.)

On the same day, I met with observers from the Organization for Security and Cooperation in Europe. They had operated with great courage inside Kosovo and had been interviewing the refugees in Macedonia and Albania. Their interview notes and observations about what was occurring inside Kosovo were chilling and destined for the tribunal as evidence. They described, for example, how Serb civilians were seen gathering at 6:00 a.m. and changing into MUP uniforms. There were eighty thousand MUPs in Kosovo. The MUP typically "cleansed" a town first, and then the VJ moved in with a support role. The Serbs moved from house to house executing people in their homes. Serb forces and paramilitary fired indiscriminately into groups of refugees streaming toward Albania. The KVM monitors sent 120 pictures of the ethnic cleansing to the tribunal, with a duplicate set passed on to Washington. In Pristina, food shelves were stripped bare and all manner of shops looted.

Witness on the Border

For the first three days of April 1999, I visited and witnessed thousands of Kosovar-Albanian refugees cross the border into Macedonia at Deneral Jankovic. I conducted scores of interviews, seeking information about expulsions, killings, ethnic persecution, burnings, rapes, torture, serious bodily or mental harm to members of the group, as well as descriptions about the Serb leadership and how it was organized. I wanted to convey to Albright and other officials in Washington, as well as to the media, as quickly as possible what the refugees had experienced. My purpose was not to compile witness testimony for the Yugoslav Tribunal, as I knew that required a different means of handling the refugees. Rather, I needed both Washington and the wider public audience to understand immediately what was transpiring on the other side of the border. We had aerial photography that we matched with what I and others were hearing from the refugees, thus forming a composite of facts and timelines of the ethnic cleansing campaign.

There was human misery everywhere. During one of my nights at the border, rain fell relentlessly. All were exposed to the elements, as tents were nowhere to be seen. No one had eaten. About ten thousand refugees huddled in that field. Some had walked three or four days to the crossing rather than wait for a crowded train. At the field hospital, many suffered from gunshot wounds. I saw the medical team spend one hour removing fragments of a sweater from the burned flesh of one child while he screamed. There were many with broken arms. One man told me he had seen, from his train window, a body burning in a field. He estimated there had been fifteen thousand Muslims at the train station in Pristina waiting to leave while he was there. There were few doctors in that crowd at the station, and many of them were overwhelmed with pleadings for help. The disabled—the frail, the injured, the ill, anyone unable to walk very far—could not get to the station; they were simply being murdered in their homes. As I walked the crowded muddy field that rain-soaked night, I came upon a baby who had just died in his mother's arms. I had never felt so helpless in my entire life.

Periodically during my days among the refugees, I used a satellite phone to call the State Department Operations Center and convey some of what I was learning to Albright, Jamie Rubin (the State Department spokesman), and other top officials. They needed to know such information in real time. I also interviewed with the media at my hotel in Skopje and conveyed to American and international audiences what I had seen and heard.

After several days in Macedonia and along the border with Kosovo, I returned to Washington to oversee the atrocity crimes monitoring that would occupy every day until the Serbs finally stood down in June. On my flight home, I wrote down my raw impressions:

> There was remarkable consistency in what the refugees told me. They described hallmarks of widespread and systematic crimes against humanity. The pattern was to kick down the door, loot, shake down the victims, beatings, five minutes to leave, drop bags, forced marches, applauding the agony of the victims. At the train station, crowds were huddled for many hours. Snipers picked off marchers. Women were separated from their children, as were men from their wives. "Leave or die" was the constant refrain. I felt like challenging Milosevic: prove us wrong. Show how the testimonies of thousands can somehow be denied by your commander. How can so many refugees, chosen at random, tell such a consistent story? These are the indicators of genocide, and intent is inferred by what has happened on the ground. I met an army of witnesses. Whatever future NATO determines for the Serbs, there is another counterforce: the thousands of witnesses of Milosevic's reign of terror and death who are relating what they experienced. The Serb leaders need to defend themselves against not only the NATO force, but also the rule of law. Just as the military campaign requires our perseverance and patience, so too will the wheels of justice. But just as NATO is determined to defeat the Yugoslav army, so too will those who have perpetrated these crimes be brought to justice. In the end the Kosovar Albanians will prevail, in the court of law and on the future of Kosovo.

No one can stand among thousands of destitute and arguing refugees, as I did, and conclude that the perpetrators will somehow evade the bar of justice. It will take years to finish that part of this outrage, and we will support the Yugoslav Tribunal and whatever competent and fair domestic courts can finally be established in Kosovo until the job is finished. I honestly do not believe President Milosevic or his colleagues in crime grasp what they have unleashed—a ceaseless campaign of justice that will bring them to their knees pleading for leniency. The sooner the people of Serbia recognize that their future honor resides with the principles of international law and not the doctrine of a leadership that has forsaken civilization, the sooner they will regain the international community's trust and friendship.

NATO is poring over the targeting issue and doing all it can to avoid civilian casualties. In contrast, Milosevic is doing everything he possibly can to inflict death, terror, and ethnic cleansing on the civilian population in Kosovo. As a government, we can reach judgments as to the criminality of the Belgrade region's actions. Prosecutor Arbour will need to undertake the investigations of particular individuals and, if the evidence warrants it, indict them. We know that the government and the military it directs are perpetrating war crimes, crimes against humanity, and ethnic cleansing. The individuals within the government and military behind this systematic slaughter will one day be held accountable. Justice necessarily lags behind the violence that spawns the need for it. But every civilized society knows the powerful force of the law. We will witness in Kosovo the arsenal of law defeat the arsenal of terror and death.

Precursors of Genocide

Back in Washington, I advised Albright that there was enough evidence publicly to associate the atrocities in Kosovo with the crime of genocide, recognizing that it would be a political rather than legal determination at that stage. Then, on April 7, Defense Secretary William Cohen exposed the issue publicly when he said, "We will reject any settlement that freezes the result of Milosevic's genocide and rewards him for his brutality."[18] If we now backed away from Cohen's statement, it would recall the anguish over describing "acts of genocide" in Rwanda in 1994 that we were determined to avoid.

I had the opportunity to articulate a similar term, *indicators of genocide*, during the opening days of the Kosovo conflict, when Serb military and paramilitary forces were crossing over into Kosovo and unleashing a violent ethnic cleansing and murderous assault on the Kosovar-Albanian population.[19] I have reached the conclusion since then that an alternative term, *precursors of genocide*, would be a more appropriate one to use in the future. The term *indicators of genocide* has evolved to mean the many political, sociological, economic, military, and diplomatic events occurring long before actual genocide occurs and which point to trends that may erupt into genocide at some point in the future.[20] That is a vital exercise, and one that I engaged in intensively as chair of the U.S. government's Atrocities Prevention Interagency Working Group in 1999 and 2000, working closely with academic experts and the intelligence community on various schematic diagrams of such *indicators of genocide*. But the exercise has been refined since then to give the term *indicators* a far more rigorous lock on a host of factors, some with long lead time, leading to genocide.

The term *precursors of genocide* refers to those events occurring immediately prior to and during possible genocide that can point to an ultimate legal judgment of genocide but which should be recognized and used in a timely manner to galvanize international action to intervene, be it diplomatically, economically, or militarily. My primary concern is to employ a term that stimulates, rather than retards, effective action by governments and international organizations, particularly the United Nations, to stem the tide of genocide (whether or not, as a matter of law, what unfolds in the field is ultimately concluded to be genocide). But in 1999, as a government official struggling with dynamic events unfolding in Kosovo, I turned to the more familiar term *indicators*, without making a rigorous distinction between long-term and short-term phenomena related to genocide, and used it in largely the same context as one now would use the term *precursors*.

Before I departed Washington to visit the Kosovar-Albanian refugees on the Macedonian border, I convened an interagency meeting of intelligence, political, and military analysts and lawyers at the State Department on March 28, 1999, for several hours of discussion about how the events unfolding in Kosovo should be described publicly. In our review at the meeting, participants came fairly rapidly to the conclusion that Serb armed forces and paramilitary units were committing crimes against humanity, given the widespread and systematic character of the actions on the ground and the particular violence being unleashed.

We turned our attention to whether genocide was being committed against the Albanian population of Kosovo. As I explained to the press on April 9, 1999, many of what I called *indicators of genocide* had become apparent, and we believed it important, as a government, to state that conclusion. I described the *indicators of genocide* as including the scorched-earth policy of death and destruction that already had been recorded from the spring, summer, and fall of 1998 in Kosovo. I said, "The pattern was established in 1998. Indeed, one might consider what happened in 1998, as a practice run for what was unleashed with remarkable speed and thoroughness in the last few weeks [of March and April 1999]. Milosevic and the Serb leadership are trying to bring to closure what they began in 1998. Now, the events of the last few weeks exceed in magnitude and ferocity all that occurred in 1998. Without question Serb assaults on the civilian population of Kosovo are widespread and systematic."[21] I reminded the press of the definition in the statute of the Yugoslav Tribunal for crimes against humanity and our conclusion that many such crimes were being committed in Kosovo. I also pointed to war crimes, including the destruction of civilian property.

I extended the analysis to events that, when viewed within the context of ongoing crimes against humanity and war crimes, pointed to the crime of genocide as well. These *indicators* [*precursors*] *of genocide* occurring within a very short period of time (namely the prior three weeks) included:[22]

> 1. *The forced expulsion of large segments of the ethnic Albanian population on a scale not seen in Europe since World War II.* I showed a map demonstrating that the sites of internal population displacement and the destruction of towns were almost entirely in the ethnic Albanian regions of Kosovo. It revealed the systematic character of assaulting the Albanian areas of Kosovo "without much appreciable damage or internally displaced populations from those areas that are largely populated by Serbs." As part of the destructive pattern, I noted the "forced removal of Albanians from their homes at gun point; destruction of all official and identifying documents; cramming of Albanians into trains; infliction of unsanitary conditions on the trains, etc." At the time we saw this kind of conduct as reflecting, at a minimum, an Article 4(2)(c) violation of the Yugoslav Tribunal statute, namely "deliberately inflicting on the group conditions of life calculated to bring about its physical destruction in whole or in part."
>
> 2. *The detention and summary execution of military-age men and mass executions.* Refugees had provided accounts of summary executions in at least fifty towns and villages throughout Kosovo. I reported that "some accounts refer to large numbers of Kosovars being killed in apparent massacres." The killings included targeting of intellectuals and leaders; separating fighting-age men from the group and killing them; causing serious bodily harm; and mass executions. These events reflected the possibility of Article 4(2)(a) ("killing members of the group") and 4(2)(d) ("imposing measures intended to prevent births within the group") violations of the Yugoslav Tribunal statute.
>
> 3. *The "burning and destruction of civilian homes and villages."* I presented a map of Kosovo showing 220 sites of village destruction and said that as of April 9, the number had increased to 250 sites and continued to rise. (By mid-May 1999 the number had risen to well over 600.) I described the character of destruction in

the villages: the lack of any battle damage and the ethnic objective that appeared evident in the pattern of destruction. This destruction pointed to Article 4(2)(c) of the Yugoslav Tribunal statute ("deliberately inflicting on the group conditions of life calculated to bring about its physical destruction in whole or in part") as well as Article 4(2)(b) of the statute ("causing serious bodily or mental harm to the members of the group"). Washington had many reports of injuries and killings, some of a sadistic character, occurring during these destructive sweeps of villages and towns, and officials logically inferred from such events that serious mental harm was being inflicted on the fleeing Kosovar-Albanians.

"If you take the totality of this information that we have acquired so far," I concluded, "we believe that it creates the basis for stating that there are indicators of genocide unfolding in Kosovo." Toward the end of the press briefing on April 9, a reporter asked what difference it made that what was unfolding in Kosovo must reflect a planned operation executed pursuant to a policy. I responded, "Let's just say that obviously, if you can demonstrate a well-thought-out plan that has an intent behind it, then—that's why we point to indicators of genocide. But I want to emphasize that regardless, you can have a very well planned campaign of crimes against humanity, and there is no question that that's what's unfolded in Kosovo."

Following my use of the term *indicators of genocide*, the pressure from the media to describe the Kosovo events as genocide dissipated. As long as there was a credible acknowledgment that genocide might be unfolding, the media and the public did not insist on definitive findings of genocide quickly or as a predicate to action by a government or organization. They wanted to know that the genocide factor was being acknowledged, recognized in some fashion, and kept in the forefront of policy-making and decision making during the Kosovo conflict. When a government, such as the United States in 1999, can confirm that indicators, or precursors, of genocide are apparent, and that there is a credible response to these alerts, then the pressure to conclude immediately that the crime of genocide has occurred or is occurring becomes far less significant. *What becomes important is the action being taken to prevent genocide rather than the search for the crime of genocide.* In the case of Kosovo, the debate in April and May 1999 shifted to whether to send in ground troops,[23] not whether the crime of genocide was literally occurring.

It is that determination of *indicators* or *precursors of genocide* that permits a political as opposed to legal judgment to surface far more rapidly among public officials. As shown by my own remarks during the Kosovo conflict, one can state more definitively the legal judgment of crimes against humanity and war crimes in real time, but the specific-intent requirements of the crime of genocide make legal judgments about genocide far more difficult to arrive at quickly. Governments should be liberated to use *precursors of genocide* in their public statements once these predictive factors begin to emerge and thus trigger the Genocide Convention's obligation, under Article 1, to act to prevent genocide as quickly and effectively as possible. What logic would that obligation convey if a government had to wait until the crime of genocide was established to prevent it?

Thus, our goals for the April 9 press briefing, following an opening salvo by Albright, were twofold. First, we needed to lay down the predicate for genocide. We continued to study the incoming data, and it all pointed in the same direction, of widespread and systematic crimes. The same patterns of criminality cropped up in areas where Albanians traditionally held the majority. Second, we wanted to reassure people that we were doing everything in our power to assist the Yugoslav Tribunal, subject to protection of sources and methods of intelligence collection. We undertook steps to accelerate and facilitate the technological transmission of data to the court.

At her press briefing, Albright showed two aerial photos of mass graves and said there were more like them. She also described the fate of the IDPs, which numbered an estimated 700,000. They were being decimated by starvation and other deprivations. This, she said, was just as serious as killing them in cold blood. Lives were being put at risk with abandon. Albright challenged the Serbs, "Feed your people." Since March 24, 413,000 refugees had streamed out of Kosovo.[24]

Later that day Phyllis Oakley, who headed the State Department's Bureau of Intelligence and Research, told me of progress on the aerial imagery front. One image of a cemetery with a hundred fresh new graves southwest of Pristina had just come in and would be shared with the Yugoslav Tribunal. She confirmed to me that efforts finally were under way to order European Command to get more imagery of this character, which would be essential in identifying atrocity sites and the numbers of victims.

The Tribunal Demands More

Problems arose from our internal machinations over how to convey the mass of information being collected by the U.S. KDOM team, our witness interviewing, and our aerial photography to the Yugoslav Tribunal fast enough for Arbour and her team to examine it for further investigation and preparation of indictments. Prodded by the media and mindful of our own sense of importance in warning the Serbs about atrocities and reporting crimes to the tribunal, we probably left the impression that a lot of information already was flowing to the tribunal. With respect to Kosovo that was not yet the case, as it simply took time, that early in the military campaign, to properly collect the data and in many cases declassify it or convey such information in approved classified channels, followed by transmittal to the tribunal. A logjam was fast developing on Washington's end of the evidence trail.

The Yugoslav Tribunal's deputy prosecutor, Graham Blewitt, told me that Arbour was encouraged by the reports that we had evidence and were handing that information over to the prosecutor. But the postman had not delivered it! He said, "We'd rather handle the deluge of paper ourselves than have you try to sort it out." If the United States was concluding that genocide may be occurring, he said, would Washington please get that information to the tribunal? They wanted a "daily dump" of evidence from us. Blewitt asked me to minimize classifying information under the tribunal's Rule 70 as lead evidence, which meant information that could not itself be used in the courtroom because of its classified or sensitive nature but would help the prosecutor know where to look to generate fresh evidence for use in the trials.[25] "David, the leads are obvious. Give us what we need in the courtroom," he pleaded. It was a tall order, and we may have deserved the scolding from Blewitt. The call inspired more intensified daily reporting on information from numerous assets until the end of the conflict in June 1999.[26]

The State Department released daily "Ethnic Cleansing in Kosovo" reports, which provided as much information as we could disclose in unclassified form regarding the atrocity crimes occurring, in real time, in Kosovo.[27] This exercise became an unprecedented dissemination of information about ongoing atrocity crimes on a daily basis regarding an armed conflict in modern times. For example, in the March 31 report, there were details on forcible displacement of ethnic Albanian civilians, the looting and widespread burning of homes and businesses, reported detentions of ethnic Albanian men, accounts of summary executions, and more detailed reporting of atrocities and war crimes and the locations where they had occurred. All this was followed by a statement I drafted of U.S. policy:

Milosevic's forces are clearly committing crimes against humanity in Kosovo. There are indicators that Yugoslav forces also are engaged in genocide. The departure of international non-governmental organizations, press and other independent sources of information has complicated international efforts to determine precisely the scale of the crimes being committed by Yugoslav forces against ethnic Albanians. International personnel are interviewing refugees to help collect evidence for possible war crimes indictments. We will make a decision on whether Yugoslav actions against ethnic Albanians constitute genocide once we have sufficient information on which to base a judgment....

The United States reminds those responsible for the actions of the Yugoslav army and the Ministry of Internal Affairs in Kosovo that these attacks directed against the civilian population and the summary execution of detained persons are war crimes under international law. Commanding officers and political leaders will be held responsible for the actions of their subordinates as well as those committing the crime.[28]

During NATO's long bombing campaign, the atrocities unfolding within Kosovo became the primary justification for further air strikes, and Washington went into overdrive to disclose as much information as possible. This stood in stark contrast to the Rwandan genocide. Never before had there been such a concerted effort by the U.S. government to record in real time atrocities unfolding "in theater" so that policy-makers could make more informed judgments and build public support for the military campaign. One small example was Easter Day, April 4, when I received a cell phone call, while in church, from my office informing me of just-received aerial photography showing an imminent massacre of men and boys corralled in some farm fields. I hurried outside and called General Clark in NATO headquarters immediately. Over the next few hours we sought to move air assets into the region to disrupt the massacre. But we were too late. We could report the massacre with great speed, but we learned once again how difficult it was to stop such slaughters in progress.

Each day the Office of War Crimes Issues worked with an interagency team to prepare an "Update on Ethnic Cleansing in Kosovo" that was used by the spokespersons at the State and Defense Departments and White House and applied in discussions with journalists and others. (Soon we labeled these "Press Input on Kosovo War Crimes.") Meanwhile, every day we also obtained confidential reports from U.S. KDOM personnel in the field who were obtaining constant streams of information from the KLA and refugees.

On April 13, I spoke with Arbour by phone while visiting Oslo. It was our first conversation about tribunal access to Kosovo as soon as a cease-fire agreement could be arranged. We began working on the responsibilities of NATO troops to cooperate with and report evidence of atrocity crimes to the tribunal. She wanted tribunal investigators to have right of access to Kosovo and NATO to accept an obligation to arrest suspects. Arbour cast aside the old "only if encountered" philosophy of the Implementation Force (IFOR) and the Stabilization Force (SFOR) in Bosnia. I told her I was accelerating information on a daily basis to the tribunal and focusing U.S. attention on Milosevic. She rightly praised the work of my deputy, Tom Warrick, who labored hard on getting information to the tribunal. On imagery, she was upset that she was not notified first regarding release of images and that the tribunal had not gotten a lot of information on Kosovo from the United States or anyone else so far. She also stressed the need for the United States to honor long-standing requests for evidence arising from events that had occurred years ago in the Bosnian theater. One can never completely satisfy the customer, but there were days with Arbour when I wondered whether I would ever earn her trust that I was pushing the system as hard as possible to produce evidence for her. As prosecutor, she had to be a pit bull, and I understood that. As an ambassador, I had many bureaucracies to persuade and pressure, usually with the civil language of diplomacy.

Shuan Byrnes, a highly talented and dedicated member of the U.S. KDOM team, outlined procedures for the tribunal team arriving in Macedonia to liaise with the monitors and ensure coordination of efforts. But he went on to say that his people were not getting much information about rapes of the Kosovar-Albanian women and girls. The French and Israeli medical teams also were not obtaining rape evidence. Women and girls who had experienced rape were proving very reluctant to come forward. Many of the doctors were men; more female interviewers were desperately needed. He was paying interpreters out of his own pocket. Accounts also kept piling up of thousands of internally displaced persons and widespread destruction of settlements, burnings, lootings, and killings, as well as mass grave sites. He pleaded for a strong statement on these wandering victims in Kosovo, as it seemed his teams were the only ones trying to compile the information.

The same day, we had a bureaucratic breakthrough on imagery and other evidence, with internal agreement on freeing up the flow of such information to the tribunal. Tactical requirements still dominated what was being observed, but the intelligence community began to open up the faucet far more efficiently that day. Confidential daily atrocities updates, which brought to light so much of what was transpiring, began to circulate in the State, Defense, and Justice departments and at the White House. Warrick kept dogging the Milosevic trail internally.

The dangers of releasing some of the aerial imagery to the public were exemplified by the Germans, who released photos taken by drone aircraft revealing evidence of mass graves. This highlighted to the Serbs that we knew where the Muslim bodies were buried, thus tipping them off to return to the killing fields and destroy the mass graves in order to remove and scatter the evidence. Keeping some of the information out of the public eye proved essential at that point, but we continued to process it for transmission to the tribunal.

One Hundred Thousand Missing Men

On April 15, aerial imagery revealed a new mass grave site at Vocnjak, with 125 individual graves and a debris field of wagons, tractors, and junk—signatures of a massacre of refugees. The next day I received a call from General Clark's office at NATO. He wanted to release the Vocnjak imagery in order to counter criticism of NATO for accidentally bombing a civilian convoy on April 15. He was told that I was the only official holding up release of the imagery. Clark was desperate to keep the alliance together and needed this kind of photographic ammunition. Jim Pardew, a key State Department official on Balkans issues, amazingly said, "So what if the Serbs disturb the site [upon release of the imagery]. If there are a few bones left that's enough for the Prosecutor!" I explained that we needed to maintain the integrity of the mass grave site and that Arbour's approval would be required before we released the imagery. This would be key evidence for her, and if we prematurely released the imagery, the Serbs would destroy the site and the evidence in it. I called Arbour to see if she had any objection. She thanked me for the heads-up, gave me a conditional go-ahead following staff consultations, and noted that I was the only person around who seemed to understand what was at stake for the tribunal in that mass grave.

Fast on the heels of Vocnjak came aerial imagery of a mass burial site near the west-central Kosovo town of Izbica. It also had been detected on April 15 and appeared to confirm KLA reporting of mass executions. There were about 140 individual graves dug in three rows on farmland west of the village. Many of the farmhouses surrounding the grave site showed signs of extensive damage, including fire scorching and missing roofs. Artillery craters pockmarked the terrain along with many burned vehicles. In contrast, imagery gathered on March 9 showed an intact village with no graves whatsoever in the farmland. The KLA claimed that up to 160 Kosovar-Albanians had been killed in Izbica on April 2. They were separated into groups of 40 and then executed by selected soldiers. Many were elderly people who were unable to flee. I received other reports of atrocities, including Serb snipers taking shots at a convoy, killing a twelve-year-old boy and wounding his mother, refugee reports of a growing number of rapes, and that Serb paramilitary had shot to death 150 men suspected of KLA ties on March 27 in Izmic. The Serbs were placing their tanks and artillery near the refugee convoys to discourage NATO bombing. The preponderance of data pointed to continuing and widespread atrocities.

I appeared on *Fox News Sunday* on April 18 and emphasized the atrocities occurring in Kosovo. Side-by-side photographs of the Izbica burials demonstrated a mass killing site. I said, "The Albanians are clearly trying to bury the victims of Milosevic with respect." I called it "a classic example of ethnic cleansing.... The Serbs came in, torched the town and then proceeded with massacres of individual groups of Kosovars." I was asked about a NATO claim that ethnic Albanian refugees had reported 3,200 deaths caused by Serb security forces. I responded, "That's a very low estimate.... If you look at what refugees coming out are reporting to us, which we cannot confirm yet, you are actually looking at the possibility of tens of thousands of Kosovars who not only are at risk but also may actually have perished."

I continued, "We have upwards of 100,000 men that we cannot account for.... We have no idea where those men are now." I said that the United States would provide Arbour with "as much information as possible ... to support her investigation." After pointing out that Serbia was providing a sanctuary for indicted fugitives of the Yugoslav Tribunal, I warned, "The pressure is going to remain on Slobodan Milosevic until ... anyone indicted on his territory is in fact transferred. If there's any thought that Serbia will somehow join the new Europe or the international community until that is done, that's a false hope." I added, "One of the great challenges, I think, of the twenty-first century is to ensure that there is individual accountability for the commission of these crimes.... It's going to take a lot of hard work over the coming years to get a grip on this and to establish a principle of deterrence that, hopefully, thirty, forty, fifty years from now will begin to sink in."[29]

Secretary Cohen also stated on *Meet the Press* that day that 100,000 men remained unaccounted for in the refugee population, and that they might be dead.[30] The figure that had been provided to us, and which Cohen and I used that Sunday, followed the same calculation: Experts started with the number of refugees from Kosovo in Albania, which was 346,000 as calculated by the U.N. high commissioner for refugees. This did not include refugees who fled to Macedonia or Montenegro. From the 1981 census, 51.3 percent of the Kosovo population was male, and 59 percent of the men were between the ages of fifteen and fifty-nine. Multiplying the two percentages meant that 30.3 percent of the Albanian population consisted of men between the ages of fifteen and fifty-nine. However, according to press accounts, only 10 percent of the people coming across the border were men of those ages. If, as of April 26, there were 346,000 refugees, one would expect to see 105,000 men between fifteen and fifty-nine (30.3 percent of 346,000) and 241,000 women, children, and elderly. Instead, there were 311,400 women, children, and elderly (90 percent of the 346,000). One would expect to see 136,000 men accompanying them. Thus, 101,400 men (136,000 minus 34,600) were missing, and we had no information of their whereabouts inside Kosovo. It was a rough estimate but also extremely conservative, as it completely excluded calculations of missing men from refugees who fled to Macedonia and Montenegro.

The 100,000 figure held nearly constant to the end of April. All this was, of course, speculative but entirely justifiable as a matter of factual inquiry—we did not know what had happened to that number of Albanian men, only that they were not present in the refugee camps and could not be located by aerial imagery within Kosovo. Some U.S. intelligence reports, publicly released, estimated in late May that from 225,000 to 400,000 men were missing, the figures being so large in part because of uncertainties about the numbers of men, living or dead, among the internally displaced persons (as opposed to the refugees we were counting). But in late April the State Department estimated that, by then, the maximum number of Kosovar-Albanian men remaining in Kosovo and "at risk" was 257,000, and that perhaps 20,000 of them were "missing." Given the murderous track record of the Bosnian Serbs in the Srebrenica genocide, we had to assume the worst and sound the alarm. With so many men missing, what exactly was their fate? We never stated that they in fact were killed, only that such massacres could have occurred. I personally put the number out there with considerable emphasis, to try to deter further killings. We were sending the message that with so many men missing, we had better not find out that all or any significant number of them had been killed.[31]

Arbour Goes to Washington

Arbour called me on April 19 to request a visit to Washington to discuss tribunal investigators' access to Kosovo when the troops finally entered it following a cease-fire. She was determined that the tribunal be integrated into the military intervention. Arbour said she was probably about six weeks away from indicting Milosevic, focusing on charges of forced deportation out of Kosovo, among other crimes. I knew that if the tribunal indicted Milosevic without U.S. assistance, we would be burned publicly and in history for not having assisted. The task proved difficult, as there remained time lags in the American processing of data that meant we simply could not rush currently retrieved information about the Kosovo crimes immediately to the tribunal. I waded into another mindless bureaucratic labyrinth of individual agencies, which were not properly staffed or prioritizing the collection of data on atrocities. It was like banging on a door and yelling, "Hello, is anyone home?" On April 20, I received one small glimmer of hope when I learned that imagery of mass graves was being declassified *expeditiously.*

The following day I advised Albright of the embarrassing fact that the British were providing fifty intelligence reports to the tribunal, immediately and with public fanfare.[32] The totality of U.S. intelligence support far exceeded this, but we usually did not talk about providing "intelligence" reports. The bulk of the British product was refugee interviews, but the United States also was intensely gathering refugee interviews. I received revealing numbers that day showing considerable U.S.-generated support and information on Kosovo given to the prosecutor's office since March 1998. In that year, Washington provided 148 documents (or about 765 pages worth of information). Up to April 20, 1999, the United States had provided 191 documents for a total of about 1,010 pages worth of information. Of the information provided in 1999, 59 documents had been provided since March 31. In addition, the National Imagery and Mapping Agency had sent many score additional documents to the prosecutor's office and was working on getting a list delivered reporting on damaged/destroyed villages and towns. The grand total stood at more than 400 documents provided to the prosecutor since 1998—a number far exceeding the British count of recent weeks. But the British had beaten us to the punch with the media and thus left the impression of being far more cooperative with the tribunal's requests for information about atrocities in Kosovo.

Arbour arrived in Washington on April 28. Some administration officials wanted to ask her to seal the anticipated indictment against Milosevic rather than announce it publicly. But I cautioned that sealing the indictment would not help unless we were prepared to make a serious effort to apprehend Milosevic, as that is the rationale of a sealed indictment. (It is kept from public view to facilitate rapid arrest of the unknowing indictee.) U.S. officials were forbidden from meeting or negotiating with Karadzic or Mladic after the tribunal's July 1995 indictments of them. Presumably the same would hold for an indicted Milosevic. However, Washington's view of international law on the issue of dealing with Milosevic was less important than what Arbour would say once the indictment was issued. If she stated that international law or Security Council resolutions prohibited meetings and negotiations with him, it would be exceptionally difficult for us to oppose her publicly. I recommended against saying anything about the option of a sealed indictment, and it quickly faded as an issue with Arbour.

On the prospects of an indictment of Milosevic, Arbour told Albright that she would decide when to indict but was willing to consult about it. She was moving the case forward and needed a lot of help penetrating layers of intelligence. She said the imagery of Kosovo proved helpful and other lead evidence had been very useful. But they did not fill critical gaps in the tribunal's evidence on command and control, about which she needed a lot of inside information. "We need access to unconventional forms of intelligence," Arbour said.

"You have done a great job," Albright told her, "and you have America's full support." She wanted Arbour to have the resources she really needed. "I understand the problem," said Albright. "There are bureaucratic procedures to contend with but I will try to speed things up." On an indictment of Milosevic, Albright told Arbour "to work at your own pace, do what you have to do, recognizing that what you do is not being done in a vacuum. It is great you are willing to consult with us." Arbour said there were ways of influencing the speed of the final production of an indictment. She would act responsibly.

Arbour noted that people asked all the time whether there was a case for genocide in Kosovo. Genocide required a sophisticated analysis about special intent, she said. "It would be irresponsible," Arbour cautioned, "until we fully analyze the facts for us to say there is a case on genocide. We have to look at all of the evidence." This view contrasted with what I had argued was necessary for a government, rather than the prosecutor, to do when confronted with precursors of genocide. Washington had every right and indeed a duty at least to describe what was transpiring as atrocity crimes and, if the facts pointed in the direction of genocide, to describe *precursors of genocide* and then act to prevent full-scale genocide from being unleashed.

Albright assured Arbour that the issue regarding intelligence transmittal to the tribunal had to do with protection of sources and methods; it had nothing to do with a political calculation to speed up or slow down the conveyance of such information. Arbour challenged her relentlessly on this point.

Moral Equivalence

The Serbs were not the only ones being held accountable. NATO, too, was being accused of deliberately destroying nonmilitary structures and targeting civilians, including when bombs fell on the Chinese embassy in Belgrade and the Serbian TV headquarters. How NATO responded to such charges of war crimes would be important, Arbour counseled. The early responses of regret or talk of unavoidable collateral damage had been too dismissive of culpability, she said. NATO needed to continue its commitment to the law of war and to the fact that leaders must understand their obligation to investigate and prosecute. One example was whether the bombing attacks were generating disproportionate civilian casualties and damage. These were Geneva Convention obligations. She had raised the issue with the Germans and British and shortly would be doing so with the French. Arbour planned to say publicly that she had sought assurances on the proportional use of force by NATO. Albright replied that every air strike followed very clear instructions regarding minimal or no collateral destruction. Arbour asked, "Do subordinates depart from orders intentionally or accidentally?" Albright answered angrily, "I won't get into an argument of moral equivalence!" Arbour responded, "I am not suggesting that. The allegations of unlawful targeting arise because of misidentification or it was disproportionate.... Making a bona fide mistake is not a war crime." It was a tense exchange and a prescient one, given the allegations against the misuse of NATO airpower, discussed shortly.

At their joint press briefing, Arbour called for an immediate and robust arrest initiative in Bosnia and Herzegovina. She wanted to arrest all indictees. The mere issuance of arrest warrants in Serbia was not enough. Arbour stressed her need for unprecedented assistance "in order to respond to the kinds of allegations that are coming out of Kosovo in a time frame that will make our work relevant.... there is no immunity before our tribunal for heads of state. There's no immunity, essentially, for any individual, both in a personal or a command responsibility position.... We are operating, essentially, from exactly the same kind of open source base that is available to journalists and others. And, of course, at the same time we are trying to move forward in our command and control investigations. We cannot do that solely on the basis of refugee accounts.... deterrence, if it works, is very difficult to measure. It's measuring what did not occur. Now, frankly, in the current environment, it's pretty hard to imagine that considerably worse atrocities could have been perpetrated. So having said that, I can assure you that one of the main subjects of discussion that I raised—not only here but in all the capitals that I visited recently—is the need for an immediate, very robust arrest initiative in Bosnia.

"I believe," Arbour continued, "that the strongest deterrent message that could have been sent into Kosovo, and that could still be sent, would be the immediate apprehension, not only of the remaining indictees who are publicly indicted, but of the persons who are the subject of sealed indictments. I believe that this would bring an air of reality to those who are in positions of accountability in Kosovo who may be associated with the perpetration of the crimes that, by credible accounts, appear to be committed now. The mere issuances of indictments in a country that has never executed any of our arrest warrants in the past, frankly, would serve only as a very hypothetical or a marginal deterrent. I believe that what will show—or I think could have a very immediate impact—would be the demonstration that we have the capacity to investigate and we have partners who have the political will and the operational skills to execute arrest warrants even in hostile environments. So I am calling—and I've called in the past—but I think now the time is absolutely critical to see very robust action on the outstanding warrants."

Arbour went on to say, after noting the refugee accounts being collected: "Other pieces of information are considerably more difficult to access, and these are those that will support our investigative effort on the command and control both on the police, military, and political level. We have long-standing relationships with information providers. We are now looking at trying to accelerate the flow of that kind of information and the quality of the product. Of course, we're doing so at a time where the collection capacity of all these potential providers is taxed by the need for them to collect information relevant to their efforts in the region. So we are, of course, competing with other interests at a time when we're trying to get access for information for our purposes. It's a dialogue and a partnership that we have to maintain."[33]

During her Washington visit, Arbour requested that the U.S. government provide a forensic crime scene examination team in the event that an international military presence was deployed to Kosovo. She recommended a team of photographers, ballistics experts, mapping experts, police investigators who could conduct interviews as needed, pathologists, and other experts who could assist with war crimes documentation. Arbour predicted that such a team would be deployed to Kosovo for about four weeks and then return to the United States to complete forensic tests, draw up conclusions, and prepare a report for delivery to her. The team would be committed to support the tribunal for about three to four months.[34]

Erasing History

Mary Robinson, the U.N. high commissioner for human rights, issued her *Report on the Human Rights Situation Involving Kosovo* on April 30.[35] She questioned the legality of the NATO bombing campaign and discussed the principles that NATO should adhere to in its bombing strategy. Robinson focused on principles of proportionality and legality, which I knew were central to all our targeting decisions. But her report ostracized her from top Clinton administration officials, who thereafter had little interest in dealing with her. I remained an exception, as I knew Robinson was an ally on the broader agenda of atrocity crimes that was the core of my own mission.

Cornelia Sommaruga, the president of the International Committee of the Red Cross, confided to me that during a recent visit to Belgrade he told Milosevic that Kosovo was in shambles: homes destroyed, people being pushed across the border, families separated, summary executions, systematic rape, mass graves, and even women's jewels stolen. Milosevic denied any of this was happening *on orders*, but he told Sommaruga he must realize it was a war against terrorists. This was a fascinating exchange because it implicated Milosevic in the atrocities, showing he was given notice of them and demonstrating that he did not intend to prevent further atrocity crimes or punish any Serb perpetrators.

In early May, European Command agreed to insert war crimes as a specified task in the planning for NATO's intervention upon a cease-fire, with General Clark squarely on board. This was a critical development, as we could expect cooperation and security protection from the NATO-led Kosovo Force (KFOR) for tribunal investigators and forensics teams if the KFOR troops knew that the Yugoslav Tribunal was part of their mission. That would be a vast improvement over the strained relations between the tribunal and IFOR and then SFOR in Bosnia.

The State Department released a comprehensive report titled *Erasing History: Ethnic Cleansing in Kosovo*, which Harold Koh, the assistant secretary of state for human rights, had overseen in its drafting, on May 10.[36] In my remarks to the State Department press corps that day, I said:

> With the exception of Rwanda in 1994 and Cambodia in 1975, you would be hard pressed to find a crime scene anywhere in the world since World War II where a defenseless civilian population has been assaulted with such ferocity and criminal intent and suffered so many multiple violations of international humanitarian law in such a short period of time, as in Kosovo since mid-March. There are hideous crime scenes elsewhere recently—Sierra Leone, DROC [the Democratic Republic of the Congo], and Sudan come to mind. But Kosovo represents a government-planned campaign to eliminate, either through forced deportation or killing, most of an ethnic population from its homes. The criminal character of such an enterprise—divorced in large part from any semblance of military necessity—cannot be ignored. The list of war crimes and crimes against humanity being committed in Kosovo is diverse, covering such a wide range of criminal behavior that it represents almost a textbook example of how not to wage warfare.[37]

The use of human shields by the Serb forces in Kosovo became a daily phenomenon that Americans tracked during the entire conflict. The Serbs employed several types of human shield. One consisted of stationary groups of people positioned near military assets in towns or near artillery or anti-aircraft for protection of those assets and related troops. The second type was associated primarily with military convoys. A third category consisted of rape houses, where victims of sexual assault were known to be held as soldiers found refuge and new targets for rape. As Serb forces herded civilians around the Kosovo terrain, NATO aircraft were plunged into a game of chess whereby an entire territory was immunized from attack because analysts could not determine where the next civilian convoy might travel. Internally displaced persons also were used as pawns. The Serbs shelled their encampments, forcing them to scatter and move elsewhere. NATO bombing actually proved to be a disincentive for the Serbs to repopulate Kosovo with new arrivals from Serbia.

Examples abounded. Some 20,000 Kosovar-Albanians were force-marched from Cirez to Srbica as human shields for Serbian tanks; 500 Kosovar men were robbed, stripped naked, and forced to lie in a field for two hours while Serb artillery fired on nearby KLA positions, near Klina. At Orahovac, as many as 700 men were used as human shields in early April. They were forced to stand in front of tanks in the rain for two days with their hands tied behind their backs. A few escaped by paying soldiers ten thousand deutsche marks. On April 19, Serb forces used ethnic Albanians as human shields along the road between Podujevo and Pristina. At Srbica, detainees were being held in an ammunition factory. In Urosevac, Serb paramilitary forced Kosovar men to dig defensive positions on the southeast side of the city. Nearly 50 paramilitary troops forced 25 civilians from nearby Starosello to dig trenches for three days from April 10 to April 12. At Glodane, NATO imagery showed 500 people surrounded by Serb forces on April 5, thus creating a human shield. On April 30, refugees claimed they had left the Presevo area because they were either being conscripted or forced into military barracks. Some Serb forces disguised themselves as refugees to prevent being targeted. The Serbs continuously used human shields to protect military convoys. Young Kosovar Albanian men were removed from refugee convoys, dressed in Serb military uniforms, and forced to form a human shield around Serb convoys. Numerous refugees claimed to have witnessed and participated in this activity on roads between Ped, Dakovica, and Kosovska Mitrovica. Brothels also served as human shields, including Hotel Karagec and possibly Hotel Metohia in Pec.

Using a human shield is an act of desperation. An army cannot use human shields to completely neutralize the firepower of an opposing force. The initial war crime is the human shield, but attacking a military target surrounded by a human shield is not necessarily illegal. Otherwise, the attacking force essentially disarms its enemy by committing the original sin of deploying a human shield. The law of armed conflict is not so illogical in its construct as to stand down an opposing army, which may be acting in self-defense, because of the use of a human shield. But I maintained during the Kosovo campaign that in no other conflict in military history had there been a greater effort made by one side, NATO, to comply with the laws of war. So human shields were paramount reasons why NATO restrained its use of air-power in scores of situations. At the same time, NATO bombing proved critical in preventing the repopulation of Kosovo by Serbs from north of the Kosovo border to complete Belgrade's grand design of ethnic cleansing.

By May 14, there had been a total of 22,246 NATO air strikes in Kosovo and Serbia. Of that number, 7,793 targeted Serbian air defense facilities. The State Department's major *Erasing History* report contained maps of more than 600 damaged settlements, various isolated groups of internally displaced persons, aerial imagery, and the tribunal questionnaire for refugees. In mid-May, an updated report typical of those the State Department released frequently in a series titled "The Ethnic Cleansing of Kosovo" recorded mass executions in 75 towns and villages of Kosovo; mass graves in Dobrosevac, Drenica, Lipljan, Kaaniku, Rexala, Malisevo, Peklek, Pusto Selo, and the Pagarusa Valley; 5,000 dead in mass executions; systematic rapes in Dukovica and at Kargac and Metohia hotels in Pec; 550,000 internally displaced persons; and 225,000 unaccounted-for men (aged fourteen to fifty-nine years) from among refugee families in Albania and Macedonia who had reported their missing status. New refugee reports described widespread starvation and disease among internally displaced persons in Kosovo, especially among those who had been in the hills for weeks.

On the home front, we arranged for hundreds of refugees from Kosovo to be temporarily housed and interviewed at Fort Dix, New Jersey, for the preparation of evidence to be used by the Yugoslav Tribunal. (Thousands of Kosovar-Albanian refugees arrived at Fort Dix in 1999, but only a portion were interviewed.) My visits to Fort Dix and the interview process my office established there demonstrated a new way to collect witness information in the aftermath of atrocity crimes. Our message to the refugees was simple: Your Story Is Important. My colleagues and I soon discovered in spades how significant that message became as their harrowing stories were recorded and then sent to the Yugoslav Tribunal, where they became part of the evidence used against the Serb defendants prosecuted for the Kosovo atrocities.

Milosevic in Her Sights

Arbour told me in The Hague on May 19 that she and her staff were working day and night. They wanted the intelligence data we could provide very soon. She complained that they did not yet have videotapes of the atrocity sites, although such videos had been broadcast on C-SPAN in the United States! I promised delivery within days. Arbour said they needed access to the authors of the KDOM reports and cables. They had received twelve aerial photographs, but their quality was poorer than the imagery available from public sources. However, aerial imagery was not Arbour's priority at that stage. As we knew from her earlier visit to Washington, Arbour's highest priority was information about the chain of command in Kosovo, as she was searching for the link to Milosevic. She tried to shame us by saying that the tribunal had a very productive relationship with the British and others who had provided scant assistance to the tribunal in the past.

Arbour had Milosevic in her sights, but she did not want to issue a weak indictment that could discredit the tribunal. If she did not get help from the United States, she said she might have to issue such an indictment anyway and claim that the United States did not offer the necessary assistance for a stronger one. From a public affairs perspective alone, that would be disastrous. Because she was acting rapidly, Washington had to as well.

Anticipating Arbour's angst, I had consulted the day before with Eric Schwartz at the National Security Council and set in motion taskings aimed at forcing this critical information-sharing issue into a Deputies and perhaps Principals Committee decision as rapidly as possible. Arbour wanted us to prepare and transmit in approved channels Milosevic-specific intelligence and to permit tribunal interviews of envoy Richard Holbrooke, Ambassador Christopher Hill, and key KDOM personnel.

The events leading up to the Yugoslav Tribunal's indictment of Slobodan Milosevic in late May 1999 pointed to the difficulties in straightening out the story with the media and keeping government officials focused on the prize of accountability. Working closely with the intelligence community and the Pentagon, I sought to provide as much real-time evidence as possible about the Kosovo atrocities to Arbour. That meant aerial imagery (much of it declassified), witness statements from refugees, and other data arriving about the atrocities and about large numbers of missing persons. A few days before Arbour announced her indictment of Milosevic for the Kosovo atrocity crimes, I placed one of my staffers on a plane bound for Amsterdam to deliver another installment of evidence to the Yugoslav Tribunal because I knew how important it was to get the information to her as quickly as possible. The *Washington Post* found out about that particular delivery and linked it to her announcement about the Milosevic indictment, implying that it was critical to that indictment.[38] That was not the case. Arbour was using a lot of other evidence to build her indictment. While the American evidence might be helpful, it certainly would not be dispositive. The evidence we were able to deliver focused largely on recording ongoing atrocities in Kosovo, not on leadership ladders reaching to Milosevic. Arbour thought we had planted the idea that our information was critical to the Milosevic indictment with the *Washington Post* reporter, and sharply criticized us. While I explained that any such presumption was entirely false, the damage with the public was done.

The Milosevic indictment in late May 1999 was not entirely welcomed by some top U.S. officials at the time. They believed that it would greatly undermine the chance to negotiate with him for a withdrawal of Serb forces from Kosovo and an end to the fighting and atrocities. He would feel threatened by the indictment, dig in his heels, and seek untenable concessions from NATO. These were legitimate concerns. But I firmly believed that nothing would enhance the downfall of Milosevic more than a tribunal indictment. Albright had similar views,[39] and though we were somewhat lone voices within the administration, I reminded our colleagues of our argument that indicting Milosevic for atrocity crimes would shame him before the Serbian people, sap him of some of his authority, humble him, and force him to minimize the damage of the indictment by agreeing to a ceasefire and withdrawal. He might even view such conduct as conducive to mitigating any sentence he might ultimately receive upon conviction by the Yugoslav Tribunal, or to helping him negotiate his way to an amended indictment dropping various counts.[40]

Nonetheless, some officials wanted me to determine whether Arbour could delay her announcement of the indictment. That was not going to happen, but she did plan on alerting me as to when the announcement would be made, so that Washington would have a heads-up. Arbour informed me that her indictment of Milosevic, Milan Milutinovic, and four others would be unsealed on May 27, 1999. She had the option to keep the indictment under seal beyond then if disclosure would endanger lives. I then spread the news to a small group of top officials. Some grumbled that we had not been consulted; rather, we were being given advance notice. I was not so disturbed, as Arbour had been talking with us intensively for weeks about an impending Milosevic indictment and giving us the opportunity to persuade her to keep it sealed.

The public indictment of Milosevic was a positive development for the rule of law and deterrence of further atrocity crimes in Kosovo. We had long held that the Yugoslav Tribunal is an independent court. The prosecutor had pursued evidence wherever it was located and to whomever it guided her, just as we had always said she should do. Keeping the indictment under seal would be plausible only if the United States demonstrated a serious intent to arrest Milosevic soon, which was impractical.

Meanwhile, aerial imagery confirmed that the Serbs had bulldozed the Izbica mass grave site and dug up the bodies there. I alerted Arbour that the Serbs were trying to destroy the evidence at Izbica. NATO soldiers had to enter Kosovo soon or more forensic evidence certainly would be destroyed.

Entering Kosovo

On the first day of June, Albright received a letter from eleven members of Congress (ten Democratic and one Republican) alerting her that the 1999 Emergency Supplemental Appropriations Act recommended $13 million above the administration's request for the Yugoslav Tribunal and $10 million more than the request for the State Department's Human Rights and Democracy Fund. They recommended that these additional resources be used to support "a more effective human rights response to the Kosovo crisis.... We believe that the $18 million in funding for the War Crimes Tribunal will enable it to expand its investigative efforts." I lived for such days, when Congress actually volunteered *additional* funds for war crimes work.

Yugoslav Tribunal deputy prosecutor Graham Blewitt requested that the United States take the lead in any Security Council resolution dealing with the tribunal's investigative work in postconflict Kosovo. Blewitt advised that the resolution include language recognizing the Yugoslav Tribunal's jurisdiction over Kosovo and ensuring that tribunal staff would be granted an unequivocal right of immediate and unimpeded access to Serbia and Kosovo. His aim was to correct the mistakes that arose after the Dayton Peace Agreement, which lacked specific mandates for tribunal work in Bosnia and Herzegovina, including arrests of indictees. Blewitt requested that the tribunal be authorized to work alongside the international military presence in Kosovo.

The North Atlantic Council of NATO in mid-June addressed the level of KFOR cooperation and support for the Yugoslav Tribunal in Kosovo. The U.S. representative, Sandy Vershbow, weighed in strongly that support for the tribunal should be among the most important of KFOR's tasks. In the end, the North Atlantic Council tasked KFOR to assist the tribunal "as a key supporting task of great importance."[41] Vershbow won an important battle for us that day.

The Kosovo conflict ended on June 3 when Milosevic agreed to a cease-fire and the withdrawal of Serb forces. I entered Kosovo on June 23. The tribunal already had some thirty-five people in the province, including twenty-five investigative and ten support personnel. I visited their outpost in Pristina at the old Yugoslav Army headquarters building behind the Grand Hotel, which had become the U.N. mission building. A U.S. Marines helicopter then transported me to Dakovica and two atrocity sites identified there in the Milosevic indictment and assigned to the FBI team for forensic work. I visited the smaller site and saw where three victims had been murdered in the prayer room adjacent to the house and three had been murdered in the cement courtyard in front of the house. The six victims were buried in the backyard of the home next door.

Dakovica was a partially destroyed town, with obvious signs of ethnic cleansing. The Albanian neighborhoods were devastated. There were some people in the streets, and they waved greetings to us. From the air, I witnessed more widespread devastation. The FBI team I had linked up with was heavily armed despite prohibitions on civilians bringing arms into Kosovo. They just ignored the rule. But they were otherwise highly professional, and their presence only demonstrated to me what an enormous difference the United States can make when it decides to engage.

On a street lined with ruined homes and shops in the center of Dakovica, I stood before the international press corps and, as CNN aired me live worldwide, I said that the worst assumptions about the atrocity crimes in Kosovo were becoming fact and that "indicators of genocide" remained apparent. The United States was meeting Arbour's request for crime scene investigators with an unprecedented FBI contingent of sixty personnel, including forensic pathologists, anthropologists, and photographers. The FBI team was investigating two crime scenes in Dakovica that were central to Arbour's indictment against Milosevic and other top Serbian officials. A Yugoslav Tribunal investigator accompanied the FBI operation. I emphasized that the KFOR mandate recognized such efforts on tribunal investigations to be a "key supporting task of great importance," which was an improvement over the immediate post-Dayton mandate of IFOR in Bosnia and Herzegovina.

Christiane Amanpour of CNN asked me about arresting Karadzic and Mladic and why that had not occurred yet. I replied, as always to such questions, that it was the responsibility of those in control of the Bosnian sectors to follow through on the Dayton Peace Agreement and Security Council resolutions to arrest indicted fugitives in their respective sectors.[42]

Upon my arrival at Camp Able Sentry in Macedonia that evening, I returned a call from Albright, who was quite agitated about my response to Amanpour's question in Dakovica. Albright complained that I had upset the French with my remarks and that she was burdened with phone calls from them scolding me, and by extension her, about blaming France for not capturing Karadzic. I told her that what I said in Dakovica was exactly what I had been saying publicly for a long time, namely that each NATO force deployed in Bosnia needed to ensure arrests of indicted fugitives in its respective sector.[43] It was the mildest possible way of stating the obvious, namely that the French had to step up to the plate and get the job done. But Albright told me to stop criticizing the French. She showed little interest in anything else I was discovering in Kosovo. I was distressed afterward that she had not stood up for me and, frankly, the Yugoslav Tribunal. She seemed influenced by French displeasure on the issue, as it no doubt complicated other dealings she had with them at that time. But atrocity crimes work always complicates other issues between governments. Too often policymakers in Washington and at the United Nations trotted out the old line "This is not the right moment" whenever I needed to press hard to achieve an atrocity crimes objective.

Kosovo had become one of the largest crime scenes in the world. By the end of the summer in 1999, tribunal investigators were examining about 300 reported atrocity crimes sites, while KFOR was compiling a database of information on over 240 of those sites. International agencies estimated between 2,000 and 5,000 Albanians were still being held in Serbia, an action that in itself constituted a war crime. Approximately 75 percent of the 1,800 villages surveyed in Kosovo had suffered moderate to severe levels of damage. The State Department estimated that Serb forces had killed over 10,000 civilians during a coordinated campaign of atrocities. The final death count may have been higher.[44]

Tribunal investigators quickly became very active in Kosovo. The United States, along with France, Germany, Canada, the United Kingdom, Switzerland, Austria, Belgium, Denmark, Sweden, and Iceland, fielded forensic teams to collect evidence from atrocity crime sites designated by the tribunal. The FBI efficiently investigated the two sites assigned to it from the Milosevic indictment as well as five other sites before returning home on July 5. They deployed to Kosovo again in mid-September 1999. Clinton released $5 million from the Defense Department to transport the FBI and provide logistics support. The FBI teams on this second mission joined the American forces and worked on a mass grave and then several more crimes scenes. Their highly professional forensic work proved invaluable in the Yugoslav Tribunal's Kosovo trials years later.

Accusing NATO

In December 1999, the new prosecutor of the Yugoslav Tribunal, Carla Del Ponte, told a British reporter that she and her staff were examining a dossier of allegations against the NATO bombing campaign—Operation Allied Force—during the Kosovo conflict. She said, "'So I will read it very attentively and I will decide what to do. I must do my job because otherwise I am not independent and the independence of the prosecutor is the most important element."[45] Her statement ignited a firestorm in Washington and other NATO capitals that I spent months damping and finally resolving. I was ripped away from my Christmas vacation and returned to Washington to explain that Arbour had long ago informed us that some Canadian law professors had lodged a plea with the Yugoslav Tribunal to investigate NATO because, in their view, the bombings had been illegally targeting and hitting civilian populations and property. Such concerns were no secret following the April 30, 1999, report of Mary Robinson, the U.N. high commissioner for human rights. But I had to peel National Security Adviser Sandy Berger off his West Wing ceiling when he read Del Ponte's interview. I explained to him that the filing of such a complaint by a third party—a common occurrence—does not mean the prosecutor will investigate or indict anyone. Such accusations require some study to determine whether there is any basis for initiating a formal investigation. Arbour had not reached any such judgment and indeed had alerted Albright and me to the accusation in her April 1999 visit to Washington during the Kosovo campaign. Nor had Arbour's successor, Carla Del Ponte, arrived at any decision, although she left the impression that she had or was about to do so!

A twenty-five-person internal committee of the Office of the Prosecutor, set up by Arbour in May 1999, reviewed documents submitted by critics of NATO's campaign in Kosovo and Serbia as well as public documents from NATO, the Defense Department, the British Defense Ministry, Human Rights Watch, Amnesty International, the U.N. Environmental Program, media reports, and NATO secretary-general George Robertson. To address the allegations, Arbour's in-house committee asked (a) whether the designated air strikes actually were violations of international law, and (b) whether the facts alleged were credible enough to show crimes were committed.

Following Del Ponte's ill-timed remark, I negotiated arrangements with NATO headquarters and with my Pentagon colleagues to respond to a host of specific questions raised by the prosecutor's staff. The United States was subject to the jurisdiction of the Yugoslav Tribunal for actions its forces undertook on or over the territory of the former Yugoslavia, which included Kosovo. This surprised many in Washington at the time, as they had no idea American forces would fall under the Yugoslav Tribunal's jurisdiction.

The military fiercely resisted this particular prosecutorial initiative. The Pentagon and NATO allies objected to any effort by an international court to force them to reveal targeting decisions and the process and procedures behind selected decisions in order to comply with law of war and international humanitarian law principles, which involve considerations of military necessity, distinction between combatants and civilians, and the proportionality of military actions. But the questions pertaining to a list of targets during the bombing campaign eventually were addressed by NATO and Washington. If we had not gone through the exercise, then we would have been accused of practicing a double standard with war crimes. If we had not complied with the prosecutor's requests for information, she might have concluded that the absence of information required the opening of a formal investigation. In the end, however, she and her staff concluded that there was insufficient evidence or justification under the law to proceed to a full-scale investigation of the NATO bombing campaign.[46]

During the entire period that Washington responded to the Kosovo bombing inquiry and up until the report issued by Del Ponte announcing the decision not to investigate NATO or the United States, Del Ponte was persona non grata in Washington. She was not welcome to visit high-ranking officials. I had to carry that message to her and enforce it, while at the same time working closely with her to answer her staff's questions about the Kosovo bombing campaign. I understood but disagreed with the strategy of Berger, Albright, and Cohen to isolate and annoy Del Ponte at a time when we needed to cultivate a cooperative spirit during a highly sensitive and potentially risky inquiry into the NATO targeting strategy over Kosovo and Serbia. They decided to play hardball with her, clearly resenting how she had shamed the United States for what we all considered to be a singular achievement in liberating Kosovo from the clutches of Serb criminality. I ran interference for both sides during many long months in 2000.

Great powers, even superpowers, can have their feelings hurt and in turn become oversensitive to the slightest challenge. It was left primarily to me to ensure that NATO (and the United States) sustained a cooperative relationship with the Yugoslav Tribunal in order to resolve the lingering questions about NATO actions. The effort paid off as NATO explained each bombing run in enough detail and with persuasive explanations to prevent a full-scale war crimes investigation. Shortly after the release of the prosecutor's report on June 24, 2000, concluding that no investigation of NATO's actions would be required, Del Ponte boarded a plane for Washington and another, albeit considerably delayed, round of consultations.

Passing the Test

The Kosovo episode in the life of the Yugoslav Tribunal demonstrated that impunity would not prevail in the Balkans, particularly following the brazen assault on hundreds of thousands of civilians more than three years after the Dayton Peace Agreement and the launch of tribunal indictments and trials. By 2010, nine Serb civilian and military leaders had been prosecuted before the tribunal; only one—Milan Milutinovic—was acquitted of the charges against him. Other Serb perpetrators of atrocity crimes, including some of those whom State Department spokesman Jamie Rubin and I had named for their potential culpability on April 9, 1999, were convicted by the tribunal and are serving lengthy sentences in European prisons. Six Kosovar-Albanians from the Kosovo Liberation Army were prosecuted; four were acquitted at the trial level (although the Appeals Chamber partially quashed three of the acquittals and ordered retrials in July 2010), and two were found guilty of war crimes and were given significant sentences. (Haradin Bala was sentenced to thirteen years and Lahi Brahimaj received a six-year sentence.) One accused former Serb leader of the MUP, Vlastimir Dordević, remained on trial while appeals for seven of the accused were outstanding in 2010. In no small measure, justice has been rendered for the atrocity crimes in Kosovo, recognizing that the most prominent defendant, Slobodan Milosevic, died just prior to judgment being rendered in his trial.

The experience reminded everyone of how fragile the weapons of international justice can be when confronting political and military interests and, of course, legal challenges by skeptical governments and seasoned defense counsel. For months the jurisdiction of the Yugoslav Tribunal hung in the balance as arguments swirled about diplomatic circles that the war in the Balkans was over and so too was the relevance of the tribunal, particularly for any confrontation with "terrorists." But the original vision for the Yugoslav Tribunal, that it would capture the needs of justice throughout all of the former Yugoslavia, including Kosovo, and that no endgame was yet in sight, prevailed to ensure that neither Milosevic nor his collaborators had any blank check to ethnically cleanse the Kosovar-Albanians.

The Kosovo conflict showed how a sharp focus on atrocity crimes during the fighting can galvanize public opinion and be a potent weapon against the enemy. The collection and explanation of raw data arriving every day from intelligence, nongovernmental sources, and monitors became a primary policy activity that deeply influenced the military campaign and the marshaling of public support for it. Such information about atrocity crimes, on a daily basis, provided powerful justification for NATO air strikes to retard the Serbian advance and thus diminish the opportunities for more atrocities. The news briefings at the State and Defense departments ultimately contributed to evidence bound for the Yugoslav Tribunal, and they relentlessly reminded the Serbian leadership that their day of reckoning was approaching. Never before had the State Department, the Pentagon, and the intelligence community worked so closely together to produce a daily narrative of how massive criminal conduct had to be confronted immediately with military action.

The flaw in our efforts, however, became self-evident after several weeks. Without a ground intervention of armed forces to directly confront Serb military and paramilitary troops inside Kosovo, there was a high probability that atrocities would continue at least for some period of time until the air campaign crippled Serbia's capabilities and dissuaded its leadership from continuing the fight. Meanwhile, many civilians would die and many more would endure great hardship. Clinton, the Pentagon, and NATO allies had no stomach for the ground option,[47] but at least they mustered the political will to act militarily and to sustain the NATO air campaign until the Serbs capitulated in June 1999.

The fact that the Yugoslav Tribunal prosecutor never indicted anyone for genocide in Kosovo might suggest a reckless and hasty judgment by me in late March 1999 that *indicators of genocide* were unfolding in the region. While, in hindsight, I would now prefer to have used the term *atrocity crimes* to describe the situation in Kosovo, as that would have been accurate and yet flexible enough for future investigations and prosecutions, the term simply did not exist in 1999. (I introduced it in 2001 after I left office.) Nonetheless, there was good reason to identify factors in the Kosovo conflict that could point ultimately to a legal finding of genocide, and at minimum to crimes against humanity and war crimes. Evidence that pointed to a specific intent on the part of Milosevic and others to destroy all or a substantial part of the Kosovar-Albanian population never emerged, and the prosecutor chose not to infer such intent.

But governments must have the flexibility to speculate, based on information streaming in from an atrocity zone, about the meaning of how certain criminal conduct relates to genocide or other atrocity crimes. That is the first step to prevention of genocide and to ending the massacres already occurring. Rarely in the heat of a conflict can one fathom the specific intent of the masterminds of mass slaughter. The only way to ensure the best possible outcome, once a determination has been made that precursors of genocide exist, is to take their predictive character seriously and then act to prevent full-scale genocide from succeeding. So I have no regrets about how I evaluated the information and labeled Serbian conduct at the time. The United States and its NATO allies acted boldly, despite their restraint on deploying ground forces, and ultimately succeeded in preventing genocide.

Arbour's angst over the slow transmission of evidence from Washington to The Hague was understandable. My deputy, Tom Warrick, and I pushed the bureaucracy as hard as we could to collect, analyze, declassify when possible, and prepare for submission to the tribunal large bodies of evidence of the atrocity crimes in Kosovo and whatever could be pinpointed regarding Milosevic's responsibility. The intelligence community remained understaffed and stuck in procedures that sometimes made expedited conveyance of information extremely difficult to manage. But the experience informed everyone in Washington and The Hague that lessons still needed to be learned and applied to more efficient and useful sharing of information with the prosecutor while violence raged. Nonetheless, in the aftermath of the ethnic cleansing, the United States led the multinational endeavor to enter Kosovo, investigate individual crime scenes, and provide forensic evidence to the prosecutor.

The indictment of Milosevic on May 24, 1999, symbolized the triumph of justice over expediency. The arguments arrayed against Arbour's decision to indict at such a critical point in the NATO air campaign were formidable because they rationalized suspending judicial action in order to negotiate a cease-fire and withdrawal of Serb forces from Kosovo. But the dire warnings of the skeptics, including those in Washington, proved false. The charges of crimes against humanity and war crimes shamed Milosevic and further diminished his credibility internationally. Although certainty will always be elusive, the indictment usefully complemented the air campaign, in that the combination of both probably compelled Milosevic to restrategize and, within days, begin to move toward a settlement. In short, the indictment threw the power punch after the long and debilitating air bombardment of Serbia.

It had taken six years and many missteps, but by 1999 the Yugoslav Tribunal and the U.S. government discovered they each had the spine to stand up to atrocity crimes together and in real time.

CHAPTER ELEVEN
FREETOWN IS BURNING

> Go show this to Kabbah. Tell Kabbah to help you now. Kabbah
> is our enemy.
>
> *The chant of rebels after they "chopped" limbs off their victims,*
> *as told to the author by survivors in Freetown*

THE TRIAL OF CHARLES TAYLOR, THE CHARISMATIC AND DIABOLICAL FOR-
mer president of Liberia, before the Special Court for Sierra Leone in recent
years was the closing chapter of an eighteen-year journey: atrocity crimes in
Sierra Leone stretching from 1991 to 2001, a flawed peace agreement in
July 1999, negotiations that built the war crimes tribunal, and finally three
joint trials and the Taylor case, which brought to justice men who had
waged a uniquely evil assault on a forsaken people.

Sierra Leone, a country about the size of South Carolina, lies on the
western tip of northern Africa facing the Atlantic Ocean, wedged between
Guinea to the north and east and Liberia to the southeast. An estimated
fifty thousand people were killed there during a civil war in the 1990s, and
tens of thousands of survivors were hideously mutilated or otherwise scarred
or wounded. As charged in the trial of Charles Taylor and concluded in
the judgments of the Special Court for Sierra Leone, the conflict in that
country was characterized by extreme brutality because such demonstrative
atrocities were used to terrorize and suppress any civilian opposition to the
rebels. Taylor, who allegedly backed the Sierra Leone rebels while simultaneously acting as president of Liberia, was indicted for "terrorizing the
civilian population." Central to the prosecution theory was that the crimes
committed by the rebels, namely the Revolutionary United Front (RUF) and

the ex-army insurgent Armed Forces Revolutionary Council (AFRC), were intentionally brutal. The leaders of the rebel groups strategized to gain control over territory they sought, especially diamond-rich areas, with minimal resistance from the civilian population. The campaigns of mutilations, rape, and other assaults on life and property served to terrorize the people into submission. The mutilations, as the special court later concluded, "served as a visible lifelong sign to all other civilians" not to resist the rebels and not to back President Ahmed Tejan Kabbah or his supporters.[1] The suffering arose from a "joint AFRC/RUF campaign to strengthen their 'government' through brutal suppression of perceived opposition by killing and beating civilians" and a "concerted campaign against civilians" by AFRC/RUF rebels.[2]

The limbless were not amputees per se, which would suggest a medical procedure, but were mutilated victims of drug-crazed boys and their rebel masters. I was dazed by the cruelty inflicted upon children and women, as well as so many innocent men, in the vast forests and so brazenly on the streets of Freetown. Nowhere else were child soldiers recruited and used so cruelly and for such power-driven purposes—to achieve political dominance and control over "blood diamonds"—during the 1990s. Every time I visited Sierra Leone, I was so outraged I wanted the full weight of the law to come crashing down on the leaders of such atrocities. There was a plan for "truth and reconciliation," but I was determined—as were many others—that tough justice would be inflicted against warlords who had so smugly cast an entire nation into the fires of hell.

Operation No Living Thing

My own experience with Sierra Leone began in February 1998, when Freetown, the capital, was engulfed in atrocities. Nigerian forces in the Military Observer Group (ECOMOG), the West African peacekeeping force deployed by the Economic Community of West African States, were fighting to retake the capital city and capture the leaders of the rebel junta. I did not realize at first how prominent the country would become on my own watch, but it did not take long. "Operation No Living Thing," the merciless assault launched by the RUF and the AFRC, which aligned itself with RUF, targeted civilians in a rampage that seemed unstoppable. The scale of the atrocities in Sierra Leone kept growing.

As the war crimes ambassador, I had to determine whether the United States would call the atrocities either war crimes or crimes against humanity.

The RUF did not appear to be targeting any particular ethnic group, so genocide did not seem to be the relevant crime for Sierra Leone. The rebels were eliminating anyone who was of no use to them in a campaign of terror that unleashed both war crimes and crimes against humanity. Atrocities spread from east to west in the country as a systematic effort unfolded to terrorize civilians and devastate the countryside. There were no accurate numbers of dead and wounded, but we had a fair amount to go on with reports from the media and such nongovernmental groups as Doctors Without Borders. Hundreds of victims reportedly were being treated at hospitals. The pattern of killing was bound to continue. The rebels clearly wanted media attention to intimidate ECOMOG, composed primarily of Nigerian soldiers.

Pressure mounted upon neighboring states to negotiate with the RUF out of fear for their own survival. RUF rebels had seized enough territory to force the Sierra Leone government to enter talks. But U.S. diplomats in West Africa advised me and other State Department officials as early as May 1998 that a sharp message had to be sent to the rebels: that they risked standing before a war crimes tribunal for their atrocities against civilians and that Sierra Leone would be no exception to the march of justice in Africa. I never forgot that early warning as we challenged the rebels time and again to stop their criminal conduct, only to be spat in the face as more mutilated bodies wandered through the bloody terrain of that country.

During the summer of 1998, more reports of atrocities landed on my desk. At least 500 victims lay in Freetown hospitals. For every surviving victim who made it to a hospital, four or five died in the forests. Six hundred thousand refugees struggled to survive in Liberia, Guinea, and Nigeria. At least 70,000 civilians were displaced within Sierra Leone. At the time it was the biggest refugee crisis in Africa. No domestic criminal law had been leveled against any captured rebel perpetrator to render him accountable for the atrocities. Talk abounded in Freetown of amnesty for child soldiers and for the government soldiers who were rebelling but not for adult rebels who were committing so many of the atrocities.

The embattled but standing president of Sierra Leone, Ahmad Tejan Kabbah, visited Washington on July 31, 1998, and spoke with me and others about the situation in his country following the rebels' unsuccessful coup. He told us that messages acquired from the rebel leaders prior to the attempted coup instructed their soldiers to massacre every living thing (hence, Operation No Living Thing). He said messages intercepted by his government probably had been destroyed along with other files during the coup attempt. He did not believe the rebels had any real political agenda. Kabbah told us that the mutilations of hands—followed by arms, feet, legs, and ears—started during the election when the rebels wanted to remove evidence of voting because a voter's hands were stamped. Kabbah firmly believed President Charles Taylor of Liberia was linked directly to the Revolutionary United Front, and that his influence led to the atrocities. He wanted Taylor publicly to make it clear that the massacres must end. I reviewed with him a list of rebel leaders who should be apprehended, if they were still alive. At least Foday Sankoh, the leader of the RUF, already was jailed.

In his meeting with Susan Rice, the assistant secretary of state for African Affairs, and me, Kabbah noted that people wanted to lynch Sankoh out of vengeance, but he believed it essential to follow principles of law and to bring him to justice. "There should be reconciliation, but there also must be justice," he told us. He recognized how small his country was and the difficulty of attracting media coverage to the atrocities, but he hoped that someday the extent of them would be revealed. Kabbah needed judicial assistance, particularly qualified foreign judges, to hold trials of rebels and renegade military commanders. The Commonwealth of Nations (formerly the British Commonwealth) promised to respond to his plea, so we did not consider that particular issue as a U.S. priority. Kabbah wanted us to provide computers, plain stationery for court personnel to use, and buses for transport of prisoners. He also sought funding for the mutilated victims trying to resume life without one or more of their limbs.

Freetown in Peril

Six months later, in the final days of 1998, a rebel takeover of Freetown and of the government, which could only lead to more atrocities, appeared imminent. Our response remained limited to finding ways to support ECOMOG and its Nigerian peacekeepers with additional funding and military supplies. Susan Rice pleaded at a senior staff meeting that if sufficient funds could be raised for ECOMOG, the Nigerian soldiers could force the rebels to stand down. U.S. logistical support at that critical moment would be both responsive to the atrocities and prevent more from occurring. But the federal budget crunch buried our hopes for helping ECOMOG even while we plotted ways to raise the profile of Sierra Leone with the public to elicit more support on Capitol Hill. "Fat chance," one official remarked to me at one of the morning senior staff meetings in the State Department. Who, I muttered, in Bill Clinton's middle America, much less among the Republican majorities on Capitol Hill, gave a damn about Sierra Leone? As our efforts to secure additional funding for ECOMOG crashed, the rebels marched on.

Within only a couple of weeks, by mid-January 1999, battles were raging on the streets of Freetown. Negotiations had stalled. ECOMOG was taking serious losses, but the deaths of Nigerian peacekeepers did not register strongly in Western capitals. In Washington, we knew the Nigerian troops required much more support, and Susan Rice kept lobbying hard for action. The situation deteriorated further, with brutality and atrocities unleashed everywhere and government forces failing to stem the tide. Washington tried to encourage the Nigerians to beef up their military forces in ECOMOG, but it was a pathetic plea when we ourselves had so little to offer. Kabbah lost the backing of many of his traditional supporters in Sierra Leone, and his real power ebbed. No one predicted the situation would improve soon.

In late January, I convened the first meeting of the Atrocities Prevention Interagency Working Group, which had been established by President Clinton the month before when he designated me as the chairman of it. The working group's objective was to examine emerging scenarios of killings and try to formulate policies to prevent them from exploding into full-scale atrocities. The first meeting had the dual focus of Sierra Leone and the Democratic Republic of the Congo. Experts reported that both RUF and ECOMOG soldiers had committed human rights abuses in Sierra Leone. The overall situation had deteriorated substantially. The Nigerians planned to withdraw their forces before the May 29 Nigerian elections. Gathering information about the RUF and the atrocities its soldiers were committing deep within the countryside was almost impossible. We concluded that the United States, at a minimum, had to ratchet up the Sierra Leone crisis at the United Nations while we explored ways to sustain ECOMOG's presence there despite reports of their own abusive behavior.

The Nigerian peacekeepers held parts of Freetown and two major towns. The RUF rarely occupied territory; it just kept moving. The illicit diamond industry fueled purchases of arms and the hiring of mercenaries for the rebellion, but the RUF had no broad base of popular support. Foday Sankoh, RUF's leader, remained in custody but would be a key player in future talks. Johnny Paul Koroma headed the AFRC and remained at large. The dead from the January killings in Freetown alone numbered at least three thousand. Nigeria was spending $500,000 a day in Sierra Leone to sustain its ECOMOG force there. The United States had provided $55 million for humanitarian aid since October 1997. Over the previous year Washington had provided a measly $5 million to ECOMOG. The State Department was having a hard time on Capitol Hill securing $2.7 million of additional funds. The United States could not provide military weapons to ECOMOG because of congressional prohibitions on supplying Nigerian troops owing to their poor human rights record.[3]

By the first week of February, ECOMOG had failed to repel the rebels. The fate of Freetown hung in the balance. An estimated 150,000 civilians had fled into the capital city, 80 percent of which was destroyed or damaged. Sixty-five percent of the city's buildings were damaged. The World Food Program warehouse had been looted, with stocks that would have fed 170,000 people for two weeks wiped out. Three hundred rotting corpses lay on the sun-baked streets of Freetown. Ten thousand people were without shelter, and the number was expected to rise as high as 50,000. The ever-growing number of displaced civilians throughout Sierra Leone had reached 250,000 souls.

Rumors circulated that the rebels would launch another attack on Freetown in the first week of February. ECOMOG was not taking prisoners, and mob justice ruled whole neighborhoods. Indescribable mass rapes and forcible mutilations of limbs swept across the city. The two thousand attacking insurgents were predominantly former Sierra Leone troops—the AFRC—challenging a much larger but outmaneuvered force of about fifteen thousand ECOMOG soldiers. Few imagined that ECOMOG, even if it ultimately prevailed to save Freetown, would seek to retake territory outside the capital. There was only one U.N. helicopter operating between Freetown and Conakry, Guinea. Security for civil society workers remained very precarious. The United Nations evacuated all its staffers to other countries.

Washington appealed for a dialogue that could lead to national reconciliation; even Kabbah was willing to talk. If the rebels won the entire struggle, there could be a domino effect, with Guinea falling next. We worried about whether the U.N. Security Council would muster the will to ban the illicit diamond trade in the region. Although the nongovernmental watchdog Global Witness had tracked the diamond trade in conflict-ridden Angola, no one was urging an embargo on diamonds transported out of Sierra Leone—at least not yet. It would be very difficult to accomplish such an embargo.

I joined another meeting on Sierra Leone on February 5 where a dual-track policy emerged. First, the United States would support ECOMOG so that it could get the upper hand over the rebels. Second, we would do everything we could to get the warring parties to the negotiating table. We discussed the use of mutilation as a tactic of war and as a war crime and decided that we would publicly condemn the atrocities, hope that the parties could come together, and, in the meantime, strongly support ECOMOG, recognize Kabbah's authority, and seek negotiations in good faith. We wanted Sankoh and the RUF to denounce the atrocities. There was no doubt of Liberia's deep involvement. We strongly suspected that Charles Taylor had his sights on the diamonds. U.S. officials visited Taylor in Monrovia to deliver a plea for cooperation. They told him he was suspected of being responsible for the commission of atrocities in Sierra Leone and that there would be a price to pay. He was overseeing the dispatch of child soldiers and mercenaries into the depths of Sierra Leone; the U.S. officials told him to bring his surrogates back to Liberia. By all appearances, Taylor ignored the plea.[4]

Witness to the Mutilated

I decided to travel to Sierra Leone on the first possible day following the Freetown massacres. U.S. policy centered on condemning Liberian participation in the atrocities, pushing for regional diplomacy, seeking increased support for ECOMOG, pressing for cessation of external support for the RUF, and expediting resumption of humanitarian assistance. I had a public message for RUF's patrons, namely Liberia, Libya, and Burkina Faso (formerly Upper Volta): "Any government that supports RUF is a collaborator in the atrocities." A small army of criminals had hijacked much of Sierra Leone and was terrorizing, torturing, and murdering its civilian population, and we needed to end that carnage.

Flying to Freetown, I scribbled down some of the points that I soon articulated privately and publicly about accountability and peace: The RUF could take the opportunity Kabbah had offered them (a cease-fire, negotiated peace, and amnesty for all except top leaders, who might be exiled instead) and essentially save themselves. The alternative, we could guarantee, was that the United States, joining with other governments and regional bodies, would ensure that RUF and AFRC leaders were held accountable before a competent court of law, that there would be no statute of limitations, and that their crimes would be prosecuted. In my view, this was the battleground for democracy, for humanity, and for the security of West Africa. The rebels had left us no choice but to bring them to justice. We would explore prospects for an international tribunal. This was the rebels' last chance before they lost the prospect of an international amnesty. The last assault on Freetown, like the Račak massacre in Kosovo, had exhausted the international community's patience. But where was the rest of Africa when it came to ending the armed conflict in Sierra Leone? Where were the Arab countries? Where was Asia? Where was Latin America?

Arriving in Freetown on February 9, 1999, I immediately met with the sleep-deprived American ambassador, Joseph Melrose, and stressed to him that the rebel leaders must not be part of any amnesty package for rebel soldiers and that there were about six leaders of greatest interest to Washington. I believed that while the world's attention had been focused on the massacre in January of forty-five civilians at Račak and the resulting Rambouillet talks unfolding in France,[5] the atrocities in Sierra Leone were far greater in number and severity. Melrose agreed that the peace process in Sierra Leone required much more international attention than it had received. The magnitude of the massacres, mutilations, torture, rapes, and destruction of civilian property within the prior six weeks was so large that its full extent was unknown to the international community. While thousands of civilians had been slaughtered in Freetown in January alone, that number almost certainly represented a fraction of the casualties in the two-thirds of Sierra Leone then under rebel control. If past experience held true, the darkness that swept over Sierra Leone since 1998 had killed and mutilated countless victims whose identities or precise locations in the remote countryside we simply did not and could not know.

My first destination was Netland Hospital in Freetown, where mutilation victims were crowded into its small wards following the massacres. The victims' stories there, and at several sites in Guinea I visited later where the wounded and mutilated had fled, fit a familiar pattern: The AFRC and RUF rebel forces had pillaged, burned down entire neighborhoods, lined up men, women, and children, and then, one by one, chopped off their hands, arms, or feet, or some combination of any or all those appendages. Many of the rebels were child soldiers, typically smoking dope, and weak enough or employing implements so dull that the "choppings" often left hands dangling from arms, requiring the victim to finish the job alone. Most victims told me that the rebels shouted after mutilating them, "Go show this to

Kabbah. Tell Kabbah to help you now. Kabbah is our enemy." Some boys were spared mutilation, at least for a while, and abducted to serve as slave labor to the rebels and as soldiers themselves. Large numbers of young girls and women were raped and kept in sexual slavery until killed. Some victims told me of doing everything the rebels told them to, including surrendering all their property and performing menial chores for days, only to be chopped anyway (and the unluckiest among them, they said, were killed). Gunshot victims were everywhere, marking those who tried to escape or were fired upon within their homes. As I describe in the introduction of this book, I visited with one teenage girl, "Nancy," whose eyes had been burned out by pouring heated plastic into them. She was still traumatized from being gang-raped and refused to speak to anyone.

Netland Hospital normally was a maternity hospital. It had been transformed into a nightmarish crush of atrocity victims. Dr. Kojo Carew, a middle-aged man with a gracious and understanding approach to his patients, showed me around. He was caring for eighty patients in the small hospital, with about ten children among them. The International Committee of the Red Cross had developed a unique technique for rehabilitating amputees, called the Krukenberg procedure,[6] which was available at Netland Hospital. It involved the use of "pincers" attached to the stump of a mutilated forearm to enable the victim to regain partial use of the limb. But the procedure required many skin grafts and could be very painful. In addition, Dr. Carew did not want the hospital too closely associated with the ICRC for fear of rebel retribution.

As we walked through the wards, I spoke with many of the victims. One very articulate man described how he gave rebels everything and then was lined up with others as the rebels started chopping, sparing no one. He pleaded, but they chopped off one of his arms anyway. Then the rebels started to kill some of the captured villagers, and he ran for his life with two others. They got to a hill, and his companions shoved his mutilated body up it. He was one of the lucky ones, for he reached the hospital within two hours of the chopping and received treatment to stop the bleeding and prevent further infection. Most of the "chopped" victims in Sierra Leone did not get to a hospital quickly or to any medical care. Within days the wounded stumps or gunshot wounds became hideously infected, and many victims perished.

One man had a bullet lodged in his head that had entered from the top and rested near the base of his brain. Dr. Carew showed it to me on an

X-ray; he was trying to arrange an airlift for a special operation elsewhere. I was reminded again of the critical need for an international medevac capability in atrocity areas to handle difficult cases. A young girl, desperately hanging onto life despite a terrible gunshot wound, told me how she was shot while trying to put out the fire that rebels ignited in her home. Another young girl was severely burned across her entire front. She had been thrown into her burning home headfirst by the rebels and yet managed to survive, hideously scarred for life. Two young brothers stared at me, one with his left arm chopped off, the other with his right arm mutilated. The rebels had apparently thought that was funny. Another small boy had a severely broken arm and a hideously disfigured face from the impact of mortar fragments. He moaned without end. I no longer held back my tears.

As I made my way through Freetown, the devastation, extreme poverty, and seemingly aimless wanderings of those displaced by the fighting, many of them showing signs of mutilation and scarring, created a deeply depressing and almost suffocating environment. I had to suppress my rising anger and get on with the job of diplomacy.

Kabbah's Hilltop

When I arrived later that day at President Kabbah's residence, perched atop a hill overlooking Freetown to the north and east and the Atlantic Ocean to the west, I felt I had walked into an enclave of cowardly retreat from the horrors outside. I entered a room with both Kabbah and his finance minister, James Jonah, who was a former U.N. undersecretary-general, sitting comfortably. Kabbah evoked none of the impressive leadership characteristics one would imagine for someone battling a massive rebel assault on his government and people. His military assessments were too optimistic. His concerns for his own people seemed disingenuous. His insularity within his own residence demonstrated a withdrawal from the plight of the tens of thousands struggling for their lives at the bottom of his hill and beyond.

Nonetheless, Melrose and I had business to do with him. Kabbah's recent offer of peace talks gave Melrose an opening to the rebels. The American ambassador had plunged into round-the-clock efforts to address the humanitarian crisis and orchestrate the peace, and now he sought a location and funding for the talks. The U.N.'s special representative for Sierra Leone, Francis Okello, had earlier told me he was very skeptical of Kabbah but also realized that Kabbah and the peace talks must be supported. Kabbah's gesture would be credible, however, only if the rebels realized that ECO-MOG was strong enough to prevail against them.

Kabbah explained to me that the November 1996 Abidjan Peace Accord gave all RUF fighters an amnesty for crimes committed prior to the signing of the agreement. But five days after the accord had been signed, RUF leader Foday Sankoh sent a message disavowing it and pledging to continue the fight. Kabbah would consent to another amnesty provided there was no renewal of fighting. He would not agree to an amnesty for the top ten rebel leaders. He wanted them to live outside Sierra Leone and might consent to their returning in a few years. He did not regard five of them as true Sierra Leoneans and described them as really Liberians. However, Kabbah pulled me aside and privately confided that if negotiations went well, the top leaders also could benefit from the amnesty. The minister of justice, Solomon Berewa, told me later that the rebels had to perform well at the negotiating table and stick to the terms of the agreement for the amnesty to hold. If they reneged on the agreement, thus unleashing more atrocities, the amnesty would be canceled. I countered that the leadership of RUF and AFRC had to be removed from any amnesty deal. That would complicate the negotiations, but how could such individuals be shielded from accountability at this stage, I asked? No one wanted to answer that question.

Kabbah then led me into another room and showed a short video about the atrocities. The film began with a rally of presumably Kabbah supporters urging Sankoh's death. Then there were interviews describing boys, seven to ten years old, being abducted and forced to fight. They were injected with drugs and told how to use guns and kill people. One boy, separated from his parents, was injected with cocaine regularly. He said he had killed two children. The video continued with scenes of mutilated victims, burning bodies, and enormous damage inflicted on the Kissy neighborhood in eastern Freetown, which the rebels had hit very hard. The boys were rescued by ECOMOG troops. I thanked Kabbah for showing me the video but told him I had just seen similar examples of mutilation and destruction only a few blocks away. I did not have the guts to ask him if he had walked his capital's streets yet and visited perhaps a hospital or two, but I regarded it as remarkable that he put so much stock in the crude video he was showing on his television. All he had to do was have the courage to wade into the horrors his own people were experiencing and then bring that firsthand story to the world far more dramatically than he could standing before his television set in the residence on the hill.

Later the same day, I discussed with the ECOMOG commander, Major General Timothy Shelpidi from Nigeria, the reported summary executions carried out by his soldiers, as well as other human rights abuses ECOMOG stood accused of by the United Nations and civil society. I pressed him on the need for military discipline and enforcement of the rule of law, which he said, with an astonishingly straight face, would be administered against any soldiers found to be guilty of war crimes. A report by the U.N. Observer Mission in Sierra Leone, prominently unveiled to the press several days earlier, criticized summary executions of rebels and other abuses attributed to ECOMOG soldiers.[7] These incidents had to be kept in perspective when compared with the magnitude and systematic nature of atrocities committed by the rebels, which were the focus of most of the U.N. report.

Shelpidi told me that Liberian and other foreign influences were pervasive in Sierra Leone among the rebels. Ships from Monrovia were carrying arms and ammunition to them, he claimed. Charles Taylor, counseled Shelpidi, opposed the Kabbah government because it permitted ECOMOG troops to be stationed there. So he started a civil war. "Taylor seized the diamond area, and he is determined to carry out his crusade of a 'greater Liberia,'" Shelpidi noted. "Can you say Taylor is democratic? He's not democratic. He still sees himself as a rebel," the commander continued. I asked him to ensure that records be kept of atrocities committed by the rebels. He assured me that ECOMOG kept reports of destruction and killing that could be used for future war crimes prosecutions.

Spillover into Guinea

I took the same request to Conakry, Guinea, following my visit in Freetown. The Office of the U.N. High Commissioner for Refugees (UNHCR) had a sizable operation in that country owing to the flood of refugees arriving from across the border with Sierra Leone. UNHCR had begun to record refugee statements regarding the atrocities, and it was critical they continue to do so. I later brought back to Washington the request that at least our qualified volunteers, perhaps drawn from the Peace Corps Crisis Corps, be sent to the refugee camps in Guinea along with vehicles, digital cameras, and other technical assistance to properly record the stories of the refugees.

I entered UNHCR headquarters in Conakry, only to hear endless criticism of Kabbah. One UNHCR official believed Kabbah would not consider reconciliation and would hide behind others fighting for him. Kabbah's amnesty offer only demonstrated his own weakness. The people of Sierra Leone, the official said, were deeply disillusioned with Kabbah's failure to lead or govern. "There is a huge gap between Kabbah and his people," he said. The government had to build up its credibility. He said Kabbah never visited the hospitals in Freetown, including Connaught Hospital, which cared for so many atrocity victims. "What is happening in that country," the weary UNHCR representative said, "is beyond imagination."

At a press briefing following my visits to a hospital and rehabilitation center and several sessions with government ministers, I told journalists that Sierra Leone was a test for democracy, a test for the rule of law, a test for humanity, and a test for regional security, peacekeeping, and stability. The international community needed to understand the severity of the situation in Sierra Leone and that a withdrawal of Nigerian troops could lead to far more atrocities and a rebel conquest. There was not much time left to resolve the problem. Regarding peace talks, the top priorities were to stop the fighting and the atrocities. The talks would not be easy, but there was a window of opportunity. A major component of the talks likely would be amnesty. Any domestic amnesty must be conditioned on the sustained commitment by rebels—all of them—not to commit further atrocities, and any such amnesty must be revoked the moment there was a breakdown. Nor would the amnesty necessarily cover the ringleaders, who might be subject to special additional conditions and might need to live outside Sierra Leone to avoid the legal process within Sierra Leone. Nothing Sierra Leone did, however, could immunize the RUF or AFRC from an international legal process or the courts of other states. This point was identical to the condition U.N. secretary-general Kofi Annan placed on the Lomé Peace Agreement later that year. In the meantime, I said, U.N. agencies, governments, and ECOMOG needed to maintain good records of atrocity crimes, because they could serve as evidence at an international court.[8]

Flying aboard a UNHCR helicopter, I visited a refugee camp on the border of southeast Guinea and Sierra Leone the next day. Polio was sweeping through the camp, a phenomenon that resurrected ancient demons long ago defeated elsewhere in the world. My mother was one of the last polio victims in America, contracting it in late 1953 shortly after my birth and a few months before the Salk vaccine was made available throughout the United States and much of the world. An exceptionally brave and proud woman, she lived a full life even though she remained paralyzed from the waist down until her death in 1995. (I too had polio as a newborn but luckily beat it back.) She would have been shocked at what I saw in the camp as crippled refugees crawled around from one hut to the next. I felt I had entered a time warp; these polio victims had never had access to vaccines in Sierra Leone. Not only had they been struck down with resurgent polio; many also had been brutally attacked by the rebels.

One victim told me of being caught during a cross-border rebel attack on the refugee camp. The Guinea soldiers fled when the rebels attacked. Rebels bound him and others with ropes and intended to slaughter them. But their leader decided to wait until the next morning, when instead they were beaten and tied up again. Three men slugged him and chopped off his hands, the stumps later becoming infected and requiring amputation. The rebels, including mostly young boys smoking marijuana, told him to go tell the president of Guinea that the rebels had arrived. Four men were abducted, and six others were mutilated. Remarkably, the women escaped. The rebels had also tortured him by scraping his back with a red-hot knife. The refugee complained he was not getting adequate medicine for his pain. I saw many in the refugee camp who had "RUF" carved into their chests. No one in the camp had been spared some kind of injury. Some even had padlocks inserted into their lips by the rebels as a cruel signal to shut up.

Thinking Ahead with Atrocities Prevention

Upon my return to Washington, on February 19, 1999, I convened an Atrocities Prevention Interagency Working Group meeting on Sierra Leone. There were many questions to examine. Would a well-structured domestic amnesty in fact stop the atrocities? What kind of amnesty should the United States support? Should the amnesty cover only crimes falling short of atrocity crimes? Should it be amnesty for all perpetrators or a more limited amnesty, perhaps excluding the leadership? I argued for isolating some leading individuals to face criminal justice procedures and channeling the rest into a truth and reconciliation process. As I had advised in Sierra Leone and Conakry, there should be an automatic withdrawal of the amnesty if atrocities resumed. Another atrocities prevention meeting in early March continued the examination of policy choices, particularly on the diamond trade and an amnesty.

Susan Rice and I explored policy options for Sierra Leone that emerged from these meetings. We recommended a U.N. Security Council resolution that would establish the threat to international peace and security in Sierra Leone, acknowledge and condemn violations of atrocity law, threaten individual criminal accountability for offenders, call upon states to support ECOMOG, and request the secretary-general to conduct a one-month review of foreign influence and mercenary involvement in support of the RUF. We wanted his report to examine ways to restrict the access of foreign governments supporting the RUF, to focus on possible mechanisms for restricting access to the diamond wealth controlled by the RUF, and to explain how to prohibit trade in diamonds with the RUF.

As for Kabbah's proposal of an amnesty in a new peace deal with the rebels, if that were found to be essential for an agreement, the United States would consider supporting a limited amnesty if it was carefully structured, provided that it did not immunize anyone from *international* prosecution for serious violations of atrocity law. (Once again, this advice previewed what the United Nations tacked onto the Lomé Peace Agreement several months later.) The amnesty would terminate automatically for anyone who committed fresh atrocities after a specified date. Regional experts would begin to assess the impact an amnesty might have on RUF behavior. I also proposed consideration of bilateral sanctions against Liberia, Burkina Faso, and other nations known to be supporting the rebels and that Washington should further explore providing qualified investigators to compile reported incidents and evidence related to the atrocities.

I was advised, however, that an amnesty offer to the RUF would be unlikely to *seal* a peace deal. There was no convincing rationale for why the RUF would cease committing their atrocity crimes even if appeased by an amnesty for past crimes. I thus recommended that any amnesty offer had to be smartly conceived and limited in scope regarding whom it covered and what would trigger its revocation. My mistake was not to insist on a clear division between judicial accountability for the rebel leadership and some form of amnesty for the lower ranks. That ambiguity opened the door to disastrous drafting in the peace agreement months later.

On March 25, Dr. Kojo Carew from Netland Hospital in Freetown visited me in Washington. He had guided me through his hospital of mutilated victims in early February and now reported that the security and medical situations remained dire. There were constant fears of rebels lurking on the outskirts of Freetown. The RUF and AFRC had continued their atrocities without slowing down a beat. He and many others believed Charles Taylor was deeply involved in the entire enterprise of killing and mayhem. Dr. Carew said he still had seventy mutilation patients in Netland Hospital, which had a normal capacity for twenty as a specialized maternity hospital. "Nancy," whom I had visited at the hospital and who had been gang-raped and then blinded with molten plastic, had just been discharged. She had a son and a family who could look after them. "Everybody bears their own pain," Dr. Carew sighed, and continued: "We are just ordinary citizens who had such confidence, and then we were attacked! We are still in a state of shock. We can't even have our own weapons. Professionals are fleeing the country in big numbers." Rather than remain, he was relocating his own family to Gambia. When he departed, my mind froze on the image of Nancy lying on the hospital porch and how she epitomized our pathetic failure to stop crimes we knew were still being committed throughout Sierra Leone.

Amnesty in Lomé

The peace talks finally began, but the rebels refused to continue until they were given an unconditional amnesty or pardon (the terms were used interchangeably) relating to past crimes. Attorney General Solomon Berewa, who headed the Sierra Leone government's delegation at the talks, stated on May 29 that if the release of Sankoh was required to achieve peace, he would be granted an absolute and free pardon. As *The Economist* reported on June 3, "That allowed the talks to begin in earnest. The rebels are demanding a four-year transition period during which they will share power with the existing government and will launch the RUF as a political party. They also want an amnesty, the release of prisoners and the integration of their fighters into the national army. Knowing that time now may be on its side, the government is likely to discuss these conditions at length."[9] But the talks did not drag on very long.

On July 7, 1999, the warring parties concluded a peace agreement in Lomé, Togo. I had not been privy to the final days of negotiation, which Jesse Jackson had facilitated as Clinton's special envoy, and was taken aback to read the breadth of its terms on pardon and amnesty. Berewa and his deal making with Sankoh had prevailed. The government of Sierra Leone agreed to an "absolute and free pardon" for Sankoh and to an "absolute and free pardon and reprieve to all combatants and collaborators in respect of anything done by them in pursuit of their objectives, up to the time of the signing of the present Agreement." The government further ensured "that no official or judicial action is taken against any member of the RUF/SL, ex-AFRC or CDF [Civil Defense Forces] in respect of anything done by them in pursuit of their objectives as members of those organizations, since March 1991, up to the time of the signing of the present Agreement. In addition, legislative and other measures necessary to guarantee immunity to former combatants, exiles and other persons, currently outside the country for reasons related to the armed conflict shall be adopted ensuring the full exercise of their civil and political rights, with a view to their reintegration within a framework of full legality."[10] The Lomé Peace Agreement was signed by Kabbah and its greatest beneficiary, Sankoh. Remarkably, Charles Taylor, who stood to gain mightily by the immunity provision, was recorded as a witness along with Francis Okello, the U.N. representative. The United States and United Kingdom issued a statement in Lomé congratulating the Sierra Leone government and the RUF and expressing their "support for the agreement, which will bring to an end the tragic war of Sierra Leone." That proved to be an absurdly optimistic statement.

The priority for the Africa specialists in the State Department was a peace deal, apparently at whatever cost to justice. The moment exemplified years of confrontation that I typically had with the regional bureaus. The quest for accountability always complicated their work, which was the "realism" of political negotiations and peace agreements. I spent much of my time lobbying all the regional bureaus to take international justice seriously. Albright usually let me fight those battles alone or with the occasional help of the human rights assistant secretary, John Shattuck, or his successor, Harold Koh. Though she had created the war crimes ambassadorship when she became the secretary of state, Albright had other priorities in her everyday work, and they usually centered on the larger geopolitical issues. My corner of the foreign policy pie was still experimental, and I had to sink or swim, usually on my own.

The Lomé Peace Agreement stank and, sure enough, backfired within months as the rebels violated the peace terms and continued inflicting their grim atrocities. The State Department publicly hoped for the success of the agreement and placed great reliance on its provision for a truth and reconciliation commission to "address impunity." As for the full "domestic pardon" of Foday Sankoh, the public line was that it would become the chance to transform the RUF from a rebel movement into a political party and advance the interests of reconciliation and reconstruction. I found such gobbledygook almost unbearable, and the best I could achieve for a judicial process was guidance that spoke to the establishment of an objective international fact-finding mission to document evidence of atrocities and provide that information to the truth and reconciliation commission as a basis for its work. The United States would remain committed to the pursuit of accountability for serious violations of international humanitarian law, wherever they occurred.

Unfortunately, these were naive sentiments now that the fate of the country had been conceded to the rebels. I had not been invited to join the Lomé talks and in retrospect regretted not forcing my way into them, but I simply did not imagine so much would be conceded so readily to the rebels. The only positive outcome to the debacle was that when, in the next year, Sierra Leone predictably imploded again into violence and atrocities, I had a fairly strong hand to play in U.S. policy-making (as in Kosovo) as the issue of accountability took its rightful place on center stage. Upon the signing of the Lomé Peace Agreement, Okello filed a handwritten reservation to it on behalf of the United Nations disavowing part of the amnesty in these words: "The United Nations holds the understanding that the amnesty provisions of the Agreement shall not apply to international crimes of genocide, crimes against humanity, war crimes and other serious violations of international humanitarian law."[11]

The Fruits of Impunity

It was not surprising that, in early January 2000, researchers from Human Rights Watch met with me about the "dismal domestic situation" in Sierra Leone, as they described it. The whole peace process had eroded, and it appeared to be in large part because of the impunity granted to the rebel leaders. The rebels believed they had won. Sankoh even admitted he opposed a truth and reconciliation commission because it would impinge on the "heroic" image of his fighters. Almost all common people said they did not need justice, but on an individual level they sought informal retribution. They saw no formal justice system functioning in Sierra Leone and thus could not believe there would be true punishment of the perpetrators.

The Security Council sought to resurrect the Lomé aspirations with a resolution that reiterated the need to foster accountability and respect for human rights in Sierra Leone, in part through seeking enough international support to establish the Truth and Reconciliation Commission called for in the peace agreement. The council also noted "with concern the continuing human rights violations against the civilian population of Sierra Leone" and emphasized "that the amnesty extended under the Peace Agreement does not extend to such violations committed after the date of its signing."[12] The peace process had completely derailed. I argued that Washington should follow up the council's edict and state publicly, and more emphatically, that war criminals would be held accountable for past crimes and that there would be no amnesty for any crimes committed after July 7, 1999. In an effort to jump-start the parallel truth and reconciliation process, I passed on to Mary Robinson, the U.N. high commissioner for human rights with the lead on the process, the U.S. "nonpaper" outlining draft domestic legislation for the Sierra Leone Truth and Reconciliation Commission.

In early February 2000, Albright sent letters to Sankoh and Koroma making clear that violations of the peace agreement and any atrocities against civilians would not be tolerated, and that those responsible for ordering or committing such acts would be held accountable. Her letter also informed them that I would be visiting Freetown on February 21 and 22 to voice American concerns over the peace agreement and human rights violations. At a senior staff meeting on February 11, one crisis after another seized our attention, including Sierra Leone, where we concluded that the peace process was in deep trouble. Everyone at the table was grim-faced. Tom Pickering, the undersecretary of state for political affairs, conceded, "We should take solace in the fact that we are involved in all of these awful projects." Then Deputy Secretary Strobe Talbott's secretary opened the door and said, "Secretary Pickering, it's [U.N. secretary-general] Kofi Annan on the phone for you." The room burst into laughter. Talbott concluded, "That's a Pickering moment!" And we poor souls laughed some more. The world was going to hell in a handbasket and Pickering was going to speak to God (Kofi Annan) to solve everything.

Later that day I convened another atrocities prevention meeting on Sierra Leone. The numbers of killings and mutilations continued to grow, with at least a thousand new mutilated victims a month. There were more kidnappings of boys for use as child soldiers and greater RUF illicit diamond-mining activity within the atrocity-burdened triangle of northwest Sierra Leone. We still knew very little of what was occurring in the eastern half of the country. The U.N. Mission in Sierra Leone (UNAMSIL), a peacekeeping force, had no real capability or will to hold back large-scale atrocities if they swept throughout the country again. The U.N. peacekeepers could guard key strategic areas but could not stop the atrocities or otherwise protect civilians. And they failed to exercise any control over the diamond areas, which provided cash for and emboldened the rebels. Like a cruel joke, the Lomé Peace Agreement had awarded rebel leader Foday Sankoh the chairmanship of the critical new Commission for the Management of Strategic Resources, National Reconstruction and Development, an agency that managed the exploitation of the country's gold and diamonds. As one analyst told me, "The quickest way to get rid of U.N. peacekeepers is to challenge them by imposing casualties." RUF militia were being trained at camps in Liberia, which likely would place Charles Taylor in direct violation of the peace deal.

Our atrocities prevention team decided that the rebels' access to diamond resources had to be curtailed. UNAMSIL eventually would need to occupy the mining areas, and the international diamond industry would have to place an embargo on trading rebel gems. U.N. peacekeepers already in-country showed no real signs of actively challenging armed rebel forces, however, having made clear their strong desire to avoid taking casualties. Several instances of U.N. units turning over their arms to rebels fully illustrated this posture. We believed that the disparate makeup of the UNAMSIL force likely would cause serious command and control problems. Poor logistical support for peacekeepers also exacerbated the problem.

The team's greatest fear, about which we alerted senior State Department officials, was that the RUF would decide that inflicting casualties on UNAMSIL would be a quick way of getting it out of the country. We speculated that the Guinea soldiers in UNAMSIL would leave if they began to take casualties. It was a prophetic fear, although the outcome was not what the RUF expected. A few months later their kidnapping of about five hundred U.N. peacekeepers, and the murder of some of them, galvanized the United Nations and key governments, including Britain and the United States, to act decisively to bring the conflict to an end and to negotiate the creation of an international criminal tribunal.

But first, in February 2000, my atrocities prevention interagency group concluded that the international community would have to assist the government of Sierra Leone in documenting, investigating, and eventually prosecuting perpetrators of atrocity crimes committed since the Lomé signing date of July 7, 1999. As I headed toward Sierra Leone in mid-February, the U.S. National Security Council confirmed to me that atrocities committed after Lomé were not covered by the amnesty. That interpretation helped take the State Department off the hook for at least some of the botched terms of the Lomé agreement. My job was to drive home the point, both privately and publicly in Freetown, that war criminals must not assume that they could act with impunity.

My visit to Sierra Leone proved both enlightening and deeply frustrating. This was my third meeting with President Kabbah, who was joined by his foreign minister. Kabbah remained hopeful about the intentions of Foday Sankoh, Johnny Paul Koroma, and the RUF, as if he was defending the worth of Lomé. Sankoh had just left the country in violation of the terms of the Lomé agreement. Seeing him was a primary purpose of my trip, namely, to deliver a tough atrocity crimes message to him. Kabbah told me Sankoh sounded confused and, with his rudimentary education, did not understand the prohibitory travel language of the agreement. In fact, Sankoh was prohibited from traveling outside the country without the permission of the U.N. sanctions committee. He traveled anyway. While I was en route to Freetown, the Security Council Committee on Sanctions concerning Sierra Leone held an urgent meeting and, noting that Sankoh was outside Sierra Leone without the committee's authorization, requested that he return to Sierra Leone immediately, and the committee reminded all governments of the travel ban against him.[13] Sankoh was promptly expelled from South Africa and flown to Cote D'Ivoire for his rapid return to Freetown, albeit after I had departed the city.[14]

Sankoh's connections with Charles Taylor continued to be a matter of deep concern. Kabbah said, "Charles Taylor is a rebel, and you can't change a rebel overnight." Sankoh's attempt to visit South Africa occurred, Kabbah said, because Taylor had connections with some shady characters. Sankoh apparently wanted to negotiate some diamond business while there.

An important part of my job, gathering the information that ultimately compelled the creation of a war crimes tribunal, was to hear testimonies of the victims firsthand. This trip to Freetown was no exception. One moment I was listening to the president's detached perspective from his hilltop home, elevated above the seething poverty of Freetown, and the next moment I was in a modest home on an obscure street of that city listening to a group of victims brought together for me by Corrine Dufka of the local Human Rights Watch outpost. They all had names, loved ones, and homes they wanted desperately to defend.

Before me sat Possch Kargbo, a weak, weeping teenage girl who was abducted by the RUF while she was going to her father's funeral. She had to take them to her house, which they looted, and then "Commander Blood" told her she was going to be mutilated. She begged him not to do it. He relented, only to take her and ten other girls to a village unfamiliar to them where, for three days, Commander Blood and three other men raped her. All the girls met similar fates. Posseh had been a virgin. She escaped with one other girl while eight others remained captive.

Aminta Mansaray, another young rape victim, had been held for one year by the rebels. She carried the child of a rebel rapist and had escaped only the month before. Pahassan Kamara had been captured in December, flogged mercilessly, stripped naked, and marched to another village, Mabaii, where about five hundred rebels were camped. He was told to sit on the ground, where he was repeatedly kicked until he became unconscious. One rebel lit a stick and scraped it along his back. Then he was stabbed in his arm and left to make his way back to his village. I heard stories from many others that day who had suffered from the madness of the Sierra Leone conflict.

Oluyemi Adeniji, the U.N. secretary-general's new special representative, and Major General Vijay Kumar Jetley, the force commander of UNAMSIL, conceded to me that the RUF still considered a vast chunk of Sierra Leone to be under their exclusive control and that the only weapons being turned in (a requirement of the peace agreement) were so antiquated it was farcical. Commander Jetley said that they had almost no capacity to protect witnesses for the planned Truth and Reconciliation Commission and, with so many weapons flooding the country, no one would emerge to testify anyway. Both men resented the United States urging them to be more proactive while Washington refused to contribute troops to the U.N. peacekeeping force. They believed that Foday Sankoh had to be pressed to comply with the terms of the Lomé Peace Agreement and that he might crater and comply under even greater diplomatic pressure. But they argued that removing Sankoh would increase their problems. "Sankoh is the best devil to deal with," said Jetley. He thought UNAMSIL could not begin to move into the rebel-held diamond areas for at least two months. I left their command bunker thinking the U.N. officials were clueless (or dismissive) about the larger goals of justice and reconciliation. They were in strict survival mode, even if it meant a pact with the devil himself.

But my discussions with Solomon Berewa, the attorney general and minister of justice, convinced me that Sierra Leone had no capability to hold trials of the rebel leaders now or in the future, and certainly no capacity to prosecute thousands of individual perpetrators of atrocity crimes, even those committed only since the Lomé Peace Agreement was signed. There were hardly any courts in the provinces. The rebel leaders simply assumed the inability of the government to do anything about their more recent crimes. Berewa labeled the challenge as "addressing impunity," meaning he wanted to find a way to minimize the effects of the Lomé amnesty on the rebel perpetrators of atrocities. Later efforts, particularly by British officials, to persuade me that somehow Sierra Leone's courts, with some assistance, could render credible justice against war criminals, including Charles Taylor, flew in the face of what I learned during that visit to Freetown in February 2000.

When I met Johnny Paul Koroma, the leader of the rebel Armed Forces Revolutionary Council (and years later the sole remaining fugitive indictee of the Special Court for Sierra Leone), he sought to assure me that all was being done to investigate alleged crimes by his forces. He even claimed that he was trying to persuade some of his commanders, such as the one called "Commander Savage," to come out of hiding in the forests by the next day. Koroma argued that domestic prosecutions "would not be good at this time due to the needs of disarmament. After disarmament, the soldiers will be in camps and their names can be registered. Then you can 'twist' them and identify war criminals one by one." He was prepared to lead in identifying perpetrators in the camps. But he told me that there had been a recent attempt on his life by his own men, "orchestrated by politicians." Koroma criticized Sankoh's travel to South Africa, accusing him of trying to sell diamonds there. He said Sankoh would keep emphasizing RUF control of the diamond-mining areas and other economic regions of the country as part of the implementation of Lomé.

My meeting with A. K. Kamera, the deputy minister of labor and a close associate of Foday Sankoh, turned acrimonious. (Under the dreamy terms of the Lomé Agreement, governmental power was shared between the Kabbah supporters and Sankoh's rebel leaders.) I told Kamera that Sankoh should not travel outside the country. I had flown all the way to Sierra Leone, at the direction of the White House and Albright, to meet with Sankoh, and he had essentially stood me up. I said his work was in Sierra Leone, particularly on disarmament and reintegration, and warned that I would press for his indictment by an international or foreign court outside Sierra Leone if he traveled again without U.N. authorization. There was great judicial risk in his traveling anywhere. I requested he tell Sankoh personally that I was deeply disappointed that he was not there to see me and that I had planned the trip on the assumption he would not violate U.N. sanctions. Then I said to Kamera, "I will make it my mission in life to track him down and bring him to justice. Tell him that's my message." A rather startled Kamera responded that he was on the phone regularly with Sankoh and would do so.

Afterward, on the ride to the helicopter pad for my departure from Freetown, Ambassador Melrose was visibly upset that I had taunted Kamera, as Melrose felt he needed to coax Sankoh back into compliance with Lomé. But I had strong reasons to speak as I did and told Melrose, "Look, this guy is spitting in our face, violating Lomé, and perpetuating war crimes. Enough. He needs the riot act read to him, and frankly he needs to be more scared of us than he is." Sankoh was the poster child for impunity, and I had reached my breaking point in tolerating his antics. Perhaps the threat of real prosecution, somehow and somewhere, would persuade him to start cooperating. No one could convince me at that stage that any other approach would work.

Kidnappings and the Ascent of Accountability

Very little was achieved on the many challenges in Sierra Leone during the following two months. But in early May, hundreds of U.N. peacekeepers were kidnapped by the RUF, which renounced the Lomé cease-fire. As many as twenty-five hundred peacekeepers had been cut off from communicating with headquarters in Freetown, and we did not know their fate. Melrose reported on May 8 that there were ten thousand demonstrators outside Foday Sankoh's compound in Freetown, enraged at the RUF's brazen resurgence, and that there had been shooting and some casualties. Several of Sankoh's ministers had been arrested the night before. Jesse Jackson spoke with Charles Taylor, although I did not learn exactly what he told him or learned in that conversation. Earlier, ECOMOG handed over its remaining troops to UNAMSIL, but the U.N. force commander, in a bid to bolster the peace process, spread out his troops in small groups in various parts of the country. That made them vulnerable regarding equipment, communications, and even rescue. UNAMSIL was forced to hunker down and try to consolidate its remaining forces in Freetown.

We all knew, in Washington and London, that international troops had to be increased. British ships were scheduled to arrive by May 13 to evacuate foreigners. Disaster or a much larger commitment to engage loomed. Julia Taft, the assistant secretary of state for refugees, asked at a senior staff meeting the most logical question: "How in the world did the peace process allow Foday Sankoh to hold such a prominent position [namely, chairmanship of the diamond-mining commission]?" I agreed with her: it was astonishing.

Reports arrived in Washington that atrocities were occurring in the northern sector of Sierra Leone. There were rumors that Koroma had ordered the arrest of RUF ministers. There also were reports that Sankoh had ordered his troops into Freetown. Harold Koh, the assistant secretary for human rights, launched his staff on a systematic mapping of the atrocities in Sierra Leone. He asked me to consider whether, if the peacekeeper hostages were released, the RUF perpetrators would go unpunished or be prosecuted.

On May 10, 2000, I shared with senior State Department officials my views on Sierra Leone accountability. I posited three scenarios, from best to worse, for possible outcomes to the situation. Under each of the three scenarios, I counseled that the question of accountability loomed large.

Under the first scenario, where the Lomé Peace Agreement was salvaged and security and safety returned to the country, the only reasonable response available, in order to preserve the credibility of peacekeeping operations as a whole, was that those responsible for the hostage taking and other post-Lomé violations must be held accountable. That would send a message to nations being encouraged to send peacekeepers to Sierra Leone and to future potential violators that attacks of this nature will not be tolerated and that measures must be taken to hold perpetrators responsible.

Under the second scenario, if the RUF succeeded in running the peacekeepers out of a significant part of Sierra Leone and began a rampage of killing similar to that experienced in the past, if not worse, we would have to determine the appropriate response to the violations of international humanitarian law. Since the signing of the Lomé Peace Agreement, the U.S. policy toward accountability had been to encourage and support the early implementation of the Truth and Reconciliation Commission and to be open to a call by the parties or the international community for an independent international fact-finding mission. Our posture was to give the peace agreement a chance to mature and bear fruit. Any discussion about an international criminal tribunal for Sierra Leone was viewed as premature. If gross violations erupted, our policy had to adapt. We needed to find forums and mechanisms that would allow for credible justice and accountability for both pre-Lomé and post-Lomé violations. I proposed some advance thinking about this approach. We had to send a message that gross violations would not be tolerated and violators would be punished.

The third scenario envisaged Freetown falling to the rebels. We would be faced with the decision of whether to strengthen the mandate of a U.N. force or a multinational force and granting it the power to restore peace and recapture Freetown. If that occurred and such a force recaptured Freetown, we would have to follow through on punitive measures against war criminals and seek to deter future violators.

In considering all these scenarios, I advised that Washington not limit itself only to a Security Council war crimes tribunal in the mold of the Yugoslav and Rwanda tribunals. Other judicial options, some regional, also should be considered. I recommended that the Security Council authorize any U.N. or multinational force in Sierra Leone to apprehend known war criminals and to collect and document evidence of atrocity crimes and human rights abuses. We had to start talking privately with other Security Council members about issues of accountability, collection of evidence, and apprehension as matters to be factored into any U.N. peacekeeping or multinational force mandate. We should be ready to discuss prospects for an international or regional criminal tribunal.

The diplomacy to build the court for Sierra Leone began on May 11, 2000, when I sat down with Hans Corell, the U.N.'s top legal counsel. He confided that U.N. secretary-general Kofi Annan was very upset, again, over the amnesty awarded in the Lomé Peace Agreement. Annan had no intention for the United Nations to accept or endorse amnesties for such crimes. If any perpetrators were caught outside Sierra Leone, Annan and Corell believed no mercy should be shown and they should be prosecuted. But no one knew how to build or use the right court.

One week later, British intervention forces arrested Sankoh and put him under the custody of the Sierra Leone government. That act signaled the possibility that if a criminal tribunal were created, at least one likely defendant already was in custody. I quickly sent a memorandum of possible options for accountability and justice forward to Susan Rice and Harold Koh, the two State Department officials most directly focused on the unfolding crisis in Sierra Leone. I predicted that upon the safe release of the U.N. peacekeepers, a broad consensus would emerge to hold Sankoh and other hard-line RUF leaders accountable for atrocity crimes. The issue would not be whether to do it, but how. While a domestic prosecution was theoretically possible, I was deeply skeptical of the Sierra Leonean courts' capabilities. The country's death penalty would make it impossible for European governments to provide expertise, funding, and logistical support, which were desperately needed. The other option would be some kind of regional or international tribunal similar to the Yugoslav and Rwanda tribunals. I suggested that such a regional court (perhaps forged by the Economic Community of West African States) could still benefit from U.N. Security Council engagement in a joint enterprise of legal authority, expertise, and funding.

There were basic questions, however, still to answer: How broad would the scope of the court be in terms of the individuals it could prosecute? Would just Sierra Leoneans be held accountable, or would foreign nationals (such as Charles Taylor) who had allegedly committed crimes on Sierra Leone territory also be accountable? What would be the chargeable offenses, and would there be a way to bring the blood diamond trade into the realm of criminal conduct? Would international forces in Sierra Leone have the authority to investigate and arrest suspects?

Pressing for an International Tribunal

I began to sketch out the option with which I felt most comfortable—a Security Council international tribunal—given the clear threat to peace and security in Sierra Leone and its devastated judiciary. There had not been any movement at Foggy Bottom, but on June 3 the U.S. ambassador to the United Nations, Richard Holbrooke, called me to recommend that we press for a full-fledged international criminal tribunal for Sierra Leone. That was the green light I had been waiting for, and I plunged into the task.

I dispatched one of my new staffers, Justice Department and former Rwanda Tribunal prosecutor Pierre-Richard Prosper, to Freetown to talk with President Kabbah about establishing a tribunal. If we could obtain Kabbah's support for an international tribunal, that would facilitate the proposal immensely within the Security Council. Within days, Prosper reported that Kabbah preferred a Security Council tribunal. Both Kabbah and Attorney General Berewa saw tremendous difficulties with any domestic trial. The biggest issue was security, which would be almost impossible to assure in war-torn Sierra Leone. Local police could not protect either the defendants or witnesses or any courtroom adequately. Sankoh was hidden at a secure location for the time being, but Sierra Leone had inadequate prison facilities. The domestic courts, Kabbah and Berewa predicted, would only deal with post-Lomé crimes. In their view, because of all the biases built up among the people of Sierra Leone, it would be impossible to have a fair trial in the country. The two leaders suggested to Prosper some kind of mixed tribunal, perhaps with nationals who were practicing law in London sitting on the bench. A tribunal should at least begin legal proceedings in Sierra Leone, which they considered absolutely essential. Then, because of security, the tribunal could exercise an option to move to another West African country.

Attorney General Berewa cautioned that Sierra Leone's antiquated law had its limitations, and that crimes committed against UNAMSIL troops, for example, might not be open to prosecution. The tribunal would have to apply international law, but he also wanted Sierra Leone law to play a significant role in the proceedings. He boldly suggested that he could serve as a coprosecutor. He confirmed that Sierra Leone would approach the United Nations for a U.N. court rooted in the Sierra Leone legal system and seek flexibility about moving the trial elsewhere in West Africa. Berewa wanted a Security Council resolution soon. In his opinion, once Sankoh's trial was finished, there would be resources to take on a second tier of perpetrators.

Prosper and I explored whether to expand the Rwanda Tribunal to absorb Sierra Leone. There were problems: First, the Rwandan government would resent any dilution of the Rwanda Tribunal mandate. Second, Burundi had been asking for an expansion of the tribunal's jurisdiction for years, as had some nongovernmental organizations, but that had never been achieved. The Burundi government would not be happy with Sierra Leone trumping Burundi. Third, could the Rwanda Tribunal, long troubled with charges of maladministration and even corruption, handle an entire new mandate administratively? If jurisdiction went to the Rwanda Tribunal, then all the combatants—rebels, government soldiers, and regional and U.N. peacekeepers—would have to be included, and that prospect was a political nonstarter for the government in Freetown and the major donor nations of those peacekeepers.

I began to formulate policy that pointed to an initial Sierra Leone indictment of Sankoh that would leave our options open. The second phase would be international in character. With Freetown's consent in hand, I planned to launch an initiative in the Security Council and soon began drafting a council resolution.

The kidnapping of several hundred U.N. peacekeepers clearly were the major grounds for stoking international support for a Security Council-sponsored tribunal, even though the magnitude of atrocity crimes in Sierra Leone for years, including a number of unlawful killings, far exceeded anything done to the peacekeepers. But the kidnapping was a direct slap at the United Nations, it angered everyone, and it had the fortunate by-product of finally focusing attention on prosecuting the atrocity crimes writ large.

Berewa told Prosper in Freetown that he had evidence Sankoh ordered the taking of U.N. peacekeepers as hostages. The possible escape of Sankoh was a major concern, as he would be lynched if he appeared on the streets. I told Prosper that Holbrooke needed to know the precise position of the government on an international tribunal. Prosper confirmed again that the Kabbah government would support a Security Council tribunal. The British, for reasons of both tribunal fatigue and maintaining the tribunal-building focus on establishment of the International Criminal Court, spoke only of domestic justice, eventually. But I suspected, as did colleagues, that if Washington could get a fair proposal before the Security Council, London would support it.

Kabbah's Bid to the Security Council

The concept paper Prosper and I drafted proposed that the Security Council create a "special court," with the power to enforce cooperation by relevant governments and with financing drawn from voluntary contributions from interested governments. It was utterly unrealistic to propose the type of assessed contributions that funded the Yugoslav and Rwanda tribunals, as most Security Council members and woefully few other U.N. member states had any interest in being compelled to pay for the Sierra Leone tribunal. The court's statute would blend international and domestic law. This would create flexibility in charging suspects, give Sierra Leone a greater stake in the court, and allow the court to prosecute crimes against the peacekeepers. There would be coprosecutors, one from Sierra Leone and the other a foreign prosecutor. Initially there would be a single trial chamber of three judges. There would be an additional chamber to hear pretrial motions. If more chambers were needed, then they would be appointed as circumstances required. The objective was to start with a lean and robust judicial strike force.

Under our proposal, the mandate of the existing Appeals Chamber for the Yugoslav and Rwanda tribunals would be expanded to include Sierra Leone. The special court would sit in Sierra Leone for pretrial and trial proceedings but have the power to move them out of the country for security purposes. In the meantime, the United States and other key governments would try to rehabilitate the domestic judicial system. Sentences likely would be served outside Sierra Leone. This contingency arose partly because when the RUF invaded any area, they first went to the prisons to liberate their soldiers. The alternative would be to create a maximum-security prison inside the country, for which funding would be extremely difficult to raise.

To garner sufficient international support, the mandate of the special court needed to be narrow, thus pointing to those "most responsible and the leadership." We suspected that would limit the reach of the tribunal to a few dozen suspects. I was undecided whether the special court's temporal jurisdiction must be limited to post-Lomé violations, but suggested that the Security Council allow the mandate to continue indefinitely until peace and security was established in Sierra Leone. Such an open-ended jurisdiction might deter future crimes, and was the model adopted for the Yugoslav Tribunal. The mandate needed to remain silent on limiting the nationality of the suspects so that the special court could investigate Charles Taylor. We had to get UNAMSIL on board to assist with apprehensions and security for tribunal investigators and other court personnel, as well as any special court offices. Finally, the Kabbah government wanted U.S. assistance in sponsoring the Security Council resolution.

In a brief interlude from our collaboration on the special court, Prosper told me that he had in his possession shocking photographs of atrocities. The RUF documented their crimes by photographing them and sending the prints to Sankoh to show him that they were doing their job. Some photographs even showed Sankoh directing the atrocities. The photographer who gave the pictures to Prosper was terrified. He had a family of five and stayed at home out of fear for his life. In one photograph, a severed head was placed on the hood of a car, with the RUF cheering as they stood nearby. The photographer clearly would be a material witness for the prosecution of the RUF. Eventually, the photographs were published by war correspondent Sebastian Junger in *Vanity Fair*.[15]

I spoke with Prosper, still working in Freetown, on June 7, 2000. He told me that the Sierra Leone government had reconfirmed the U.S. approach. They also knew it would be subject to some revision in the process. At an interagency meeting the next day, I achieved consensus on invoking the U.N. Charter's enforcement provisions (Chapter VII) to build a special court for Sierra Leone. We hoped to call for investigators to begin work immediately in Sierra Leone. I had the lead on the resolution and would be in New York for the next three weeks anyway for further negotiations related to the International Criminal Court.

A few days later I met with Holbrooke. He wanted me to negotiate a single resolution that would marry some of the personnel and other resources of the Rwanda Tribunal with a special court for Sierra Leone. He saw that kind of formula as potentially more saleable among his council colleagues. Holbrooke's bottom line was to maintain the international jurisdiction of the Security Council over whatever was built. British-born Ralph Zacklin, the deputy legal counsel at the United Nations, viewed the situation quite differently and urged me to opt for strictly national trials in Sierra Leone. He thought the vast shortcomings of the Sierra Leone courts could be overcome if the United States, United Nations, and international community assisted the government. He also had little stomach for the cost implications of a third ad hoc tribunal following the Yugoslav and Rwanda tribunals.

So far, however, U.N. officials had not discussed any of their plans with Kabbah or the attorney general or other government officials. All they knew was Kabbah's intention to put Sankoh on trial. I told Zacklin to contact Freetown immediately to ascertain their intentions. What, for example, would be the best way to prosecute crimes committed against U.N. peacekeepers? Would the court's jurisdiction extend to crimes that occurred prior to the Lomé Peace Agreement and to crimes against humanity, and would a domestic court accept such jurisdiction? Does Kabbah want national trials?

Kabbah acted faster, however, and sent Annan a letter on June 12 accompanied by a "Suggested Framework"[16] that finally triggered serious consideration in New York of a special court for Sierra Leone. It followed closely the concept paper Prosper and I had drafted and which Prosper had presented to Kabbah and Berewa during his visit several days earlier. Kabbah wrote in his letter of the special court for Sierra Leone, which sounded very familiar to me by then:

> With regard to the magnitude and extent of the crimes committed, Sierra Leone does not have the resources or expertise to conduct trials for such crimes. This is one of the consequences of the civil conflict, which has destroyed the infrastructure, including the legal and judicial infrastructure, of this country. Also, there are gaps in Sierra Leonean criminal law as it does not encompass such heinous crimes as those against humanity and some of the

gross human rights abuses committed by the RUF. It is my view, therefore, that, unless a court such as that now requested is established here to administer international justice and humanitarian law, it will not be possible to do justice to the people of Sierra Leone or to the United Nations peacekeepers who fell victim to hostage-taking.

In the framework document attached to his letter, Kabbah asked for a special court created by the Security Council:

> This will be a special court for Sierra Leone created by the United Nations Security Council that will take into account the special needs and requirements of the Sierra Leone situation. It should be a court that is flexible in law and venue.
>
> A court created under the Security Council's authority will have the advantage of strong enforcement powers that will call for cooperation from States in investigations, arrests, extradition and enforcement of sentences. It will also call for voluntary financial contributions to a trust fund that will pay for the investigations, the operations of the court and the enforcement of its sentences.
>
> Immediately after the adoption of the resolution now requested establishing the court, the Security Council should send a rapid response team of inquiry to Freetown to explore the extent of the violations and the facilities necessary in Sierra Leone to bring credible and secure justice. This will at once send the right signals to the perpetrators of the violations that they will not continue committing atrocities with impunity, and the population of Sierra Leone too will be assured that the process to address those atrocities and to do justice to them has commenced.[17]

The Kabbah letter set the stage for serious talks in the council and particularly between Washington and London, the two permanent members with the strongest engagement in Sierra Leone.

Breaking the Logjam

However, on June 14, the British informed me that they would not commit to a Security Council tribunal like the Yugoslav or Rwanda tribunals. In fact, they wanted to stand down on any resolution and await a report by a Security Council mission to the country before determining how to structure a court with a two-year mandate that would transform into a regional criminal court. Mali, a regional power, was keen on the prospect for such a court. The Sierra Leone court could serve as the template for a West African court, or so the British believed.

Holbrooke pushed back, telling the Security Council on June 20 that RUF leaders must be brought to justice. I joined him in the Security Council chamber that day, and watched as he made the case for an international tribunal. All eyes turned to him as he pointed to Kabbah's own request of June 12 and called for some form of international umbrella, perhaps as an expansion of the Rwanda Tribunal, and he urged that it be done quickly to defeat the influence of impunity over Sierra Leone's rebels. Holbrooke described as "farsighted" the reservation Kofi Annan had made to the Lomé Peace Agreement leaving open international accountability for atrocity crimes, and said the United States highly approved of it. But there needed to be a vigorous international mechanism or an extension of an existing one to accomplish this, he said. Holbrooke looked forward to a partnership with Freetown to render justice.

In the following days I worked through details of how the special court could be structured, including its legal character internationally and its jurisdiction. The key remained for the Security Council to establish the tribunal, even if it had hybrid characteristics with Sierra Leone participation, so that it could share the existing Appeals Chamber of the Yugoslav and Rwanda tribunals, compel cooperation of governments, enforce sentences, and require U.N. selection of key staff, particularly a lead prosecutor and the judges. Kabbah wanted the Sierra Leone attorney general to be the "chief or co-chief prosecutor of the court." But in New York we knew such a lead role for the attorney general was highly unlikely if the Security Council was going to create the tribunal to begin with. Most council members would insist on an international prosecutor selected by the secretary-general to head up the prosecutions.

In late June, one of Holbrooke's deputy ambassadors at the United Nations, Nancy Soderberg, and I were still slogging through concept drafts with council delegations, particularly with the British, whose colonial heritage in Sierra Leone and military presence there following the kidnapping of U.N. peacekeepers had thrust upon them a primary duty to engage. We were getting bogged down over whether the special court would be of an international origin and character (namely, created by the Security Council under its enforcement powers) or would be established within the Sierra Leone judicial system with a heavy dose of international assistance (the British preference). London still wanted to see the secretary-general's experts' report first before making any final decisions on the structure of the court.

An innovative approach had to break the logjam. I was nearing the end of weeks of negotiations at the United Nations over the rules of procedure and evidence and the elements of crimes for the International Criminal Court. During a break in the talks, I was lost in thought walking along Second Avenue when the idea struck me: If the International Criminal Court was to be created by treaty among governments, why not also establish the special court for Sierra Leone as an international criminal court with a *treaty* between the United Nations and the government of Sierra Leone? International law permits international organizations to enter into treaties with governments, and that was certainly being contemplated for the Cambodia Tribunal, albeit with a domestic court the fulcrum of that particular treaty. Surely we could create an *international* court, with Sierra Leone participation, by treaty between the United Nations and the government and thus avoid having to use the Security Council's enforcement authority, which the British so firmly opposed given the recent arrival of the International Criminal Court and the collective desire in New York, mostly for financial reasons, to remove the council from tribunal-building ventures.

I began to draft the treaty language and talk up the idea back in Washington. We would lose the powerful enforcement authority of the Security Council that the Yugoslav and Rwanda tribunals benefited from, at least in theory and in law, because the special court would not be established as a subsidiary organ of the council as had been those tribunals. But the proposal suggested an easier pathway toward political acceptance by skeptical and tribunal-fatigued council members and those Non-Aligned governments (such Mexico and Brazil) that despised empowering the Security Council to build more courts. It also had the advantage of giving the U.N. secretary-general the upper hand in staffing the court with international prosecutors, judges, and administrators and thus ensuring international control of the proceedings. This was far different from the Cambodian negotiations at the time (described in the next chapter), where Phnom Penh was insisting on a Cambodian court staffed mostly with its own nationals. Freetown refrained from making those kinds of demands during the negotiations.

Soderberg called me from New York on July 6 to report that until the captured Indian peacekeepers in UNAMSIL were released, there was little

chance of making headway in the Security Council on a court-building resolution. The fate of the peacekeepers had to remain the only priority until
the crisis was resolved. Carolyn Willson, our deputy legal counsel in New
York, weighed in with more negative feedback from various delegations
rejecting the concept of a conventional Security Council tribunal and
seeking the views of the experts' mission before going any further. The pattern I had long experienced with Cambodia—tribunal fatigue and passing
the buck to "experts" who would take their time making reports and recommendations—had taken hold as well with Sierra Leone.

A Treaty-Based International Court

By mid-July 2000 Washington approved my proposal for a Security Council resolution authorizing negotiation of a treaty between the United Nations
and the government of Sierra Leone to create an international criminal
court. My proposal would authorize Kofi Annan to enter into an agreement
with the Kabbah government to create a special court under both international law and Sierra Leone law that would act independently to ensure
full investigation and prosecution of leading suspects. I called it the "coestablishment concept." In principle, my approach proved acceptable, although
one of my colleagues described it as a Rube Goldberg machine, namely a
deliberately overengineered apparatus that performs a very simple task in
a very complex fashion. The same could be said of what emerged in Cambodia shortly thereafter. But that was the nature of the beast, and it worked.
The proposal calmed the nerves of those opposed to a Security Council
tribunal and assured a significant buy-in by Sierra Leone.

Harold Koh and I held a videoconference with British officials sitting in
London on July 14 to introduce the proposal and hammer out our differences. London wanted a domestic Sierra Leone court with international
assistance, and was not very concerned about international law governing
the court's jurisprudence. In the British view, Sierra Leone law could incorporate customary international law (as if that were guaranteed, particularly
in a devastated nation). They realized that a regime change in Sierra Leone
might wipe out any strictly domestic court process, but did not seem to care.
Koh and I pushed back hard, arguing the whole issue arose because of international law and the need for its enforcement, particularly by the United
Nations. Justice was not the sole equity of the embattled government of Sierra Leone.

The British countered with a simple formula: "Justice is an absolute. It doesn't matter about the court being local as long as it's fair and credible, with all the help it needs from the international community. International assistance can ensure fairness in the Sierra Leone courtroom. After all, the Rome Statute of the International Criminal Court encourages domestic jurisdiction!" They also objected to the Security Council setting up the court, which "would mean we own it." We had to impress upon them that our proposal was a coestablishment concept that did not require creation by the council or assessed payments drawn from the U.N. budget to pay for it. The coestablished court would have what international lawyers call "international legal personality," with the legal power to stand as an international (judicial) organization independently of any other organization or government. The British rejected our proposal, but Koh and I were confident we had set their minds to pondering it.

Meanwhile, Kabbah informed me that he was comfortable with my coestablishment concept, which required an international prosecutor, international judges, and some Sierra Leone jurists. Kabbah expressed confidence that such an independent court could work in both Sierra Leone and internationally. He also knew that the option of a Security Council–mandated tribunal under Chapter VII of the U.N. Charter, similar to the Yugoslav and Rwanda tribunals, was losing traction in New York.

High-level contacts were launched with British officials. Albright called Foreign Secretary Robin Cook. Still smarting from the Yugoslav Tribunal prosecutor's review of NATO bombing decisions during the Kosovo campaign, Cook did not want another Carla Del Ponte in charge as prosecutor. He refused to offer his own country as an available site for any trials that might need to be held outside Sierra Leone for security reasons. The hard slogging continued.

Then, on July 19, the U.S. deputy permanent representative to the United Nations, James Cunningham, called me with the breakthrough we sought. He had just left a reasonably good conversation with British diplomats who suddenly were in the mood to settle differences over the structure of the special court. He needed a short concept paper on how coestablishment would work so that he could circulate it to relevant officials. I drafted the paper immediately and shot it up to Cunningham in New York. Within a week word came back that the British could work on the basis of our concept paper and the text of the Security Council resolution and treaty we had prepared.

Konari's Solar Energy Offer

Over the next few weeks, continuous discussions took place in New York, Washington, London, Paris, Bamako (the capital of Mali), and Freetown to review and refine the U.S. proposal into an acceptable document. U.N. lawyer Ralph Zacklin signaled on August 2 that he preferred the U.S. proposal, which was an important development for us. I flew to West Africa in early August to consult with a key player, President Omar Konari of Mali, who was also the head of the Economic Community of West African States, and once again with Kabbah and his cabinet in Freetown.

I obtained Konari's support for the U.S. approach but also emphasized to him that the Special Court for Sierra Leone, as we were then calling it, could mature into a regional court following its mandated work in Sierra Leone. I told Konari that because of the precarious security situation in that country, we needed to ensure that the special court could meet outside Sierra Leone, preferably in the region, if security proved to be a problem in Freetown. I asked him if he had any suggestions. Konari broke a huge smile, invited me into his limousine, and drove me along dusty roads to a lone hill on the outskirts of Bamako where an abandoned institute for the study of solar energy sat in all its sun-baked loneliness. The money had run out for its continued operation. Here, Konari told me proudly, is where you will house the Special Court for Sierra Leone.

All the buildings and security facilities—an auditorium that could be converted into a courtroom, a tall office building, a dormitory complex, a cafeteria, a building that could be converted into a prison, and even a barbed wire fence surrounding the entire hill—already were there and probably could be powered by solar energy! I had found our alternative site for the court. However, when I returned home and brought the idea to the United Nations, the lawyers there killed it with the excuse that all documents and court proceedings would have to be translated into Mali's primary European language, French, and that would be too expensive. Nothing dictated the necessity for French, as the court would operate with Sierra Leone and international staff, but such was their reasoning. The fact that years later the one high-profile trial that needed to be held outside Sierra Leone for security reasons, namely, the prosecution of Charles Taylor, was held in The Hague rather than Bamako—a West African site that might have been more meaningful to the victims of that region—resulted from that pointless bureaucratic angst over translation into French of the court proceedings.

Security Council Endorsement

My talks in Freetown further consolidated the government's support for our drafts, although certain issues would crop up soon enough for further negotiation. More negotiations followed once I returned to the United States, and on August 14 the Security Council adopted Resolution 1315, which became the launching pad for the ultimate establishment of the Special Court for Sierra Leone.[18] The council still viewed the situation in Sierra Leone as threatening international peace and security, hence validating its initiative to set up the special court to achieve the Kabbah government's "objectives of bringing justice and ensuring lasting peace." The resolution requested that Annan negotiate an agreement with the Sierra Leone government "to create an independent special court consistent with this resolution," with jurisdiction over atrocity crimes and several categories of crimes under Sierra Leone law. This was my Second Avenue idea formally endorsed by the Security Council.

The council recommended that the special court "should have personal jurisdiction over persons who bear the greatest responsibility for the commission of the crimes ... including those leaders who, in committing such crimes, have threatened the establishment of and implementation of the peace process in Sierra Leone." The Security Council, following Kabbah's lead from his June 12 letter, requested Annan to send a team of experts to Sierra Leone to prepare a report on how precisely to establish the special court. Key issues the experts had to address included the tribunal's temporal jurisdiction (between what dates would the court's authority to prosecute crimes extend?), how to set up an appeals chamber and whether to share the one used by the Yugoslav and Rwanda tribunals, and where else the special court could sit if Sierra Leone proved too dangerous. The critical issue of how voluntary contributions could support the special court's operations loomed as a major challenge for the experts to address in their report, which was delivered on October 4, 2000.[19]

Negotiating a Novel Court

As the newly minted team of U.N. experts explored the judicial terrain in Sierra Leone, I met in early September with Zacklin and one of his top U.N. lawyers, Daphne Schraga. They recognized that we were proposing a sui generis, or entirely unprecedented, court that would derive its authority and legitimacy from the treaty between the United Nations and Sierra Leone rather than from a Security Council resolution. Zacklin and Schraga wanted more Security Council support for the court even though it would not be the literal creation of the council. They also worried about how to finance the court for the next several years. There would need to be some kind of board of trustees to oversee the administration and budget of the court. Although it would not be a U.N. court per se, they understandably pondered whether they would be held responsible for ensuring an adequate flow of funds to pay staff and run the trials.

During the next few months, an intensive debate took place between Security Council members and the U.N. lawyers over how to finalize key provisions of the governing statute of the Special Court for Sierra Leone and ensure they mirrored sections in the agreement to be entered into between the United Nations and the government of Sierra Leone to establish the court. I was the American point man for that debate, shuttling between Washington and New York in order to try to establish the court before the end of the Clinton administration. I was surprised at times over how certain parties dug in their heels on issues that seemed easily resolvable, but that is the nature of the negotiating game, particularly when pride and political agendas influence the process.

I spent weeks negotiating the scope of the special court's personal jurisdiction, namely who would be subject to investigation and prosecution by the court. Corell and Zacklin wanted prosecutors to go after a relatively broad group of individuals who were "the most responsible" for the atrocity crimes. The United States and most of its Security Council partners wanted a smaller set of possible suspects given the special court's limited capacity and reliance on voluntary contributions. We also wanted to focus on those individuals who had violated the Lomé Peace Agreement. So council members insisted on "persons who bear the greatest responsibility" for the atrocity crimes, and that language prevailed in the final text. There were humorous moments when the difference between "most responsible" and "greatest responsibility" descended into distinctions without a difference, but the dueling definitions dogged countless discussions. The Security Council also prevailed with explicit reference to "those leaders who, in committing such crimes, have threatened the establishment of and implementation of the peace process in Sierra Leone." While their crimes reaching back to November 30, 1996, were fair game for an international prosecutor to investigate, leaders who failed to abide by the Lomé Peace Agreement had to know they were primary targets for the court.[20]

Another highly sensitive issue was how to deal with the largely Nigerian ECOMOG peacekeepers who allegedly had committed their own crimes and human rights abuses against rebel forces and civilians during their long deployments in Sierra Leone. The issue of peacekeeper liability also focused on the UNAMSIL forces then deployed in large numbers throughout Sierra Leone. The UNAMSIL soldiers came from across the globe, particularly Bangladesh, Ghana, India, Indonesia, Jordan, Kenya, Nigeria, and Zambia. The governments of these nations had zero interest in their own military personnel falling under the special court's jurisdiction. But nongovernmental organizations and the U.N. lawyers argued that the prosecutor could not credibly pursue only certain categories of top perpetrators while ignoring the past or contemporary conduct of the peacekeepers, be they of ECOMOG or UNAMSIL identity. While logic pointed to inclusion, political reality dictated exclusion. The controversy also involved the International Criminal Court and whether troops from countries not party to that court should be subject to its jurisdiction under any circumstances. Most of the contributors of troops in Sierra Leone were not party to the International Criminal Court and thus did not want the special court to pretend to exercise jurisdiction the same way some were arguing the International Criminal Court should be able to if atrocity crimes were committed on the territory of a country (like Sierra Leone) that had joined that court.

The compromise that eventually emerged held that "any transgressions by peacekeepers and related personnel present in Sierra Leone" under agreement with or with the consent of the government of Sierra Leone would be within the primary jurisdiction of the government that sent the particular soldiers, meaning, for example, that the courts of Nigeria would be responsible for investigating and prosecuting Nigerian peacekeepers deployed in Sierra Leone.[21] However, in a nod to the complementarity principle firmly lodged in the Rome Statute, the governing statute and treaty for the special court required that, "in the event the sending State is unwilling or unable genuinely to carry out an investigation or prosecution, the Court may, if authorized by the Security Council on the proposal of any State, exercise jurisdiction over such persons."[22] This potentially exposed peacekeepers to the special court's jurisdiction. The U.N. lawyers long argued that the secretary-general, rather than the Security Council, should make the determination of whether a nation was "unwilling or unable" to investigate or prosecute, but the Security Council insisted that it retain that authority even though there proved be no political will to reach any such decision in subsequent years.

The third major issue of contention involved whether juveniles, namely boys and girls under the age of eighteen, could be investigated and prosecuted by the special court. The Kabbah government insisted that teenagers between fifteen and eighteen years of age when the alleged crimes were committed be subject to the court's scrutiny. The rebels used tens of thousands of child soldiers, and some of them had clearly led others in committing atrocities. Indeed, the crime of conscripting or enlisting or using child soldiers eventually was charged against Charles Taylor and other defendants. Yet the United States and other governments invested in the creation of the Special Court for Sierra Leone found the idea of prosecuting child soldiers repugnant. I consulted with Carol Bellamy, the head of the United Nations Children's Fund, who strongly urged me to resist the idea. The official U.S. position, which I advocated tirelessly in New York, opposed the jurisdiction of the special court reaching anyone under the age of eighteen when the crimes were committed. The Western and international law tradition simply forbade such harsh scrutiny and punishment of minors, although the United States has not been the best example of keeping minors out of the adult criminal law system.

But the Kabbah government pointed to the popular will of its own people and the thousands of survivors of atrocity crimes, who insisted on holding accountable the drugged-up teenage ringleaders who had orchestrated mutilations, rapes, killings, and further kidnappings of children to serve in the rebel ranks. This was make or break for them, similar to the death penalty imperative for the Rwandan government in 1994 that led to its negative vote in the Security Council on the creation of the Rwanda Tribunal. Some formula had to be found to bring Sierra Leone back from the brink of opposing the special court that Kabbah had sought since the early summer.

The compromise that we finally negotiated included several components. First, the Special Court could prosecute the crime of "conscripting or enlisting children under the age of 15 years into armed forces or groups or using them to participate actively in hostilities."[23] We had hoped for sixteen- and perhaps seventeen-year-olds to be included among the children covered by this provision, but the international standard, confirmed in the Rome Statute, that attracted broad support remained at the threshold of fifteen-year-olds. Second, the Sierra Leone domestic law criminalizing abuse of young girls and their abduction for immoral purposes was incorporated as an offense in the special court's statute.[24]

Third, the jurisdiction of the special court did not reach anyone under the age of fifteen at the time of the alleged crime. Children between fifteen and eighteen years of age at the time of the alleged crime could be prosecuted, but with several key caveats: "[H]e or she shall be treated with dignity and a sense of worth, taking into account his or her young age and the desirability of promoting his or her rehabilitation, reintegration into and assumption of a constructive role in society, and in accordance with international human rights standards, in particular the rights of the child."[25] Further, the punishment for any juvenile offender convicted by the court was limited to "care guidance and supervision orders, community service orders, counseling, foster care, correctional, educational and vocational training programmes, approved schools and, as appropriate, any programmes of disarmament, demobilization and reintegration or programmes of child protection agencies."[26] There would be no imprisonment as punishment of juvenile offenders.[27]

The Kabbah government agreed to these provisions; we bit our tongues on some of them and approved their incorporation. In reality, the first prosecutor, David Crane, and his successors never charged anyone under the age of eighteen when the alleged crimes took place in Sierra Leone. That use of the prosecutor's discretion to indict only older leaders probably reflected his American background and a correct application of the jurisdictional limitation to prosecute those who bore the greatest responsibility. If the prosecutor had been a citizen of Sierra Leone, there might have been a different strategy employed to snare one or more teenage mutilators. The deputy prosecutor always was of Sierra Leone citizenship, as required by the special court's statute,[28] but the chief prosecutor had the power to determine against whom to seek indictments.

The notorious amnesty clause of the Lomé Peace Agreement, which Kofi Annan had disowned after the document was signed, was buried for purposes of the special court, and the Kabbah government never objected to the reality of having to do so. But the negotiations centered on ultimately limiting the no-amnesty principle to atrocity crimes and not to the specific violations of Sierra Leone law also forming part of the court's jurisdiction. The Lomé amnesty was litigated by defense counsel in cases that came before the special court in later years, but was never successfully invoked to shield a defendant from criminal charges or conviction.

The final major contention between the Security Council and U.N. lawyers centered on how to fund the special court. Since it would not be a Security Council tribunal established under Chapter VII, and there was no interest among most council members to finance the court through U.N.-assessed contributions, the only way it would be funded rested on voluntary contributions of interested governments. We all knew this was far more problematic than the kind of funding enjoyed by the Yugoslav and Rwanda tribunals, but either the special court would be voluntarily financed or there would be no such court established. Tribunal fatigue in the Security Council had one irreversible reality: there would be no more assessed funding for war crimes tribunals. U.N. lawyers fought this reality for months, trying to convince most council members to create a guaranteed stream of funding for the special court. I understood their pain and the logic of their arguments, but I also knew it was utterly futile. Russia, China, France, and even Britain flatly refused assessed obligations, and the U.S. Congress did not even want to imagine the idea. My hands were tied. But I recognized that there would be intense lobbying ahead by me and my successor to secure sufficient voluntary financing from Washington and other governments.

Having lost the funding battle, Kofi Annan wrote a letter to the Security Council on January 12, 2001, with a very restrictive view of how the special court would be established, thus delaying its creation by at least one year. He believed the voluntary contributions would be neither viable nor sustainable. Annan reiterated to the council "the risks associated with the establishment of an operation of this kind with insufficient funds, or without assurances of continuous availability of funds." He refused to conclude the essential treaty with Sierra Leone until cash was on hand to finance the first year of operations and pledges covered the second and third years of work.[29] Annan thus nailed shut any possibility of a rapid launch of the special court by holding it hostage to even more guaranteed funding than was afforded to the Yugoslav and Rwanda tribunals, which depended on periodic budget deliberations in New York. The council was not going to force Annan to sign the treaty with the Kabbah government before he was prepared to do so, but the consequence of this virtual standoff was to delay justice in Sierra Leone.

If justice delayed is justice denied, Sierra Leone paid a large price for the delay in concluding the treaty. Sankoh died in 2003 before he could be put on trial. Top defendant Sam Hinga Norman of the Civil Defense Forces, whose trial I attended in May 2006, died in 2007 just before judgment was to be rendered. Their fates would likely have been different if Annan and the Security Council had reached an accelerated accommodation on funding in 2001, but no effort to achieve that was attempted by the George W. Bush administration following my departure from office. Judgments against Sankoh and Norman probably would have contributed to national reconciliation. Like the Cambodia Tribunal, where delays meant that likely prominent defendants died naturally or by violence before they could face justice, the Special Court for Sierra Leone was undermined by a dispute over money that could have been resolved if key policy-makers had exercised political will and recognized the critical need for timely justice.

Punishment

The accomplishments of the Special Court for Sierra Leone to date remain largely faithful to its original design and purpose, despite the crippling delay over funding that undermined the objective of bringing the leading perpetrators of atrocity crimes in Sierra Leone to justice. Financial crises remained the norm for the court as it struggled to raise voluntary funds throughout its years of operation. As difficult as that task became, particularly for the staff of the court, there was no practical alternative to that means of funding its work.

The special court convicted eight leaders—spread among the Revolutionary United Front, the Armed Forces Revolutionary Council, and the Civil Defense Forces—of atrocity crimes in Sierra Leone. The trials held in Freetown resulted in no acquittals. Charles Taylor, the president of Liberia and alleged mastermind of the criminalization of an entire nation, was successfully indicted, arrested, and put on trial before the special court—no mean feat. Taylor's verdict one day will be rendered, and an appeal (by either Taylor or the prosecutor) doubtless will follow. As noted, Sankoh and Norman failed to reach their judgment days in court. Sam Bockarie, the battlefield commander of the RUF, was indicted on seventeen counts of atrocity crimes but met a violent death in Liberia while a fugitive from justice in May 2003. Some speculate that Charles Taylor had something to do with his murder.[30] Johnny Paul Koroma was indicted on war crimes and crimes against humanity and as of this writing remains at large. If he is alive, I would like to see him—the man who told me that war criminals could be identified one by one, and who made such a sweeping claim that he was prepared to investigate and bring to justice his own soldiers in the AFRC—brought to justice. Like so many war criminals, he was a thuggish hypocrite. Finding a legal mechanism to deal with his open case may be one of the special court's final tasks.

The rulings of the Special Court for Sierra Leone included many historic "firsts" in atrocity law. Domestic amnesties were confirmed to be no shield to international criminal prosecutions of atrocity crimes.[31] The absence of immunity for heads of state before international courts was confirmed.[32] Defendants were convicted for recruiting and using child soldiers,[33] for attacks on U.N. peacekeepers,[34] and for acts of terrorism in internal armed conflicts.[35] The court also convicted defendants for forced marriage as a crime against humanity and for sexual slavery.[36]

Although the special court remained faithful to its pursuit of those "with the greatest responsibility" for the atrocity crimes in Sierra Leone, and thus a fairly small number of war criminals, in the end it did the job it was created to do. Was it worth it? For international justice, the answer is an unequivocal yes. For the victims in Sierra Leone, nothing will return their hacked body parts or their families. But the high-ranking men who orchestrated the horror were brought very low and punished. That fact will resonate for generations to come in Freetown and into the depths of Sierra Leone's glorious forests. "Nancy" can tell her son that some justice was rendered for his mother's missing eyes and tormented nights.

CHAPTER TWELVE

THE TOUGHEST COCKFIGHT

I am standing there when he enters the jail cell. That's it. Just standing there. (*Pol Pot enters the cell.*) A feeling washes over me. I am flying.

An American "war crimes" diplomat in 1998 speaking to a reporter,
in Catherine Filloux's play Silence of God[1]

INTERNATIONAL JUSTICE IS THE ART OF THE POSSIBLE, AND NOWHERE WAS that demonstrated more profoundly than in Cambodia. Whenever impatience or frustration engulfed the Office of War Crimes Issues, I reminded all, "Welcome to my life with Cambodia."

My journey with Cambodia reaches back much further than anything I witnessed in the Balkans or Africa. As a high school and college student, I came of age with revelations about the secret bombing of Cambodia during the Vietnam War. Launched by President Richard Nixon and his top foreign policy official, Henry Kissinger, the B-52 strikes on eastern Cambodia inspired even stronger dissent among Americans, including myself, to the war. As a college senior, I followed the early months of Pol Pot's takeover of the Cambodian government in 1975 and read Sydney Schanberg's dispatches for the *New York Times* (which later inspired the award-winning film *The Killing Fields*[2]). But during my years of law studies, I lost track of developments in Cambodia as it fell into the darkness of Democratic Kampuchea.

Then, one crisp November morning in 1978, I awoke to an interview on National Public Radio with Senator George McGovern, a decorated World War II aviator who had unsuccessfully run for the presidency against Nixon in 1972 on an antiwar platform. He condemned the mass killings in Cambodia and, perhaps paradoxically for his isolationist image, called for an international military intervention to stop them. His was a very lone voice at the time, but he reminded me that a massive atrocity was occurring in my lifetime while the U.S. government largely ignored it. When Pol Pot's regime collapsed shortly thereafter and its horrors began to be revealed, I realized that "never again" had been contradicted with profound ambivalence by the international community.

Six months later the international law firm Coudert Brothers asked me to join its Singapore office. I arrived in Singapore in December 1979 during the aftermath of Pol Pot's reign of terror. Cambodians were starving. An international charity required legal advice on chartering barges to ship rice up the Mekong River to Phnom Penh. I grabbed the chance to work pro bono on the project. After months of such shipments, the situation improved somewhat. During the 1980s, I was one of only a few American voices advocating normalization of relations with Vietnam,[3] a position that kept me immersed in the unfolding drama in Cambodia, which was occupied by the Vietnamese Army. By the time I arrived to work in the Clinton administration, which recognized the government of Vietnam in 1995, I had forged a special bond with the fate of Cambodia.

Today, the Extraordinary Chambers in the Courts of Cambodia (the "Cambodia Tribunal") is a uniquely designed national Cambodian court with a statutory mandate to bring to justice surviving senior leaders of Democratic Kampuchea, the formal name for Cambodia under Pol Pot's rule. It also has a mandate to bring to justice those who were "most responsible" for atrocity crimes and certain other Cambodian crimes during the Pol Pot era (April 17, 1975, to January 6, 1979). An estimated 1.7 million Cambodian citizens perished because of atrocities committed by the Khmer Rouge during that period, and millions more were victimized. (Khmer Rouge was a name given to followers and members of the Communist Party of Kampuchea, led by Pol Pot.) A Cambodian law adopted in 2001 and amended in 2004 (the "tribunal law"),[4] along with a 2004 treaty between the United Nations and the government of Cambodia (the "UN/Cambodia agreement"),[5] together established the Cambodia Tribunal. It is a special court requiring the participation of both international and Cambodian judges, prosecutors, and administrators. Both documents were negotiated largely on my watch, but their implementation was delayed for years owing to a complex fusion of Cambodian and U.N. politics, a one-year slog by newly appointed judges to draft the internal rules of the court, and the search for adequate funding.

The creation of the Cambodia Tribunal—spanning 1997 to 2006— took longer than the creation of any other international or hybrid criminal tribunal in the post–Cold War era, although the far more complex modern negotiating history of the permanent International Criminal Court extended through different forums for about a decade as well. The Cambodian endeavor began long after the atrocities of the Pol Pot era. There were complex political, security, and legal reasons for the decade-long journey in Cambodia that culminated with the creation of the Cambodia Tribunal as a new national court of limited jurisdiction over specific crimes for a set period of time and over a small class of likely suspects. Cambodian society remained fragile and politically explosive for years after the Agreements on a Comprehensive Political Settlement of the Cambodia Conflict, signed in Paris on October 23, 1991, with the primary aim of free and fair elections for the people of Cambodia. The negotiations that finally began in 1997 to create the tribunal never occurred in a vacuum. Efforts to perfect the constitutional character of the Cambodia Tribunal were doomed to fail as the nationalistic insularity of Cambodian officials locked horns with the stubbornness of U.N. lawyers and diplomats. Nonetheless, the end result achieved a credible institutional character that meets, at least on paper and perhaps ultimately in practice, adherence to international standards of due process.

I am often asked why the United States took such a focused and sustained interest in creating the Cambodia Tribunal. No other government was so determined to launch a tribunal-building initiative, and no other government became so deeply involved for four years (1997 through 2000) in negotiations leading to the constitutional documents of the Cambodia Tribunal. I honestly would like to write that there was a coherent policy, fully backed by the top officials in Washington, to accomplish this particular task in Cambodia. However, that was not the case. Albright inspired and supported my efforts; Tom Pickering, the under secretary of state for political affairs, was always there when I needed him; Senator John Kerry brilliantly intervened on several occasions to move the negotiations forward; and the American ambassadors to Cambodia on my watch, Kenneth Quinn and Kent Wiedemann, courageously pressed Cambodian officials to achieve the objective of a tribunal.

But this was a personal mission that I translated into an American mission once I became the war crimes ambassador. I was determined to negotiate, against all odds at times, judicial accountability for the major perpetrators of atrocity crimes during the Pol Pot era. So I prodded everyone. I kept searching for a methodology that would achieve enough support, both within the Cambodian government and at the United Nations, to build a court that could deliver credible justice respectful of international standards of due process. I could not rationalize building the other war crimes tribunals and then ignore a reckoning for the Khmer Rouge and their decimation of the Cambodian people. This sometimes did not sit well with major civil society groups and U.N. lawyers who were seeking a near-perfect model of justice and were prepared to abandon the endeavor, which both sometimes did. The building of the Cambodia Tribunal is a story of innovation, risk taking, and perseverance in which some of my colleagues deserve enormous credit, while others in Washington or at the United Nations played the role of spoiler time and time again.

"We're Advancing to the Rear"

As early as February 20, 1993, Cambodia and the challenge of accountability appeared on my agenda while working for Albright. Only weeks into her new job as the U.S. ambassador to the United Nations, she hosted a working dinner in her Georgetown residence with Cambodia wonks to mind-bend the upcoming elections there in May. I debated former Iowa senator Dick Clarke over the value of seeking accountability for the Khmer Rouge leaders, a goal he thought was eclipsed by the enormous political and security challenges then confronting Cambodians. My sometimes heated discussion with Clarke inspired me to dig in and try, when the time arrived, to pursue a tribunal to prosecute the Pol Pot regime.

One year later, Senator Chuck Robb, a Vietnam veteran from Virginia, successfully pushed through to passage the Cambodian Genocide Justice Act, which called for the president "to encourage the establishment of a national or international criminal tribunal for the prosecution of those accused of genocide in Cambodia."[6] He had raised his hopes for the bill in his first conversation with Albright and me during her courtesy calls for Senate confirmation in January 1993. State Department lawyers concluded that a domestic Cambodian trial with significant international assistance and even participation offered the best option and that an ad hoc international tribunal, based on the Yugoslavia Tribunal, also would be an effective forum in which to bring legal action against the Khmer Rouge. But, they cautioned, the first priority had to be the apprehension of the Khmer Rouge leadership. That requirement, for prior apprehension, meant that concrete thinking about a tribunal did not progress until the arrest of Pol Pot became plausible. Even then, the high priority of apprehension became a millstone as well as a lodestone, as governments did not want to participate in arrest or detention operations prior to the existence of a tribunal to prosecute the alleged war criminals. That paradox dogged the effort for many long years.

The most significant initial step toward the building of the Cambodia Tribunal occurred on June 19, 1997, when the prospect of gaining custody of Pol Pot improved dramatically. Reports began to arrive in Washington that Pol Pot was being detained by someone within his own Khmer Rouge. This made it much more likely that he could be located, as his captors would seek to leverage his surrender for their own safety. Prior to that date, the Cambodian Genocide Justice Act had provided funding for the documentation of the Pol Pot–era atrocity crimes. In early 1997, while serving as senior adviser to Secretary of State Madeleine Albright and awaiting Senate confirmation hearings for my war crimes ambassadorship, I helped marshal State Department efforts in the U.N. Commission on Human Rights to formulate a request that U.N. secretary-general Kofi Annan examine seriously any request from Cambodia for assistance to develop a mechanism of accountability for the atrocity crimes of the Pol Pot era. The commission did so in April of that year.[7] Meanwhile, in Cambodia, both major parties called for the establishment of an "international tribunal" but were silent about whether it should be a Security Council tribunal. The Cambodian co–prime ministers verbally expressed to the U.N. special representative for Human Rights in Cambodia, Thomas Hammarberg, their support for an international tribunal to prosecute the Khmer Rouge leaders. By early June 1997 American efforts were underway to propose to the Cambodian government the creation of a commission of inquiry or truth commission as an initial step that ultimately might lead to a criminal tribunal. But with Pol Pot's capture suddenly possible later that month, interest in finding or building a court with jurisdiction to competently and credibly prosecute him rose rapidly.

On June 21, Cambodia's first prime minister, Prince Norodom Ranariddh, and second prime minister, Hun Sen, signed a letter to Kofi Annan asking "for the assistance of the United Nations and the international community in bringing to justice those persons responsible for the genocide and crimes against humanity during the rule of the Khmer Rouge from 1975 to 1979." They continued, "Cambodia does not have the resources or expertise to conduct this very important procedure. Thus, we believe it is necessary to ask for the assistance of the United Nations. We are aware of similar efforts to respond to the genocide and crimes against humanity in Rwanda and the former Yugoslavia, and ask that similar assistance be given to Cambodia."[8] The cosigned letter represented a significant leap for the Cambodian government, and it served as a lasting premise for international engagement to achieve accountability.

There was considerable activity all that weekend over the fate of Pol Pot. A host of State and Justice Department officials examined options. While Albright attended the Summit of the Eight (government representatives of the world's largest economies, "the group of eight," or G8) in Denver, Colorado, I drafted and circulated to her and others in Washington an informal paper titled "Proposed Plan for Dealing with Pol Pot and Khmer Rouge Accountability." I advised that it would be desirable to remove Pol Pot and perhaps other Khmer Rouge leaders from Cambodia, that they be transported to a country that exercised universal (or near-universal) jurisdiction over crimes against humanity, and that they ultimately be brought to justice before some sort of U.N.-constituted or U.N.-approved judicial body. The paper examined how to render Pol Pot and other surviving Khmer Rouge leaders from Cambodia to another country, what countries should be approached to receive Pol Pot, the deployment of a Justice Department prosecutor to New Haven to review the Yale University data project's files and make them available for any such country that received Pol Pot or others, and the options for prosecution. These included expanding the jurisdiction of the Yugoslav Tribunal, having the U.N. Security Council create a new international criminal tribunal for Cambodia, having the U.N. General Assembly create a judicial tribunal for Cambodia, forging a multilateral tribunal, or providing U.N. support for a national or multilateral prosecution.

Albright suggested options for accountability to the foreign ministers of the governments convened for the G8 Summit. Drawing from my paper, she stressed two primary options: establishing a multilateral criminal tribunal as a G8 treaty initiative, with Cambodian government consent and cooperation, or a Security Council international criminal tribunal. The foreign ministers reached no agreement on this sudden initiative introduced in Denver, but it served the purpose of sensitizing major governments to the accountability challenge in Cambodia.

On the same day, Prince Ranariddh announced, "I confirm that Pol Pot has already been arrested." He said that Pol Pot's former comrades had detained him and that the Khmer Rouge thereby ceased to exist politically and militarily. A Khmer Rouge radio broadcast also reported the capture of Pol Pot, calling it an "historic event."[9] This was very encouraging news, but where, precisely, was Pol Pot?

Ranariddh suggested that Pol Pot was being held at Anlong Veng, a Khmer Rouge stronghold in northern Cambodia, and that he should be moved soon to the capital, Phnom Penh, "for security reasons."[10] But there were considerable obstacles to overcome, not least of which was how to pry Pol Pot away from his Khmer Rouge captors and isolate him from supporters who might try to liberate him. Meanwhile, the other copremier, Hun Sen, said he had received a report that Pol Pot was dead. He helpfully added, "Even if he cannot be handed over alive, even his dead body, we would accept it. And we can keep his body by injecting serum into it so that people can view him." However, Pol Pot was indeed alive but not, in fact, arrested by any government authorities. He remained at large in northwestern Cambodia for many months to come.

On June 22, White House spokesman Mike McCurry told reporters covering the Denver summit that Pol Pot had to be brought to justice. "We clearly have taken the position that those responsible for heinous crimes ought to be brought to justice and that would be true in the case of Cambodia and Pol Pot, as well," he said. He confirmed that setting up an international tribunal to accomplish that task was discussed among the leaders at the summit. I was working closely with Albright on the issue as she presented it to the summit diplomats. She confirmed on ABC's *This Week* television show that the United States would be "seeking ways to make sure there is international justice carried out against this major war criminal." If Pol Pot were to be captured, she said, "then just imagine what a sense of justice and relief could come." New Jersey senator Robert Torricelli called for the United States "to extract Pol Pot from Cambodia and place him under protective custody."[11]

I inquired about where, outside Cambodia, Pol Pot could be prosecuted if captured. The State Department's lawyer in The Hague, Sean Murphy, checked with Adriaan Bos, the legal adviser of the Dutch Foreign Ministry, and with the Danish Legal Department. Both countries had nominal universal jurisdiction over certain categories of crimes including, between them, genocide, torture, terrorism, and hijacking. But neither had universal jurisdiction for crimes against humanity, the likeliest set of charges that would be brought against Pol Pot. Further, a Dutch or Danish court would need to proceed on the assumption of a full trial and then transfer him to an international tribunal if one were to be set up, but domestic legislation probably would have to be enacted to make that possible. Finally, a political decision at the highest level would have to be made even to start any such process. Such initiatives were practically insurmountable barriers in these countries.

Hans Corell, the undersecretary-general for legal affairs at the United Nations, also sent a memorandum to Secretary-General Kofi Annan outlining similar issues and options, although favoring a tribunal established by the General Assembly or possibly by the Security Council if that could prove politically feasible. On June 23, the State Department inquired with about fifteen foreign governments to determine whether they would be both legally able and politically willing to take temporary custody of Pol Pot and perhaps other senior Khmer Rouge leaders if they were arrested and detained. The Cambodian government had asked us for assistance in holding Pol Pot in custody outside Cambodia until a tribunal or court could be established or located to prosecute him. We were struggling to determine a legal basis for holding Pol Pot in the United States, but so far none had been found.

I discussed with Prosecutor Louise Arbour in The Hague the possibility of the Yugoslav Tribunal being expanded to incorporate Cambodia and the Pol Pot regime atrocities. (This was similar to the initial U.S. proposal in the summer of 1994 to prosecute the perpetrators of the Rwandan genocide.) She responded positively but with the usual caveats about sufficient resources, limited mandate, and the like. Meanwhile, back in Washington, the State Department's Tom Pickering dined with Australian prime minister John Howard and spoke with him about Australia as a possible venue for Pol Pot's custody. Howard told Pickering that his lawyers had done their homework and there was no legal authority to hold Pol Pot or to try him, even though there was a large enough Cambodian refugee community in Australia to make it a politically attractive option domestically. He was willing to weigh in with China to help facilitate its support or at least abstention for expansion of the jurisdiction of one of the ad hoc tribunals to cover Cambodia.

On June 28, Marc Richard of the Justice Department's Criminal Division discussed prosecution options with me. We explored possibilities for holding Pol Pot in the United States. Alternatively, I wanted to know whether the Cambodians would agree to hold Pol Pot in custody while we worked out options for the longer term. Albright instructed me to follow through on military contingency planning for an arrest and extraction of Pol Pot from Cambodia, determine if there was a U.S. legal basis for custody, accelerate planning at the United Nations on an international tribunal, and arrange for her to talk to U.S. ambassador Kenneth Quinn in Phnom Penh directly.

Quinn fielded reports that Chhit Choeun (alias Ta Mok) was prepared to turn Pol Pot over to Cambodian or even U.S. authorities. Ta Mok had been one of two military commanders functioning as the "hammer" of the Central Committee during Pol Pot's regime; he also became known as "the butcher" for his oversight of mass killings. Ta Mok had taken custody of Pol Pot earlier in June, perhaps as a bargaining chip for his own fate. If Pol Pot were to be handed over, Quinn wanted U.S. Air Force assets available to move him out of the country quickly. But he was deeply skeptical that the Chinese would ever allow a transfer of Pol Pot to an international tribunal and for good reason. Beijing had supported and collaborated with the Pol Pot regime.[12] China had a long and confrontational relationship with Vietnam, which invaded Cambodia in December 1978 to end Pol Pot's rule. The Chinese had nothing to gain from a criminal prosecution of senior Khmer Rouge leaders and much to fear from the possible disclosure in the trials of links between Pol Pot and Beijing. Unless the court was limited in its jurisdiction, China's leaders probably feared possible prosecution of some of their own for complicity in the atrocity crimes of the Pol Pot era.

I spoke with a Norwegian official on June 30 about the prospect of our flying Pol Pot to Oslo if he were captured. He was doubtful Norway would find a basis for prosecuting Pol Pot but he said we could count on his country to fund a tribunal and send lawyers and investigators to it. The Netherlands, Australia, Denmark, and Canada also responded negatively to our inquiries.

The National Security Council convened an interagency meeting to focus on capturing and detaining Pol Pot. The Justice Department concluded that the United States had no criminal jurisdiction over him. But efforts were under way to determine if any of the four Americans killed in Cambodia during his regime had been U.S. employees. (They were not.) A Defense Department lawyer rejected Wake Island and Guantanamo as possible detention sites because the necessary legal authority to prosecute was untested, and it was likely that no universal jurisdiction would be found in the executive orders covering those locations.

Suddenly, as quickly as it had risen to the fore, the air began to escape from the strategy balloon we had floated to capture Pol Pot. Politics overtook any strategy to apprehend him as the joint leadership of Hun Sen and Ranariddh began to unravel. Marc Richard reconfirmed to me (as I kept pressing for more innovative thinking) that there was no U.S. jurisdiction over Pol Pot and that federal criminal law was not applicable to U.S. personnel who might have been detained during the Pol Pot regime. We talked about creating a war crimes commission at the Pentagon, but it had never before been done when the United States was not an occupying power. The Defense Department would oppose such a broad application.

Nonetheless, we speculated that there might be immigration law authority to "parole" Pol Pot into the United States with the intention of surrendering him to an international tribunal. This approach required that we be certain a tribunal would be created quickly. Marc Richard worried about what constitutional rights could be invoked by Pol Pot. He thought it would be better if the Cambodian government formally handed him over to U.S. authorities and then, with limited jurisdiction under parole, we would keep him in custody for a very short period. I suggested that a U.N. Security Council resolution requesting states to provide assistance on detention might be sufficient legal cover. In sum, we concluded that Pol Pot would not be prosecuted in U.S. courts, that there was no viable option for prolonged detention in the United States, that there was some ambiguity regarding U.S.-controlled areas, and that a Cambodian government request would certainly help in conjunction with a parole of Pol Pot into U.S. custody for no more than ten days.

On July 3, a top State Department official in the East Asian Affairs Bureau concluded, "We're advancing to the rear." He doubted there would be any successful outcome to the negotiations on Pol Pot. On Independence Day, the State Department again inquired with various governments to secure their help with Pol Pot if he were to be captured. Foreign officials were asked whether their countries would be legally able and willing to take temporary custody of Pol Pot and possibly up to ten other top Khmer Rouge leaders if they could be arrested. The confinement, we proposed, would be without prejudice to considerations of what forum might ultimately try the case. The costs would be borne by the accepting state until other arrangements for trial and financing could be made. Our embassies were asked to ascertain whether the host country had identified a specific legal basis for confinement and whether prosecution would be an option in any case.

Unfortunately, Hun Sen's coup in July 1997, during which Ranariddh was ousted from the government, derailed serious discussions between Cambodia and the United Nations and deflated our efforts with other governments. Nonetheless, on November 27, Hun Sen and Ung Huot, the new first prime minister and minister of foreign affairs and international cooperation, sent President Clinton a letter stating, "The Royal Government of Cambodia would be most grateful to the United States government if help could be provided, according to US laws, to set up an international criminal tribunal and to bring to trial the Khmer Rouge leadership while they are still alive. We should not forget, nor delay, nor avoid taking this historic responsibility."[13] The Cambodian letter reenergized American efforts both to search for a means to find or build a court that could hold the senior Khmer Rouge leaders accountable and to apprehend Pol Pot and others who remained in hiding. I pressed forward.

Yale Law School professor Ben Kiernan, a foremost scholar on the Pol Pot regime, alerted me to the fact that when Youk Chhang, head of the Documentation Center of Cambodia, and he had an audience with King Norodom Sihanouk in July 1996, the king supported accountability and called for an international tribunal on Cambodia akin to the Yugoslav and Rwanda tribunals. But he wanted it held in Phnom Penh and believed Cambodian lawyers should participate in, but not dominate, the proceedings. He was adamant that the United Nations and the international community should run the tribunal. Sihanouk's views always were important, particularly on the issue of Khmer Rouge accountability. Indeed, they were so important that the French wanted to keep hearing his views reconfirmed again and again as the months and years dragged on.

Meet You in Palau

In late March 1998 the prospects for detaining senior Khmer Rouge suspects suddenly rose again. Pol Pot, Ta Mok, Khieu Samphan, and others appeared set to flee to Thailand from their hideouts on the Cambodian side of the border. We gambled that the Thai would hold Pol Pot briefly until we could pin down another country willing to hold him, at least temporarily. I hoped to secure Security Council approval to expand the Yugoslav Tribunal's jurisdiction to include a relatively limited number of Khmer Rouge leaders. Others in the State Department were very skeptical that the Chinese would ever permit this to happen.

On March 27, I reported to the Deputies Committee of the National Security Council the results of our renewed inquiries with five governments as to whether any of them would accept even temporary custody of Pol Pot if the United States helped capture and fly him out of the region. Sweden's response was encouraging, but it needed a much better sense of the endgame, namely what international tribunal would definitely prosecute Pol Pot. Spain wanted a written guarantee from the United States that Pol Pot would be transferred to another jurisdiction within thirty days of arriving in Spain, which we could not yet provide. It also wanted to find a Spanish victim of Pol Pot's regime. Germany doubted it would muster the political will unless Pol Pot were captured. Israel confirmed the theoretical possibility of prosecuting Pol Pot in its courts under a theory of universal jurisdiction. But the collapsed prosecution of John Demjanjuk, the SS guard from the Sobibor extermination camp in Poland during World War II, when the Israeli Supreme Court overturned his conviction on crimes against humanity in 1988, had left a bitter taste with Israeli officials. Further, officials feared that such a trial might complicate Israeli relations with the Non-Aligned and Arab worlds, particularly if Pol Pot was viewed as a victim of high-handed Israeli justice. Finland also discouraged the United States from pursuing the inquiry.

The White House believed that our efforts to prepare for Pol Pot's capture would boost Clinton's credibility as he embarked on his long-awaited trip to Rwanda to confront the memory of genocide there. Advice flowed on how to deal with the Chinese, who would have to be approached at the highest levels if we were to make any headway on prospects for a tribunal. Eric Holder, the deputy attorney general, explained how Pol Pot might be prosecuted if we had to bring him to U.S. soil and keep him there. The *ex post facto limitation analysis* he set forth would have to succeed, but he could not guarantee it. Under Holder's plan, U.S. adherence to the Genocide Convention and the Torture Convention would reflect America's "buy-in" to long-standing principles of customary international law that would arguably justify prosecution of Pol Pot. Holder, however, strongly preferred temporary detention on U.S. soil under the president's foreign affairs power followed by rapid transfer to another country or an international tribunal to stand trial. The Thais had assured us that they had ordered local commanders to detain Pol Pot and other Khmer Rouge leaders if they attempted to cross the border.

The deputies also discussed the possibility of detaining Pol Pot on U.S.-controlled territory covered by the Immigration and Nationality Act (such as Guam) and certain places (like Wake and Kwajalein islands) where that law does not apply. They examined expanding the Yugoslav Tribunal to cover Cambodia following Arbour's consent to a limited supplemental mandate. We speculated at the Situation Room table that we might avoid a Chinese veto of such a resolution in the U.N. Security Council if we could obtain explicit Cambodian government consent to the idea. The deputies agreed to seek an amendment of the Yugoslav Tribunal statute and instructed me to continue consultations immediately with Arbour.

Facts on the ground in Cambodia changed rapidly as the Khmer Rouge began to collapse as a fighting force that could continue to challenge the Cambodian government. One faction of Khmer Rouge troops seized the Anlong Veng base, about fifteen kilometers from the Thai border. Ta Mok and other Khmer Rouge leaders, including Pol Pot, fled north to higher ground adjoining the Thai border.

On March 30 I met with Arbour, who requested that she be involved in drafting the mandate of the proposed Security Council resolution on the Cambodia Tribunal. She wanted to ensure that the number of suspects would be limited and that it operated largely independent of the Yugoslav Tribunal. Arbour also requested that the tribunal have a separate deputy prosecutor.

A few days later, I received a fax from Ben Kiernan with a list from 1979 of the foreigners who had died in Tuol Sleng prison. Among them were four American tourists not employed by the U.S. government. James William Clark, Lance Manamara, Michael Scott Deed, and Christopher Edward Delance. They were seized from their sailing boat offshore Cambodia and were executed at the prison in April 1978.

The prospects of apprehending Pol Pot greatly improved in April and inspired American initiatives with a small group of governments and the U.N. Security Council to ensure that a captured Pol Pot (and other senior Khmer Rouge leaders) in fact could be brought to justice in a timely manner. The Cambodian government reaffirmed its desire for an international tribunal to prosecute Pol Pot and senior Khmer Rouge leaders. U.S. diplomats, including myself, inquired once again with seven governments about their capabilities (under either domestic criminal law or principles of universal jurisdiction over atrocity crimes) and political willingness either to detain Pol Pot temporarily or prosecute him if the United States transported him to their jurisdiction. All declined the opportunity for their own legal and political reasons. U.S. officials had determined that there was no firm basis under American law to proceed with a successful prosecution of Pol Pot or other senior Khmer Rouge leaders if they were held on U.S. territory. But there was enough confidence that if any of these suspects could be detained under joint custody by the United States and a foreign government (including Cambodia) on foreign territory, preferably with Cambodian consent, then the United States could participate in an apprehension and detention strategy.

Among Security Council members, several had questions about an expanded Yugoslav Tribunal, but none opposed the idea outright. Arbour and President Gabrielle McDonald of the Yugoslav Tribunal raised no objections to the proposal so long as sufficient resources were provided. Three countries in addition to the United States indicated their willingness to provide substantial financial support.

The reality was a chicken-and-egg dilemma. We needed the Security Council resolution establishing the Cambodia Tribunal before we could persuade various governments to make their jurisdictions available for temporary detention of Pol Pot and other leading Khmer Rouge suspects. But we could not persuade them to build the tribunal without having Pol Pot in custody, as that would be the political stimulus to move the issue forward in New York.

Meanwhile, the pursuit of Pol Pot quickened. U.S. diplomats pressed Thai officials about whether they would detain Pol Pot and other Khmer Rouge leaders should they come under Thai control, and then transfer them to another country or an appropriate tribunal. Rumors circulated that Pol Pot already was in Thailand under the control of the Royal Thai Army. We warned government officials that were Pol Pot to reside in Thailand for any period of time without being detained, and that fact became known, it could be misinterpreted by the international community that Thailand had let him slip through the net. We assured them that the United States stood ready to take custody of Pol Pot and fly him out of Thailand to another location.

The Justice Department confirmed that U.S. marshals or U.S. military personnel would have clear legal authority to transport and detain the Khmer

Rouge leaders if President Clinton issued an executive directive to that effect. That kind of presidential intervention would make the critical difference to confirm the legality of the operation. There were credible legal grounds for American detention of the Khmer Rouge leaders for an indefinite period as long as we continued to engage in good-faith negotiations for a prosecution in some other country or before an international tribunal. Regarding where Pol Pot and others could be detained, Justice Department lawyers preferred someplace like Diego Garcia in the Indian Ocean, where U.S. courts had no jurisdiction. Their second preference was a U.S. insular possession where federal immigration law did not apply directly (such as Wake Island or Guantanamo Bay). The ultimate fallback was detention in the continental United States. Justice Department officials expressed their concern about the captured suspects exercising the full panoply of rights if they were within range of U.S. courts. They concluded there was only a 50-50 chance that they could successfully convict Pol Pot in federal court under the *ex post facto limitation analysis* introduced by Holder at the Deputies Committee meeting. The lawyers viewed prosecution in the United States only as a last resort.

By the end of the first week of April 1998, U.S. officials in Washington, Phnom Penh, and Bangkok knew that defections by units of the remaining Khmer Rouge units had opened the possibility that Pol Pot and his senior cadre might be exposed to apprehension, perhaps in Thailand. Clinton signed a presidential determination on April 4 authorizing the Departments of Defense and Justice to take the necessary steps to detain the Khmer Rouge leaders.[14] The Justice Department agreed to deploy U.S. marshals for this purpose. The Pentagon had to be ready to assist with the transport of any captured suspects. The location of the prospective detention and determination of who, precisely, should be detained for trial remained critical unresolved issues. Exhaustive discussions with several countries virtually precluded detention or trial by a third country. The best option seemed to be detention by the U.S. government (location still undetermined) while awaiting expansion of the mandate of the Yugoslav Tribunal to accommodate the trials of a small number of the most culpable senior Khmer Rouge leaders.

We again canvassed U.N. Security Council members regarding an amendment to the Yugoslav Tribunal mandate. Their responses were largely equivocal. The options for temporary detention included the Commonwealth of Northern Mariana Islands, where there was one federal judge and three

U.S. attorneys. This would be an advantage if a habeas corpus brief was filed because Pol Pot and any other detainees would not have to be moved elsewhere, particularly to the continental United States, to appear before a federal court. Another option was distant Wake Island, which had an adequate U.S. military facility and access to a federal judge, but it was a costly option. Guantanamo was the third option, with an adequate detention facility for ten or more detainees, and it would be the least expensive. However, the Justice Department speculated the Fourth Circuit courts might seek to exercise jurisdiction over the detainees there.

I joined an exhaustive interagency meeting in Washington on April 7 to discuss strategy on how to negotiate with China and the rest of the Security Council so as to seek their support for building the Cambodia Tribunal. There was agreement among all to aim for a council resolution the next week so as to broaden the jurisdiction of the Yugoslav Tribunal. We would also stress to the Thai government and military that the United States was prepared to transport Pol Pot and other senior Khmer Rouge leaders from Thailand to a facility outside the country for temporary custody pending their turnover to an international tribunal or national court for prosecution. We targeted Pol Pot, Ta Mok, Khieu Samphan, and Nuon Chea as the high-priority suspects for such action.

Then, on April 9, the *New York Times* reported on U.S. planning for spiriting Pol Pot, if captured, out of Thailand.[15] It was an unfortunate article, as it spooked Thai officials and, we feared, caused them to back off cooperating with us. There was no confirmation of Pol Pot's actual presence in Thailand yet. We also were not convinced that Thai military authorities were committed to apprehending Pol Pot and suspected that they might just push him back across the border if necessary. The Thai military border units operated with a certain degree of autonomy, and we could not determine with any degree of certainty precisely what was happening on their side of the border. Journalists had long reported that some local commanders probably profited from the lumber trade out of Cambodia facilitated by the Khmer Rouge.[16] I suspected that what happened at the border under their eyes might not necessarily reach headquarters in Bangkok.

Meanwhile, Robert Rosenstock, the legal adviser at the U.S. Mission to the United Nations, quickly prepared a draft resolution for the Security Council and circulated it internally for review on April 9. It called for acting under the U.N. Charter's enforcement authority and establishing a third chamber in the Yugoslav Tribunal, installing three additional judges, limiting the tribunal's personal jurisdiction to the senior Khmer Rouge leaders, authorizing transfer of suspects to The Hague, recommending voluntary funding, and proposing a range of amendments to the Yugoslav Tribunal to accomplish the task. We knew that if we could apprehend Pol Pot, the Security Council had to be primed to act immediately to set up the court that would try him.

However, the competing interests of different federal agencies vastly complicated the issue of where the U.S. military might fly Pol Pot even if he were captured. We continued to look closely at the Northern Mariana Islands for a temporary detention site. The advantage of these islands was that federal immigration law did not apply there, so Pol Pot or someone acting on his behalf could not make use of the provisions and protections of federal law that could lead to his release. But the Interior Department strongly objected, arguing that bringing Pol Pot to the Northern Mariana Islands would undermine a political and legislative priority of *extending* federal immigration law to cover the islands. Their objective was to combat the growing problem of sweatshops using cheap Asian labor in the islands.

Interior Department officials proposed, as an alternative, the Freely Associated States (FAS), which included the Marshall Islands, Palau, and the Federated States of Micronesia. But the State Department opposed that idea. The FAS countries are independent despite their security ties to the United States. If Pol Pot was detained there, we would not have the same degree of influence on any judicial proceedings introduced on his behalf. Also, renegotiations of the compact status of the FAS were imminent, and U.S. objectives could be seriously compromised if we put ourselves in their political debt by asking them to take Pol Pot.

On April 11 and 12, possibilities began to open up dramatically for achieving custody of Pol Pot at the Thai-Cambodian border. We were learning of several plans afoot at the border. We could not confirm whether other senior Khmer Rouge leaders would be turned over with Pol Pot. In fact, any attempt to require a group transfer might have jeopardized our securing Pol Pot's apprehension.

With this news in hand, the deputies met with me on April 14 to decide on the apprehension of Pol Pot and possibly others. Anlong Veng had just fallen to Cambodian government troops, and Ambassador Quinn had reached it in the company of Cambodian military officials. He heard reports that Ta Mok, Pol Pot, Kieu Samphan, and other Khmer Rouge leaders were ten kilometers inside Thailand and that Nuon Chea was heading to

Thailand's Trat Province for sanctuary. The deputies were apprised of the earlier conversations near the border. Many key decisions had to be made rapidly, including what we should communicate to the Thai government, whether we should inform both civilian and military officials, and how we should respond to the offer from the Khmer Rouge officials holding Pol Pot and whether we should be holding any talks with them. Additional pending decisions included how to respond to any other offer that might be made to capture and turn over Pol Pot, what we should say to the Cambodian government since its military might reach Pol Pot first, and finally how to accelerate rollout of the authorizing resolution in the Security Council for expanding the Yugoslav Tribunal to absorb a new chamber devoted to Khmer Rouge atrocities.

The deputies agreed to initiate indirect communications with the Khmer Rouge on the future of Pol Pot. President Clinton would urge the Thai prime minister to cooperate fully with the U.S. objective to apprehend Pol Pot and other senior Khmer Rouge leaders. Similar appeals by U.S. officials would be made to Thai civilian and military counterparts. The deputies wanted Hun Sen to reaffirm his government's support for an international tribunal to try Pol Pot and other senior Khmer Rouge leaders and to order Cambodian troops to detain Khmer Rouge leaders for trial if the opportunity arose. The deputies instructed that consultations be launched at the United Nations and with Paris, London, and Moscow to garner support for the draft resolution expanding the Yugoslav Tribunal's jurisdiction to cover Cambodia.

Following the deputies' meeting, the East Asian Affairs Bureau in the State Department opposed even indirect communications with the Khmer Rouge for the purpose of detaining Pol Pot, a position at odds with the deputies' decision and one that I strongly opposed. Even though Washington's long-standing policy was not to deal with the Khmer Rouge, Quinn and I believed we could risk minimal contact with them in exchange for the apprehension of Pol Pot. Nor did we have to get drawn into agreeing to any de facto amnesty for other senior Khmer Rouge leaders or to a Khmer Rouge sanctuary in Thailand.

On the morning of April 15, the principals urgently tasked various actions. We continued to coordinate an operations plan to take Pol Pot and other senior Khmer Rouge leaders into custody and transport them out of Thailand. Hun Sen was notified of our willingness to take custody of Pol Pot. Moreover, the Security Council intensified consultations. The island of

Palau, despite the Interior Department's concerns, became the Justice Department's favored destination and would be readied as the detention site, but only after further consultations with Palau officials to confirm their willingness to receive Pol Pot.

Albright placed an urgent call to Thai prime minister Chuan Leekpai and asked for immediate Thai cooperation to detain and transfer Pol Pot and any other Khmer Rouge leaders. She told him that the situation on the border was evolving very rapidly and we needed Thai assistance to bring the senior Khmer Rouge leaders to justice. The United States would take custody of them and transport them out of the country as quickly as possible. Clinton would send Leekpai a message the same day. I believed at the time that, with Clinton's unifying message to the bureaucracy and to Thai officials, we had all arrived at a now-or-never window of opportunity to bring the Khmer Rouge leaders, particularly Pol Pot, to justice. For the first time, I saw the entire U.S. government galvanized for the apprehension effort. Everyone seemed to recognize that the Khmer Rouge were responsible for more than twice the number of deaths in the Rwandan genocide and seventeen times more than were estimated in Bosnia and Herzegovina, and their day of reckoning was long overdue.

Clinton and Albright weighed in heavily with the Thai government, but hit roadblocks over Bangkok's insistence on following time-consuming extradition procedures if Pol Pot were captured on Thai territory.[17] Meanwhile, Thomas Hubbard, the American ambassador to the Philippines and the South Pacific island nation of Palau, requested the assistance of the highest officials of Palau in providing a secure detention block on their territory for the imminent arrival of Pol Pot and perhaps other Khmer Rouge leaders. U.S. marshals would retain direct custody of the suspects, and Washington would pay the full costs of the detention.

But events were spiraling out of control. On the same day, U.S. diplomats in Bangkok phoned Washington about unconfirmed reports that Pol Pot already had died. The news was devastating. My pursuit of Pol Pot had begun in June 1997 and intensified for much of early 1998, only to collapse upon the ring of a distant phone call. The countless hours of planning suddenly seemed a colossal waste of time.

At an interagency meeting on the morning of April 16, the best information indeed pointed toward Pol Pot's death. We awaited transmission of photographs of his corpse. But we determined, despite this setback, to stay the course and continue to seek the apprehension or surrender of other senior Khmer Rouge leaders. I was surprised that it did not take much effort on my part to keep everyone focused on the prize of apprehending other top suspects. The previous days of intensive efforts on Pol Pot seemed to have intoxicated Washington with the prospect of finally achieving some small measure of justice in Cambodia. American ambassador Nancy Soderberg, a political appointee who covered the Security Council in New York, received instructions to begin consultations on our draft resolution for adding Cambodia to an expanded Yugoslav Tribunal mandate. I joined her on April 17 in New York, where our talks with council members continued for several days thereafter.

American officials in Bangkok could not confirm Pol Pot's death as the day stretched on. Rumors floated that the Thai Army had ordered his murder. Some journalists reportedly crossed the border and saw Pol Pot's body. There was speculation that the body would be cremated on April 17. One story had it that Pol Pot ate a poison pill supplied by the Chinese late at night on April 15. In Washington, we were not able to provide independent confirmation of Pol Pot's death, nor the cause of his presumed death.

I advised Albright on April 16 that the planning to bring senior Khmer Rouge leaders to justice continued, despite the reports of Pol Pot's death. We supported the Cambodian government's call for an autopsy. I believed that Pol Pot's demise removed him as a bargaining chip that other Khmer Rouge leaders, Ta Mok in particular, had likely hoped to exchange for guarantees of safe haven or even amnesty. We prepared to request that the Cambodian military commit to detain and turn over to us, for prosecution before an international tribunal, senior Khmer Rouge leaders, including Ta Mok, who came under their control. The key pieces of our plan for transporting detained Khmer Rouge leaders for prosecution also were falling into place. Ambassador Hubbard secured agreement with the Palau government to permit the temporary detention of a small number of such individuals, and U.S. marshals already had been dispatched to Palau and were prepared to help take custody of them on the island.

The Associated Press later ran a story titled "Khmer Rouge Leader Pol Pot Committed Suicide" in which it reported on a *Far Eastern Economic Review* press release claiming that Washington had turned down the chance to take Pol Pot into custody because it was unprepared to arrest and try him.[18] This was misleading and essentially false reporting. We never "refused" custody of Pol Pot. U.S. officials were deeply engaged at that time in seeking

Pol Pot's arrest and transfer out of Cambodia or Thailand to stand trial, not necessarily in the United States but certainly elsewhere.

Much activity occurred on April 17 over whether and how to conduct an autopsy of Pol Pot's body. Both the Khmer Rouge and Royal Thai Army contacted U.S. officials in Thailand to ask if the United States wanted the body for an autopsy. After an initial misstep, Washington confirmed its interest in a professional autopsy. However, control over the body seemed to evade everyone at that point and, with every passing moment, it seemed more certain we had lost our opportunity to ascertain the fate of Pol Pot's corpse.

Failure in the Security Council

Following Pol Pot's untimely and mysterious death, Clinton reaffirmed the U.S. resolve to bring the senior Khmer Rouge leaders to justice. He said, "Although the opportunity to hold Pol Pot accountable for his monstrous crimes appears to have passed, senior Khmer Rouge, who exercised leadership from 1975 to 1979, are still at large and share responsibility for the monstrous human rights abuses committed during this period. We must not permit the death of the most notorious of the Khmer Rouge leaders to deter us from the equally important task of bringing these others to justice."[19]

Among Security Council members, Soderberg and I heard some diplomats begin to speak more favorably about a freestanding criminal tribunal that nonetheless could draw on the infrastructure of the Yugoslav and Rwanda tribunals. The British informed us that they expected Foreign Minister Robin Cook to support our proposal for expanding the Yugoslav Tribunal's mandate to try a limited number of senior Khmer Rouge leaders. They would be "taking this decision with their hearts, not their heads," one of their officials conceded. The French Embassy also told us that they had questions but were not hostile to the U.S. proposal. However, Paris threw another barrier onto our path. The French wanted the Cambodian government to confirm its request for assistance from the U.N. Security Council, particularly by demonstrating the unequivocal consent of King Sihanouk. The prosecutor would have to draw up a list of some of the persons who would be accused, although the French did not want the tribunal's competence limited to a set number of suspects, as that would appear to violate the prosccutor's independence. They also expressed concerns about how to determine that Cambodia still had a prolonged conflict threatening peace so as to fully utilize the Yugoslav Tribunal's enforcement authority under Chapter VII of the U.N. Charter.

Elizabeth Becker of the *New York Times* reported on April 17: "Since 1994 the Clinton administration has actively promoted insuring that Cambodians responsible for mass killings are brought to justice either in national or international courts. Those efforts, however, are late, according to legal experts on Cambodia. 'Particularly since the appointment of David Scheffer as ambassador for war crimes issues, the United States has made bringing major human-rights violators to justice an integral part of finding peace,' said [Steve] Heder. 'But in order to do this in Cambodia they've had to undo the legacies of old American policy and that has required that they start from scratch.'"[20]

By April 20 we still did not have independent confirmation of Pol Pot's death or of its cause. We had seen videotape and photographs of his purported remains. We were concerned about reports that the Khmer Rouge had cremated the body because this precluded any forensic examination to determine the cause of death.

At an interagency meeting we discussed what evidence the Justice Department would need for seizing and prosecuting the top seven suspects. All agreed that Justice Department lawyers probably would need to travel to Phnom Penh. For the purpose of detaining suspects, evidence meeting the standard of probable cause would be sufficient. Obviously, prosecuting them would require a higher evidentiary standard. If the suspects were taken to Palau, we anticipated they could file a habeas corpus petition in federal court because they would still be under the control of the U.S. marshals. But Justice Department lawyers would contest the petition because of Palau's independent status.

To its credit, the Palau government cooperated with the U.S. marshals in developing a secure detention site on Palau's territory that could be used to temporarily detain senior Khmer Rouge leaders. Our plans in that regard had not changed.

Two days later, at another interagency meeting on Cambodia, Justice Department lawyers reported they lacked sufficient evidence in the United States on Khieu Samphan and Ieng Sary and would need to send prosecutors with me to Cambodia during my forthcoming trip there to cxamine other documents. We also discussed how to secure U.N. Security Council approval for the American resolution proposing to add the Cambodian crimes to the Yugoslav Tribunal's mandate. China was firmly opposed and, we surmised, did not want any sort of criminal investigation that might unearth its own links to Pol Pot.

I lobbied Security Council members to garner support for our proposal. The Swedes did not want to take the lead in the council but understood our approach. The British still had no instructions from London but suspected that linking the Cambodian prosecutions into the Yugoslav Tribunal might work. Kenya pledged to be as supportive as possible. Some speculated that in the end Russia would not oppose a separate Cambodia chamber in the Yugoslav Tribunal. Brazil would not commit and remained skeptical of Security Council involvement in the building of war crimes tribunals. The Brazilian diplomat at the United Nations viewed the American proposal as disingenuous, and wondered whether it was an American tactic to back away from the International Criminal Court, which was steaming toward the Rome Conference to be held in a few months. France wanted more input from Southeast Asian governments and a paper from me defending the Security Council's use of Chapter VII enforcement authority to expand the Yugoslav Tribunal's jurisdiction to cover Cambodia. French diplomats predicted Chinese intransigence. Japan was skeptical the Security Council would act on a Cambodian resolution by month's end.

On April 24, Thai authorities advised that any transfer of Khmer Rouge leaders from Thai territory likely would require us to produce an indictment in order to achieve an extradition to a foreign venue and court. We began to shift our focus to Cambodia as the likelier and easier jurisdiction from which to extract the leadership.

I headed to Phnom Penh and Bangkok to explore apprehension and tribunal issues. Two tiers of suspects for the Cambodia Tribunal occupied my attention. Ideally, the United States had to be prepared to detain at least some of the suspects and then transfer them in short order to an expanded Yugoslav Tribunal.[21]

Several Justice Department lawyers arrived in Phnom Penh at the same time to review evidence filed at the Documentation Center of Cambodia. I continued to use as a platform, in my consultations with Cambodian officials, their repeated requests to the international community and the United Nations for help in bringing Khmer Rouge leaders to justice before an international tribunal. My discussions in Phnom Penh were long and arduous, with a wide cast of players, including government officials and U.N. human rights officers. All eyes focused on Ta Mok, who had held Pol Pot until the latter's death, and on whether it might be possible to seize him. We were developing enough evidence against Ta Mok to believe an indictment could be rendered against him. We began to strategize transport modalities if he were apprehended and turned over to U.S. authorities. I had to garner regional support for a tribunal and persuade Cambodian authorities repeatedly to request such a tribunal so as to convince everyone they really meant it. At my meetings in Bangkok, I learned a great deal about Ta Mok and strategized with Thai officials how to capture and fly him out of the region. I made my way home through Malaysia and Indonesia, where views about the United Nations or the United States pursuing justice in Cambodia were hardly enthusiastic. Nonetheless, they acquiesced to our general approach.

U.S. diplomats in New York circulated a draft U.N. Charter Chapter VII (enforcement) resolution on April 28 aimed at establishing the "International Criminal Tribunal for Cambodia" as a subsidiary organ of the Security Council and headquartered in the Netherlands. The rapid advance of the resolution stemmed from the ongoing disintegration of the Khmer Rouge and the resulting possibility that senior Khmer Rouge leaders suddenly could be held accountable for their actions. In order to maximize efficiency and limit expenditures, the proposed tribunal would share much of the infrastructure and resources of the Yugoslav Tribunal. We modified our proposal to take account of the strong sentiment among some council members for a separate tribunal dedicated to Cambodia, but left intact our vision of shared components with the Yugoslav Tribunal.

The draft resolution required the cooperation of all nations and authorized them to detain and transfer to the custody of the tribunal any suspects designated by the prosecutor. It also invited the General Assembly to consider a voluntary funding scheme for the tribunal. In the annexed draft statute, the Cambodia Tribunal prosecutor would be the same person as the Yugoslav Tribunal prosecutor, who at that time was Louise Arbour, and the tribunal on Cambodian prosecutions would share the Appeals Chamber of the Yugoslav and Rwanda tribunals and the registry of the Yugoslav Tribunal. The primary argument for setting up the International Criminal Tribunal for Cambodia was to ensure that when senior Khmer Rouge leaders were apprehended or voluntarily surrendered, there would be at least the shell of a tribunal authorized by the Security Council to proceed relatively quickly with prosecutions (preceded by ongoing investigations and indictments prepared by the prosecutor).

The U.S. Justice Department team in Phnom Penh advised me that it would make their job much easier if the Security Council adopted the resolution soon, as then access to evidence and the prospect of apprehensions would be facilitated by clear legal authority. Also, we explored in Bangkok the idea of deploying a small planning team from the Pentagon to assist the American embassy in working out the myriad details of a successful extraction of other senior Khmer Rouge leaders if they reached Thai territory. However, I was becoming more convinced that extraction using only Cambodian airspace appeared more likely to yield success. We needed a small special operations planning team in the region that could work through the logistical details arising in any extraction operation through Thai or Cambodian territory or airspace. U.S. diplomats also communicated to foreign officials that Washington wanted to see Ta Mok stand trial before an international tribunal. If he were made available to us, U.S. authorities would be prepared to accept custody provided we worked closely with Thai or Cambodian officials.

Back in New York, Soderberg and I had a tough challenge explaining the rationale for the International Criminal Tribunal for Cambodia as a creature of Chapter VII of the U.N. Charter, which requires a threat to international peace and security in order to mandate compliance by governments and to establish such criminal tribunals as the Yugoslav and Rwanda tribunals. Our argument went something like this:

> In the absence of Chapter VII authority, defense counsel could challenge the establishment of the tribunal, its jurisdiction over the accused, and the enforceability of any decision, verdict, or sentence. Reliance on Chapter VII authority may also prove important for countries involved in the posttrial imprisonment phase for those convicted by the Yugoslav and Rwanda tribunals. Some countries have argued that, in the case of Cambodia, the fact that the crimes to be tried before an international tribunal occurred two decades ago undermines the credibility of any such finding. It is inherent in the very nature of accountability that it must come after the fact of the crimes committed, and often, as in the case of the Rwanda Tribunal, after the most acute phase of the threat to international peace and stability has subsided. Only at that point are alleged perpetrators likely to surrender or to be captured and therefore to be available to defend themselves in a judicial proceeding. The passing of the acute phase does not mean, however, that the threat to international peace and security has disappeared altogether. To the contrary, despite

the passage of time, the crimes committed and as yet unpunished by the Khmer Rouge remain a festering wound that is exacerbating political tensions in Cambodian society and could lead to clashes with the remaining Khmer Rouge elements. Moreover, impunity for senior Khmer Rouge leaders—who are still the authority figures within the Khmer Rouge troop units now dispersed within the Cambodian army—means that the threat of serious use of force by the Khmer Rouge remains real. Indeed, this very threat has been invoked perversely as a reason to delay establishment of a tribunal. Either scenario—clashes with or coordinated attacks by the Khmer Rouge—makes clear that a failure to act at this juncture would leave Cambodia with great potential for instability and violence, which in turn could easily affect or spill over into the surrounding region, and which therefore constitutes a threat to international peace and security.

Days earlier, during my meeting with Thai officials on April 29, I had sought their support for our resolution and explained that an element that would help Thailand—and would assist the United States given the probability that habeas corpus writs could be filed by those detained by U.S. authorities— was language in the resolution text authorizing and encouraging states to detain Khmer Rouge leaders in preparation for their transfer to the tribunal to stand trial. Having the resolution and this language in place as soon as possible would give both Bangkok and Washington legal cover to take custody of the suspects and transfer them quickly out of Thailand and ultimately to The Hague.

Yet, with no one in custody and with Pol Pot, the kingpin suspect, recently deceased, Security Council members balked at the U.S.-sponsored resolution. Some, in particular China, held fast to their belief that there was no longer any threat to international peace and security in Cambodia and therefore the Security Council had no legal authority to set up a judicial body as a means of nonmilitary enforcement to maintain or restore peace and security.

The American proposal was pushed to the extreme back burner when, on May 6, the Cambodian government released a statement noting Pol Pot's death, expressing the desire to still try Khmer Rouge leaders, committing itself to hold "free, fair and democratic elections for 26 July 1998," and requesting the setting up of "a national or international court of justice after the 26 July 1998 general elections in Cambodia."[22] Some council members also wanted to delay further consideration of the American proposal until after the elections.

It was clear that support for creating the International Criminal Tribunal for Cambodia was shallow within the Security Council. France, Russia, China, and others had raised serious concerns about the advisability of creating such an institution from a political standpoint and particularly as an enforcement measure under Chapter VII of the U.N. Charter, for in their view no threat to international peace and security existed in Cambodia. They also had conditioned their support for a tribunal on receipt of fresh letters from the Cambodian government expressing its consent for such a court.

Pursuing Khmer Rouge Leaders

Suddenly there arose the prospect of arresting at least three senior Khmer Rouge leaders. Hun Sen mentioned their names—Ta Mok, Nuon Chea, and Khieu Samphan—in a May 17 phone call to Ambassador Quinn, who responded that if they were detained by Cambodian soldiers, the United States was prepared to assist in their detention pending their transfer to an international tribunal. We needed seventy-two hours notice and thus wondered whether Cambodia could hold them that long. Quinn requested that Cambodian law enforcement authorities accompany the detainees to their detention site outside Cambodia. We also were prepared to assist in the detention of three other leading suspects: Ieng Sary, Ke Pauk, and Kaing Guek Eav (alias Duch). Quinn asked Hun Sen to make a public request for an international tribunal once they were in custody. The Justice Department confirmed that the United States had legal authority to assist Cambodian law enforcement officials in maintaining custody of the detainees. To help matters, President Clinton weighed in with instructions to assist Cambodia in maintaining custody of Ta Mok, Nuon Chea, and Khieu Samphan pending their rendition or delivery to a tribunal having proper jurisdiction.

Two teams of U.S. marshals departed on May 19, 1998, one team bound for Thailand and the other for Palau. Since commercial flights to the region were difficult to arrange, we did not know exactly when the teams would be in place. But the prospects were so encouraging that Quinn and I planned for how the detainees would be handled until they could arrive.

Quinn met with Hun Sen, who agreed to deploy Cambodian law enforcement officials with the detainees to Palau. He also told Quinn that the three suspects were in hiding in Thailand about two kilometers from the border near a Thai military base. His plan was that either the Thai military would turn them over or they would be captured by a Cambodian team and then handed over to U.S. marshals by the Royal Cambodian Air Force after a helicopter flight into Cambodia. Hun Sen expected the capture within the week. He arranged for an adviser to visit with Quinn to work out procedures for a turnover, including a memorandum of understanding. The memorandum would refer to the November 1997 letter to Clinton requesting assistance to bring senior Khmer Rouge leaders to justice before an international tribunal, acknowledge difficulty in keeping them in Cambodia, and request U.S. assistance in maintaining their safety until an international tribunal could be established. The plan called for a turnover at the airport in Phnom Penh, where four or five Cambodian officials would join the flight, reserving the right to question detainees on national security issues. We stressed the need for the Cambodian government to affirm its support for an international tribunal so as to advance the resolution in New York. The wild card remained Hun Sen's true thoughts about how all this would play with the Chinese.

The U.S. marshals arrived in Bangkok on May 20, 1998. Enough priority had been given to their mission that the assistant director of the service accompanied them. Washington worried about the Thai role, for any misstep there would endanger the Cambodian initiative. Several more U.S. marshals flew into Phnom Penh in the following days. But on May 26, Quinn learned that the Cambodians had encountered difficulties in moving the capture forward, perhaps meeting some resistance from Thai elements.

Meanwhile, I met with U.N. diplomats and learned that Latin American governments generally opposed setting up the Cambodia Tribunal. Mexico believed that the Yugoslav and Rwanda tribunals lacked legitimacy and so too would this one. The tribunal's retroactive jurisdiction, stretching all the way back to 1975, seemed more like high-stakes poker than international justice to some in New York. Several foreign diplomats, particularly from Europe, accused me of undermining the forthcoming Rome negotiations on the International Criminal Court by pressing forward with another ad hoc tribunal. They could not have been more mistaken, but presumptions are hard to kill on short notice. The senior Khmer Rouge leaders could never be prosecuted before the permanent court, because its jurisdiction would only cover crimes committed after the court became operational, which under any scenario ruled out atrocity crimes in the 1970s. Even among the

Europeans, walking and chewing gum at the same time sometimes proved difficult for the most fervent advocates of international justice. When their chants of "No more Pol Pots!" echoed in Rome two months later, I wondered why that sentiment had not seized them over the prior year to ensure that the leadership of the Pol Pot regime would be brought to justice.

In the final days of May 1998, the apprehension plans once again unraveled. Frustrated with the failure to apprehend Ta Mok and expending scarce funds, the U.S. marshals began to pull out of Bangkok, Phnom Penh, and Palau. The capture of the Khmer Rouge leaders no longer appeared imminent. The U.S. Navy had called the exercise Operation Curtain Call. I just wish the curtain had fallen for the suspects rather than for the U.S. marshals.

Our diplomats' efforts with Thai officials proved inconclusive and demonstrated once again lack of resolve by the Thai government. They seemed far more worried about what an apprehension might mean for the July elections in Cambodia. Our next step was to circulate a U.S. position paper at the United Nations on the rationale for a Security Council resolution to establish an International Criminal Tribunal for Cambodia.

I engaged in a round of consultations on May 29, 1998, with Security Council members and discussed line by line the content of the draft U.S. resolution and points raised in our position paper. I wanted to work on the resolution text with them in anticipation of proceeding with it right after the July 26 election or sooner if any of the suspects were apprehended prior to that date. Officials from Brazil, China, France, Russia, and the United Kingdom questioned me about whether a threat to international peace and security existed, which is a requirement to invoke Chapter VII authority. Although Washington still considered a tribunal under Chapter VII to be preferable, we were prepared to examine whether it would be feasible to proceed under Chapter VI instead, where a threat to international peace and security would not be required, but such a tribunal would lack the type of enforcement authority enjoyed by the Yugoslav and Rwanda tribunals. The diplomats reiterated their concerns that the statute must contain a precise description of those sought in order to narrow the group and avoid implicating thousands. At the same time, they said, the description could not appear to prejudge the suspects.

U.N. delegations also repeated requests for a clear indication that the Cambodian government supported creating the tribunal. They suggested that the descriptions of crimes to be prosecuted be refined more precisely to fit the situation in Cambodia. Kenya, Portugal, and Britain expressed support for the U.S. proposal. The French were very concerned about proceeding to establish the tribunal prior to the Cambodian elections, but were prepared to engage in technical discussions. The Brazilians expressed their fundamental objection to the Security Council establishing international criminal tribunals. The entire group of Latin American governments opposed *ex post facto* prosecutions. The Russians continued to take a firm stand against the proposal.

Also driving the delay in any council vote on the resolution was the appointment of three senior experts to examine accountability options for Cambodia and deliver recommendations.[23] This Group of Experts was formally established by Secretary-General Kofi Annan on July 31, 1998, "to evaluate the existing evidence, to assess the feasibility of bringing Khmer Rouge leaders to justice, and to explore options for bringing them to justice before an international or national jurisdiction."[24] They would take seven months to complete their work, further delaying creation of a tribunal for Cambodia.

Trying to Salvage an International Tribunal

Over the summer of 1998 various tracking efforts, particularly by the Cambodian government, appeared to locate Ta Mok and others inside Thailand, but no major effort was undertaken by Cambodian authorities to capture any of them. Interest subsided as the July 26 elections drew near. On July 20, however, I received a faxed map from Cambodia scholar Steve Heder purporting to show Ta Mok's location. This set off another futile effort to confirm his whereabouts. In mid-July, Hun Sen confirmed it remained the policy of the government to capture Ta Mok and others and welcomed coordination with the United States to fly them to an international tribunal after their capture. Quinn valiantly kept raising the issue with Hun Sen and other Cambodian leaders throughout his tour there.

I met with Kofi Annan and his deputy legal counsel, Ralph Zacklin, on August 4 in New York to explain the U.S. initiatives and our commitment to bringing senior Khmer Rouge leaders to justice as soon as possible. I told them we were concerned about the sincerity of Hun Sen in apprehending the top Khmer Rouge leaders and in holding a credible trial in Cambodia. We had a good working relationship with Hun Sen and sensed his priorities. Hun Sen's first preference was to have the senior Khmer Rouge leaders fade away as long as their troops were neutralized. His second choice seemed to be a trial that he controlled. Obviously, if this were to happen, given his track record, it would be seen as lacking credibility and would taint everyone associated with it. I told Annan that Quinn had recently met with Hammarberg, the U.N. special representative for human rights in Cambodia, who was working with the Group of Experts and who seemed intent on a largely indigenous Cambodian legal process, which would apparently target midlevel people. Our concern was that Hammarberg's approach would bring to justice only those Khmer Rouge officers Hun Sen wanted to see removed from society rather than the leaders who had given the orders back in 1975–1979. Hun Sen could end up controlling the process to the detriment of credible accountability for the top Khmer Rouge leaders.

We also were concerned that Hammarberg was diverting the process away from the Security Council and what our resolution sought to achieve. On August 10, I emphasized to Hammarberg the continuing role of the Security Council and the utility of a council role merging, in the future, with whatever might develop from his approach. He agreed on a role for the council and for an ultimate merger of the two approaches. He did not confirm whether his approach would target primarily midlevel officials, but implied that the scope of the target list would be left to the experts.

I returned to New York on September 9 to hold discussions with Hammarberg and other UN officials. I mentioned the possibility of establishing a judicial tribunal for top Khmer Rouge leaders and a truth and reconciliation process for mid- and low-level Khmer Rouge cadre who had participated in the Pol Pot regime atrocities. Judge Ninian Stephen, who was one of the chosen "experts," was very taken with this approach and returned to it through the afternoon of meetings. U.N. assistant secretary-general for political affairs Alvaro de Soto stressed that some Security Council members still had concerns about a Chapter VII premise and wanted a formal Cambodian government request for the tribunal. If both of these issues could be resolved, he indicated the usefulness of a Security Council tribunal.

Drawing from my trip to Cambodia the week before, I shared some ideas, including the possibility for a nonvoting Cambodian judge, a Cambodian prosecutor as an adviser to the tribunal's international prosecutor, the option to hold trials in Cambodia, and the possibility of a trial located somewhere in the region. I described the origin and rationale for the U.S. strategy that Soderberg and I had used with the Security Council earlier that year, and why a Security Council role remained critical to the ultimate legal process. I stressed that the U.S. approach (which had been driven by the prospect of imminent custody earlier that year) could be merged with another viable process determined by the experts. But I felt that it would be folly to follow any course that eliminated the Security Council, which could provide clout to the tribunal. I also discussed a Chapter VI basis for Security Council action and noted that it would require full Cambodian government cooperation. But a Chapter VI basis could not mandate cooperation by other states, particularly China, which might be very resistant to working with the tribunal. I conceded that getting China's consent to any Security Council procedure would be difficult, but it would not be impossible (particularly if the procedure was not under Chapter VII authority).

It is characteristic of U.N. practice to await the delivery of the report of a group of experts or commission of inquiry, once one has been formed, before the council takes any further steps on a contentious issue. That is precisely what happened at the United Nations with the report of the Group of Experts for Cambodia, which was not delivered to U.N. member states until March 1999.[25] No proposals were considered or actions taken at the United Nations, and no U.N. negotiations were entered into with Cambodian authorities, prior to the release of that report. The momentum behind a post–Cambodian election accountability initiative had lost much of its steam by the time the experts weighed in, largely because everyone in New York was waiting for delivery of their report.

Defections and Hun Sen's Gambit

During the final days of 1998 two top Khmer Rouge leaders, Khieu Samphan (Pol Pot's right-hand man) and Nuon Chea ("Brother No. 2" under Pol Pot), defected to Cambodian authorities and were warmly greeted by Prime Minister Hun Sen. The public impression at the time was that amnesty of some sort had been offered in order to neutralize these Khmer Rouge leaders and bring them in from the forests. However, Hun Sen denied this, explaining that he had prioritized talking about "peace" and "reconciliation" in his initial welcoming statement. That did not mean he was reversing his position on the need for trials of Khmer Rouge leaders.[26] The United States was the first country following the defection episode to comment publicly and unambiguously on accountability. Other senior Khmer Rouge leaders were still in hiding, and Ta Mok remained the object of intensive American efforts aimed at securing his surrender or apprehension.

King Sihanouk issued a statement on December 30 confirming that he would grant a royal pardon to the two defectors. He went on to say that an international tribunal nevertheless had a "perfect right" to take up the case of genocide in Cambodia because it concerned crimes against humanity, which involved the conscience of the world community. We still intended to build an international consensus in support of the position that the door to prosecution of these individuals remained open. American diplomats in the key countries approached the highest possible officials to request that they maintain a firm line on accountability of the Khmer Rouge with immediate expressions of support for justice to be rendered against Nuon Chea and Khieu Samphan. Such support, coupled with direct communications to the Cambodian government, would be vital to help forestall any actions or statements that could complicate efforts or close the door on options intended to hold the most senior Khmer Rouge leaders accountable.

On January 4, 1999, Hun Sen assured Quinn that criminal proceedings against Nuon Chea and Khieu Samphan were still possible. He had every intention of moving against them whenever a proper court was established and then, if they did not volunteer to appear, he would arrest them when a warrant was issued by a proper court.

Speculation persisted that the two defectors and Ta Mok had been staying in Thailand for a long time. Hun Sen publicly stated the week before that an unidentified "neighboring country" had sheltered Khmer Rouge leaders in the past. He said the neighboring country should have handed the men over to an international court while it had them in its grasp.[27]

While Hun Sen did not arrest Nuon Chea and Khieu Samphan when they surrendered, he did not exempt them from any future trial or grant either one immunity for crimes committed during the Pol Pot regime. The defectors' appearance on television might convince many average Cambodians who still lived in fear of the Khmer Rouge that the movement was no longer a threat. However, Hun Sen wanted Ta Mok arrested and prosecuted. If he surrendered, Ta Mok would be arrested and turned over to the United States until he could be brought to trial. Hun Sen asked Quinn to send a legal expert from Washington, namely me, to work with his senior adviser on how to structure the tribunal and integrate that process with Hammarberg's work with the Group of Experts.

I advised Albright that the U.S. goal should be to establish a tribunal that met the fundamental requirements for international justice in accordance with international standards of due process. We had to avoid any attempts to immunize the Khmer Rouge leaders from prosecution or to try them in an easily manipulated judicial system that lacked international legitimacy or credibility. We should keep pressing for a Security Council–created tribunal. We also needed to develop a new plan to seek the apprehension or surrender of Ta Mok. If we could help bring Ta Mok into custody, that alone might trigger a Security Council process that would force Hun Sen to focus more intently on accountability for senior Khmer Rouge leaders and to cooperate with international efforts.

Russia responded publicly that it supported the goal of bringing "Pol Pot warlords to justice in any format—international, national or combined." But stability was paramount, and Moscow believed that the initiative for the tribunal should come from the Cambodian people and their leaders.[28] On January 11, 1999, we followed up with the Russians and learned that they saw no practical possibility of bringing Khmer Rouge figures to account before an international tribunal. The French were in a holding pattern until the experts' report was released. Indonesia opposed international accountability and considered the matter entirely up to the Cambodians to decide.

Hun Sen told the press that "nobody should escape justice" and the Khmer Rouge should be brought to trial, "but those who supported them should appear as well." He continued, "There is the period from 1970 to 1975—should we consider nearly 1 million dead to be a crime?" with apparent reference to when American B-52 bombers pounded the country in an effort to hit Vietcong supply routes. He said, "We should find justice for those who died from 1970 to 1975, from 1975 to 1979, and from 1979 to 1998. The dead from each period demand the same justice.... The international community should not forgive and forget certain periods for their political gain." He proclaimed that no amnesty had been given to Nuon Chea and Khieu Samphan, casting doubt on King Sihanouk's December 30 promise of a pardon. ("Pardon" and "amnesty" often were used interchangeably by the Cambodians in the long process of negotiating the Cambodia Tribunal.) "Many people have proclaimed what is morality and law. If you talk like this, you have to be transparent, and you cannot hide one fact that is intrinsically linked to another." Hun Sen all but confirmed that Thailand was hosting Ta Mok. "I do not want to say where he [Ta Mok] is," he said, "but I can tell you he is not on Cambodian soil." Hun Sen favored a trial in Cambodia. "A tribunal must be linked both to justice and reconciliation," he concluded.[29]

Intensified Efforts to Build a Tribunal

Arriving in Phnom Penh on January 19, 1999, I strategized with Quinn on how to achieve a Ta Mok handover. Then I visited with Hun Sen, who told me that the time had arrived for Thailand to deal with the issue. He had discussed the capture of Khmer Rouge leaders during his May 1998 visit there. Hun Sen believed that the new Thai leader and military commander should be able to accomplish the task, as they were not tied to past policy and had fewer ties to the Khmer Rouge.

Hun Sen said that the Cambodians tried to pay for Ta Mok's capture but so far had lost a lot of money. They had spent a lot to bribe the Thai officials at border checkpoints to ensure the crossing of Khieu Samphan and Nuon Chea. If Ta Mok were to be captured secretly (that is, by avoiding public knowledge of Thai involvement), it would take a lot of money to bribe the Thai military. But if the Thais could just capture Ta Mok by whatever means, he said, then Cambodia possibly could sign onto an option for a tribunal. The capture would accelerate the judicial process. Hun Sen told me that his paramount objective was to put an end to the Khmer Rouge. The key symbol of the enemy was Ta Mok, whose remaining troops could revitalize Khmer Rouge fighters and sympathizers in the countryside and pose a direct threat to the Hun Sen regime.

In Bangkok I visited General Terrawat Putamanonda, director of the Thai Defense Ministry's Office of Planning. I told him on January 20 that the emergence of Khieu Samphan and Nuon Chea in late December had taken us only "halfway there" as far as Washington was concerned. Ta Mok's continued presence on the Thai-Cambodian border was a "lingering irritant" that hurt the U.S.-Thai bilateral relationship. Prospects for his arrest were receiving the highest attention in Washington. Putamanonda reacted visibly to the message that Ta Mok's remaining uncaptured was damaging the relationship. He repeated what had been Thailand's long-standing position: the Thai military stood ready to take Ta Mok into custody should he enter Thai territory. He claimed Ta Mok was not in Thailand but assured me that the military would act "decisively" if that changed. I pressed him to follow through, as I had my private doubts about whether he even knew what all his own men were doing on the border.

Hun Sen had asked me during our earlier meeting in Phnom Penh to act as a mediator on Cambodian cooperation with the Thais and to convey three scenarios of arrest. The first would be an arrest of Ta Mok by the Thais, who would hand him over to U.S. officials directly for transport to another country. The second would be a Thai arrest of Ta Mok followed by a public announcement and then his transfer to Cambodian authorities, while the United States coordinated his transport out of Cambodia for detention in another country. Third, Thai authorities would arrest Ta Mok secretly and hand him over to Cambodian authorities, followed by a joint U.S. and Cambodian transport of Ta Mok to another country while Phnom Penh announced the arrest without mentioning any Thai role.

Putamanonda said the third scenario was "most likely to be accepted" by Thai authorities should Ta Mok be found in Thailand. This would avoid Thai legal issues, but he was skeptical that Hun Sen would play along and keep the Thai role secret. After I explained the U.S. position rejecting a General Assembly tribunal, Putamanonda noted that the Thai position on a future Cambodia Tribunal centered on the issue being an "internal matter for Cambodia ultimately to decide." But Thailand would not oppose an international tribunal should Cambodia opt for one.

On January 21, Hun Sen forwarded to Kofi Annan an "Aide Memoire and Analysis" on bringing Khmer Rouge leaders to trial. The document raised many questions about methodology and scope of investigations, and noted: "Should there be an international court, it would be established by the United Nations. Would the United Nations Security Council be able to establish it?"[30] That was my continuing challenge to answer.

I visited Cambodia, Thailand, China, France, and the Netherlands in mid-January 1999 to press forward with accountability and explore several approaches, including an international criminal tribunal that would be established by the Security Council under its U.N. Charter Chapter VI authority at the request of the Cambodian government and with its full cooperation. Such an approach would avoid the criticism that Cambodia was no longer a threat to international peace and security and hence outside the realm of a Chapter VII ad hoc international criminal tribunal. Rather, the council's action would be responsive to its U.N. Charter Chapter VI powers to deal with any dispute, the continuance of which might lead to international friction or give rise to a larger dispute.[31] Under a Chapter VI tribunal, the cooperation of other governments would not be mandatory; the Cambodian government would maintain custody over the suspects and enforce penalties in cooperation with the tribunal. The concept I advanced opened the door for continued efforts to explore options outside the conventional Chapter VII approach, which was making no progress in the Security Council even though it remained the preferred option of the American government.

China's assistant foreign minister, Wang Yi, listened to my argument that it was in the interest of the permanent members of the Security Council, which includes China, to ensure that the council supervised the tribunal-building process. Otherwise, the process could spin out of control with negative consequences for both China and the United States. Wang questioned the inevitability of the tribunal and said that the Cambodians should make that judgment themselves, free of external pressure. He uttered the standard Chinese line not to interfere in the internal affairs of other countries.

But I needed to press Wang further. I described the relevant factors in how the process I was proposing could unfold:

- Cambodia would file a specific request under Chapter VI of the U.N. Charter for the establishment of a special tribunal.
- No other country would be required to cooperate with the tribunal.
- The scope of the tribunal's jurisdiction would be for those actions committed from March 1975 through January 1979.
- The tribunal's targets would be about ten of the senior most Khmer Rouge leaders.
- Cambodia could even suggest names of such leaders to the tribunal.
- Cambodia would request that the tribunal include at least one Cambodian judge and that there be Cambodian lawyers in the Prosecutor's Office.
- Cambodia would request that the trials be held in Phnom Penh though some, out of concern for national security, could be held in The Hague.
- Cambodia would approve the country of detention for any Khmer Rouge found guilty.
- Cambodia would reject the possibility, within the bounds of reason for an international court, that the tribunal examine the conduct of any foreign country during the Pol Pot regime. (I explained that if this point were not stipulated, any tribunal examination of the period would imperil the national character of the proceedings and the peaceful evolution of Cambodia's relations with its neighbors. In addition, the defense counsel for any of the accused might seek to describe that person's relationship with a foreign country. Judges should not allow any such inquiry to go that far.)
- Cambodia could ask that the National Assembly of Cambodia approve the statute governing the tribunal before its creation.

- The Security Council would receive the request from Phnom Penh and know that any broadening or change would result in the loss of Cambodian cooperation. If such cooperation were lost, the proposal would fall back to the General Assembly, placing the process in jeopardy. Following strictly these guidelines, the Security Council would be able to manage the effort with a single objective: a tribunal circumscribed by the necessary parameters.

In further dialogue with Wang, I focused on the desire to limit the examination of the tribunal to Khmer Rouge actions from 1975 to 1979. I noted that the United States had bombed Cambodia in the early 1970s and while the United States acknowledged that reality, we wanted to avoid giving any individuals an excuse for using the bombing to justify their own actions in Cambodia. However, if we did not maintain such a condition, China's actions in Cambodia after 1979 would be fair game as well.

The American view remained that the process was inevitable and that the U.N. experts' forthcoming report would set the process into full gear. Wang asserted that even if the experts issued their February report calling for an international tribunal, the overarching principle in the U.N. Charter was noninterference in the internal affairs of others. No matter what the report contained, the principle of noninterference would determine whether the process proceeded or not. The judgment, he reiterated, must be made by the Cambodians themselves with no external pressure.

I flew to Paris and repeated my concerns that if the accountability process veered into a General Assembly process, it could spin out of control. I thought any international tribunal would need to be established by the Security Council, but I explored the possibility of establishing a tribunal under Chapter VI of the U.N. Charter. This would be a novel approach, but it would allow for a tribunal with an international imprint. Such a tribunal would rely on a request by the government of Cambodia, on the voluntary cooperation of states, and it might allow for participation of Cambodian judges and staff.

On January 29, U.S. embassy officials in Phnom Penh met with Hun Sen adviser Om Yentieng to explore further the details of the Chapter VI initiative I had discussed in my talks a week earlier. My bottom line was that a Cambodian request for a Chapter VI tribunal could greatly increase Cambodia's stake in the entire process. It also avoided the precedent of a General Assembly–generated tribunal. Om Yentieng volunteered what was really on his mind, namely that he was flabbergasted that the United States was not able to elicit Thai cooperation to arrest Ta Mok.

Meanwhile, Putamananda met with U.S. diplomats in Bangkok on January 26 to follow up on my request that he investigate the whereabouts of Ta Mok. He was supposed to confirm to me that the Thais had not found Ta Mok in any of the locations identified by the United States. Instead, Putamananda said he was convinced Ta Mok was not in the custody of the Thai military and in fact was on the Cambodian side of the border. But he added that he would plan on taking U.S. officials to the border soon to inspect for any sign of Ta Mok.

Final Pursuit of Ta Mok

In Washington and at our embassy in Phnom Penh, we continued to focus on how to root out Ta Mok, including whether, with sufficient cash, we could induce someone to turn Ta Mok over to us and get him out of Indochina. The Thais made clear to us that they would seek to prevent Ta Mok's entry into Thailand or would apprehend him and turn him over to Cambodia if he were discovered within Thailand's borders. Alternatively, should Ta Mok fall into Thai hands, U.S. officials would transport Ta Mok out of Thailand for trial before an international or foreign tribunal. The Cambodian government confirmed in writing that it would ask for U.S. assistance to take custody of Ta Mok. In our view, the United States could legally take custody of Ta Mok and detain him pending his delivery to a tribunal with jurisdiction to adjudicate the crimes committed by the Khmer Rouge. American diplomats had thoroughly discussed this framework with Thai officials when it appeared that Pol Pot might be apprehended, and U.S. marshals and military personnel still remained on standby to take custody of any other suspects.

All our laborious planning to apprehend Ta Mok and use him as a catalyst for the Security Council to establish the International Criminal Tribunal for Cambodia collapsed on March 6, 1999, when Cambodian authorities captured him and brought him to Phnom Penh to await domestic rather than foreign prosecution. The arrest of Ta Mok may have been the result of cooperation between Thailand and Cambodia following direct U.S. and Japanese pressure. Albright told a news conference during a visit to Thailand shortly before Ta Mok's capture that she had discussed his status during hcr meetings with Thai leaders. "We did speak about the importance of rendering Ta Mok to Cambodian authorities," she said, adding that Washington sought establishment of an international tribunal. Jamie Rubin, Albright's spokesman, told reporters in London: "We are encouraged that we now have the opportunity to bring one of the most notorious war criminals in the recent past to justice and we will now be focusing our efforts on working with the Cambodians to that end. Apparently he has been arrested. We welcome this arrest."[32]

The State Department sent out demarches two days later to those governments with the greatest interest in Cambodian accountability in order to seek support for an international tribunal. We wanted to build on Ta Mok's arrest to achieve a more comprehensive approach to Cambodian justice, with the tribunal as the linchpin. But two days later I spoke with Quinn by phone. He told me there was no flexibility among Cambodian officials. They had made up their minds and would proceed with investigations before a domestic court.

At the time I was not too alarmed. In the absence of an international tribunal, Cambodia proceeded with the investigation of Ta Mok. He was charged with violations of a 1994 Cambodian law outlawing the "Group of Democratic Kampuchea" and thus focusing any further proceedings on post–Pol Pot crimes. No decision had been made yet whether he would be tried in a military or civilian court, and we did not know yet whether Ta Mok would also be charged with atrocity crimes. None of this precluded prosecution by an international tribunal in the future, which was Washington's long-standing preference and the formal recommendation of the U.N. Group of Experts. But our original plan to spirit Ta Mok out of Cambodia in the hope that it would accelerate action to create an international tribunal was extinguished by the reality that Khieu Samphan, Nuon Chea, and now Ta Mok were in the control of Cambodian authorities, thus creating substantial pressure upon Hun Sen to handle their fates himself.

Shifts in the U.S. and U.N. Positions

While the Ta Mok saga was unfolding in Thailand and Cambodia, the National Security Council convened a meeting in Washington on February 8, 1999, to discuss my Cambodia strategy paper on the Chapter VI Security Council approach. Nancy Soderberg threw a wrench into my efforts when she argued we should stick to our guns and try to set up the tribunal under

Chapter VII authority (the difficulty of finding a "threat to international peace and security" notwithstanding) and that we should settle for nothing less for the time being. Her view prevailed, and I was instructed to continue pressing for a Chapter VII resolution.

Quinn, notably agitated after he learned about the outcome of the meeting, complained that suddenly the whole Chapter VI approach was being abandoned, the very one I had discussed in January with Hun Sen and others. He was exaggerating, but it put me in a very tight spot. I called Quinn and told him that Chapter VII remained the preferred approach and that what I presented in Cambodia was the makings for a fallback position in the event the Chapter VII effort failed, but that was cold comfort to Quinn. This was an instance where I had to take a risk to move the process forward with the Chapter VI option. I knew that the idea was premature and likely to elicit someone's disapproval. But without it, I was left with the much maligned Chapter VII approach. As is often the case in negotiations, my task in this situation was to push the envelope to find an acceptable means to a desired end. But I recognized that there was always the risk someone in the bureaucracy would dig in and say no.

The U.N. Group of Experts for Cambodia delivered their report to the General Assembly and the Security Council in March 1999.[33] In line generally with U.S. policy preferences and diverging from the negative view among certain Security Council members about any council role in the process, the three experts concluded that the best approach for accountability in Cambodia would be for the Security Council to establish a Chapter VII international criminal tribunal in the mold of the Yugoslav and Rwanda tribunals. The experts concluded that the Cambodian legal system failed to meet three essential conditions: a trained cadre of judges, lawyers, and investigators; an adequate infrastructure; and a culture of respect for due process. In their view, only an international tribunal would guarantee international standards of justice, fairness, and due process of law. They recommended that "the independent prosecutor appointed by the United Nations limit his or her investigations to those persons most responsible for the most serious violations of international human rights law.... that the Security Council establish this tribunal or, should it not do so, that the General Assembly establish it ... that the Prosecutor of the Yugoslav Tribunal and of the Rwanda Tribunal serve as Prosecutor of the new tribunal, with a Deputy Prosecutor specifically charged with responsibility for this tribunal.... that the tribunal, including the office of the Deputy Prosecutor, be established in a State in the Asia-Pacific region, but not in Cambodia; that the Prosecutor establish an investigations office in Cambodia."[34]

The experts' report did not sit well with Hun Sen, who stressed in a letter to Kofi Annan that his aide-mémoire and analysis of January 21 sought "more comprehensive justice for Cambodia and her people" and called for a full investigation of crimes committed from 1970 to 1998. Hun Sen wrote in the letter that "we are now studying the South African case and the experience of the South African Truth and Reconciliation Commission in dealing with justice for the Cambodian people, and peace and national reconciliation."[35]

The Hun Sen letter temporarily undermined efforts to forge an international tribunal of some workable character.[36] On March 4, Albright rejected the South African–style commission as any kind of plausible alternative to criminal accountability for the Pol Pot–era atrocities.[37] With the arrest of Ta Mok on March 6 by the Cambodian military,[38] the challenge of actually bringing to justice a leading figure in the atrocities of the Pol Pot era suddenly became a reality, albeit not in the way we had envisaged with a U.S. transport of suspects out of the region. Everyone realized that the likes of Ta Mok would have to be tried, somehow and somewhere.

I joined a National Security Council meeting on March 17, 1999, to review the state of play. We agreed to press for an international criminal tribunal with a high-level strategy. We would restate our position on an international tribunal and refuse to abandon our position on bringing suspects to justice. But we could not be perceived as the lone ranger and would shun any confrontational style. We had to keep the matter out of the control of the General Assembly, which could, by majority vote, create a tribunal with wide-ranging jurisdiction. (In retrospect, it was the General Assembly that saved the tribunal by pressing the U.N. Office of the Legal Counsel to resume talks with the Cambodian government in 2002.)

The Chinese government demarched me in my State Department office two days later. It claimed that the Pol Pot years were an entirely internal affair for Cambodia and that the experts' report had not fully reflected the position of the Cambodian government. Cambodia no longer constituted a breach or threat to international peace and security, so the Chinese opposed creating any international tribunal for Cambodia. It would constitute, in their view, a bad precedent. They bluntly described their own tribunal fatigue. I knew the Chinese had a considerable trump card with the amount of foreign assistance they were funneling that year to Cambodia compared with the far smaller American aid program. We had to assume this gave the Chinese considerable leverage with Hun Sen and his government.

During a visit to the United Nations, the Cambodian foreign minister Hor Nam Hong rejected the recommendations of the Group of Experts for Cambodia, including the establishment of an international criminal tribunal. He said Cambodia would try Khmer Rouge leaders in its own courts.[39] My meeting with him proved contentious and revealed his seeming misunderstanding of various points of law relevant to prosecuting the Khmer Rouge.

U.S. senator John F. Kerry, a decorated Vietnam veteran and chairman of the East Asian subcommittee of the Senate Foreign Relations Committee, visited Phnom Penh in early April 1999 and proposed to Hun Sen that a tribunal of mixed composition be established and staffed with international and Cambodian judges. The international judges and prosecutors would work with their Cambodian counterparts in a manner that remained to be negotiated.

Kerry's proposal took hold. Hun Sen sent a letter to Annan on April 28 stating that there would be a domestic trial of Ta Mok with "assistance from foreign countries, in which foreign judges and prosecutors would be allowed to take part fully, thereby ensuring that [the] trial [will] meet international standards of due process." Hun Sen announced that there would be a draft law submitted to the Cambodia's National Assembly to make it possible for foreign judges and prosecutors to take part in the judicial proceedings.[40] Although the Clinton administration still formally supported the creation of a conventional Chapter VII tribunal for Cambodia, some Security Council members were leaning toward a mixed tribunal authorized by the council. Indeed, by May 1999 Hammarberg shifted his own position from one supporting the U.N. experts' recommendations to one supporting a mixed tribunal created under Cambodian law.[41]

I held a series of meetings at the United Nations on May 5 to try once again to advance the U.S. proposal for a tribunal, but they proved inconclusive. By the end of June several discussions in Washington had led to a shift in the U.S. position: we would advocate a mixed tribunal created under both Security Council and Cambodian government authority. The new American position, which was briefed to Hun Sen in July, proposed that a "Special Tribunal" would be authorized by the Security Council under an enabling resolution (outside Chapter VII and thus reflecting my concept

on Chapter VI explored earlier in the year) that would define the tribunal's
temporal, personal, and subject matter jurisdiction. But the court would be
established in Cambodia pursuant to a new Cambodian law that confirmed
the Security Council's mandate for the tribunal and authorized Cambodian
enforcement of arrest powers, incarceration, and penalties. The United Nations would retain unambiguous decision-making authority and control
over the appointment of individual judges, and the U.N.-appointed prosecutor was to control the indictment and prosecution of suspects. The number of international judges in the trial and appellate chambers would have
to be in the majority, and the Cambodian judges in the minority. The chief
prosecutor and the director of investigations would be international, with
the deputy positions being filled by Cambodians. In short, the Cambodian
government would have to agree to the key principle of U.N. control of the
mixed tribunal on Cambodian soil.[42]

I visited Hans Corell, the U.N. legal counsel, in New York on July 12. He
asked for our paper on a mixed tribunal and said his lawyers would compare it against their own draft concept for a mixed tribunal. On July 30, two
U.N. assistant secretary-generals, Alvaro de Soto (political affairs) and Ralph
Zacklin (legal affairs), briefed Security Council members. They introduced
the U.N. Secretariat's concept of a mixed tribunal for Cambodia that would
be established under domestic law, pursuant to Cambodia's request, and
with the assistance of the secretary-general. This proposal was a sharp departure from the Group of Experts for Cambodia Report and abandoned
Security Council engagement under Chapter VI (Washington's new position) or Chapter VII. Its main features included:

- A mixed tribunal established under Cambodian law, the provisions of which
  would govern the tribunal.
- Applicable law that draws upon the statutes of the Yugoslav and Rwanda Tri-
  bunals including the crime of genocide and other crimes against humanity.
- Temporal jurisdiction of 1975 to 1979.
- Personal jurisdiction reaching the major political and military leaders of the
  Khmer Rouge and those most responsible for the most serious violations of
  human rights.
- A Trial Chamber of first and last instance comprised of five or seven judges, with
  the majority being non-Cambodian. There would be no Appeals Chamber.
- Non-Cambodian judges would be appointed by the Secretary-General. Cam-
  bodian judges would be appointed by the Cambodian government.

- The U.N. Secretary-General would appoint the Chief Prosecutor.
- The prosecution strategy would be based, to the extent possible, on a Nuremberg-type joint trial of major Khmer Rouge political and military leaders.
- The financing of the mixed tribunal would be from voluntary contributions and the Cambodian government. Interested states would be expected to contribute personnel as seconded or "gratis" personnel.[43]

Russia and China argued that this new concept for a tribunal was not germane to Security Council business, as the council was no longer seized with a threat to international peace and security in Cambodia. Such objections, long voiced and repeated emphatically at this meeting, effectively killed any prospect for a Chapter VI or VII international criminal tribunal for Cambodia. It had been a long journey, but my efforts to keep the Security Council in the driver's seat were swept aside. Nonetheless, there was an implicit green light for the Secretariat to forge ahead on its own authority as proposed by the U.N. officials.

Upon receipt of the Secretariat's proposal, the Cambodian government responded cryptically on August 4 with a reminder of its need for international assistance in drafting the domestic law and in sending foreign judges and prosecutors to participate in the trial.[44] Later that month, Hun Sen publicly and categorically rejected the U.N. plan, which had been leaked to the press on August 17. He insisted that the majority of judges must be Cambodian and criticized the U.N. call for the arrest of twenty to thirty Khmer Rouge leaders, the plan for a Nuremberg-style trial, and the absence of any appeals chamber. Hun Sen pronounced a position that he maintained during all future negotiations. As reported at the time: "Suggesting Cambodia's sovereignty was at stake, Hun Sen called it a question of 'whether Cambodia should be cooperating with the UN or the UN should be cooperating with Cambodia.'"[45] A late August 1999 visit to Phnom Penh by Zacklin only confirmed the divergent approaches, including Cambodia's insistence on a Cambodian chief prosecutor.[46] Both sides dug in deeply.

Time to Innovate

During his visit to New York in mid-September 1999, Sok An, the chairman of Cambodia's Council of Ministers and Hun Sen's senior adviser on Khmer Rouge accountability, met with me to discuss the state of play. Sok

An had just visited with Zacklin, and it had gone poorly. Annan threatened to walk away if he did not like how the U.N.'s mixed tribunal proposal fared. Sok An cited the Kerry–Hun Sen meeting, which had left the question of Cambodian versus international dominance open, and how the idea of a mixed tribunal had evolved. He insisted that the Cambodian judges make the decisions and that the tribunal focus on a small number of Khmer Rouge leaders. Two days later, on September 19, I spoke with Tom Pickering to prepare him for his meeting with Hun Sen the next day. I proposed to him that he suggest a special chamber of an existing Cambodian court that could be tailored with sufficient international character and standards of due process.

Hun Sen met with Annan in New York on September 20 and presented him with an aide-mémoire listing three options: (1) provide a legal team and participate in a tribunal conducted in Cambodia's existing courts; (2) provide a legal team that would not participate in the tribunal; (3) withdraw completely from the proposed tribunal.[47] None of these options proved attractive to Annan, and the meeting between the two men did not go well. There was a strongly held concern among diplomats at the time that the entire accountability enterprise would sink. In an effort to salvage it, I engaged with the visiting Cambodian officials in New York and proposed that both sides (1) drop the terminology of "mixed tribunal," as it was offending Cambodian sensitivities regarding sovereignty; (2) properly understand between them such legal issues as applicable law and international standards of due process; and (3) recognize the limited character of what was being sought by the international community. I suggested that a "special chamber" be created in the Cambodian courts that would meet U.N. concerns and be empowered only to prosecute those most responsible for the atrocity crimes of the Pol Pot regime.

Hun Sen and Sok An then consulted with Undersecretary of State for Political Affairs Tom Pickering and me. Pickering pressed Hun Sen to walk back from the three options he had presented to Annan earlier and instead move toward endorsing a "special chamber" or "special session" in the Cambodian courts that would have a majority of international judges. Pickering suggested that some dual national Cambodian jurists, particularly those residing in France, might be good candidates to satisfy the numerical quotas for either the international or Cambodian judges.

Shortly after the New York meetings, I prepared a concept paper reflecting some of what Pickering and I had discussed with the Cambodian delegation. I expanded the concept with more detail: A new Cambodian law would create a two-part special chamber of the existing trial and appeals court structure, with a special trial chamber and a special appeals chamber exercising narrow jurisdiction—subject matter (atrocity crimes and some Cambodian crimes), temporal (1975–1979), territorial (Cambodia only)—and focusing only on the senior leadership of the Khmer Rouge and those most responsible for the most heinous crimes committed during the Pol Pot regime. There would be appropriate foreign participation regarding judges and prosecutors selected by the U.N. secretary-general and other due process safeguards common to international practice.

Decisions at the trial and appeals levels would require supermajority votes if the law required that the majority of the judges be Cambodian (even though the U.S. and U.N. preferences were for a majority of international judges). I introduced the supermajority vote rule because I was convinced that some formula had to be developed to ensure the participation of Cambodian judges in the court, but in a way that preserved international influence and oversight. That formula arose in my thinking as a way to manage the fusion of Cambodian and international judges in the Cambodia Tribunal. There was no magical historical reflection or precedent that brought it to mind. I simply tried to figure out how to manage a Cambodian majority on the bench (if that proved to be the endgame) and determined that requiring the vote of at least one international judge could establish the minimum threshold of international oversight in the decision-making process of the judges.

One analogy deeply influenced my thinking at the time: the requirement for unanimous jury verdicts in common-law criminal trials. In civil-law jurisdictions, the judge-rendered verdicts typically require only a majority vote. But this would be a hybrid court, located somewhere between common-law and civil-law principles. The supermajority rule logically fell within that hybrid concept. Why should not a ruling in a criminal trial require more than a bare majority of judges' votes, when American criminal trials require all twelve jurors to render "guilty" verdicts before a defendant in fact is found guilty? The supermajority vote would be a lower threshold than required in the United States and yet an appropriately higher bar to surmount than that found in civil-law jurisdictions, where one is not juggling both domestic and international judges. Furthermore, I had to find some formula that addressed the corruption concerns that everyone had about Cambodian judges, whether such corruption was fact or presumption.

There simply was no way either the United Nations or Washington would buy into an internationally supported domestic court in Cambodia ruled by the simple majority vote of possibly corrupt judges.

There also would be an international coprosecutor and international coinvestigating judge. The U.N. secretary-general would appoint a "Group of Monitors" who would monitor the Cambodian government and offer nonbinding advice to the special chambers regarding the proceedings. Assuming there would be a U.N. trust fund for Cambodian trials, the release of money from that fund would require the approval of the Group of Monitors. I shared the concept paper with Corell and with the Cambodian government through the constructive interventions of Kent Wiedemann, the new U.S. ambassador to Cambodia who had succeeded Kenneth Quinn.

At the end of September, Hun Sen reacted favorably to his meeting with Pickering and me and to the concept paper. He also believed the Cambodian government would consider the use of at least some ethnic Cambodian judges holding citizenship in other countries. In early October the United States formally conveyed the "special chamber" proposal to the Cambodians. The U.S. position reflected the requirement that a majority of judges in each chamber be of foreign nationality.

Hun Sen agreed with the overall plan, including the supermajority vote rule for each level of the special chamber. But he insisted on Cambodian judges being in the majority. The Trial Chamber would have three Cambodian judges and two foreign judges, with four votes required for a decision. The Appeals Chamber would have four Cambodian judges and three foreign judges, with five votes required for a decision. The Supreme Court chamber would have five Cambodian judges and four foreign judges, with six votes required for a decision. On October 20, I met with Corell and his legal team in New York, and after lengthy discussion Corell began to move toward the evolving concept of the special chamber. There were a host of caveats, however, and he asked me to mediate during my forthcoming visit to Cambodia so that the U.N. positions were fully understood in Phnom Penh. Corell wanted me to "push back" on the idea of a supermajority vote and to press for foreigners to hold the majority of the judgeships, which I knew would be a difficult sell given Hun Sen's views. He also wanted me to convey his demand that there be viable government assurances that Khmer Rouge leaders would be arrested or surrendered to the Cambodia Tribunal and that due process standards would be honored.

At Hun Sen's invitation, I visited Cambodia in late October 1999. First I labored for hours with his adviser, Om Yentieng, over each provision of the tribunal law. I told Om Yentieng that the suspect list should include about twenty to thirty individuals (which fit Corell's thinking) and that the prosecutor should be mandated to take fully into account the twin goals of individual accountability and national reconciliation. The decision of whom to indict must rest solely with the prosecutor, I stressed. His or her independence and integrity would be critical. We also talked at length about the supermajority rule. I pressed for the U.N. secretary-general to appoint the investigating judge of the tribunal.

Sok An invited me to visit his jackfruit farm about thirty minutes drive outside Phnom Penh on October 23. We trudged through a long walking tour in sweltering heat. The farm produced thousands of chicken eggs each day and had well-stocked fish ponds. For most of the entire day we sat in a gazebo in the middle of one of his large fish ponds to hammer out the provisions of the tribunal law. Not surprisingly, he strongly objected to the use of the term "mixed tribunal," as it suggested something less than a Cambodian court. He wanted the crime of genocide to cover politicide, namely intending to destroy all or part of a political group (which the Genocide Convention does not cover). I told him that crimes against humanity probably could serve that purpose within the court's jurisdiction. Despite Corell's demand, Sok An insisted on the majority of judges being Cambodian and embraced a supermajority vote locking in at least one international judge's affirmative vote. He also wanted coprosecutors, one Cambodian and one international. As for custody issues, he agreed that the government would reaffirm the responsibility of judicial police to arrest anyone indicted by the tribunal. I proposed using "Extraordinary" rather than "Special" in the title of the court, which Sok An found far more attractive.

There was, at times, an almost surreal character to our discussions in the gazebo. Sok An described his beloved hobby—cockfighting, which is legal in Cambodia but outlawed in the United States. He owned scores of roosters trained for fighting, and he proudly had his farmworkers arrange a cockfight for me to witness. During lunch, which was set out exquisitely with fine chinaware on our negotiating table in the gazebo, we ate large portions of fish and vegetables while Sok An and Om Yentieng spoke of the atrocities during the Pol Pot era. Om Yentieng had witnessed his relatives shot in front of him. Sok An's son had died at the age of two because they could not save him from illnesses brought on by near starvation. He had smuggled his sick son to a doctor who was trying to keep his identity unknown from the Khmer Rouge, who were killing all professionals. Sok An and his had son visited the doctor for five nights. On the sixth night, he saw the doctor being led away with his hands tied and knew that the doctor would be killed.

Sok An described how the Khmer Rouge had instilled terror in the people. They would gather people and indiscriminately kill one of them in full view of others. This traumatized them into full submission. He said people had shielded his true identity as an upper-class businessman for fear he would be killed. So they described him as a taxi driver. Sok An later became a member of parliament representing the people who had helped him during the Pol Pot years. Om Yentieng spoke of how, to this day, he could go to a nearby village of two hundred residents and, if they were to speak of the past, within fifteen minutes they would be in tears. The memory still ran that deep with everyone. I asked him how they sustained hope during those years. He laughed, as did Sok An. Om Yentieng admitted: "There was no hope. Hope had died. The task was to live each day and to survive for the next day."

Sok An had regarded himself as nothing more than slave labor during the Pol Pot years, as was everyone else. He said that the "new people" in the work fields were those driven from the cities and towns. The "old people" were those already on the land, the agrarian class. The latter were more often spared the wrath of the Khmer Rouge. Om Yentieng described "auto-genocide" or "autocide" in Cambodia. He believed the definition of genocide needed to be broadened to include going after the elite class, of which he and Sok An were both members.

We agreed at the end of the day to meet the next morning at Sok An's office in Phnom Penh to continue our talks. In the interim, I drafted a "concept" law that incorporated our various positions. This initial draft tracked the ideas in the U.S. concept paper shared with Hun Sen earlier in the month and was modeled in large part on the statutes of the Yugoslav and Rwanda tribunals. It included a *ne bis in idem* (double jeopardy) provision that was designed to address the unique situation of Ieng Sary, the foreign minister during the Pol Pot regime. The clause ensured that the Cambodia Tribunal could prosecute him for any crime different from that for which he was convicted (genocide) in 1979 in Cambodia. It also ensured that the Cambodia Tribunal could determine whether the prior trial met the international standards of justice and due process existing at the time and that, if it did not, even the genocide charge could be prosecuted again.

The draft law proposed two coprosecutors, one Cambodian and the other international, who would work jointly to investigate, prepare indictments, and prosecute cases. The supermajority voting requirement was set forth in detail for a court comprising a majority of Cambodian judges. Corell's request that I withdraw the supermajority vote proposal landed like a lead balloon on Sok An's gazebo. I knew that the only plausible way to make any progress with Sok An and Om Yentieng would be to preserve the supermajority concept in the draft. If I had left it out of the draft I shared with Sok An in his office, he would have been taken aback, and I was concerned that he would then reject other critical provisions both Corell and I wanted. After all, the supermajority vote was a U.S. proposal I had introduced a month earlier, so abandoning it would have undercut my own negotiating credibility at that stage. In any case Sok An already knew that Corell wanted only a majority vote requirement with a majority of the judges being non-Cambodians selected by the U.N. secretary-general, and I reminded Sok An of that fact.

Cambodian officials set to work on finalizing a draft law for the U.N. Secretariat's consideration, although Hun Sen took a firm line with the United Nations in public comments.[48] The Cambodian government informally floated their draft law with U.N. lawyers in late December. It contained some new and troublesome provisions (which had not appeared in the late October draft), which I discussed with U.N. officials on November 10 in New York. They remained opposed to the construct of a majority of judges being Cambodian and a supermajority vote rule, even though that formula meant that the vote of an international judge would always be required for any affirmative decision. U.N. officials wanted a majority of the judges to be international jurists and to operate under a majority vote rule. They also were concerned about funding, and how disagreements between the two coprosecutors would be handled. The draft included a requirement for only one investigating judge, although I had proposed to the Cambodians two coinvestigating judges, one being international, to reflect consistency with the two coprosecutors. The reaction of the U.N. lawyers to the draft was largely negative, and I was constantly on the phone with our diplomats in Phnom Penh and with Corell's office during the following month to resolve outstanding issues.

Trench Warfare

I flew to New York on December 22, 1999, for another meeting with Corell, who stated his main concerns. These included his continuing opposition to the supermajority vote as the compromise for permitting a majority of the judges to be Cambodian. As lawyer Robert Rosenstock at the U.S. Mission to the United Nations, Eric Schwartz of the U.S. National Security Council, and I had been pointing out to him since our last meeting, Corell's fear that a supermajority vote might not be obtained for a conviction rang a bit hollow to common-law lawyers, such as ourselves, accustomed to persuading all twelve jurors in a criminal trial for any conviction. Nevertheless, Corell and Zacklin were concerned that no convictions would be achieved and wanted a simple majority of the judges, the majority of whom they thought should be international jurists, to render the verdicts. I had to keep pointing out that this was not going to be an easy sell in Cambodia. Corell and his colleagues also worried that with funding approved by the U.N. General Assembly, there would have to be a formal treaty between the United Nations and Cambodia as well as national implementing legislation. They believed a "recipe for paralysis" was being concocted and only the clearest of agreements would avoid it. I stressed that once again they appeared to be trying to scuttle the project rather than working their way toward a solution to an admittedly difficult challenge.

Sitting in that room, I wondered: does anyone here give a damn about 1.7 million dead, or is this just a game of who can win the prize for arguing the perfect formula for justice rather than building a court that can *deliver* such justice? The easiest point to make at the table is the cautious one that cynically demands a perfect outcome. The real challenge is how to make an imperfect world work reasonably well.

The next day I spoke with our ambassador in Phnom Penh, Kent Wiedemann, who remarked: "In principle, the best case will be that international justice can be served. The only way to know is after the proceedings get under way. So let it begin. If the United Nations does not like it, it can walk away." He also told me that King Sihanouk had said that day that Ieng Sary was not amnestied for war crimes committed during the Pol Pot regime, which was further confirmation of what we knew was Ieng Sary's continued exposure to prosecution by the Cambodia Tribunal.

The deputy permanent representative at the U.S. Mission to the United Nations, James Cunningham, called U.N. undersecretary-general for political affairs Kieran Prendergast, who was unreceptive and annoyed at the way the Cambodians were moving the issue, "trying to jam us." Then Ambassador Richard Holbrooke, whose interventions on atrocity crimes had often helped me, spoke to Annan directly and told him to instruct his guys to "play ball." Annan said he had to have an indication that Phnom Penh would wait on passage of the country's new law for establishing an "extraordinary" mixed court so that the United Nations and Cambodia could resolve the remaining issues. Long discussions ensued with Sok An, who was surprised that Corell still opposed the supermajority rule and wanted to give me more time to mediate with U.N. officials. Corell sent a letter to Sok An that the Cambodian described as "not a promising message." The tone of Corell's letter, which bluntly outlined five areas of serious concerns, was not well received in Phnom Penh.

Nonetheless, further revisions to the draft law followed, and on December 29, 1999, Sok An formally submitted it to Annan.[49] Hun Sen soon agreed to the requirement of two coinvestigating judges, one a Cambodian and the other an international judge nominated by the U.N. secretary-general. His agreement came first during a meeting with Wiedemann and then in a meeting with Japanese prime minister Keizo Obuchi.[50] Hun Sen also agreed in his meeting with Wiedemann to resolve all remaining obstacles, including confirmation that Ieng Sary would not be excluded from the jurisdiction of the Cambodia Tribunal despite the domestic pardon and amnesty accorded him in 1996.[51] On January 10, 2000, Wiedemann met with Sok An and Hun Sen to discuss the evolving draft. Hun Sen told Wiedemann that there was no outstanding issue that could not be resolved with the United Nations. Both Hun Sen and Sok An invited me to come back to Cambodia to advance the process.

I submitted to the U.N. lawyers an informal document on January 12, 2000, that included a proposal on how to resolve disputes between the two coprosecutors over whether or not to indict a suspect, which was one of Corell's major concerns. The answer, I suggested, would be found in requiring a review of the dispute by an "extraordinary session" of the Trial Chamber (which eventually would be called the Pre-trial Chamber). A supermajority vote of the judges sitting in that extraordinary session would be required in order to uphold the particular coprosecutor's decision *not* to indict. In the absence of that supermajority vote, the other coprosecutor's decision to indict would stand, and the case would move forward to trial. In a further nonpaper, I floated the proposal that disagreements between the two coinvestigating judges be similarly resolved by the "Extraordinary Chamber [replacing 'session']" of the Trial Chamber. This would mean that a supermajority vote of that Extraordinary Chamber would be required to uphold a coinvestigating judge's decision not to proceed with an investigation or to recommend to the coprosecutors that sufficient evidence existed to indict a suspect. In the absence of the supermajority vote, the investigation or recommendation to indict would proceed. I introduced this concept to U.N. lawyers in late January 2000.

Further drafts, nonpapers, and analyses circulated among Cambodian, U.N., Japanese, and U.S. officials in the weeks that followed.[52] On January 18, Wiedemann told me by phone that Hun Sen had assured him that Ieng Sary would be arrested. Wiedemann suggested that the best move would be for Corell to visit Phnom Penh and talk to Hun Sen in person. Hammarberg confirmed to me that Hun Sen had told him that he had personally drafted the pardon and amnesty for Ieng Sary in 1996 and intended it to apply only to one prior conviction in 1979, so that Ieng Sary would still be subject to prosecution for the Pol Pot–era crimes. The Japanese also weighed in, supporting the supermajority voting rule.

The following month, four U.S. senators (Patrick Leahy, John Kerry, Mitch McConnell, and Edward Kennedy) urged Annan in a letter to send a negotiating team "as soon as possible" to Cambodia. A week later Annan sent Hun Sen a letter identifying several key issues to be clarified in the draft law. Annan, at this point, was essentially repeating the U.N. lawyers' line that the Cambodians had been hearing all along. He discouraged resort to coprosecutors and coinvestigating judges and instead sought an independent prosecutor, who would be non-Cambodian, and an independent investigating judge, who also would be non-Cambodian. Annan requested a majority vote rule in chambers where foreign judges would sit in the majority. He wanted Cambodian government guarantees for the arrest and surrender of indictees of the Cambodia Tribunal. He also required that there be an international agreement between the United Nations and Cambodia and that the Cambodian law be consistent with that treaty.[53] Sok An felt the tone of the letter from the United Nations was imperious, and he resented it. He basically told the United Nations to take a hike.

Annan met with Hun Sen in Bangkok on February 12 and stressed the need for "minimum international standards" while agreeing to send a U.N. negotiating team to Phnom Penh in March. Immediately prior to the U.N. team's trip to Cambodia, Washington intervened with my proposal that a separate chamber of judges be constituted to break any deadlock between the two coprosecutors.

On March 20, 2000, Sok An provided a letter to Corell regarding the pardon and amnesty of Ieng Sary in 1996. In the letter, Sok An indicated that the Cambodian government would seek no more amnesties. He also clarified that the amnesty granted to Ieng Sary applied only to his 1979 conviction in absentia for the crime of genocide.[54] But the next day Corell rejected a set of compromises in the talks, and they ground to a halt.[55] Significantly, Corell reluctantly had accepted the supermajority voting rule—a major step forward with the Cambodians—but only on the condition that the international coprosecutor would be completely independent. In a March 24 letter to Sok An, Corell stressed the need to limit the personal jurisdiction of the Cambodia Tribunal to the senior Khmer Rouge leaders and those "most responsible" for the crimes committed during the Pol Pot era (rather than the Cambodian formulation of "those who were responsible for crimes and serious violations"). He also proposed an independent third-party mechanism to settle differences between the coprosecutors or between the coinvestigating judges, which he labeled the "Article 5 bis" proposal.[56]

A few days later Corell called to ask me to travel to Cambodia to try to bridge the remaining differences, and provided me with proposed amendments to the draft law. He confirmed that he could live with the supermajority vote rule, but he was still pressing for his alternative proposal of a majority vote with most of the judges being international. "We know who came up with the idea of supermajority," he told my colleague Pierre Prosper. He stressed with me what he had already told Sok An, that the Cambodian law should reflect the U.N. agreement and not vice versa. On March 28, I met in person with Corell, who was very critical of the Cambodian responses to his latest missive. The French government weighed in with a proposal for a special chamber within the Cambodia Tribunal to resolve disagreements concerning indictments and investigations by supermajority vote. This proposal largely mirrored the American proposal of the previous month and was a constructive influence on the outcome of the talks between Sok An and Corell.

I departed for East Asia on March 30 and met with the Cambodian negotiators over the next four days in both Phnom Penh and Bangkok. We labored intensively through many formulations to bridge the remaining differences, particularly on how to resolve a dispute between the coprosecutors or between the coinvestigating judges. Once again Sok An and I hammered out details at his jackfruit farm, this time slogging through nine options for structuring a chamber to adjudicate disputes. The next day we continued negotiations at his residence in Phnom Penh. I told Sok An that Hun Sen would have to reach a compromise with Kofi Annan when they met the next month in Havana. Then I flew to Bangkok to work on more options with Om Yentieng, who was visiting there. Again, the main issue was how to manage the working relationship of the two coprosecutors and what to do when they disagreed with each other. I shuttled back to Sok An in Phnom Penh for further talks.

Corell learned from me on April 6 that Sok An viewed any dispute between the coprosecutors over approving a new indictment as requiring a supermajority vote to deny the indictment moving forward, which had been my original proposal. Corell responded that the United Nations "would hold our ground" and that he had the nongovernmental organizations and a *New York Times* editorial to back him up. Furthermore, the suspects to be indicted must be only those of Cambodian nationality, the secretary-general would be responsible for selection of the international coprosecutor, and the United Nations must reserve the right to back down if insufficient financing for the tribunal resulted from the voluntary funding requirement—three positions that were essentially sustained in the final drafting. I then spoke with Senator Kerry to help prepare him for his trip to Miami, where he would meet with Hun Sen.

The month of April 2000 proved decisive. In addition to my own visit with the Cambodian negotiators, Kerry engaged Annan, Corell, and Hun Sen directly by phone and with personal visits. He met with Hun Sen in Miami on April 11 prior to Hun Sen's meeting with Annan in Havana the next day. Thus ensued a range of meetings and discussions involving all the major players over how to set up a dispute resolution chamber for the tribunal and whether a supermajority vote would dictate the outcome or whether Corell's insistence on a majority vote with most of the judges being international would prevail.

Then, on April 20, there seemed to be a breakthrough with the United Nations. I spoke with Corell, who indicated he *might* accept a pretrial chamber in the Cambodia Tribunal with two international judges selected by the secretary-general and three Cambodian judges selected by the Cambodian government, and that none of those selections could be challenged by the other party. If disputes between coinvestigating judges or coprosecutors were not submitted to the pretrial judges for resolution, then the investigation or prosecution would proceed. If a dispute was brought to the Pretrial Chamber, then a supermajority vote would be required to end the investigation or prosecution. However, if such a vote was not achieved, or if a supermajority of the judges voted to go ahead with the work, then the investigation or prosecution would proceed unhindered. This was the formula, originally advanced by the United States months earlier, that would be agreed upon in the final text of the Cambodian tribunal law and the U.N./Cambodia treaty. Corell told me that the formula had been conveyed to Hun Sen and that Kofi Annan had approved it. Corell said that when I contacted Sok An, he must understand that the United Nations had made a major concession and they had to accept this solution. Sok An understood. I also conveyed the news to Senator Kerry.

In late April 2000, Kerry traveled to Cambodia. He knew exactly what the U.N. lawyers had already agreed to subsequent to my own visit earlier in the month.[57] They were willing to accept that the dispute resolution mechanism for the coprosecutors and coinvestigating judges occur within the Extraordinary Chambers, which would have a majority of Cambodian judges but be governed by the supermajority rule. But there remained uncertainty over how the supermajority rule would be used—either to terminate or to approve an investigation or indictment.

Kerry and Wiedemann called me on April 29 to discuss their meeting with Hun Sen. Kerry spoke of getting Hun Sen to put in writing his agreement to the U.N. proposal. He complained about Corell, whom Kerry had called earlier. Corell had asked whether the Cambodians had agreed to everything else in the negotiations, a task that had not been Kerry's to achieve. Corell had sounded agitated over the phone and voiced deep suspicions about the Cambodians. But at the airport Kerry spoke to the press and laid out the whole deal. He heaped praise on Corell and said he, Kerry, was not a negotiator. He acted on behalf of no one. He was just an interested party and had consulted with the United Nations closely. Kerry announced upon his departure from Phnom Penh the commitment of the Cambodian government to reach agreement with the United Nations by June 15, 2000.[58]

Corell told me on May 10 that Annan was deeply concerned over the behavior of the Cambodians: the way they were treating the United Nations, Annan said, was unacceptable. Annan would not send any letter to Hun Sen, despite Kerry's statement that the Cambodians were "committed" to reaching an agreement by June 15. Rather, Annan expected a letter from

Sok An to Corell. Furthermore, Corell told me, Annan had retreated on his earlier interest in the Pretrial Chamber and said the Cambodians must accept the Article 5 bis proposal, which would set up an independent review board outside the court to review disputes. Corell summed up Annan's view: "In the United Nations, we've come to the end of the road. If erratic behavior is the norm, then that is unacceptable."

I called Wiedemann immediately. He said the last thing Hun Sen wanted to do was to please Kofi Annan. Kerry spoke to Annan, who wanted the Cambodians to accept Corell's proposed language for Article 1 on personal jurisdiction. He got the impression that Annan was nervous and did not want our interference.

On May 11, Wiedemann reported that there was a meltdown of trust between the Cambodians and the United Nations. Everything was dominated by each side's pride. I spoke with Kerry, who lamented that "the United Nations is capable of really screwing this up." Kerry agreed to call Hun Sen, who was expecting a letter from the United Nations. "The U.N. is silly not to write the letter," Kerry muttered.

Sok An wanted to hear that the United Nations concurred with what had been agreed upon with Kerry in April. I called Corell, once again mediating between Phnom Penh and New York. He said Annan was upset, as he had proposed a very simple procedure and asked for a short letter confirming the Article 5 bis proposal and the temporal jurisdiction of 1975 to 1979. Corell said that if Hun Sen "goes erratic again," Annan would publicly vent his own angst. They needed a letter from Phnom Penh. Corell said Annan was not trying to pick a quarrel with Sok An, but "this is a test."

Kerry, Holbrooke, and I met with Annan in the latter's office at U.N. Headquarters to discuss how to move forward. Kerry nudged Annan toward writing a letter to Hun Sen that stressed the importance of accepting the Article 5 bis proposal and the 1975 to 1979 time frame of temporal jurisdiction. He proposed that Annan set June 15 as the deadline for closure and offer to send a negotiating team. Hun Sen then would have to respond, and if he did not, the game would be over. Kerry said this was not a time to have form triumph over substance. But for Annan, the issue was more than form; indeed it was substance. There had been eighteen months of discussions, and he cited unhelpful statements by Hun Sen in the past, including one insisting on a 1970–1999 jurisdictional period. Now it seemed it was up to the National Assembly to decide. Writing a letter and sending a negotiating team would be wrong, Annan argued. He wanted Hun Sen to reflect the

U.N. terms in the bill he would submit to Cambodia's National Assembly, and then the U.N. team could go to Phnom Penh to finalize the provisions.

Kerry responded that they were talking past each other. Stubborn vanity by Annan and Hun Sen, I thought, seemed to be swamping the exercise. The U.N. secretary-general asked Zacklin if an exchange of letters and the minutes of the Kerry talks in April would be an appropriate way to proceed. Zacklin advised against it. They agreed that Kerry would send a letter to Hun Sen describing the deal, with a copy to Annan. Annan then would go to Hun Sen and express gratitude for his confirmation of the Kerry letter. If Hun Sen did not confirm the terms of the Kerry letter, then that would be the end of it. So the minutes of the Kerry talks reflecting all the issues he and Hun Sen had discussed would be attached to an exchange of letters between Sok An and Corell. Shortly thereafter, Sok An admitted he was very pleased with the news and impressed with our meeting at the United Nations.

Progress was made, and on June 13 Corell set the dates for his team's visit to Phnom Penh in early July. During the U.N. talks with Cambodia that summer some outstanding issues were resolved, including acceptance of the supermajority voting rule, a majority of Cambodian judges sitting in the chambers, and the establishment of a Pretrial Chamber that would resolve disputes between the coprosecutors or between the coinvestigating judges. Thus Corell finally dropped his Article 5 bis proposal and accepted the Pretrial Chamber. The U.N. mission team negotiated a draft memorandum of understanding governing the cooperation between the United Nations and Cambodia for the establishment and operation of the Cambodia Tribunal. The team created a marked-up copy of Cambodia's draft tribunal law to ensure its conformity with the draft memorandum of understanding.

Complications arose over the next several months between what the U.N. lawyers sought to include in Cambodia's tribunal law and what the Cambodian government was willing to adjust, on such issues as how to handle amnesties and pardons (particularly regarding Ieng Sary) and the scope of personal jurisdiction. American diplomats, including myself, remained intensively engaged in discussions with Cambodian authorities and U.N. lawyers. The twin objectives in making these contacts were to move the draft tribunal law toward adoption in the National Assembly and to ensure its symmetry with the draft U.N./Cambodia Agreement, a version of which I had prepared in conjunction with U.N. lawyers. The latter document was intended to be signed shortly after approval of the tribunal law.

Final Passages

Ambassador Wiedemann told me on October 12, 2000, that an impasse had been reached again in Phnom Penh. He continued to get assurances that the tribunal law was on track for passage. But in fact there had been no real movement. Sok An was waffling on the timing of National Assembly action. He speculated the delay arose from new Khmer Rouge threats that they would cause trouble if the bill went forward. The Chinese also appeared determined to frustrate progress on the bill. Maybe they were waiting for results of the fast-approaching 2000 presidential elections in the United States to bury the project. If the Republicans won, then U.S. policy toward Cambodia could possibly shift away from this particular endeavor. Republicans appeared far more antithetical than the Clinton administration to Hun Sen and his government.

Kerry visited Hun Sen once more in Phnom Penh on November 20 and discussed his own hopes for early passage of a tribunal law that would be consistent with the U.N./Cambodia Agreement. Hun Sen and Kerry agreed to a timetable for passage of the law by mid-December.

Sok An and the Legislative Committee examined every article of the bill during the first week of December. Sok An's team put together a revised version, which they claimed incorporated Corell's requested changes. The amnesty provision was left intact just as Corell had requested. Regardless, no amnesty was likely to be forthcoming. The 1994 amnesty law specifically excluded senior Khmer Rouge leadership, and its six-month period had expired in December 1994; and the one-time pardon pertained only to the 1979 genocide convictions of Ieng Sary and Pol Pot. The Cambodian government moved forward legislatively with the draft tribunal law and, on January 2, 2001, it was adopted by the National Assembly.

Following approval in the Cambodian National Assembly, Corell raised several concerns about the content of the law in a letter to Sok An dated January 9.[59] I visited Phnom Penh shortly thereafter, witnessed the Cambodian Senate debate the tribunal law, met with Hun Sen and other officials, clarified discrepancies between the draft tribunal law and the draft U.N./Cambodia Agreement, and sought appropriate language to bridge the two documents. On January 15, the Cambodian Senate unanimously passed the tribunal law. The rest of 2001, following my departure from government service, was spent in sporadic exchanges between Cambodian and U.N. officials over requests for an official translation of the law and the lack of total consistency between the law and the draft U.N./Cambodia Agreement. The Cambodian Constitutional Council required that the law be amended to prohibit the death penalty by explicitly imposing a maximum sentence of life imprisonment. By midsummer 2001, the Cambodian Constitutional Council had acted following further legislation by both the National Assembly and the Senate, and the tribunal law was finalized and signed into law by King Sihanouk on August 10, 2001.

Decline and Resurrection

With my departure at the end of the Clinton administration and the new priorities of the George W. Bush administration in late January 2001, Washington's attention to the judicial process in Cambodia waned. Throughout 2001, the talks faltered badly between U.N. and Cambodian officials over substantive provisions of the required international agreement between the United Nations and Cambodia. The U.N. team was distressed that the tribunal law was adopted before its consistency with the U.N./Cambodia Agreement could be assured. A high U.N. priority had been to ensure that certain provisions intended for the latter would be reflected in the former as domestic law, and thus raise no question as to their applicability and enforceability for the Cambodia Tribunal. In their view, the cart had now been placed before the horse, and that could spell doom for the minimal threshold of international standards of due process and the necessary protection of international personnel required by the United Nations.[60]

The failure of both parties to arrive at acceptable language for the U.N./Cambodia Agreement, particularly with respect to the Ieng Sary pardon and amnesty of 1996, certain rights of the accused, privileges and immunities, protection of victims and witnesses, and the status of the U.N./Cambodia Agreement as compared to the tribunal law, led to a U.N. withdrawal from the talks in February 2002. Corell issued a statement at a U.N. press briefing on February 8 in which he stated his strongest objection to the Cambodian view, expressed in Sok An's November 23, 2001, letter to him, that the U.N./Cambodia Agreement would not prevail over the tribunal law under domestic law. Corell said: "it has been the consistent position of the United Nations that the [tribunal law] would have to conform to the contents of the agreement.... Given the Cambodian Government's position in this matter, it is not likely that the parties would resolve it through further negotiations.... the United Nations has come to the conclusion that the Extraordinary Chambers, as currently envisaged, would not guarantee the independence, impartiality and objectivity that a court established with the support of the United Nations must have.... Therefore, having carefully considered these concerns, the United Nations has concluded that the proceedings of the Extraordinary Chambers would not guarantee the international standards of justice required for the United Nations to continue to work towards their establishment and have decided, with regret, to end its participation in this process."[61] The U.N. walkout appeared at the time to slam the door on the Cambodia Tribunal before it even could be established.

However, some U.N. member states found the decision of Annan and Corell surprising, and they called for resumption of the negotiations.[62] If the United Nations had been capable of engaging vigorously in accountability mechanisms for the Balkans, Rwanda, Sierra Leone, East Timor, and Kosovo, why was Cambodia so difficult that its people were to be denied justice for atrocity crimes that, in some respects, far exceeded those experienced elsewhere? A core group of governments, including Japan, France, Australia, the United States, Canada, and the United Kingdom began to question Corell's judgment to shut down the negotiations. Alternatives were explored and, in July 2002, Hun Sen said Cambodia could amend the tribunal law in light of the long-standing U.N. concerns. Momentum gathered in the U.N. General Assembly to reengage on Cambodian accountability. Finally, in resolution 57/228 of December 18, 2002, the General Assembly welcomed the promulgation of the tribunal law and requested that Annan resume negotiations, without delay, to conclude an agreement with the Cambodian government and to base those efforts on previous negotiations on the establishment of the Cambodia Tribunal consistent with the terms of resolution 57/228.[63]

Thus, under General Assembly instruction, Annan and Corell had no choice but to resume the negotiations with Cambodia.[64] But their initial effort, with a nonpaper dated January 6, 2003, was so regressive in character that the endeavor would prove a difficult one for all concerned—the Secretariat, Cambodia, and the interested U.N. member states. The nonpaper walked back on a number of issues that had been resolved between U.N. lawyers and the Cambodians on my watch, prior to 2001.[65] Few of the newly stated U.N. positions survived in subsequent negotiations. I directly intervened, as a private citizen, to clarify what had previously been agreed upon and what was being cast aside in the U.N. nonpaper.

A further exchange of letters between Hun Sen and Annan set the stage for additional talks. A resurrected draft U.N./Cambodia Agreement was negotiated by U.N. and Cambodian officials during talks in Phnom Penh in March 2003. Annan delivered a lengthy report about the negotiated U.N./Cambodia Agreement to the General Assembly on March 31, 2003.[66] Several changes in the Cambodia Tribunal were agreed to and were reflected in the secretary-general's report: (1) the UN/Cambodia Agreement would apply as law within Cambodia; (2) there would be only one Trial Chamber and the Supreme Court Chamber, thus eliminating the Appeals Chamber; and (3) there would be improved adherence to international standards of due process.[67]

The progress achieved during the U.N.-Cambodia talks of March 2003 led to the General Assembly approving the U.N./Cambodia Agreement on May 13 and urging the secretary-general and the Cambodian government to take all the measures necessary to bring it into force and implement it. On June 6, 2003, the text was finalized, and the agreement was signed by both parties. The General Assembly also directed that the expenses of the Cambodia Tribunal be borne by voluntary contributions from the international community.[68] The funding task proved to be a long and laborious one given its voluntary character, and it resulted in significantly delaying the entry into force of the U.N./Cambodia Agreement. The Open Society Justice Initiative took the lead among nongovernmental organizations to build financial and other support for the Cambodia Tribunal, and, in my private capacity, I engaged often with U.N. officials and government missions to the United Nations to press for budgetary support. A technical assessment team led by Karsten Harrel, the coordinator for United Nations assistance to the Khmer Rouge trials, visited Cambodia in December 2003 and March 2004. Following many meetings with the group of interested states in New York, the team's findings were reflected in the "Report of the Secretary-General on Khmer Rouge Trials" in late 2004.[69]

By May 2004, work had began in earnest to amend the tribunal law in order to conform its provisions with the U.N./Cambodia Agreement. I once again dove into this endeavor during months of consultations with Cambodian officials.[70] The U.N./Cambodia Agreement finally was ratified by Cambodia's National Assembly on October 4, 2004, and officially promulgated on October 19 following amendment of the tribunal law to ensure that the two documents would be mutually consistent.[71] The tribunal law had to be amended so as to track provisions in the U.N./Cambodia Agreement of critical importance to the U.N. negotiators.

A significant bump in the road to U.N. implementation of the treaty revealed itself in the "Report of the Secretary-General on Khmer Rouge Trials" on November 29, 2004, in which Kofi Annan stated that the United Nations would withhold its notification to the Cambodian government that the legal requirements for entry into force had been complied with, as required by Article 32 of the U.N./Cambodia Agreement, until such time as "pledges for the full three years of the Extraordinary Chambers' operations as well as actual contributions for its first year of operations have been received."[72]

Legal interpretations may differ on whether the financial pledge constituted a legal requirement for entry into force, but the U.N. Secretariat used it as leverage to press for contributions from the international community despite the fact that it delayed establishment of the Cambodia Tribunal for many months. Nonetheless, the strategy worked. By March 2005, most of the international community's voluntary share of the tribunal's three-year budget was pledged. On April 28, 2005, Annan notified Hun Sen that the legal requirements for entry into force by the United Nations had been complied with, and thus the U.N./Cambodia Agreement entered into force for both parties on the next day.[73]

The Cambodian and international judges, coprosecutors, and coinvestigating judges were sworn into office in July 2006, when the coprosecutors began their preliminary investigative work in earnest. I chaired a private group of experts who reviewed a draft body of Internal Rules (essentially the rules of procedure and evidence) of the Cambodia Tribunal prepared by Gregory Stanton, a retired U.S. foreign service officer, and which was delivered to Phnom Penh that year. A group of judges under the leadership of the international coinvestigating judge, Marcel LeMonde from France, was tasked to further draft and negotiate the Internal Rules. Through several rounds of contentious sessions, often pitting the Cambodian judges against the international judges, scores of issues were negotiated and resolved. It was not until June 2007, practically one year after they started, that the judges in plenary session approved the Internal Rules. The coprosecutors refrained from filing anything with the coinvestigating judges until the Internal Rules were adopted and began to regulate the proceedings.

Top suspects Son Sen[74] and Ke Pauk[75] died before the Cambodia Tribunal became operational. So did Ta Mok, who remained in Cambodian custody for seven years before passing away in July 2006. The first defendant to stand trial was the commandant of Tuol Sleng Prison, Kaing Guek Eav (alias Duch), who was imprisoned in a military jail beginning in 1999 and entered the Cambodia Tribunal for the first day of his prosecution in February 2009. Four other defendants—Khieu Samphan, Nuon Chea, Ieng Sary, and his wife, Ieng Thirith—were imprisoned in 2007 and were scheduled for a joint trial starting in 2011. Additional suspects were under investigation by the Cambodia Tribunal by the summer of 2009 with the prospect that a total of ten individuals would stand trial, precisely the number I had proposed in early 1999.

The Cambodia Tribunal suffered from charges of corruption during its start-up phase. The allegations centered on suspected up-front payments to government coffers by the Cambodian staff essentially as gratitude for being hired for their jobs. If proven, these charges will have to be addressed so that the integrity of the court can be affirmed and strengthened. But the allegations alone should not detract from the impressive trial work in the Duch case, which has more often than not demonstrated the professionalism and thoroughness of the judicial experiment, mixing international and national law and procedure in novel ways. There has been dedicated representation of victims' rights and vigorous defenses of the accused.

The long negotiating history of the Cambodia Tribunal leaves a clear message: setbacks that burden the operation of the court must be addressed with patience and persistence and with the overriding goal of ultimately achieving credible justice for the millions of victims of the Pol Pot era. The trial of Duch demonstrated that the Cambodia Tribunal is establishing a historical record of profound importance for the people of that scarred nation and for a global audience, and justice is being rendered in its courtroom. In the end, the Cambodia Tribunal is an exercise in retribution for atrocity crimes. That is precisely what any leading perpetrator found guilty in a fair trial deserves for such an outrage against humanity.

PART IV

CHAPTER THIRTEEN

NO TURNING BACK

I closed my eyes, closed my ears. I did not want to see the real situation.... I think it was beyond cowardice.

Defendant Kaing Guek Eav speaking before the
Cambodia Tribunal on June 15, 2009

In November of 2009, I observed the closing arguments at the Cambodia Tribunal in the trial of Kaing Guek Eav, or "Duch," the warden from Tuol Sleng Prison. I had last seen the auditorium on the outskirts of Phnom Penh being renovated in anticipation of the Cambodian trials several years earlier and wondered whether my vision of accountability for the senior Khmer Rouge leaders finally would come to pass. In the joust between justice and evil, which would prevail? Total accountability for the deaths of 1.7 million Cambodians would be impossible to achieve. But I hoped that Cambodia no longer would stand silent as the nation that feared seeking justice after having experienced some of the worst atrocities of the twentieth century.

Before me, behind a bulletproof glass shield that stretched across the courtroom, sat Duch as a frail, pitiful, and deeply conflicted man. Nothing about him shocked me, but he was no symbol of banality. I noticed, as I had with other defendants before the war crimes tribunals, how Duch appeared detached from the reality of the court of law. The ceiling lights blazed, but for Duch there was nothing to see anymore. He acknowledged his responsibility, advanced rationales, blamed others, and sought refuge in the fantastical arguments of his Cambodian defense counsel. In the final moments, he boldly sought an acquittal and release as a free man. But justice had the last word when, on July 26, 2010, the trial judges rendered a verdict of guilty for the crime against humanity of persecution and for war crimes.[1] One dominant thought took hold of me that November day: there must be blindness in evil, or else the Devil resides in us all.

I wondered whether Duch had blocked out the memory of sheer terror he had instilled upon his victims. Evil's blindness must have enveloped Milosevic, Krajisnik, Krstic, and Karadzic when they stood before the Yugoslav Tribunal. I witnessed a similar distant gaze in Hutu leaders at the Rwanda Tribunal and in the eyes of rebel and militia leaders during their trials in Freetown before the Special Court for Sierra Leone. These masterminds of the atrocity crimes who tore asunder their own societies were beacons into the darkest episodes of our times.

The complete legacy of the five war crimes tribunals has yet to be fully recorded because they all remain hard at work as this story concludes. Scores of treatises have been written about their emerging jurisprudence, which will keep evolving to define the atrocity law of the tribunals, including the International Criminal Court, for the indefinite future. But so far, from 1993 through December 31, 2010, the individuals, mostly leaders, charged with atrocity crimes before the tribunals already number in the hundreds (see table 1): 266 indictees surrendered or were captured, 21 fugitives from arrest warrants remained on the run, 131 defendants were tried and convicted while 20 were acquitted, and 45 defendants remained on trial as 12 others awaited the judge's opening gavel. A total of 44 indictees either had indictments withdrawn or died while in custody prior to verdict. Thirteen cases were transferred by the Yugoslav Tribunal to Sarajevo for domestic prosecution, while the Rwanda Tribunal transferred two cases to Kigali for trial. In comparison, the Nuremberg Tribunal prosecuted 22 Nazi defendants and the Tokyo Tribunal 28 Japanese leaders during their initial, major trials following World War II.

A new era of international justice resulted from the eight bloody but pathbreaking years on my watch. The jurisprudence of atrocity law emerged to shape the judicial landscape of the twenty-first century. The war crimes tribunals brought an impressive number of the leaders of atrocity crimes to trial and to justice. The presumption of impunity for the elite among policy-makers and generals was buried. Some nations began to modernize their criminal codes to prosecute atrocity crimes in their own courts. The United States earned a reputation for leadership in building the five war crimes tribunals, even though the creation of the International Criminal

TABLE 1

A Scorecard of the War Crimes Tribunals

Outcomes (numbers of indictees)	Yugoslav Tribunal	Rwanda Tribunal	Cambodia Tribunal	Special Court for Sierra Leone	International Criminal Court
Surrendered or captured	159	82	5	12	8
At large	2	10	0	1	8
Convicted	77	45	1	8	0
Acquitted	12	3	0	0	0
On trial	18	21	0	1	5
Awaiting trial	3	2	4	0	3
Withdrawn or dead before judgment	36	4	0	3	1
Transferred to national jurisdiction	13	5	0	0	0

Sources: http://www.icty.org/sections/TheCases/KeyFigures; http://www.unictr.org/Cases/StatusofCases/tabid/204/Default.aspx; http://www.icc-cpi.int/Menus/ICC/Situations+and+Cases/Cases/; http://www.sc-sl.org/CASES/tabid/71/Default.aspx.

Note: The data are current as of December 31, 2010. Among the eight International Criminal Court suspects taken into custody by December 31, 2010, the charges against Bahar Idriss Abu Garda were not confirmed, and there had not yet been any confirmation of charges against Abdallah Banda Abakaer Nourain, Saleh Mohammed Jerbo Jamus, or Callixte Mbarushima. Four of the charged persons before the Cambodia Tribunal—Khieu Samphan, Nuon Chea, Ieng Sary, and Ieng Thirith—had charges against them confirmed in a Closing Order by the coinvestigating judges on September 16, 2010.

Court proved to be a turbulent journey through the Clinton administration that concluded with my signature on the Rome Statute.

Missteps

There were, however, serious missteps on my watch. In this book I have described the most significant among them: There could have been a more effective strategy to find an acceptable prosecutor for the Yugoslav Tribunal, and thus accelerate the work of that court, if we had better anticipated the opposition to our favored choices. The actual delivery of useful evidence to the tribunal never fully matched our promises, even though there were countless efforts to prod the intelligence community to rise to the challenge. Too many thousands of Bosnian and Croatian civilians perished before President Clinton used the power of his office to compel a peace settlement and a military intervention to stop the fighting. There were opportunities in 1993, 1994, and early 1995 that would have entailed significant diplomatic and military risks but also might have prevented the final genocide at Srebrenica. The anemic pursuit of indicted fugitives Radovan Karadzic and Ratko Mladic became a five-year debacle that scarred the Clinton administration's commitment to international justice. The death and destruction that enveloped the people of Kosovo should have been confronted sooner during the air bombardment campaign with the introduction of ground troops to confront the advancing Serbian troops and paramilitary.

Few doubt how egregiously the United States, as well as the United Nations and our European allies, failed to react to the Rwandan genocide. I have sought to relate how this abdication of responsibility came to pass in Washington and New York. But excuses do not resurrect the dead. After I labored over creating the Rwanda Tribunal, there should have been more focus on tough-minded oversight of its administration to avoid the mismanagement and corruption charges of the early years. Leading donor nations, including the United States, could have expended more time and diplomatic clout to improve the dissemination of information about the tribunal's work among the Rwandan people, which would be critical to that country's resurrection. The American role in sanctioning impunity in the Lomé Peace Agreement, which only reenergized the atrocities that plagued Sierra Leone, revealed a shortsightedness in diplomacy that history will never vindicate. Perhaps I could have done more in late 2000, if I had had better foresight, to secure financial support for the Special Court for Sierra Leone so as to jump-start its operations. The delay of the operational launch of the special court until 2002 can be attributed primarily to the reluctance of major governments to pledge sufficient voluntary funding. As a result trials were delayed, and some defendants died before judgment could be rendered.

Timing is everything, and nowhere was that more true than in Cambodia. Pol Pot needlessly died on the Thai-Cambodian border. Washington could have acted even faster than it did to track and capture him before he met his fate. The long-standing policy focus on a Security Council–created tribunal delayed more realistic concepts from emerging sooner. My best efforts to launch the court simply were not good enough, and as a result the Cambodia Tribunal did not start its real work until 2007. Perhaps there really was no other path to take in Cambodia than the one that emerged year after year, but I wonder to this day whether there could have been a more expeditious outcome.

The winding trail of missteps and missed opportunities in the making of the International Criminal Court will long color perceptions about the U.S. commitment to international justice. I struggled to avoid the train wreck at Rome only to embrace certain defeat. I would have risked my own removal from the negotiations if I had pressed too openly or too hard on the Pentagon or on Senator Jesse Helms, so I had to maneuver in ways that steadily built broader circles of support for the policies that stood any chance of adoption at Rome. But decision making in Washington proved far too cumbersome and depressingly tardy to ensure success in the international negotiations. The stubbornness of various Washington agencies and officials in seeking full immunity from prosecution for American soldiers and other citizens, regardless of whether the United States joined the International Criminal Court, seemed at times to be forged in Alice's Wonderland. As with so many other international treaties of great importance, the Rome Statute fell prey to Washington's endless conflicts between sovereignty and global responsibilities. American exceptionalism prevailed, but Rome's verdict was a Pyrrhic victory for the United States overseas. How much longer will Americans be lulled into false security by the echo chambers of Washington's nativist proponents?

Several proposals have examined how the United States can move toward a stronger cooperative relationship with the International Criminal Court.[2] Some imagine a day when the president and the Senate can consider ratification of the Rome Statute. I hope such initiatives finally nudge political and military leaders and members of Congress toward a resumption of U.S. leadership in atrocity law.

One corrective process has been spearheaded by U.S. Senator Richard Durbin of Illinois in recent years. Durbin has led the way toward enactment of three bipartisan laws that speak well of the American intent to ensure that perpetrators of atrocity crimes will find no sanctuary in the United States.[3] Any U.S. citizen or foreigner who arrives on U.S. territory and who has committed genocide or participated in the recruitment or use of child soldiers or has engaged in human trafficking anywhere in the world can now be prosecuted in federal courts. The next step, the Crimes Against Humanity Act, which Durbin introduced in July 2009, would hold criminally liable any U.S. citizen or any alien in the United States who has committed a crime against humanity anywhere in the world.[4] If that legislation becomes law, then the United States will be well on the way to modernizing its criminal code to require our own courts to embrace the same mandate as that of the International Criminal Court, namely to bring the perpetrators of atrocity crimes to justice.

No Turning Back

There is no turning back now. Following the Cold War, the world of law and politics changed fundamentally. The first decade of the twenty-first century confirmed that transformation in the dockets of the war crimes tribunals. Impunity for atrocity crimes has been shorn of any legitimacy even though some leaders doubtless will continue to escape the jaws of justice. The oldest rules of diplomacy and sovereignty will succeed at times in shielding a leader from accountability, but that will be because of the limitations of a court's jurisdiction and not because there is any justification in law for a prime minister or army general or corporate propagandist to use his or her position of authority to assault a civilian population or violate the laws of war. There remains no plausible argument for any privileged right, under law, to use the mantle of leadership or elevated power to incite, plan, or carry out atrocity crimes. No theory of exceptionalism should immunize those who plot and oversee atrocity crimes under the guise of national security, somehow expecting the rest of the world to understand unique reasons why there must be torture, ethnic cleansing, or the disappearance of the "enemy" for the love of country.

Exceptionalism resides not only within the borders of the United States. As the Rome Statute gained the ratified participation of scores of African governments, and as three of its initial situations resulted from submissions by the African nations that would themselves be investigated, one could be forgiven for assuming that the referral of the Darfur situation to the International Criminal Court by the Security Council in 2005 might have been accorded additional support by African leaders. A nonparty state, Sudan, launched massive ethnic cleansing and perhaps genocide against several of its own African tribes in the western region of Darfur, partly in response to an insurgency. Hundreds of thousands of civilians were forced from their villages and were dying.[5] What occurred was no accident; it was systematically planned and widespread throughout Darfur. The Security Council, relying on an experts' report about the atrocity crimes in Darfur,[6] adopted a resolution referring the situation of Darfur to the International Criminal Court for investigation and prosecution of political and military leaders responsible for the atrocity crimes.[7] The United States, still locked into President George W. Bush's anticourt campaign driven by the exceptionalist and alarmist rhetoric of his ambassador to the United Nations, John R. Bolton, nonetheless abstained on the resolution. The self-evident rationale for judicial action in the face of such monstrous crimes, coupled with pressure from evangelical groups in the United States, left Bush with no viable choice but to enable the court to intervene.

However, when Prosecutor Luis Moreno-Ocampo sought an arrest warrant against President Omar Hassan Ahmad al-Bashir of Sudan on atrocity crimes charges in 2008,[8] the African Union (comprising governments most of which are party to the Rome Statute) lashed out at the International Criminal Court and rallied around al-Bashir to shield him from the court's jurisdiction. African leaders accused the court of bias against their continent, as all the court's official investigations and prosecutions concerned African situations (Darfur, the Democratic Republic of the Congo, Uganda, the Central African Republic, and more recently Kenya and Libya).[9] Heads of state, such as al-Bashir, required exceptional protection from the anti-African bias of the prosecutor, or so the argument went. In that vein, the African Union, supported by Arab leaders, appealed to the Security Council to invoke the power granted by Article 16 of the Rome Statute (the Singapore compromise) to suspend the court's investigation and prosecution of al-Bashir for at least one year, and to consider according the same favor to other top Sudanese and militia officials under indictment for the Darfur crimes and who also were fugitives from international justice.[10]

To its credit, the Bush administration had finally rid itself of Bolton and decided to block the African Union's initiative by ensuring that the Security Council would not derail the prosecutor's pursuit of al-Bashir.[11] In August 2008, a Bush appointee asked me, as the lead U.S. negotiator of the Rome Statute, how the Security Council should interpret the wording of Article 16 under these circumstances. I explained, and then published an essay circulated among the council members, that the Singapore compromise resulting in Article 16 was intended to block a referral by a state party or by the prosecutor that the Security Council considered to be politically motivated or that should be suspended to permit peace efforts to proceed unhindered by judicial action for a while.[12] The Singapore compromise arose following the failure of the American position to restrict referrals only to the Security Council or states parties subject to council oversight of their referrals. Article 16 was never intended to act as a restraint on a Security Council referral, such as Darfur. Negotiators of Article 16, myself included, were not aiming to throttle back the council once it had referred a situation to the prosecutor, as that kind of referral was precisely the kind many of us wanted to see successfully carried out. Our concern centered on other kinds of referrals, namely by states parties and by the independent prosecutor.[13] Yet Article 16 does not make that distinction, and thus, using the bare words of the provision, the African Union sought to derail the Darfur indictments and reassert African sovereignty to shield its leaders from accountability.

In short order, the United States gained the support of permanent members France and the United Kingdom to ensure that there would be no Article 16 resolution to halt the court's investigation of atrocity crimes in Darfur. But the African Union initiative, which continued into 2011, demonstrated that exceptionalism appears in many guises, including an anticolonial nationalist viewpoint shared by many African leaders to the point of shielding the prosecutor's prime target—a nation's president—for prosecution of atrocity crimes against his own people.

This episode in the early history of the International Criminal Court tested the resilience of impunity, and the court prevailed. The fact that President al-Bashir remained in power in Khartoum and evaded arrest, as did his coindictees charged with masterminding the ethnic cleansing in Darfur, revealed the practical difficulties of enforcing atrocity law, particularly in a nonparty state, but did not prove that impunity had triumphed. On July 12,

2010, al-Bashir was indicted for genocide in Darfur as well.[14] Al-Bashir's fate demonstrated how the assault on impunity often will be waged, namely, by forcing an indicted fugitive into isolation and by stoking his or her fear of ultimate apprehension.[15] Though such fear can turn to violence, more often it probably will result in constraining the indictee's criminal conduct. Neither Karadzic nor Mladic were indicted by the Yugoslav Tribunal until immediately *after* the Srebrenica genocide—on July 25, 1995—for genocide and other atrocity crimes against civilians throughout Bosnia and Herzegovina. The assault on Srebrenica was added several months later to an amended indictment. But relatively few major atrocity crimes were launched under their leadership following the July 1995 indictment, and the two men were powerless to stop the signing of the Dayton Peace Agreement in December of that year.

Conduct Unbecoming of a Great Nation

It never occurred to me during the 1990s that the United States, which as a diplomat I had proudly trumpeted for its dedicated support of the war crimes tribunals and its adherence to the law of war and accountability for atrocity crimes, so quickly would embrace conduct unbecoming of a great nation in the following decade. The George W. Bush administration's descent into torture and denial of the Geneva Conventions, coupled with the invasion and military occupation of Iraq in defiance of wide swaths of international law, put U.S. officials on a collision course with atrocity law even though no war crimes tribunal had jurisdiction over the United States for its actions in Iraq or Guantanamo Bay. This book concerns events that preceded the so-called war on terror, but the exceptional phenomenon of the Bush administration years is how little impact either the court-building leadership of the United States during the 1990s or the growing jurisprudence of those tribunals had on the strategists of the Bush era. Its officials essentially ignored the tribunals' work. In their opposition to the International Criminal Court, they waged a highly organized campaign to deride and delegitimize the court and browbeat other countries into choosing between the court and Washington.

Then, in a perverted contortion of the rule of law, advocates of the Bush administration's military policies rolled out their "lawfare" charges against international organizations, European governments, and international lawyers who criticized the United States for failing to adhere to either traditional precepts of international law or the fast-evolving principles of atrocity law being articulated by the war crimes tribunals. Bush administration apologists accused their critics of using foreign conceptions of international law to thwart the projection of American military power in the face of international terrorists, rogue nuclear powers, and despots.[16]

My efforts were focused on building civilian-administered criminal tribunals to render justice against indicted war criminals, many of whom had far more blood on their hands than the international terrorists of al-Qaeda or even the Taliban of Afghanistan following 9/11. Yet, to the best of my knowledge, not a single indictee of the war crimes tribunals has been tortured or subjected to cruel, inhumane, or degrading treatment during interrogations or detentions controlled by the tribunals. Each arrested indictee has been brought to justice in a nonmilitary criminal court with the assistance of tough-minded defense counsel (or by voluntary self-representation) each step of the way and in compliance with international standards of due process. Many have pled guilty to genocide, crimes against humanity, or war crimes. War criminals have been convicted and sentenced to imprisonment for terms reflecting the gravity and culpability of their crimes.

The notion that terrorist suspects should be denied the full range of due process rights that are granted to indicted war criminals before the tribunals perversely elevates them to some higher level of evil, as if that were possible, and only makes sense if the intent is to deprive them of a fair trial. But I would challenge any advocate of such a policy to stand before the families of victims of the Rwandan and Srebrenica genocides, the mutilated masses of Sierra Leone, practically the entire population of Cambodia decades following the deaths of 1.7 million citizens there during the Pol Pot era, the victims of ethnic cleansing in Darfur, the women raped en masse in the Central African Republic, the millions whose kin have perished in the Democratic Republic of the Congo, and the slave children of the Lord's Resistance Army in Uganda, and then pronounce that the terrorists represent some greater evil requiring a novel regime of law that retreats from due process and humane treatment. The evidence regarding the value of interrogations points toward according suspects humane treatment[17] and full access to defense counsel, who see the value of their clients providing information in exchange for more lenient prosecutions and sentences. The methodology employed in the campaign against terrorism has emerged as deeply flawed and shameful for a nation otherwise committed to the rule of law.

A Nonpartisan Imperative

I always described the building of the war crimes tribunals and the challenge of preventing atrocity crimes during the 1990s as the most bipartisan and nonpartisan work in Washington. How could there be a political divide over bringing war criminals to justice, whatever might be their rank or political cause? Surely, on this issue, Americans would stand united because of their steadfast commitment to the rule of law and to the rights of all accused to due process and fair trials.

As the war crimes ambassador, I enjoyed strong support from most Republicans and Democrats on Capitol Hill. Often key Republican and Democratic lawmakers wanted more aggressive efforts on my part than the Clinton administration was prepared to endorse, such as in apprehension efforts against leading indicted fugitives. Congress stood united in withholding economic support to Serbia until there was better cooperation with the Yugoslav Tribunal, and it supported significant funding for the Yugoslav Tribunal's investigative needs in Kosovo following the bombing campaign in 1999. Lawmakers of both political parties insisted on voluntary funding for the Special Court for Sierra Leone, which initially handicapped my efforts in New York to jump start the creation of the tribunal, but ultimately Democrats and Republicans joined in providing substantial U.S. contributions to the special court.

Congressional views on the International Criminal Court danced across the political spectrum, with some in each party sympathetic to the objectives of the court and others from within both parties opposed to or deeply skeptical of it. The bipartisan vote for the American Service-Members' Protection Act of 2002, which ran counter to the Clinton administration's policies, reflected both parties' concerns about the court in the aftermath of 9/11, when preserving the freedom of the U.S. military to act boldly overseas to confront international terrorism dominated congressional attitudes.[18] In large measure, Senator Jesse Helms and House majority leader Tom Delay led a frontal assault by Republicans on any American cooperation or participation in the court, while Senators Patrick Leahy and Christopher Dodd guided other Democrats in supporting gradual American engagement with the court. Helms's extreme "dead on arrival" opposition to the court defined the Republican view over the years, while Democrats waited to see how important American equities were finally addressed. The International Criminal Court has no business being a partisan issue in American politics, but sadly it probably will be as the political parties gravitate toward more polarized positions across the spectrum of public and foreign policy.

The American view of the International Criminal Court invariably is framed by concern over how exposed U.S. service personnel, political and military leaders, and average citizens will be to the jurisdiction of the court. While that concern is commendable, and something I have addressed repeatedly above all other issues since 1993, I always have found it remarkable that very few of the critics of the court spend any time trying to understand what the court actually stands for, how it embodies so many American values, and why America's national security can be strengthened by supporting the court's pursuit of war criminals who are perpetuating atrocity crimes in other regions of the world that so often require our blood and treasure to defeat, not to mention the hundreds of millions of dollars required of the American taxpayers to rebuild the societies those war criminals have destroyed.

The policy of the United States should be the pursuit of an international justice that deters war criminals and removes them from the means of inflicting their barbarity. The world should expect from the United States the same leadership that built the Nuremberg and Tokyo tribunals, the Yugoslav, Rwanda, and Cambodia tribunals, and the Special Court for Sierra Leone. Fear of prosecution of American leaders before the International Criminal Court reveals misunderstandings about how nations manage their relationships with the court, insecurity in American adherence to the rule of law, and how the nation's military wages war, and it reveals an unwillingness to understand how law is evolving in the jurisprudence of the war crimes tribunals. Will the United States become the intimidated nation? Or will the American people join the citizens of other nations in defeating impunity for atrocity crimes with courage, determination, and perseverance?

This I know: Every day that the war crimes tribunals are open, holding trials, and rendering judgments is a good day for civilization. An even better day will be when the International Criminal Court locks the doors of its chambers, if only temporarily, for lack of atrocity crimes to prosecute. I look forward to standing in The Hague to witness that affirmation in the future of humankind.

CHAPTER FOURTEEN
POSTSCRIPT ON LAW, CRIMES, AND IMPUNITY

<small>CHAPTER FOURTEEN</small>

Bᴏɴᴅᴇᴅ ᴛᴏɢᴇᴛʜᴇʀ ɪɴ ᴀ ᴅᴇᴀᴛʜ ɢʀɪᴘ ᴅᴜʀɪɴɢ ᴛʜᴇ 1990s ᴡᴇʀᴇ ᴛᴡᴏ ᴘʜᴇ-
nomena that at first seemed beyond the will of humankind to defeat: the
surge of atrocities and the impunity that shielded political and military
leaders as they plotted Hell on earth. Neither reality disappeared on my
watch. But they were boldly confronted in ways not seen since the Nuremberg and Tokyo trials by tribunals that challenged master criminals seeking
to destroy the lives of millions in their pursuit of power and dominance.
The atrocities erupted so rapidly and so furiously that everyone fumbled
over what precisely to call the actual crimes that were consuming entire societies. The confusion infected debates at the United Nations and retarded
effective government action to stop the killings. There also lingered the
presumption that political and military leaders enjoy sovereign immunity
from prosecution by international criminal tribunals. That theory imploded
as the tribunals targeted one leader after another.

The war crimes tribunals were built to prosecute a relatively narrow range
of heinous crimes planned by political and military leaders who should fear
the rule of law. In this postscript we explore the crimes, the law, and the
challenges to impunity that have molded the tribunals.

The Lieber Code

When Francis Lieber, a wounded Prussian soldier, witnessed horrific
carnage at the Battle of Ligny and then at Waterloo in 1815, he wrote that
he "had the strange and vital discipline of lying long on the battlefield in

expectation of death."[1] The memory of that experience never faded after Lieber immigrated to the United States and eventually became a professor at Columbia University in New York City in 1856. Several years later, the American Civil War erupted. Lieber knew U.S. army general Henry Halleck, who had published his own treatise on international law. Army regulations were almost entirely devoid of guidance on the laws of war, offering only two paragraphs on the subject of prisoners of war. Lieber proposed to Halleck that rules of conduct for the Union forces needed to be drafted and that he, Lieber, would be prepared to put those rules on paper. Halleck agreed, and Lieber set out to craft a code of discipline for the Union Army.

The Code for the Government of the Armies of the United States in the Field, issued on April 24, 1863,[2] was the end product of Lieber's work. The Lieber Code, as it became known, was the first codification of rules for the conduct of land warfare "in the field," and the practical guide became the model for similar codes in many European nations, which adopted them in short order. Even parts of the Confederate Army were known to use the Lieber Code. It underpinned the international conventions forged in The Hague at the end of the nineteenth century and in Geneva during the twentieth century.

The Lieber Code set forth in 157 succinct paragraphs the rules concerning such matters as martial law, military necessity, retaliation, protection of civilians and of religion, traitors, armistice, insurrection, civil war, rebellion, and treatment of deserters, prisoners of war, and hostages. Interestingly, Lieber demonstrated an expansive view of military necessity and retaliation. He defined military necessity as "those measures which are indispensable for securing the end of the war, and which are lawful according to the modern law and usages of war."[3] Lieber conceded that "military necessity does not admit of cruelty—that is, the infliction of suffering for the sake of suffering or for revenge, nor of maiming or wounding except in fight, nor of torture to extort confessions."[4]

Most military officers today still would agree with Lieber's observation that "the more vigorously wars are pursued the better it is for humanity. Sharp wars are brief."[5] Nonetheless, the Lieber Code's principles on the rights of civilians affirmed what the great European legal theorists Francesca Victoria, Roberto Gentili, and Hugo Grotius struggled to mandate centuries earlier.[6] In his code, Lieber wrote, "as civilization has advanced during the last centuries, so has likewise steadily advanced ... the distinction between the private individual belonging to a hostile country and the hostile country itself, with its men in arms. The principle has been more and more acknowledged that the unarmed citizen is to be spared in person, property, and honor as much as the exigencies of war will admit."[7]

In his views on military necessity and retaliation, Lieber was highly pragmatic. One hundred forty years later the corpus of his principles remained largely intact. They assumed new importance and urgency as the George W. Bush administration launched its doctrine of preemptive use of military force[8] and confronted new challenges in the Iraqi and Afghanistan theaters of combat with the so-called war on terror.

Thus, fundamental precepts guiding the conduct of soldiers in warfare were first codified during the American Civil War by a Columbia University professor who sought to bring more discipline to the conduct of Union soldiers. Scorched-earth operations in Virginia and Georgia that pointed to a devastating, but less murderous, strategy to defeat the Confederate army squarely tested the Lieber Code.[9]

A European initiative, spearheaded by a Swiss businessman named Jean-Henri Dunant, paralleled Lieber's work. Dunant had witnessed the Battle of Solferino between Austrian and Franco-Italian forces in June 1859, where close to forty thousand soldiers died. Most were lost to untended wounds, a phenomenon that Dunant could not accept. He worked tirelessly to create the International Committee of the Red Cross in 1863 and to convene an international conference that resulted in the Geneva Convention of 1864, the purpose of which was to ameliorate "the conditions of the wounded on armies in the field."[10]

Thus began a century-long drafting exercise, embodied in conventions and in war manuals, tested by the horrors of two world wars, and ultimately enforced by the Nuremberg and Tokyo military tribunals following World War II. One track of law evolved as "Hague Law," which was embodied in regulations agreed to in 1899 and 1907 to regulate the conduct of warfare. It identified permissible weapons and how to occupy conquered territory. The other track of law became known as "Geneva Law," focusing on how to protect noncombatants and civilians in time of war and occupation. Starting with the Geneva Convention of 1864, subsequent Geneva conventions and protocols were finalized in 1929, 1949, and 1977. In practice, Hague Law and Geneva Law increasingly overlapped, so the distinction is rarely applied anymore.[11] Both are now encompassed under international humanitarian law and the law of war. American negotiators deeply influenced each and every one of these pathbreaking exercises, which, by the 1990s, would fuse into atrocity law in the work of the war crimes tribunals.

The charters of the Nuremberg and Tokyo international military tribunals were the templates for the drafting endeavors of the modern tribunals.[12] They confirmed the core definitions of crimes against humanity and war crimes and set the stage for the Geneva Conventions in 1949.[13] The military tribunals deprived leaders of any immunity from prosecution and soldiers of the defense of superior orders. Their charters insisted on due process protections for the defendants, regardless of how repulsive or guilty they appeared. Although they constituted a popular forum for victor's justice, the military tribunals nonetheless handed down acquittals and sentences that fell far short of life imprisonment or the death penalty.[14] In fact, only one convicted defendant at the original Nuremberg trials who escaped the death penalty was behind bars after 1966. Rudolf Hess died in Spandau Prison in Berlin in 1987 only because the Soviet Union refused to release him.

The legal precedents of the military tribunals never had the chance to bind together as a law governing the prosecution of alleged war criminals. There soon arose the Geneva Conventions of 1949 and other treaties that dominated the landscape of war crimes work for more than four decades thereafter. It was not until the middle of the 1990s that a more effective embodiment of the law, forged in the crucible of major war crimes trials, began to emerge at the Yugoslav and Rwanda tribunals.

I propose a simple way to describe the law and the particular crimes being prosecuted by the Yugoslav Tribunal, the Rwanda Tribunal, the Special Court for Sierra Leone, the Cambodia Tribunal, and the International Criminal Court. My terms have not appeared in the *Oxford English Dictionary* yet, but they are commonsensical and accurate.[15]

Atrocity Law

Oddly, international law employs two, sometimes three or more, legal disciplines to cover the same megacrimes consuming an entire patch of earth. Diplomats, jurists, lawyers, and journalists describe the law governing atrocities as international criminal law, international humanitarian law, international human rights law, or the laws and customs of war.[16] Yet none of these long-standing fields of international law suffice to describe comprehensively the legal framework of the war crimes tribunals.

Why care? Because clarity and simplicity in law promote public understanding and support for the pursuit of justice. Such a goal is not unprecedented for international lawyers. The English legal theorist Jeremy Bentham unveiled the term *international law* in 1789 in order to modernize
theories about the "law of nations" that had wandered in the intellectual
wilderness for hundreds of years.[17] Raphael Lemkin, an obscure Polish-
American lawyer canonized by Samantha Power in *A Problem from Hell*, recognized the need for a new word to describe the type of human destruction
that no other legal term adequately covered during the Holocaust.[18] His
introduction of the term *genocide* filled a gap in terminology and has had a
profound impact on law, culture, history, and politics since the late 1940s.
Our task is less ambitious, but it is essential for understanding what has
confronted the war crimes tribunals since 1993, most of which started their
work either in the middle of war or in the immediate aftermath of violent
upheavals.

For example, the field of law known as *international criminal law* ranges
far beyond atrocities and is codified in more than 270 international treaties. Fewer than half of twenty-four standard categories of international
criminal law pertain to atrocities. Other crimes include aircraft hijacking,
drug trafficking, destruction or theft of national treasures, counterfeiting,
and bribery of foreign public officials.[19] Though entirely accurate, the term
international criminal law is misleading as a precise description of the kind of
actions and law that directly concern the war crimes tribunals. Most of international criminal law fails the substantiality test, seeks out common criminals rather than criminal warlords, and diminishes the unique character of
the crimes prosecuted before the war crimes tribunals.

International humanitarian law establishes norms to protect certain categories of persons and property and prohibits attacks against them only during the course of an international armed conflict or a civil war and any military occupation that may follow.[20] But it can exclude some parts of the laws
of war whose primary purpose is not humanitarian, and it does not cover
situations where genocide or crimes against humanity are committed in the
absence of a war. Most of international humanitarian law cannot be prosecuted against an individual; rather, it seeks to regulate the conduct of nations at war or as occupiers and to establish a government's responsibility
for how armed conflicts and military occupations are waged.

International human rights law also is inadequate, as it traditionally concerns the political responsibility of states for violations against individual

victims and how to redress them domestically, and not solely the criminal responsibility of individual perpetrators.[21] Considerable tension has erupted in recent years as to the status of human rights law during time of war. One theory holds that when there is war, only one field of law—international humanitarian law—should govern the treatment of civilians and wounded soldiers. Human rights law, which protects a vast array of civil, political, and often economic and social rights during peacetime, thus would be unenforceable until hostilities cease or any subsequent military occupation ends. The alternative theory argues that a balance must be struck between the two fields of law during wartime and military occupation, such that in some instances international humanitarian law would prevail and in other cases the broader tableau of human rights law would be enforceable.[22]

Much of human rights law requires the breathing space afforded by the absence of criminal penalties and by the absence of war. Governments need to adhere to human rights law and be shamed if they do not, but holding officials criminally responsible for any infraction is not the optimal way of protecting human rights across the spectrum of each society. The war crimes tribunals impose criminal sanctions for those human rights violations that can be prosecuted as crimes on a scale and under circumstances that only skim the surface of the law that seeks to protect the full range of human rights.

The laws and customs of war pertain solely to rules governing the conduct of warfare, despite the notion that regulating warfare may appear as a contradiction of terms. Legal scholars and military specialists have been crafting "good behavior" rules on warfare for hundreds of years.[23] It is an entirely unsatisfactory body of law, however, to address the criminality of individual perpetrators, including civilian leaders, for most of the crimes prosecuted before the war crimes tribunals.

Therefore, I know of no way to accurately describe what law is truly on deck in the realm of atrocities and before the war crimes tribunals other than to label it *atrocity law*. The targeted criminal conduct causing the horror may be a mixture of several of the conventional fields of law described above. For any particular atrocity situation and the war crimes tribunal investigating it, one body of law—*atrocity law*—marries parts of each of these well-established fields of law into its rapidly growing body of jurisprudence. *Atrocity law* is applied primarily by the war crimes tribunals to these categories of conventional law that cover the crimes prosecuted by the tribunals some of the time, but no single category does so all the time. As the drawing

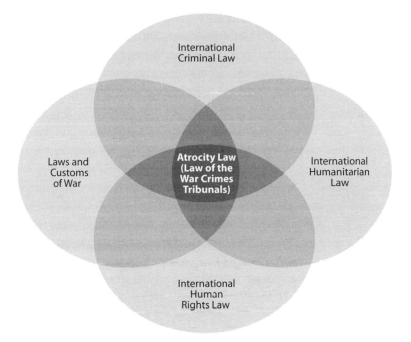

Figure 5. Venn diagram. Atrocity law is the intersection of four disciplines of international law that comprise the evolving law of the war crimes tribunals.

in figure 5 demonstrates, *atrocity law* is the core of a kaleidoscope of systems of law joined by the common thread of the war crimes tribunals.

The types of suspects prosecuted under *atrocity law* are typically political and military leaders whose numbers are limited either because of the substantiality test used by the tribunal and by the court's practical limitations or because the tribunal's statute explicitly narrows the field of likely suspects to a particular category of leaders.

Despite the distinctions among these fields of law, there has long been and there remains an unfortunate inaccuracy that appears repeatedly in United Nations Security Council and General Assembly resolutions, in legislation by the U.S. Congress and European parliaments, and in the public pronouncements of governments and civil society groups. These public institutions typically refer to the law at stake on atrocities as *international humanitarian law* and to the mass killings and devastation as *violations of international humanitarian law*. But the facts of a particular megacrime, particular genocide, or a crime against humanity often will not qualify as *international humanitarian law*, especially if the act occurs absent warfare.

The law applied by the war crimes tribunals is not only international criminal law, international humanitarian law, international human rights law, or the law of war. The law used by the tribunals draws upon all these fields but requires a unifying term: *atrocity law.*

Atrocity Crimes

> Over and again we find the lawyers' issue of "genocide or not genocide" becoming the issue, when the real issue is the need to act to protect when atrocity crimes of any kind are being committed.... I have long been attracted by the proposal of David Scheffer ... that in order to avoid these unedifying and often (as in Darfur) counterproductive semantic arguments, which constantly distract attention from the need for effective action, we should all just use the generic expression "atrocity crimes" and leave it to the prosecutors and judges in the international courts, or courts exercising international jurisdiction, to work out which one of the various well-established branches of international humanitarian law has been breached in any particular case.
>
> *Gareth Evans, president, International Crisis Group (April 30, 2006)*

In the realm of atrocities any deficiencies in the lexicon of how to describe the actual crimes can become deadly serious. Confusion about the use of words can lead to paralyzing fear, acquiescence, and judicial hairsplitting in the face of sheer evil. Was it genocide or just mass murder in Rwanda? Did civilians in Sierra Leone suffer from war crimes or crimes against humanity? Were women and girls in Darfur victims of mass rape as a war crime or as genocide? When these crimes are unleashed, should we refrain from responding effectively until we figure out the precise nature of the offense under international law?

In conventional legal terminology, no term describes how the crimes being prosecuted by the tribunals should be described *collectively.* Where is the term that easily and accurately describes the totality of these crimes so that both dialogue and action can coexist? If we can discover such a term, it might help avoid the paralysis that overtakes bureaucracies mired in definition hunting rather than effective responses to evil. The devastating consequences of this terminological charade were evident in the inaction of governments and the United Nations when confronted with atrocities in Bosnia and Herzegovina and in Rwanda in the early 1990s and remarkably once again in Darfur at the dawn of the twenty-first century.

These acts are not only genocide or crimes against humanity or war crimes. Like the law of the tribunals, these crimes need their own unifying term: *atrocity crimes*. In recent years, the term *atrocity crimes* has begun to take hold in the writing of legal scholars, reports from nongovernmental groups such as the International Crisis Group, and articles by journalists. I suspect it will take much longer for *atrocity law* to attract the support of experts schooled in the conventional terminology. Even Gareth Evans, who endorses the usage of "atrocity crimes," still finds refuge in international humanitarian law to describe the law of such crimes.

Atrocity crimes describe particularly heinous crimes suitable for criminal prosecution before international tribunals and special national courts and for which leaders of nations, armies, and rebel groups must be held responsible. The war crimes tribunals have created a new body of jurisprudence that encompasses the following definitional characteristics, *all* of which must exist, in my view, in order for the term *atrocity crimes* to be used accurately:

- The crime must be of significant magnitude, meaning its commission is widespread or systematic or part of a large-scale commission of such crimes. It must involve a relatively large number of victims (such as a fairly significant number of deaths or casualties), or impose other very severe injury upon noncombatant populations (such as massive destruction of private property), or subject a large number of combatants or prisoners of war to violations of the laws and customs of war.

- The crime can occur in time of war, or in time of peace, or in time of violent societal upheaval of some organized character, and be committed either across sovereign borders or strictly within one nation.

- The crime at least has the appearance of the crime of genocide, a war crime, a crime against humanity (including ethnic cleansing), or the crime of aggression.

- The crime must have been led in its execution by a ruling or otherwise powerful elite in society (including rebel leaders) who planned the commission of the crime and were the leading perpetrators of the crime.

- The law applicable to such crime, while it may cover the responsibility of nations, is also regarded under the long traditions of international law or the established practice of the war crimes tribunals as holding *individuals* criminally liable for the commission of the crime.

A crime that meets all five of these criteria should be called an *atrocity crime*. In short, these are high-impact crimes of severe gravity that are of an orchestrated character, shock the conscience of humankind, result in a significant number of victims or large-scale property damage, and merit an international response to hold at least the top war criminals accountable under the law. Tribunal judges speak of "significant magnitude," "high threshold," "extreme gravity," and "significant numbers." The preamble of the Rome Statute of the International Criminal Court refers to "unimaginable atrocities that deeply shock the conscience of humanity," "such grave crimes [that] threaten the peace, security and well-being of the world," and "the most serious crimes of concern to the international community as a whole."

Public officials, military officers, journalists, scholars, victims, and others should describe erupting events that may be genocide, crimes against humanity (including what is commonly known as ethnic cleansing), or serious war crimes as *atrocity crimes* and then get on with the critical task of ending them. Associating individual acts with specific crimes through painstaking study of mountains of evidence is an exercise—for crimes against humanity and war crimes as well as genocide—that can take years to accomplish, particularly in complex litigation before the war crimes tribunals. The victims—past, present, and future—cannot wait that long for actions to achieve peace and stability in war-torn and devastated societies. Nonetheless, all manner of official documents, news articles, public statements, and scholarly works struggle to find the right terminology for the range of crimes associated with atrocities, and we are left with fragmentary and very often inaccurate descriptions of the range of crimes involved.

The first characteristic of atrocity crimes above speaks to the threshold of criminal conduct for atrocity crimes. The simple reality is that until the atrocity crime reaches a high level of killing, wounding, or property destruction that decimates a society, tribunals will not prosecute the crime and the international community typically will not react to it. There may be plenty to do in prosecuting essentially common crimes for years to come before domestic courts, but such lesser crimes do not burden the war crimes tribunals. A growing number of national courts are being strengthened to prosecute atrocity crimes, however, and that is an encouraging trend for the future. But here we focus on the international and hybrid tribunals where most of the prosecutions for atrocity crimes have occurred since the early 1990s.

Why the Lexicon Matters

If *atrocity law* and *atrocity crimes* were to become the lexicon for the crimes and law of the war crimes tribunals, these terms would help in several ways. First, while the war crimes tribunals rightly act with great precision to prosecute each of the atrocity crimes, there remains the need to elevate once again the responsibility of governments not to commit these crimes. An effective way of doing that would be to invoke *atrocity crimes* to describe what a nation appears to have done rather than get mired in the technical legal requirements of genocide or any one of the scores of crimes against humanity or war crimes while thousands are being slaughtered or routed from their villages.

Second, use of the terms *atrocity law* and *atrocity crimes* would enhance the unique character and accuracy of the conventional terminology, which otherwise risks becoming blurred with overlapping applications and incomplete stories about what the war crimes tribunals actually enforce. Diplomats, scholars, and journalists need not mischaracterize either the crimes or the law to describe the reality of events leading to prosecution before the war crimes tribunals.

Third, the guiding principle of the war crimes tribunals is that the leading perpetrators of the atrocity crimes will be prosecuted, whereas the mid- and lower-level perpetrators will be brought to justice either before competent domestic courts or handled through nonjudicial or quasi-judicial mechanisms, such as a truth and reconciliation commission, determined at the national or local level. By focusing on *atrocity law* and *atrocity crimes* in describing the jurisdiction of the war crimes tribunals, one can more clearly delineate between the international and domestic mechanisms of justice that are evolving. Theoretically, of course, a tribunal should have the legal tools to prosecute a foot soldier for a grave breach of the 1949 Geneva Conventions, or a local policeman for participating in mass rape during a genocidal rampage. But the international community and national governments have drawn a different line, using scarce resources for war crimes tribunals that prosecute warlords responsible for crimes of substantial character and encouraging alternative mechanisms at the national level for the typically much larger number of mid- and low-level perpetrators. Using the terms *atrocity law* and *atrocity crimes* would better distinguish between these two levels of justice and rehabilitation.

Finally, it remains tempting to leave the crime of genocide untethered as a powerful public rationale for humanitarian intervention or some other action to protect imperiled civilians. But history teaches us of crippling struggles by governments and the United Nations to respond to genocide and of being utterly intimidated by the prospect of that particular term obligating them to do anything. We need a powerful and accurate term that can be readily understood—within minutes—as justifying an effective response by governments and by the United Nations to protect civilian populations at risk. That term is *atrocity crimes*. And we need an accurate term to describe what law the war crimes tribunals are enforcing. That term is *atrocity law*.

Once we have crossed that threshold to more accurate and accessible language for what is transpiring on the killing fields and in the tribunals, we still need to understand how the major categories of atrocity crimes—namely, genocide, crimes against humanity, and war crimes—have been interpreted by the tribunals.

Genocide

Not surprisingly, Raphael Lemkin's bold invocation of *genocide* in the aftermath of World War II has proven insufficient and at times counterproductive when dealing with the full range of atrocity crimes in the modern era. The criminal conduct that involves assaults on civilian populations and the misuse of military power in armed conflict extends far beyond the relatively narrow confines of the crime of *genocide*. Nonetheless, the term *genocide* has been commonly used, particularly in political dialogue, to describe atrocities of great diversity, magnitude, and character. We have reached the inconvenient stage where every mass killing, whether immediate or prolonged, soon evokes the language of *genocide*, which tragically slams the brake on effective responses. As an almost perverse methodology, governments and institutions seem incapable of effectively responding to atrocities because they have not yet been determined to be *genocide*. If they embrace the word *genocide*, enormous pressures build to commit many soldiers and much treasure and stay the course long enough to end the *genocide*.

The crime of *genocide* identified by Lemkin arose from his concern that the Holocaust could not be properly defined or prosecuted as simply a *crime against humanity*, a term which begged for its own proper definition.[24] The constituent parts of the crime of *genocide* are unique, for they require the *specific intent* to destroy all or part of a national, ethnic, religious, or racial group. The Nuremberg Military Tribunal relied upon *crimes against humanity* as the basis for many of its prosecutions of the Nazi regime, but it became clear that a newly defined crime would be required. Thanks in large measure to Lemkin's perseverance, the treaty he inspired, the Convention on the Prevention and Punishment of the Crime of Genocide, defined the crime of *genocide* in 1948.[25]

For example, the crime of genocide, which in a technical sense can be found with the specific intent to kill one member of a designated group, in practice requires a larger number of victims. The resulting substantiality test provides a better understanding of atrocity crimes and the magnitude required to reach such a level of criminality. The war crimes tribunals have focused on how substantial the crime—be it genocide, crimes against humanity, or war crimes—must be to qualify for prosecution.

For genocide, the calculus for "the intent to destroy in whole or in part" a national, racial, religious, or ethnic group can center on acts of genocide occurring only within a limited geographic area of an entire country with the massacres of men and boys, as at Srebrenica in 1995,[26] or the mass rape of women in order to terminally disrupt the group's viability for reproduction in the future, as in Rwanda in 1994[27] and, as argued before the International Criminal Court, in Darfur in recent years.[28] Genocide can occur as part of a civil war or an international armed conflict. It can arise as the diabolical design of a dictator to eliminate an entire group within society, such as Adolf Hitler's plan to eliminate all the Jews in Europe, which the Wannsee Conference confirmed in January 1942.[29]

Destroying part of a targeted group must entail a *substantial* part of that group, which clearly happened in Rwanda. The part destroyed must be significant enough to have an impact on the targeted group as a whole. This means exterminating a large number of the members of the group or destroying a smaller number of them in such a way as to imperil the survival of the group itself. The latter formulation took hold at Srebrenica in July 1995[30] and perhaps in Darfur beginning in 2003.[31]

Crimes against Humanity

When a crime against humanity is committed, there need be no specific intent, as in genocide, to target a designated group for destruction. Rather, the crime must be committed as a widespread or systematic attack, either in time of war or peace, against enough civilians in a sufficiently concentrated number to represent the civilian population. The widespread character of the attack is the "cumulative effect of a series of inhumane acts or the singular effect of an inhumane act of extraordinary magnitude."[32] The Rwanda Tribunal found that "a widespread attack is one that is directed against a multiplicity of victims"[33] and thus is of a "collective nature."[34]

The systematic nature of an attack on a civilian population is usually joined with a widespread action but also can exist independently as a trigger for a crime against humanity. The judges of the Yugoslav Tribunal have referred to the four horsemen of a systematic attack: First, there must exist a political objective, a plan or an ideology pursuant to which the attack is perpetrated to destroy, persecute, or weaken a community. Second, the crime must be committed on a very large scale against a group of civilians or it must be a continuous eruption of inhumane acts linked to one another. Third, the crime must involve the preparation and use of significant public or private resources, whether military or otherwise. Fourth, high-level political and/or military authorities must be implicated in defining and establishing the methodical plan.[35] The Yugoslav Tribunal found a way of calculating "widespread or systematic" by looking at "the number of victims"[36] and at "the employment of considerable financial, military or other resources and the scale or the repeated, unchanging and continuous nature of the violence committed against a particular civilian population."[37]

The range of offenses covered by crimes against humanity has continued to grow since the first prosecution of these crimes at Nuremberg. During the negotiations to establish the International Criminal Court, I joined other negotiators to further define the individual offenses that make up crimes against humanity. It is a long list: murder, extermination, enslavement, deportation or forcible transfer of population, imprisonment or other severe deprivation of physical liberty in violation of fundamental rules of international law, torture, rape or sexual slavery, enforced prostitution, forced pregnancy, enforced sterilization, or any other form of sexual violence of comparable gravity, persecutions on political, racial, and religious grounds, and other inhumane acts of a similar character intentionally causing great suffering, or serious injury to body or to mental or physical health. The Rome Statute also added enforced disappearance of persons and apartheid to the roster of crimes against humanity.[38] Each one of these crimes against humanity has deep origins in the law and in the realm of atrocities, but here we briefly mention two of particular interest to the war crimes tribunals.

Ethnic cleansing, which ravaged the Balkans and Darfur, is a popularized term grounded in persecution as a crime against humanity.[39] The Rome Statute explains that persecution is an act of discrimination that must be associated in its execution with one of the other crimes in the treaty (such as murder, deportation, attacking undefended villages), and it widens the scope for persecution "against any identifiable group or collectivity on political, racial, national, ethnic, cultural, religious, gender ... or other grounds that are universally recognized as impermissible under international law."[40] That scope is far broader than the four specific groups under the crime of genocide, at least one of which must be targeted. It leaves the field fairly wide open for the rationales guiding ethnic cleansing and the capability of the International Criminal Court, in particular, to investigate this most insidious crime against humanity.

The crime against humanity of extermination, which may look like genocide, does not require the prosecutor, as with genocide, to prove the defendant's specific intent to destroy a group of people. The Yugoslav Tribunal ruled that only those individuals responsible "for a large number of deaths, even if their part [in the crime] was remote or indirect," could be prosecuted for extermination. "Responsibility for one or a limited number of such killings is insufficient," and "extermination must be collective in nature rather than directed towards singled out individuals."[41]

War Crimes

War crimes obviously occur only during armed conflicts, although the range of such conflicts can span across internal insurgencies, all-out civil wars, cross-border raids, military operations authorized by the United Nations Security Council, international wars, military occupations, and, lately, various concoctions of the campaign against international terrorism (though with great controversy). The number and variety of war crimes is far too extensive to record here. When I was negotiating the Rome Statute, my colleagues and I spent years creating and editing lists of war crimes for both international and internal wars that we concluded were unquestionably illegal under international law. In other words, these war crimes had entered the domain of an enforceable branch of law called *customary international law* by the summer of 1998, and therefore all nations and their militaries were bound *not* to commit such offenses in time of war.[42] Although customary law prohibiting uncivilized treatment of civilians in particular is often violated by nations waging warfare, there is little dissent from the view that the offending nation indeed is breaking the law.

Specifically, soldiers must not commit "grave breaches" of the 1949 Geneva Conventions, which means they must not torture or inflict inhumane treatment on "protected persons or property" (mostly civilians and their property), or willfully deprive a prisoner of war or other protected person of the rights of fair and regular trial. Nations and their militaries, particularly the commanders and political leaders, must not intentionally direct attacks against the civilian population or nonmilitary objects or against humanitarian aid workers or U.N.-authorized peacekeeping forces, or attack an undefended town of no military value. They must not declare abolished, suspended, or inadmissible in a court of law the rights and actions of enemy nationals, or pillage a town, or employ poison or poisoned weapons. Soldiers must not perpetrate "outrages upon personal dignity," or commit rape or sexual slavery, or intentionally starve civilians as a method of warfare, or conscript or enlist children under the age of fifteen years into the national armed forces or use them to participate actively in hostilities.

The full list for what constitutes war crimes during "an armed conflict not of an international character" (a civil war) is shorter because legal regulation of strictly internal conflicts has not yet caught up with the law governing wars between nations. The discrepancy between the two types of armed conflicts (international and internal) no longer has much of any rational justification.[43] But given the number of dictatorial, authoritarian, and isolationist regimes still populating the world and resistant to any legal regulation of their internal rule, it probably will take many more years before judges label a war crime a war crime regardless of whether it occurs during an international armed conflict or a civil war. However, it does not matter whether a soldier is in uniform, fights as a guerrilla, or is labeled a "lawful" or "unlawful" enemy combatant; any of these warriors can commit a war crime and be held responsible for it. Such distinctions only become relevant in terms of the suspected perpetrators' specific rights once detained by enemy forces, and even then international law progressed long ago to accord all of them fundamental rights of humane treatment and judicial due process regardless of their alleged crimes or their identities.[44]

The substantiality test for war crimes follows the same logic as for genocide and crimes against humanity. In general, for war crimes to be prosecuted as atrocity crimes before the war crimes tribunals they must be "serious violations,"[45] meaning they have "grave consequences for the victim"[46] and perhaps even "constitute a breach of a rule protecting important values."[47] The tribunals prosecute crimes committed by high-level leaders, and such violations demonstrate, in the context of war crimes and other atrocity crimes, a substantial amount of illegal conduct.

Final Days for Impunity

> Never before in history have leaders sacrificed their customary right to sovereign immunity as have those who lead their countries into union with the International Criminal Court. This act of self-denial, essential for the elimination of impunity for those who would unleash atrocity crimes, is the biggest step forward in law since the Magna Carta.
>
> *Prince Zeid Ra'ad Zeid al-Hussein, the first president of the Assembly of States Parties of the International Criminal Court (December 6, 2007)*

The most significant advancement in confronting impunity—the avoidance of prosecution and punishment—has been a single treaty provision: Article 27 of the Rome Statute of the International Criminal Court. It reads in part: "This Statute shall apply equally to all persons without any distinction based on official capacity. In particular, official capacity as a Head of State or Government, a member of a Government or parliament, an elected representative or a government official shall in no case exempt a person from criminal responsibility under this Statute." The Nuremberg and Tokyo military tribunals and the war crimes tribunals of the 1990s had similar language denying the defense of "official capacity" in their constitutional statutes. The fact that a denial of impunity was reaffirmed in the tribunal statutes of the 1990s and is now accepted as perpetual law by the countries (numbering 118 in 2011) that have joined the permanent International Criminal Court means something quite significant has occurred on the world stage. The end of impunity, and hence the end of amnesties fortifying impunity, is in sight for political and military leaders who commit atrocity crimes.

Princes and warlords may escape justice in the turbulent world of the twenty-first century. But the die has been cast. Each and every political and military leader, and even every corporate and media tycoon who joins the killing cartels, is on notice of the actual and potential reach of atrocity law. They are learning that policy-making and military strategizing cannot proceed in a vacuum from legal consequences and that the world is watching more intently every day. Those leaders intimidated by this emerging reality are most likely to seek refuge in manipulative reinterpretations of the law, defensive exceptionalism, territorial isolation, or the sheer clout of their nation's power on a regional or global stage. But those tactics increasingly will be seen for what they seek to hide and will be judged against the Article 27 standard of accountability.

Amnesties fulfill a function in those societies that cannot possibly bring to justice the thousands, sometimes hundreds of thousands, of low-level perpetrators of the crimes who usually determine the fate of each victim. Sometimes such amnesties are heavily conditioned with confessional and punitive options, as well as with obligations to join with others in what is optimistically called "restorative justice." They should be distinguished from leadership amnesties, which remain so tempting to the peace negotiators (as we have seen occurred in Sierra Leone in 1999) but which are incompatible with international justice and cast ominous spells on the future of societies that fail to account for what has transpired in the past.

The fact that governments committed to the Rome Statute have embraced the "no impunity" pledge of Article 27 is a testament to civilization in our time. The U.S. signature of the Rome Statute on December 31, 2000, confirmed the intent of the United States to end leadership impunity. The record of the Bush administration almost buried that aspiration as high officials appeared to bask in claims of impunity. Their attitudes were almost surreal for the carpenters of the war crimes tribunals and in the wake of the rapid evolution of atrocity law since 1993. How could it be that in the opening decade of the twenty-first century there was serious debate in the United States over whether the government should and in fact did orchestrate policies of torture? Or that there were no legal consequences for senior officials involved in the commission of what legal scholars and jurists globally viewed with disgust and bewilderment as blatant disregard for the law? Yet impunity still remains an option many people are willing to use to protect their leaders from legal accountability.

The political and military leaders held responsible under the law for the commission of atrocity crimes still remain a fairly exclusive club. As data emerges recording the number of officials thrown out of power or prosecuted for atrocity crimes, we know that the disciplining of military officers has occurred frequently and that during the last century political leaders (as well as some business, judicial, and media leaders) have faced the bar of justice, either at home or before international tribunals. Until the 1990s, the numbers were not impressive enough to signal the beginning of the end of impunity. Nuremberg and Tokyo had become aberrations in an otherwise fairly wide-open field for the likes of mass murderers.

Joseph Stalin of the Soviet Union, Idi Amin of Uganda, Mengistu Haile Marium of Ethiopia, Kim Il Sung of North Korea, Suharto of Indonesia, rebel leader Jonas Savimbi of Angola, Robert Mugabe of Zimbabwe, and even Richard Nixon and Henry Kissinger of the United States—none of these men were ever prosecuted. Each one escaped the jaws of justice, partly because the legal doctrine of "head-of-state immunity" shielded them. That doctrine, one of the oldest in the arsenal of international law, insulated heads of state and high government officials from any prosecution by foreign courts for any crime they might commit while in their elevated office of power. The theory was that prime ministers and presidents and foreign and defense ministers must have the freedom to conduct public and foreign policies without the threat of criminal prosecution.[48] If there was to be responsibility, it must be attached to the government and the nation—not to the leaders. After they left office, high public officials had immunity for what they had done as part of their official duties while in power.

But head-of-state immunity flew in the face of atrocity crimes, for how could any leader be excused for planning atrocity crimes while his subordinates followed orders to commit them and then were prosecuted? The result was two contesting principles of law: official or sovereign immunity (thus, impunity) and liability for atrocity crimes. If they were to coexist, then the law truly would be an ass.

An opening wedge appeared in the Convention Against Torture[49] in the 1980s. Since torture under the convention required, by definition, the guiding hand of a public official, it would be counterintuitive to grant immunity to a head of state or senior minister who orchestrated a policy of torture. His or her participation is critical to defining the crime that must be punished. The same logic applies to atrocity crimes. How could top leaders take a pass under head-of-state immunity for crimes that largely were planned and executed with the active participation of the highest leaders of the government? Yet international law invited such impunity for leaders by immunizing them from prosecution. The Nuremberg and Tokyo tribunals shattered the shield of impunity temporarily but did not amend international law to end it altogether. The International Court of Justice made this clear as recently as 2002 in a ruling that reconfirmed the head-of-state immunity doctrine, but left a window open for the war crimes tribunals to deny it.[50]

This is because the tribunals have represented a truly international counterattack on impunity for the worst possible crimes, a mission that has gathered strength with each passing year. Top defendants, including Serbia's Slobodan Milosevic and Radovan Karadzic, Liberia's Charles Taylor, and Sudan's Omar Hassan Ahmad al-Bashir, invoked the immunity defense, but their arguments proved futile. Each tribunal's statute rejected head-of-state immunity.[51] In the negotiations creating the war crimes tribunals in the 1990s, no one seriously defended the theory that senior government officials could act with impunity. It just made no sense to preserve head-of-state immunity in the face of atrocity crimes.

The entire legal framework of the so-called "war on terror" was premised on ignoring or rejecting the jurisprudence of the war crimes tribunals and the evolution of atrocity law during the 1990s, for they presented inconvenient rules of conduct in the face of an unconventional enemy.[52] The result was a uniquely and perversely crafted American interpretation of legal prohibitions on torture and cruel, inhumane, and degrading treatment of detainees. The exercise, advanced by politically appointed Justice Department lawyers, sought to shield U.S. officials and their subordinates in the field from any liability for actions that clearly violated years of standard-setting in the tribunals and in treaties that the United States had ratified.

But this book has not been the story of how the United States marched over to the dark side of torture and other human rights violations during the George W. Bush years. The American experience simply emphasizes how fragile the assault on impunity can be when leaders are determined to reinterpret the law or hide behind a shield of impunity. Fortunately, impunity fared poorly as each of the war crimes tribunals was built and began to indict the architects of atrocity crimes.

ACKNOWLEDGMENTS

Often I am asked what inspired me to pursue a career in international law and, more particularly, international justice. The answer is fairly simple: three professors. As an undergraduate at Harvard, I read *How Nations Behave* (New York: Columbia University Press, 1968) by one of the great international law professors, Louis Henkin, who passed away in 2010. His writing exposed me to the political realities behind the theory of international law. I recall sitting in Widener Library reading that book cover to cover and becoming fascinated with the world Henkin so masterfully described.

During my sophomore year, Professor Michael Walzer was writing his seminal book, *Just and Unjust Wars* (New York: Basic Books, 1977), and we, his students, were his sounding board. Benazir Bhutto, who later became prime minister of Pakistan, sat next to me in Walzer's class and joined in the turbulent debates. (She and I also attended Oxford University together. Shortly before her assassination in December 2007, Bhutto and I bumped into each other in the Washington studios of CNN. She volunteered to me that Walzer was right, and she was wrong, about the injustices of Pakistan's conduct during the Indo-Pakistani War of 1971—an issue she had hotly contested during our class.) Walzer, who is now professor emeritus at the Institute of Advanced Study in Princeton, demonstrated to me that the search for truth and justice in the conduct of warfare is a worthy endeavor. He inspired me to enter that arena. And ultimately I did.

Finally, as a law student at Oxford University, I was tutored in several subjects, including international law, by a young Paul Craig, now a distinguished professor of English law. Our weekly sessions at Worcester College, where I lived, were the high point of my entire legal education. Craig convinced me by the sheer force of his intellect that there was no turning back from the direction Henkin and Walzer had unwittingly set for me.

The writing of this book began with some initial drafting while I was a Randolph Jennings Senior Fellow at the U.S. Institute of Peace in Washington, D.C., during 2001 and part of 2002. I am grateful for the support I received there. The writing resumed in 2007 after a phone call from Professor Eric Weitz, a renowned scholar on genocide at the University of Minnesota and editor of a series of books on human rights for Princeton University

Press. Professor Weitz asked me to write about atrocity crimes and atrocity law, terms I had already introduced in articles for the *Suffolk Transnational Law Review* and *Genocide Studies and Prevention*. I told him I had long intended to write a personal history of my years in the State Department and that perhaps we could accomplish both goals. Following discussions with Brigitta van Rheinberg, the editor in chief of Princeton University Press, I embarked upon a three-year journey backward into the 1990s and much that transpired on my watch. I owe both of these individuals my gratitude and respect for their guidance and expert editing through every stage of the drafting. I also want to thank the anonymous peers who reviewed the manuscript for PUP and Sarah Wolf, Nathan Carr, and other staffers at PUP for their unfailing assistance. I was fortunate to have Will Hively as my copy editor and to use the cartography skills of Dmitri Karetnikov.

I resumed work on the book without the benefit of any fellowship or sabbatical that would relieve me of my full-time teaching duties at Northwestern University School of Law or my directorship of the Center for International Human Rights and its many programs. I owe special thanks to other professors at the center and the law school's Bluhm Legal Clinic—particularly Sandra Babcock, Bridget Arimond, Steve Sawyer, Juliet Sorensen, and Tom Geraghty—for putting up with my secluded days of writing.

There are many colleagues, students, friends, and State Department officials who helped in one way or another through the years. I will not prioritize them, but they all should know that I value their help immensely and that this book simply would not have been finished without their assistance. These individuals include Caroline Kaeb, Nicholas Martinez, Ronit Arié, Catherine Peterson, Danielle Goldman, Virginia Richardson, Michael Saliba, Anthony Dinh, Andrew Strong, Elizabeth Jun, Grant Dawson, Gregory Townsend, Mark Harmon, Sara Sanoushivani, Victoria Enaut, Bianca Bulliner, Dan Swistel, Alice Phillips, Oceanna Holton, Andrew Furer, Samuel Anderson, Mark Leib, Steve Saudek, Doug and Joan Scheffer, Dolores Scheffer, John Shattuck, Mike Pan, Anne Pham, William Schabas, John Hagan, William Romans, Heidi Hansberry, Louis Stejskal, Xander Meise Bay, William Pace, Roger and Imelda Huhnke, Marie Huhnke, and Matthew Huhnke. Heather Scheiwe undertook the laborious task of conforming my endnotes to proper style and assisting with source citation, two tasks for which I am deeply grateful to her. I also appreciate the labors of the State Department reviewers of the manuscript, including Paul Hilburn, Natalie Kolb, and Alden Fahey. The opinions and characterizations in this book are those of the author, and do not necessarily represent official positions of the United States government.

I owe special thanks to my father, Dr. Walter Scheffer, professor emeritus at the University of Oklahoma, who read and commented on my drafts with his deep perspective on politics and long experience in the academic world. I also value the encouragement of my sisters, Paula Lader, Nicole Tousley, and Claudia Gallo.

Finally, three individuals deserve special acknowledgment. My wife, Michelle Huhnke, never wavered in her support for me and this book. She ensured that I had the time at home to work on it and encouraged me to labor onward while the children and she exited the house. I owe her more than I can write here. My daughter, Kate, and son, Henry, endured years of my tapping away in the study rather than being "out there" with them. They took it all in stride, with great maturity, and always with smiles for me. I feel less guilty knowing that my family understands why this book is so important.

David Scheffer
April 17, 2011

APPENDIX
Comparison of Modern War Crimes Tribunals

	Yugoslav Tribunal, est. 1993 (ICTY)	*Rwanda Tribunal, est. 1994 (ICTR)*
Personal jurisdiction		
Who can be investigated and prosecuted	Natural persons responsible for serious violations of international humanitarian law (atrocity law).	Natural persons responsible for serious violations of international humanitarian law (atrocity law).

Special Court for Sierra Leone, est. 2002 (SCSL)	Cambodia Tribunal, est. 2006 (ECCC)	International Criminal Court, est. 2002 (ICC)
Persons who bear the greatest responsibility for serious violations of international humanitarian law (atrocity law) and Sierra Leonean law, including those leaders who, in committing such crimes, have threatened the establishment of and implementation of the peace process in Sierra Leone. This jurisdiction extends to any person who at the time of alleged commission of the crime was a juvenile offender between 15 and 18 years of age, but special considerations must be followed in prosecuting and sentencing any such juvenile offender.	Senior leaders of Democratic Kampuchea and those who were most responsible for the crimes and serious violations of Cambodian penal law, international humanitarian law and custom (atrocity law), and international conventions recognized by Cambodia.	Natural persons.

(*continued*)

	Yugoslav Tribunal, est. 1993 (ICTY)	*Rwanda Tribunal, est. 1994 (ICTR)*
Subject-matter jurisdiction		
Atrocity crimes that can be investigated and prosecuted	Grave breaches of the Geneva Conventions of 1949, violations of the laws or customs of war, genocide, and crimes against humanity when committed in international or internal armed conflict and directed against any civilian population. Crimes against humanity include murder, extermination, enslavement, deportation, imprisonment, torture, rape, persecutions on political, racial, and religious grounds, and other inhumane acts.	Genocide, violations of Article 3 Common to the Geneva Conventions of 1949 and of Additional Protocol II of 1977, and crimes against humanity when committed as part of a widespread or systematic attack against any civilian population on national, political, ethnic, racial, or religious grounds. Crimes against humanity include murder, extermination, enslavement, deportation, imprisonment, torture, rape, persecutions on political, racial, and religious grounds, and other inhumane acts.

Special Court for Sierra Leone, est. 2002 (SCSL)	Cambodia Tribunal, est. 2006 (ECCC)	International Criminal Court, est. 2002 (ICC)
Violations of Article 3 Common to the Geneva Conventions of 1949 and of Additional Protocol II of 1977; other listed serious violations of international humanitarian law (intentionally directing attacks against the civilian population as such or against individual civilians not taking direct part in hostilities; intentionally directing attacks against personnel, installations, material, units, or vehicles involved in a humanitarian assistance or peacekeeping mission in accordance with the U.N. Charter, as long as they are entitled to the protection given to civilians or civilian objects under the international law of armed conflict; conscripting or enlisting children under the age of 15 years into armed forces or groups or using them to participate actively in hostilities); crimes under Sierra Leonean law (abuse of girls, wanton destruction of property, setting fire to dwelling or public buildings or other buildings); crimes against humanity, including murder, extermination, enslavement, deportation, imprisonment, torture, rape, sexual slavery, enforced prostitution, forced pregnancy and any other form of sexual violence, persecution on political, racial, ethnic, or religious grounds, and other inhumane acts.	Specific crimes (homicide, torture, and religious persecution) set forth in Cambodia's 1956 Penal Code; genocide as defined in the Convention on the Prevention and Punishment of the Crime of Genocide of 1948; crimes against humanity as part of a widespread or systematic attack directed against any civilian population on national, political, ethnic, racial, or religious grounds, such as murder, extermination, enslavement, deportation, imprisonment, torture, rape, persecutions on political, racial, and religious grounds, and other inhumane acts (the U.N.-Cambodia treaty describes "crimes against humanity as defined in the 1998 Rome Statute of the International Criminal Court," which is broader in scope); grave breaches of the Geneva Conventions of 1949; destruction of cultural property during armed conflict pursuant to the 1954 Hague Convention for Protection of Cultural Property in the Event of Armed Conflict; and crimes against internationally protected persons pursuant to the Vienna Convention of 1961 on Diplomatic Relations.	Limited to the most serious crimes of concern to the international community as a whole: (a) genocide; (b) crimes against humanity; (c) war crimes; (d) aggression (no earlier than 2017). The Rome Statute codifies a much more comprehensive list of war crimes for international and noninternational armed conflicts and a more comprehensive set of precisely defined crimes against humanity, with no express linkage to armed conflict, than available to the other tribunals. Among the crimes against humanity are forcible transfer of population; severe deprivation of physical liberty in violation of fundamental rules of international law; sexual slavery, enforced prostitution, forced pregnancy, enforced sterilization, or any other form of sexual violence of comparable gravity; persecution against any identifiable group or collectivity on national, ethnic, cultural, gender, or other grounds that are universally recognized as impermissible under international law; other inhumane acts of a similar character intentionally causing great suffering, or serious injury to body or to mental or physical health.

(continued)

	Yugoslav Tribunal, est. 1993 (ICTY)	*Rwanda Tribunal, est. 1994 (ICTR)*
Temporal jurisdiction		
Period of time during which the atrocity crimes must have been committed	Extends over the period beginning on January 1, 1991.	Extends over the period beginning on January 1, 1994, and ending on December 31, 1994.
Territorial jurisdiction		
National territory in which the atrocity crimes must have been committed	The territory of the former Socialist Federal Republic of Yugoslavia, including its land surface, airspace, and territorial waters. This encompasses present-day Bosnia and Herzegovina, Croatia, Serbia, Kosovo, Macedonia, and Slovenia.	The territory of Rwanda including its land surface and airspace as well as to the territory of neighboring states in respect of serious violations of international humanitarian law (atrocity crimes) committed by Rwandan citizens.

Special Court for Sierra Leone, est. 2002 (SCSL)	*Cambodia Tribunal, est. 2006 (ECCC)*	*International Criminal Court, est. 2002 (ICC)*
Extends over the period beginning November 30, 1996.	Extends over the period from April 17, 1975, to January 6, 1979.	Begins July 1, 2002, for states parties to the Rome Statute as of that date and extends to any other nation for crimes committed at least 60 days after the entry into force of the Rome Statute for that nation. However, temporal jurisdiction can be retroactive for a nonparty state if it files an Article 12(3) declaration inviting the jurisdiction of the court (and perhaps, though untested, over any nation that at the time was a nonparty state committing atrocity crimes on the territory of such nonparty state), or if the Security Council approves an enforcement resolution consistent with Article 13(c) authorizing the jurisdiction of the court over a nonparty state or a state party for crimes that occurred as early as July 1, 2002, or any other subsequent date designated by the Security Council.
The territory of Sierra Leone.	No territorial jurisdiction was codified for the ECCC. (The ECCC is a national court of Cambodia; a national court's reach is confined by the territorial boundaries of the nation unless some extraterritorial basis for jurisdiction is claimed, which has not occurred with the ECCC.)	Extends to the territory of any state party; by special agreement to the territory of any other state; or to territory of a nonparty state as stipulated in a Security Council referral pursuant to Article 13(c).

NOTES

Introduction: Ambassador to Hell

[1] Isaiah 2:17 (King James).

[2] Ian Buruma, *The Wages of Guilt: Memories of War in Germany and Japan* (New York: Farrar, Straus & Giroux, 1994), 137–176.

[3] Skylight Pictures, Inc., 2008.

[4] I am particularly indebted to Zachary D. Kaufman, whose Ph.D. research at the University of Oxford into the creation of the Rwanda Tribunal greatly assisted my own recollections of 1994. I also benefited from references to declassified cables in John Shattuck, *Freedom on Fire: Human Rights Wars & America's Response* (Cambridge, Massachusetts: Harvard University Press, 2003).

[5] President Barack Obama stated, "I do not bring with me today a definitive solution to the problems of war. What I do know is that meeting these challenges [nuclear proliferation, terrorism, ethnic or sectarian conflicts, secessionist movements, insurgences, and failed states, and the killing of more civilians than soldiers] will require the same vision, hard work, and persistence of those men and women who acted so boldly decades ago [the Marshall Plan and the United Nations]. And it will require us to think in new ways about the notions of just war and the imperatives of a just peace." "Remarks by the President at the Acceptance of the Nobel Peace Prize," December 10, 2009, Oslo City Hall, Oslo, Norway, http://www.whitehouse .gov/the-press-office/remarks-president-acceptance-nobel-peace-prize. See also David E. Sanger, "Obama Outlines a Vision of Might and Right," *New York Times*, December 11, 2009, http://www.nytimes.com/2009/12/12/world/12sanger.html?_r=1&scp=6 &sq=David%20E.%20Sanger%20and%20Nobel%20Peace%20Prize&st=cse.

Chapter One: An Echo of Nuremberg

[1] Population Loss Project 1991–1995 (Sarejevo: Research and Documentation Centre, 2007).

[2] Strobe Talbott, "America Abroad," *Time*, November 25, 1991, 56.

[3] Roy Gutman, *A Witness to Genocide* (New York: Macmillan Publishing Company, 1993).

[4] United Nations Security Council, Resolution 780, October 6, 1992. Chaired by Professor Cherif Bassiouni, the Commission of Experts delivered extensive reports and data on the atrocity crimes in the former Yugoslavia that greatly assisted the Yugoslav Tribunal in its investigations and prosecutions. See "Final Report of the Commission of Experts Established pursuant to Security Council Resolution 780 (1992)," U.N. SCOR, Annes, U.N. Doc. S/1994/674 (May 27, 1994); M. Cherif

Bassiouni and Peter Manikas, *The Law of the International Criminal Tribunal for the Former Yugoslavia* (Irvington-on-Hudson, New York: Transnational Publishers, 1996), 1–198.

[5] William Schabas, *The UN International Criminal Tribunals: The Former Yugoslavia, Rwanda and Sierra Leone* (New York: Cambridge University Press, 2006), 15; Rapporteurs (Corell—Türk—Thune), "Proposal for an International War Crimes Tribunal for the Former Yugoslavia." CSCE Moscow Human Dimension Mechanism to Bosnia—Herzegovina and Croatia, February 9, 1993.

[6] Schabas, *UN International Criminal Tribunals*, 15–16.

[7] Ibid., 18.

[8] Clifford Krauss, "U.S. Backs Away from Charge of Atrocities in Bosnia Camps," *New York Times*, August 5, 1992, A12.

[9] Elaine Sciolino, "U.S. Names Figures It Wants Charged with War Crimes," *New York Times*, December 17, 1992, A1.

[10] United Nations Security Council, Resolution 712, September 25, 1991.

[11] Elaine Sciolino, "U.S. Moves Ahead with War-Crimes Tribunal," *New York Times*, January 27, 1993, A3.

[12] Hearing before the Committee on Foreign Relations, "Nomination of Madeleine K. Albright to be United States Ambassador to the United Nations," U.S. Senate, 103rd Congress, 1st session, January 21, 1993, 24–25.

[13] Ibid., 62.

[14] Gary Jonathan Bass, *Stay the Hand of Vengeance* (Princeton: Princeton University Press, 2000), 207, 214–215; Samantha Power, *A Problem from Hell: America and the Age of Genocide* (New York: Basic Books, 2002), 484, 491; Aryeh Neier, *War Crimes: Brutality, Genocide, Terror, and the Struggle for Justice* (New York: Random House, 1998), 112.

[15] John Shattuck, *Freedom on Fire: Human Rights Wars and America's Response* (Cambridge, Massachusetts: Harvard University Press, 2003), 130.

[16] Ibid., 141–142.

[17] Allison Marston Danner, "When Courts Make Law: How the International Criminal Tribunal Recast the Laws of War," *Vanderbilt Law Review* 59 (2006): 1–65.

[18] International Tribunal for the former Yugoslavia, *Prosecutor v. Dusko Tadic*, case no. IT-94-1-T, May 7, 1997, paras. 2–3.

[19] These reports complied with United Nations Security Council, Resolution 771, August 13, 1992.

[20] United Nations Security Council, Resolution 808, February 22, 1993. See also Paul Lewis, "Immunity Sought for Bosnian Serb," *New York Times*, February 23, 1993, A8.

[21] See Julia Preston, "U.N. Security Council Establishes Yugoslav War Crimes Tribunal; Judicial Panel Is 1st Such Body since Nuremberg," *Washington Post*, February 23, 1993, A1.

[22] The governments of the United States, France, Canada, Brazil, Russia, the Netherlands, Italy, Mexico, Slovenia, and even the suspected mastermind of the entire conflict, the Federal Republic of Yugoslavia (Serbia and Montenegro), weighed in quickly with proposed language for it. A number of organizations, including the Conference on Security and Cooperation in Europe, the International Committee

of the Red Cross, the Organization of the Islamic Conference, the National Alliance of Women's Organizations, and the Lawyers Committee for Human Rights, also submitted drafts. Virginia Morris and Michael P. Scharf, *An Insider's Guide to the International Criminal Tribunal for the Former Yugoslavia: A Documentary History and Analysis* (Irvington-on-Hudson, New York: Transnational Publishers, 1994), 209–480.

[23] Ibid., 451–457.

[24] Albright conveyed the U.S. draft to the U.N. secretary-general on April 12, 1993. Ibid., 455, Articles 15–16.

[25] Telford Taylor, *Anatomy of the Nuremberg Trials* (New York: Alfred A. Knopf, 1992).

[26] Louis Henkin, *How Nations Behave* (New York: Columbia University Press, 1979).

[27] David Scheffer, "Nuremberg Trials," in *Proceedings of the First International Humanitarian Law Dialogs,* ed. David M. Crane and Elizabeth Anderson (Washington, D.C.: The American Society of International Law, 2008), 155, 171–173; Whitney R. Harris, *Tyranny on Trial* (Dallas: Southern Methodist University Press, 1999), 509–513.

[28] Alexander Zahar and Göran Sluiter, *International Criminal Law* (New York: Oxford University Press, 2008), 204–205; Schabas, *UN International Criminal Tribunals,* 187–189.

[29] *Tadic* (see note 18 above), para. 4.

[30] United Nations Security Council, "Updated Statute of the International Tribunal for the Former Yugoslavia," Resolution 827, May 19, 1993, Article 4.

[31] Ibid.

[32] "Provisional Verbatim Record of the Three Thousand Two Hundred and Seventeenth Meeting," U.N. Doc. S/PV.3217, May 25, 1993, 17.

[33] Albright registered several U.S. interpretative statements on the charge of conspiracy to commit war crimes and on the defense of superior orders that did not stand up well in the jurisprudence of the Yugoslav Tribunal.

[34] *Tadic* (see note 18 above), para. 4.

[35] See, e.g., Helena Cobban, "Think Again: International Courts," *Foreign Policy* 153 (March/April 2006): 22–24, 26, 28, and, in response, David Scheffer, "Jostling over Justice," *Foreign Policy* 154 (May/June 2006): 4.

[36] Louise Story, "Wall Street Pay," *New York Times,* updated March 3, 2011, http://topics.nytimes.com/top/reference/timestopics/subjects/e/executive_pay/index.html.

[37] David Wippman, "The Costs of International Justice," *American Journal of International Law* 100 (2006): 861.

[38] Taylor, *Anatomy of the Nuremberg Trials,* 39–40, 45.

[39] Richard J. Goldstone, *For Humanity: Reflections of a War Crimes Investigator* (New Haven: Yale University Press, 2000), 21. John Shattuck, the State Department's top human rights official, was instrumental in securing the Russian vote endorsing Goldstone. See Shattuck, *Freedom on Fire,* 143–144.

[40] "United Nations Fact Finding Mission on the Gaza Conflict," September 29, 2009, http://www2.ohchr.org/english/bodies/hrcouncil/specialsession/9/FactFindingMission.htm. See "Understanding the Goldstone Report," http://www.goldstonereport.org/, and Human Rights Watch, "US: Endorse Goldstone Report on Gaza,"

September 27, 2009, http://www.hrw.org/en/news/2009/09/27/us-endorse-gold stone-report-gaza.

[41] Goldstone, *For Humanity*, 82.

[42] See International Tribunal for the former Yugoslavia, "Judgement," *Prosecutor v. Radoslav Brdanin*, case no. IT-99-36-T, September 1, 2004, para. 629: "At first, real property certificates were issued in order to justify the confiscation. Later on certificates were no longer issued. In contrast, Bosnian Serb residents did not have their property confiscated." See also International Tribunal for the former Yugoslavia, "Judgement," *Prosecutor v. Momcilo Krajišnik*, case no. IT-00-39-T, September 27, 2006, para. 821: "Muslims were given no option but to sign over their property to the Serb municipality, receiving nothing in exchange except for written authorization to leave the area."

[43] Three types of ethnic cleansing typically were identified: radical, selective, and subtle. The radical ethnic cleansing was a three-part process: first, artillery attacks would terrorize the village; second, the Bosnian Serb Army would advance and occupy territory; third, the actual cleansing would be carried out by paramilitary forces. Selective ethnic cleansing often employed a three-part process as well, but the destruction would be limited to discrete areas. Subtle ethnic cleansing proved less discernible. Often the destruction of a mosque was the only evidence. This type of ethnic cleansing usually occurred in large urban areas already controlled by the Serbs and with comparably small Muslim populations.

[44] See Goldstone, *For Humanity*, 90: "Its complex terms were necessary to provide the assurances required by the United States. That experience made our office a lot more efficient when conducting similar discussions with other governments." The tribunal judges had paved the way a few months earlier when they amended Rule 70 of the tribunal's Rules of Procedure and Evidence to read:

> A. Notwithstanding the provisions of Rules 66 and 67, reports, memoranda, or other internal documents prepared by a party, its assistants or representatives in connection with the investigation or preparation of the case, are not subject to disclosure or notification under those Rules.
> B. If the Prosecutor is in possession of information which has been provided to him on a confidential basis and which has been used solely for the purpose of generating new evidence, that initial information and its origin shall not be disclosed by the Prosecutor without the consent of the person or entity providing the initial information.

[45] The Goldstone statement of understanding with the U.S. government remained critical to the flow of information to the tribunal. Five years later the third prosecutor, Carla Del Ponte, confirmed its continued applicability and that it remained the policy of her office relating to information provided on a confidential basis to the prosecutor.

[46] Robert M. Hayden, "Genocide Denial Laws as Secular Heresy: A Critical Analysis with Reference to Bosnia," *Slavic Review* 67 (Summer 2008): 384, at 395–396.

[47] Anthony Lewis, "Abroad at Home: Crimes against Humanity," *New York Times*, July 28, 1995, A27.

[48] The legislation became law in early 1996. See U.S. Public Law 104-106, February 10, 1996, 1342(a)(1).

[49] The outer wall's demand for cooperation with the Yugoslav Tribunal meant (1) compliance with tribunal orders (since the tribunal's orders were discrete and well-defined requests for specific actions, the tribunal should have the final word on whether authorities have complied); and (2) avoiding efforts to impede the tribunal's work. The latter element meant that no entity should enter the international community if it underwrote attacks on the tribunal, its personnel, or its witnesses, or if it harbored fugitives from the tribunal. Active cooperation would include full cooperation with the tribunal, such as by volunteering information, providing access to witnesses, and permitting the tribunal to operate freely in its territory. Serbia-Montenegro could apply for membership in the United Nations as a successor to the former Yugoslavia, but that step would require at least a nominal showing that the state was peace-loving, and Serbia had not yet met that standard.

Chapter Two: It's Genocide, Stupid

[1] I had previously traveled to Rwanda with Albright.

[2] Steven Lee Myers, "Making Sure War Crimes Aren't Forgotten," *New York Times*, September 22, 1997, A1, http://www.nytimes.com/1997/09/22/world/making-sure -war-crimes-aren t forgotten.html?scp=1&sq=Scheffer%20Rwanda&st=cse.

[3] United Nations, Security Council, "Report of the Independent Inquiry into the Actions of the United Nations during the 1994 Genocide in Rwanda," U.N. Doc. S/1999/1257 (December 16, 1999): 3.

[4] John H. Cushman Jr., "5 G.I.'s Are Killed as Somalis Down 2 U.S. Helicopters, *New York Times*, A1, October 4, 1993, http://www.nytimes.com/1993/10/04/world/5-gi-s -are-killed-as-somalis-down-2-us-helicopters.html?scp=1&sq=October%204,%20 1993%20Black%20Hawk&st=cse; Mark Bowden, *Black Hawk Down: A Story of Modern War* (Berkeley, California: Atlantic Monthly Press, 1999).

[5] "After Rwandan Terror, Albright Promises Greater Vigilance," *New York Times*, December 10, 1997, A7, http://www.nytimes.com/1997/12/10/world/after-rwandan -terror-albright-promises-greater-vigilance.html?pagewanted=1.

[6] William J. Clinton, "Remarks to Genocide Victims in Kigali, Rwanda, March 25, 1998," *Public Papers of the Presidents of the United States: William J. Clinton* (1998), book 1, 431.

[7] The prime minister of Belgium, Guy Verhofstadt, apologized in March 2000. The U.N. Security Council accepted responsibility for failing to prevent the Rwandan genocide during its session on April 15, 2000, in response to the secretary-general's report on the Rwandan genocide. A decade later, French president Nicholas Sarkozy acknowledged French mistakes during the genocide but did not apologize. He said, "What happened here is unacceptable, but what happened here compels the international community, including France, to reflect on the mistakes that stopped

it from preventing and halting this abominable crime." Philippe Alfroy, "Excuses but No Sarkozy Apology for Rwanda Genocide." AFP (Agence France-Presse), February 25, 2010. South African president Thabo Mbeki offered a "sincere apology" for South African inaction on April 7, 2004, and U.N. secretary-general Kofi Annan accepted personal and institutional blame for the United Nations on the same tenth anniversary date of the genocide.

[8] "Peace Agreement Between the Government of the Republic of Rwanda and the Rwandese Patriotic Front," August 4, 1993, http://www.incore.ulst.ac.uk/services/cds/agreements/pdf/rwan1.pdf.

[9] United Nations Security Council, International Commission of Inquiry for Burundi: Final Report, S/1996/682, June 7, 2002.

[10] Ibid., para. 496.

[11] Roméo Dallaire, *Shake Hands with the Devil* (New York: Carroll & Graf Publishers, 2003), 141–146; "Outgoing Code Cable," in *The US and the Genocide in Rwanda 1994: Evidence of Inaction*, ed. William Ferroggiaro (Washington, D.C.: National Security Archive, 2001), doc. 1, 2, http://www.gwu.edu/~nsarchiv/NSAEBB/NSAEBB53/index.html.

[12] Dallaire, *Shake Hands with the Devil*, 146–149.

[13] United Nations Security Council, Resolution 893, January 6, 1994, http://www.unhcr.org/refworld/type,RESOLUTION,RWA,3b00f1380,0.html; United Nations, "Statement by the President of the Security Council," February 17, 1994, http://daccess-dds-ny.un.org/doc/UNDOC/GEN/N94/084/07/PDF/N9408407.pdf?OpenElement.

[14] U.S. State Department Communication 086165, April 1, 1994 (declassified).

[15] United Nations Security Council, Resolution 909, April 5, 1994.

[16] Alison Des Forges, *Leave None to Tell the Story* (New York: Human Rights Watch, 1999); Dallaire, *Shake Hands with the Devil*.

[17] United Nations Security Council, "Report of the Independent Inquiry into the Actions of the United Nations during the 1994 Genocide in Rwanda," December 15, 1999, 19, http://daccess-dds-ny.un.org/doc/UNDOC/GEN/N99/395/47/IMG/N9939547.pdf?OpenElement.

[18] See Taylor Branch, *The Clinton Tapes: Wrestling History with the President* (New York: Simon & Shuster, 2009), 133: "Of the ongoing rampage against Rwanda Tutsis in central Africa, Clinton commended the U.S. ambassador there for a remarkable job evacuating American citizens. This was not a very positive mission, he added, but it was all that could be done in the midst of the chaotic tribal warfare"; Samantha Power, *"A Problem from Hell": America and the Age of Genocide* (New York: Basic Books, 2002), 351–353.

[19] United Nations, "Statement by the President of the Security Council," April 7, 1994, http://daccess-dds-ny.un.org/doc/UNDOC/GEN/N94/170/30/PDF/N9417030.pdf?OpenElement.

[20] U.S. Mission to the United Nations cable 1473, April 9, 1994 (declassified). The four-stage plan for authorizing the evacuation of both foreign nationals and UNAMIR in the absence of a cease-fire within a few days was described as follows: "First, the

member states inform the SYG that they are very concerned about the safety of their foreign nationals, that they will take whatever actions are necessary to protect their nationals, and that they seek UNAMIR's assistance in this evacuation effort. Annan added that it was very important that the member states, and not the SYG, initiate the request; otherwise, it might appear that the SYG was abandoning Rwanda. Second, the SYG would use this letter from the member states to approach the Security Council, and recommend that UNAMIR also be evacuated because of the threat to the lives of the peacekeepers and because the original conditions for having the mandate no longer exist. Annan made it clear that UNAMIR should not be left behind, and that those states who are involved in the evacuation effort also make plans to evacuate the 2500 UNAMIR troops. Third, the Security Council convenes to discuss the evacuation of foreign nationals and UNAMIR by member states. Finally, the Security Council authorizes the aforementioned requests, either by a responding letter to the SYG, a presidential statement, or, possibly, a resolution."

[21] U.S. Mission to the United Nations, Geneva, Cable 03437, April 12, 1994 (unclassified).

[22] Des Forges, *Leave None*, 628.

[23] United Nations Secretary-General, "Letter Dated 13 April 1994 to the President of the Security Council Concerning Developments which may Necessitate the Withdrawal of UNAMIR," in *The United Nations and Rwanda, 1993–1996* (New York: U.N. Department of Public Information, 1996), 259. See also U.S. Mission to the United Nations, Cable 1553, April 14, 1994 (declassified): "The sentiment prevailed that the UN could not take either of the two extreme options—it could not take on Chapter VII peace enforcement duties, and it could not abandon Rwanda by total withdrawal. Almost all Council members criticized the Secretariat for not presenting an options paper with a few options for proceeding within the middle ground between those two extremes.... Several members of the Council, including Ambassador Albright, criticized the SYG's letter of 4/13 for laying the blame on the Belgians, rather than on the Rwandans, for the inability of UNAMIR to fulfill its mandate." The council instructed the Secretariat to prepare more detailed options, eventually submitted on April 21 in a report to the Security Council.

[24] U.S. Mission to the United Nations, Cable 001533, April 13, 1994 (declassified). The U.S. Mission reported: "The Africans have argued that the UN will lose all credibility as a peacekeeper if they run away when they are needed the most. The Chinese support this African position. The Africans claim, with no thought of the conditions on which UNAMIR was established, that a withdrawal would be perceived as a betrayal by the UN. They contrast pulling out UN forces from Rwanda, where 20,000 have died in 4 days, to reinforcing UN forces in Bosnia, where less than one hundred have died in Gorazde over a similar period." The U.S. Mission recommended: "It is especially important for the Africans to keep 'UNAMIR' alive, even if only on paper. A skeletal staff of perhaps a dozen (SRSG plus support staff) might be enough to pursue political reconciliation. If it becomes too dangerous for the skeletal staff to remain in Kigali, perhaps they might be temporarily relocated to some nearby location."

[25] Madeleine Albright with William Woodward, *Madam Secretary* (New York: Miramax Books, 2003), 150.

[26] U.S. State Department Communication 098085, April 14, 1994 (declassified).

[27] See the publicly released version of PDD-25 at David Scheffer, introduction to "United States: Administration Policy on Reforming Multilateral Peace Operations," *International Legal Materials* 33 (1994): 795.

[28] U.S. State Department, "Talking Points on UNAMIR Withdrawal," in *The US and the Genocide in Rwanda 1994*, ed. Ferroggiaro, doc. 4, http://www.gwu.edu/-nsarchiv/NSAEBB/NSAEBB53/index.html.

[29] U.S. Mission to the United Nations, Cable 1588, April 15, 1994 (declassified).

[30] See Albright with Woodward, *Madam Secretary*, 150–151: "Belgium, shocked by the murder of its peacekeepers, announced its intention to withdraw, thereby depriving Dallaire of his best-equipped troops. Authorities in Brussels had appealed to the United States, as a NATO ally, to support the termination of the entire U.N. mission.... The Belgians wanted a full UN pullout to cover their own withdrawal."

[31] See, for example, Paul Quiles, Pierre Brana, and Bernard Cazeneuve, "Mission D'information Sur Le Rwanda," December 15, 1998, http://www.assemblee-nationale.fr/dossiers/rwanda/r1271.asp, the report that investigated France and the Rwandan genocide; the Belgian investigation into the Rwandan genocide was released in 1997 in Belgian Senate session of 1997–1998, "Report, Parliamentary Commission of Inquiry Regarding the Events in Rwanda," December 6, 1997, http://www.senate.be/english/rwanda.html; the Rwandan government's investigation accusing the French of complicity in the genocide is found in the Mucyo Commission, *Report of an Independent Commission to Establish the Role of France in the 1994 Rwandan Genocide*, November 17, 2007, http://www.assatashakur.org/forum/breaking-down-understanding-our-enemies/35471-mucyo-report-role-france-1995-rwandan-genocide.html; several books lend credence to France's complicity and include Linda Melvern, *Conspiracy to Murder: The Rwandan Genocide* (London: Verso, 2006); Andrew Wallis, *Silent Accomplice: The Untold Story of France's Role in the Rwandan Genocide* (London: I. B. Taurus & Co., 2006); Daniela Kroslak, *The Role of France in the Rwandan Genocide* (London: Hurst & Co., 2007); an additional report by the Organization of African Unity discusses the role of France and Belgium with respect to the Rwandan genocide, Organization for African Unity/African Union, *Rwanda: The Preventable Genocide*, The International Panel of Eminent Personalities to Investigate the 1994 Genocide in Rwanda and the Surrounding Events, July 7, 2000, 133–144, http://www.africa-union.org/Official_documents/reports/Report_rowanda_genocide.pdf.

[32] Albright with Woodward, *Madam Secretary*, 150.

[33] United Nations Security Council, "Report of the Independent Inquiry into the Actions of the United Nations during the 1994 Genocide in Rwanda," U.N. Doc. S/1999/1257 (December 16, 1999): 20, http://www.un.org/ga/search/view_doc.asp?symbol=S/1999/1257.

[34] United Nations Security Council, Resolution 912, April 21, 1994.

[35] "Groups Protest UN Pullout from Rwanda," *Chicago Tribune*, April 23, 1994, 3.

[36] The publicly released summary of PDD-25 described the factors as follows:

> The Administration will consider the factors below when deciding whether to vote for a proposed new UN peace operation (Chapter VI or Chapter VII) or to support a regionally-sponsored peace operation:
>
> - UN involvement advances U.S. interests, and there is an international community of interest for dealing with the problem on a multilateral basis.
> - There is a threat to or breach of international peace and security, often of a regional character, defined as one or a combination of the following:
>   - International aggression, or;
>   - Urgent humanitarian disaster coupled with violence;
>   - Sudden interruption of established democracy or gross violation of human rights coupled with violence, or threat of violence.
> - There are clear objectives and an understanding of where the mission fits on the spectrum between traditional peacekeeping and peace enforcement.
> - For traditional (Chapter VI) peacekeeping operations, a ceasefire should be in place and the consent of the parties obtained before the force is deployed.
> - For peace enforcement (Chapter VII) operations, the threat to international peace and security is considered significant.
> - The means to accomplish the mission are available, including the forces, financing and a mandate appropriate to the mission.
> - The political, economic and humanitarian consequences of inaction by the international community have been weighed and are considered unacceptable.
> - The operation's anticipated duration is tied to clear objectives and realistic criteria for ending the operation.
>
> These factors are an aid in decision-making; they do not by themselves constitute a prescriptive device. Decisions have been and will be based on the cumulative weight of the factors, with no single factor necessarily being an absolute determinant....
>
> The Administration will continue to apply even stricter standards when it assesses whether to recommend to the President that U.S. personnel participate in a given peace operation. In addition to the factors listed above, we will consider the following factors:
>
> - Participation advances U.S. interests and both the unique and general risks to American personnel have been weighed and are considered acceptable.
> - Personnel, funds and other resources are available.
> - U.S. participation is necessary for operation's success.
> - The role of U.S. forces is tied to clear objectives and an endpoint for U.S. participation can be identified.
> - Domestic and Congressional support exists or can be marshaled.
> - Command and control arrangements are acceptable.

Additional, even more rigorous factors will be applied when there is the possibility of significant U.S. participation in Chapter VII operations that are likely to involve combat:

- There exists a determination to commit sufficient forces to achieve clearly defined objectives.
- There exists a plan to achieve those objectives decisively.
- There exists a commitment to reassess and adjust, as necessary, the size, composition, and disposition of our forces to achieve our objectives.

Any recommendation to the President will be based on the cumulative weight of the above factors, with no single factor necessarily being an absolute determinant.

David J. Scheffer, "United States: Administration Policy on Reforming Multilateral Peace Operations," *International Legal Materials* 33 (1994): 795, 802–804.

[37] Senator Carl Levin, a Democrat from Michigan, wisely pushed hard for inclusion of this factor in PDD-25.

[38] A revised copy of her testimony from this January 20, 1995, closed session on Capitol Hill appears in Madeleine K. Albright, U.S. Permanent Representative to the United Nations, "Testimony to the Subcommittee on International Operations and Human Rights," U.S. House of Representatives, Washington, D.C., February 8, 1995.

[39] Christine Shelly, "United States State Department Press Briefing," April 28, 1994, http://dosfan.lib.uic.edu/ERC/briefing/daily_briefings/1994/9404/940428db.html.

[40] U.S. Mission to the United Nations, Cable 1817, April 30, 1994 (declassified). The full membership of the Security Council in 1994 consisted of the five permanent members—the United States, France, United Kingdom, China, and Russia—and the ten nonpermanent members, being Nigeria, Rwanda, Djibouti, Oman, Pakistan, Argentina, Brazil, New Zealand, Spain, and the Czech Republic.

[41] For example, "Statement by the President: The Deaths of the Presidents of Rwanda and Burundi," Office of the White House Press Secretary, April 7, 1994, http://www.gwu.edu/~nsarchiv/NSAEBB/NSAEBB119/Rw6.pdf.

[42] "Statement by the Press Secretary," Office of the White House Press Secretary, April 22, 1994, http://www.gwu.edu/~nsarchiv/NSAEBB/NSAEBB53/rw042294.pdf.

[43] A critical weapon of the Rwandan genocide was the use of hate radio to stir up anti-Tutsi anger among the Hutu-majority Rwandan population. We were far too conservative in concluding, as our legal advisers did many weeks after the genocide began, that there were insurmountable legal impediments to "taking out" hate-radio transmissions. Hate radio was inciting the population to commit the crime of genocide in Rwanda, and we should have found a way despite legal risks to silence it. See a general discussion of these impediments in Jamie Frederic Metzl, "Rwandan Genocide and the International Law of Radio Jamming," *American Journal of International Law* 91 (October 1997): 628. See also Power, *"A Problem from Hell,"* 371–372.

[44] National Intelligence Daily (April 26, 1994), 8 (declassified), in *The US and the Genocide in Rwanda 1994* ed. Ferroggiaro, http://www.gwu.edu/~nsarchiv/NSAEBB/NSAEBB117/Rw35.pdf; "Rwanda: Genocide and Partition," written brief by Bureau of Intelligence and Research, U.S. State Department, April 26, 1994 (declassified), in ibid., http://www.gwu.edu/~nsarchiv/NSAEBB/NSAEBB117/Rw23.pdf; see also Albright with Woodward, *Madam Secretary*, 151.

[45] The statement skated fairly close to alleging genocidal attacks: "The Security Council condemns all these breaches of international humanitarian law in Rwanda, particularly those perpetrated against the civilian population, and recalls that persons who instigate or participate in such acts are individually responsible. In this context, the Security Council recalls that the killing of members of an ethnic group with the intention of destroying such a group in whole or in part constitutes a crime punishable under international law." United Nations, "Statement by the President of the Security Council," April 30, 1994, 3, http://daccess-dds-ny.un.org/doc/UNDOC/GEN/N94/199/86/PDF/N9419986.pdf?OpenElement.

[46] Ibid.

[47] Jose Ayala Lasso, "Press Statement," Office of United Nations High Commissioner for Human Rights, May 4, 1994.

[48] Jose Ayala Lasso issued the report of his May 11–12 visit to Rwanda on May 19, in which he characterized the killings as "a human rights tragedy of unprecedented dimensions" and noted "the indiscriminate and large-scale killing of civilians including political opponents of the dead President." He declined to describe the massacres as genocide. Jose Ayala Lasso, "Report from the United Nations High Commissioner for Human Rights on his Mission to Rwanda, 11–12 May 1994," E/CN.4/S-3/3, May 19, 1994.

[49] U.S. Mission to the United Nations, Cable 1856, May 3, 1994 (declassified); Mark Huband, "Rwanda Rebels Talk Tough on Peacekeepers," *The Observer*, May 21, 1994, 21.

[50] John Shattuck, *Freedom on Fire: Human Rights Wars and America's Response* (Cambridge, Massachusetts: Harvard University Press, 2003), 49.

[51] United Nations Security Council, Resolution 918, May 17, 1994, para. 3, http://daccess-dds-ny.un.org/doc/UNDOC/GEN/N94/218/36/PDF/N9421836.pdf?OpenElement.

[52] See William A. Schabas, *Genocide in International Law*, 2nd ed. (New York: Cambridge University Press, 2009), 520–592.

[53] Resolution 918, n. 51, para. 18.

[54] The memorandum stated in part: "A USG statement that acts of genocide have occurred would not have any particular legal consequences. Under the Convention, the prosecution of persons charged with genocide is the responsibility of the competent courts in the state where the acts took place or an international penal tribunal (none has yet been established); the U.S. has no criminal jurisdiction over acts of genocide occurring within Rwanda unless they are committed by U.S. citizens or they fall under another criminal provision of U.S. law (such as those relating to acts of terrorism for which there is a basis for U.S. jurisdiction). Although lacking in legal consequences, a clear statement that the USG believes that acts of genocide

have occurred could increase pressure for USG activism in response to the crisis in Rwanda. We believe, however, that we should send a clear signal that the United States believes that acts of genocide have occurred in Rwanda. If we do not seize the opportunity presented by the UNHRC to use the genocide label to condemn events in Rwanda, our credibility will be undermined with human rights groups and the general public, who may question how much evidence we can legitimately require before coming to a policy conclusion." Assistant Secretary of State for African Affairs George E. Moose, Assistant Secretary of State for Democracy, Human Rights and Labor John Shattuck, Assistant Secretary of State for International Organization Affairs Douglas J. Bennet, and Department of State Legal Adviser Conrad K. Harper, "Action Memorandum to Secretary of State Warren Christopher: Has Genocide Occurred in Rwanda?" May 21, 1994 (declassified), in *The US and the Genocide in Rwanda 1994*, ed. Ferroggiaro, doc.14, 2–3, http://www.gwu.edu/~nsarchiv/NSAEBB/NSAEBB53/rw052194.pdf.

[55] "There can be little question that the specific listed acts have taken place in Rwanda.... The second requirement is also clearly satisfied.... The Tutsis are an ethnic group.... It also appears that the third element has been satisfied. At least some of the prohibited acts have apparently been committed with the requisite intent to destroy, in whole or in part the Tutsi group, as required by the [Genocide] Convention.... here, given the context of the overall factual situation described by INR [Intelligence and Research Bureau], it seems evident that killings and other listed acts have been undertaken with the intent of destroying the Tutsi group in whole or in part." Assistant Legal Adviser for African Affairs Joan Donoghue, "Draft Legal Analysis," Office of the Legal Adviser for the Department of State, May 16, 1994 (declassified), in *The US and the Genocide in Rwanda 1994*, ed. Ferroggiaro, doc. 16, http://www.gwu.edu/~nsarchiv/NSAEBB/NSAEBB53/rw051694.pdf.

[56] Christine Shelly, "U.S. Department of State Daily Press Briefing," June 10, 1994, 4–7, http://dosfan.lib.uic.edu/ERC/briefing/daily_briefings/1994/9406/940610db.html.

[57] U.S. State Department press guidance, June 10, 1994:

Q. What is the distinction between saying that "acts of genocide may have occurred" and that "genocide has occurred"?

A. Under the definition of genocide contained in the 1948 Convention, not all killings are genocide. As the UN Human Rights Commission noted in a resolution that the United States strongly supported, genocidal acts may have occurred in Rwanda. On May 25, the UN Human Rights Commission, with strong support from the United States, appointed a Special Rapporteur for Rwanda to compile information on possible violations of human rights and acts which may constitute breaches of international humanitarian law and crimes against humanity, including acts of genocide. His preliminary report, which is due later this month, will provide additional information about human rights violations in Rwanda.

Q. Do we avoid our legal obligations by saying that acts of genocide may have occurred instead of saying that genocide has occurred?

A. No. Under the Convention, the prosecution of persons charged with genocide is the responsibility of the competent courts in the state where the acts took place or of a competent international tribunal. Parties to the Convention may also call upon the competent UN organs to take appropriate action to prevent and suppress acts of genocide. The actions of the UN Security Council and the UN Human Rights commission's designation of a Special Rapporteur are such actions.

[58] United Nations Security Council, "Report of the Secretary-General on the Situation in Rwanda," S/1994/640, May 31, 1994, para. 36, http://daccess-dds-ny.un .org/doc/UNDOC/GEN/N94/234/12/IMG/N9423412.pdf?OpenElement.

[59] United Nations Security Council, Resolution 925, June 8, 1994.

[60] Special Rapporteur of the Commission on Human Rights Rene Degni-Ségui, "Report on the Situation of Human Rights in Rwanda," United Nations Economic and Social Council, June 28, 1994, http://www.unhchr.ch/Huridocda/Huridoca.nsf/ TestFrame/d32234b56f13245580256716003356b6?Opendocument.

[61] Boutros-Ghali wrote the Security Council that "it should be noted that none of those Governments possessing the capacity to provide fully trained and equipped military units have offered so far to do so for the implementation of the Security Council's resolutions to deal with the situation in Rwanda.... UNAMIR may not be in a position, for about three months, to fully undertake the tasks entrusted to it by those resolutions. Meanwhile, the situation in Rwanda has continued to deteriorate and the killing of innocent civilians has not stopped." United Nations Secretary General, "Letter to the President of the United Nations Security Council," S/ 1994/728, June 19, 1994, para.10.

[62] United Nations Security Council, Resolution 929, June 2, 1994.

[63] "Operation Support Hope," Global Security, http://www.globalsecurity.org/ military/ops/support_hope.htm.

[64] See Bill Clinton, *My Life* (New York: Random House, 2004), 593: "With a few thousand troops and help from our allies, even making allowances for the time it would have taken to deploy them, we could have saved lives. The failure to try to stop Rwanda's tragedies became one of the greatest regrets of my presidency."

Chapter Three: Credible Justice for Rwanda

[1] U.S. Mission to the United Nations, Cable 02491, June 15, 1994 (declassified), "Rwanda: Bringing the Guilty to Justice."

[2] United Nations Security Council, Resolution 935, July 1, 1994.

[3] Special Rapporteur R. Degni-Ségui, "Report on the Situation of Human Rights in Rwanda," United Nations Commission on Human Rights, June 30, 1994, http:// daccess-dds-ny.un.org/doc/UNDOC/GEN/G94/131/47/PDF/G9413147.pdf ?OpenElement.

[4] Indeed, in cable instructions to Embassy Paris on July 12, 1994, the State Department reconfirmed that "it will support establishing a war crimes tribunal along the

lines of the UN's Yugoslavia ad hoc tribunal." "Consultations with France and Others on Rwanda," U.S. State Department Communication 184612, July 12, 1994 (declassified).

[5] Ibid.

[6] "Next Steps in Addressing War Crimes in Rwanda," U.S. State Department Communication 188919, July 15, 1994 (declassified). U.S. foreign service officer Gregory Stanton was instrumental in early drafting of a Security Council resolution to create an international criminal tribunal for Rwanda.

[7] Dee Dee Myers, White House Press Secretary, "Statement on the Close of the U.S. Embassy in Rwanda," Washington, D.C., July 15, 1994.

[8] U.S. Mission to the United Nations, Cable 02952, July 19, 1994 [Rwanda: 18 Jul 94 Security Council Meeting] (declassified).

[9] "British Response Muted in Considering Next Steps in Addressing War Crimes in Rwanda," U.S. State Department Communication, Embassy London 11339, July 19, 1994.

[10] "Rwanda War Crimes," U.S. State Department Papers 198848, July 26, 1994 (declassified).

[11] U.S. Mission to the United Nations, Cable 03228, August 4, 1994 (declassified) [SC Discussion of Rwanda, 4 Aug 94]. See also "Report of the Secretary-General on the Situation in Rwanda," United Nations Security Council, August 3, 1994, 27(c), http://daccess-dds-ny.un.org/doc/UNDOC/GEN/N94/308/97/IMG/N9430897 .pdf?OpenElement.

[12] Paul Lewis, "Rwanda Agrees to a U.N. War Crimes Tribunal," *New York Times*, August 9, 1994, A6, http://www.nytimes.com/1994/08/09/world/rwanda-agrees-to-a -un-war-crimes-tribunal.html?pagewanted=1.

[13] "Statement by the President of the Security Council," United Nations, August 10, 1994, http://daccess-dds-ny.un.org/doc/UNDOC/GEN/N94/323/81/PDF/ N9432381.pdf?OpenElement.

[14] John Shattuck, *Freedom on Fire: Human Rights Wars and America's Response* (Cambridge, Massachusetts: Harvard University Press, 2003), 62–63.

[15] "Shattuck's Meeting with French on Rwanda War Crimes Tribunal and Burundi," U.S. State Department Communication, Embassy Paris 22245, August 12, 1994 (declassified). See also Shattuck, *Freedom on Fire*, 68.

[16] "Shattuck's Discussion on the proposed Rwanda War Crimes Tribunal with HMG," U.S. State Department Communication, Embassy London 12901, August 15, 1994 (declassified). By September 30, 1994, the British had modified their position, noting the importance of the work regarding the Rwanda domestic legal system proceeding in parallel but also recognizing that progress toward a tribunal should not be held hostage to progress on the other front. U.S. Mission to the United Nations Cable 04112, September 30, 1994 (declassified) [Resolution and Statute Establishing War Crimes Tribunal for Rwanda].

[17] "Demarche for International Tribunal in Rwanda," U.S. State Department Communication 228408, August 24,1994 (declassified).

[18] The plan was to incorporate the following provisions in the Security Council resolution on Rwandan accountability:

- Three preambular clauses describing "acts of genocide" having been committed in Rwanda, noting that the situation "continues to constitute a threat to international peace and security," and stating the conviction that prosecuting the war criminals in Rwanda "would contribute to the restoration and maintenance of peace" and ensure "that such violations are halted and effectively redressed," which combined both how justice would support the peace process and how it would serve as a deterrent to further atrocity crimes.
- Extend the jurisdiction of the Yugoslav Tribunal to cover atrocity crimes in Rwanda since April 6, 1994.
- Require additional prosecutorial staff for the Rwanda cases, an expansion of the registry staff to meet the increased workload, the election of additional judges, and "any other measures to ensure" that the tribunal receives sufficient support and resources.
- Establish the seat of the tribunal as The Hague although it could sit elsewhere when necessary.
- Change the name of the court to "The International Tribunal for the Prosecution of Persons Responsible for Serious Violations of International Humanitarian Law" or, in short-hand, "The International Tribunal."
- Expand the tribunal's territorial jurisdiction to include Rwanda and states bordering Rwanda and related to the crisis there since April 6, 1994."Resolution Establishing War Crimes Tribunal for Rwanda," U.S. State Department Communication 237220, September 1, 1994 (declassified).

A "nonpaper" attached to the draft explained why the two sets of prosecutions should be joined in one expanded tribunal: "It is also important to treat the two situations on an equal footing, applying the same principles of international law and the same procedural protections. This is best guaranteed by dealing with the two situations under the same statute and rules of procedure. It is also important to have uniformity in the application of the law to the two situations. This is best ensured by having common trial and appellate chambers, which would hear cases arising from both conflicts. It would be useful to have common overall direction of the two prosecution efforts, so as to encourage equal treatment, an efficient management of the workload, and coordinated development of common legal issues. This is best done by having both prosecution teams report to a single chief prosecutor. (This would also avoid the need for another potentially prolonged search for a second Chief Prosecutor.) We believe a strong, experienced prosecutor should be selected to head up the Rwanda prosecution team. As part of his duties, the prosecutor will need to work with the Rwandan Government to determine which cases merit international prosecution, and which cases should be subject to domestic prosecution." Ibid.

[19] "UN War Crimes Prosecutions for Rwanda," U.S. State Department Communication 251046, September 16, 1994 (declassified).

[20] U.S. Mission to the United Nations, Cable 03594, August 30, 1994 (declassified), [War Crimes Tribunal for Rwanda]. See also Raymond Bonner, "U.N. Commission Recommends Rwanda 'Genocide' Tribunal," *New York Times*, September 29, 1994,

http://www.nytimes.com/1994/09/29/world/un-commission-recommends-rwanda
-genocide-tribunal.html?scp=1&sq=china+rwanda+tribunal&st=nyt.

[21] David Scheffer, "Official-Informal: Eyes Only Ambassador Albright," U.S. State
Department Communication 238830, September 3, 1994 (declassified).

[22] "Visit by UN Commission of Experts; Recommendation for U.S. Assistance," U.S.
State Department Communications in Kigali 01509, September 7, 1994 (declassified). See Commission of Experts, "Report." S/1994/1125, October 1, 1994.

[23] U.S. Mission to the United Nations, Cable 04101, September 29, 1994 (declassified) [A/S Shattuck Discussions with Secretariat, ICRC, and Missions Regarding Haiti,
Rwanda, Burundi, China, Turkey, and Funding for UN Human Rights Activities].

[24] Commission of Experts, "Report," S/1994/1125, October 1, 1994.

[25] U.S. Mission to the United Nations, Cable 04112, September 30, 1994 (declassified) [Resolution and Statute Establishing War Crimes Tribunal for Rwanda].

[26] Barbara Crossette, "Rwanda Asks Quick Start of Tribunal," *New York Times*, October 9, 1994, A19, http://www.nytimes.com/1994/10/09/world/rwanda-asks-quick
-start-of-tribunal.html?scp=1&sq=rwanda%20tribunal%20october%201994&st=cse.

[27] "Rwanda Position on Rwanda War Crimes Tribunal," U.S. State Department
Communications in Kigali 01872, October 19, 1994 (declassified).

[28] U.S. State Department Communications in Kigali 01883, October 20, 1994 (declassified) [Follow-up Demarches on Rwanda War Crimes Tribunal Resolution:
Prime Minister and Justice Minister]. Faustin Gacinya, "What Is 'Justice' after Genocide," *New Times*, May 1, 1996, http://www.nacdl.org/CHAMPION/ARTICLES/
97may01.htm.

[29] The aim was to incorporate the targeting purpose of the crime of genocide
against national, ethnic, racial, or religious groups into the definition of crimes
against humanity. There was also the precedent in Article 6(c) of the Nuremberg
Charter, where crimes against humanity included persecutions "on political, racial
or religious grounds." Given the primary targeting of Tutsi on ethnic grounds in
Rwanda in 1994, the Rwandan government insisted on a similar formulation for the
statute of the Rwanda Tribunal.

[30] See Alison Des Forges, *"Leave None to Tell the Story": Genocide in Rwanda* (New York:
Human Rights Watch, 1999), 222–262.

[31] Telford Taylor, *The Anatomy of the Nuremberg Trials* (New York: Alfred A. Knopf,
1992), 583–587.

[32] Rwanda Tribunal Statute, Article 27.

[33] United Nations Security Council, Resolution 955, November 8, 1994.

[34] United Nations Security Council, Resolution 977, February 22, 1995.

Chapter Four: Abandoned at Srebrenica

[1] See Madeleine Albright with William Woodward, *Madam Secretary* (New York: Miramax Books, 2003), 186.

[2] See, e.g., "Mortar Shell Hits Headquarters of U.N. Peacekeepers in Bosnia," *New
York Times*, July 3, 1995.

[3] Elaine Sciolino, "3,500 G.I.'s Going to Italy In Case U.N. Force Needs Aid," *New York Times*, June 6, 1995, http://www.nytimes.com/1995/06/06/world/conflict-balkans -us-forces-3500-gi-s-going-italy-case-un-force-needs-aid.html; "DoD News Briefing," Mr. Kenneth Bacon, July 13, 1995, http://www.defenselink.mil/transcripts/transcript .aspx?transcriptid=148.

[4] The Balkan Institute, "A Review of Weekly Events," *Balkan Watch*, July 10, 1995, http://www.hri.org/news/misc/misc-news/1995/95-07-11_1.misc.txt.

[5] "Serbs Overrun UN 'Safe Haven'," BBC, July 11, 1995, http://news.bbc.co.uk/ onthisday/hi/dates/stories/july/11/newsid_4080000/4080690.stm.

[6] John Shattuck, *Freedom on Fire: Human Rights Wars and America's Response* (Cambridge, Massachusetts: Harvard University Press, 2003), 154: "Our plan would involve publicly highlighting the tribunal's indictments of Karadzic and Mladic; having the United States issue a new 'no-negotiation-with-indicted-war-criminals' statement; urging European governments to arrest any indicted war criminals entering their jurisdictions; holding congressional briefings on the tribunal; and arranging for the tribunal's chief prosecutor, Richard Goldstone, to visit Washington and New York at the end of July. These ideas would all be implemented over the next few weeks. The most important part of the strategy—no negotiation with indicted war criminals— would be put into play by Richard Holbrooke in a stormy meeting in Belgrade on August 30 with Slobodan Milosevic."

[7] See Albright's account of this meeting in Albright with Woodward, *Madam Secretary*, 187.

[8] Ibid., 187–188.

[9] 1995 WL 607521 (F.D.C.H.) (July 17, 1995).

[10] Elaine Sciolino, "Defiant Senators Vote to Override Bosnian Arms Ban," *New York Times*, July 27, 1995, http://www.nytimes.com/1995/07/27/world/conflict-balkans -washington-defiant-senators-vote-override-bosnian-arms-ban.html?pagewanted =all

[11] 5 CFR 2641.204.

[12] Samantha Power, *"A Problem from Hell": America and the Age of Genocide* (New York: Basic Books, 2002), 419–420; Albright with Woodward, *Madam Secretary*, 188.

[13] Richard Holbrooke, *To End a War* (New York: Random House, 1998), 107–108.

[14] For Richard Holbrooke's published account of this meeting, see ibid., 148–151.

Chapter Five: The Pastor from Mugonero

[1] "Consultations with France on Rwanda War Crimes Issues," U.S. State Department Communications in Paris 19216, July 13, 1994 (declassified).

[2] The Security Council authorized Operation Turquoise on June 22, 1994. See "UN Authorizes 'Operation Turquoise' to Protect Displaced Persons," *U.N. Chronicle Online* 4 (1994): 4, http://www.un.org/Pubs/chronicle/1994/issue4/0494p4.asp; "Report of the Independent Inquiry into the Actions of the United Nations during the 1994 Genocide in Rwanda," December 15, 1999, http://daccess-dds-ny.un.org/ doc/UNDOC/GEN/N99/395/47/IMG/N9939547.pdf?OpenElement.

[3] United Nations Security Council, Resolution 978, February 27, 1995, 2, http://www.un.org/ictr/english/Resolutions/978e.htm.

[4] International Criminal Tribunal for Rwanda, "Prosecutor Louise Arbour Confirms the Transfer of Four Major Accused as a Capital Turning Point for the Rwanda Tribunal," ICTR Press Releases, January 23, 1997.

[5] International Criminal Tribunal for Rwanda, "Judgement and Sentence," *The Prosecutor v. Jean Kambanda*, ICTR 97-23-S, September 4, 1998.

[6] Significantly, Idelphonse Nizeyemana, a top Hutu military official during the genocide, was arrested in Uganda and transferred to the Rwanda Tribunal in October 2009. See International Criminal Tribunal for Rwanda, "Idelphonse Nizeyemana Arrested and Transferred Today to Arusha," ICTR Press Releases, October 6, 2009.

[7] James C. McKinley, "Killing at Refugee Camp at Mudende Underscores Growing Violence in Rwanda," *New York Times*, December 12, 1997, A1.

[8] Douglas Martin, "Rosamond Carr, 94, Dies; Loved Africa and Orphans," *New York Times*, October 8, 2006, 42.

[9] Spokesman James P. Rubin, "Statement on the Massacre at Mudende Refugee Camp, Rwanda," December 18, 1997, http://secretary.state.gov/www/travels/971218jrubin.html.

[10] The Prosecutor of the International Criminal Tribunal for Rwanda, "Amended Indictment," *Prosecutor v. Elizaphan Ntakirutimana and Gérard Ntakirutimana*, ICTR-96-17-T, July 7, 1998; The Prosecutor of the International Criminal Tribunal for Rwanda, "Amended Indictment," *Prosecutor v. Elizaphan Ntakirutimana and Gérard Ntakirutimana*, ICTR-96-17-T, October 20, 2000.

[11] International Criminal Tribunal for Rwanda Trial Chamber I, "Judgement and Sentence," *Prosecutor v. Elizaphan and Gerard Ntakirutimana*, ICTR-96-10 and ICTR-96-17-T, February 21, 2003.

[12] U.S. Public Law 104-106, February 10, 1996, 1342(a)(1).

[13] U.S. District Court for the Southern District of Texas, Laredo Division, "In the Matter of Surrender of Elizaphan Ntakirumtimana," *Federal Supplement* 988 (December 17, 1997): 1038.

[14] Genocide Convention Implementation Act of 1987, U.S. Public Law 100-606, November 4, 1988, § 1091(d)(2).

[15] U.S. Department of Justice Immigration and Naturalization Service, "Arrival/Departure Record," M-447, September 1998, C, http://ublib.buffalo.edu/libraries/e-resources/ebooks/records/eel9502.pdf.

[16] Genocide Accountability Act of 2007, Public Law 110-151, December 21, 2007, § 1091(d)(3) and (4). See David Scheffer, "Closing the Impunity Gap in U.S. Law," *Northwestern University Journal of International Human Rights* 8 (2009): 30. This article received Honorable Mention for the National Institute of Military Justice's 2009 Kevin J. Barry Award for Excellence in Military Legal Studies.

[17] U.S. District Court for the Southern District of Texas, Laredo Division, "In re Ntakirutimana," *Westlaw* 655708, August 6, 1998, 17.

[18] U.S. Court of Appeals, Fifth Circuit, "Ntakirutimana v. Reno," *Third Federal Reporter* 184 (August 5, 1999): 431.

[19] U.S. Supreme Court, "Ntakirutimana v. Reno," *U.S.* 528 (January 24, 2000): 977.

[20] See note 11 above.

[21] See, for example, International Criminal Tribunal for Rwanda Trial Chamber, "Judgement," *The Prosecutor v. Athanase Seromba* (December 13, 2006).

Chapter Six: Unbearable Timidity

[1] Dan Bilefsky and Marlise Simons, "Bosnian Serb Under Arrest in War Crimes," *New York Times*, July 22, 2008; International Criminal Tribunal for the former Yugoslavia, "Press Release: Tribunal Welcomes the Arrest of Radovan Karazdic," July 21, 2008, http://www.icty.org/sid/9952.

[2] Rule 47(b) of the ICTY Rules of Procedure and Evidence.

[3] Rule 87(1) of the ICTY Rules of Procedure and Evidence.

[4] Elaine Sciolino, "Bosnian Talks Snag on Fate of Two Serbs," *New York Times*, November 17, 1995, http://www.nytimes.com/1995/11/17/world/bosnian-talks-snag -on-fate-of-two-serbs.html.

[5] David Scheffer, "International Judicial Intervention," *Foreign Policy* 102 (1996): 34.

[6] John Shattuck, *Freedom on Fire: Human Rights Wars and America's Response* (Cambridge, Massachusetts: Harvard University Press, 2003): 206–213.

[7] Wesley Clark, *Waging Modern War: Bosnia, Kosovo, and the Future of Combat* (New York: Public Affairs, 2001), 65.

[8] General Framework Agreement for Peace in Bosnia and Herzegovina, B.A.-H.R.-Y.U., December 14, 1995, 35 *International Legal Materials* 75.

[9] William J. Clinton, "Remarks at the Dedication of the Thomas J. Dodd Archives and Research Center in Storrs, Connecticut, October 15, 1995," *Public Papers of the Presidents of the United States: William J. Clinton* (1995), books 1 and 2, 1593.

[10] Ambassador Madeleine K. Albright, U.S. Representative to the United Nations, "Symposium on Human Rights and the Lessons of the Holocaust," Senator Thomas J. Dodd Research Center, Storrs, Connecticut, October 17, 1995, http://dosfan.lib .uic.edu/ERC/democracy/releases_statements/951017.html.

[11] "General Assembly Hears Calls for Adequate Funding of International Criminal Tribunal for the former Yugoslavia," GA/8988, November 7, 1995, http://www .scienceblog.com/community/older/archives/L/1995/A/un950269.html.

[12] Article IX of the General Framework Agreement reads, "The Parties shall cooperate fully with all entities involved in implementation of this peace settlement, as described in the Annexes to this Agreement, or which are otherwise authorized by the United Nations Security Council, pursuant to the obligation of all Parties to cooperate in the investigation and prosecution of war crimes and other violations of international humanitarian law."

[13] United Nations Security Council, Resolution 1022 (November 22, 1995): "Noting that compliance with the requests and orders of the International Tribunal for the former Yugoslavia constitutes an essential aspect of implementing the Peace Agreement."

[14] U.N. SCOR, 3595th mtg. at 14–16, U.N. Doc. S/PV.3595 (1995).

[15] "Imperfect Peace Dogs US in Bosnia," *Christian Science Monitor*, December 4, 1995.

[16] Dayton Peace Agreement, Article VI.3(d) of Annex 1-A.

[17] *Case Concerning the Application of the Convention on the Prevention and Punishment of the Crime of Genocide* (*Bosnia and Herzegovina v. Serbia and Montenegro*), February 26, 2007.

[18] Under the Dayton Peace Agreement, IFOR had the authority to (1) help create secure conditions for the conduct by others of other (nonmilitary) tasks associated with the peace settlement; and (2) respond appropriately to deliberate violence to life and person, within the limits of its assigned principal tasks and available resources. It might also implement additional directives decided by the North Atlantic Council. United Nations Security Council Resolution 1031 reaffirmed the obligation of all states (including those contributing forces to IFOR) to cooperate with the tribunal and recognized that the parties, having acknowledged that they must cooperate with the tribunal, authorized IFOR "to take such actions as required, including the use of necessary force, to ensure compliance with Annex I-A of the Peace Agreement." The North Atlantic Council decision of December 16, 1995, stated: "It was important to cooperate actively with the work of the Tribunal within the context of the IFOR Mission.... IFOR should detain any persons indicted by the International Criminal Tribunal who come into contact with IFOR in its execution of assigned tasks in order to assure the transfer of these persons to the International Criminal Tribunal." On December 27, the Yugoslav Tribunal relied on this NAC decision and a supplemental rule of engagement to issue an order for the transfer of persons detained by IFOR to the tribunal. The tribunal's order noted "that the North Atlantic Council on 16 December 1995 agreed that, having regard to U.N. Security Council resolutions 827 (1993) and 1031 (1995) and Annex 1-A of the General Framework Agreement for Peace in Bosnia and Herzegovina, the multinational military implementation force (IFOR) should detain any persons indicted by the International Criminal Tribunal who come into contact with IFOR in its execution of assigned tasks in order to assure the transfer of these persons to the International Criminal Tribunal." The tribunal also noted in its order that the Bosnian government authorized the members of IFOR to carry out arrest warrants of the tribunal on Bosnian territory. Some European delegations argued that fresh authorization would be required, which finally was reconfirmed.

[19] David Halberstam, *War in a Time of Peace: Bush, Clinton, and the Generals* (New York: Touchstone, 2002), 362–363: "His forces, [Smith] insisted, would not go after indicted war criminals."

[20] I rested our case on the authority of United Nations Security Council, Resolution 827, May 25, 1993; 1031(4), December 15, 1995; and 1088, December 12, 1996; the United Nations, Statute of the International Criminal Tribunal for the former Yugoslavia, May 25, 1993, Article 19(2); United Nations, "International Criminal Tribunal for the former Yugoslavia: Rules of Procedure and Evidence," U.N. Doc. IT/32/Rev. 7 (March 14, 1994), rule 37, 55–59, and 59 bis; The Republic of Bosnia and Herzegovina, the Republic of Croatia and the Federal Republic of Yugoslavia, General Framework Agreement for Peace in Bosnia and Herzegovina, December 14,

1995, Articles IX, X, II(8); Bosnia and Herzegovina's consent to IFOR deployment in December 1995 (each country had to consent to the presence of IFOR troops, per Annex 11 of the Dayton accord); Michael J. Dziedzic and Andrew Bair, "Bosnia and the International Police Task Force," in *Policing the New Disorder*, ed. Robert B. Oakley, Michael J. Dziedzic, and Eliot M. Goldberg (Washington D.C.: National Defense University Press, 1998); and the exchange of letters of January 30 and February 16, 1996, between the International Tribunal for the former Yugoslavia and the Bosnian government.

[21] United Nations Security Council, Resolution 1088, December 12, 1996, para. 20.

[22] United Nations Security Council, Resolution 827, May 25, 1993.

[23] International Criminal Tribunal for the former Yugoslavia, "Apprehension and Transfer to The Hague of an Accused Under Sealed Indictment," June 27, 1997, http://www.icty.org/sid/7497.

[24] International Criminal Tribunal for the former Yugoslavia, "Rules of Procedure and Evidence," U.N. Doc. IT/32/Rev. 12, November 12, 1997, Rule 59 bis, http://www.icty.org/x/file/Legal%20Library/Rules procedure_evidence/IT032_rev12_en.pdf.

[25] Chris Hedges, "NATO Troops Kill a Serbian Suspect in War Atrocities," *New York Times*, July 11, 1997, A1.

[26] R. Jeffrey Smith described the folly in "Secret Meetings Foiled Karadzic Capture Plan; U.S. Says French Jeopardized Mission," *Washington Post*, April 23, 1998, AO1:

> Gourmillon, the army major at the center of Washington's ire, was the French military's principal liaison officer to the Serbs within his military sector and operated out of the French military headquarters just outside the city of Mostar in central Bosnia. His meetings with Karadzic occurred over a lengthy period in 1997, and were discovered by Washington after someone tipped U.S. intelligence officials, according to several sources.
>
> At a minimum, the meetings were a violation of NATO's policy of shunning any official contact with indicted war criminals such as Karadzic....
>
> The officials declined to provide details of the operation that was planned last year, but said that the discovery of Gourmillon's meetings with Karadzic immediately provoked suspicions that the purpose was to help Karadzic evade capture. "We know, definitely, that he passed information about NATO operations related to efforts to eventually get Karadzic," a senior U.S. official said, without offering details.
>
> The decision to suspend the attempted capture was reportedly made by U.S. Army Gen. Wesley Clark, the Supreme Allied Commander of NATO, who concluded that the French contact with Karadzic could have exposed Western forces to undue risk by "stripping away" their defenses against a Serb counterattack, according to another official. Clark demanded an explanation for the contacts from the French military leadership, which responded that the meetings had indeed taken place but without authorization from the Defense Ministry in Paris.
>
> But U.S. officials say this claim was undercut when the French government later acknowledged that memoranda summarizing the meetings had been writ-

ten by Gourmillon and transmitted to his superiors. "It is perplexing" one official said.

French officials declined to comment yesterday on the case. Aides to President Jacque Chirac and Foreign Minister Hubert Vedrine referred inquiries to the Defense Ministry, which did not respond to telephone calls seeking comment.

[27] Taylor Branch, *The Clinton Tapes: Wrestling History with the President* (New York: Simon & Schuster, 2009), 466.

[28] U.S. State Department, "Press Briefing," October 3, 1997, http://secretary.state .gov/www/briefings/9710/971003db.html.

[29] International Criminal Tribunal for the former Yugoslavia, "Rules of Procedure and Evidence," U.N. Doc. IT/32/Rev. 12, November 12, 1997, Rule 70, http://www .icty.org/x/file/Legal%20Library/Rules_procedure_evidence/IT032_rev12_en.pdf.

[30] The indictment eventually arrived: International Criminal Tribunal for the former Yugoslavia, "Indictment," *Prosecutor v. Seselj*, January 15, 2003, http://www.icty .org/x/cases/seselj/ind/en/ses-ii030115e.pdf.

[31] Steven Lee Myers, "Making Sure War Crimes Aren't Forgotten," *New York Times*, September 22, 1997, A1.

[32] "Bringing War Criminals to Justice," CNN, June 24, 1999, http://www.cnn.com/ WORLD/europe/9906/24/kosovo.01/index.html.

[33] Richard Holbrooke, U.S. Ambassador to the United Nations, "Testimony before the United Nations Security Council," November 21, 2000.

[34] Steven Erlanger and Carlotta Gall, "The Milosevic Surrender: The Overview; Milosevic Arrest Came with a Pledge for a Fair Trial," *New York Times*, April 2, 2001, http:// www.nytimes.com/2001/04/02/world/milosevic-surrender-overview-milosevic -arrest-came-with-pledge-for-fair-trial.html?scp=2&sq=April%202,%202001%20 Milosevic&st=cse.

[35] Steven Erlanger, "The Handover of Milosevic: News Analysis; Milosevic Trial: Test on Many Levels," *New York Times*, June 29, 2001, A12, http://www.nytimes.com/ 2001/06/29/world/the-handover-of-milosevic-news-analysis-milosevic-trial-test-on -many-levels.html?scp=1&sq=Milosevic%20transfer&st=cse.

[36] International Criminal Tribunal for the former Yugoslavia, "Press Release: Slobodan Milosevic Found Dead in His Cell at the Detention Unit," March 11, 2006, http://www.icty.org/sid/8794.

Chapter Seven: The Siren of Exceptionalism

[1] Robert D. Kaplan, *Warrior Politics: Why Leadership Demands a Pagan Ethos* (New York: Vintage, 2003); Caleb Carr, *The Lessons of Terror: A History of Warfare against Civilians; Why It Has Always Failed and Why It Will Fail Again* (New York: Random House, 2002); Jack L. Goldsmith, *The Terror Presidency: Law and Judgment inside the Bush Administration* (New York: W. W. Norton & Company, 2007); John Bolton, *Surrender Is Not an Option: Defending America at the United Nations* (New York: Threshold Editions, 2007); Lee A. Casey and David B. Rivkin Jr., "The International Criminal Courts

v. The American People," *The Heritage Foundation Backgrounder*, February 8, 1999; Transcript of Palin, Biden debate, October 3, 2008, http://edition.cnn.com/2008/POLITICS/10/02/debate.transcript/.

[2] C. F. Amerasinghe, *Principles of the Institutional Law of International Organizations*, 2nd ed. (Cambridge, Massachusetts: Cambridge University Press, 2005), 315–317.

[3] J. L. Brierly, *The Law of Nations: An Introduction to the International Law of Peace*, 6th ed. (Oxford: Oxford University Press, 1963), 130–133.

[4] United Nations, *Convention on the Law of the Sea*, December 10, 1982, http://www.un.org/Depts/los/convention_agreements/texts/unclos/closindx.htm.

[5] The United States signed the treaty on August 21, 1996. "Chronological Lists of Ratifications of, Accessions and Successions to the Convention and the Related Agreements as at 08 January 2010," United Nations, Division for Ocean Affairs and the Law of the Sea, http://www.un.org/Depts/los/reference_files/chronological _lists_of_ratifications.htm.

[6] U.S. Department of State, "Fact Sheet: U.S. Oceans Policy and the Law of the Sea Convention," Bureau of Oceans and International Environmental and Scientific Affairs, May 28, 1998, http://www.state.gov/www/global/oes/oceans/fs_oceans _los.html; Marjorie Ann Browne, "CRS Issue Brief for Congress IB95010: The Law of the Sea Convention and U.S. Policy," Foreign Affairs, Defense, and Trade Division, February 14, 2001, http://www.ncseonline.org/nle/crsreports/marine/mar-16.cfm. The Pentagon has long strongly supported ratification of the Law of the Sea Convention, in part because it guarantees rights of passage for the U.S. Navy on the global ocas.

[7] John Luddy, "The Law of the Sea Treaty: Unwise and Unnecessary," Heritage Foundation Executive Memorandum no. 386, August 10, 1994.

[8] United Nations, General Assembly Resolution 44/89 (1989); P. Robinson, "The Missing Crimes," in *The Rome Statute of the International Criminal Court: A Commentary*, ed. Antonio Cassese, Paolo Gaeta, and John R.W.D. Jones (New York: Oxford University Press, 2002), 497–521.

[9] M. Cherif Bassiouni, *International Criminal Law Conventions and Their Penal Provisions* (Dobbs Ferry, New York: Transnational Publishers, 1997).

[10] M. Cherif Bassiouni, *The Institutionalization of Torture by the Bush Administration: Is Anyone Responsible?* (Mortsel, Belgium: Intersentia Publishing, 2010); Philippe Sands, *Torture Team: Rumsfeld's Memo and the Betrayal of American Values* (New York: Palgrave, 2008); Jordan J. Paust, *Beyond the Law: The Bush Administration's Unlawful Responses in the "War" on Terror* (New York: Cambridge University Press, 2007); Jane Mayer, *The Dark Side: The Inside Story of How the War on Terror Turned into a War on American Ideals* (New York: Doubleday, 2008); Goldsmith, *The Terror Presidency*.

[11] United Nations General Assembly International Law Commission, "Establishment of an International Criminal Court: Draft Resolution," A/C.6/49/L.24, November 29, 1994; J. Crawford, "The Work of the International Law Commission," in *The Rome Statute of the International Criminal Court*, ed. Cassese, Gaeta, and Jones, 23–34.

[12] William Schabas, *An Introduction to the International Criminal Court*, 4th ed. (Cambridge: Cambridge University Press, 2011), 16–17, notes 54, 56.

[13] Article 98(2) of the Rome Statute reads: "The Court may not proceed with a request for surrender which would require the requested State to act inconsistently with its obligations under international agreements pursuant to which the consent of a sending State is required to surrender a person of that State to the Court, unless the Court can first obtain the cooperation of the sending State for the giving of consent for the surrender."

[14] See note 12 above, 190–199; *The Oxford Companion to International Criminal Justice*, ed. Antonio Cassese (New York: Oxford University Press, 2009), 346–48; J. T. Holmes, "Complementarity: National Courts Versus the ICC," in *The Rome Statute of the International Criminal Court*, ed. Cassese, Gaeta, and Jones, 667–686.

[15] Larry Rohter, "Cedras Will Step Down Today, Haitian Military Officials Say," *New York Times*, October 10, 1994, http://www.nytimes.com/1994/10/10/world/cedras-will-step-down-today-haitian-military-officials-say.html?scp=1&sq=Raoul+Cedras&st=nyt.

[16] William J. Clinton, "Remarks at the Dedication of the Thomas J. Dodd Archives and Research Center in Storrs, Connecticut, October 15, 1995," *Public Papers of the Presidents of the United States: William J. Clinton* (1995), books 1 and 2, 1593.

[17] "No prosecution may be commenced under this Statute arising from a situation which is being dealt with by the Security Council as a threat to or breach of the peace or an act of aggression under Chapter VII of the Charter, unless the Security Council otherwise decides." Working Group on a Draft Statute for an International Criminal Court, "Report of the Working Group," United Nations General Assembly International Law Commission, July 14, 1994, Article 23(3).

[18] U.S. State Department, "U.S. Delegation Draft: State Practice Regarding Amnesties and Pardons" (August 1997), http://www.iccnow.org/documents/USDrafton AmnestiesPardons.pdf.

[19] William J. Clinton, "Remarks to Genocide Victims in Kigali, Rwanda, March 25, 1998," *Public Papers of the Presidents of the United States: William J. Clinton* (1998), book 1, 431.

[20] Barbara Crossette, "Helms Vows to Make War on U.N. Courts," *New York Times*, March 27, 1998, A9.

[21] Eric Schmitt, "Pentagon Battles Plans for International War Crimes Tribunal," *New York Times*, April 14, 1998, A11, http://www.nytimes.com/1998/04/14/world/pentagon-battles-plans-for-international-war-crimes-tribunal.html?pagewanted=1.

[22] United Nations, Rome Statute of the International Criminal Court, July 17, 1998, Article 5(2) and 123(1). Such amendments were achieved at the Kampala Review Conference of the Rome Statute of the International Criminal Court, convened from May 31 to June 11, 2010. See "The Crime of Aggression," Resolution RC/Res. 6 (June 28, 2010), adopted by the Assembly of States Parties of the International Criminal Court on June 11, 2010; David Scheffer, "States Parties Approve New Crimes for International Criminal Court," *ASIL Insights* 14(16) (June 22, 2010), http://www.asil.org/insights100622.cfm; David Scheffer, "Aggression Is Now a Crime," *International Herald Tribune*, July 1, 2010, 8; David Scheffer, "The Complex Crime of Aggression under the Rome Statute," *Leiden Journal of International Law* 23 (2010): 897; David Scheffer, "The Crime of Aggression," in *Beyond Kampala: Next*

Steps for U.S. Principled Engagement with the International Criminal Court, ed. Rachel Gore, 87 (ASIL Discussion Paper, November 2010), http://asil.org/pdfs/2010_beyond_Kampala.pdf.

[23] United Nations, Rome Statute of the International Criminal Court, July 17, 1998, Article 8.

[24] "Report of the Preparatory Commission for the International Criminal Court, Addendum: Finalized Draft Text of the Elements of Crimes," U.N. Doc. PCNICC/2000/INF/3/Add.2 (2000).

[25] United Nations, Rome Statute of the International Criminal Court, July 17, 1998, Article 13(c) and 15.

[26] See the original American Service-Members' Protection Act. See also the amended acts: John Warner National Defense Authorization Act for Fiscal Year 2007, U.S. Public Law 109-364, October 17, 2006, § 1222 (amending the act to remove International Military Education and Training [IMET] restrictions); National Defense Authorization Act for Fiscal Year 2008, U.S. Public Law 110-181, January 28, 2008, § 1212 (amending the act to eliminate restrictions on Foreign Military Financing [FMF] assistance laws). The prohibition on the provision of economic support funds for countries that supported the International Criminal Court, Consolidated Appropriations Act, U.S. Public Law 108-447, December 8, 2004, § 574 (the "Nethercutt Amendment") expired on September 30, 2008, and was not renewed in the Fiscal Year 2009 Omnibus Appropriations Act, U.S. Public Law 111-8, which was signed into law by President Barack Obama on March 11, 2009.

[27] Mary Beth Sheridan, "Clinton Regrets U.S. Not Part of Court," *Washington Post*, August 7, 2009, http://www.washingtonpost.com/wp-dyn/content/article/2009/08/06/AR2009080603763.html.

Chapter Eight: Futile Endgame

[1] William Richardson, U.S. Ambassador to the United Nations, "Remarks at the Opening Plenary Session of the United Nations Diplomatic Conference of Plenipotentiaries on the Establishment of an International Criminal Court," Rome, Italy, June 16, 1998.

[2] U.S. Delegation to the Rome Conference, "Statement Expressing Concerns Regarding the Proposal for a Proprio Motu Prosecutor," June 22, 1998, 147–149, http://www.iccnow.org/documents/1stSesPrepComSenatecfr.pdf.

[3] See David Scheffer and Caroline Kaeb, "The Five Levels of CSR Compliance: The Resiliency of Corporate Liability under the Alien Tort Statute and the Case for a Counterattack Strategy in Compliance Theory," *Berkeley Journal of International Law* 29 (2011): 334–397; Ralph G. Steinhardt, Paul L. Hoffman, and Christopher N. Camponovo, *International Human Rights Lawyering: Cases and Materials* (Eagan, Minnesota: West, 2008), 661–743.

[4] United Nations, Rome Statute of the International Criminal Court, July 17, 1998, Article 8(2)(b)(xxvi) and 8(2)(e)(vii).

[5] Ibid., Article 8(2)(b)(viii).

[6] See Geneva Convention IV Relative to the Protection of Civilian Persons in Time of War, August 12, 1949, Article 49: "The Occupying Power shall not deport or transfer parts of its own civilian population into the territory it occupies."

[7] U.S. Delegation to the Rome Conference, "Statement on Article 11bis—Preliminary Rulings Regarding Admissibility," April 3, 1998, 145–146, http://www.iccnow.org/documents/1stSesPrepComSenatecfr.pdf; United States of America, Preparatory Committee on the Establishment of an International Criminal Court, Working Group on Complementarity and Trigger Mechanism, "Proposal on Article 11bis Preliminary Rulings Regarding Admissibility," March 25, 1998, 147, http://www.iccnow.org/documents/1stSesPrepComSenatecfr.pdf.

[8] See note 4 above, Article 77.

[9] United Nations Diplomatic Conference of Plenipotentiaries on the Establishment of an International Criminal Court, "Consideration of the Bureau Discussion Paper on Part 2: Jurisdiction, Admissibility and Applicable Law," Rome, Italy, July 9, 1998, 209.

[10] United Nations, "Draft Statute for an International Criminal Court," *Report of the International Law Commission on the Work of its Forty-Sixth Session*, U.N. Doc. A/49/10, July 22, 1994, 83.

[11] United Nations Diplomatic Conference of Plenipotentiaries on the Establishment of an International Criminal Court, *Summary Records of the Plenary Meetings and of the Meetings of the Committee of the Whole Official Records*, vol. 2 (Rome: United Nations, 1998), 298.

[12] "Undermining an International Court," *New York Times*, July 15, 1998, A18.

[13] David J. Scheffer, "Status of Negotiations on the Establishment of an International Criminal Court," U.S. Department of State, July 15, 1998, http://www.state.gov/www/policy_remarks/1998/980715_scheffer_icc.html; Alessandra Stanley, "U.S. Presses Allies to Rein in Proposed War Crimes," *New York Times*, July 15, 1998, A8.

[14] United States of America, "Proposal Regarding Article 7ter," in *Official Records*, vol. 3, *United Nations Diplomatic Conference of Plenipotentiaries on the Establishment of an International Criminal Court* (Rome: United Nations, 1998), 249.

[15] Ibid., 361.

[16] "Annan Faults U.S. and 9 Other Lands in Debate in Court," *New York Times*, July 14, 1998, A7.

[17] United States of America, "Proposal," U.N. Doc. A/CONF.183/C.1/L.70, July 14, 1998.

[18] United States of America, "Proposal," U.N. Doc. A/CONF.183/C.1/L.90, July 16, 1998, Article 7.

[19] United States of America, "Proposal Regarding Article 7ter,", 362.

[20] William Schabas, *An Introduction to the International Criminal Court*, 4th ed. (Cambridge: Cambridge University Press, 2011), 21.

[21] "Resolution E," in *Official Records*, vol. 1, *United Nations Diplomatic Conference of Plenipotentiaries on the Establishment of an International Criminal Court* (Rome: United Nations, 1998), 71–72.

[22] "Final Act of the United Nations Diplomatic Conference of Plenipotentiaries on the Establishment of an International Criminal Court," in ibid., 65–79.

Chapter Nine: Rome's Aftermath

[1] Alessandra Stanley, "U.S. Presses Allies to Rein in Proposed War Crimes," *New York Times*, July 15, 1998, A8.

[2] David J. Scheffer, U.S. Ambassador at Large for War Crimes Issues, "Address before the University of Oklahoma College of Law, Norman, Oklahoma," February 24, 1998, http://www.state.gov/www/policy_remarks/1998/980224_scheffer_crimes.html.

[3] Anthony Lewis, "At Home Abroad: A Turn in the Road," *New York Times*, July 20, 1998, A15, http://www.nytimes.com/1998/07/20/opinion/at-home-abroad-a-turn -in-the-road.html?pagewanted=1.

[4] Madeleine Albright with William Woodward, *Madam Secretary* (New York: Miramax Books, 2003).

[5] Hon. David J. Scheffer, Ambassador-at-Large for War Crimes Issues, "Is a U.N. International Criminal Court in the U.S. National Interest?" Hearing before the U.S. Senate Subcommittee on International Operations of the Committee on Foreign Relations, July 23, 1998, 12.

[6] These included the Rules of Procedure and Evidence, the Elements of Crimes, the Relationship Agreement between the International Criminal Court and the United Nations, the Agreement on the Privileges and Immunities of the International Criminal Court, the Headquarters Agreement, the Financial Regulations and Rules, the Rules of Procedure of the Assembly of States Parties, and the Rules of Procedure of the Committee on Budget and Finance.

[7] See David Scheffer and Ashley Cox, "The Constitutionality of the Rome Statute of the International Criminal Court," *Journal of Criminal Law and Criminology* 98(3) (Spring 2008): 983–1068.

[8] Barbara Crossette, "U.S. Gains a Compromise on War Crimes Tribunal," *New York Times*, June 30, 2000, A6, http://www.nytimes.com/2000/06/30/world/us-gains-a -compromise-on-war-crimes-tribunal.html?scp=1&sq=June%2030,%202000%20 David%20Scheffer&st=cse.

[9] See David J. Scheffer, "Staying the Course with the International Criminal Court," *Cornell International Law Journal* 35(1) (November 2001–February 2002): 47, 74–87, 99.

[10] Ibid., 78–80. The proposed U.S. text read: "The United Nations and the International Criminal Court agree that the Court may seek the surrender or accept custody of a national who acts within the overall direction of a U.N. Member State, and such directing State has so acknowledged, only in the event (a) the directing State is a State Party to the Statute or the Court obtains the consent of the directing State, or (b) measures have been authorized pursuant to Chapter VII of the U.N. Charter against the directing State in relation to the situation or actions giving rise to the alleged crime or crimes, provided that in connection with such authorization the Security Council has determined that this subsection shall apply."

[11] David Scheffer, Ambassador at Large for War Crimes Issues, "Evolution of U.S. Policy toward the International Criminal Court," Address at American University, Washington, D.C., September 14, 2000, http://www.state.gov/www/policy _remarks/2000/000914_scheffer_au.html.

[12] David J. Scheffer, "The International Criminal Court: The Challenge of Jurisdiction," *American Society of International Law Proceedings, March 24–27, 1999,* 93 (1999): 70–72.

[13] See, e.g., Madeline Morris, "The Jurisdiction of the International Criminal Court over National Non-Party States," *ILSA Journal of International and Comparative Law* 6 (2000): 363–369.

[14] See, e.g., Michael Scharf, "The ICC's Jurisdiction over the Nationals of Non-State Party: A Critique of the U.S. Position," *Law and Contemporary Problems* 64 (2001): 67–114; Jerry Fowler, "The Rome Treaty for an International Criminal Court: A Framework of International Justice for Future Generations," in *International Criminal Law and Its Enforcement: Cases and Materials,* ed. Beth Van Schaack and Ronald C. Slye, 2nd ed. (New York: Foundation Press, 2010), 70.

[15] United Nations, Rome Statute of the International Criminal Court, July 17, 1998, Article 125(1).

[16] See Scheffer, "Staying the Course,", 96–97.

[17] "Report of the Preparatory Commission for the International Criminal Court, Addendum, Finalized Draft Text of the Elements of Crimes," U.N. Doc. PCNICC/2000/INF/3/Add.2, fn. 44.

[18] See Scheffer, "Staying the Course,", 96–97.

[19] Florida Supreme Court, *Gore v. Harris,* December 8, 2000.

[20] "Helms Opposes Clinton's Approval of the ICC Treaty," *Washington File,* January 2, 2001.

[21] Patrick Leahy, U.S. Senator from Vermont, "Statement on the International Criminal Court," December 15, 2000, http://leahy.senate.gov/issues/foreign%20policy/icc-statement.html.

[22] Robert S. McNamara and Benjamin B. Ferencz, "For Clinton's Last Act," *New York Times,* December 12, 2000, A33.

[23] William J. Clinton, "Statement on the Rome Treaty on the International Criminal Court, December 31, 2000," *Public Papers of the Presidents of the United States: William J. Clinton* (2000–2001), book 3, 2816; Alan Baker, Israel Foreign Ministry Legal Advisor, "International Criminal Court Press Briefing," Jerusalem, January 3, 2001, http://www.mfa.gov.il/MFA/MFAArchive/2000_2009/2001/1/International%20Criminal%20Court%20-%20Press%20Briefing%20by%20I.

[24] Steven Lee Meyers, "U.S. Signs Treaty for World Court to Try Atrocities," *New York Times,* January 1, 2001.

[25] Jesse Helms, U.S. senator from North Carolina, "Press Release on Clinton Signature of the Rome Treaty," Washington, D.C., December 31, 2000.

[26] John Bolton, Under Secretary of State for Arms Control and International Security, "Letter to Kofi Annan, Secretary-General for the United Nations," May 6, 2002, http://www.amicc.org/docs/bolton.pdf; Neil A. Lewis, "U.S. Rejects All Support for New Court on Atrocities," *New York Times,* May 7, 2002, A11, http://www.nytimes.com/2002/05/07/world/us-rejects-all-support-for-new-court-on-atrocities.html?scp=2&sq=May+7%2C+2002+bolton&st=nyt.

[27] Clinton, "Statement on Signature of the International Criminal Court Treaty."

[28] See David J. Scheffer, "How to Turn the Tide Using the Rome Statute's Temporal Jurisdiction," *Journal of International Criminal Justice* 2 (2004): 26–34.

[29] Clinton wrote in his memoirs, "Finally, on the last day of the year, I signed the treaty by which America joined the International Criminal Court. Senator Lott and most Republic senators were strongly opposed to it, fearing that U.S. soldiers sent to foreign lands would be hauled before the court for political purposes. I had been concerned about that, too, but the treaty was now drafted in a manner that I was convinced would prevent that from happening. I had been among the first world leaders to call for an International War Crimes Tribunal, and I thought the United States should support it." Bill Clinton, *My Life* (New York: Random House, 2004), 942–943.

[30] See "Address by former President Bill Clinton before the National Democratic Convention," Boston, July 26, 2004, http://www.americanrhetoric.com/speeches/convention2004/billclinton2004dnc.htm; "Address by former President Bill Clinton before the Democratic Leadership Council," New York University, New York, December 3, 2002, http://www.amicc.org/docs/ClintonDec3_02.pdf; Bill Clinton, "Our Shared Future: Globalization in the 21st Century," Council on Foreign Relations, New York, June 17, 2002, http://www.amicc.org/docs/WJC_CFR.pdf.

[31] Marc Grossman, Under Secretary for Political Affairs, "Remarks to the Center for Strategic and International Studies," Washington, D.C., May 6, 2002, http://www.coalitionfortheicc.org/documents/USUnsigningGrossman6May02.pdf; Pierre-Richard Prosper, U.S. Ambassador for War Crimes Issues, "Foreign Press Center Briefing," Washington, D.C., May 6, 2002, http://www.coalitionfortheicc.org/documents/USProsperUnsigning6May02.pdf; Donald Rumsfeld, Secretary of Defense, "Statement on the ICC Treaty," Washington, D.C., May 6, 2002, http://www.amicc.org/docs/Rumsfeld5_6_02.pdf; Richard Boucher, Spokesman for the U.S. State Department, "Daily Press Briefing," May 6, 2002, http://www.amicc.org/docs/Boucher.pdf; U.S. State Department, Press Release to the United Nations, "Demarche on the US Government Policy on the International Criminal Court from Secretary of State to Ambassadors," May 6, 2002, http://www.amicc.org/docs/Demarche_US.pdf; David E. Sanger, "Bush Renews Pledge to Strike First to Counter Terror Threats," *New York Times*, July 20, 2002, http://www.nytimes.com/2002/07/20/politics/20PREX.html?pagewanted=1.

[32] American Service-Members' Protection Act of 2002, U.S. Public Law 107-206, August 2, 2002; Bush's presidential signing statements prior to signing the act indicate his assault on the court. See "Statement by President George W. Bush upon Signing H.R. 3338," *Weekly Compilation of Presidential Documents* 38 (January 10, 2002): 46; "Statement by President George W. Bush upon Signing H.R. 2500," *Weekly Compilation of Presidential Documents* 37 (November 28, 2001): 1723.

Chapter Ten: Crime Scene Kosovo

[1] See, e.g., International Criminal Tribunal for the former Yugoslavia, "Judgement Summary For Milutinović et al.," United Nations Press Release, February 26, 2009, http://www.icty.org/x/cases/milutinovic/tjug/en/090226summary.pdf.

[2] The Honorable David J. Scheffer, U.S. Ambassador-at-Large for War Crimes Issues, "U.S. Policy on International Criminal Tribunals," *American University International Law Review* 13 (1998): 1383, 1389–1400.

[3] David Binder, "Bush Warns Serbs Not to Widen War," *New York Times*, December 28, 1992, A6, http://www.nytimes.com/1992/12/28/world/bush-warns-serbs-not-to-widen-war.html?scp=48&sq=December%201992%20Milosevic&st=cse.

[4] International Criminal Tribunal for the former Yugoslavia, "Communication from the Prosecutor to the Contact Group Members," Office of the Prosecutor, July 7, 1998, http://www.icty.org/sid/7656.

[5] Mike O'Connor, "Kosovo Assault Steps Up, Making Thousands More Homeless," *New York Times*, August 4, 1998, A3, http://www.nytimes.com/1998/08/04/world/kosovo-assault-steps-up-making-thousands-more-homeless.html?scp=22&sq=August%201998%20fighting%20kosovo&st=cse.

[6] Philip Shenon, "U.S. Says It Might Consider Attacking Serbs," *New York Times*, March 13, 1998, http://www.nytimes.com/1998/03/13/world/us-says-it-might-consider-attacking-serbs.html.

[7] Human Rights Watch, "Human Rights Watch Condemns Yugoslav Obstruction of War Crimes Investigations," October 9, 1998, http://www.hrw.org/en/news/1998/10/09/human-rights-watch-condemns-yugoslav-obstruction-war-crimes-investigations.

[8] "Mutilated Kosovo Bodies Found after Serb Attack," *New York Times*, January 17, 1999, 11, http://www.nytimes.com/1999/01/17/world/mutilated-kosovo-bodies-found-after-serb-attack.html?scp=3&sq=Racak&st=cse.

[9] "Belgrade Hints at 'New Decision' on Walker Expulsion," Agence France Presse, January 21, 1999.

[10] Jane Perlez, "U.S. to Push NATO to Issue Ultimatum to Serb Leader," *New York Times*, January 21, 1999, A3, http://www.nytimes.com/1999/01/21/world/us-to-push-nato-to-issue-ultimatum-to-serb-leader.html?scp=1&sq=Arbour%20border%20Macedonia&st=cse.

[11] United Nations Security Council, "Security Council Strongly Condemns Massacre of Kosovo Albanians in Southern Kosovo," Press Release 6288, January 19, 1999, http://www.un.org/News/Press/docs/1999/19990119.sc6628.html.

[12] "Finnish Experts to Probe Massacre," *Tribune India*, January 21, 1999; see the report at "Report of the EU Forensic Expert Team on the Racak Incident," March 17, 1999, http://web.archive.org/web/19991116063236/http://www.usia.gov/regional/eur/balkans/kosovo/texts/racak.htm.

[13] Statement by the North Atlantic Council, cited in Tim Judah, *Kosovo: War and Revenge* (New Haven: Yale University Press, 2000), 195.

[14] Carlotta Gall, "U.S. Official Sees 'Collision Course' in Kosovo Dispute," *New York Times*, March 10, 1999, A1.

[15] Madeleine Albright with William Woodward, *Madam Secretary* (New York: Miramax Books, 2003), 406–410.

[16] Independent International Commission on Kosovo, "The Kosovo Report" (2000), 4, http://www.reliefweb.int/library/documents/thekosovoreport.htm.

[17] In February 1999, I participated in the U.S. Pacific Command's annual conference for military legal officers from throughout the Pacific theater, including America's allies there. A Defense Department lawyer offered a rationale to justify the use

of military force in Kosovo if that became necessary. He conceded that there was no Security Council resolution expressly authorizing use of force in Kosovo. But the lawyer from the general counsel's staff invoked several factors: First, if the Security Council cannot act effectively, then a regional group like NATO should not be prevented from acting. He cited the Uniting for Peace resolution, the Organization of American States' resolution during the Cuban missile crisis in 1962, and the Organization of Eastern Caribbean States' request for intervention into Grenada in 1982. Second, there was a threat to regional peace and security in Kosovo. The entire area could erupt in sustained armed conflict. This threat had already been recognized by the Security Council, and Resolution 1199 invoked Chapter VII authority while affirming the threat to international peace and security. Third, the presence of NATO forces in Bosnia gave NATO a special role in the crisis in Kosovo. There was a real threat of a humanitarian catastrophe. While the United States was leery of humanitarian interventions because they could lead to a slippery slope for illegal armed interventions, there was no longer any doubt that a real humanitarian threat had emerged in Kosovo. He argued that all these factors provided a persuasive argument for the use of force by NATO.

[18] U.S. Defense Department, "Secretary Cohen's Press Conference at NATO Headquarters," April 7, 1999, http://www.defense.gov/transcripts/transcript.aspx?transcriptid=582.

[19] See Samantha Power, *"A Problem from Hell": America and the Age of Genocide* (New York: Basic Books, 2003), 467–468.

[20] U.S. Department of State, "Report on the Visit of Ambassador Scheffer to the Border Between the Former Republic of Macedonia and Kosovo April 1–2 and Refugee Accounts of Atrocities," April 7, 1999; "The Ground War," *Washington Post*, March 28, 1999, B06; John K. Roth, "After-Words: Post Holocaust Struggles with Restitution and Genocide Prevention," *Whittier Law Review* 24 (Summer 2003): 899, 905.

[21] David Scheffer, Ambassador-at-Large for War Crimes Issues, "On-the-Record Briefing on Atrocities in Kosovo Released by the Office of the Spokesman," U.S. Department of State, Washington, D.C., April 9, 1999, http://www.state.gov/www/policy_remarks/1999/990409_scheffer_kosovo.html.

[22] The information conveyed in the next four paragraphs was reported in my April 9, 1999, briefing with the press. Ibid.

[23] Wesley Clark, *Waging Modern War: Bosnia, Kosovo, and the Future of Combat* (New York: Public Affairs): 268–292.

[24] Ibid.

[25] International Criminal Tribunal for the former Yugoslavia, "Rules of Procedure and Evidence," U.N. Doc. IT/32/Rev. 12, November 12, 1997, Rule 70, http://www.icty.org/x/file/Legal%20Library/Rules_procedure_evidence/IT032_rev12_en.pdf.

[26] Marlise Simons of the *New York Times* accurately portrayed the dilemma faced by tribunal prosecutors and American officials and others: "Tribunal officials have said that even as Western political leaders were promising to provide detailed evidence

to the court, the tribunal found itself hampered by a lack of information about the Yugoslav high command that only government agencies can supply, like orders issued to commit atrocities. In many cases, such orders can be best documented through classified intelligence, like electronic surveillance, that governments have either been reluctant to share or have hesitated to allow to be presented in open court because of their fear of exposing intelligence-gathering methods. Prosecutors have been gathering such classified evidence to indict President Slobodan Milosevic and the Yugoslav high command.... In recent weeks ... tribunal officials have been saying that they cannot work effectively unless they get more cooperation. They say it is one thing for politicians to say who is in command and who is responsible for war crimes in Kosovo, as American and NATO spokesmen have done recently, but it is another thing to demonstrate that in court. Prosecutors need to provide the evidence to establish responsibility." Marlise Simons, "Crisis in the Balkans: The Tribunal; U.S. and Britain, after Complaints, Vow to Give War Court Data on Top Yugoslavs," *New York Times*, April 18, 1999, A14.

[27] See, for example, U.S. Department of State, "Fact Sheet: Ethnic Cleansing in Kosovo," April 1, 1999, http://www.ess.uwe.ac.uk/kosovo/Kosovo-Ethnic_Cleansing1 .htm; an archive of most of the reports may be found in the U.S. Department of State, *Erasing History: Ethnic Cleansing in Kosovo*, May 1999, http://www.state.gov/ www/regions/eur/rpt_9905_ethnic_ksvo_toc.html.

[28] U.S. Department of State, "Report: Ethnic Cleansing in Kosovo," March 31, 1999.

[29] David Scheffer, interview, *Fox News Sunday*, April 18, 1999.

[30] William S. Cohen, interview, *Meet the Press*, April 18, 1999.

[31] See Power, *"A Problem from Hell"*, 468–470.

[32] T. R. Reid, "NATO Builds 'Slaughterhouse' Case," *Washington Post*, April 21, 1999, A20.

[33] Secretary of State Madeleine K. Albright and Justice Louise Arbour, "International Criminal Tribunal for the Former Yugoslavia Joint Press Conference," U.S. Department of State, Office of Spokesman, Washington, D.C., April 30, 1999.

[34] "FBI to Send Forensic Team to Kosovo," CNN, June 12, 1999, http://www.cnn .com/US/9906/12/war.crimes.02/.

[35] Mary Robinson, High Commissioner for Human Rights, Report on the Human Rights Situation Involving Kosovo, submitted to the United Nations General Assembly, April 30, 1999, http://www.unhchr.ch/Huricane/Huricane.nsf/60a520ce334aaa 77802566100031b4bf/06d1ffba87251da1802567630038ce3b?OpenDocument.

[36] U.S. Department of State, *Erasing History*.

[37] Julia Taft, Harold Koh, and Ambassador David Scheffer, "Briefing Upon the Release of the Report *Erasing History: Ethnic Cleansing in Kosovo*," U.S. State Department, Washington, D.C., May 10, 1999.

[38] William Brannigan, "Secret U.S. Information Helped Tribunal Indict Yugoslav Officials," *Washington Post*, May 28, 1999.

[39] See Albright with Woodward, *Madam Secretary*, 419: "There were those who were nervous about Milošević's indictment, feeling that it would mean we couldn't negotiate with him. I was not in that camp. I was gratified by the indictments."

[40] See Taylor Branch, *The Clinton Tapes: Wrestling History with the President* (New York: Simon & Schuster, 2009), 550: "[Clinton] thought the indictment of President Milosevic for war crimes, on May 27, reinforced Serbia's isolation from world standards."

[41] North Atlantic Treaty Organization, "NATO's Role in Kosovo," http://www.nato.int/cps/en/natolive/topics_48818.htm.

[42] "NATO's Clark, Solana Make First Visit to Kosovo," CNN, June 24, 1999.

[43] See, e.g., Scheffer, "On-the-Record Briefing on Atrocities in Kosovo."

[44] U.S. Department of State, *Ethnic Cleansing in Kosovo: An Accounting* (Washington, D.C.: U.S. Department of State, December 1999), http://www.state.gov/www/global/human_rights/kosovoii/homepage.html; "UN Gives Figure for Kosovo Dead," *BBC News*, November 10, 1999, http://news.bbc.co.uk/2/hi/europe/514828.stm.

[45] Emma Daly, "Dossier of 'NATO' Crimes Lands in Prosecutor's Lap," *The Observer*, December 26, 1999, http://www.guardian.co.uk/world/1999/dec/26/theobserver2.

[46] Office of the Prosecutor, "Final Report to the Prosecutor by the Committee Established to Review the NATO Bombing Campaign against the Federal Republic of Yugoslavia," International Criminal Tribunal for the former Yugoslavia, June 13, 2000, http://www.icty.org/sid/10052.

[47] See David Halberstam, *War in a Time of Peace: Bush, Clinton, and the Generals* (New York: Simon & Schuster, 2001), 423–425, 462–466, 473–478; Wesley K. Clark, *Waging Modern War* (New York: Public Affairs, 2001), 268–292.

Chapter Eleven: Freetown Is Burning

[1] AFRC Trial Chamber decision, para. 1463.

[2] RUF Appeals Chamber decision, para. 353.

[3] 105th U.S. Congress, 2nd session, "African Growth and Opportunity Act," U.S. Library of Congress, July 31, 1998, §§ 1004(a)(1) and (a)(1)(B), 1009 (18).

[4] See Nicolas Cook, "Liberia: Current Issues and United States Policy," CRS Issues Brief for Congress, September 26, 2000, http://www.ncseonline.org/NLE/CRS reports/international/inter-66.cfm?&CFID=8576637&CFTOKEN=34834956.

[5] Madeleine Albright with William Woodward, *Madam Secretary* (New York: Miramax Books, 2003), 397–405; David Halberstam, *War in a Time of Peace: Bush, Clinton, and the Generals* (New York: Simon & Schuster, 2001), 420–421.

[6] The Krukenberg procedure was used with many mutilated victims in Sierra Leone. F. Irmay, B. Merzouga, and D. Vettorel, "The Krukenberg Procedure: A Surgical Option for the Treatment of Double Hand Amputees in Sierra Leone," *Lancet* 356(9235) (September 23, 2000): 1072–1075.

[7] U.N. Security Council, "Special Report of the Secretary General of the United Nations Observer Mission in Sierra Leone," January 7, 1999, http://daccess-dds-ny.un.org/doc/UNDOC/GEN/N99/002/20/IMG/N9900220.pdf?OpenElement.

[8] *Sierra Leone News*, February 11, 1999, http://www.sierra-leone.org/Archives/slnews 0299.html; Embassy of Sierra Leone, Press Release, February 15, 1999, http://www.sierra-leone.org/GOSL/Embassy-Statements.pdf, 68.21.

[9] "Sierra Leone Talks Peace," *Economist*, June 5, 1999, 44.

[10] The Government of the Republic of Sierra Leone and The Revolutionary United Front of Sierra Leone, Lomé Peace Agreement, July 7, 1999, IX; see also the United Nations Security Council, Resolution 1260, August 20, 1999, which welcomed the Lomé Agreement and commended the Sierra Leonean government for it.

[11] U.N. secretary-general Kofi Annan rejected the amnesty provision: "As in other peace accords, many compromises were necessary in the Lomé Peace Agreement. As a result, some of the terms which this peace has been obtained, in particular the provisions on amnesty, are difficult to reconcile with the goal of ending the culture of impunity, which inspired the creation of the United Nations Tribunals for Rwanda and the Former Yugoslavia, and the future International Criminal Court. Hence the instruction to my Special Representative to enter a reservation when he signed the peace agreement stating that, for the United Nations, the amnesty cannot cover international crimes of genocide, crimes against humanity, war crimes and other serious violations of international humanitarian law." U.N. Doc. S/1999/836 (July 30, 1999), para. 54. The reasoning behind the amnesty reservation is outlined in Priscilla Hayner, *Negotiating Peace in Sierra Leone: Confronting the Justice Challenge* (Geneva, Switzerland: Center for Humanitarian Dialogue, 2007), 17, http://www.ictj.org/static/Africa/SierraLeone/HaynerSL1207.eng.pdf. The U.N. reservation was reaffirmed by the U.N. Security Council in the establishment resolution of the Special Court for Sierra Leone. See United Nations Security Council, Resolution 1315. "On the Situation in Sierra Leone," August 14, 2000, fifth preambular clause: "*Recalling* that Special Representative of the Secretary-General appended to his signature of the Lomé Agreement a statement that the United Nations holds the understanding that the amnesty provisions of the Agreement shall not apply to international crimes of genocide, crimes against humanity, war crimes and other serious violations of international humanitarian law."

[12] United Nations Security Council, Resolution 1289, "Expansion of Sierra Leone Mission," February 7, 2000, 5.

[13] United Nations Security Council, Resolution 1171, June 5, 1998, 5, http://daccess-dds-ny.un.org/doc/UNDOC/GEN/N98/157/81/PDF/N9815781.pdf.

[14] *Sierra Leone News*, February 29, 2000, http://www.sierra-leone.org/Archives/slnews0200.html; Press Release, "No Country Found to Take Sankoh for Medical Treatment," Special Court for Sierra Leone, June 11, 2003, http://www.sc-sl.org/LinkClick.aspx?fileticket=8zYVLpYWViU%3D&tabid=114.

[15] Sebastian Junger, "Terror Recorded," *Vanity Fair*, October 2000, http://www.vanityfair.com/politics/features/2000/10/junger200010.

[16] Ahmad Tejan Kabbah, President of Sierra Leone, "Letter to Kofi Annan, United Nations Secretary-General," S/2000/786, annex, June 12, 2000.

[17] Ibid.

[18] United Nations Security Council, Resolution 1315, August 14, 2000, http://www.ictj.org/static/Africa/SierraLeone/sres.1315.2000.eng.pdf.

[19] Ibid., 8(c); Secretary-General Kofi Annan, "Report of the Secretary-General on the Establishment of a Special Court for Sierra Leone," U.N. Doc. S/2000/915, October 4, 2000.

[20] The statute explicitly targeted such actions. See United Nations and the Government of Sierra Leone, Statute of the Special Court for Sierra Leone, January 16, 2002, Article 1(1), annex to United Nations and the Government of Sierra Leone, "Agreement between the United Nations and the Government of Sierra Leone on the Establishment of a Special Court for Sierra Leone," January 16, 2002.

[21] Ibid., Article 1(2).

[22] Ibid., Article 1(3).

[23] Ibid., Article 4(c).

[24] Ibid., Article 5(a).

[25] Ibid., Article 7(1).

[26] Ibid., Article 7(2).

[27] Ibid., Article 19(1).

[28] Ibid., Article 15(4).

[29] Annan wrote: "in the absence of any indication as to whether funds are likely to be made available for the start-up of the Court and its sustained operation thereafter ... I would, therefore, propose that the process of establishing the Court shall not commence until the U.N. Secretariat has obtained sufficient contributions in hand to finance the establishment of the Court and 12 months of its operation, and pledges equal to the anticipated expenses of the following 24 months. This extension by a further 12 months of the Council's proposal would provide a basis for a functioning Court over three years which, in my view, is the minimum time required for the investigation, prosecution and trial of a very limited number of accused. I suggest, therefore, that as soon as an agreement in principle is reached between Members of the Security Council, the Secretary-General and the Government of Sierra Leone, I will launch an appeal to all States to indicate, within a reasonable period of time, their willingness to contribute funds, personnel and services to the Special Court for Sierra Leone and to specify the scope and extent of their contributions. Upon receipt of concrete information, I will be able to assess whether the process of establishing the Special Court may commence or whether the matter should revert to the Council to explore alternate means of financing the Court." Kofi Annan, Secretary-General of the United Nations, "Letter to the United Nations Security Council," S/2001/40, January 12, 2001, para. 12.

[30] "The Mysterious Death of a Fugitive," *The Perspective*, May 7, 2003, http://www.theperspective.org/fugitivebockarie.html. One witness at Charles Taylor's trial testified how she found out that Sam Bockarie was dead and that Charles Taylor had ordered him killed. *Prosecutor of the Special Court for Sierra Leone v. Charles Ghankay Taylor*, "Transcript," Trial Chamber II, September 9, 2008, 15766:8–15769:29, http://www.sc-sl.org/LinkClick.aspx?fileticket=qa8o6VIePBg=&tabid=160.

[31] *The Prosecutor of the Special Court for Sierra Leone v. Morris Kallon et al.*, SCSL-2004-15-AR72(E), "Decision on Challenge to Jurisdiction: Lomé Accord Amnesty, March 13, 2004.

[32] *Prosecutor v. Taylor*, SCSL-04-04-I, "Decision on Immunity from Jurisdiction," May 31, 2004, para. 53 (Appeals Chamber), http://www.sc-sl.org/CASES/Prosecutorvs CharlesTaylor/AppealsChamberDecisions/tabid/191/Default.aspx.

[33] *Prosecutor of the Special Court for Sierra Leone v. Sesay*, "Judgement," Trial Chamber I, March 2, 2009, 651–654, http://www.sc-sl.org/LinkClick.aspx?fileticket=D5HojR8 FZS4%3d&tabid=215.

[34] Ibid., 23.

[35] Ibid., 320, 344, 401, 477, 581.

[36] Ibid., 391.

Chapter Twelve: The Toughest Cockfight

[1] Catherine Filloux, *Silence of God* (2007), reprinted from Catherine Filloux, *Silence of God and Other Plays* (New York: Seagull Books, 2009), 212. All rights reserved. Used by permission. Seagull Books © 2009.

[2] *The Killing Fields*, Warner Brothers, 1984.

[3] David Scheffer, "Letter: The Benefits of a U.S. Presence in Hanoi," *New York Times*, July 19, 1984, A22; David Scheffer, "Should the U.S. Recognize Vietnam?" *Asian Wall Street Journal*, May 15, 1984, 8 (republished as "Reagan's Do-Nothing Vietnam Policy," in *Asian Wall Street Journal Weekly*, May 28, 1984, 10); David Scheffer, "Normalization: Time for a U.S. Initiative," *World Policy Journal* 3(1) (Winter 1985/1986): 127–141.

[4] "Law on the Establishment of Extraordinary Chambers in the Courts of Cambodia for the Prosecution of Crimes Committed during the Period of Democratic Kampuchea," Reach Kram NS/RKM/0801/12, August 10, 2001, amended by "Law on Amendments to Article 2, Article 3, Article 9, Article 10, Article 11, Article 14, Article 17, Article 18, Article 20, Article 21, Article 22, Article 23, Article 24, Article 27, Article 29, Article 31, Article 33, Article 34, Article 35, Article 36, Article 37, Article 39, Article 40, Article 42, Article 43, Article 44, Article 45, Article 46, and Article 47 of the "Law on the Establishment of the Extraordinary Chambers in the Courts of Cambodia for the Prosecution of Crimes Committed during the Period of Democratic Kampuchea," NS/RKM/1004/006, October 5, 2004, http://www.cambodia .gov.kh/krt/pdfs/Kram%20and%20KR%20Law%20amendments%2027%20 Oct%202004%20—%20Eng.pdf [Tribunal Law].

[5] The United Nations and the Royal Government of Cambodia, "Agreement Between the United Nations and the Royal Government of Cambodia Concerning the Prosecution Uunder Cambodian Law of Crimes Committed Dduring the Period of Democratic Kampuchea," June 6, 2003, http://www.eccc.gov.kh/english/cabinet/ agreement/5/Agreement_between_UN_and_RGC.pdf [U.N./Cambodia Agreement].

[6] 103rd U.S. Congress, "Cambodian Genocide Justice Act," Public Law 103-236, April 30, 1994, section 572(b)(2).

[7] United Nations Commission on Human Rights, "Situation of Human Rights in Cambodia," Resolution 1997/49, April 11, 1997, http://www.unhchr.ch/Huridocda/ Huridoca.nsf/TestFrame/ee74e24f4834b57a8025664800550026?Opendocument.

[8] Prince Norodom Ranariddh and Hun Sen, "Letter to Kofi Annan, United Nations Secretary-General," U.N.Doc. A/51/930-S/1997/488, June 24, 1997, http://www .khmerinstitute.org/docs/UNKRreportx.htm.

[9] "Rebels Again Claim Pol Pot Arrested," *Advertiser*, June 21, 1997.

[10] "General: Pol Pot Is Still Alive; The Khmer Rouge Leader Is Being Held at the Rebels' Base, He Said, and Would Be Turned Over Soon," *Philadelphia Inquirer*, June, 23, 1997, A03.

[11] "Tyrant Pol Pot Alive and to be Handed Over Shortly," *The Observer*, June 22, 1997, 3.

[12] See Elizabeth Becker, *When the War Was Over: Cambodia and the Khmer Rouge Revolution* (New York: Public Affairs, 1998), 268–269, 294–295, 304, 307–308.

[13] Cambodian Prime Ministers Ung Huot and Samdech Hun Sen, "Letter to United States President Bill Clinton," November 27, 1997, http://www.embassy.org/cambodia/pressrelease/press97/1201.htm.

[14] Philip Shenon and Eric Schmitt, "U.S. Is Planning a Move to Seize Pol Pot for Trial," *New York Times*, April 9, 1998, A1.

[15] Ibid.

[16] Puangthong Rungswasdisab, "Thailand's Response to Cambodian Genocide," http://www.yale.edu/cgp/thailand_response.html.

[17] Chris Fontaine reported in "US Sets Its Sights on the Remaining KR Cadre," *Phnom Penh Post*, April 24, 1998, 9, the following: "Should Ta Mok, Nuon Chea and Khieu Samphan be flushed out by the government army, Thai Prime Minister Chuan Leekpai has pledged that they will be arrested if they cross into Thailand. On April 17 Chuan appeared to suggest that was as much as his nation could help since Thailand had a policy of non-interference in Cambodia's internal affairs. But Chuan's words rang hollow on the Thai-Cambodian border where the Thai military was a constant presence inside Cambodia as the events of Pol Pot's death unfolded. Non-interference may keep the Thais from arresting rebel leaders on Cambodian soil, but it did not stop them from arranging media coverage of Pol Pot's corpse and cremation, taking and hoarding flimsy forensic evidence or remaining in apparent constant friendly contact with Pol Pot's KR keepers."

[18] "Pol Pot Committed Suicide," Associated Press, in *Tribune India*, January 22, 1999, http://www.tribuneindia.com/1999/99jan22/world.htm#6: "Khmer Rouge sources told [Nate] Thayer in this week's *Review* that Ta Mok, the one-legged general who became Khmer Rouge leader, offered to turn Pol Pot over to the United States last March. The offer came as the last Khmer Rouge strongholds were falling under government attack. Lacking an indictment, an arrest warrant or a court order on which to try the aged rebel leader, the Americans refused, the *Review* said." The press release continued, with greater accuracy: "The offer set off a furious behind-the-scenes effort in Washington to establish grounds for an arrest and find a country willing to hold Pol Pot while a trial could be arranged. But in mid-April, Pol Pot died. The Khmer Rouge said the cause was a heart attack, though there was speculation he was murdered by former followers. His body was cremated without an autopsy. Khmer Rouge sources recently told Thayer, however, that Pol Pot committed suicide after hearing of Ta Mok's plans to turn him over on the Voice of America radio. According to the *Review*, Pol Pot took an overdose of anti-malarial pills and tranquilizers April 15 to avoid being taken alive."

[19] "Clinton to Pursue Khmer Leaders," Associated Press, April 17, 1998.

[20] Elizabeth Becker, "Pol Pot's Death Won't End U.S. Pursuit of His Associates," *New York Times*, April 17, 1998, A15.

[21] The first tier consisted of Nuon Chea (Pol Pot's right-hand man), Ta Mok, Khieu Samphan (president of Democratic Kampuchea, who controlled the prisons), Ieng Sary (foreign minister, "Brother No. 2"), Ke Pauk (commander of the Northern Zone), and Kang Kek Iev (alias Duch). The second tier consisted of Khun Vat (Duch's deputy, who carried out executions at Tuol Sleng Prison), Mam Nai (interrogator at Tuol Sleng), Than Sin Hean (deputy interrogator at Tuol Sleng), Ieng Therith (Ieng Sary's wife, who directed a death camp), Ny Korn (first chief of Tuol Sleng), Sau Met (oversaw S-21), Khat Raen (chairman of Route 1 Battlefield), Khe Muth (commanded death troops), and Sam Bith (commanded death troops).

[22] The statement began as follows: "The Royal Government of Cambodia had earlier requested the UN Secretary General and President Bill Clinton [on November 27, 1997] to help setting up an international tribunal to try the Khmer rouge [*sic*] leadership responsible for crimes of genocide committed between 1975 and 1979, crimes against humanity and other related war crimes." The statement concluded as follows: "The Royal Government of Cambodia is most grateful to the international community for any assistance designed to bring about a successful conclusion for … the long overdue trial of the Khmer Rouge leaders responsible for crimes of genocide in Cambodia." Office of the Spokesman of the Royal Government of Cambodia, "Statement," Phnom Penh, May 6, 1998; Office of the Spokesman of the Royal Government of Cambodia, "Supports [*sic*] for the International Tribunal to Try Pol Pot," in *Cambodia in Review*, Royal Embassy of Cambodia to the United States, vol. 3 (June 1998), 28, http://www.embassy.org/cambodia/newsletter/June98.htm#polpot.

[23] United Nations Commission on Human Rights, Resolution 1998/60, U. N. Doc. E/CN.4/1998/60, April 17, 1998.

[24] United Nations General Assembly, Resolution 52/135, December 12, 1997.

[25] "Report of the Group of Experts for Cambodia Pursuant to General Assembly Resolution 52/125," U.N. Doc. A/53/850, February 18, 1999.

[26] See Samdech Hun Sen, Prime Minister of the Royal Government of Cambodia and Commander-in-Chief of the Cambodian National Armed Forces, "Declaration," Phnom Pehn, Cambodia, January 1, 1999, cited in Seth Mydans, "Cambodian Denies He Opposed Trial for Khmer Rouge," *New York Times*, January 2, 1999, http://www .nytimes.com/1999/01/02/world/cambodian-denies-he-opposed-trial-for-khmer -rouge.html?pagewanted=1: "It is not that I forget to mention about [the trial of the Khmer Rouge leaders]. But I have yet to say because I am now having to talk about peace before anything else in accordance with the need of the nation and people for peace.… My position is that the trial of the Khmer Rouge is a fait accompli and to be proceeded.… To be proceeded, I mean a court that is to be set up at the recommendation of the national and foreign jurists who are actually doing the job. I am one of the people who supports the investigation on the crimes of the Pol Pot's genocide that it definitely be punished. But I am not acting as a plaintiff to accuse this or that person on behalf of the prosecutor seconded to the court. We have to seek answers to various questions such as what type of court to be set up, national or

international? Where shall it be located, in Cambodia or abroad? Will they use Cambodian or foreign judges and prosecutors, or a mixture of both? Will the trial be based on the Cambodian or international laws?, etc. Based upon my minor knowledge, only the prosecutor is entitled to impeach this or that individual.... Based upon the reasons listed above, I decided to welcome Khieu Samphan and Nuon Chea back into the fold of the nation for the sake of putting an end to the war, moving forward the national reconciliation, and also annihilating the political and military organization of the Khmer Rouge."

[27] "Thailand Says Won't Protect Khmer Rouge Leaders," Reuters , January 5, 1999.

[28] ITAR-TASS, January 6, 1999.

[29] Stefan Smith, "PM Asserts Support for Wide-Reaching Tribunal," *Cambodia Daily*, January 18, 1999, 1.

[30] Hun Sen, Samdech Prime Minister of Cambodia, "Letter and Aide Memoire to Kofi Annan, United Nations Secretary-General," January 21, 1999, http://www.cnv.org.kh/cnv_html_pdf/cnv_14.htm.

[31] United Nations Charter, June 26, 1945, Articles 33–38.

[32] Sutin Wannaovorn, Reuters, March 6, 1999. The State Department issued a confirming statement: "Cambodian Prime Minister Hun Sen has informed the U.S. Ambassador in Phnom Penh that former Khmer Rouge leader Ta Mok was captured March 6 near the town of Anlong Veng along the Thai-Cambodian border. Ta Mok has been transported to Phnom Penh where he is now being held by military/judicial authorities. The United States welcomes the capture of Ta Mok as a very positive step by the Cambodian government. The U.S. and Cambodia have been in close contact on this subject for many months. We congratulate the Cambodian government on the success of its operation to apprehend this hardline Khmer Rouge leader. The United States looks forward to further cooperation with the Cambodian government that will bring Ta Mok to justice as soon as possible. As the Secretary of State said recently, it is important that work proceed now on establishment of an international criminal tribunal covering the atrocities of the Pol Pot regime of 1975."

[33] Group of Experts for Cambodia, "Report of the Group of Experts for Cambodia Established Pursuant to General Assembly Resolution 52/135," U.N. Doc. A/53/850, S/1999/231 (March 16, 1999).

[34] Ibid., Annex, 71–72.

[35] Hun Sen, Prime Minister of Cambodia, "Letter to Kofi Annan, United Nations Secretary-General," March 3, 1999, http://www.ngoforum.org.kh/aboutcambodia/Resource_Files/Tribunnal/your_excellency.htm.

[36] Other factors included the negative views of the Chinese government. See Elizabeth Becker, "U.N. Panel Urges Tribunal for Khmer Rouge Leaders," *New York Times*, March 2, 1999, A8.

[37] Keith B. Richburg, "U.S. Wants Tribunal for Top Khmer Rouge; Cambodian Says Trials Could Renew War," *Washington Post*, March 5, 1999, A27: "'We want these top leaders to be brought to justice, and we support an international tribunal,' Albright said at a news conference in Bangkok.... 'We disagree with the point that Hun Sen

and others have made that bringing these people to justice would be destabilizing. To the contrary ... we think it is the only way to reconciliation.' ... Albright, however, said the United States would reject the truth commission formula for the top leaders. It 'is not a substitute for an international tribunal,' she said."

[38] "Last Khmer Rouge Arrest," *New York Times*, March 7, 1999, 15.

[39] On March 19, 1999, Hun Sen issued a declaration welcoming "assistance, including legal experts, from various countries to be able to assist the court of Cambodia in order to try the Khmer Rouge leaders in accordance with the international standard for the sake of justice for all the victims." He reiterated this point in a letter to Annan dated March 24, 1999. Samdech Hun Sen, "Letter to United Nations Secretary General Kofi A. Annan," March 24, 1999, http://www.cnv.org.kh/cnv_html_pdf/cnv_16.htm. See Elizabeth Becker, "Cambodia Spurns U.N. Plan for Khmer Rouge Tribunal," *New York Times*, March 13, 1999, A4.

[40] Hun Sen, Prime Minister of Cambodia, "Letter to Kofi Annan, United Nations Secretary-General," April 28, 1999.

[41] Ambassador Thomas Hammarberg, "Statement to the Press," May 20, 1999, http://cambodia.ohchr.org/download.aspx?ep_id=142: "I have now again met the Prime Minister and his leading advisors on this important issue.... What has emerged is a resolve by the Government that a trial be organized in Cambodia which would meet international standards. The tribunal would be Cambodian and at the same time international in character. The teams of judges and prosecutors would be 'mixed,' both foreigners and Cambodians would be appointed"; Joe Cochrane, "Khmer Rouge's Top Killer Ordered into Protection," *Australian*, May 11, 1999, 9: "Mr. Hammarberg, in an apparent shift of position, said the UN was now flexible on prosecuting rebel leaders under Cambodian law if process met international standards."

[42] Assistant Secretary of State for Public Affairs James Rubin alluded to this American concept in his press briefing of August 12, 1999, when he said: "We believe that credible justice would be best achieved if senior Khmer Rouge leaders were brought before an international tribunal endorsed by the UN. We are continuing our ongoing consultations with the Cambodian Government and in the United Nations on this issue.... We will continue to press for a speedy trial on these charges under international auspices." He went on to describe the United Nations proposal as "a constructive idea" and said that the United States was "working within the UN system to be supportive of it." That meant U.S. officials were exploring how to maintain sufficient international control, preferably through Security Council action, of the tribunal. U.S. Department of State, "Daily Press Briefing" August 12, 1999, http://secretary.state.gov/www/ briefings/9908/990812db.html.

[43] Drawn from a working paper circulated among Security Council members at the July 30, 1999, meeting and shared with the Cambodian government. See Human Rights Watch, "U.N. Should Insist on International Standards for Khmer Rouge Trial," August 24, 1999, http://www.hrw.org/en/news/1999/08/24/un-should-insist-international-standards-khmer-rouge-trial.

[44] Ouch Borith, Permanent United Nations Representative of Cambodia, "Letter to Ralph Zacklin, Deputy Director of the United Nations Office of Legal Affairs,"

August 12, 1999. See "Yale University Cambodia Genocide Project," http://www
.yale.edu/cgp/chron_v3.html.

[45] "Hun Sen Rejects Foreign Majority for Khmer Rouge Trial," Kyodo News Service,
August 17, 1999; Kay Johnson, "UN Team Arrives for Khmer Rouge Talks," *Straight
Times* (Singapore), August 26, 1999, 24: "Said the [Cambodian] government team's
vice-chairman Om Yen Tieng, 'We never said anything about a mixed tribunal. This
is not the affair of the UN. This is a national affair of Cambodia'"); Joe Cochrane,
"Khmer Rouge Trial Hope," *Australian*, August 23, 1999, 7: "Cambodian prime minister Hun Sen has rejected proposals floated by the UN to have the majority of
judges and prosecutors on the tribunal be foreigners."

[46] Cambodia Office of the United Nations High Commissioner for Human Rights,
"Unofficial Transcript of the Press Conference Given by the United Nations Legal
Experts," August 31, 1999.

[47] United Nations Office of Legal Affairs, "History of the Negotiations on the Khmer
Rouge Tribunal between the United Nations and Cambodia: A Chronology," February 8, 2002; "Hun Sen, Annan Hold 'Frank' Talks about Tribunal," Reuters, September 16, 1999; "Putin's Comments Came as the Government Is under Mounting
Pressure to Crack Down on Violence in the Caucasus and around the Country; Co-
lombian Mayor Slain," *Pittsburgh Post-Gazette*, September 20, 1999, A4: "The prime
minister delivered a memo that took a take-it-or-leave-it stance on Cambodia's demand for an existing Cambodian court to try the Khmer Rouge."

[48] Denis Gray, "Cambodian Premier Ready to Try Khmer Rouge with or without
U.N.," Associated Press, November 4, 1999: "The United States has been struggling
to bridge a gap between Cambodia and the United Nations on how to conduct a
tribunal. U.N. experts say the Cambodian court system is underdeveloped and too
politicized to provide a fair trial. Hun Sen endorsed U.S. recommendations that the
contentious issue of control during the trial can be minimized by creating a panel
of judges with a Cambodian majority that would require agreement by at least one
U.N.-supported judge to pass rulings. 'I want to stress that this issue does not need
the approval of the U.N. secretary-general. This law requires no ratification in New
York,' Hun Sen said. 'If the U.N. would like to help us, we would welcome it. But it
cannot be the master of this issue,' Hun Sen said."

[49] I sent a letter dated December 28, 1999, to Hans Corell discussing in detail the
changes that we understood the revised draft included to respond to U.N. concerns.

[50] Kay Johnson, "Compromise Offered on Trial Judges," *South China Morning Post*,
January 12, 2000. I and other U.S. officials had intervened with the Japanese prior
to Prime Minister Obuchi's visit to encourage him to propose creation of a second
coinvestigating judge selected by the U.N. secretary-general.

[51] Hun Sen reconfirmed this with me personally during my meeting with him in
January 2001. The text of Ieng Sary's pardon/amnesty reads in full: "a pardon to Mr.
Ieng Sary, former Deputy Prime Minister in charge of Foreign Affairs in the Govern-
ment of Democratic Kampuchea, for the sentence of death and confiscation of all
his property imposed by order of the People's Revolutionary Tribunal of Phnom
Penh, dated 19 August 1979; and an amnesty for prosecution under the Law to

Outlaw the Democratic Kampuchea Group, promulgated by Reach Kram No. 1, NS 94, dated 14 July 1994." Royal Decree (Reach Kret) NS/RKT/0996/7, September 14, 1996, Article 1 (unofficial translation), http://www.cambodia.gov.kh/krt/pdfs/pardon%20for%20ieng%20sary.pdf.

[52] The United States submitted three nonpapers to the U.N. lawyers during this time period: "Revised Cambodian Draft Legislation for the Cambodian Extraordinary Chamber," January 2, 2000, "Non-paper on the Draft Cambodian Law for Extraordinary Sessions," January 12, 2000, and "Analysis of Draft Law on the Establishment of Extraordinary Chambers in the Courts of Cambodia for the Prosecution of Crimes Committed during the Period of Democratic Kampuchea," February 2, 2000.

[53] Kofi Annan, United Nations Secretary-General, "Letter to Hun Sen, Prime Minister of Cambodia," February 8, 2000; United Nations Legal Counsel, "Press Briefing," February 8, 2000. On February 10, 2000, Hun Sen sent a letter to Annan in which Hun Sen expressed surprise at the gap between the positions of the United Nations and Cambodia and invited U.N. officials to Cambodia for further talks. See "Composite Chronology of the Evolution and Operation of the Extraordinary Chambers in the Courts of Cambodia," *Cambodia Tribunal Monitor*, http://www.cambodia tribunal.org/images/CTM/eccc%20chronology%201994-may%202009.pdf?phpMy Admin=KZTGHmT45FRCAiEg7OLlzXFdNJ4 ["Chronology"].

[54] See "Chronology," note 53 above; Sok An, Chairman of the Council of Ministers of Cambodia, "Letter to Hans Corell, United Nations Under-Secretary for Legal Affairs," March 20, 2000.

[55] Hans Corell, Head of the United Nations Delegation, "Statement to the Press," Phnom Penh, Cambodia, March 22, 2000; Seth Mydans, "Terms of Khmer Rouge Trials Still Elude U.N. and Cambodia," *New York Times*, March 23, 2000, A3.

[56] Hans Corell, United Nations Under-Secretary for Legal Affairs, "Letter to Sok An, Chairman of the Cambodian Council of Ministers," March 24, 2000. See "Chronology," note 53 above. In the annex to the letter, Corell proposed a new Article 5 bis to the draft law that read as follows:

ARTICLE 5 BIS: SETTLEMENT OF DIFFERENCES BETWEEN THE CO-INVESTIGATING JUDGES AND THE CO-PROSECUTORS

1. In case the Co-Investigating Judges or the Co-Prosecutors, as the case may be, are unable to agree, they shall submit a written statement of facts and the reasons for their different positions to the Supreme Council of the Magistracy. The difference shall be settled forthwith by a panel of three persons, one selected by the Supreme Council of the Magistracy, one by the Secretary-General and one [to be discussed [Different solutions could be considered, such as nominated jointly by the Presidents of the Yugoslav and the Rwanda Tribunals or by the Secretary-General of the Asian-African Legal consultative Committee. Do you have alternative solutions?]].

2. The Panel will examine the difference, applying the standards of a diligent investigating judge or prosecutor, as the case may be. If necessary, they shall meet to deliberate.

3. The decision of the Panel shall be by majority and shall be communicated to the Director of Administration, who shall publish it and communicate it to the Co-Investigating Judges or the Co-Prosecutors who shall proceed accordingly.

[57] U.N. lawyers had agreed to (a) the use of coprosecutors (one Cambodian and one foreign) and coinvestigating judges (one Cambodian and one foreign), (b) the supermajority voting principle provided other priorities were agreed upon, (c) an exchange of letters with an attached memorandum of understanding in lieu of a treaty between the United Nations and Cambodia (a position that ultimately succumbed to the treaty format), and (d) general satisfaction on the issues of Ieng Sary's pardon and amnesty and of a governmental guarantee to arrest the indictees of the Cambodia Tribunal.

[58] On April 8, 2000, Sok An sent a letter to Corell setting forth six options for how to resolve Cambodia Tribunal disputes. There followed several exchanges of letters between Annan and Hun Sen, among which Annan commented on the six options and then proposed a pretrial mechanism for resolving a Cambodia Tribunal dispute (April 19, 2000), Hun Sen proposed a "special chamber" to settle disagreements between the coprosecutors (April 22, 2000), Annan urged acceptance of the U.N. proposal of a pretrial mechanism (April 25, 2000), Hun Sen requested a change in the Cambodia Tribunal's's temporal jurisdiction to commence in 1970 (April. 27, 2000), Annan sought Hun Sen's acceptance of the April 19, 2000, proposal and a limitation of the temporal jurisdiction to 1975–1979 (May 17, 2000), and Hun Sen confirmed the mechanism to resolve Cambodia Tribunal disputes (May 19, 2000). See "Chronology," note 53 above; Colum Lynch, "Kerry Tackles Deadlock in Khmer Rouge Trial," *Washington Post*, April 28, 2000, A26; "News Summary," *New York Times*, April 30, 2000, 2.

[59] Kay Kimsong and Gina Chon, "Senators Begin Approval of KR Draft Law," *Cambodia Daily*, January 12, 2001: "Meanwhile, Minister of Cabinet Sok An told senators he received a letter from UN Deputy Secretary-General Hans Corell, who questioned parts of the law"; see United Nations Office of Legal Affairs, "History of the Negotiations," note 47 above.

[60] Corell set forth his comments and suggestions regarding the tribunal law and the proposed U.N./Cambodia Agreement in a letter to Sok An dated October 10, 2001, which Sok An responded to in a letter dated November 23, 2001. See, generally, Documentation Center of Cambodia, "Chronology," http://www.dccam.org/Archives/Chronology/Chronology.htm.

[61] Hans Corell, United Nations Legal Counsel, "Press Briefing: Negotiations between the UN and Cambodia Regarding the Establishment of the Court to Try Khmer Rouge Leaders," February 8, 2002; "UN Withdraws from Plan to Try Khmer Rouge Leaders," Reuters, February 8, 2002; Colum Lynch, "U.N. Ends Negotiations on Khmer Rouge Trials," *Washington Post*, February 9, 2002, A24; Seth Mydans, "U.N. Ends Cambodia Talks on Trials for Khmer Rouge," *New York Times*, February 9, 2002, A4; Matt McKinney, "After Talks Break, Tribunal for Cambodia is Put into Doubt," *Boston Globe*, February 17, 2002, A20.

[62] Barry Wain, "U.N. Is Pressured to Restart Dialogue on Cambodian War Crimes Tribunal," *Wall Street Journal*, February 11, 2002, 4: "Mr. Corell surprised governments that have taken a close interest in the process, primarily because they expected another round of talks to resolve remaining differences. He also irritated them by not informing them in advance of the decision to pull out. Cambodia's U.N. ambassador was given only half an hour's warning of the public announcement"; "Annan, Negroponte Discuss Cambodia," Associated Press, February 12, 2002; "US Pressures UN on Khmer Rouge Panel," Associated Press, February 24, 2002.

[63] United Nations General Assembly, Resolution 228, U.N. Doc. A/57/228 (2002); David Scheffer, "Justice for Cambodia," *New York Times*, December 21, 2002, A35.

[64] "United Nations and Cambodia Wrap Up Exploratory Talks on Special Court for Khmer Rouge," UN News Service, January 14, 2003. The Cambodian government explained its position at the end of the January 2003 talks in Cambodian Delegation to the United Nations, "Statement Regarding the Establishment of Extraordinary Chambers within the Courts of Cambodia," January 13, 2003.

[65] The Secretariat's nonpaper rejected coprosecutors and coinvestigating judges, thus eliminating any dispute resolution mechanism. It also required that the majority of judges be non-Cambodian, rejected the supermajority voting principle, and reduced the total number of judges in each chamber. The nonpaper overreached General Assembly Resolution 228, which welcomed the domestic law of the tribunal, "noting with appreciation the general provisions and competence of the Law and its provision for a role for the United Nations." Instead, the nonpaper sought fundamental revision to the domestic law of the tribunal. The contents of the nonpaper were reproduced in "Report of the Secretary-General on Khmer Rouge Trials," U.N. Doc. A/57/769 (March 31, 2003), para. 16. See also Tom Fawthrop, "Khmer Rouge: 'Last Chance' for Justice," *Asia Times Online*, February 19, 2003.

[66] "Report of the Secretary-General on Khmer Rouge Trials," U.N. Doc. A/RES/ 57/228B (May 22, 2003).

[67] Ibid., paras. 24–27. An explanation of the draft U.N./Cambodia Agreement is set forth in paras. 31–51 of the report.

[68] United Nations General Assembly, Resolution 57/228, U.N. Doc. A/RES/57/228B (May 22, 2003), http://daccess-dds-ny.un.org/doc/UNDOC/GEN/N03/358/90/ PDF/N0335890.pdf?OpenElement.

[69] United Nations Secretary General, "Report on the Khmer Rouge Trials," U..N Doc. A/59/432 (October 12, 2004).

[70] See, e.g., David Scheffer, "A Rare Chance to Try These Architects of Atrocity," *Financial Times* (London), August 16, 2004, 13.

[71] See note 66 above. The three-year budget of the Cambodia Tribunal is projected to reach almost $57 million (ibid., para. 45).

[72] United Nations Secretary General, "Report on the Khmer Rouge Trials," U.N Doc. A/59/432/Add.1 (November 29, 2004).

[73] Kofi Annan, Untied Nations Secretary-General, "Letter to Hun Sen, Prime Minister of Cambodia," April 28, 2005. See "Chronology," note 53 above.

[74] Son Sen was deputy prime minister and defense minister. See "Chronology," note 53 above.

[75] Ke Pauk was deputy chief of the general staff, Revolutionary Armed Forces of Democratic Kampuchea, and commander in chief, Central Zone armed forces. Ibid.

Chapter Thirteen: No Turning Back

[1] See David Scheffer, "Cambodia's Precedent for Humanity: The First Khmer Rouge Genocide Conviction Lays the Legal Groundwork for Bringing Other Offenders to Justice," *Wall Street Journal*, July 26, 2010, http://online.wsj.com/article/SB1000142 405274870370090457539219028379650.html.

[2] *U.S. Policy toward the International Criminal Court: Furthering Positive Engagement, Report of an Independent Task Force* (Washington, D.C.: The American Society of International Law, March 2009); Lee Feinstein and Tod Lindberg, *Means to an End* (Washington, D.C.: Brookings Institution, 2009); David Scheffer and John Hutson, *Strategy for U.S. Engagement with the International Criminal Court* (New York: The Century Foundation, 2008); Vijay Padmanabhan, *From Rome to Kampala: The U.S. Approach to the 2010 International Criminal Court Review Conference* (New York: Council on Foreign Relations Press, 2010).

[3] Genocide Accountability Act, 18 U.S.C. § 1091 (2007); Child Soldiers Accountability Act, 18 U.S.C. §§ 118, 213 (2008); Trafficking Victims Protection Reauthorization Act of 2008, Publ. L. No. 114-457, § 223, 122, Stat. 5044 (2008); See David Scheffer, "Closing the Impunity Gap in U.S. Law," *Northwestern University Journal of International Human Rights* 8 (Fall 2009): 30–35.

[4] Crimes Against Humanity Act of 2009, S. 1346, 111th U.S. Congress. See Scheffer, "Closing the Impunity Gap," 36–45.

[5] John Hagan and Wenona Rymond-Richmond, *Darfur and the Crime of Genocide* (New York: Cambridge University Press, 2009).

[6] "Report of the International Commission of Inquiry on Darfur to the United Nations Secretary-General, Pursuant to Security Council Resolution 1564 of 18 September 2004," Geneva, January 25, 2005, http://www.un.org/News/dh/sudan/com_inq_darfur.pdf.

[7] U.N. Security Council, Resolution 1593, March 31, 2005.

[8] The prosecutor's application for an arrest warrant on July 14, 2008, was issued (in part) by the Pretrial Chamber on March 4, 2009. "Warrant of Arrest for Omar Hassan Ahmad Al Bashir," in *Prosecutor v. Omar Hassan Ahmad Al Bashir ("Omar Al Bashir")*, ICC-02/04-01/09, March 4, 2009, http://www.icc-cpi.int/iccdocs/doc/doc639078.pdf.

[9] See Katherine Iliopoulos, "The African Union and the ICC," Crimes of War Project, July 10, 2009, http://www.crimesofwar.org/onnews/news-darfur10.html; Robert Marquand, "African Backlash against International Courts Rises," *Christian Science Monitor*, October 6, 2009, 14; Kofi Annan, "Africa and the International Court," *New*

York Times, June 30, 2009, http://www.nytimes.com/2009/06/30/opinion/30iht -edannan.html?_r=1.

[10] Communique, "African Union, Peace and Security Council, 142nd Meeting, July 21, 2008, Addis Ababa, Ethiopia," PSC/MIN/Comm(CXLII) Rev. 1: "... requests the United Nations Security Council, in accordance with the provisions of Article 16 of the Rome Statute of the ICC, to defer the process initiated by the ICC, taking into account the need to ensure that the ongoing peace efforts are not jeopardized, as well as the fact that, in the current circumstances, a prosecution may not be in the interest of the victims and justice"; Michael Slackman and Robert E. Worth, "Often Split, Arab Leaders Unite for Sudan's Chief," *New York Times,* March 31, 2009, A5; "Decision on the Meeting of African States Parties to the Rome Statute of the International Criminal Court (ICC)," Doc. Assembly/AU/13(XIII) Rev. 1, July 3, 2009.

[11] Neil MacFarquhar, "U.N. to Keep Darfur Force, but U.S. Withholds Its Vote," *New York Times,* August 1, 2008, A11.

[12] David Scheffer, "The Security Council's Struggle over Darfur and International Justice," *Jurist,* August 20, 2008, http://jurist.law.pitt.edu/forumy/2008/08/security -councils-struggle-darfur.php.

[13] Rome Statute, Article 13(a) and (c).

[14] "Second Warrant of Arrest for Omar Hassan Ahmad Al Bashir," in *Prosecutor v. Omar Hassan Ahmad Al Bashir ("Omar Al Bashir"),* ICC-02/04-01/09, July 12, 2010), http://www.icc-cpi.int/iccdocs/doc/doc907140.pdf.

[15] Marlise Simons, "Wanted: Sudan's President Cannot Escape Isolation," *New York Times,* May 2, 2010, A8.

[16] David B. Rivkin and Lee A. Casey, "Lawfare," *Wall Street Journal,* February 23, 2007, A11; Jeremy Rabkin, "Lawfare: The International Court of Justice Rules in Favor of Terrorism," *Wall Street Journal,* July 17, 2004 (online); David Kennedy, *Of Law and War* (Princeton University Press, Princeton, 2006); Major General Charles J. Dunlap, Jr., USAF, "Lawfare Today: A Perspective," *Yale Journal of International Affairs* (Winter 2008): 146–154. Compare with David Scheffer, "Whose Lawfare Is It, Anyway?" *Case Western Reserve Journal of International Law* 43 (Fall 2010): 215–227.

[17] Sharon Begley, "The Tortured Brain: Extreme Pain and Stress Can Actually Impair a Person's Ability to Tell the Truth," *Newsweek,* September 21, 2009, http://www .newsweek.com/id/215922; Shane O'Mara, "Torturing the Brain: On the Folk Psychology and Folk Neurobiology Motivating 'Enhanced and Coercive Interrogation Techniques,'" *Trends in Cognitive Science: Science and Society,* December 1, 2009, 497–500; Scott Shane and Mark Mazzetti, "In Adopting Harsh Tactics, No Inquiry into Past Use," *New York Times,* April 22, 2009, A1; "Why Bush's 'Enhanced Interrogation' Program Failed," ThinkProgress.org, the blog of the Center for American Progress Action Fund, http://thinkprogress.org/why-enhanced-interrogation-failed/; "Inquiry into the Treatment of Detainees in U.S. Custody," Report of the Committee on Armed Services, U.S. Senate, 110th Congress, 2nd session, November 20, 2008, 47–51.

[18] U.S.C. §§ 7421–33 (2006). During a key roll call vote on June 6, 2002, in the U.S. Senate, 45 Republicans and 30 Democrats (including Senator Hillary Rodham Clin-

ton) voted yea while 17 Democrats and only one Republican (Senator Arlen Specter) voted nay. In a similar key vote on May 24, 2002, in the U.S. House of Representatives, 196 Republicans and 84 Democrats voted yea, while 20 Republicans and 116 Democrats voted nay.

Chapter Fourteen: Postscript on Law, Crimes, and Impunity

[1] Elihu Root, "Francis Lieber," *American Journal International Law* 7 (1913): 453, 459.

[2] U.S. War Department, "Instructions for the Government of Armies of the United States in the Field, General Orders No. 100," April 24, 1863, http://www.civilwar home.com/liebercode.htm (hereinafter, The Lieber Code).

[3] Ibid., para. 14.

[4] Ibid., para. 16.

[5] Ibid., para. 29.

[6] Francisci de Victoria, *De Indis Et De Ivre Belli Relectiones*, ed. Ernest Nys (Washington, D.C.: Carnegie Institution of Washington, 1917); Alberico Gentili, *De Iure Belli Libri Tres* (Oxford: The Clarendon Press, 1933); Hugo Grotius, *De Jure Belli Ac Pacis Libri Tres* (Oxford: The Clarendon Press, 1925).

[7] The Lieber Code, para. 22.

[8] The White House, "The National Security Strategy of the United States of America," September 2002, http://georgewbush-whitehouse.archives.gov/nsc/nss/2002/ nss.pdf.

[9] But see Burrus M. Carnahan, "Lincoln, Lieber and the Laws of War. The Origins and Limits of the Principal of Military Necessity," *American Journal of International Law* 92 (April 1998): 213, note 86, for an analysis of Sherman and his troops' actions in light of military codes in place at the time.

[10] Introduction, "Resolutions of the Geneva International Conference" (1869), http://www.icrc.org/IHL.nsf/INTRO/115?OpenDocument.

[11] M. Cherif Bassiouni, "The Normative Framework of International Humanitarian Law: Overlaps, Gaps, and Ambiguities," in *International Criminal Law*, 3rd ed., vol. 1, ed. M. Cherif Bassiouni (Leiden: Koninklijke Brill NV, 2008), 493, 505–519.

[12] "Agreement for the Prosecution and Punishment of the Major War Criminals of the European Axis," *United Nations Treaty Series* 82 (August 8, 1945), 279; "Charter of the International Military Tribunal for the Far East" (January 19, 1946), http://www .ibiblio.org/hyperwar/PTO/IMTFE/IMTFE-A5.html.

[13] Edoardo Greppi, "The Evolution of Criminal Responsibility under International Law," *International Review of the Red Cross* 835 (September 30, 1999): 531–553.

[14] See generally Telford Taylor, *The Anatomy of the Nuremberg Trials: A Personal Memoir* (New York: Alfred A. Knopf, 2002); Neil Boister and Robert Cryer, *The Tokyo International Military Tribunal: A Reappraisal* (Oxford: Oxford University Press, 2008).

[15] The general arguments, and the critiques of them, are set forth in David Scheffer, "The Future of Atrocity Law," *Suffolk Transnational Law Review* 25 (2002): 389–432; David Scheffer, "Genocide and Atrocity Crimes," *Genocide Studies & Prevention* 1 (2006): 229–250; David Scheffer, "The Merits of Unifying Terms: 'Atrocity Crimes'

and 'Atrocity Law,'" *Genocide Studies & Prevention* 2 (2007): 91–95; "A Symposium on David Scheffer's 'Genocide and Atrocity Crimes,'" *Genocide Studies & Prevention* 2 (2007): 31–90.

[16] See Scheffer, "The Future of Atrocity Law," 402–414.

[17] Jeremy Bentham, *An Introduction to the Principles of Morals and Legislation* (Oxford: Clarendon Press, 1907), 25.

[18] Samantha Power, *A Problem from Hell: America at the Age of Genocide* (New York: Basic Books, 2002), xix. See also David Scheffer, The Legacy of Raphael Lemkin, in Catherine Filloux, *Silence of God and Other Plays* (New York: Seagull Books, 2009), 4–8.

[19] M. Cherif Bassiouni, *International Criminal Law Conventions and Their Penal Provisions* (Dobbs Ferry, New York: Transnational Publishers, 1997), 20–21.

[20] See M. Cherif Bassiouni, "The Normative Framework of International Humanitarian Law: Overlaps, Gaps and Ambiguities," *Transnational Law & Contemporary Problems* 8 (1999): 199, 200.

[21] See Louis Henkin et al., eds., *Human Rights,* 2nd ed. (New York: Foundation Press, 2009), 413–415:("International human rights conventions typically require States Parties not only to respect the rights recognized in the treaties, but also to ensure that those rights are protected.... Ordinarily, when an international tribunal or monitoring body establishes a breach of human rights, the state is the responsible actor. However, international law also imposes certain duties directly on individuals, and subjects them to criminal punishment for violating those obligations."

[22] See Henry J. Steiner, Philip Alston, and Ryan Goodman, *International Human Rights in Context: Law, Politics, Morals,* 3rd ed. (New York: Oxford University Press, 2008): 395–471.

[23] Geoffrey Best, *War & Law Since 1945* (New York: Oxford University Press, 1994).

[24] Power, *A Problem from Hell,* 49.

[25] United Nations General Assembly, "Convention on the Prevention and Punishment of the Crime of Genocide," *United Nations Treaty Series* 78 (January 12, 1951), Key Provisions.

[26] International Criminal Tribunal for the former Yugoslavia, "Judgement," *Prosecutor v. Krstic* (April 19, 2004), para. 37, http://www.icty.org/x/cases/krstic/acjug/en/krs-aj040419e.pdf; Scheffer, "Genocide and Atrocity Crimes," 239–242.

[27] See generally International Criminal Tribunal for Rwanda, "Judgement," *Prosecutor v. Akayesu* (September 2, 1998), http://www.ictrcaselaw.org/docs/doc15154.pdf.

[28] International Criminal Court Pretrial Chamber 1, "Decision on the Prosecution's Application for a Warrant of Arrest Against Omar Hassan Ahmad Al Bashir," *Prosecutor v. Omar Hassan Ahmad Al Bashir* (March 9, 2009), paras. 105–108, http://www.icc-cpi.int/iccdocs/doc/doc639096.pdf; International Criminal Court Pretrial Chamber 1, "Second Decision on the Prosecution's Application for a Warrant of Arrest against Omar Hassan Ahmad Al Bashir," *Prosecutor v. Omar Hassan Ahmad Al Bashir* (July 12, 2010), paras. 25–31; David Scheffer, "Rape as Genocide: Sudan and the ICC," *International Herald Tribune,* December 3, 2008, 6.

[29] The genocides of the twentieth century, as Eric Weitz has explored, can arise under a wide range of national and international circumstances. Eric Weitz, *A Century of Genocide: Utopias of Race and Nation* (Princeton: Princeton University Press, 2003).

[30] "Judgement," *Prosecutor v. Krstic* (see note 26 above, para. 37).

[31] "Decision on the Prosecution's Application for a Warrant of Arrest," *Prosecutor v. Omar Hassan Ahmad Al Bashir* (see note 28 above), paras. 162–163.

[32] International Criminal Tribunal for the former Yugoslavia, "Judgement," *Prosecutor v. Kordic and Cerkez* (February 26, 2001), para. 179.

[33] International Criminal Tribunal for Rwanda, "Judgement," *Prosecutor v. Kayishema and Ruzindana* (May 21, 1999), para. 123.

[34] International Criminal Tribunal for Rwanda, "Judgement," *Prosecutor v. Baglishema* (June 7, 2001). para. 80.

[35] International Criminal Tribunal for the former Yugoslavia, "Judgement," *Prosecutor v. Blaskic* (March 3, 2000), para. 203.

[36] International Criminal Tribunal for the former Yugoslavia, "Judgement," *Prosecutor v. Kunarac, Kovac and Vokovic* (June 12, 2002), para. 95.

[37] International Criminal Tribunal for the former Yugoslavia, "Judgement," *Prosecutor v. Jelisic* (December 14, 1999), para. 53.

[38] International Criminal Court, *The Rome Statute* (July 17, 1998), Article 7(1)(i), (j).

[39] Antonio Cassese et al., eds., *The Oxford Companion to International Criminal Justice* (New York: Oxford University Press, 2009), 312–313; Roger Cohen, "Ethnic Cleansing," in *Crimes of War: What the Public Should Know*, 2nd ed., ed. Anthony Dworkin, Roy Gutman, and David Rieff (New York: W. W. Norton & Company, 2007), 175–177.

[40] *The Rome Statute* (see note 38 above), Article 7(1)(h).

[41] International Criminal Tribunal for the former Yugoslavia, "Judgement," *Prosecutor v. Vasiljevic* (November 29, 2002), para. 227.

[42] See list of war crimes in *The Rome Statute* (note 38 above), Article 8; William Schabas, *An Introduction to the International Criminal Court*, 4th ed. (Cambridge: Cambridge University Press, 2011), 122–146.

[43] Cassese et al., *International Criminal Law*, 96–97; Bassiouni, *International Criminal Law*, 505–519.

[44] See generally Jean-Marie Henckaerts and Louise Doswald-Beck, eds., *Customary International Humanitarian Law* (Cambridge: International Committee of the Red Cross, 2006); "Protocol Additional to the Geneva Conventions of 12 August 1949, and relating to the Protection of Victims of International Armed Conflicts" (Protocol I), June 8, 1977, Article 75 of Protocol I (1977).

[45] This is the description set forth in the statutes alongside "grave breaches."

[46] International Criminal Tribunal for Rwanda, "Judgement," *Prosecutor v. Akayesu* (September 2, 1998), para. 616; International Criminal Tribunal for Rwanda, "Judgement," *Prosecutor v. Rutaganda* (December 6, 1999), para. 106.

[47] International Criminal Tribunal for Rwanda, "Judgment," *Prosecutor v. Kunarac, Kovac and Vokovic* (June 12, 2002), para. 66.

[48] Cassese et al., *International Criminal Law*, 302–314; Cassese et al., *The Oxford Companion*, 368–369.

[49] United Nations General Assembly, "Convention Against Torture and Other Cruel, Inhuman, or Degrading Treatment or Punishment," *United Nations Treaty Series* 1465 (December 10, 1984): 85

[50] International Court of Justice, "Democratic Republic of the Congo v. Belgium (Arrest Warrant Case)," *ICJ Reports* (February 14, 2002).

[51] "Agreement for the Prosecution and Punishment of the Major War Criminals of the European Axis," *United Nations Treaty Series* 82 (August 8, 1945): 279, Article 7; Charter of the International Military Tribunal for the Far East, Article 6; International Criminal Tribunal for the former Yugoslavia, Article 7(2); International Criminal Tribunal for Rwanda, Article 6(2); Statute for the Special Court for Sierra Leone (January 16, 2002), Article 6(2); Law on the Establishment of the Extraordinary Chambers in the Courts of Cambodia for the Prosecution of Crimes Committed during the Period of Democratic Kampuchea, Article 29.

[52] See generally M. Cherif Bassiouni, *The Institutionalization of Torture by the Bush Administration: Is Anyone Responsible?* (Portland: Intersentia, 2010); Philippe Sands, *Torture Team: Rumsfeld's Memo and the Betrayal of American Values* (New York: Palgrave Macmillan, 2008); Jane Mayer, *The Dark Side: The Inside Story of How the War on Terror Turned into a War on American Ideals* (New York: Anchor Books, 2008); Jordan J. Paust, *Beyond the Law: The Bush Administration's Unlawful Responses in the "War" on Terror* (New York: Cambridge University Press, 2007); Jack L. Goldsmith, *The Terror Presidency: Law and Judgment inside the Bush Administration* (New York: W. W. Norton and Company, 2007).

FURTHER READING

Students of the war crimes tribunals built during the 1990s now have a wealth of scholarly books and other source material to read. I have drawn from and used all the following books, journal articles, and Web sites in the preparation of this book or my other publications or in my teaching of international criminal law at Northwestern University School of Law. However, some of what is described below covers the work of the tribunals after I left government service in 2001, and thus only occasionally pertains to the focus of this book's story. I apologize for omitting any outstanding treatments of this subject by scholars who deserve to be recognized but whose works I may have overlooked.

Histories of the Atrocities

Among the best histories of the actual atrocities that swept through the 1990s, as well as Cambodia in the 1970s, are the following books, some of which offer a distinctly American point of view.

Cambodia

Becker, Elizabeth. *When the War Was Over: Cambodia and the Khmer Rouge Revolution.* New York: Public Affairs, 1998.

Kiernan, Ben. *The Pol Pot Regime: Race, Power, and Genocide in Cambodia under the Khmer Rouge, 1975–79.* 2nd ed. New Haven: Yale University Press, 2002.

Power, Samantha. *A Problem From Hell: America and the Age of Genocide.* New York: Basic Books, 2002: 87–154.

Short, Philip. *Pol Pot: The History of a Nightmare.* London: John Murray, 2004.

The Balkans and Kosovo

Clark, Wesley K. *Waging Modern War: Bosnia, Kosovo, and the Future of Combat.* New York: Public Affairs, 2001.

Gutman, Roy. *A Witness to Genocide.* New York: Macmillan Publishing Company, 1993.

Halberstam, David. *War in a Time of Peace: Bush, Clinton, and the Generals.* New York: Simon & Schuster, 2002.

Holbrooke, Richard. *To End a War.* New York: Random House, 1998.

Ignatieff, Michael. *Virtual War: Kosovo and Beyond.* New York: Henry Holt and Company, 2000.

Maas, Peter. *Love Thy Neighbor: A Story of War.* New York: Vintage Books, 1996.

Power, Samantha. *A Problem From Hell: America and the Age of Genocide.* New York: Basic Books, 2002: 247–327, 391–473.

Rohde, David. *Endgame: The Betrayal and Fall of Srebrenica, Europe's Worst Massacre since World War II.* New York: Farrar, Straus and Giroux, 1997.

Shattuck, John. *Freedom on Fire: Human Rights Wars and America's Response.* Cambridge, Massachusetts: Harvard University Press, 2003: 113–220.

Rwanda

Dallaire, Roméo. *Shake Hands with the Devil: The Failure of Humanity in Rwanda.* New York: Carroll & Graf Publishers, 2003.

Des Forges, Alison. *Leave None to Tell the Story: Genocide in Rwanda.* New York: Human Rights Watch, 1999.

Gourevitch, Philip. *We Wish to Inform You That Tomorrow We Will Be Killed with Our Families: Stories from Rwanda.* New York: Farrar Straus and Giroux, 1998.

Kinzer, Stephen. *A Thousand Hills.* Hoboken, New Jersey: John Wiley & Sons, 2008.

Neuffer, Elizabeth. *The Key to My Neighbor's House: Seeking Justice in Bosnia and Rwanda.* New York: Picador, 2001.

Power, Samantha. *A Problem From Hell: America and the Age of Genocide.* New York: Basic Books, 2002: 329–389.

Prunier, Gérard. *The Rwanda Crisis: History of a Genocide.* New York: Columbia University Press, 1995.

Shattuck, John. *Freedom on Fire: Human Rights Wars and America's Response.* Cambridge, Massachusetts: Harvard University Press, 2003: 21–76.

Sierra Leone

Beah, Ishmail. *A Long Way Gone: Memoirs of a Boy Soldier.* New York: Farrar, Straus and Giroux, 2007.

Campbell, Greg. *Blood Diamonds: Tracing the Path of the World's Most Precious Stones.* Boulder: Westview Press, 2004.

Gberie, Lansana. *A Dirty War in West Africa: The RUF and the Destruction of Sierra Leone.* Bloomington: Indiana University Press, 2005.

Mosele, Fr. Victor F. M. *Running For My Life: Captive of the RUF Rebels of Sierra Leone.* Tucson: E. T. Nedder Publishing, 1999.

The War Crimes Tribunals

There exists a virtual explosion of books, law review articles, and Ph.D. dissertations about the five war crimes tribunals covered in this book—the

International Criminal Tribunals for the former Yugoslavia and Rwanda, the Special Court for Sierra Leone, the Extraordinary Chambers in the Courts of Cambodia, and the International Criminal Court. These scholarly works focus primarily on the constitutional structure of the tribunals, their practice, and their jurisprudence. The list below is but a sampling of the published material.

Bass, Gary Jonathan. *Stay the Hand of Vengeance*. Princeton: Princeton University Press, 2000.

Bassiouni, M. Cherif, ed. *The Legislative History of the International Criminal Court: Introduction, Analysis, and Integrated Text*. Ardsley, New York: Transnational Publishers, 2005.

Bassiouni, M. Cherif, ed. *The Statute of the International Criminal Court: A Documentary History*. Ardsley, New York: Transnational Publishers, 1998.

Bassiouni, M. Cherif, and Peter Manikas. *The Law of the International Criminal Tribunal for the Former Yugoslavia*. Irvington-on-Hudson, New York: Transnational Publishers, 1996.

Broomhall, Bruce. *International Justice & the International Criminal Court: Between Sovereignty and the Rule of Law*. New York: Oxford University Press, 2003.

Cassese, Antonio, Paola Gaeta, and John R.W.D. Jones, eds. *The Rome Statute of the International Criminal Court: A Commentary*. New York: Oxford University Press, 2002.

Goldstone, Richard J. *For Humanity: Reflections of a War Crimes Investigator*. New Haven: Yale University Press, 2000.

Hagan, John. *Justice in the Balkans: Prosecuting War Crimes in the Hague Tribunal*. Chicago: University of Chicago Press, 2003.

Knoops, Geert-Jan Alexander. *An Introduction to the Law of the International Criminal Tribunals: A Comparative Study*. Ardsley, New York: Transnational Publishers, 2003.

Knoops, Geert-Jan Alexander. *Theory and Practice of International and Internationalized Criminal Proceedings*. The Hague: Kluwer Law International, 2005.

Lee, Roy S., ed. *The International Criminal Court: The Making of the Rome Statute*. Boston: Kluwer Law International, 1999.

Mettraux, Guénaël. *International Crimes and the Ad Hoc Tribunals*. New York: Oxford University Press, 2005.

Moghalu, Kingsley Chiedu. *Global Justice: The Politics of the War Crimes Trials*. Westport: Greenwood Publishing Group, 2006.

Morris, Virginia, and Michael P. Scharf. *An Insider's Guide to The International Criminal Tribunal for the Former Yugoslavia*. Irvington-on-Hudson, New York: Transnational Publishers, 1995.

Morris, Virginia, and Michael P. Scharf. *The International Criminal Tribunal for Rwanda*. Irvington-on-Hudson, New York: Transnational Publishers, 1998.

Paris, Edna. *The Sun Climbs Slow: Justice in the Age of Imperial America*. Toronto: Alfred
    A. Knopf Canada, 2008.

Peskin, Victor. *International Justice in Rwanda and the Balkans*. New York: Cambridge
    University Press, 2008.

Romano, Cesare P. R., André Nollkaemper, and Jann K. Kleffner, eds. *International-
    ized Criminal Courts*. New York: Oxford University Press, 2004.

Sadat, Leila Nadya. *The International Criminal Court and the Transformation of Interna-
    tional Law*. Ardsley, New York: Transnational Publishers, 2002.

Schabas, William A. *The International Criminal Court: A Commentary on the Rome Stat-
    ute*. New York: Oxford University Press, 2010.

Schabas, William A. *An Introduction to the International Criminal Court*. 4th ed. New
    York: Cambridge University Press, 2011.

Schabas, William A. *The UN International Criminal Tribunals: The Former Yugoslavia,
    Rwanda and Sierra Leone*. New York: Cambridge University Press, 2006.

Scharf, Michael. *Balkan Justice: The Story Behind the First International War Crimes Trial
    since Nüremberg*. Durham, North Carolina: Carolina Academic Press, 1997.

Scharf, Michael, and Paul Williams. *Peace with Justice? War Crimes and Accountability in
    the Former Yugoslavia*. Lanham, Maryland: Rowman & Littlefield, 2002.

Sewall, Sarah B., and Karl Kaysen. *The United States and the International Criminal
    Court*. New York: Rowman & Littlefield Publishers, 2000.

Shattuck, John. *Freedom on Fire: Human Rights Wars and America's Response*. Cam-
    bridge, Massachusetts: Harvard University Press, 2003: 51–76.

Stahn, Carsten, and Göran Sluiter, eds. *The Emerging Practice of the International Crimi-
    nal Court*. Leiden: Brill, 2009.

Stromseth, Jane E. *Accountability for Atrocities: National and International Responses*.
    Ardsley, New York: Transnational Publishers, 2003.

Atrocity Law

The principles of law underpinning the war crimes tribunals, and which I
write about in chapter 14 as "atrocity law," are described in a rich body of
scholarly works. Some of these books record the modern origins of the discipline in the Nuremberg and Tokyo trials, while others focus on textbook
treatments of both customary and codified international law.

Bassiouni, M. Cherif. *Crimes Against Humanity in International Criminal Law*, 2nd ed.
    The Hague: Kluwer Law International, 1999.

Bassiouni, M. Cherif, ed. *International Criminal Law*, 3rd ed. Leiden: Brill, 2008.

Bellelli, Roberto, ed. *International Criminal Justice: Law and Practice from the Rome Stat-
    ute to Its Review*. Burlington, Vermont: Ashgate Publishing Company, 2010.

Best, Geoffrey. *War & Law Since 1945*. Oxford: Oxford University Press, 1994.

Cassese, Antonio. *International Criminal Law*. 2nd ed. New York: Oxford University Press, 2008.

Cassese, Antonio, ed. *The Oxford Companion to International Criminal Justice*. New York: Oxford University Press, 2009.

Detter, Ingrid. *The Law of War*. 2nd ed. New York: Cambridge University Press, 2000.

Drumbl, Mark. *Atrocity, Punishment, and International Law*. New York: Cambridge University Press, 2007.

Dworkin, Anthony, Roy Gutman, David Rieff, and Sheryl A. Mendez, eds. *Crimes of War 2.0*. New York: W. W. Norton & Company, 2007.

Fleck, Dieter, ed. *The Handbook of International Humanitarian Law*. 2d ed. Oxford: Oxford University Press, 2008.

Green, Leslie C. *The Contemporary Law of Armed Conflict*. 2nd ed. Manchester: Manchester University Press, 2000.

Harris, Whitney R. *Tyranny on Trial: The Trial of the Major German War Criminals at the End of World War II at Nuremberg, Germany, 1945–1946*. Revised edition. Dallas: Southern Methodist University Press, 1999.

Henckaerts, Jean-Marie, and Louise Doswald-Beck. *Customary International Humanitarian Law, Vol. 1: Rules*. New York: Cambridge University Press, 2005.

Knoops, Geert-Jan Alexander. *Theory and Practice of International and Internationalized Criminal Proceedings*. The Hague: Kluwer Law International, 2005.

Meron, Theodor. *War Crimes Law Comes of Age: Essays*. Oxford: Clarendon Press, 1998.

Osiel, Mark J. *Obeying Orders: Atrocity, Military Discipline and the Law of War*. New Brunswick: Transaction Publishers, 1999.

Sands, Philippe, ed. *From Nuremberg to The Hague: The Future of International Criminal Justice*. Cambridge: Cambridge University Press, 2003.

Schabas, William A. *Genocide in International Law: The Crime of Crimes*. 2nd ed. New York: Cambridge University Press, 2009.

Schabas, William A., and Nadia Bernaz, eds. *Routledge Handbook of International Criminal Law*. New York: Routledge, 2011.

Taylor, Telford. *The Anatomy of the Nuremberg Trials*. New York: Alfred A. Knopf, 1992.

Tuck, Richard. *The Rights of War and Peace: Political Thought and the International Order from Grotius to Kant*. New York: Oxford University Press, 1999.

Zahar, Alexander, and Göran Sluiter. *International Criminal Law*. New York: Oxford University Press, 2008.

Other Books on Atrocities, Memory, and Justice

Another group of books, listed below, should be foremost in the study of atrocity crimes and accountability for them.

Bassiouni, M. Cherif. *The Pursuit of International Criminal Justice: A World Study on Conflicts, Victimization, and Post-Conflict Justice.* Mortsel, Belgium: Intersentia Publishing, 2010.

Biggar, Nigel, ed. *Burying the Past: Making Peace and Doing Justice after Civil Conflict.* Washington, D.C.: Georgetown University Press, 2001.

Buruma, Ian. *The Wages of Guilt: Memories of War in Germany and Japan.* New York: Farrar Straus Giroux, 1994.

Chuter, David. *War Crimes: Confronting Atrocity in the Modern World.* Boulder: Lynne Rienner Publishers, 2003.

Cobban, Helena. *Amnesty after Atrocity? Healing Nations after Genocide and War Crimes.* Boulder: Paradigm Publishers, 2007.

Minow, Martha. *Between Vengeance and History after Genocide and Mass Violence.* Boston: Beacon Press, 1998.

Neier, Aryeh. *War Crimes: Brutality, Genocide, Terror, and the Struggle for Justice.* New York: Random House, 1998.

Paris, Edna. *Long Shadows: Truth, Lies and History.* New York: Bloomsbury, 2000.

Sikkink, Kathryn. *The Justice Cascade: How Human Rights Prosecutions Are Changing World Politics.* New York: W.W. Norton & Company, 2011.

Teitel, Ruti G. *Transitional Justice.* New York: Oxford University Press, 2000.

Tuck, Richard. *The Rights of War and Peace: Political Thought and the International Order from Grotius to Kant.* New York: Oxford University Press, 1999.

Weitz, Eric D. *A Century of Genocide: Utopias of Race and Nation.* Princeton: Princeton University Press, 2003.

Memoirs and Clinton Era Histories

The most relevant memoirs and historical treatments of the Clinton administration's eight years of governance relevant to the atrocities and war crimes tribunals of that era comprise a small but important list; they provide other insights and points of view about what transpired on my own watch. Several of these books already appear above under other areas of study.

Albright, Madeleine, with William Woodward. *Madam Secretary.* New York: Miramax Books, 2003.

Branch, Taylor. *The Clinton Tapes: Wrestling History with the President.* New York: Simon & Schuster, 2009.

Clark, Wesley K. *Waging Modern War: Bosnia, Kosovo, and the Future of Combat.* New York: Public Affairs, 2001.

Clinton, Bill. *My Life.* New York: Random House, 2004.

Dallaire, Roméo. *Shake Hands with the Devil: The Failure of Humanity in Rwanda.* New York: Carroll & Graf Publishers, 2003.

Goldstone, Richard J. *For Humanity: Reflections of a War Crimes Investigator.* New Haven: Yale University Press, 2000.

Halberstam, David. *War in a Time of Peace: Bush, Clinton, and the Generals.* New York: Simon & Schuster, 2002.

Holbrooke, Richard. *To End a War.* New York: Random House, 1998.

Power, Samantha. *A Problem from Hell: America and the Age of Genocide.* New York: Basic Books, 2002.

Shattuck, John. *Freedom on Fire: Human Rights Wars and America's Response.* Cambridge, Massachusetts: Harvard University Press, 2003.

David Scheffer's Relevant Publications

Among my prior publications in books, law journals, and magazines that may prove useful to examine in the context of this book, the following list offers a sampling, in chronological order by year of publication, starting with the most recent. My public speeches as ambassador at large for war crimes issues (1997–2001) can be accessed at www.state.gov/www/global/swci/index.html.

"International Criminal Court." In *Routledge Handbook of International Criminal Law,* ed. William Schabas and Nadia Bernaz, 67–83. New York: Routledge, 2011.

"Whose Lawfare Is It, Anyway?" *Case Western Reserve Journal of International Law* 43 (Fall 2010): 215–227.

"The Complex Crime of Aggression under the Rome Statute." *Leiden Journal of International Law* 23 (2010): 215–227.

"The Crime of Aggression." In *Beyond Kampala: Next Steps for U.S. Principled Engagement with the International Criminal Court,* ed. Rachel Gore, 87–107. ASIL Discussion Paper, November 2010. http://asil.org/pdfs/2010_beyond_Kampala.pdf.

"Atrocity Crimes: Framing the Responsibility to Protect." In *Responsibility to Protect: The Global Moral Compact for the 21st Century,* ed. Richard H. Cooper and Juliette Voïnov Kohler, 77–98. New York: Palgrave Macmillan, 2009.

"Closing the Impunity Gap in U.S. Law." *Northwestern University Journal of International Human Rights* 8 (2009): 30–52.

"The Legacy of Raphael Lemkin." In *Silence of God and Other Plays* (Catherine Filloux). New York: Seagull Books, 2009: 4–8.

"The Constitutionality of the Rome Statute of the International Criminal Court." *The Journal of Criminal Law and Criminology* 95 (2008) (with Ashley Cox): 983–1068.

"For Love of Country and International Criminal Law: Further Reflections." *ASIL Proceedings* 102 (2008): 12–16.

"Nuremberg Trials." In *Proceedings of the First International Humanitarian Law Dialogs,* ed. David M. Crane and Elizabeth Anderson, 155–182. Washington, D.C.: American Society of International Law, 2008.

"Policy Issues under the UN Charter and the Rome Statute." In *Conference on International Criminal Justice*, ed. Roberto Bellelli, 48–52. Torino: AGAT, 2008.

"The End of Exceptionalism in War Crimes." *ILSA Quarterly* 16 (October 2007): 16–23.

"The Merits of Unifying Terms: 'Atrocity Crimes' and 'Atrocity Law.'" *Genocide Studies and Prevention* 2 (2007): 91–95.

"Genocide and Atrocity Crimes." *Genocide Studies and Prevention* 1 (2006): 229–250.

"Jostling over Justice." *Foreign Policy* 154 (2006): 4.

"Memorandum on the Application of International Standards of Due Process by the Extraordinary Chambers in the Courts of Cambodia." Open Society Justice Initiative, New York, 2006. www.osji.org/db/resource2?res_id=103267.

"Article 98(2) of the Rome Statute: America's Original Intent." *Journal of International Criminal Justice* 3(2) (2005): 333–353.

"Blueprint for Legal Reforms at the United Nations and the International Criminal Court." *Georgetown Journal of International Law* 36 (2005): 683–701.

"The Future U.S. Relationship with the International Criminal Court." *Pace International Law Review* 17 (2005): 161–178.

"How to Turn the Tide Using the Rome Statute's Temporal Jurisdiction." *Journal of International Criminal Justice* 2(1) (2004): 26–34.

"Lessons from the Rwandan Genocide." *Georgetown Journal of International Affairs* 5 (2004): 125–132.

"Three Memories from the Year of Origin, 1993." *Journal of International Criminal Justice* 2 (2004): 353–360.

"Advancing U.S. Interests with the International Criminal Court." *Vanderbilt Journal of Transnational Law* 36 (2003): 1567–1578.

"Arresting War Criminals: Mission Creep or Mission Impossible?" *Case Western Reserve Journal of International Law* 35 (2003): 319–324.

"Restoring U.S. Engagement with the International Criminal Court." *Wisconsin International Law Journal* 21 (2003): 599–609.

"The Future of Atrocity Law." *Suffolk Transnational Law Review* 25 (2002): 389–432.

"Staying the Course with the International Criminal Court." *Cornell International Law Journal* 35 (2002): 47–100.

"War Crimes and the Clinton Administration." *Social Research* 69 (2002): 1109–1117.

"A Negotiator's Perspective on the International Criminal Court, Fourteenth Waldemar A. Solf Lecture in International Law Delivered at the Judge Advocate General's School (Feb. 28, 2001)." *Military Law Review* 167 (2001): 1–19.

"The Tool Box, Past and Present, of Justice and Reconciliation for Atrocities." *American Journal of International Law* 95 (2001): 970–977.

"The U.S. Perspective on the International Criminal Court." *McGill Law Journal* 46 (2000): 269–274.

"Blaine Sloan Lecture: War Crimes and Crimes against Humanity." *Pace International Law Review* 11 (1999): 319–340.

"The United States and the International Criminal Court." *American Journal of International Law* 93 (1999): 12–22.

"U.S. Policy and the International Criminal Court." *Cornell International Law Journal* 32 (1999): 529–534.

"U.S. Policy on International Criminal Tribunals." *American University International Law Review* 13 (1998): 1389–1400.

"International Judicial Intervention." *Foreign Policy* 102 (1996): 34–51.

Web Sites of the War Crimes Tribunals

Any study of the jurisprudence of the war crimes tribunals relics heavily on access to each tribunal's official Web site, where the indictments, decisions, judgments, and press releases are recorded and easily accessible. These Web sites also provide the most current information about the status of indicted fugitives, defendants, trials, and the administration of each tribunal.

Extraordinary Chambers in the Courts of Cambodia: www.eccc.gov.kh. (See also www.cambodiatribunal.org, a Web site that I coedit.)

International Criminal Court: www.icc-cpi.int.

International Criminal Tribunal for Rwanda: www.unictr.org.

International Criminal Tribunal for the former Yugoslavia: www.icty.org.

Special Court for Sierra Leone. www.sc-sl.org.

LIST OF ILLUSTRATIONS

Figures

Photographs (Insert with photos begins after page 218)

INDEX

Note: The photos referred to in this index can be found in the insert following page 218

HUMAN RIGHTS AND CRIMES AGAINST HUMANITY

This series provides a forum for publication and debate on the most pressing issues of modern times: the establishment of human rights standards and, at the same time, their persistent violation. It features a broad understanding of human rights, one that encompasses democratic citizenship as well as concerns for social, economic, and environmental justice. Its understanding of crimes against humanity is similarly broad, ranging from large-scale atrocities like ethnic cleansings, genocides, war crimes, and various forms of human trafficking to lynchings, mass rapes, and torture. Some books in the series are more historically oriented and explore particular events and their legacies. Others focus on contemporary concerns, like instances of forced population displacements or indiscriminate bombings. Still others provide serious reflection on the meaning and history of human rights or on the reconciliation efforts that follow major human rights abuses. Chronologically, the series runs from around 1500, the onset of the modern era marked by European colonialism abroad and the Atlantic slave trade, to the present. Geographically, it takes in every area of the globe. It publishes significant works of original scholarship and major interpretations by historians, human rights practitioners, legal scholars, social scientists, philosophers, and journalists. An important goal is to bring issues of human rights and their violations to the attention of a wide audience and to stimulate discussion and debate in the public sphere as well as among scholars and in the classroom. The knowledge that develops from the series will also, we hope, help promote human rights standards and prevent future crimes against humanity.